The Baltimore Sun
1837–1987

THE BALTIMORE SUN
1837–1987

Harold A. Williams

The Johns Hopkins University Press
Baltimore and London

Photographs, except where noted otherwise, courtesy of the *Baltimore Sun* Library

The Johns Hopkins University Press
701 West 40th Street
Baltimore, Maryland 21211
The Johns Hopkins Press Ltd., London

The paper used in this publication meets the minimum requirements
of American National Standard for Information Sciences—Permanence of Paper
for Printed Library Materials,
ANSI Z39.48-1984.

Library of Congress Cataloging-in-Publication Data

Williams, Harold A., 1916–
The Baltimore Sun, 1837–1987.

Bibliography: p.
Includes index.
1. Sun (Baltimore, Md. : 1837) I. Title.
PN4899.B35S84   1987   071′.52   87-2796
ISBN 0-8018-3516-X (alk. paper)

For all *Sun* men and women,
past and present

"A newspaper is at once a product
of long tradition and instant decision,
but it is most of all a product of the
individuals who give it its special
character."

—A *Sun* editorial, October 18, 1973

and for John Koenig,

Hal William

Contents

Contents

Preface

In 1976, William F. Schmick, Jr., president of the A. S. Abell Company, which published the *Sun,* the *Evening Sun,* and the *Sunday Sun,* asked me to begin collecting material for the 150th anniversary of the *Sun,* to be commemorated in 1987. Ever since I joined the *Sun* in 1940 as a rewriteman, I had been casually collecting *Sunpaper* ephemera and lore. With 1987 as a goal, my collecting became more organized, and stealing time now and then from my work as Sunday editor, I began interviewing the oldest retired editors and reporters, some of whom had worked for the *Sunpapers* in the 1930s. At the time I had no idea how the material would be used.

A 430-page history, *The Sunpapers of Baltimore,* had been published for the *Sun*'s centennial in 1937. The authors, all old *Sun* hands, were Gerald W. Johnson, Frank R. Kent, H. L. Mencken, and Hamilton Owens, with Mencken serving as general editor.

The possibility of republishing that history with a postscript encompassing the years 1937–1987 was rejected because the 1937 perspective would not be viable in 1987. A *Sun* chronicle limited to the years between 1937 and 1987 would lack a historical context. I suggested a new history covering 150 years. Schmick agreed, and so did Reg Murphy when he became president and publisher of the A. S. Abell Publishing Company in 1981. Neither made any suggestions or imposed any restrictions regarding the content or tone of the history. I had a free hand. I began writing the history after my retirement in December 1981.

I'm indebted to a great many people for their help. First to be thanked are those who through interviews or with letters, diaries, and dog-eared mementos retrieved from desk drawers and attics provided the sinews and soul of *Sun* history. They were fountainheads of great stories—enough for a separate book of anecdotes. They are named in the Sources at the end of this book.

A number of men and women deserve special thanks and mention:

The *Sun* Library staff, each and every one. It probably would have been an insurmountable task to produce this history without their help and the library's vast files. They were willing, resourceful, indefatigable. Illustrations for this book come from the *Sun* Library.

Darryl Hart, a doctoral student in American history at Johns Hopkins University, served as my researcher, skillfully ferreting out answers to my questions—and more.

Joseph R. L. Sterne, editorial-page editor of the *Sun*, John H. Plunkett, an assistant managing editor of the *Sun*, and Richard P. O'Mara, foreign editor of the *Sun*, agreed to read portions of the manuscript and made valuable suggestions.

Janice E. Dice, of the "TBS" staff of *The Baltimore Sun*, typed the finished manuscript, sometimes working at night and on weekends to meet deadlines.

James H. Bready, a member of the *Evening Sun* from 1945 to 1985 and amazingly steeped in *Sun* and Baltimore history, and Peggy Hoover, a copy editor for the Johns Hopkins University Press, edited the manuscript and immeasurably improved it.

And finally, the men and women of the Johns Hopkins University Press for their care and expertness in producing this book, with special thanks to Barbara Lamb, the managing editor, Nancy C. Essig, the assistant director, and, especially, J. G. Goellner, the director, for his guiding hand and encouragement every step of the way.

The Baltimore Sun,
1837–1987

ONE

---•---

The Beginnings
1837–1839

Arunah S. Abell's Baltimore *Sun,* the first penny paper in town, was only sixteen weeks old when with foresight and ingenuity Abell beat six established competitors on the biggest story of the day and, what is more significant, found ways to get the news faster.

His enterprise had Baltimoreans buzzing with excitement on September 6, 1837, when the *Sun* printed President Martin Van Buren's message to Congress in its entirety the day after it was delivered—an unprecedented feat. The 12,000-word message dealt with the nation's volatile commercial crisis, and to present it Abell shrewdly used all of pages one, two, and three of his four-page paper. On page four he explained: "The President's message, which will be found entire in this day's paper, was received in our office at 2 o'clock precisely—the transmission from Washington to Baltimore occupying less than two hours. Its great length has excluded almost everything previously prepared for publication. Advertisements crowded out will hereafter be attended to. We, of course, have neither time nor room for a word of comment upon this important document."

The President's message was important because it affected everyone. The Panic of 1837, the most severe in the history of the nation, had resulted in a tidal wave of inflation, forced banks to close, shut down factories and businesses, and put thousands out of work. Baltimoreans had been waiting impatiently and anxiously to learn what the President had said and what relief he might be able to promise. They wanted to read and study every word of the long message.

Abell, perhaps in his haste, did not point out these aspects of his enterprise: First, the *Sun* would probably be at least twenty-four hours ahead of its competitors. In those days the President's message was usually printed by a Washington, D.C., paper in the form of a circular and sent by mail to Baltimore and other out-of-town papers, which would imprint their own name plates before distributing it a day or two later. The *Sun* did note that the message had arrived in two hours, but failed to say that such speed was achieved by having its courier pick up the text at the Capitol and rush it to Baltimore by train, a novel and personal way of delivering news. (The Baltimore & Ohio Railroad [B&O] had completed its line to the nation's capital only two years earlier, and Abell was evidently one of the first to see its potential in communications.) And getting the 12,000-word message at 2:00 P.M. and having it set in type for the morning paper was an astounding achievement in itself. An undertaking of this scope would require forethought, precise planning, and organization. Abell undoubtedly had to hire extra compositors both inside and outside his small plant. Part of the President's message was set in a type size different from what the paper ordinarily used, which probably meant that it had been set in a job shop. These were the first of many ways in which Abell contrived to get the news out faster than his competitors.

Abell did even better on Tuesday, December 7, with another Van Buren message. That morning the *Sun* announced that it would get the President's message by railroad express and hoped to distribute Wednesday's paper that same afternoon. Consequently, a competitor, the Baltimore *Federal Gazette,* announced, "This will render it unnecessary for us to issue an extra, as formerly, at great inconvenience and expense."

According to reminiscences in the *Sun*'s fiftieth anniversary issue, the extra was produced this way: "Mr. Wilde brought the document to Baltimore on the 'William Cook' in one hour and seventeen minutes—making the actual time (by deducting four minutes for taking water) one hour and thirteen minutes, or 34 miles per hour." B&O trains were not permitted closer to the center of the city than Mount Clare Station in the western section. There the paper's messenger, "on a Canadian pony, nimble as a goat and fleet as the wind," met the special and raced with the message to the *Sun* office, "where 49 compositors stood ready at their cases for the 'takes' of copy." (Setting type was still a laborious hand craft. A compositor picked every tiny letter from a type case that was divided into upper- and lower-case letters and placed them in a composing stick held in one hand, justifying each line to make it flush on both sides. When the stick was full, he put the lines in a galley tray to draw a proof and make corrections of typographical errors. Finally he locked the columns in a form for printing. After the pages were printed the compositor had to disassemble the page, picking each letter from each line and replacing it in its slot in the case.) Papers came off the press a few minutes after 5:00 P.M. for "a tremendous crowd of persons, who had collected in and about our office, and a part of the carriers were enabled to supply their patrons with the paper before 9 o'clock that evening. Between 5 o'clock on Tuesday afternoon and 9 o'clock yesterday morning were delivered upwards of 15,000 copies." The venture cost Abell $600.

Abell was 31 years old when he published the first issue of the *Sun* on the morning of May 17, 1837. A photograph made in 1836 portrays him as shorter than his partners, with mutton-chop whiskers and a broad forehead; he was dressed in a cutaway and a waistcoat, flowing tie, and gray beaver. His expression was serious and resolute.

Little is known about the man himself. He did not write an autobiography or even keep a journal. None of his letters have turned up. The vanity biographical sketches of his time are littered with platitudes and reveal little of what Abell was really like. Many of the personal bits and pieces about his life come from the jottings of *Sun* men who heard about Abell from those who worked with him in his later years.

"The Abell Family in America," a genealogy, sets forth this family history: Arunah Shepherdson Abell was born in East Providence, Rhode Island, on August 10, 1806, the son of Caleb Abell and Elona (Shepherdson) Hodges and the seventh of nine children. The Abells were descended from Puritans who had settled in New England around 1630. His father had served in the War of 1812 as a quartermaster with the rank of captain and was a town clerk for fifty years. It was said of Caleb Abell, "He wrote a round distinct hand and the language is grammatical and terse."

At age 14, after a few years of plain schooling, Arunah became a clerk in a store owned by P. Bishop, a dealer in "West India Goods." But young Abell's ambition was to be a printer, and in October 1822 he was apprenticed by his father to the *Providence Patriot,* a Democratic journal of the Jeffersonian school. When his apprenticeship ended—known as "out of his time"—he journeyed to Boston, taking "a seat on the outside of the coach." With letters of introduction to two influential newspapermen, he got a job as a journeyman and before long became foreman of a printing shop.

About 1828, when he was 22 years old, the young Abell gravitated to New York, where printers were in demand. There he befriended two, Azariah H. Simmons, 21, a native of Connecticut, and William M. Swain, perhaps in his mid-twenties, a friend of Benjamin H. Day. Day had worked as a printer on the *Springfield Republican,* and in 1831 moved to New York at the age of 20. For two years he ran a printing shop, but business was never brisk. To take up the slack and attract attention, Day talked about publishing a penny paper. He knew about penny papers that had been tried in Boston and New York, and even though they had failed he thought he could succeed with one. Swain tried to dissuade him from risking money on such a venture, and Abell, who had met Day through Swain, ridiculed the idea. Years later Day recalled that in planning his paper he struck off a headline and showed it to Abell, who was working on the *Mercantile Advertiser.* "He made no end of fun of it," Day said. "Every time he met me he would say, 'Well, Day, how is that penny *Sun?* Ha, ha! Ho, ho!' His jokes on the penny *Sun* were eternal."

But Day was determined, and his New York *Sun* appeared on the morning of September 3, 1833. (Swain became foreman of its composing room.) The *Sun* was tiny compared to other papers, 7½ by 10 inches, less than the size of business stationery. Its four pages were packed with local happenings and accounts to titillate and shock the reader—stories of ghosts, monstrosities, miracles, murders, and, its most popular feature, humorous and crude descriptions of police court news patterned after the *London Morning Herald*'s reports of the Bow Street Court. Day hired as court reporter a printer whose vivid descriptions contributed so much to the success of the *Sun* that within a year Day made him a co-owner.

In 1833 most papers were still either mercantile or political and, since they were intended for people of means, usually conservative in their outlook. Mercantile papers—largely advertising—concentrated on trading and shipping news. They usually had the words "advertiser," "mercantile," or "commercial" in their titles. Political papers owed support and allegiance to a political party, a faction, or even a candidate. They emphasized a viewpoint and opinion rather than fact and news. Their editorials were partisan, personal, and quarrelsome. Penny papers stressed local news from the police, the courts, city government, and even social and cultural life. They made a point of being not only politically independent but even indifferent to politics.

The traditional papers were sold mainly by the year, $8 or $10 in advance, and cost more than a skilled worker earned in a week. Some were never sold as single copies. The papers were known as "six-pennies" or "fippennies," even though they cost 6¼ cents. The odd price resulted from a lack of standard coinage. Because the United States mint could not meet the needs of the rapidly expanding population, foreign coins were accepted as legal tender. British, Spanish, and Mexican coins were all welcomed for pocket change. The Spanish and Mexican half real were also known as a fippenny, or fip. The fip in Baltimore and Philadelphia, the sixpence in New York, and the picayune in New Orleans were worth 6¼ cents.

The penny paper emerged during the time of political, economic, social, and technological turmoil. Jacksonian Democracy had swept the nation, popularizing political equality and broadened economic opportunity. The labor and middle classes gained in power as mechanical inventions proliferated; cottage work gave way to factory work; towns turned into cities. With the spread of public schooling came more readers, more social awareness. In newspaper shops the cylinder press replaced hand-operated wooden and iron flatbed presses, and Henry Fourdrinier's papermaking machine reduced the price of newsprint. Faster means of communication gave more timeliness and immediacy to news, even news from great distances.

The penny press, as analyzed by Frank Luther Mott in his history of American journalism, was a revolutionary development. The first such paper in America was probably the *Cent* of Philadelphia, which appeared in 1830 but lasted only a few issues. The forerunners of the pennies were known as $4-a-year-papers. One of these was published in Portland, Maine, and several were published in Boston, between 1830 and 1833. In the summer of 1833, two Boston printers tried penny papers, but both soon suspended. They were probably trying to duplicate the success of the English *Penny Magazine,* founded in 1832, which within a year had a circulation of 160,000 and was reprinted in the United States. The first inexpensive paper in New York was started by Horace Greeley and a Dr. H. D. Shepard, who wanted a penny paper but were persuaded to charge two cents. Known as the *New York Post*, it appeared on January 1, 1833, but lasted only a short time, even though in its final days it sold for one cent.

Day's penny *Sun* was an immediate success. He had imported the "London plan" of circulation, by which newsboys both hawked the paper on the street and delivered it to homes on a route system. Because Day charged subscribers less for cash, he got circulation money in advance. In fourteen months he was selling 10,000 papers a day; in less than two years, 15,000; within four years, 30,000. Mercantile and political papers averaged fewer than 1,200 copies daily.

Day's example inspired printers to found rival papers, particularly in New York, where at least twelve started up between 1833 and 1837, some lasting only a few weeks. The most important, and the *Sun*'s direct competitor, was James Gordon Bennett's *Morning Herald,* appearing on May 6, 1835. Bennett was a cut above the ordinary entrepreneur. He was not a printer, but a reporter, a Washington correspondent, and a news editor. Putting out a paper of his own, Bennett then initiated personal journalism, becoming as well known to readers as his paper. The *Herald* offered better and broader coverage of the city than the *Sun* did, objective political reporting, national and international news, and a money column that Bennett wrote about Wall Street, forerunner of the financial page. The *Herald* also featured theatrical and social chitchat and sensational crime stories covering the courts, reproducing testimony in question-and-answer fashion. The *Herald* dubbed itself "spicy" and "saucy," and it was that and more. In addition, Bennett made himself notorious by writing about himself and his exploits.

Impressed with the success of the *Sun,* the *Herald,* and another penny paper, the *Transcript,* Abell, Swain, and Simmons talked about starting one of their own. Swain and Simmons wanted to publish it in New York, but Abell, believing that market too competitive, proposed Philadelphia, and they assented. Simmons had become a proprietor of the *New York Morning Star,* a new paper; Swain was making $12 a week as foreman at the *Sun;* and Abell, a printer, was making less than that. But with the plentiful paper money of "wildcat" banks (between 1835 and 1837 some $80,000,000 was circulated), venture capital was available for those risking new enterprises.

On February 29—Leap Year Day—1836, the three partners signed a twenty-one-line agreement in New York to publish a daily paper in Philadelphia that was "neutral in politics": "Said parties are to appropriate each an equal amount in money and are each to devote his time and energy either as printer or in such other capacity as shall be deemed most conducive to the interest of said firm, to the commencement, establishment and success of said paper. In case of a difference of opinion with regard to any measure of policy to be pursued, not expressed above, the views of two shall be the governing principle." Years later, this framed agreement hung in Abell's home.

Their capital was $1,033.37, each partner putting up less than $350. The paper was to be called the *Times* and to sell for one cent, but the name was deemed inappropriate because a paper so named had just failed. At Abell's suggestion, the *Public Ledger* was the name adopted. The first issue, printed on a hand press, 15½ by 21½ inches in size, four columns to a page, appeared on March 25, 1836. Its objectives were expressed in an "Opening Address":

> . . . to render it a vehicle of general and useful intelligence, adapted to the wants and interests of the community generally. While its cheapness places it within reach of the poorest artisan or laborer, we shall endeavor to furnish to the merchant and manufacturer the earliest and most useful information relating to their respective interests. . . . We shall give place to no religious discussions, nor to political discussions involving questions of merely partisan character. The *Ledger* will worship no men, and be devoted to no parties. On all political principles and questions involving the common good it will speak freely, yet temperately. The common good is its object, and in seeking this object it will have special regard to the moral and intellectual improvement of the laboring classes, the great sinew of all civilized communities. While this paper shall worship no man, it shall vituperate none. It will be fearless and independent, applauding virtue and reproving vice whenever found, unawed by station, uninfluenced by wealth.

An early account said the *Public Ledger* was "coldly received and two of the partners became so discouraged as to propose to discontinue publication," but Abell argued so strenuously for holding on at least until their money was gone that they did persevere. Gradually the paper got readers, and before long it bought its struggling rival, the *Transcript*. The *Public Ledger* had little local news except for lurid police reports and other sensational matter. The traditional Philadelphia papers denounced it as "that virulent little sheet." There were libel suits, which at least helped circulation. In editorials the paper denounced local abuses and supported Catholics when their churches were burned during the Know-Nothing riots. Swain was the editor, a hardworking man who supposedly read every word that went into the paper. Abell and Simmons probably were the printers and handymen.

At the end of the first year, Abell proposed that they start a paper in Baltimore. Swain and Simmons, although less than enthusiastic, agreed. Abell visited Baltimore for the first time in April 1837 (the trip by coach took nine-and-a-half hours), bringing letters of introduction to Baltimore editors. They told Abell that the town was overcrowded with six-pennies, but Abell liked what he saw and in short order convinced his partners to put up their share of the venture. Here were three young printers of limited means, just a little more than a year from New York composing rooms, enterprising and daring enough to start their second paper in a town that two had never seen and the third had visited for less than seven weeks. Because Abell had pushed for the second paper, his partners made him responsible for it, although

Simmons came to Baltimore to help get it under way. The preparations took about seven weeks, in which Abell surveyed the town, assessed its possibilities and limitations, rented an office, hired printers and other staff, secured a press, equipment, and paper, solicited advertising, and attended to perhaps hundreds of other details, routine and unforeseen.

On Wednesday, May 17, 1837, the *Sun* appeared. The logotype resembled that of the New York *Sun*. The paper was four pages, each four columns wide, 13½ by 9 inches, somewhat smaller than today's tabloid size, printed on rag paper. The price was one cent.

The *Sun*'s reason for publication and what it hoped to accomplish were specified in a declaration "TO THE PUBLIC," on page two, more than a column-and-a-half long. The last paragraph was the most significant:

> We shall give no place to religious controversy, nor to political discussions of merely partisan character. On political principles, and questions involving the interest or honor of the whole country, it will be free, firm and temperate. Our object will be the common good, without regard to that of sects, factions or parties; and for this object we shall labor without fear or partiality. The publication of this paper will be continued for *one year at least,* and the publishers hope to receive, as they will try to deserve, a liberal support.

The reference to "one year at least" might have been an Abell nudge for his partners to recall their timidity in the first year of the *Public Ledger.* The statement was similar in tone and philosophy to that announcing their first paper, but there were more references to the successes of the penny paper.

Baltimore had been selected because it "offers a favorable prospect to a new paper, upon a foundation different from that of the papers already established here." The *Sun* continued, "With the numerous and ably conducted papers of this city, the affluent are well supplied. . . . But, as in all the northern cities, a large portion of our population, with a laudable desire of knowledge, have not access to that fertile source of improvement, a newspaper." The answer, said the *Sun,* was to be found in the penny press. It referred to the beginnings of the penny press in England and subsequently in New York and Philadelphia, adding, "We have resolved upon the experiment of publishing a penny paper, entitled '*THE SUN.*' . . . We shall strive to render it a channel of useful information to every citizen in every department of society . . . whether literary, professional, mercantile, manufacturing or miscellaneous."

And a channel of useful information it was, that Wednesday. At the top of the right-hand column on page one was a report on the City Council's extraordinary session on Monday afternoon. The two branches authorized the issue of city scrip not to exceed $100,000 to supply change in the absence of real coin in sums of 5 cents, 10 cents, 25 cents, 50 cents, one dollar, and two dollars. This was important because gold and silver had practically disappeared from circulation. On May 10, New York banks had suspended specie payments, followed by about 800 other banks, including those in Baltimore on

May 12. Gold and silver were scarce because of the financial panic sweeping the nation. The *Sun* was telling its readers how they could pay bills and buy groceries.

There were six other local items. Two dealt with specie. The Post Office, on orders from the Postmaster General, could accept nothing but specie for postage, and "The Messrs. Cohen of this city have not suspended specie payment. They say that they are abundantly able to redeem all their bills, and will do so." News included a fire on Monday night at the coach manufactory of Mr. William Simpson, North Calvert Street, in which numerous coaches were destroyed; the Maryland Jockey Club races, which began the day before, with $9,000 going to the winner of the Dorsey Stakes; the arrival of Mr. Pontis, "minister of the King of the French at Washington," on his way north, and a favorable mention of Marden's scale's, which were advertised. It listed one marriage, three deaths, and marine intelligence, including the arrival of the "Brig Dido, 29 days from Rio Nunez, coast of Africa, 116 days from the Cape de Verde Islands, hides, ivory, camwood, &c. to J. I. Corner."

One-paragraph items mentioned the proclamation for an extra session of Congress, and the visit of Colonel R. M. Johnson, the Vice President of the United States, to General Andrew Jackson, the former President, at the Hermitage, Jackson's home in Tennessee. Eight items came by Northern Express Mail. The New York Stock market list for Monday included fifteen stocks for banks, trusts, railroads, the Morris Canal, and an insurance company. Specie was bringing an 8 to 10 percent premium, and "uncurrent money" a discount of up to 2.5 percent.

Much of the reading material was similar to that in other papers. Page one had a poem, "O Fairest of the Rural Maids." Other papers were quoted at length: the *New York Gazette* on Paganini, "the greatest prodigy that ever touched a violin" and his anticipated visit to the United States, the *Norfolk Beacon* on Indians, the *New York Star*'s spoof on domestic life, and the *New York American* on a 9-year-old "from the West Indies whose head measured 31 inches in circumference and 23 inches from ear to ear over the crown, the weight being 50 pounds." Though it also quoted from the *London Herald,* the *Sun* apologized for its limited selections: "Being new in the field, we of course have not yet established an exchange list, and cannot make our sheet so varied as we could wish. In a few days, however, the evil will be remedied, and we doubt not that we shall then be found quite as interesting as our neighbors."

Nearly two of the four pages were filled with ads—for the B&O Railroad, West Nottingham Academy, carriages, stoves, parasols, shovels, nails, segars, carpeting, butter boxes "in which butter may be transported with perfect safety by land or water," and a patent husk-splitter, "a very valuable and useful machine for splitting corn husks into fine fibres for mattresses." Most of the ads, though, were for palliatives and nostrums. Brandreth, with two offices in the small downtown area, sold vegetable universal pills, and Dr. William Evans dispensed medicine for dyspepsia and "hypochondriasm." They were the biggest advertisers.

The first issue, Vol. 1, No. 1, is a rarity today. The Library of Congress was consulted so often about copies of this issue which turned out to be reprints that it prepared a circular telling how to determine the difference: On page one of the original the last paragraph in the second column begins "The Public Hotels in New York . . ." and the last paragraph in the third column begins "The Mayor of New York. . . ." In reprints the two paragraphs are both in the third column, "The Public Hotels in New York" being at the bottom. One of the reprints is identified by the word "facsimile," but the reprint made in 1887 on the *Sun*'s fiftieth anniversary is not.

The *Sun* office, next to a stove manufacturer, was at 21 Light Street, a block below Market (later Baltimore) Street. Type was set by hand in lamplight, and the paper was printed on a single-cylinder hand-cranked Napier press with a capacity of 1,000 copies an hour. The *Sun* boasted that its first printing consisted of 15,000 "specimen" copies, which were then distributed to nearly every doorstep. Pressmen had to turn the press for fifteen hours. Abell advertised for "eight to ten sturdy men" as carriers and "active, thorough-going boys" to hawk the paper on the street. He was following the "London plan," which Day had introduced in New York. It was unique for Baltimore, both in newsboy street sales and in getting vendors to set up an independent carrier system. Other papers had apprentice printers deliver papers to subscribers. They were not paid for this, but traditionally on New Year's Day subscribers gave "a small pecuniary gratuity which in aggregate amounted to a snug equivalent for his labor. To evade the unpleasantness of personal solicitation" a rhymester printer would furnish a string of verses that coyly requested a gift.

On Thursday, Friday, and Saturday, the *Sun* repeated its long statement "To THE PUBLIC." The first cultural note was a paragraph on the performance of *Macbeth* at the Opera House to a "very intelligent and discriminating audience." Ads began appearing on page one on Monday, the same day the paper began reporting city court proceedings in the humorous but crude manner of the New York *Sun,* lampooning blacks and especially the Irish. The court was described as "a motley congregation of people who had assembled either to be tried themselves for petty offenses, or to witness the disgrace of their more indiscreet and unfortunate neighbors." One was "a small matter of difficulty between two colored gemmen." Another involved a domestic case: "Mrs. Day, an Irishwoman, neat and respectable in her appearance, came to enter a complaint against her husband, a gentleman also from the *ould* country, a weaver by profession and a brute by practice. He had treated her with great unkindness, and neglected all the soft and tender offices of love." The report ended:

Prosecuting attorney: Did you kick her?
Accused: O yes, I kicked her.
Court: Stand aside.
(*Accused bowed low and retired.*)

The court report, usually two columns long, got more space than any other news—even the first live event the *Sun* covered, a meeting of 10,000 to 15,000 citizens in Monument Square to listen to speakers discuss the banking and paper currency quandary. The reporter described at length the "brilliant, lucid and eloquent" talks, "blended with unanswerable arguments," but gave almost nothing of the content.

In these first days, editorials and news accounts, national and local, dwelt on the specie question ("We are a bankrupt nation"), land speculation, comment and letters about Harriet Martineau (an English novelist-economist who had written a book about the United States and was going to write about her travels on her next visit), and the burning of the steamboat *Ben Sherrod* with 200 passengers on board when it raced with the *Prairie* on the Mississippi. The accident occurred, the *Sun* reported in a censuring tone, after the crew was encouraged to drink whiskey as an inducement to maintain excessive fires in the boilers. It printed a number of editorials on temperance.

On June 13, less than a month after it began publication, the *Sun* published its first letter "From our Correspondent" in Washington, D.C. "Without intending to violate the Sabbath," it began, "I avail myself of this moment to drop you a line by a friend who is leaving here early in the morning for Baltimore." The dispatch dealt with mandamus proceedings against the Postmaster General, to compel him to accept banknotes instead of specie at the post offices, although this was not clear in the article. The report concluded:

> The city is exceedingly dull; the hotels and boarding houses are empty and all hands are looking forward for the commencement of the extra session, with the hope that it will relieve them from all embarrassment. The new furniture of the Palace is now going in. It is very splendid, and I am happy to say is of American manufacture. You will recollect that the late Mr. Monroe raised a breeze by importing his chairs from England. The President is well and, for aught I know, is happy. Yours truly.

Though not signed, the letter was written by James Lawrenson, a Post Office Department clerk. Before long he was writing once or twice a week, and he continued until the Civil War.

Abell had many obstacles to overcome with the President's message of 1839, which was delayed day after day because of "squabbling among the members" of Congress. On December 6 the paper warned: "The President's message of last year has been clandestinely reprinted at the office of one of the New York papers, and hawked about the streets by the boys as the real message of this year. Look out for such tricks. The true document will be delivered to our desk—that is, if it ever be delivered in Washington."

The *Sun* finally received the message, but it had to publish its first extra—on Christmas Day! Van Buren delivered the message on Monday, December 23, and the *Sun* expected the text by train that afternoon. But a windstorm, "which had almost blown the dome off the rotunda," was followed by a snowstorm that blocked all traffic. Abell realized that the message would not arrive until Christmas Eve. In anticipation of its arrival, extra printers were rounded up from other shops. Abell waited and waited and at "midnight dismissed our hands."

> We had scarcely navigated as far as the depot, when the jingling bells of a car were heard, and as the clock struck one we received our copies of the message. By this time every printer had gone to bed . . . dreaming of eggnog and a Christmas holiday. Scouts—fellows who are not afraid of a drop too much—were sent out and after wallowing in gutters and floundering through snow drifts, until they were drenching, they succeeded in disturbing the repose of some score of families and collecting some 17 compositors from different quarters of the city.

By 7:00 A.M. "an immense edition" was on the press. Then the forms were taken back to the composing room "for the purpose of making alterations necessary for printing the extras ordered by a large number of our country contemporaries, the inner form was knocked into pi [type mixed together indiscriminately] and we were left with an awkward predicament. Grieving, however, would not mend the matter and we succeeded yesterday [December 26] in obtaining the assistance of other offices, by which we were able to overcome the difficulties."

On its fiftieth anniversary, the *Sun* recalled that when it began it had "but eight men in all departments, exclusive of the editorial." Abell was editor, probably business manager, circulation director, and possibly a printer too. He was a no-nonsense man, and a week after his paper began it was clear that he considered himself an experienced, tough editor, judging from this item: "Individual who forwarded an 'Ode to the *Sun*' to this office for publication is informed that his attempt did not succeed. If he wishes to impose upon us he must study a little originality, and get up rather early in the morning. We are not so young with the press as not to be familiar with all the acts that are attempted to be practiced on it by asses."

In a book of not-always-reliable reminiscences published in 1877, John H. Hewitt, a poet-musician and editor, claimed that John D. Reed, "a man of very ordinary talent," was

> attached to the *Sun* from the day of its first issue up to the time of his death; generally in the capacity of reporter attending mostly to court cases. He was 61 years of age when he died and did not "die in harness," as some papers stated; but, more probably broke down in harness. In his later years he became almost useless to the *Sun* establishment, the duties of his department requiring younger and more active men. Mr. Abell, the proprietor, assigned him to no particular station, but allowed him to be at the office and come and go when he pleased,

leaving orders that he should receive his pay regularly. Reed was sincerely attached to the journal that carried him along, and bitter against its rival establishment, the *Clipper.* He fought many a hard battle.

If Hewitt was correct, Reed was the *Sun*'s first reporter and must have been more highly regarded by Abell than by Hewitt. One of the first reporters disappeared, according to a note in the December 6, 1837, issue: "One of our reporters a few days since reported himself as having been taken up the night before, and put in the watch house, for getting drunk and trying to break into a porter house to get more liquor, and what is more singular, has not been here since to correct the error."

In those days printers not only set type but also selected items from exchange papers to put into type. News items were often gathered by the editor by chance, not by design, or were handed to him by outsiders who had an interest in a particular event. The first reporters concentrated on covering courts for human interest stories, imitating the *New York Sun.* Gradually they widened their coverage to include police stations, city government, business, churches, and cultural and other news, following the lead of Bennett's *New York Herald,* a pioneer in directing reporters to systematically uncover news and write about it objectively. At first the work of the *Sun*'s reporters was typical of the time— casual and haphazard. In his account of the City Council action authorizing city scrip, the reporter wrote that an amendment "was offered by a member whose name we could not learn." At another meeting he concluded, "For want of time and room we are compelled to omit for the day the further report of the proceedings of the City Council, which by the way were not of unusual importance." But through trial and error and the need to be competitive, the reporting improved. When a devastating thunderstorm flooded Jones Falls in June 1837, inundating a large section of the town, taking nearly twenty lives, some squatters, the *Sun* was able to identify a number of those lost and the circumstances of their deaths and give a factual, graphic account of the damage in two-and-a-half columns, noting that water in the Presbyterian church rose to the cushion in the pulpit seat.

The *Sun* competed with seven or more dailies, seven weeklies, five semi-weeklies and two monthlies. Most of the dailies had been published for at least eighteen years. The *Federal Gazette* was forty-six years old. The *American and Commercial Daily Advertiser,* thirty-eight years old, was the most prestigious paper. In addition to covering city affairs, it had an entree to the social life— tea parties and formal dinners—that the *Sun* did not have. The others were the *Patriot,* the *Chronicle,* the *Transcript,* and the *Republican.* All were "six-pennies," selling for a fip, six times the cost of the *Sun.* They were also known as "blanket sheets" because of their size. (The *New York Journal of Commerce* was 35 inches wide and 58 inches high; when opened it was about 6 feet across.)

Eight days after the *Sun* appeared, another daily paper started. Abell welcomed it, at the same time chiding his competitors, "In obedience to that well known maxim of the press, which teaches that we should treat new candidates for public favor with courtesy and kindness, instead of a jealous and envious disposition, we announce a new paper by Gen. Duff Green, called the *Merchant*. It is of the largest class of city newspapers published at $8 a year and as its title indicates is devoted to the interests of *political* merchants." Two days later, in an editorial on the penny press, the *Sun* took a harder line on the established papers: "Since we commenced operations in Baltimore, our sheet has been noticed by all the papers of the city excepting two." It was annoyed that its competitors demeaned it by referring to it as a "little daily" and "a paper of the penny tribe." The *Sun* described the penny press—with this aside:

> We do not of course speak of the *Sun* in this instance, for we are not capable of so much egotism—without an exception, sustained with more spirit, managed with more industry, regulated by nobler principles and desires, guided by a purer morality, conducted with a better feeling, and propelled by a loftier talent, than its contemporaries of the larger size, and which, by the way, too often estimates its utility and morality, and talent, not by the quantity and quality of the matter it contains, but by the number of square feet of paper that is spread over its surface.

Then, at length, it attacked its competitors as lacking independence, owing their existence to a party—"prostrated, prostituted, enslaved, disgraced."

The *Sun* was soon boasting about its circulation. The day it began it had "to double its corps of carriers." Then on June 19, in an item headed "Great Edition," it proclaimed: "The largest edition ever issued from any newspaper press in the city of Baltimore was issued from the *Sun* office on Saturday and disposed of before 10 o'clock in the forenoon. The success of the *Sun* is unparalleled. What a field for advertisers." In February 1838 it claimed that its circulation was 11,000, "three times that of any Baltimore paper," adding that it was read mainly by the "mechanic class." Later it offered a $1,000 forfeit if it did not print daily as many copies as all other Baltimore dailies combined.

Growth pushed the *Sun* on February 16, 1838, into larger quarters at the southeast corner of Gay and Baltimore streets, closer to the center of the city. Five dailies were on Gay Street, and another was nearby. In announcing its move, the *Sun* made punning reference to five of them: "While we give a transcript of all that is of interest to an American and endeavor to aid the patriot, we hope we shall never chronicle what will injure the hopes of a true republican."

Abell operated a job shop in conjunction with his newspaper, and on April 15, 1838, he introduced the *Weekly Sun*, "containing all the domestic news of the week, foreign intelligence by the Great Western, Review of the Market, Prices current, Communications, Miscellany, Poetry, &c. Subscription $1.50, always in advance." Later it solicited original stories, offering prizes ranging from $300 to $1,000.

The year 1837 was not a propitious time for a new business—newspaper or other. The nation was struggling through another financial crisis of the machine-production age. The first was in 1819, the second in 1829. The third, of 1837, would drag on for several years. It was caused by inflated land values, speculation, wildcat banking, collapse of state banks, and suspension of specie. In some cities there were bread riots. Prices jumped unbelievably. For example, flour went from $5 to $11 a barrel. "Best" beef cost ten cents a pound. Those who had jobs worked fourteen hours a day, six days a week, often for only $1 or $2 a day. Many were paid in wildcat money of dubious value, called "foul rags" or "shinplasters."

Baltimoreans remembered the violence that followed the bank failures of 1835, when the "Bank of Maryland mob" ransacked the homes of bank trustees, burning furniture and books, and set fires at the Athenaeum and the Maryland Academy of Fine Arts in five days of rioting. Volunteer fire department quarrels, labor protests, and elections often resulted in riots erupting in destruction and death. White mobs on occasion attacked blacks to drive them from their homes and their jobs in the shipyards. Baltimore's nickname was "Mobtown."

But in the city's early days and those turbulent times, the population increased through immigration from Germany and Ireland and the influx of rural families seeking urban employment: from 35,000 in 1810, to 62,000 in 1830, to 90,000 in 1837 and 102,000 by 1840. Its growth was even more spectacular when measured between 1837 and 1860: It doubled its population, its work force, the number of houses, its built-up area, and its street mileage. About the time the *Sun* appeared, one-third or more of the population had been born in Germany or Ireland or were Afro-American. This mix gave the city the characteristics of both a northern and a southern city. According to the census of 1840, Baltimore still had about 3,000 slaves (with nearly 90,000 in Maryland, most of them on the Eastern Shore and in the southern counties). The city still carried on slave trading with the South. Many of the Baltimore slaves worked as house servants or artisans and craftsmen. Some hired themselves out, paying part of their wages to their owner. With what they could keep they provided their own food and quarters. At times as many as two-thirds of the prisoners in the penitentiary were black. To control the number, a state law stipulated that second offenders could be sold into slavery and shipped out of state. In her history of Baltimore, Sherry H. Olson also said that without judicial proceedings masters could privately take their black servants and slaves to the city jail to be whipped.

The overgrown village of 1729 had spread out from the waterfront. In retrospective view, the *Sun*, on its fiftieth anniversary, described the Baltimore of 1837 this way:

On Calvert Street its houses did not extend beyond Madison Street, at which point commenced Howard's Woods, extending back to the Belvidere estate of Col. John Eager Howard and westward to Cathedral Street, blocking progress in both directions. Paca and Lexington streets was the limit to the northwest. Of that part of the city known as Southwest Baltimore, as well as of the area west of Poppleton and Franklin streets and south to Spring Gardens, the whole was open fields and marsh lands. Across the Basin, from Federal Hill south to Fort McHenry, was vacant land except by the waterside. Eastward there were no houses beyond Baltimore Street and Broadway, nor any buildings north of the falls.

The most prosperous lived in the north central section. The *Sun* recalled that the houses had "large brass knockers which, when used, would wake the whole neighborhood. This was before door bells and gas were fashionable. Bootblack Henry Jakes every morning made his calls at doors of his customers for boots placed there the night before." After he married, Abell lived at 42 North Front Street, between Baltimore and Lexington streets, east of the Fallsway. Shipbuilders and dockworkers lived around Fells Point, laborers and wagoners in the central section, free blacks and slaves south of the city in wooden shacks.

Houses and commercial buildings had two or three stories. The low skyline was broken by shot towers, the Byzantine dome of the Cathedral, and the graceful Doric pillar of the Washington Monument. The monument had been planned for a square surrounded by mansions owned by aristocrats, but it was feared that the 180-foot tower, the tallest in the nation, might topple and crush the houses, so the monument was placed on a ridge in Howard's Woods.

The port bustled with a prosperous South American trade, exporting flour for coffee, and grain and flour going to Liverpool and Bremen—a busy, diversified trade in the Chesapeake Bay and up and down the coast. More than 2,000 vessels, mostly sail, were engaged in the coastal trade. Baltimore-built vessels were in demand here and abroad, including sloops of war for South American republics. The expanding B&O and Baltimore and Susquehanna railroads carried Baltimore goods north and west. Manufacturing was diversified. The immense water power of Jones Falls drove seventy-seven mills. The city had iron foundries; chemical, copper, and glass works; brick kilns; and factories that made agricultural implements, coaches, coach fringe and lace, carpets, soap, candles, combs, and castor oil. Unscrupulous operators, capitalizing on the profitable guano (bird manure) imported from Peru for truck farmers, sold guano-colored earth from Hampstead Hill. Factories were clustered on the periphery of the port, smaller ones on "work" streets such as Pratt, Howard, Fleet, and Central, and Pennsylvania and Fremont avenues. Cottage work shops mushroomed in lanes and alleys, where the working people lived.

Cobbled thoroughfares and muddy side streets were crowded. Edward Sachse's lithograph of the 1850s still shows Baltimore (Market) Street with a stage coach, Conestoga wagon, stylish vehicles, drays, and carts. Busy streets were used for herding cattle and swine through town. Water came from 800 town pumps. Used water and slop jars were dumped in the streets. When it rained, pedestrians crossed at intersections on raised stepping stones. Intestinal diseases, especially in the hot months, took many lives. The "night watch," established in 1775, was still the only police force. Watchmen strolled the streets with lanterns, calling out the quarter-hour from 10:00 P.M. until daybreak. The cry "12 o'clock and all is well" was heard until 1843, when the *Sun* explained that such a practice alerted thieves "and other evil-disposed persons" and made it easy for them to go where the watchmen were not. At the *Sun*'s suggestion the practice was abandoned.

In this town Abell had selected, his paper was an immediate success, with influence beyond Baltimore. With three other leading penny papers it had attracted a new audience reaching all corners of society. Frank Luther Mott, the newspaper historian, observed: "the great and influential penny dailies of the '30s were the *Sun* and the *Herald* in New York, the *Philadelphia Public Ledger,* and the Baltimore *Sun.* . . . What these papers did, primarily, was to make newspaper readers of a whole economic class which the six-cent dailies had scarcely touched. They enlarged America's newspaper-reading tremendously. This constituted a great societal change."

A year-and-a-half after the *Sun* began, and after unremitting work on his part, Abell, at the age of 33, took time on December 23, 1839, to marry a widow, Mrs. Mary (Fox) Campbell, a native of Philadelphia who had moved to Baltimore. Although he was not a Catholic (he remained "somewhat vaguely" a Protestant), they were married with all formalities by Archbishop Francis A. Kendrick in Philadelphia. Abell had met Mrs. Campbell by rescuing her daughter Rose from being run over by an out-of-control wagon.

TWO

Enterprise and the War
1841–1858

Because of Abell's drive to get news faster than traditional methods, and with Baltimore's proximity to Washington, D.C., it was expedient for him to supply news from the nation's capital and the South to the *Public Ledger,* allied through identical ownership, and at the same time to New York papers, because they in turn could relay news from the north and from abroad more quickly than the spotty mails. This was one of the first, if not the first, sustained and extensive systems of swift cooperative news-gathering. It was ingenious and costly, involving complicated combinations of pony express, four-horse post coaches, special locomotives, chartered ships—even carrier pigeons at times—linked when possible to the slowly expanding lines of the magnetic telegraph. Men conveying the news made heroic efforts battling winter storms, floods, and other obstacles and dangers. In those precedent-setting times, which changed the nature and significance of news, Abell was an innovator and a leader.

The *Sun* forwarded President William Henry Harrison's inaugural address of March 4, 1841, to Philadelphia and New York faster than any presidential message had ever been delivered. It was presented at noon. The *Sun* had it on a special train by 12:45 P.M. An hour-and-a-quarter later it was in Baltimore and the *Sun* published an extra. Meeting the train at the Mount Clare depot on the edge of town was "a most distinguished express rider" who took the packages for Philadelphia and New York to the Canton depot on the eastern side of town, where another special locomotive waited. The packages arrived in Philadelphia at 6:00 P.M. Because the railroad did not extend to New York, the rest of the journey was made by horse express. The *Sun*'s special delivery beat the mails by more than twenty-four hours.

The *Sun* not only cooperated in news-gathering, it also, like other resourceful papers, sold copies of its extras to its exchange papers in Maryland, Ohio, and Kentucky. These supplements enabled those papers to beat their competitors by a day or more. Finding it difficult to believe how quickly President Harrison's message had appeared in print, the *Cincinnati Advertiser* thought the *Sun* extra might be a hoax, claiming that it sounded like the President's stump speeches. (Newspaper hoaxes were not uncommon, and readers were wary of unexpected news. On April 1 a Boston paper proclaimed a major victory by U.S. forces in the Mexican War. Previous dispatches had implied that the same units might be annihilated. Readers did not believe the good news, accusing the paper of an April Fools' Day joke. What is often thought of as the greatest newspaper hoax was perpetrated in 1835 by the *New York Sun*. In a four-part front-page series it described life on the moon as seen through an immense new telescope. In absorbing detail it portrayed flora and fauna, "strange amphibious creatures of a spherical form," and "man-bat inhabitants." The articles created a sensation, sending circulation soaring. Yale University sent professors to the paper for more information. The series concluded with a report that the telescope had suddenly shattered, ending the observations.)

The *Sun* not only printed supplements for its exchanges; on at least one occasion it also bought one from the *Washington Union* containing a long official message from President James K. Polk; it sold these on the street while preparing its own extra. *Sun* presses then ran for seven hours to supply the fifteen or twenty papers in its exchange network. Unlikely to meet his rail and mail deadlines for lack of composing room personnel, Abell once recruited actors from a troupe at the Holliday Street Theater, actors who were former printers. Later, anticipating an extra with news from England on the volatile Oregon Territory question, the paper announced: "Agents of the *Sun* in different cities who desire to be furnished with extras containing the news should send in their orders immediately." And then, showing enterprise in still another way, it added, "The immense additional circulation, through the neighboring cities, as well as the West and South . . . will render it unusually important to our merchants and business men to [advertise in the extra]."

In October 1841 the *Sun* arranged for special coverage of the Alexander McLeod trial in Utica, New York. Great Britain had threatened war if McLeod were convicted. A Canadian citizen, he had been accused of murder during a rebellion in Canada and had escaped to the United States. England demanded his return; the United States refused. McLeod was acquitted—it turned out that he was not involved, just a braggart—and the war cloud disappeared.

Although the *Sun* boasted about beating its competitors, claiming, "Never before was there brought to this city from so great a distance so large a quantity of original reporting," the trial report undoubtedly came from the *New York Sun,* which had run a special train from Utica to Schenectady and a horse express to the Albany–New York boat. Then the route was by horse express to Philadelphia and by train to Baltimore.

On other occasions the *New York Sun* used carrier pigeons to fly bulletins from Washington, Albany, and the environs of New York City with slips of tissue paper under their wings. That paper said some of its flock had been used by the *London Morning Chronicle* to carry news from Dublin and Paris. The Baltimore *Sun* also had carrier pigeons. In his *History of Baltimore City and County,* J. Thomas Scharf wrote: "Mr. Abell organized a carrier pigeon express for the transmission of news between the cities of New York, Philadelphia, Baltimore and Washington. The pigeons for this service, about 400 or 500 in number, were kept in a house on Hampstead Hill, near the old Maryland Hospital for the Insane, and were carefully trained."

In January 1846 the *Sun* was the first to inform the President of the United States and congressional leaders that the British ministry of Sir John Peel had unexpectedly resigned. The event had commercial overtones. Peel favored free trade; his successor might be a protectionist. The news was being carried by the ship *Liberty,* and to get it even before it docked in Boston, the *New York Herald*'s fast dispatch boat met the ship 100 miles offshore and rushed the bundles of British newspapers to New York. The *Sun*'s "extraordinary express" brought copies of the papers to Baltimore, and the *Sun* immediately "threw off an Exclusive Extra considerably in advance of the mails." Characteristic of the time, the resignation story was secondary in the play given it to a breathless account of how the *Sun* got the story, and to a repetition of Abell's dedication: "We thus present our claim to a sleepless enterprise before the citizens of Baltimore, in whose interests we are engaged." After the extra was printed,

> The intelligence was thrown into an abridged form and dispatched from this office to Mr. Polk, the President of the United States, the President of the Senate, the Speaker of the House of Representatives, and other distinguished gentlemen, through the agency of the magnetic telegraph.
>
> In consideration of the importance of the news, Mr. Woodside, the energetic superintendent of the Baltimore and Ohio Railroad, consented to run down a locomotive to Washington with a large package of the Extra *Sun,* for the convenience of the Government, the Departments, and the citizens of the District generally, and thus we have enjoyed the gratification, though at an outlay far beyond what such an enterprise can possibly compensate in a mere pecuniary point of view, of contributing to the relief of that anxiety which prevails at this period with reference to foreign intelligence.

When war threatened between the United States and Great Britain over the Oregon Territory, stretching from the Rockies to the Pacific and from Mexican California to Russian Alaska, sixteen papers, dubbed the "Holy Alliance" by a paper excluded from the group, set up the Halifax Express. Halifax was the first port of call for mail steamers from Liverpool, and the Express was formed to outrace the steamers to Boston and New York. A horse express would travel the 130 miles across Nova Scotia to Annapolis on the Bay of Fundy. There a steamer with a handpicked crew would carry the bundles of British papers to Portland, Maine, where a locomotive express would take them to Boston.

Then it would be by rail to New York, horse express again to Philadelphia, and rail to Baltimore. The 1,070 miles were to be covered in fifty-five hours.

The *Sun* was the only Baltimore paper enrolled in the cooperative. Anxiously, late in February 1846, staff members awaited arrival of the first express, bearing London newspapers from the mail steamer *Cambria*. The *Sun* averred that "the news will be the most important in years." First word from the *Cambria,* though, came not from the Halifax Express but from another newspaper express and the stouthearted efforts of a Captain Wolfe, in charge of the *Sun*'s chartered locomotive. The *Philadelphia United States Gazette* had set up its own express to connect with the steamer when it docked in Boston. When the rival relay was the first to reach Philadelphia, Wolfe, who had been waiting for the Halifax Express, grabbed a bundle of English papers and sped off at 8:00 P.M. "in the greatest storm of the season." "The impediment to the track from the mass of snow and slush," the *Sun* reported, "compelled him to abandon the locomotive within a few miles of the city, and he finished the task on foot," arriving at 3:00 A.M.

Before dawn, the *Sun* had an extra on the street. It printed a second extra when the package from the Halifax Express arrived. As told by George Ormiston, who devised and managed that news relay, it was one of the stirring sagas of the time in newspaper enterprise: British authorities in Halifax, informed of his plan, were hostile, reflecting the tension over the Oregon dispute, "so much so," he wrote afterward in a letter printed in the *Sun,* "that I began to fear even for my personal liberty." Not finding the proper harness for his horses, he had to have them made to order.

When the *Cambria* docked at Halifax, the port captain hailed her captain, Judkins, and told him to prevent all papers and letters from being landed without permission. Ormiston, who was not allowed on board, related, "But soon a hand which he [Judkins] did not see tossed a bundle at my feet. I grasped it and started at once to my sled a few rods off where concealed in the bottom I found more papers . . . brought ashore and placed there by a friendly passenger, under his coat." Because the road to Annapolis—Nova Scotia— was blocked by four feet of snow, the express had to go by way of Windham, nearly forty miles farther. Ormiston wrote:

> We had a horn to blow and warn travellers of our approach, so as to clear the track and also to give notice when we came to where changes of horses were to be made. Beyond Windsor the road was hardly broken and we were frequently sent rolling among the drifts. One drift, worse than the rest, took the sleigh body completely off, leaving us the runners only. My driver then took one, and I the other runner, and thus we rode for the last 50 miles—a picturesque sight truly, but we thus got along with less difficulty than before.

The trip took ten hours and ten minutes. The temperature was twelve degrees below zero. At Annapolis, Ormiston found that Halifax authorities had sent instructions that were the opposite of those he had issued. But the inhabitants were cooperative and had followed his agent's request, breaking "a road specifically for me, down to nearly opposite to where the steamer lay, a distance of about fourteen miles. This occupied them nearly three days." Arrangements had been made to fire a cannon from the fort when *Ormiston* approached, so the chartered steamer *Kennebec*, "the finest vessel between Cape Cod and Nova Scotia," could sail immediately. But the ice was eight inches thick. "This was an uncommon occurrence—so swift the tide here, that during the coldest winters of the last 70 years this bay has been frozen only once." It took the steamer two hours and five minutes to break her way out of the Bay of Fundy; the 280-mile run to Portland took seventeen-and-a-half hours. Near Portland, the *Kennebec* "telegraphed" its position, and "the whole city literally turned out to meet and welcome us. The piers, streets and railroad depot swarmed with human beings of all ages and sexes." A chartered locomotive was standing by, "belching forth from her iron nostrils." It made the trip to Boston in less than three hours—arriving two hours before the *Cambria,* though Captain Judkins had boasted that he would beat the express by three hours even if he "had to burst his boilers." "Heavy" bets had been made on the race. *Ormiston's* role ended at Boston. Between there and Hartford the express was delayed—the *Sun* hinted at treachery—which lost the time that had been gained. From Hartford the package was sent by locomotive to New Haven, by horse the eighty miles to New York in deep snow in four-and-a-half hours, then by horse express to Philadelphia and train to Baltimore.

As another means of getting the first news from Great Britain, the *Sun* joined with newspapers from New York, Boston, Philadelphia, and Washington in chartering the New York pilot-boat *William J. Romer,* a vessel of extraordinary speed, which was expected to cross the Atlantic faster than the *Cambria.* Boasting of the costly venture, the *Sun* said: "This is one of the great newspaper enterprises, furnishing the public important foreign news days in advance of when they would otherwise have received it." But the *Cambria* won the race, and no more was heard of the *Romer* as a dispatch boat. The Halifax Express made more than one trip, but without the excitement of its first frenzied dash.

Newspapers were using a horse express as far back as the early days of the nineteenth century. David Hale, a New York newspaperman, introduced one to gather state news. In 1830, Richard Haughton, an editor of the *New York Journal of Commerce,* adopted the idea. He later founded the *Boston Atlas* and linked relays of horses with short rail-lines to gather Massachusetts election returns and print them the next morning. James W. Webb, editor of the *New York Courier and Enquirer,* started frequent horse expresses to Philadelphia in 1832, and in 1833 the *Journal of Commerce* developed a regular service to that city with eight relays. After the *Courier and Enquirer* sold its line to the Post Office Department, the *Journal of Commerce* extended its line to Washington, covering the 227 miles in twenty hours with twenty-four horses. When they had to compete with the penny press, the two papers established an express to Washington one winter, but the cost was too great. In May 1848 six New York papers formed the New York Associated Press to share the costs of telegraphing the foreign news from Boston when mail steamers arrived. The papers were the *Sun,* the *Herald,* the *Tribune,* the *Express,* the *Courier and Enquirer,* and the *Journal of Commerce.* That summer, the organization, which became the Associated Press, began selling its dispatches. The *Philadelphia Public Ledger* and the *Sun,* though not yet members (the New York group restricted that privilege), were the first paying clients. The *Sun* became a member of the Associated Press in October 1893.

The magnetic telegraph at first only supplemented the horse express but in short order supplanted it. Telegraphy was invented by Samuel Finley Morse, a portrait painter of note and a founder of the National Academy of Design, who had become intrigued with the possibilities of electricity while still a student at Yale. Beginning in 1832, at the age of 41, after studying the old masters in Europe for three years, Morse spent twelve years perfecting his invention and petitioning Congress for money to fund a practical demonstration. Finally he got the attention of John Pendleton Kennedy of Baltimore, a businessman, lawyer, novelist, and member of Congress. Through Kennedy's influence, Congress appropriated $30,000 to build an experimental telegraph line from Washington, D.C., to Baltimore. On May 24, 1844, from the Supreme Court room in Washington, Morse sent a message along a wire wrapped in rope yarn and tar to an assistant in the B&O Mount Clare station on Pratt Street. The message—a series of dots and dashes registered on a paper tape—when decoded read "What hath God wrought?" Thus began one of the most momentous advances in communication, not to say the biggest news story of that age. Even though A. S. Abell was understood to have been encouraging Morse, the *Sun* chronicled the event in a mere two sentences under "Local Matters":

> Magnetic telegraph: Some further experiments were conducted on the new telegraph on Saturday morning, which were witnessed by a number of spectators. Several messages were sent to and fro with almost incredible dispatch, which, although unimportant in themselves, were most interesting from the novelty of the proceedings, forcing upon the mind the reality of the complete annihilation of space, in the fact that a distinct and well-defined conversation was actually going on with persons in a city forty miles distant.

The first Baltimore newspaper to print a telegraphic dispatch was the *Patriot,* a six-penny paper that often tormented the *Sun.* What was published was only a twenty-eight-word paragraph about Congress, but it appeared a few days after Morse's famous question. The dispatch read: "One o'clock. — There has just been made a motion in the House to go into committee of the whole on the Oregon question. Rejected; ayes, 79, nays 86." The *Sun,* preoccupied with using its saddlebags and steamer pouches, was slow to adapt to the telegraph, but before long the new device was being used effectively. When funds ran out after the line was opened between Philadelphia and New York, Abell and Swain joined others in underwriting an extension to Baltimore. Swain was an incorporator of the Magnetic Telegraph Company and later its president.

By June 6, 1846, a through wire was operating from Washington, D.C., to New York, and the *Sun* predicted that newspapers in Washington, Baltimore, Philadelphia, and New York would publish the news "simultaneously." But it did not always work that way. Now and then the magnetic telegraph—by this time hailed as "the Great Highway of Thought" and, more often, "the lightning line"—was inoperable because of storms or line failures. Commercial messages took precedence over press dispatches. Initial costs were high: the rate from Baltimore to Philadelphia was twenty-five cents for ten words. Sending long messages took time. Transmitting a presidential address from Philadelphia to Pittsburgh in 1847 took 15 hours and 43 minutes; the following year, sending a gubernatorial message from Albany to New York City on one wire took eight hours. The *Sun* said, "The 12,000 words, or about 72,000 letters, required over 288,000 manipulations," and the transmission was so inaccurate that many papers reprinted the message after receiving it by mail. Today the high-speed wire of the Associated Press, aided by computer printing, transmits 1,200 words a minute.

A high point occurred on May 11, 1846, when President James K. Polk sent his Mexican War message to Congress. The *Sun* ordered the message telegraphed in its entirety, a journalistic feat with international repercussions. This was the longest message that had ever been sent by telegraph, taking two-and-a-half hours and filling more than two columns in the next day's paper. Later, the French Academy reproduced the printed version alongside an authenticated copy of the original message. The Paris correspondent of the *National Intelligencer* filed this account:

> Prof. Morse had the goodness to send me an account of the recent achievements of the electrical telegraph, with a copy of the Baltimore *Sun* containing the President's message on the Mexican War, as it was magically transmitted to that paper. I sent the communications to Pouillet, the deputy author of the report, . . . and he placed them in the hands of Arago, who submitted their very interesting and decisive contents to the Academy of Science and the Chamber of Deputies. In the Chamber, on the 18th instant, when the proposed appropriation for an electrical telegraph from this capital to the Belgian frontier came under consideration, Berryer opposed it on the ground that the experiments of the new system were incomplete; that it would be well to wait for the full trial of what was undertaken between Paris and Rouen. Arago answered, "The experiment is consummated; in the United States the matter is settled irresistibly. I received three days ago the *Sun* of Baltimore, with a letter from Mr. Morse, one of the most honorable men of his country, and here is the President's message, printed from the telegraph in two or three hours; the message would fill four columns of the *Moniteur;* it could

not have been copied by the most rapid penman in a shorter time than it was transmitted. The galvanic fluid travels 70,000 leagues per minute.'' The appropriation of nearly 500,000 francs passed with only a few dissenting voices.

A week after Polk's message preparing Congress for hostilities, the *Sun* was first in Baltimore with news of the opening battle of the Mexican War. The paper's special report arrived in Washington fifteen minutes ahead of the ''Southern mail''; at once, a *Sun* representative filed the dispatch by telegraph ''exclusively for the *Sun*.'' Within minutes the *Sun* was ''throwing extras from our press at the rate of 4,000 and 5,000 an hour.'' The next day the *Patriot* accused Morse of ''wrong done to the public at large and the *Patriot* in particular'': the telegraph, supported with public funds, was public property, it said, and news of the battle should have gone to all papers. Because it did not, the *Patriot* said, Baltimore's 120,000 inhabitants were held ''in suspense and torture for two hours.'' The *Sun* replied that as soon as it received the news it placed a summary on the bulletin board of the telegraph office and another on its own bulletin board, ''from which copies were made by representatives of other papers, the *Patriot* amongst the number, and displayed at the respective offices. The whole city rejoiced, and instead of suffering 'torture and suspense,' congratulations springing from true patriotism were heard on every hand.''

This was clarified in an explanation that Morse telegraphed to the Baltimore *American,* which the *Sun* reprinted. Morse explained that he had set up two instruments and was preparing to send news from the Southern mail as soon as it arrived. The *Sun*'s message, arriving first, was sent first. But let Morse tell what happened: ''Scarcely had the communication from the *Sun* been completed, when a severe thundergust, whose greatest force was at Baltimore, induced my vigilant superintendant [*sic*] of that station to protect the instrument from possible injury during the violence of the storm by the usual mode of stopping off the magnets. The lateness of the hour at which this was done prevented any further telegraphic communication until the next morning.''

In those days spot news was not presented as it is today, with the important information usually summarized in the first paragraph and the basic questions—who, what, where, when, why, and how—answered in order of relevancy in succeeding paragraphs. In 1846 the *Sun* was first with a whale of a story—the opening battle of a war of unforeseeable proportions and effect, an American victory at that, and with a Baltimorean as a hero. Nevertheless, by modern standards the *Sun* backed into the report and took forever to give the essential facts. Its exclusive began:

We received by telegraph last evening at five o'clock, exclusively for our use, and issued in an extra, by which the city was flooded during the evening, an intelligent synopsis of the following highly important, highly gratifying and joyfully welcome news from our chivalrous and noble army—small in numbers, but great in deeds of valor and of skill. We also issued a more detailed statement in a subsequent edition, after the arrival of the mail.

The news was received at New Orleans, first and mainly by the steamship *New York* which had taken down reinforcements from the city to Point Isabel, and returned on the 8th inst. at 9 o'clock, P.M. to New Orleans.

We acknowledge our indebtedness to our brethren of the entire press at New Orleans, for their attention in furnishing us with ample means for obtaining all necessary information. In introducing this intelligence we make use of the following paragraph from the New Orleans *Tropic,* as indicative of the feeling with which it was received in that city, and also for its testimonial in favor of a gallant son of Maryland, and an officer of whom our city may be justly proud:

"We have met the Enemy and they are Ours." —After a painful suspense of several days, news has reached us of a blow being struck by the Americans. The prowess of our brave soldiers has made the perfidious Mexicans bite the dust. The serpent of the Mexican arms now writhes in death agony in the beak of the American Eagle. Victory perches upon our banner! Honor to Major Ringgold of the 3d artillery, and his brave companions for their defense of the American Camp. Cheers, nine times nine, for our country and its free institutions!

Facts about the Battle of Matamoras finally emerged near the end of that twenty-one-inch account: The Baltimore hero, Major Sam Ringgold, was an artillery commander; his four-gun battery had shelled the town, destroying a number of houses. Only one U.S. soldier was killed, but the Mexicans suffered an estimated 700 casualties.

War was declared on May 12, 1846. President Polk, after resolving the Oregon question to his satisfaction, had tried to purchase New Mexico and California from Mexico. When he was rebuffed—the Mexican government had regarded U.S. annexation of Texas the year before as an act of aggression— fighting broke out between the two countries along the Rio Grande. It continued until a peace treaty was signed in February 1848. Of the 116,000 men commissioned or enlisted in the U.S. Army, nearly 13,000 died—1,721 in action, 11,155 from disease and exposure.

News of the fighting, referred to wherever it happened as the "Seat of War," came by government courier or news messengers on horseback across miles of Mexican wilderness infested with brigands and guerrillas to Point Isabel on the Gulf of Mexico and then by ship to New Orleans, the army's base of supplies and the chief news center. When the fighting was deep in Mexico, this might take three or more days. Most of the war news came from New Orleans newspapers, the *Picayune,* the *Delta,* the *Crescent City,* the *Tropic,* and the *Bee.* The voyage from New Orleans to New York took twelve days; with adverse winds or weather it took as long as nineteen days. Most news came by the Southern mail, termed the "Great Mail" by the Post Office Department. The first leg was by water: from New Orleans across the Mississippi Sound to Mobile, and up the Alabama River to Montgomery. Then the journey was by rail for fifty-three miles to Notasulga; by four-horse post over unimproved roads (often washed out by storms that made rivers too deep to ford) to Griffin, Georgia; by rail to Charleston, South Carolina; by steamboat to Wilmington, North Carolina; by rail to Aquia Creek, Virginia; by steamboat again to Washington; and by telegraph or rail to Baltimore. This route extended more than 1,000 miles, and the Great Mail was carried over it, or variations of it, from 1844 to 1848.

The mail was expected to move about ten miles an hour—an uneventful passage would take eight or nine days—but there were so many breakdowns that the Postmaster General was ordered to investigate. Service failed most often between December and February because of "snows, ice, fogs, storms and accidents to the machinery of the cars or boats." The worst two months were in 1845 and 1846, when the mails failed 120 times. The *Sun* often carried such items as "The Southern mail failed last night from all points beyond Wilmington, N.C.," and "The Southern mail failed two nights in succession, all points beyond Petersburg, Va., and from beyond Macon, Ga." Jokes were made about mail delays and failures. The *Picayune* wrote: "It seems some of the mail riders in Wisconsin have lately been chased by wolves. It might not be a bad plan for the government to employ a pack of wolves to chase its mail carriers upon a good many routes throughout the country."

Southern mails were so slow and undependable that the *Picayune* in 1837 arranged its own private express, which, in a dig at the Post Office, was called "Our Horse." In 1844 the *New Orleans Crescent City* and the *Mobile Register* operated a private express between New Orleans, Mobile, and New York. Major O'Callaghan, a proprietor of the *Crescent City,* devised this to supplant the stagecoach link of 190 miles between Montgomery and Covington, Georgia, where a rail line ended. The four-horse stages carried six to fourteen passengers, two on the deck when crowded, and 1,100 pounds of mail, much of it newspapers. The bulkiness of the papers often overloaded a stage, and then bundles were left behind along the line, which enraged editors who depended on them for their exchanges. The stage lumbered over rutted roads at about five miles an hour, the driver blowing on his horn "Molly Put the Kettle On" to alert the next team as he approached a station. O'Callaghan's horse express rode the 190 miles at ten miles an hour, catching the mail of the previous day, sometimes even putting his letters in the mail a day-and-a-half ahead of schedule. Merchants and competing papers complained about O'Callaghan's express beating the mails, and the U.S. Senate demanded an investigation. The result was the postal reform bill of 1845 which, among other provisions, forbade private expresses to move mail. O'Callaghan continued the *Crescent City* express anyway, and was arrested for moving mail by private means. But one way or another, private expresses continued to operate.

Because the mail passed through so many hands, money was sometimes stolen from it. In reply to a complaint, one postmaster general said, "I know of but one effectual security—to cut bank notes into two parts—send one and wait an acknowledgment of its receipt, before the other is forwarded." During yellow fever epidemics in New Orleans, authorities, believing the fever was "exportable," would fumigate the mail by punching holes in letters, then placing them in earthen jars and exposing them to fumes of carbolic and sulfuric acid. Mail was sent collect, except for express mail, which was prepaid. Leonard Huber and Clarence Wagner, in their book *The Great Mail: A Postal History of New Orleans,* relate an anecdote concerning collect mail. General Zachary Taylor, a popular hero of the Mexican War then living in Baton Rouge, received so much fan mail—all collect—that he refused to pay the postage and had the letters sent to the dead-letter office. He had heard, unofficially, that he had been nominated by the Whigs as their candidate for U.S. President. When he did not receive official notification, he realized that it had been sent collect and that it too had gone to the dead-letter office. Finally he got a duplicate, but in the campaign he was ridiculed for not accepting his mail. The incident, which drew national attention, was partly instrumental in the change from collect mail to prepaid mail. In those days the exchange of newspapers between publishers was free, but this, as noted, became an increasing burden for the Post Office. In 1847 it prohibited publishers from sending papers to subscribers as freight over mail routes. The *Sun* said that this cost "upwards of $2,000 for the transmission of the *Sun* to our agents in the District of Columbia," and smaller sums to other places. To reduce the bulk of its exchange mailings, some papers, the *Sun* included, sent one-sheet extras or, more often, "news slips," which by law were limited to two news columns of a certain width.

Most of the *Sun*'s war news arrived by Southern mail, but the paper supplemented this with faster express services and, in the fall of 1846, with its own Special Overland Express—with the insignia of three pony express riders over the dispatch. This express made the trip from New Orleans to Washington, D.C., in six days. There a representative would summarize what was important in the New Orleans papers and telegraph it to Baltimore for the next edition or an extra. The packet of papers would be forwarded by rail to be quoted at length—"annexed" as the *Sun* termed it—the next day. More than once the *Sun*'s dispatches were the first to arrive. On May 25, 1846, a Washington correspondent reported that the news forwarded exclusively for the Baltimore *Sun* was copied in the telegraph office in Washington by the Postmaster General himself, who hurried with it immediately to President Polk. The Special Overland Express became famous and attracted attention along its route, papers noting its passage and informing readers that their news would be arriving the next day. For example, the *Richmond Whig* wrote: "Mr. Martin, the accommodating mail agent on the Fredericksburg Road, informed us that the Baltimore *Sun*'s 'pony express' went through yesterday—consequently we may expect some interesting intelligence by this morning's Southern mail."

The *Sun*'s Special Overland Express followed the Great Mail route, though occasionally its news package came on a steamer from New Orleans to Pensacola, Florida, instead of Mobile, then by horse express to link with the route north. Its express and the one operated by the *New York Sun* and the *Charleston Courier* were the two most important. For a while the *New York Herald* attempted its own service, but later it relied on that of the Baltimore *Sun,* although the *Herald* did have its own correspondent in Mexico.

Probably the two best correspondents were from New Orleans papers: George W. Kendall, co-founder and editor of the *Picayune,* and James L. Freaner, a native of Hagerstown, Maryland, of the *Delta.* Both were adventurers and famous for their daring. At the battle of Monterey, Freaner killed a Mexican officer for his horse. After that he signed his dispatches "Mustang," and they appeared in the *Sun* that way. Kendall has been honored as the first modern war correspondent. He was also unofficial adviser to generals. After the battle of Buena Vista, rumors got back to the nation's capital that General Taylor was cut off from the rest of the army, and President Polk sent word that Taylor was relying too much on his "advisers," including, he heard, "Mr. Kendall, editor of the *Picayune.*" (Kendall is credited with inventing General Taylor's famous order "A little more grape, Captain Bragg." Historians have uncovered several versions of the general's command, "Take that damned battery. . . . Give 'em hell. . . . And now is the time to give them a little jesse." Kendall probably cleaned up the language for home consumption and thought he could make the expression more colorful and concise.)

Kendall developed his own pony express in Mexico, which also carried official dispatches. Several riders were killed by guerrillas. (A soldier's letter described Mexico: "All plants here have thorns, all animals stings or horns and all men carry weapons.") Kendall is said to have chartered a steamer at Vera Cruz to deliver his dispatch to New Orleans at a cost of $5,000. The *Picayune* was so enterprising that it sent fast sloops carrying printers and their type cases to meet the slow steamers sailing from Vera Cruz with news. When the sloops returned to New Orleans, the news was already in type, ready for the press. For all his enterprise, Abell sent no correspondent to Mexico. He was content to rely on other papers and to concentrate on getting the news as fast as possible.

On April 10, 1847, "By Special Overland Express of Nearly 1,000 miles, Exclusively for the Baltimore *Sun,* Independent of All Telegraphic Communications, Unparalleled Effort of Newspaper Enterprise," Abell published the first news in the north of the fall of the fortress of Vera Cruz, an event that practically assured victory in the war. He beat not only the Southern mail but also the War Department's official courier. Knowing he was first, he sent a private telegraphic dispatch to President Polk to inform him of the victory. Years after, that was still being called the greatest day in the *Sun*'s history.

When its extras reached the nation's capital, the *Washington Union* reported, "the whole city was filled with enthusiasm . . . by the accounts, for which we were indebted to the Baltimore *Sun,* through its extraordinary express from Pensacola. The *Sun* must have run an express through this city last night. It shows what enterprise can do, and no press has done more in experiments of this nature than the *Sun.*" The President's private secretary, J. Knox Walker, wrote Abell:

I am directed by the President to acknowledge the receipt of your note by Telegraph announcing, in advance of the mail, the important and gratifying achievements of the American Arms at Vera Cruz—the unconditional surrender and capitulation of the city and castle. For the zeal and enterprise manifested by you in running this express, you will doubtless receive deserved commendations. I am requested by the President to thank you for your obliging kindness in communicating this information in advance of your paper.

When the *Patriot* made a snide remark about his glorious scoop, Abell responded a bit haughtily:

We may advert, with becoming diffidence, to our war news, so frequently furnished to the government—when important, by private communication—and through our columns in advance of the mail; it is not for us to say how, or to what extent, in this respect we may have been instrumental in serving national interests. It has been generally admitted that the news of the capture of Vera Cruz, arriving by our express on the very day appointed for the close of a national loan, was directly favorable to the national interests in the final negotiations.

The *Patriot* was envious of the *Sun*'s express, and on June 24, 1847, it published a telegraph dispatch from Fredericksburg, Virginia, that stung Abell more than any other *Patriot* attack:

There is no news beyond what you have already received by Riddle's Express, which runs from Mobile to Montgomery, Alabama, and thus overtakes the mail at the latter place, gaining 24 hours on the regular mail. The proprietor of this express accomplishes his purpose by keeping a relay of twelve horses which, on certain occasions, run to and from the cities mentioned. He is employed chiefly by a few speculating merchants in New Orleans, and some merchants and newspaper proprietors in the northern cities. Such is a brief history of the "Overland Express."

Abell resented the smear that the Overland Express was used by "speculating merchants" and the insinuation that he could also profit personally. He had a reputation for always posting news that might affect markets or politics on the front door as soon as it was received and making it immediately available to a wider audience with bulletins or news slips before publication. Abell printed three editorials in rebuttal, denying any link with speculators and detailing how exclusive news was announced before publication.

But the *Sun* certainly conveyed the impression that its Special Overland Express was being run with its own ponies or, as it said one time, with "60 blooded horses." The reader was given to understand that here was an unbroken chain of horsemen from New Orleans to Baltimore. After the *Patriot*'s jab, the *Sun* for the first time mentioned "our express agents"; later it admitted that the express was "managed and directed by J. C. Riddle, Esq.," the name mentioned by the *Patriot*. The Special Overland Express, obviously, operated to connect with sporadic rail lines and with the expanding telegraph line. On February 28, 1848, the *Sun* announced: "Our telegraph reporter, who formerly received a dispatch from our 'pony express' at Petersburg [Virginia], since the completion of the telegraph to Charleston, has located himself at Columbia, S.C. some 300 miles further south, consequently gaining an additional day on the mail."

Nevertheless, the Overland Express was something special. It conveys exciting and romantic images that were evoked on a larger scale in 1860 and 1861, when the famed Pony Express carried mail from St. Joseph, Missouri, then the western end of the telegraph lines, to California, across 2,000 miles of plains, desert, and mountains, where hostile Indians roamed. The *Sun's* express made better time than the Great Mail or private express, despite weather and whatever dangers lurked on primitive roads through forests or on spongy causeways across swamps. When storms washed out bridges or flooded fords, riders would cross rivers in canoes or streams on fallen logs while their ponies swam beside them. Even though packages were carried in supposedly watertight rubber sacks, they often arrived soaked and unreadable. Mentioning the rains in Alabama, the *Sun* said its package of at least sixty papers "bore evidence, in their wet and soiled appearance, to the depth of the water courses." From time to time the paper ran items about express riders traveling on improved roads between northern cities who had fallen or been thrown from their horses, sometimes fatally. Such accidents must have been more frequent still in the South, with its greater distances, worse conditions, and wartime urgency.

In July 1847, mentioning that the "mails from the South due last evening failed us from every point south of Petersburg," the *Sun* said of its pony express, "Neither wind nor weather, tide, or storm, or the heat of the Southern sun, it seems can dampen the spirits or clog the heels of our 'go-ahead' team of 'express ponies.' Although mails may unavoidably fail from the effects of contrary winds, storms or freshets, our 'ponies' pass them all unheeded and reach their destination with almost unerring certainty."

Still smarting from the *Patriot's* gibe, the *Sun* introduced a letter from the Pony Express station at Piney Woods, Alabama, by saying it contained "information from the 'ponies,' relative to certain slanders promulgated against them." The letter said the ponies had brought information from Mexico forty-eight hours in advance of the mails. It added:

> The whole country is flooded, but where the ponies cannot touch bottom they *swim,* and they now have pretty tall swimming and wading to do. . . . The weather is very hot, and many of the ponies have recently been numbered among the things that were, and many more are now in hospital [sic], undergoing *quarantine.* The *intelligent* correspondent of the Baltimore *Patriot* "per telegraph" missed the mark widely when he gave you credit for performing this heavy service with twelve horses. The fact is there is now on the road *thirty-five horses and eight riders,* besides

those held in readiness to take the place of those that may get out of condition, independent of a number of cripples in pasture—the extreme heat, and bad conditions of the roads making sad havoc among them.

All told, it was a costly venture. According to Scharf, Abell spent $1,000 a month. Freaner, the *Delta* correspondent, in a letter to a friend in Hagerstown that was quoted by the *Sun,* said the *Delta* was spending the same amount. The *Sun* never said what it spent but, commenting on the *Delta*'s expenses it wrote, "The reader may infer from this the amount of expense we so readily incur in our unrivaled 'pony express.' But when Senator Henry Johnson of Louisiana introduced a resolution in the Senate in January 1848 "to prevent the losses sustained by the public in consequence of intelligence conveyed by the daily express established by individuals to and from New Orleans," the *Sun* resoundingly responded: "We have been incurring an enormous daily expense to establish our express. If he meant to ask the government to sustain us in our losses . . . he has moved without our knowledge or desire. We go entirely on our own hook and ask no favors from individuals or government."

On November 29, 1847, though the "City of Mexico" had been occupied and peace negotiations were being discussed, Abell announced that he was starting a southern daily "Pony Express for important intelligence from the seat of war, Havana, South America, &c." But it did not operate every day because there was not enough news, though it did continue into 1848.

The *Sun* and the *Washington Union* were able to publish provisions of the peace treaty in advance of the government's announcement because of the *Picayune*'s ability in obtaining Kendall's report, and because of the dramatic arrival in the nation's capital of Freaner, who had become a government courier. As told by Tom Mahoney in his account of Kendall's career, the treaty was signed on February 2, 1848, on the altar of the cathedral in Guadalupe Hidalgo. Clutching a copy of the treaty, Freaner sped to the coast with a U.S. cavalry escort. He and the messenger carrying Kendall's account reached Vera Cruz in three days. Freaner sailed immediately for Mobile. A steamer was waiting for Kendall's dispatch, but the port captain delayed the departure for two days to assure that the government courier would arrive first. Still the ship, under forced draft, reached New Orleans about the time Freaner got to Mobile. Freaner left there forty-eight hours ahead of the express, carrying copies of the *Picayune*'s February 13 extra about the treaty. Between Mobile and Montgomery the newspaper express made up twenty-four hours. Freaner and the express both reached Charleston on February 17. From there it was almost a neck-and-neck race to Washington, D.C., without rest. Then, dirty and unkempt after his seventeen-day trek from Mexico, Freaner had trouble getting by bureaucrats to deliver the treaty to the Secretary of War. And that was how the *Sun* and the *Washington Union,* on February 21, were able to publish Kendall's account before any government announcement.

Scarcely a decade after its founding, in the mind of the public, the *Sun* was becoming one of the nation's foremost newspapers. This reputation was built partly on its first-with-the-news pony express and partly on the breadth and depth of its coverage, which on many days filled nearly a fourth of the paper. Abell was an ardent, open advocate of the Mexican War—which helped split pro- and antislavery factions in the United States. Some newspapers, particularly in the first year of the war, were not in favor of the adventure, and some later called it "a criminal war," in reference to its unconcealed aim of land seizure. As the war dragged on, Abell became clamorous and jingoistic. He thundered "for the effectual defeat, humiliation and subjection to terms of this graceless and perfidious nation." Another time his paper averred that "Mexico and the various states of South America are wholly unfit for self-government," and added: "Our future destiny depends on proving to Mexico and the world that there is but one power of the first rank on the North American continent and that is the United States." Near the end of the war, the *Sun* predicted that if the war were to be prolonged for two or three years and actively prosecuted, "the entire subjugation and annexation of Mexico will be unavoidable."

In spite of distance, still-primitive communications, lack of systematic coverage, and reliance for the most part on untrained observers, the war was reported by the *Sun* and perhaps ten other papers in greater detail than any nation's press had ever previously accomplished. It marked the beginnings of modern war correspondence.

The *Sun* published whatever government documents became public and some that were confidential. When eighteen days went by without official correspondence from the field to the War Office, the paper noted, "It leaves an inference by no means unfavorable to the soldiers that our army is quicker at fighting than writing." Casualty lists were published: "Officers, noncommissioned officers, musicians and privates." In addition to long annexes from the New Orleans papers and the camp papers put out by soldier-printers, the *Sun* offered accounts of the expeditions to Santa Fe and California, comment from British journals, translations from the Mexican press of official documents, and speeches by Santa Anna, the Mexican leader described as "an amusing writer of romance."

Columns of letters appeared, from officers and soldiers—sent free if "Belonging to the Army" were written across the envelope—which gave colorful and personal glimpses of their lives. One letter told of mosquitoes strong enough to bite through the sole of an army boot. Another, in an ideal location (most soldiers were not), exulted that he was living well off the land on quail, chicken, pork, and exotic fruits. Others told of being homesick, and the paper urged female readers to send them jellies and syrups in care of the quartermaster general. Soldiers visited the grave of Major Ringgold of Baltimore and sent back descriptions of how it was decorated with "bayonets, spears, &c., from the enemy." (Ringgold had been killed in an early battle. When the *Sun* received word of his death it printed an extra.)

The first large illustration the *Sun* ever published was a three-column War Department map of the battle of Monterey, copied from an engraving in the *Delta*. The *Sun* noted, "The draughtsman took responsibility for striking the Mexican flag although his view is prior to the battle." It published army ads for 100 to 150 artillery and dragoon horses and twenty teamsters for service in Mexico. Baltimore's reaction to an important victory was described in detail: City Hall, the courthouse, public schools, and the Washington and Battle monuments were decorated with transparencies. The *Sun* building was illuminated with 500 lights, and windows displayed the names of military and naval heroes. The town turned out to gape and cheer.

From 1846 to 1848 there was little about the war—at the seat of war, in Washington or Baltimore—that the *Sun* did not cover meticulously in regular editions and in innumerable two-cent extras, sometimes issuing more than one a day, occasionally even on a Sunday. The only war-related material omitted was the flood of "poetic efforts commemorative of the deeds and fame of gallant men who have fallen" submitted by readers, because "few specimens arrive above mediocrity."

International news, on the Oregon question and afterward, was reported at length in extracts from parliamentary debate and editorial comment of the British press. As soon as mail steamers arrived in Boston or New York with important news, the *Sun* published telegraphic summaries and followed the next day with columns of annexes from the British papers when they arrived by express mail. Particular attention was paid to market reports and other commercial news. Abell posted the Liverpool prices of flour and Indian corn on the office door before issuing slips or extras.

The Atlantic cable—or submarine telegraph as it was first called—opened in August 1858, and the first formal messages were congratulatory notes exchanged between President James Buchanan and Queen Victoria. The next day the *Sun*, "to illustrate the promptness of the management to seize upon and utilize every instrumentality for obtaining the earliest news, . . . received the first and only news telegram from London to any Baltimore paper."

Nationally, the *Sun* had daily reports from several correspondents in the nation's capital, and it covered such events as the laying of the cornerstone of the Smithsonian Institution with four columns of detail. It listed acts passed by Congress, printed tariff schedules, and compared them with previous rates. In these and other areas it was a paper of record. As the telegraph lines diverged, the *Sun* used them for reports from other cities, labeled "Things from New York," "Things from Philadelphia." The daily telegraphic report from Philadelphia was evidently a must, even though there was a dearth of news. Often these began: "We are again without any local news of the slightest importance to forward you by the lightning line," followed by several paragraphs about the weather or how attractive Philadelphians were. Abell was generous with space on church conferences, and even more so with the Sons of Temperance, particularly when they held a national jubilee in New York attended by more than 40,000. His paper was quick with election returns, both nationally and in Maryland, but it showed little interest in presidential nominating conventions even though the Whigs held them in Baltimore in 1840, 1844, and 1852, and the Democrats in 1848. In 1852, responding to newspaper reports alleging the drunkenness of presidential candidates, the *Sun* defended the character of both General Winfield Scott and Franklin Pierce and suggested that the personal lives of candidates be off-limits to the press. When Pierce was nominated, the *Sun* made no mention of him—his merits or his flaws.

The *Sun* did take notice, though, of what other papers were doing. When the *Western Continent* had hired Kate Harebell as editorial assistant for the "ladies' department," the public was assured, "She is no imaginary sprite but indeed a bona fide, young, beautiful and accomplished lady." Another time the *Sun* reported that the *New York Herald* was sending a special edition to Europe, aboard French steamships. This form of the *Herald* contained "a summary of American news printed in French for the benefit of those who are not acquainted with Anglo-Saxon. It will also print the same in English for the benefit of those in France who are not at home in French."

Change was taking place. Now in the 1850s, the paper whose original strength was its local coverage took more notice of national and international news, and trials, especially murder trials, were played up. The *Sun* was cited for contempt "for imputing to the judges corrupt motives" in one rape case. Although Baltimore was a busy port for immigrants, the paper was meager with port news: "Emigrants —Ship Richard Anderson, 230 passengers, mostly Irish emigrants [sic]." One day it printed a rumor that immigrants on one ship had been badly treated; then the paper reversed itself; they had been treated well. Evidently censured, the *Sun* then reported on how the Hibernian Society was caring for sick and distressed newcomers. It told of one family, with the father dying en route and the mother when she reached quarantine, leaving "five orphan children strangers in a strange land. . . . They started on the voyage with but 42 pounds of meal and six pounds of meat, and not a cent in the world, they having been put on board by a Mr. Barton, their landlord, who assured them they would have an abundance, and, when they got here, land would be given to them, &c."

Most Baltimore news was compartmentalized under the heading "Local Matters," a device begun back in January 1841. Local Matters consisted mainly of court reports, assaults, drownings, or workers struck by lightning or dying from heat prostration. Hangings were reported in detail with descriptions of the prisoner's death throes and the mood of the 20,000 or more men, women and children crowding the hills near the jail where the gallows stood. The *Sun* urged the legislature to make executions private.

An occurrence of later moment was the death of Edgar Allan Poe while pausing in Baltimore on his way north. Alone among local newspapers, the *Sun* marked the event in a compassionate item on October 8, 1849:

We regret to learn that Edgar A. Poe, Esq., the distinguished American poet, scholar and critic, died in this city yesterday morning after an illness of four or five days. This announcement coming so sudden and unexpected will cause poignant regret among all who admire genius and have sympathies for the frailties too often attending it. Mr. Poe, we believe, was a native of this state, though reared by a foster-father at Richmond, Va., where he lately spent some time on a visit. He was in the 38th year of his age.

Poe, born in Boston, was 40 years old, and there was no mention that *Sun* printer Joseph W. Walker had tried to help him in his last illness. Walker wrote a note to Dr. J. E. Snodgrass: "There is a gentleman, rather the worse for wear, at Ryan's 4th Ward Polls, who goes under the cognomen of Edgar A. Poe and who appears in great distress, and he says he is acquainted with you, and I assure you he is in need of immediate assistance." Response was prompt, but Poe could not be helped.

Local Matters often had the informal, chatty air of neighbors talking over the back fence. It mentioned prices in the city markets (butter 37 1/2 cents a pound, eggs 12 1/2 cents a dozen, bacon 15 1/2 cents a pound) and told of W. W. Levy of Havre de Grace "who follows duck hunting as a matter of business and pleasure," shooting 65,000 in one season, two-thirds canvasbacks; of maids stealing from their employers; and of the gullible swindled in a recurring confidence game called "The Box." Sometimes there was commentary. Someone having thrown water on several drunks, Local Matters observed: "A bucket of water on a drunken man breaks no bones, leaves no bruises and an energetic application usually cures the most obstinate cases."

Baltimore was booming. In March 1847 the *Sun* reported that more than 1,000 houses had been built the previous winter and that another 2,000 were expected that summer, along with "numerous workshops, foundries and factories." Hotels were crowded with western and southern dealers buying spring supplies. Three hundred wagons, loaded with produce, had passed through Westminster, Maryland, on the way to Baltimore. The harbor was crowded with seventy-three square-rigged vessels and an unusually large number of schooners and bay craft.

The *Sun* prospered. In June 1846 it installed a powerful steam engine on a double-cylinder Hoe machine, which was about twice as fast as its double-cylinder Napier press and "the only kind used by any other one cent paper south of Philadelphia." That same year the *Public Ledger* had purchased a revolutionary new Hoe press, which used a revolving cylinder instead of a flat bed for printing. Hoe could not induce other publishers to try one; they doubted it would work. In 1847 the new model was shipped to the *Sun*, which had a greater press run than its sister paper. The new press had a capacity of 10,000 to 12,000 impressions an hour, far beyond that of conventional presses.

Although newspapers then seldom revealed circulation figures, and when they did they were exaggerated, the *Sun* liked to boast of its sales in general terms. It would declare that its circulation was greater than the combined sales of other Baltimore dailies and equal to that of the *Times* of London, making the *Sun* "the third daily in point of circulation in the world." Such claims were questionable. When a reader asked why so many District of Columbia ads appeared in the *Sun,* it replied that its circulation there was higher than that of any Washington paper. Advertising increased to such an extent that in 1848 the *Sun* began publishing two-page supplements that were mostly ads. Some papers replaced worn type every few years, the *Sun* remarked, some only every ten years or so. But the *Sun,* because of its huge press runs, had to replace type every few months. It enjoyed printing subscribers' comments about neighbors who borrowed their *Sun.* It told of one store owner's complaint: An acquaintance kept leaning on the counter for an hour every morning to read the paper free, "to the great inconvenience of the customers." The *Sun* commented, "A man that is too mean to pay a cent a day for a newspaper is not very likely to regard the convenience or advantages of his neighbor. Turn him out."

With circulation and advertising expanding, the paper was cramped in its rented quarters at Gay and Baltimore streets. Abell resolved to have his own building and bought five old houses for $50,000 on the southeast corner of Baltimore and South streets. It was in the heart of downtown and the same location as Baltimore's first newspaper, the *Maryland Journal and Advertiser,* published by William Goddard. Abell wanted the best office building in Baltimore and the finest newspaper plant in the United States. About that time, James Bogardus came to town seeking a client. Bogardus was an inventor with a reputation as a weird genius whose patents included an eight-day clock, an engraving machine for making postage stamps, and mills for grinding rice, sugar, and lead paint. He wanted to construct an "iron" building with cast iron for the frame, floors, and supports, but businessmen were wary. Abell, who had run many a risk during the Mexican War, took a big one when he invested in the nebulous dream of Bogardus, whose only experience in construction was the erecting of an iron building for his own use in New York. In their only serious disagreement, Abell insisted the castings be made in Baltimore, not New York, Bogardus's home base.

Robert G. Hatfield, of New York, was the architect daring enough to risk his reputation on the design. He made it five stories high, a building not supported by traditional masonry walls but by cast-iron columns resting on granite pillars. The columns on the fifth level were adorned with twenty-three metal statues of Washington, Jefferson, and Franklin. Known as the *Sun* Iron Building, it was long the most famous commercial structure in Baltimore, attracting not only tourists but also architects and builders from all over the nation. A Boston magazine said it is "generally conceded to be one of the most beautiful and imposing edifices which modern architecture has ever contributed to useful or civic ornament." Later Bogardus erected the *Philadelphia Public Ledger* Building. Abell and his partners were evidently well pleased with what he had accomplished in Baltimore. When steel was substituted for cast iron in the frame, the modern skyscraper became feasible. The *Sun* Iron Building has been called the progenitor of that architectural evolution.

The new building opened on September 13, 1851. The *Sun* limited its announcement of the event to twenty lines, calling the attention of subscribers and advertisers to its new address. There was not a word about the imaginativeness of the structure or its accommodations. The paper occupied only part of the premises: the counting room (business office) was at street level on one corner, the *Sun* job shop at another corner. Other ground-floor space was rented out to a publisher-stationer, a hatter, and a coal dealer. On the second floor were three telegraph companies: the Magnetic, the Western, and the Southern. The composing room and editorial offices were on the third floor. Employees climbed stairs built at a 45-degree angle. The eight-cylinder, steam driven Hoe presses were in the basement, with the mail room and storage space for newsprint. In a basement corner was a deep hole to drain off water from the frequent floods sweeping down Jones Falls. In those days, memorable events inspired the composers of sheet music. The Iron Building was celebrated by "The Sun Quick Step" which became a popular tune nationally.

In the next few years, Baltimore was subjected to violence on a scale matching anything it had earlier undergone, by youth clubs (members of which even rioted on Christmas), volunteer fire companies disputing the rights to fires, striking railroad employees, and political parties. When one fire company's reel was damaged by a rival group, a fight among three companies ensued, the combatants using pistols, axes, picks, hooks, and bricks. Two participants were killed, and a number were wounded. In May 1857 conductors struck when the B&O gave them additional responsibilities, and the strike led to bloodshed and the stopping and derailing of trains until the governor called out the military.

In the midst of violence a controversy developed over the proposal of Dr. Thomas H. Buckler in 1858 to level historic Federal Hill and use the earth to fill in the Basin. Supposedly the city would realize $3 million to $5 million from selling the 103³/8 acres of new land, and shipping would be forced back to deep water, "where it belongs." The *Sun* was impressed: "The relation of the land to the water and the symmetry of the city would certainly be vastly improved, while the great expanse of South Baltimore, now an outlying province, to be reached only by a tour round the head of the Basin, would be brought into territorial, social and commercial relation with the body of the city." But City Council never acted on the proposal. Benjamin H. Latrobe, the distinguished architect, estimated the cost at $764,346.

Little is known of the *Sun* staff in those days. Abell did not believe, as many editors did, in being the fountainhead of his paper's opinions and the embodiment of its personality, much less in playing a role of civic prominence. Neither did he favor personal journalism on the part of his staff. No bylines appeared while he was in charge. "He suppressed the individualities," an earlier historian, Gerald W. Johnson, observed, "and, as far as possible, even the identities of his men to an extent that seems, to modern practice, unjust and even tyrannous." The *Sun* was the entity greater than the total of its parts. It is known, though, that Thomas J. Beach, who had worked on the *Transcript* and the *American,* joined the paper about the time it moved to Gay Street in 1838 and was editor at least in the 1850s and down to his death in 1864. His scant obituary in the *Sun* did not mention where he was born or whether he was married. Charles Carroll Fulton joined the paper as a printer in 1840 or 1841 after five years of owning and editing the *Georgetown Advocate.* Before long, Fulton became a reporter, one of the first such employed full-time in Baltimore. In 1842 he was appointed managing editor and served as such and as Baltimore agent of the New York, western and southern press until 1853, when he purchased an interest in the *American,* where in time he became editor and sole proprietor. John Taylor Crow, a co-owner and editor of the *Georgetown Advocate,* joined the *Sun* as assistant editor in 1847 when he was 25 years old. Crow was managing editor by 1861, when illness forced his temporary retirement; the following year he returned as the Washington correspondent.

Azariah H. Simmons, one of the three partners, died on December 9, 1855, at the age of 48. Abell's editorial said he was one "with whom we have enjoyed a season of business, social and almost fraternal intercourse." It looked back at Simmons's career: He "learned the printing business, at which he was practically engaged until he entered a proprietorship of the *Morning Star,* a daily paper in New York, and from which he retired to unite with the present publishers of the *Philadelphia Ledger* in that enterprise. Subsequently he came to Baltimore, and, with the present proprietors, commenced the publication of the Baltimore *Sun,* in which he was an indefatigable co-laborer in every department of duty." Abell and Swain purchased his interest in the two papers from his estate; Swain was now half owner of the *Sun,* Abell half owner of the *Public Ledger.*

Swain and Abell were rich men. Baltimoreans believed that the *Sun* alone netted Abell $1,000 a day, but that figure may have been closer to his gross income than his net. On the fortieth anniversary of the *Sun,* the *Maryland Journal,* a Baltimore weekly, said: "It is not generally known, probably, that A. S. Abell, Esq., is the wealthiest newspaper publisher in the world, not excepting the proprietor of the *London Times.*" That was undoubtedly an exaggeration, but it was how part of the public perceived the publisher of the *Sun.*

About the only personal glimpse of Abell from this period is in a date book compiled by James W. Dove, a *Sun* business executive who recorded reminiscences of those who had worked with the Founder or his sons. One of Abell's favorite haunts, they recalled, was Barnum's City Hotel, frequented by Southern Maryland tobacco planters and once hailed by Charles Dickens as "the most comfortable of all the hotels of which I had any experience in the United States." Abell carried a supply of quarters, which he passed out to blind shoestring peddlers, newsboys, and others who appealed to his sympathy. He also used the coins at Barnum's. Stopping on his way to work, he would place a quarter on the bar, calling for his whiskey and glancing around to see if an acquaintance were present to drink with him (drinks were two for twenty-five cents). There generally was, but if not Abell would drink alone and tell the barkeep to hold the change, and he would be back in the afternoon to collect the second drink.

THREE

The Civil War
1859–1865

The first news came by telegraph from Frederick, Maryland: "Information has been received here this morning of a formidable negro insurrection at Harpers Ferry. An armed band of abolitionists have full possession of Harpers Ferry and the United States arsenal. One of the railroad hands, a negro, was killed whilst trying to get the train through town."

Realizing what that might portend, the editors of the *Sun* responded with speed and enterprise. The next morning, October 18, 1859, the paper had reports from the B&O Railroad, statements from the baggagemaster of the train that had been detained, a description from a passenger ("a gentleman well known in this city") who estimated that 250 to 300 insurgents were "plundering and robbing the government funds that had been deposited on Saturday," details of troops entraining from Baltimore ("Thousands wended their way to Camden Station to witness the dispatch of three companies. . . . Hundreds wanted to go but there were no arms for them. Telegraphic operators accompanied the military expedition to use it [the wire] from points where it was not cut"). Officers included R. E. Lee and J. E. B. Stewart [*sic*]." In the nation's capital, President James Buchanan and the secretaries of war and the navy watched a marine detachment depart by special train. Government authorities believed the insurrection burst forth when the "contractor for the government dam absconded, largely indebted to several hundred employees, who may have taken this step to indemnify themselves by the seizure of government funds." These reports were followed by one wild rumor after another from Monocacy, Frederick, Martinsburg, Plane No. 4 on the railroad, and, at midnight, from the Monocacy bridge: Harpers Ferry had been plundered by 500 to 600 blacks and whites, the whites painted as blacks, and joined by 600 runaway blacks. One report followed another chronologically, the newspaper practice of the day. At the end of the three columns was the headline

"Latest and Highly Important" — "Troops have landed and are in the town. The insurrectionists are willing to surrender, but on terms of safe conduct out of difficulty. . . . The plan has been concocting for a year or more, the parties rendezvoused at a farm four miles from here, rented for the purpose by Capt. [John] Brown, of Kansas notoriety, under the name of Smith." The account concluded: "At this hour (2:00) we are compelled to go to press." In its last bulletin it was finally getting the facts.

A *Sun* reporter was sent with the troops. His dispatch the next day was vivid, detailed, accurate (except for still misspelling J. E. B. Stuart's name), and judgmental. Brown was identified as the commander-in-chief of the Army of the Provisional Government of the United States with a force of seventeen white men and five blacks. The reporter was close to the enginehouse when Brown was captured. He described Brown as "a monomaniac, possessing a strong will, superior firmness and resources of mind," whose followers "possessed a weakness of mind and character which enabled him to obtain the ascendancy over them which led to their destruction." In the pocket of a victim the reporter found twenty-five pages of a constitution which "would be treasonable were it not ridiculous." The reporter included this vignette:

> Aaron D. Stevens, a captain of the rioters, shot at the bridge, was taken to the Carroll Hotel, where his dreadful wounds were dressed by Dr. McGarrity. Heavy bullets passed through his breast, head and arm. He said to those around him that as he expected to die before morning he wanted somebody to telegraph his father, at Norwich, Conn., to say to him that his son died at Harpers Ferry, in an attempt at high treason against the state of Virginia. He was alive at 4 o'clock yesterday morning. He is represented as a remarkable, fine-looking man, 6 foot, 6 inches high, and possessed of great nerve. While lying in bed a number of outraged citizens crowded into the room and attempted to dispatch him, pointing cocked muskets at his head, but Stevens, as he lay helpless, folded his arms and looked them calmly in the eye, without uttering a word.

It was the only time the *Sun* sent a reporter out of Baltimore, other than to the nation's capital, through the Civil War.

For the trial of Brown and his men in Charles Town, Virginia, and Brown's execution by public hanging on December 2, the paper relied on telegraph dispatches and reprinting reports from other papers, a practice continued during the war.

The *Sun* was concerned with the fall elections because of growing violence at the polling places. The American (Know-Nothing) Party, an outgrowth of the nativist movement, became a force in Maryland in the 1850s, pledged to correct election abuses, restrict immigration, combat "foreign influences," and preserve "American" ideals. Because of its reform aspects the party attracted well-meaning, often prominent citizens, but unscrupulous leaders gained control. It became a secret society; when a member was asked about its goals he would reply, "I know nothing." Know-Nothing clubs flourished, with links to the police and names such as Rip-Raps, Blood Tubs, Tigers, Red Necks, Gladiators, Wampanoags, and Plug Uglies. At election time, the objective of the members was control of the polls by means of marked ballots, intimidation, and violence. In 1856 the Know-Nothing candidate, Thomas Swann, a former president of the B&O, was elected mayor after the bloodiest battle yet. Eyewitnesses said "gunfire was as regular as if it were by platoons." In the presidential election, that November, rioters fought with shoemaker awls (the symbol of the party), muskets, pistols, knives, clubs, bricks, even small cannon on wheels. So many bricks were used as missiles that streets looked as if cartloads had been dumped.

Guerrilla warfare raged through streets and alleys. Citizens stayed away from the polls; some cowered all day in their cellars. Ten persons were killed, some 150 wounded. Millard C. Fillmore, the American Party's presidential candidate, carried every Baltimore ward, but his only electoral votes were from Maryland. James Buchanan of Pennsylvania was the nation's choice for President. In 1858, Swann was reelected mayor, not so much by violence as by intimidation. Immigrants were threatened with being thrown into tubs of bloody water. Others who did not proffer the party's striped ballot were kept from voting by Know-Nothings brandishing awls. A City Reform Association, encouraged by the *American,* was founded in 1859 and had limited success that fall. The *Sun* endorsed it, but not vigorously. November's state and congressional elections were again marred by violence. The Know-Nothings paraded with banners emblazoned with awls; one showed a would-be voter fleeing with an awl in his back, another showed a sign, "The Awl is Useful in the Hands of an Artist." The awl was a "disappearing weapon," attached to a rubber band fastened at the elbow. After being flashed or used, the weapon vanished up the assailant's sleeve. At Know-Nothing rallies a blacksmith forged awls for members. The *Sun,* in a panorama of the polls, had Regulators attacking Reformers, Tigers assaulting Reformers, a man dying from apoplexy after being pressed by roughs, and a voter, after being stabbed with an awl, shooting the attacker in the head, which precipitated more gunfire. The *Sun* lamented, "A whole city is literally disenfranchised, defied and laid helpless and prostrate at the feet of violent men."

The national American Party had collapsed from defections and internal fights over slavery, and the state party too began to fall apart. Know-Nothings "alleged to have been elected from Baltimore" were expelled from the legislature. That body, acting on recommendations of the Reform Committee, passed a historic law taking control of the police commissioners away from the city and giving it to the governor. The *Sun* reported all this but said little editorially. A turning point came in 1860 with the election of George William Brown, a leader in the Reform movement, as mayor; the defeat proved fatal for the Know-Nothings as a force in Maryland politics. Yet the rifts and estrangements in the citizenry only went on growing, locally and nationally.

After the April 1860 Democratic National Convention in Charleston,

South Carolina, split over North-South issues, it reconvened in Baltimore in June. The *Sun* said the shift in setting showed the South's conciliatory spirit, and it called for a compromise candidate. The paper covered this home-city convention almost verbatim except for prolonged debate. When Stephen A. Douglas of Illinois was nominated on a platform of preserving the Union by not allowing congressional intervention in the territories, the Southern Democrats moved to another hall and nominated John C. Breckenridge of Kentucky. Southern conservatives, fearing the consequences of sectionalism, had met earlier in Baltimore and formed the Constitutional Party with John Bell of Tennessee as its candidate.

Maryland had long had strong bonds, economically, socially, and politically, with the South. It was a slave state, although black servitude had become abhorrent to a growing number of Marylanders, particularly middle-class city-dwellers. But when Arunah S. Abell came south in 1837, he had identified himself with the Southern tradition, and from the start his paper reflected that viewpoint. It consistently maintained that Maryland's interest lay entirely with the South, once adding flippantly, "Aside from a few peck of tomatoes and peaches which go to New York."

An 1849 editorial on "The Territorial Question" declared: "Slavery is a domestic institution. It belongs to the states, each for itself, to decide whether it shall be abolished or not. . . . Here is the true ground and upon this the South must take her final position." Therefore, the *Sun* was determinedly anti-Republican, claiming a decade later that "as a party, the Republican organization lives solely upon the existence of slavery." The editorial writer foresaw, in the unlikely election of a Republican to the Presidency in 1860, that "collision between the North and South would be almost inevitable."

That summer, when the newly formed Republican Party met in Chicago, the *Sun* relied on other papers for its coverage and knew so little about the candidate that it reported the nomination of "Abram" Lincoln and Hannibal "Hamblin" of Maine for Vice President. It supplied a sketch of Lincoln's life because he was relatively unknown, and an even briefer one of Hamlin.

In November, Breckenridge carried Maryland, barely defeating Bell. Lincoln got only 2,294 of the 92,421 votes cast, but carrying the northern states with 180 electoral votes, he won the election. The *Sun* said sourly that Lincoln would be expected to "rule with authority over the people of sovereign states who reject his principles and avowed policy as in direct conflict with their constitutional rights, their institutions, their interests, their equality in the general confederacy, their honor, dignity and self-respect."

At once the *Sun* began contemplating a breakup of the Union. It delved editorially into the "doctrine of secession," which the *Sun* said had its roots in the Tariff Act of 1829. "We love the union and the Constitution," the *Sun* asserted, "and we desire to live under the broad shadow of the first and within the protection of the other. But it is not from those who have willfully sought to destroy its guarantees and to abrogate its rights that we can today ask the people of Maryland to take counsel. Her counsel must be taken at home, and from herself, and from her sister states of the South. She is one of them, and with them, and her destiny is cast with them."

The *Sun* believed that the seceding states were more faithful to the Constitution "than those who remain." It was in the North "that the spirit of disunion exists and is cherished." The paper asked its readers to suggest practical ways of preserving the Union, but none of the ideas was deemed to be feasible. Then the *Sun* rashly predicted: "If the future of the Republican Party is truly foreshadowed by the declaration of its present recognized leaders 'that the election of Lincoln is the end of slavery,' the Union will be positively at end before the fourth of March, and Mr. Lincoln will never go to Washington."

"The National Crisis," a standing headline, appeared almost daily. There was an outcry, the *Sun* joining, for Governor Thomas Holliday Hicks to convene a special session of the legislature and have it call for a state convention as the southern states had been doing. The *Sun* urged this: "Not to pass an act of secession, never to dream of such a thing as that, but to provide for election of a sovereign convention, so as to elicit the will of the people and determine the position of the state." Hicks refused. He said that while Maryland must stand or fall with the South he did not want hasty action, which would endanger Maryland's interests. Angered, the *Sun* called him "faithless" to his obligations. After the war began, Hicks continued to vacillate. In a Baltimore speech he said he "would rather have his right arm hewn from his body than lift it in any way against the South." Two months later, in a speech at Williamsport to a Union brigade, the paper quoted him as saying, "Go forth and let this great rebellion be crushed as it deserves to be crushed." The *Sun* mocked him in an editorial headlined "Governor Hicks's Double."

As the southern state legislatures voted, one by one, to leave the Union, stories, reports, opinion, speculation, and rumors swirled through Baltimore. The *Sun* printed a reporter's tip that students at St. Timothy's Hall in Catonsville had revolted "because of extreme feelings in relation to present disturbed conditions" and that a number had left for their homes in the South while others held possession of the armory. However, a later paper reported that three students had become disgruntled and gone home; four others, to show their support, fired a salute. They were expelled. The affair had no connection with national affairs. Meanwhile, Lincoln was on the slow journey from his home in Illinois to Washington, D.C., and inauguration into office. The *Sun* printed his Springfield farewell speech, adding, "Towards the conclusion of his remarks himself [sic] and audience were moved to tears." At Indianapolis, it explained, "Mr. Lincoln made the speech given yesterday by telegraph, which we reproduced today in a corrected form." Precautions were taken on the journey. "Flag men were stationed at every cross road displaying an American flag as a signal that all was right." At Cincinnati the crowd was disappointed to find Lincoln not "so atrociously ugly as he has been represented." In an unforgiving editorial on his wayside speeches, the *Sun* remarked that Lincoln approached the capital "more in character of a harlequin," and spoke of his qualifications as a "bar-room 'Phunny-Phellow.'"

Crowds had gathered out of "curiosity" to see Lincoln pass through Baltimore. Allan E. Pinkerton, a well-known private detective, warned of a conspiracy to assassinate the President-elect at that time. Pinkerton advised that Lincoln hurry through town after midnight while the city slept, and this was done early on the morning of February 22, 1861. The *Sun* said the crowds were indignant that Lincoln should have traveled "upon the first Southern soil incognito" and called the decision "stupendous folly." The paper was not alone. Much of the East ridiculed that furtiveness of the journey's end. Whether there was a plot has never been established.

Reactions to Lincoln's inauguration reflected partisan passions. Predictably, the historic significance and rhetorical greatness of his First Inaugural Address were altogether lost upon the *Sun,* which fumed: "If the North will sustain him he will coerce and subjugate the South. The argumentation is puerile. Indeed, it has no quality entitled to the dignity of an argument. It is a shaky specimen of special pleading. . . . Unhappily we can find in the message only that prevailing disunionism which is the animating spirit of black republicanism—that disunionism which insists upon the humiliation and submission of the South." The next day it added that after reading and rereading the address "we regard it with the most repugnance and horror."

And the *Sun* belittled Lincoln about his inauguration parade—his riding in a "bullet-proof" carriage, the route guarded by soldiers not only on the streets but on rooftops as well. It implied that so many were needed to guard him that not enough would be left to fight a war.

On page one in February it had reported the inauguration of Jefferson Davis in Montgomery, Alabama, as president of the provisional government of the Confederacy. The *Sun* underscored the differences between the constitutions of the United States and the Confederacy. It reported the recruiting of 200 to 300 Baltimoreans and their departure for "Dixie's land." As war loomed, business was bad, shipping was off, unemployment was high. A dry-goods merchant said that not within the memory of the oldest merchant had trade been so depressed. Visitors from the South declined to buy until they knew what the future would bring. The city appropriated $20,000 to give the unemployed one week's work in the city parks. The pay was 75 cents a day for a six-day week, which often had to support a large family.

Later that March, the *Sun* was still predicting that an invasion of the South was "not within the contemplation of anybody. Everybody, except a few foolish fanatics, knows this is impracticable and moreover that it would not be tolerated by the most Union-loving of the border states. A blockade then is the only real remedy left to the federal government." And if there were a blockade, the South would retaliate with privateers, it assumed, adding, "We could not object to the resort of this system of offense because the government has never agreed to abandon the right of carrying on public war by private exertions." Abell was thinking with his hopes or fears rather than with his brain.

Upon the bombardment of Fort Sumter on April 12, 1861, by encircling Southern batteries, the *Sun* assayed the news accurately. Its headline was "Opening of Civil War." It cautioned readers that "an orderly forbearance in view of differences of opinion is absolutely essential to the preservation of the peace, with excitement running high and demagogues and mischief-makers employing every means to increase it." The *Sun* was still protective of the rights of the South: "In the issues which have been presented in this national crisis, we have directed the attention of our readers to the simple and single matter of Southern rights. The slavery question, secession, coercion and all abstract matters we have avoided, and based our argument and comments upon the practical issues of Southern rights. On this point we cannot err."

Maryland's position was instantly precarious. Roads, shipping, telegraph lines, the railroad between the North and Washington, D.C.—all traversed Maryland. Were Maryland to secede, the nation's capital, adjoining it, would be vulnerable or even untenable. Central and Western Maryland, influenced by their agriculture not dependent on slavery and much of their population newly immigrated, sided with the North. The Eastern Shore and Southern Maryland, a mosaic of ancestral farms and tobacco plantations, used slave labor and had strong ties with the South, socially and politically. Baltimore, with intertwining allegiances, was a divided city. The Protestant Episcopal bishop warned clergymen who were omitting the prayer for the President that they were willfully violating their ordination vow by "mutilating" the worship service. Throughout the long, grievous, savage war, friends, even relatives, with opposed loyalties would not speak. John Pendleton Kennedy, one of Baltimore's distinguished citizens and loyal to the North, was rebuffed when passing old acquaintances who blurted, "No, Sir! No, Sir!" At Front Royal, Virginia, in 1862, the First Regiment of Maryland Volunteers fought the First Maryland Infantry of the Confederate army.

Many Baltimoreans felt that the federal government should not move troops through the city when the purpose was to subdue seceding states. On April 18, 1861, the day Virginia seceded, two companies of U.S. artillery and four companies of Pennsylvania militia bound for Washington, D.C., were hooted and hissed as they marched between protective files of police. The city was so tense that Mayor George William Brown pleaded with partisans to refrain from violence. Referring to Lincoln's call for volunteers, Governor Hicks announced that no Maryland troops would be sent out of state except to defend the nation's capital.

The next day, Friday, without adequate warning to authorities, 1,700 men of the Sixth Massachusetts Infantry arrived at President Street Station. They then had to cross some twenty blocks to Camden Street Station. Because a city ordinance prohibited locomotives from pulling passenger trains through downtown, cars were customarily drawn by horses between stations. As the first seven cars moved along Pratt Street, onlookers began jeering and throwing bricks. But the cars reached Camden Station, where Mayor Brown had ordered police to mass in case of trouble. Trouble was elsewhere. Onlookers had erupted into mobs on Pratt Street, barricading the tracks by upsetting a cart loaded with sand and dragging anchors from the abutting wharves. This action forced the cars back to President Street Station. The soldiers, untrained but with loaded muskets, then headed toward Camden Station on foot at double-quick time. Mayor Brown, apprised, reached the troops as they started down Pratt Street. He ordered the mob to disperse but was ignored. Then, running alongside the commanding officer, the mayor convinced him that the double-quick order indicated panic; the order was changed to a marching step. The plucky mayor joined the commander at the head of the column, hat in hand, brandishing his umbrella at the mob and ordering it to push back. But members of the mob, waving a Confederate flag, were undeterred. They threw stones and bricks, grabbed the regiment's flags and guidons, even wrestled a musket from a frightened soldier. A gun was fired. The *Sun* quoted Policeman No. 71 as saying it came from a soldier. The troops presented arms and fired. The mob responded by firing pistols into the column. About fifty policemen on the run, led by Marshal George P. Kane, put themselves between the column and the rioters. With drawn revolvers they got the troops to Camden Station. While they were entraining, the mob pushed against the car windows, taunting, cursing, spitting, waving knives and guns. In those two hours, four soldiers and eleven citizens were killed, and thirty-six soldiers and an uncounted number of civilians were wounded. As the troop train passed the outskirts, several businessmen, unaware of the rioting, cheered for Jefferson Davis. Angry soldiers leveled their muskets from windows and killed one of the men.

Governor Hicks had three prominent citizens carry a message to President Lincoln by special train, appealing that no more troops be sent through Baltimore. The city militia was called up. The North was outraged by the rioting and clamored for revenge. Northern troops, on their way south, promised to get even with "Mobtown." Mayor Brown, the board of police commissioners, and Governor Hicks were determined to keep more federal troops from Baltimore. They ordered police and the City Guard to burn the railroad bridges that connected the city with the North.

The day after, the *Sun*'s coverage of the rioting filled more than three columns. The account—graphic, detailed, objective and, in the light of history, surprisingly accurate despite the tumult and the conflicting eyewitness versions—began, "It is with profound regret that we record this morning the scenes of bloodshed which took place in our city yesterday. . . . The results of the unequal conflict, in which the blood of our citizens and their lives sacrificed, has had the effect to obliterate almost every shade of difference among us, and to unite as one people, zealously devoted to the honor, the interests and the welfare of our State.''

Monday morning's paper drew a striking portrait of the city: Thousands were on the street around City Hall, headquarters for defense with a volunteer un-uniformed corps. The sight of firearms, a reporter wrote, drew no more attention than an umbrella. Bars had been closed. Urchins sold secession badges and Confederate flags. Artists sketched scenes where the rioting had occurred. Souvenir hunters searched among the Pratt Street cobblestones for cartridge shells. Crowds around bulletin boards of newspaper offices were so dense that those close to them were called upon to read the news as loud as they could.

Because the bridges were now burned, mail from the North was interrupted, but an enterprising news vendor had a horseback rider fetch the Northern papers, which had reached Havre de Grace. The papers denounced Baltimore and called for revenge, to lay the city in ashes. The *Sun* responded, unrealistically, ''But there was no premeditation, no plan, no purpose of bloodshed, and the whole matter was a temporary and sudden ebullition of feeling which might have occurred in any city of the world under similar circumstances.''

Heeding the city's plea, Lincoln agreed that federal troops would thereafter bypass the city. Rumors spread: The North was readying an attack; Jefferson Davis with 100,000 men was marching toward Maryland. A run started on a bank. The paper noted, ''Individuals whose political opinions had grown obnoxious to public sentiment at this crisis had left . . . for fear of personal violence.'' The Massachusetts Eighth Regiment, commanded by General Benjamin F. Butler, on its way to Washington, D.C., bypassed Baltimore by moving down the Chesapeake Bay on a commandeered ferry. Governor Hicks refused Butler permission to land in Annapolis, but Butler did anyway. Army authorities established a military department at Annapolis with Butler in command. He had orders to put down any uprising in Maryland and, if necessary, to suspend the writ of habeas corpus. A suspected spy named Grandval was arrested. The report was that he worked for the *Sun*. The paper called it slanderous: Grandval had only applied for a job with the *Sun* as a reporter in Annapolis and been promptly turned down.

After temporizing, Governor Hicks finally called the General Assembly into special session in Frederick because General Butler had occupied Annapolis. ''Over and over,'' the *Sun* said on April 30, we have urged that the legislature be called into special session, ''not to pass an act of secession, never to dream of such a thing as that, but to provide for election of a sovereign convention, so as to elicit the will of the people and determine the position of the state.'' A few days later it said, ''There is no doubt, and our experience confirms the belief, that the great majority of our citizens, would today, if the independence of the Confederate states, including Virginia, were about to be recognized, vote to unite the state of Maryland and the city of Baltimore with the Southern nation." Soon after convening, the legislature decided it was without authority to take any such action. It did declare the war unjust and unconstitutional, and called for recognition of the Confederacy's independence. But Maryland was not going to join the Confederate States of America.

Later the *Sun* would say, even more unrealistically than ever, "We could select one-half dozen journals of the North and a half-dozen of the South whose editorial staffs would meet in Baltimore and settle this national difficulty to the satisfaction of the whole country in 24 hours." One letter-writer asked the *Sun* to define the duty of a Marylander in the crisis. On May 22, 1861, it replied, "We are living under the constitution and laws of the United States. That in itself is the answer. . . . It is the duty of every good citizen to support the constitution and the laws." It was a point made over and over. Northern papers saw it otherwise. Many attacked the *Sun* as a troublemaker for its Southern and anti-Union viewpoint. Replying, it did not answer directly; it just said, "It has been the fashion of several journals of the North, systematically and persistently to abuse, misrepresent and slander the *Sun*."

After Butler informed General Winfield Scott, commander of the Union forces, that some Baltimoreans were suspected of aiding the Confederacy, he was encouraged to seize and examine them. Butler used that as a reason to occupy Baltimore with 1,000 troops, including the Sixth Massachusetts Regiment. He set up camp on Federal Hill, which was the site of a lager beer garden but overlooked the harbor and much of the city. Butler authorized the Fort McHenry commandant to fire its cannon on the city if he were attacked. (After the April 19 riot, an officer at the fort threatened to destroy the Washington Monument with cannon fire if the garrison was attacked.) Butler was soon removed from his command; the *Sun* reported, almost with glee, that the government had not approved Butler's proclamation: "The removal of General Butler from this station is owing to the fact that he has not managed his command here in a manner likely to conciliate the people or serve the true interests of the government." But the next day it published news of Butler's promotion to major general, with added responsibilities. (In February 1863, without comment, the *Sun* reported a reception tendered Butler by the mayor and City Council, at which Butler was lauded as having "with great energy and ability devoted himself to the preservation of our glorious Union, and our citizens deeply appreciating his labors are anxious to extend to him a cordial welcome.")

John Merryman, a member of an old Maryland family and an officer of the militia that helped burn the railroad bridges on April 20, was arrested a month later without a warrant and imprisoned in Fort McHenry. The next day Chief Justice Roger B. Taney issued a writ of habeas corpus. But at the direction of President Lincoln, the fort's commanding officer ignored the writ and a later charge of contempt of court, saying the President had suspended the writ.

The *Sun* printed Taney's writ, which filled three-and-a-half columns, called it one of the most important in the history of the nation, and termed the President's action "a flagrant usurpation of power."

A month later Marshal Kane, known for his Confederate sympathies, was arrested at his home at three o'clock in the morning, when, according to the *Sun*, about 1,000 soldiers from Fort McHenry and all policemen they met along the way surrounded his house. Kane said it was unnecessary to use such a force for his arrest, that he would have complied with a note from the commandant. He was sent to Fort McHenry, where he shared a room with Merryman.

The military abolished the powers of the police commissioners, claiming Governor Hicks had uncovered a plot for them to forcibly oppose the military. The commissioners did not comply, and ordered police to remove their stars and number. That afternoon no policemen were on the street. The provost marshal appointed new police, who since they had no uniforms were identified with a ribbon in the buttonhole of their coats. The police commissioners were imprisoned in Fort Lafayette in New York harbor for more than a year without being charged or tried.

Under a small headline, "Military Occupation of the City," the *Sun* described infantry and artillery units on the main streets, with cannon in Exchange Place and Monument Square. Guards were placed around the Post Office and the customhouse. A public school was occupied after classes were dismissed.

During the spring and summer of 1861, the *Sun* published detailed accounts of military movements through Baltimore. Reporters would identify units, their strength, and their officers and describe uniforms, equipment, and arms: "The New Jersey regiment wore dark blue frock coats, light blue pantaloons, felt hats ornamented by a gilt edge eagle and black feather. Their arm is the improved percussion lock musket." This was tactical information. Often the reports commented on appearance and fitness: "Among the officers were several aged men whose whitened locks and bent appearance attracted very unusual attention." Another time a reporter remarked, "The men appeared to be very much fatigued and were several times obliged to halt and rest themselves on the curbstone."

A reporter was usually at Camden Station to report arrivals and departures. One noted that troop movements attracted several thousand spectators at times and always attracted the unemployed of both colors and all ages and sexes. "The poor colored persons and boys vending cakes, apples, oranges, lemonade and ice water. They seldom leave the station except for their meals and to obtain fresh stock in trade." One day, as the Twenty-Second New York Infantry entered Camden Station, one soldier stumbled, discharging his musket and killing the man ahead of him. A colonel thought the regiment was being attacked and ordered an entire company to fire into the air to intimidate the supposed mob. Then other companies began firing, a few men leveling their guns and wounding spectators. The crowd panicked, "men, women and children, black and white, falling over and upon each other. Several females fainted, others shrieked and the most alarming reports went forth over the city." Muskets fired into the air had pierced the tin roof of the train shed. The *Sun* said thousands went to the station the next day to view the damaged roof, "which looked like a sieve." Soon after, a similar accident occurred while another regiment was marching through. A cry of riot was raised. The regiment halted, aiming their muskets at the curbside spectators, including women and children. Fortunately an officer discovered what had happened before the soldiers fired. Evidently because of the April 19 riot, troops passing through Baltimore had their muskets loaded. Many were recruits with only a few days' training.

In July 1861 more and more Baltimoreans were arrested on charges of treason. Marshal Kane was charged and indicted for burning the railroad bridges, a number of persons for their part in the April 19 riot (one for grabbing a soldier's musket and killing him), several for recruiting Confederate soldiers, and the proprietor of a lager beer house for treasonable language (he was overheard wishing "that someone would poison all federal troops encamped in Baltimore"). Private houses were searched. When military police entered her house, Mrs. Charles Howard said they would have to break every door and drawer because she would not surrender her keys. They got a locksmith, then ransacked rooms and drawers, seizing three militia muskets and an heirloom sword. So many houses were searched that four congressmen wrote to the President, objecting. He replied the same day: "Our security in the seizing of arms for our destruction will amount to nothing at all if we are never to make mistakes in searching a place where there are none."

A steamer was stopped off Fort McHenry, and the three trunks of two women were searched. Buttons with the letter "J" were considered contraband, because the letter might stand for Jefferson, and were seized. The *Sun* quoted the women as saying that with or without the buttons the Confederates would and could whip their invaders. It printed a letter from Richmond, confiscated by the military, which said, "The Baltimore ladies are more dangerous than their men." Several times women were arrested as Confederate spies for cutting telegraph wires. The paper, unfortunately, never described how they managed this.

The *Sun* told of a colonel's seizing Confederate cards and badges from a boy selling them on the street, then threatening the boy "who wept bitterly at his loss." Witnesses "expressed their opinions without regard to choice of language. The boy was doubly indemnified for his loss." The provost marshal ordered stores to remove portraits of Confederate leaders and secession badges and emblems. The order also applied to secession cravats, "much in vogue with young men and lads." Those who refused to doff them when so ordered were sent to jail. Two young girls were arrested on the street and carried to a station house because portions of their dresses bore the combination of prohibited colors. The *Sun* observed, "Other cases, of which the above are samples, occurred during the day." Sentinels on Long Bridge in Anne Arundel County stopped a funeral procession with its somber attendants. The coffin was opened, and instead of a corpse the searchers found muskets and ammunition.

The paper's reports on Bull Run, the first major battle, were drawn from "Agents of the Associated Press" and indirectly from eyewitness accounts by three congressmen. Later it printed the South's version from Richmond papers and official reports from both sides. Printing General Pierre Beauregard's dispatch, it explained, "It contains little that is new but we give it, notwithstanding, as part of the history of our time." When European journals reached Baltimore, the *Sun* printed the newsletters of a French correspondent and of William H. Russell of the *Times* of London. Russell was a *Sun* favorite, and it often used his correspondence. The paper made a fuss when he stopped in Baltimore before duck-hunting on the Bush River.

In the summer of 1861 the economic depression intensified. The *Sun* was usually casual and weak with business and financial news, but in bits and pieces it reported that the city's $20,000 had provided one week's work for 5,378 of the unemployed, and that because employment was off more than 25 percent in most businesses the poor were suffering. Children begging at public houses were a common sight. When police put some in a house of refuge the *Sun* observed sententiously that they would there "be taught to labor for a living— a more honorable calling than that of mendicant." The largest soup kitchen was funded and served by the prominent Winans family across from their mansion in a building "with a basement for the exclusive use of the colored people." In one ward on Christmas Eve, 700 loaves of bread were passed out on a street corner. Shortages caused the price of beef to shoot up 50 percent (in two weeks some 2,000 cattle passed through Baltimore for the army). A scarcity of coal and wood for fuel was predicted.

Until that summer, the *Sun* had spoken out—moderately, to be sure—on issues that divided the North and the South, and in some ways it had tried to be the conscience of the North. It challenged and rebutted Northern papers for their attacks and what it deemed the government's attempts to coerce the South. As noted, the *Sun* was a constant defender of states' rights and strict interpretation of the Constitution. And it was a staunch defender of the city, resenting the vilification of Baltimore after April 19. A *Sun* editorial denounced the Northern press, especially the Republican papers of New York, as "an irresponsible dictatorship with regard to the whole South and most offensively to Baltimore."

But the pressure built up, as evidenced by an attack in the *Philadelphia Press,* the harassing and suspension of newspapers by federal authorities, and the arrest, jailing, or deporting of proprietors and editors to the South. Soon Abell became intimidated, the *Sun* muzzled. From then on the editorial watchword was caution. Abell was not and did not pretend to be heroic. His only objective was to keep his paper in business and himself out of jail. The *Sun* ceased expressing even mild displeasure over turns of events. It mentioned political parties by name as little as possible. The paper became extremely prudent in reporting political news, local or national. On sensitive issues the *Sun* took no stand. In fact, it seldom printed an editorial. When it did, the topic was innocuous—the glory of spring or the work of missionaries in China.

The *Press,* in an editorial entitled "Aid and Comfort to the Enemy," had said, "The Baltimore papers continue to publish daily accounts of the movements of our troops, while the papers here and the newspaper correspondents are denied a similar privilege. The Baltimore *Sun* is in Beauregard's army every morning in large numbers." In a long, sputtering editorial the *Sun* denied the charge as a "deliberate fabrication—a sheer invention." It said, "From the day that mail facilities were suspended between Northern and Southern states, not a paper has been dispatched from this office to subscribers in any portion of the seceded states." It added, "It is impossible for us to gauge the depths of that malice which seems to actuate a portion of the Northern press with respect to the Baltimore *Sun.*" But from then on, August 28, 1861, it did not give specifics on troop movements or describe their uniforms, equipment, or physical condition. It restricted reporting to such generalizations as "Several regiments moved from their camps and were occupied by others."

According to a study by Sidney T. Matthews in the *Maryland Historical Magazine* of June 1941, federal military authorities exercised more control over Baltimore newspapers and suppressed more of them in that city than in any other city under Union control. Only three were published without interruption during the war: the *American,* staunch in its loyalty, the *Clipper,* and the *Sun.*

In August 1861 the Fort McHenry commandant wrote a letter to a member of Lincoln's cabinet. It said, in part: "I have had the idea that some of the rabid Secession papers in Baltimore should be stopped. The *Sun* has, all say, changed its tone. I had an interview with the agent and informed him that the publication would not be permitted if it persisted in the course it was pursuing. The provost marshal had a visit subsequently from the proprietor, who assured him that there should be no future cause of complaint."

During the first months of the war, the authorities did not interfere no matter what papers printed. Then, as a warning to those printing facts and opinion that were deemed disloyal, the Post Office Department denied use of the mails to three using combustible language. In 1861 only the Secretary of War could take action against the papers, but thereafter the commanding general in Baltimore was empowered to act on his own in arresting editors and suppressing papers. As feelings intensified, seven papers were suppressed temporarily or permanently. They had urged Maryland to secede or, less blatant, reprinted articles from Northern or foreign papers sympathetic to the South and hostile to the North. The *Daily Exchange* and the *South* were forced to stop publishing when their respective editors, Frank Key Howard and

Thomas W. Hall, were imprisoned. The *South* reappeared six days later with a new editor, but in six months was again suspended, and its two publishers and editor were charged with treason and imprisoned.

Abell was probably both amused and frightened when Charles C. Fulton, once a *Sun* man and then publisher and editor of the *American,* was arrested and sent to Fort McHenry for forty-eight hours. Fulton, a loyal Union man, was apprehended for notifying the Associated Press of a meeting he had had with President Lincoln. Fulton's confidential memo was then inadvertently published. When this was explained, he was released.

From time to time the *Sun* reported the arrests of Baltimore editors and the suppressions of other Baltimore newspapers, but without comment. Only when Howard and Hall were released after thirteen months in three different federal prisons did the *Sun,* in its local column, not in an editorial, observe, "They returned to their own homes and their own people; to the voiceless but certain sympathy of those who know them true and faithful to the Constitution and laws of the land." That was the closest the *Sun* ventured to challenging the military censorship.

In June 1863 the provost marshal prohibited Baltimore newspapers from publishing articles from five Northern papers: the *New York World* and the *New York Express,* the *Cincinnati Enquirer,* the *Chicago Times,* and the *Caucasian,* although those journals were not censored. Baltimore papers were also forbidden in obituary notices to use the initials C.S.A. (for Confederate States of America), because, authorities said, it gave recognition to the Confederate cause.

Papers suppressed between 1862 and October 1865 were the *Maryland News Sheet* (its two editors and owner were jailed); the *Evening Transcript* (once stopped for four days, but later stopped permanently for printing an exaggerated estimate of Union losses at the battle of Spotsylvania Court House); the *Evening Bulletin* (probably for the owner's suspected disloyalty); the *Evening Post* (for posting on its bulletin board news of a riot in Cincinnati which it had copied from a Cincinnati paper); the *Evening Loyalist* (for alleging that the government had called up 300,000 more men, "thus imposing upon the people"); and the *Daily Republican* (for its sympathetic attitude toward the South and specifically for printing the poem "The Southern Cross," written in the style of the "The Star-Spangled Banner" and urging rebellion). Stephen H. Joyce, Beale H. Richardson, and his son, Francis A. Richardson, proprietors and editors, were arrested and sent by train to Winchester, Virginia, and set free at Southern picket lines. They were ordered not to return during the war under penalty of being treated as spies. Francis A. Richardson, attempting to come back, was arrested and imprisoned. He was released in March 1865 by order of President Lincoln. (Richardson joined the *Sun* in 1866 and was its Washington correspondent until 1901.) The top circulation for any of the suppressed papers was about 1,200; the *Daily Republican*'s circulation was only 700. This in a city of 230,000.

In his *History of Maryland,* J. Thomas Scharf relates this account of an attempt to suppress the *Sun* and force its sale:

> During these dark hours the Baltimore *Sun* often incurred the displeasure of the government, and at one time an order for its suppression and the arrest of Mr. Arunah S. Abell, the proprietor, was issued by the War Department in Washington, and was about to be transmitted to the commander of the Baltimore military department, when Mr. Abell received information of the fact in time to have an effective and earnest protest interposed against this high-handed proceeding, and the execution of the order was suspended. The principal motive which instigated the proceeding was betrayed the day after, when two prominent Pennsylvania politicians called upon Mr. Abell at his office, and desired to know if the *Sun* could be purchased, and if so, at what figure. They anticipated that with the fate of other newspapers, which had been suppressed and their editors incarcerated, staring him in the face, Mr. Abell would be only too willing, if not thankful, to retire from his dangerous position and be rid of his precarious property at any sacrifice. They were, however, very much surprised, if not mortified, when they found that their design was thoroughly understood, upon being told that the *Sun* was not for sale at any price which it was in their power to offer.

In addition to nine Baltimore papers temporarily or permanently suppressed, the military also arrested the editors of a number of county papers, including the *Denton Journal,* the *Marlboro Gazette,* the *Worcester County Shield,* the *Leonardtown Beacon,* and the *Rockville Sentinel.* The *Sun* also reported the arrests of editors in Harrisburg, Philadelphia, and New York and the arrest of a *New York Herald* war correspondent on orders of General William T. Sherman, charged with giving aid and comfort to the enemy and with being a spy. The *Sun* said his story of the battle of Vicksburg, in which General Sherman "was severely handled," was the reason for the correspondent's arrest and court-martial. George A. Porter—his paper was not identified—was arrested for publishing erroneous information about the Army of the Potomac "with a view to affect the stock market &c." Matthews concluded his newspaper study:

> In the arbitrary arrest of disloyal editors the action taken by the government, for the first year and a half of the war, had no support in the law. . . . The only reasonable justification, on legal grounds, for the suppression of newspapers appears to be "the doctrine that under martial law the military rule supplants the ordinary law." But in Maryland, martial law was proclaimed only once (June 30, 1863) and all cases of newspaper suppression occurred during a time when the civil authority, in theory and according to the law, was supreme.

Newspapers were intimidated not only by authorities but also by demonstrators. One day, a crowd expecting news from the Upper Potomac became unruly; ringleaders burst into a newspaper's offices, demanding that it fly the national flag, which was hurriedly done.

In the November state elections the *Sun* announced, "We have no suggestions to make." At the polls military police arrested so many for treason that police stations were jammed. Few Democrats voted, and the Union party elected its entire ticket. After the election the *Sun* said, "The report in another column furnishes a sketch of the proceedings of the day and renders comment needless, as it would be profitless and unwise."

Silenced editorially, a paper could still make a point by simply reporting the military arrests, which were often for what seemed ridiculous reasons: A house was searched to remove a small Confederate flag decorating a Christmas tree. A silk quilt, embroidered with the name of Jefferson Davis, alleged to be a present for him, was confiscated. A young man was arrested because the inside crown of his hat was embellished with a Southern flag. People were arrested for "hurrahing" for Jefferson Davis and for waving handkerchiefs when Confederate prisoners passed. Neighbors reported a boy for waving at prisoners from his home; the deputy marshal and his assistants sent him to Fort McHenry, and a guard of twenty soldiers was placed around the house. It developed that a young lady, a visitor from New York, had waved her apron at the prisoners, then gone to a window and waved the end of a lace curtain, as did the boy. The marshal had orders to arrest the woman, but decided it was a thoughtless gesture rather than premeditated disloyalty.

Military detectives roamed Baltimore to ferret out spies and acts of disloyalty. They, and overwrought neighbors, were flooding the military police with tips and names. So many citizens were arrested for disloyalty based on rumor that authorities announced this was "causing great annoyance to the general commanding and the officers having charge of such matters." Thereafter such charges had to be made in writing and attested under oath.

In September 1862, General Robert E. Lee carried the war into the North, and Baltimore prepared for an invasion by enrolling volunteer militia and throwing up defenses. Lee's army of Northern Virginia occupied Frederick, fought the battle of South Mountain, and then confronted the Union army under General George B. McClellan at Antietam. Although the battle between 75,000 Union troops and 40,000 Confederates was only seventy miles from Baltimore, Abell did not send his reporters to cover it. Instead—three days after the bloodiest one-day battle of the war, in which 23,000 were killed— the headline in the *Sun*'s Saturday paper ("War in Maryland") was based on the report of the *New York Herald* correspondent. On Monday it had "graphic and interesting particulars," but again it relied on the Associated Press and Northern papers.

New York, Philadelphia, Boston, Chicago, St. Louis, and Cincinnati papers had correspondents in the field. The most enterprising paper was the *Herald,* which at one time or another had sixty-three correspondents. It claimed that at every important battle at least one of its correspondents was an eyewitness. Its Southern department collected whatever information it could concerning the South. Most came from Southern papers—the tales of runaway Negroes, deserters, prisoners of war, refugees. The *Herald* even compiled a roster of the Confederate army. When this was published and a copy reached Richmond, the Confederate War Office suspected clerks of having furnished the information. The *Herald* spent more than $500,000 on its coverage of the war. The *American* was the only Baltimore paper to employ war correspondents, and it had three. Because of its extensive coverage, it had a large circulation in the army. Some of its best reporting was done by Fulton, who won praise for his coverage of the naval attack on Charleston in 1863.

During much of the war, Abell headed the editorial column on page two with a short piece titled "The War News." It was a news summary, and the only opinion ever risked was to describe whatever was occurring as "interesting": "The intelligence from the Upper Potomac is interesting," "The intelligence from Yorktown is interesting," "Interesting particulars of the evacuation of Norfolk by the Confederates and its occupation by Federal forces," "An interesting account of the operations of the Confederates, while in possession of the Orange and Alexandria Railroad . . . is published," "We publish an interesting account of the capture of the Federal gunboat *Indianola*." "Interesting" was safe.

The *Sun* held its peace about President Lincoln's preliminary Emancipation Proclamation freeing slaves in the Confederacy, issued a few days after Antietam, but it did print what Northern and Southern papers said. Its comment on the fall election was restricted to a coy "There is no opposition to what is known as the Union party, the reason for this being generally understood and requiring no explanation at our hands." And on New Year's Day it said, "We look forward . . . for the day when in clear light of civil supremacy we shall resume the advocacy of political truth."

In June 1863, Lee marched a second time into Maryland, and again Baltimore feared invasion. Refugees from Western Maryland flocked into the city. Martial law was declared. All stores except apothecaries and offices of daily papers had to close at 5:00 P.M., bars and restaurants at 8:00 P.M., and the railway at 10:00 P.M. Men enlisted for temporary service. The city appropriated $100,000 to dig entrenchments and appealed for 1,000 men to do it. The central city was barricaded with several thousand hogsheads filled with sand and stone (later the broken ones were given to the poor for fuel). But the only troops to enter the city were the wounded from the three-day battle of Gettysburg, when the Union force of 88,000 lost 23,000 killed, wounded, or missing and the Confederate army of 75,000 lost 28,000. For that epic battle the *Sun* was again content to use the Associated Press and to reprint a few days later eyewitness accounts from the Northern papers. The *Sun* did sketch scenes of the aftermath: 2,000 wounded soldiers streaming into Baltimore (it remarked on the number shot in the hands and arms), the Adams Express Company putting together a makeshift ambulance corps of its horses and wagons, Baltimoreans rushing to the battlefield to aid the wounded and remove the dead. Some hack drivers charged double fares for carrying the wounded; those caught were sentenced to work six days on the city's fortifications.

When the battlefield was dedicated in November, the *Sun* called the two-hour address of Edward Everett, the principal speaker, "brilliant and eloquent" and quoted more than a column of Everett's 15,000 words. The *Sun* added, "Among the distinguished persons in attendance were President Lincoln and some members of his cabinet." Two days later it printed Lincoln's Gettysburg address without comment. It did note at the end "long continued applause."

The *Sun* may not have exerted itself to cover the battles even when nearby, but the busy, observant staff did create a vivid mosaic of the divided city, both in the vicissitudes of its domestic life and in the scope of the military occupation. An August Sunday was portrayed this way: "Many sought the country, but the dust in the roads made the journey uncomfortable. The police had little else to do than seek the shady side of the streets." (If laborers suffered sunstroke it was described as "Coup de Soleil.") The absences of itinerant organ-grinders was wistfully noted; they had gone off to war, "keeping step with the music instead of making it." When a cow ran amok on Baltimore Street, trampling a wheelbarrow overloaded with mattresses and making hundreds run for their lives, 300 words of detail captured the excitement. Even on a busy day there was time to draw a touching, intimate picture of a departed citizen: "Joseph R. Foreman, many years a courteous and gentlemanly gatekeeper at Green Mount Cemetery, died at the advanced age of 77. He had been partially paralyzed for some time, and shortly before he expired was assisted out of bed and while in the act of kneeling to pray suddenly fell dead. Few citizens were better known than Mr. Foreman." They were trying times, not a time for humor, but once Abell permitted a touch—perhaps it was a gibe—in the news column when a bell was installed to signal the departure of cars to Towsontown. The item said it would not only alert travelers "but will be a ready means of the editor of the *Advocate* keeping his watch and clock correct."

The military police were still doggedly busy. Many Baltimoreans were being charged for their part in the riot of April 19, 1861. A lad was arrested for hissing the national airs at the Front Street Theatre. Proprietors of drinking houses were arrested for selling liquor to soldiers. The punishment was ten days in jail and confiscation of all liquor. In one incident, friends got to the bar before the police and removed the liquor for their own use. Often the proprietor was made to walk through town carrying a sign saying "I Sold Liquor to Soldiers." Public embarrassment was not an unusual punishment. Thirteen men, banished from Washington as thieves and sent north, during their layover in Baltimore were marched around town carrying a placard stating "We Are Thieves and Vagabonds," followed by a band playing the "Rogue's March." (When soldiers were drummed out of service they were stripped of their uniform, their heads were shaved, and they were "dismissed with the usual formalities.")

At a funeral of a Confederate officer in Green Mount Cemetery, a detachment of soldiers arrested eighteen mourners, including the officer's father, because the corpse had supposedly been dressed in a new Confederate uniform. The undertaker later testified that no changes had been made after the body arrived from Gettysburg, except for a piece of gray cloth laid over part of the torn uniform. The eighteen were asked to take the oath of allegiance. All declined. They were released, but "the declinations were noted opposite each name and kept."

When a building of a Union supporter was burned under suspicious circumstances, the military rule was to levy a tax to pay for the destroyed property on those residing within six miles who were known to be "disaffected and encouraging rebellion and treason." If the fines were not paid within three days, those owing them were jailed until payment was made.

The *Sun* carried slave-trade advertisements. In those for runaways, descriptions often included abnormalities and mannerisms, "Face full of bumps and looks down when spoken to." (When one slave escaped from Virginia on an overturned canoe, General Butler made him a servant of a fellow officer.) For-sale ads stressed skills, "First-rate meat and pastry cook," or gave length of servitude, "12-year-old Talbot County girl to serve until April 1, 1865." Black convicts were sold, one to the sheriff of Harford County for five years for $167.50. News items told of slaves hired out in Virginia as factory workers and house servants for $100 to $125 year; the price went down as the war progressed. Baltimore still had slave pens in 1863. Military authorities freed slaves in what they called a "prison" on West Pratt Street; those who were the property of rebels were enlisted in the Union army.

Free blacks did not have the same rights as whites. They could not be on the street after 11:00 P.M. without a pass, and they could not buy liquor. Frequently they were assaulted for no apparent reason, with little action taken against assailants. A black hack driver was charged with assaulting a white woman returning from a funeral. He was fined $20 and given thirty-nine lashes. The *Sun* commented: "The frequency of insults to white passengers by negroes has put upon them the severest penalty of law."

The *Sun* was still weak on business news, and for its annual January review relied on a commercial journal. In 1863 business was better than in previous war years. Communication lines to the West were opened. Shipbuilding was never more prosperous. Ship caulker's wages were up to $2.75 a day. But prices in the city markets were "beyond anything ever known in the history of Baltimore." Beef was fifteen to twenty-five cents a pound, butter $1, shad as high as $2 a pair, and vegetables—four to five times higher than at the start of war—were hard to get because the Sanitary Commission bought most for the sick and wounded. The Wilkens Hair Factory had scavengers on battlefields collect hair from the fallen for its products.

In July 1864, Baltimore again feared attack. Southern forces had moved into Maryland, and the Union army lost 1,600 men at the battle of Monocacy, near Frederick. Church bells sounded the general alarm. Militia forming new units "captured some of the citizens standing on street corners." Policemen on horseback impressed "able-bodied colored men for service." The *Sun* noted that this caused "a general skedaddling." About 10,000 men were mobilized; volunteers included veterans of the War of 1812 who were in their seventies and eighties. Evidently *Sun* men too were impressed or volunteered. Filler— type set in advance—was used to plug columns, and local items were few. One was about a well-known portrait painter charged with disloyalty. It was alleged that he said he would not cut his hair until the independence of the South was recognized. After taking an oath of allegiance, putting up $10,000 for bail, and having his hair cut to an acceptable length, he was released from Fort McHenry. During the five days the city prepared for attack, children built miniature forts, asking passersby for a penny for supplies. One responded by smashing his cane on the head of an 8-year-old boy, "inflicting injury from which he never recovered."

That spring, citizens voted to hold a convention to draw up a new state constitution. It abolished slavery, declared that the federal government was supreme over the states, and forbade anyone who had shown sympathy for the South from voting or holding office. The former constitution had declared "that the liberty of the press ought to be inviolably preserved." The new one added "that every citizen . . . ought to be allowed to speak, write and publish his sentiments on all subjects, being responsible for the abuse of that liberty." Before it was voted on, the *Sun*'s only comment was "The election is an important one and its results will be looked upon with deep interest." It appeared that the constitution would be rejected. "No" votes piled up from Southern Maryland and the Eastern Shore, but Maryland soldiers in the Union army endorsed it ringingly. The new constitution, approved by a slender 375 votes, became effective on November 1. Maryland could say afterward that it had, by a full year, preceded the federal government in abolishing slavery.

The national Union convention had met in Baltimore in June at the Front Street Theatre to nominate Lincoln for President and Andrew Johnson, a pro-Union congressman from Tennessee, for Vice President. The *Sun* printed several columns of news but no editorial comment. After the November elections, it said that many voters had stayed home, while others were challenged for alleged disloyalty and their votes refused. In Baltimore, Lincoln got 14,983 votes to 2,954 for his Democratic rival, George B. McClellan, one of the generals whom the President had to relieve from command for ineffectiveness. Lincoln carried the state, 40,171 to 32,739. When Lincoln gave an informal talk after the election, the *Sun* devoted nine paragraphs to it. In contrast, Jefferson Davis's views of the war, copied from the *New York Herald*, were deemed worth three-and-a-half columns.

Lincoln's inauguration was reported by reprinting the coverage of Washington papers. Commenting on the address, which began "With malice toward none and charity for all," the *Sun* remarked: "The unusual brevity of President Lincoln's second inaugural address affords little upon which to comment." Later the *Sun* quoted the *New York Independent,* which it identified as an administration paper, as saying Andrew Johnson had taken "the solemn oath of office in a state of intoxication."

When Petersburg and Richmond were captured, the *Sun* made no comment on the Union victories or their implications. On April 10, 1865, under the headline "Glorious News," it announced the surrender of Lee at Appomattox. The *Sun* editorial the following day was on the Baltimore United Fire Department, which had been disbanded after twenty-five years of supervising volunteer fire companies.

Arunah S. Abell's newspaper voiced no overall judgment on the bloodiest war America had known, or on the merits of either the winning or losing side. Only by reading between the lines could a subscriber gather that the *Sun* was happy at last to have peace. Four days later, its headline on the assassination of Lincoln was "A Great National Calamity." Once again the *Sun* made no editorial comment, on the event itself or on Lincoln's presidency.

The next day it reported that the band of the Fourteenth Virginia Rebel Regiment, recently captured and paroled, had been performing at the Holliday Street Theater. The City Council complained that it was offensive and asked the police to intervene. The sale of portraits of John Wilkes Booth, Lincoln's assassin, was prohibited. A woman was jailed for exulting in that assassination, and four others for sympathizing with rebel prisoners. Edward Keelan was locked up as a military prisoner on charges of rioting on April 19, 1861. Returning soldiers, who got their canteens filled with liquor in Washington, D.C., for $1, were often intoxicated and "frequently straggle behind and fall down upon the sidewalks, &c."

On April 22 the *Sun* printed a lengthy graphic description when Lincoln's funeral train stopped in Baltimore. All business in the city was suspended as Lincoln's coffin was conveyed to the Merchants Exchange, followed by a cortege of thousands, including military units and bands, relatives, members of Congress, state and city officials, and such diverse delegations as the Hebrew Literary Association and the Aged Guard of 1812. At the Exchange the coffin was opened for viewing for one-and-a-half hours. The *Sun,* a constant critic of the President during the war, observed, "All we can see of Abraham Lincoln is a mere shell. All that made this flesh vital, sentient and affectionate is gone forever." After the viewing, the procession moved to Calvert Station, where the nine-car funeral train left with "a shrill whistle, thus closing the last sad rite the city of Baltimore can pay to the beloved ruler of the country."

Using Associated Press dispatches, the *Sun* reported the passage through Maryland to Philadelphia. "Some of the most notable and affecting scenes were of exceedingly plain and poorly dressed men and women, at different places on the route, with handkerchiefs at their eyes and having the appearance of weeping." In Philadelphia the line waiting to view the President stretched for three miles. During the rest of the 1,600-mile roundabout trip to Springfield, Illinois, the *Sun* devoted only a daily paragraph to give the destination of the train and the size of the crowd. It concluded: "Our mournful duty of escorting the mortal remains of Abraham Lincoln hither is performed."

Little is known of the *Sun* staff during the war. Only a few names appeared in the paper. Two reporters were inspecting emplacements on Federal Hill when a soldier said to one, J. Marshall Hanna, "I know you're a d—— secessionist," then beat and kicked him, breaking his jaw. A Mr. Wingate, identified as the law reporter, ran for help. It was the only time the paper mentioned staff members except in short obituaries. When Thomas J. Beach, the editor, died in 1864, his obituary was only four inches long and sadly lacking in facts.

Washington dispatches appeared under two headings: "Reported for the Baltimore *Sun*" and "Correspondence of the Baltimore *Sun*." The former was mainly a congressional report, the latter a roundup of Washington and national news, sometimes about casual matters. "Correspondence" was signed by Aga, Ion, Ura, Mercury, or "M." Some days two dispatches appeared, each with a different pen name. During much of the war, often every day, the signature was "Potomac." Who was employed exclusively by the *Sun* and which ones contributed to a number of papers is not clear. The *Sun* did mention that a number of correspondents also served as congressional clerks.

Unlike the Mexican War years, the *Sun* had little to boast about. It did marvel at the speed it received presidential messages—sometimes over six wires—and how fast it could produce an extra. Once in 1862 the Associated Press (AP) sent such a message, but the transmission was so garbled that the *Sun* claimed "it could not make even readable nonsense of it [and] concluded that it was hardly worth while to perplex the public with it" in an extra. The *Sun* joined in complaints that AP dispatches on political meetings were "tinged with political coloring . . . with slang phrases or political nicknames." It objected not only because papers had different political opinions but also because it believed the duty of the Associated Press was to "consist simply in furnishing facts in plain, unvarnished language, free from political or sectarian bias, and also from the personal opinion of the agents or anyone else." (Fulton, of the *American*, was also the Baltimore agent of the Associated Press.) The *Sun*, like other papers, printed many extras—sometimes three a day. Because no regular edition was printed the day after Thanksgiving, it printed an evening edition at 2:00 P.M. for the first time on Friday, November 28, 1863.

Introducing new type, it explained that the old type was worn down after such large press runs. In an editorial on circulation, the *Sun* said some of its "slandering" competitors had claimed its circulation had "diminished to a fabulous extent." Its reply, in the next few weeks, was to claim the greatest circulation ever. The *Sun* never gave a total figure, but claimed "the paper was distributed by 31 carriers, sold in twenty bookstores, hawked on the street by 60 youths, sent to 639 post offices over a vast area of the United and Confederate States of America and sent in packages to 65 agents representing cities and villages where it is served by carrier as it is in Baltimore." This circulation, it estimated, "was from 20,000 to 25,000 greater than that of all the other daily papers in Baltimore, printed in the English language, combined." Another boast was, "The *Sun* is of infinitely more value to this community than the *London Times* to the people of London."

Many errors occurred in reporting local news. Names of prominent people were misspelled, some were misidentified, and typographical errors were more common than in previous years. The stresses and strains of wartime publication and perhaps a smaller and less-qualified staff had much to do with it. Mistakes were corrected under a heading "Review." One of the more embarrassing mistakes concerned the death of Merrick Boyfoil Field [*sic*], who had died three months before and whose body had gone unclaimed. "The deceased, whose lot it was to die among strangers, in a strange land," the *Sun* reported, "was highly connected in England, a brother being the British Secretary of War." Then the Review: "We were misinformed in some of the statements made yesterday concerning the disposal of the remains of the late Captain Meyrick Beaufoy Field. The body is to be buried in Green Mount Cemetery. The personal effects are in possession of the counsel, not the coroner. . . . The deceased is no relative of the Secretary of War, but his brother-in-law is one of the chief clerks in that department, which fact gave rise to the report."

The *Sun* was packed with ads. At times they preempted column one on page two, the editorial column. Editorials, or what passed for them during the war, were moved to page one, which often had several columns of ads. These included a series of letters to the editor extolling the astonishing healing powers of a doctor whose address and office hours would be given at the end of the letters. A large ad that appeared frequently on inside pages, headed "Disease of Imprudence," mentioned "the many thousands cured at this institution year after year and the other numerous important surgical operations performed by Dr. Johnson and witnessed by reporters of the *Sun*."

All the while, Abell was forbidding typographical exhibitionism in advertising, particularly by imposing a one-column width limit. For their part, many advertisers jammed as many words as possible into their space because they paid by the line. To attract attention, a dry-goods merchant would repeat the word "shirts" twenty or more times vertically, surrounded by white space. Then theaters and concert halls began using that style, taking half a column or more. The ads were eye-catchers on a page otherwise set solidly with small type.

The *Sun* often puffed in the news columns for its advertising successes on lost and found items: "Almost daily there is striking incidents [*sic*] of the benefits arising from advertisements inserted in the columns of the *Sun*. A woman with a helpless family came to the city from the county, and having a husband in the army, drew his bounty and also took charge of money due wives of two other soldiers, $300 in greenbacks. She dropped her pocketbook. Distressed, she resorted to a *Sun* ad and a few hours after it appeared the money was found by an honest youth."

After innumerable references to papers in other cities that were raising their street-sale price, the *Sun* on December 19, 1864, increased the price to two cents, claiming it was the last penny paper to do so. The reason, it said, was the wartime cost of newsprint—up threefold.

After Simmons's death in 1855, Abell and Swain had purchased his interest in the *Philadelphia Public Ledger* and continued their partnership, Abell as half-owner of the *Ledger* and Swain as half-owner of the *Sun*. But with secession and war, a rift developed. Swain was a staunch Union man, Abell a supporter of the South. The partnership ended, Swain keeping the *Ledger*, Abell the *Sun*. No announcement of the split was made, but on December 22, 1860, the *Sun* Iron Building was sold at public auction. "The necessity of the sale," the *Sun* said in a short local item, "originated in the adjustment of the joint estate of the proprietors, one of whom deceased some time since. It was, therefore, a bona fide offer and sale of the property, open to all. There were a large number of capitalists and many of our most wealthy and responsible business men present, besides partners from New York and Philadelphia, and among them several bidders." The building was purchased in fee by the Abell interests for $80,000. The property on the southeast corner of Baltimore and Gay streets, a former site of the *Sun*, was bought at the same time by Abell for $12,050.

In December 1864 the *Sun* announced the sale of the *Ledger*, with a two-sentence reference to the original partnership, "Established nearly 29 years ago by Messrs. Swain, Abell and Simmons. After the death of Mr. Simmons, in 1855, it was published by Messrs. Swain & Abell, and for the past four years by Messrs. Wm. M. Swain & Co." The *Ledger* was seldom quoted by the *Sun* after the partnership's dissolution, but excerpts appeared again after Swain sold the *Ledger* to George W. Childs, a native of Baltimore who had a successful printing business in Philadelphia. Childs, in his memoirs, wrote that the *Ledger* "had been sold at a cent ever since it was started in 1836, and Messrs. Swain & Abell, then the proprietors, though they had lost over $100,000 by keeping the rate at 'six and a quarter cents a week,' were averse to a change." Frank Luther Mott, the newspaper historian, said that when Swain retired he was worth $3 million.

Abell was not the enterprising, spirited publisher-proprietor he had been in the Mexican War. He had discreetly and warily avoided conflict with federal authorities so the *Sun* would not be suppressed or he himself imprisoned. Shackled editorially, he emphasized the business side, sometimes carrying so much advertising that space for news was curtailed in the four-page paper. He seemed to think of everything when it came to making money. He even ran ads selling his exchange papers for wrapping paper.

FOUR

The Last Years of the Founder
1865–1888

When the Civil War ended, Baltimore remained a divided city. Citizens were still being arrested for disloyal acts and treasonable language, one for avowing "The war is not over!" Paroled Confederate soldiers had to register and change to civilian clothing within twenty-four hours after returning home. No member of the Confederate forces could remain in Maryland unless he had lived there before the war. Parishioners had split to form new churches or denominations because of political differences. The City Council wanted the pro-South congregations closed because they were "governed by disloyal and unpatriotic purposes," but the military refused to intervene. The *Sun* reported that the Freedmen's Bureau had ordered Southern Maryland landowners to care for their aged former slaves; if they did not, their plantations would be seized. (A week later this was denied by the Bureau.) The military commander forbade boys in military schools to wear gray uniforms, because they were "offensive to loyal soldiers and citizens." Later the order was amended: they could wear gray provided it did not differ from the shade of gray used for cadet uniforms at the U.S. Military Academy.

The *Sun*, in ways both small and large, strove to be a pacifier. It suggested that citizens put out barrels of ice water along streets where returning soldiers marched, adding, "The men have seen hard service." Gradually it began to voice opinions. After Jefferson Davis was reported captured in Georgia with a train of five wagons and three ambulances, "disguised in his wife's clothing," the *Sun* said, "All considerate and dispassionate men . . . will approve the determination of President Johnson to give Jefferson Davis a trial before a civil court." It was a steady, reasoned voice for reconciliation. Editorially it declared,

> If there be anything in which political parties should vie with each other it is in the cultivation of fraternal feeling among the members of our widespread national

family and in hastening to bind up the wounds which the late struggle has inflicted upon the people. The citizens of the Southern states have been conquered and they have submitted to the results of the trial by battle with a manly readiness that must command the respect, as their stubborn resistance on the battlefield challenged the admiration of the people of the North.

The *Sun* concentrated on postwar life. The Bay Line steamers resumed their schedules, and Baltimoreans traveled to Richmond—some out of curiosity, others to search out lost relatives and friends or to bring back sick and wounded. In news and editorial columns extensive coverage was given to the Baltimore Agricultural Aid Society, raising money to provide farm implements, tools, seed, and stock to the Potomac counties of Virginia and the Shenandoah Valley, "that portion [of the South] where it was commercially connected with the city." Within two months Baltimoreans raised nearly half the $100,000 goal, helping 463 applicants with two steam sawmills, farm implements, horses, and 6,000 bushels of wheat. The Maryland Union Commission helped destitute people in the South. The *Sun* reported that parts of the new state of West Virginia had been overrun twelve times by contending armies and had been stripped bare of necessities. A general telegraphed from Macon, Georgia, that 25,000 to 50,000 people were "absolutely destitute for food." Speaking of Baltimore charity, the paper remarked, "We are not disappointed in the manifestation of kindly regard and forgiveness on this side—from all which there can flow but the one result, fraternal and permanent Union, great prosperity and renown to the American people in the future."

"Baltimore," it added, "is at last waking up from its long lethargy." Among Baltimore's priorities was the restoring of trade with the South. As early as May, four steamers were sailing to Norfolk and Richmond, and a small fleet arrived from Virginia and North Carolina with tobacco, oats, turpentine, rosin, tar, staves, shingles, and lumber. Merchants sent a "mutual trade circular" to former customers in the South. Near the end of the summer, the *Sun* noted an increase in Southern trade "to an extent hitherto unknown." Often, regular steamers were unable to carry all the freight, and agents were compelled to charter sailing vessels. "At no former period in the history of Baltimore," the *Sun* editorialized, "have her business prospects been in a more flattering condition than at present." More business with the South and Southwest was done that summer than ever before. Wholesale merchants kept clerks "busily engaged far into the night."

Finally, on January 31, 1866, the provost marshal's department was abolished. Military rule thus ended; city and state were again the master of their own fates. Then the *Sun* began to express a stronger viewpoint. It was still a stout defender of the South; now the foe was the "radical party," the Republicans, of the North. When New York merchants were reported to have discontinued postwar trade with the South because of continuing "revolutionary threats" there, the *Sun* denounced such an attitude. It said that Baltimore would continue to deal with the South and warned that basing business policy on political revenge was "monstrous idiocy." Meanwhile, the *Sun* defended Maryland against "every fanatical paper in the land" that was condemning the state for its penitentiary law allowing a convicted black to be sold into servitude for the length of his sentence. It conceded only that the law would soon be changed "for the obvious reason that such a servitude . . . is totally inadequate as a punishment for the higher grades of crime." After slavery was abolished in Maryland, the *Sun* declared, the legislature had removed "every material disability under which the black race labored," except for the penitentiary law and another forbidding a black man from testifying in any case in which a white man was a party.

The *Sun* favored a less restrictive law on naturalization and suffrage. (Foreigners "are as well informed about the obligations of good citizenship as many of those admitted to suffrage.") Commenting on a trial of Ku Klux Klan members in North Carolina, an editorial defended their right to belong to an "invisible empire" and compared its secretiveness to that of the Odd Fellows. "A loyal reader of the *Sun*" in Clyde, Kansas, asked why the paper took the side of the Indians in the frontier war. It replied that if it were located on the frontier it too would probably want to see the Indians shot, but from faraway Baltimore took the side of the Indians. "They have been rendered devilish by the habitual bad faith of the whites."

The 1864 Maryland state constitution disenfranchised those who had sympathized with the South by requiring voters to take an oath of allegiance of past and future loyalty to the United States. This provision, disqualifying many Democrats, helped the unconditional Unionists to maintain control. The *Sun* complained that more than half of Maryland's voters were thereby disenfranchised. In 1865 the legislature passed a Registry Law that required a voter to answer twenty-five questions regarding his loyalty and background. (The last four: "Have you on any occasion expressed sympathy for the Government of the United States during the rebellion?" "During the rebellion, when the armies were engaged in battle, did you wish the success of the armies of the United States or those of the rebels?" "Have you voted at all the elections held since the year 1861, and if not, give your reason why?" "Have you, in taking the oath or in answering any questions propounded to you, held any mental reservations or used any evasions whatever?") Those appointed by the Unionists were not only judges but accusers too, and had the say on registration. Of a Baltimore voting population of about 40,000, only 10,000 were registered. Throughout Maryland, 95,000 people were entitled to vote but only 35,000 were registered. Of that total, an estimated 15,000 were opposed to the controlling, but minority, Unionists. While the Registry Law was still being enforced, most Baltimoreans did not vote—in the city election of 1865 only 5,000 did so.

The *Sun* called for repeal of the Registry Law. In his *History of Maryland*, Scharf declared that the *Sun* believed that restoration of state unity required "the enfranchisement of the citizens of the State and abrogation of the Constitution of 1864." He continued:

> Steadily persevering in this course, and crystallizing public sentiment as it went on, the *Sun* succeeded in bringing about a complete transformation of our public affairs. The editorial utterances of that paper during this period were distinguished for the eloquence and logic with which they advocated the restoration of the right of suffrage to a disfranchised and powerless people, the recognition in the statutes of the State of the new political status and the changed condition of the colored race, the restoration of the revolted States to their former relations in the Union, the acceptance on all sides of the inevitable results of the war, and the resumption in all sections of amicable business and social relations.

A new state constitution was approved by a 2-to-1 vote, in the fall of 1867. The Registry Law was dropped, and only a simple oath of allegiance was required for officeholders.

Francis A. Richardson, who had been managing editor of the Baltimore *Daily Republican* when it was suppressed by the military in 1863, joined the *Sun* in 1866. One of his first assignments was to cover the Maryland constitutional convention held in Annapolis in the spring and summer of 1867.

When the question of keeping a record of the debates was raised, Judge Albert Ritchie (father of Albert C. Ritchie, who was governor of Maryland from 1919 to 1936) contended that it was not necessary because "the reports of Mr. Richardson in the *Sun* are so accurate, fair and complete that no official record is needed." In 1923, Philip B. Perlman, then Maryland secretary of state (later Solicitor General of the United States) had them printed as "Debates of the Maryland Constitutional Convention of 1867," and they have been cited by the Maryland Court of Appeals in its decisions. However, Theo Lippman, Jr., a *Sun* editorial columnist, discovered that lawyers preparing a school-aid case in 1983 decided to check the convention reporting of other Baltimore newspapers. They found that the *Gazette* was much more detailed than the *Sun*. Where Richardson only paraphrased, the meticulous *Gazette* reporter used long, direct quotations. After the constitutional convention, Richardson was permanently assigned to Washington, D.C.

The paper still had occasional difficulties getting its facts straight and had to print corrections, even on small matters. A man charged with assaulting a child was fined 25 cents, not $25, as the *Sun* first reported. Another time it published this "Review": "The statement that Charles Crook, of West Pratt Street, was knocked down and robbed between 11 and 12 at night last week was erroneous. It occurred about 7 P.M. Mr. Crook is an old gentleman and is not in the habit of keeping late hours."

It missed the biggest local story of that time when Johns Hopkins, merchant and banker, died on December 24, 1873, at his home on Saratoga Street, two doors from Abell's mansion. Hopkins was the city's leading private citizen and its most munificent philanthropist. The Johns Hopkins University had been incorporated in 1867, and his millions would endow it and provide for the hospital also to bear his name. On Christmas Eve, the *Sun* had a skeleton staff and the door of the newsroom was locked to keep out holiday well-wishers, particularly celebrants. Hopkins's physician sent a servant with a note to the *Sun* announcing the death, but he was turned away by Henry Shuck, the watchman, who had been ordered to keep out all visitors. The servant walked across the street to the *American,* where he was assured he had come to the right newspaper. The next morning, *Sun* editors read the news in their strongest competitor. Shuck, an old retainer and friend of Abell's, was not dismissed or even penalized for his misjudgment.

In the 1870s the *Sun* began to shake off its lethargy of the Civil War days. The Founder, worn by the travails of war, was letting his second son, George W. Abell, become the dominant voice in the business. And George instituted changes.

In 1870 the *Sun* became the first paper in the South to introduce stereotyping to speed the printing process. A papier-maché matrix, called a mat, is placed on each form holding a page of type. Then both pass under a heavy roller, which exerts tremendous pressure to make a sharp, positive impression on the mat of whatever is on the page. The mat goes to a casting box, where hot metal is forced over it to make the mold a duplicate of the page of type. By then the mold is no longer flat, but a half-cylinder shell of solid metal type to fit on the cylinders of the rotary presses. The major advantage of stereotyping is that two or more molds can be made of each page and the presses can print two or more papers simultaneously. When it added stereotyping, the *Sun* also purchased two double-capacity rotary presses capable of printing 40,000 copies an hour.

In its first national promotion stunt, the paper sent 5,000 copies of the June 1, 1876, edition on the Jarrett and Palmer special train, which was attempting to set a transcontinental record. The exploit was contrived by Henry C. Jarrett and Harry Palmer, well-known New York theater managers. The *Sun* chartered Engine No. 123, "one of the best equipped and most improved locomotives of the Northern Central Railway," and Directors' Coach No. 1 to carry the papers to Harrisburg, Pennsylvania, to meet the Jarrett-Palmer train. Traveling in the cab of the engine, W. H. Whitty, a reporter, wrote a detailed account of the eighty-four-mile trip. "The exhilaration of riding in an engine cab," he wrote, "is a hundred-fold more intense than behind the fastest roadsters out of Charles Street Avenue." He was impressed with the night scenes: the burning lime kilns, the flaming iron furnaces, and the moonlit rivers, especially the broad Susquehanna, reached at daybreak—"all formed indelible pictures in the memory."

Precise arrangements had to be made to load the papers at Harrisburg. The Pennsylvania Railroad was determined to run the special from New York to Pittsburgh, 444 miles, without a single stop so it would be the longest continuous run ever made by an engine or a train. But at George Abell's urging the railroad agreed to reduce the speed to twenty miles an hour at Harrisburg.

Five mail pouches, each containing 1,000 *Suns* that had been folded and "enveloped" en route from Baltimore, were given to uniformed baggagemen, each "thoroughly experienced and accustomed to transferring articles to and from passing trains." They stood forty feet apart along the tracks, and as the special glided by each man launched his bag at the open door of the baggage car. Not one missed.

The *Sun* had no reporter aboard, as the special headed on west, but the *Times* of London, Paris papers, and the *New York Herald* did. The *Sun* reprinted the graphic descriptions of the *Herald* correspondent. Crowds gathered at depots along the way and "cheered themselves hoarse at our safe arrival." On the Great Plains, passengers would see a horseman galloping in the distance "although his mustang's legs could not compete with the driving wheels of our iron horse." At Omaha the train took on water. "When we washed for dinner, everybody was surprised to find the water yellow with the mud of the Missouri." At Cheyenne, Jarrett sent up rockets and Roman candles, "the crowd on the platform cheered lustily, the brass band played something full of crashing notes but the screams of the locomotive and the yells from the crowd drowned the music." Passengers ate in the hotel car, sometimes when "running at the rate of 50 miles per hour." One morning they dined on mountain trout and antelope steak. The train reached San Francisco in 83 hours and 34 minutes. Normally the trip took a week. Jarrett sent a telegram to the Abells: "Thanks be to God we arrived safely this morning. We are ahead of time. One grand ovation attended our trip from the Atlantic to the Pacific. Thursday morning's Baltimore *Sun* illuminates a thousand homes in San Francisco this beautiful sabbath morning." The *Sun*'s comprehensive coverage was breathless and intense. It called the trip "the greatest railroad feat of any age or any country."

In 1876, George Abell founded the *Sun Almanac*, "to freshen patriotism and treasure up those stirring incidents of the past which illustrate the history of Maryland." A year-end statistical compendium, the almanac was a gift to every subscriber. It appeared annually until 1915 and grew in size from a 32-page pamphlet to 256 pages in its last years. The year the almanac began, the *Baltimore Weekly Sun* printed its $500 prize story, "The Great Wheel."

In 1879 a telephone was installed in the *Sun* Iron Building. It hung on the city room wall, and one who remembered it said, "It worked so badly that reporters were not allowed to take weddings and deaths over it, but had to go to the homes by trolley to get the facts." If the assignment were urgent, transportation was by hack or horse from a livery stable. (Frank Brown, Jr., son of Governor Brown, got a job on the *American* and had the family coachman drive him to work and sometimes on his rounds. He did not last long as a reporter.) Telephones were scarce in the city. At night about the only place a reporter could use one was at a livery stable or undertaker's establishment. Reporters telephoned only in emergencies or when it was close to their deadline.

By 1879 two-page supplements, in occasional use since 1848, were appearing more frequently, and the size of the paper had increased to 19½ by 25 inches, with nine columns to the page. An editorial headlined "The Paper of the People" declared that from October 1885 to May 4, 1886, the *Sun* had printed 121 supplements.

> On Saturday last the number of separate advertisements in the *Sun* was 1,069, contained in 20½ columns, and on Monday there were 833 separate advertisements in 30⅞ columns, leaving in each issue over seventeen columns for news of the day. . . . the *Sun*'s advertisements "are all fresh, all genuine, and all brought to the office of the *Sun* by those who desire their insertion or by their representatives, for the *Sun* employs no solicitors, nor does it resort to tricks or subterfuges, or in any way aspire to notoriety by playing upon the credulity of the public."

It claimed its circulation was larger than that of all the other daily morning papers combined. This was a lesser boast than that made during the war, when its circulation was "greater than that of all the other daily papers in Baltimore, printed in the English language, combined."

On October 12, 1882, the Iron Building was the first office in Maryland to be illuminated by electricity. This was described in a two-column article headed "Always in the Lead—the *Sun* Building Lighted with Edison's Electric Lamps." It enumerated how many lights were in each room, for example, six in the mail room, three lamps in the managing editor's office, and three in the Abells' office, "two of them double swinging brackets." Power was generated by a dynamo run by the same steam engine that powered the presses. "The present improvement," the article explained, "not only benefits the office and all concerned in the multiplicity of details of its work, but will instruct the general public and allow all to judge of the desirability of the introduction of the Edison system into their places of business or households."

In the summer of 1882, the *Sun* for the first time took a vigorous part in local politics. The paper denounced the Democratic organization led by Senator Arthur Pue Gorman, the state boss, Isaac Freeman Rasin, the ward-machine boss of Baltimore, and Mayor William Pinkney Whyte, the nominal party leader, who had been governor and U.S. Senator. Boss rule included a controlled legislature and a mismanaged Baltimore—it was the largest city in the nation without sewers, its streets were rutted, and its public school system was inadequate. Arunah S. Abell, who believed it best to stay above the nitty-gritty of politics, had long ignored most of these problems. But his son George was changing the paper's persona. When the machine, which had been running the city for years, manipulated the renomination of the city judges to perpetuate its power in the courts, an independent movement countered with a "new judge" ticket. The *Sun,* under George Abell's prodding, was the only paper in the city to offer all-out support to the independents. It encouraged all reformers to unite, saying the only way to attack corruption in Maryland was to start locally. "The success of this effort," an editorial asserted, "will effectively crush the machine and the dying throes of this machine will be a trumpet-warning to machine politicians outside the city of their fate." It added, "Let us secure a judiciary that will not wink at crime nor spare a criminal who might be useful as a ward politician." Mayor Whyte rejoined that no lawyers or clients had complained about the courts for fifteen years, and the machine fought hard. But thanks to the indefatigable reformers, the Baltimore Bar Association, and the *Sun*'s intense news coverage and slam-bang editorials, Baltimore elected an independent judiciary by a majority of 11,000 votes. The *Sun* hailed the victors with the headline "The Bosses Beaten at the Polls — The Ring Machine Smashed." The campaign was so effective that ever since then the Baltimore judiciary has been largely free of machine domination.

The *Sun*, consistently supporting Democrats, was not as effective a voice in national politics between 1868 and 1880, when the Republicans won four presidential elections. On the eve of the presidential election of 1868, the *Sun* believed it detected a tendency in the nation toward conservatism and hoped that this would be a factor in the election. It was not. Its man, Horatio Seymour of New York, the Democratic candidate, lost to General Ulysses S. Grant, a "Radical Republican" in the *Sun*'s eyes. But it was a good loser: "The result, however much it may disappoint those who had anticipated any other conclusion, and however unsatisfactory it may be to all the opponents of the successful candidate, . . . will be acknowledged by them, as good citizens, to be decisive, and, as the declared verdict of the people, to be universally submitted to." The *Sun* was a good loser again in 1870, when Grant won reelection against Horace Greeley of New York; in 1878, with Rutherford B. Hayes electorally defeating Samuel J. Tilden of New York; and in 1880, as James A. Garfield beat General Winfield S. Hancock.

In the presidential election of 1884, Democrat Grover Cleveland, a former mayor of Buffalo and governor of New York, defeated James G. Blaine of Maine, the Republican candidate. Cleveland was the kind of Democrat the Abells admired. They liked his conservative political philosophy, found him a leader who could be trusted, and admired the man himself. The *Sun* was a Cleveland cheerleader from the time he came on the national scene until he left office in 1897. And during those years the Abells and Cleveland became good friends.

In the municipal election of October 1887, the *Sun* surprised independents and others by reverting to the Democratic fold. Even though that party was as boss-controlled as ever, the *Sun* with straight face denounced the Reform League for damaging the city by attacking the Democrats:

> The *Sun*'s prediction months ago that the efforts of self-styled "reformers" to make political capital for themselves by presenting the city of Baltimore as being under

the domination of "criminal classes" would have an injurious effect upon the city's reputation is being amply verified. . . . The accusation has been seized upon with avidity . . . by those who hope to throw discredit upon the Cleveland administration by representing the President as in alliance with disreputable elements of the community. . . . The state of Maryland and the city of Baltimore have prospered for years under democratic rule.

John K. Cowen, general counsel and later president of the B&O, and an anti-Gorman, anti-machine Democrat during the 1880s, derided the *Sun* by quoting from its 1882 editorials denouncing bosses and their machine when it campaigned for an independent judiciary. The *Sun* replied, not convincingly, by describing the 1882 fight as "non-partisan" and maintaining that this "Republican reform combination" sought "to delude the public . . . that the present campaign bears some resemblance to the real reform movement of 1882."

The only way Cowen could get his letters to the editor printed was to pay for them as advertisements. Here is a sample:

You have attacked, without reason or evidence, the motives of my political action. Let us see how disinterested has been your political career. I assert that it has been time-serving and selfish always, and that you have never opposed with vigor any bad administration—Know-Nothingism, Republicanism, Democracy, or Gormanism—so long as you received what you demanded of it. In the days of Know-Nothing misrule, when the Democratic Party needed the vigorous support of every real Democrat, the *Exchange* [a rival daily paper], right across the street from you, conducted by Mr. Wallis and other real Democrats, was mobbed time and again by the Know-Nothings, but your "Democracy" was never so offensive as to incur their anger. It was not of that kind. Your plant was as well protected then as now by the party in power. When the war came on, and outspoken Democracy again meant danger, when the *Exchange* and other Democratic papers were suppressed, you never gave trouble. When the City Ring, after the frauds of 1875, became more rotten than ever, you were silent and did the public printing. When Mayor Whyte [William Pinkney Whyte] took away the printing from you before the New Judge campaign, you were inoculated with virtuous indignation, and attacked Mr. Rasin and Mayor Whyte as vigorously as you now support them. Whyte was beaten. Gorman came into power. The city printing was restored. You were silent again. Gormanism—the combining and organizing of the city's different criminal elements for mutual advantage—became a feature of our city, and, in a measure, of our state politics, but even as it grew, your perquisites grew also, and the national printing was added to the rest. Though controlling a great public journal, you have never entered protest against this blot of blood and grease upon the history of our state and city. You did assume a somewhat menacing tone on the eve of the late convention, when it seemed likely that Baughman [Victor L. Baughman, the son-in-law of A.S. Abell], a recent candidate for the Governorship of Maryland, and the nominee of the Regular Democratic Organization for the state comptrollership), would be dropped, and so Baughman was not dropped entirely. Is it too much to say that your protest is never heard unless some perquisite or other is being taken from you? "Doth the wild ass bray when he hath grass, or loweth the ox over his fodder?"

Has this not been your case? And now, for some time past, you have been the apologist, open or silent, for the most disgraceful regime that the city every knew. . . . Election after election has been carried by bare-faced fraud. . . . Is it possible for us not to connect your silence as to all this with the fact that you have both city, state and national printing? Is it this that silences your protest against this saturnalia of blood and crime? Such is the common report. I do not say that it is true—I should dislike to believe such a thing of any journal—but if it be so, if that be the consideration for your support of such an abomination, verily, it comes within the old Levitical prohibition—it is "the hire of an harlot and the price of a dog." Such is your time-serving record; such is your "Democracy."

The Wallis he referred to was Severn Teackle Wallis, lawyer and public servant, whose statue stands in Mount Vernon Place. Wallis too had to pay to get his letters published; he complained that when he sent one the *Sun* seemed to make a point of publishing it among its advertisements for venereal-disease remedies. The *Sun* called the paid letters "cards" and during political campaigns often printed several columns of them, some on the front page.

The municipal campaign of 1887 attracted more national attention than any off-year election since the Civil War because Republicans hoped to embarrass the President himself by defeating his party. But the Democrats, aided by the state party boss (and friend of Cleveland), Senator Gorman, prevailed; their candidate for mayor, Ferdinand C. Latrobe, won handily in the October election.

"The only serious affair of the day," the *Sun* reported, "was the killing of Edward Dailey, a Democrat, in the 17th Ward. The general calm was a surprise to a number of New York, Philadelphia and other newspaper correspondents who came over, as one expressed it, expecting to see men killed all over the city and blood flowing in the gutters." The election was "as free from corruption or suspicious influence as even the most exacting 'reformers' could demand," said the *Sun*. It did print the opinion of the *New York Times* that the "Gorman ring bought a great many legal votes" and the *New York World*'s comment that the Democratic success came with the "aid of Negro repeaters" and "other fraudulent ways."

In the November state elections the *Sun* called for a new constitution to replace that of 1867, pointing out that "the greater number living under its provisions today had no voice in its framing or adoption." It also spoke out for labor unions: "The rights of laboring men to combine as wage earners for their own protection ought no longer rest upon the provisions of an alterable law, but ought to be guaranteed by an article in the new bill of rights." The call for a constitutional convention was defeated, but the Democratic state ticket was elected. Democratic victories in Maryland, Virginia, and New York, the *Sun* said, are a "signal triumph for the national administration"; it predicted Cleveland's renomination and reelection in 1888.

To cover the off-year election, a *Sun* representative was present at each of the several hundred state precincts, and there was a *Sun* part-time correspondent in each county seat. "Scores of telegraph operators" were used, and the results were telegraphed in words rather than figures for greater accuracy. The paper, under George Abell, was once more showing some of the enterprise of its early years. Obtaining election returns in Southern Maryland was unusually difficult because of the many names on the ticket "and the unprecedented scratching and alteration of them to suit the fancy of the many individuals who did not vote the full party tickets." To report returns, the *Sun* chartered four special trains and engaged a number of fast horses.

> The count at St. Inigoes, the most remote polling place in Southern Maryland, was completed between 2 and 3 o'clock Wednesday morning, and a race against time began. Mr. J. T. H. Allston, the best whip in Southern Maryland, carried the *Sun*'s representative over the first 25 miles of the course, when Mr. T. R. Farrell's team took the courier in charge and whistled him along at the usual fast pace to Mechanicsville, the terminus of the Southern Maryland Railroad. . . . While the work of gathering the remote districts of Charles County was done by mounted carriers, the most hazardous service was performed by steeds of steam. That at a rate of a mile a minute carried the returns from LaPlata to Marlboro.

"To sit behind a locomotive going at such a rate of speed, and prepare dispatches from returns in hand, and to be in readiness at the beginning of the telegraphic communication to place the copy on the operator's desk" was evidently not only a trying task, but a thrill as well.

Assisting the office staff was "a strong corps of experts" and compositors who "were heavily reinforced."

> The ten columns of figures published would strike even the superficial eye as a work of great magnitude, but it is only those who have a practical knowledge of type setting and the difficulties of tabular work who can fully realize the great work done in the composing room and the expense it entailed. Under the rules of the Typographical Union, tabular work, such as the *Sun*'s election returns, is charged at double the rate of composition, but in this instance, owing to the changes and corrections necessary in revising returns, the cost of composition was more than four times that of plain matter.

The *Sun* was enterprising not only in elections but also for dramatic events that generated intense excitement across the nation. It followed the Chicago trial of three prominent anarchists who were convicted of murder, and the day they were executed it had an exclusive wire running from the Illinois jail to its composing room. Twenty-two minutes after the men were hanged, it had an extra in the hands of hundreds of waiting newsboys. Baltimore had an anarchist's club, and feeling ran high about the executions. The *Sun* implied that it had prevented demonstrations by its enterprise: "When the news of the execution was so fully and definitely supplied, as it was by the *Sun* extra, the crowd dispersed, the excitement measurably abated, and affairs of the business centres of the city resumed their accustomed channels." In these decades the paper, with a tinge of sensationalism, dwelt on spectacular accidents and gory deaths resulting from train wrecks, steamboat explosions, or mob violence (in one of Maryland's several lynchings the victim was impaled on a drawbridge prong). Suicides, often headlined "Weary of Life," were reported in vivid detail: a new mother cutting her throat, a man jumping from a moving train, another plunging off a bridge. A fourth Chicago anarchist, about to be hanged, committed suicide by placing a dynamite cap in his mouth and lighting the fuse with a candle.

On the light side, the *Sun* also had time to respond to a Pennsylvania farmer who disputed its report that a load of hay weighing 12,925 pounds had passed through Baltimore. The farmer maintained that such a load could not be hauled out of any barn, moved on any road, or weighed on any scale. A reporter, sent to interview the deputy weighman, quoted him as saying that Pennsylvania farmers probably did not have the skill to stack such a load but that he knew Baltimore County farmers who could do it any time they felt like it. The reporter then interviewed B. T. Ridgely, the farmer with the big load. He said he had hauled the hay sixteen miles and had thrown off a ton when he reached the city limits, rain having dampened the top of it; he wanted a dry load because it brought a better price. Then he had the load weighed. He still had the weighbill to prove it.

Francis A. Richardson, head of the Washington (D.C.) bureau, spent part of his summers at the ocean resorts of Cape May and Long Branch, New Jersey. Long Branch, where Grant had a summer home, was popular with politicians. Richardson forwarded long pieces from the resorts, though they were seldom about politics. He was a good storyteller and much caught his attention—from the "bare arms and shoulders and fine busts" at the Proprietors' Ball, to a New York journalist "whose income is close to $100,000 per annum and who as a rule cares nothing for expense." After watching 200 men bet large sums, Richardson dubbed Long Branch "the Monte Carlo of America." The bathhouses of Cape May were so dilapidated that their doors would not close, "but good breeding and chivalry are too prevalent to develop any Peeping Toms." He pictured two friendly rivals, the Philadelphia publishers Frank McLaughlin of the *Times* and George Childs of the *Public Ledger*. Childs strolled down one day from his handsome cottage to the West End Hotel, where he spied McLaughlin sitting on the porch, sunning his gouty foot on a chair. Childs complimented McLaughlin on his appearance: "Why, you are looking better than when I saw you last; maybe you will live as long as I do but, old fellow, when you do die, you shall have a splendid obituary in the *Ledger*. It is all prepared now." McLaughlin was so overcome, Richardson wrote, that he could only express his appreciation by looks. He lacked the voice to tell Childs that his obituary had not only been written in the *Times* office but was in type.

The *Sun* added another dimension to its news pages by engaging Professor Richard T. Ely of Johns Hopkins University, a prominent economist, to write a series of twenty-five letters for the front page on "Problems of the Day," dealing with industry, taxation, commerce, and other current matters. This was followed by a series on national affairs by Senator Zebulon B. Vance of North Carolina. And the paper devoted full pages to promotions for Baltimore and Maryland ("Make Way for Baltimore — Progress of a Solid City").

The *Sun* also broadened its coverage by hiring a woman. In the fall or early winter of 1887, May Garrettson Evans, a student at the Peabody Conservatory of Music, applied for a job on the *Sun*. Her experience was limited. She had helped her brother, Henry Ridgeway Evans, who worked for another paper, cover musical events. She was engaged on a trial basis and paid space rates for her work. Though she was not identified as a reporter, her presence was soon apparent to the reader: five columns describing the music to be played in churches at Christmas; descriptions of debutante receptions, teas, and parties; hints for home dressmakers; columns about fashion; a shopper's directory prepared with a woman's eye. Before long she was submitting so much copy that she was hired as a staff member. She was the first female reporter in Baltimore, and probably one of the first in the nation to cover not just "women news" but general assignments. She said later that this "created a commotion, both inside and outside the office." Once when she arrived unexpectedly in the office she noticed the city editor trying to stop laughing. The assistant city editor had been sitting with his coat off and his shirtsleeves and suspenders showing. When he saw a woman coming he crawled under the desk, embarrassed by his informal appearance.

On her first assignments Evans was more interviewed than interviewing. Everywhere she had to explain herself: "I had to tell what my family thought of my 'hazardous undertaking' and why I was permitted to engage in anything so full of pitfalls for the unwary." At first, Evans's mother chaperoned her on night assignments, waiting downstairs while her daughter wrote upstairs in the newsroom. Later, while going home alone one night after work, she noticed a man following her. When he was only a few steps behind her as she neared her home, Evans jerked out her long bonnet pin. Just as she turned to jab him she noticed that he was a relative. He thought she had recognized him and knew he was joking. When that story got back to the *Sun*, Harold E. West, a member of the staff, placed a small stiletto in a leather case on Evans's desk. It was the right length to conceal in her sleeve. She carried it for years on night assignments but never had to use it.

Evans was probably responsible for the *Sun*'s comprehensive coverage of the International Council of Women, assembled in 1888 by the National Woman's Suffrage Association, to celebrate the fortieth anniversary of the first women's rights convention. The week-long council in Washington, D.C., discussed suffrage, higher education, and expanding job opportunities for women. One speaker dealt with medicine as a profession, saying that 1,000 women were practicing throughout the nation, some making as much as $50,000 a year. Laura C. Holloway, "a practical journalist," talked about women in journalism, asserting that across the nation there were 200 female staff members, "an army of female correspondents and writers, though few reporters." She added that she "never knew of an editor who opposed women journalists who did not lose his position."

The *Sun* reported that the hall, which seated 2,000, was packed for every session, with women and men standing in the aisles. Susan B. Anthony announced that men would not be admitted to the last session, which would deal with "strong views on the relations of husband and wife." At this closed session, women were admonished that "sons and daughters alike should be taught the awful power of sex—young girls should be taught the sacredness of marriage and to hold control of their persons against their husband's lust."

Editorially the *Sun* predicted that "the suffrage question will not occupy the prominent place it once did," but noted with approval the advances made by womankind: "She is finding employment in decorative art work, in illustrating books, in telegraphy, in type-writing, as cashiers, as bookkeepers in stores and in many light branches of industry from which not long ago she was almost completely excluded." Then, however, reflecting the viewpoint of older male subscribers and its own conservative views, the editorial concluded, "But above all others, the home ought to be considered, for the crown of glory to all but a few belongs to her who is a good wife, a good mother and an excellent housekeeper."

But the significant event for the *Sun* in 1887 was its fiftieth anniversary. The headlines of May 17 reflected how the Abells looked back upon the years:

THE SUN'S GOLDEN JUBILEE
HALF A CENTURY IN HARNESS
THE HISTORY OF A MOST EVENTFUL AGE
A Period of Industrial and Political Progress
Brilliant Retrospect of *The Sun*'s Career — Its Life Work in the Arena of Social Advancement and Political Reform — Dangers and Difficulties that Beset Its Path — Triumphs that Rewarded Its Constancy and Devotion to the People

The paper reviewed those fifty years in four-and-a-half columns, beginning with its founding during the Panic of 1837, when "men were more actively engaged in winding up old than in laying the foundations of new ventures."

It stretched some truths. It claimed to be the third penny paper in the United States, but the *New York Sun* and the *Herald* were established and successful earlier, as was the *Philadelphia Public Ledger.* Between 1830 and 1837, some fifteen penny papers were started in Boston, New York, and Philadelphia, though most lasted only a short time. The *Sun* of 1887 reiterated that its pony express had been established and conducted "without consultations or previous arrangements with any other paper," but that claim remains unproven. The paper's first pony expresses were probably run in part with the cooperation of New Orleans and New York papers. Not until later did the *Sun* have its own horse couriers. It also claimed that its "firm stand . . . against the ostracism and violence of the Know Nothing Party of 1854–59 never knew any abatement or cessation until that party went out of existence." The implication was that the paper, by itself, deserved the full credit. The *Sun* indeed helped—even though it often did not mention the party by name— but the paper was only one of the many forces that led to the collapse of the Know-Nothings. Comment on the Civil War was brief: "When the War Between States began, newspapers in this latitude which did not fawn upon the federal power and crook the knee to military satraps were, like the laws of the state, its people and even its judges, compelled to be silent."

For the anniversary celebration, the *Sun* building was painted in three tints of "yellow drab with the relief castings of the lower story done in gold." Potted plants were placed in second-floor windows, and baskets of flowers hung beneath them. "On the roof waved the large flag which is only shaken to the breeze upon Washington's birthday, the Fourth of July or other high occasion." The article immodestly declared, "The decorations of the *Sun* Iron Building were the subject of much comment, and the general verdict was that for taste and beautiful effect they exceeded anything else of the kind that has ever been done in the city."

The printers presented Abell with a gold-headed cane. In their testimonial they recalled that when the paper began he "performed the work of a journeymen printer in addition to [his] other labors." In 1837, they remembered, the paper had but eight men in all departments, excluding editorial. In 1887 it had sixty-five men in the composing room alone, including four who had been with Abell for forty-five years. The machinery, press, and mailing departments gave him a California armchair, and the editorial and city staffs gave him a solid gold medal, ten inches in circumference, engraved with the *Sun*'s logotype vignette and the words "Light for All." The reporter describing the medal—perhaps the same one who wrote about the *Sun* building—said it is "considered the most artistic and perfect piece of engraving ever done by that famous house (Samuel Kirk & Son). This is saying a great deal, for the firm was started in 1817."

Baltimore papers added their congratulations. The *German Correspondent* referred to Abell as the "aged, storm-tried manager," and the *Evening News* emphasized Abell's enterprise and industry, saying, "His large wealth has been won wholly in the field of legitimate business enterprise." The *Argus* predicted what Baltimore would be like on the *Sun*'s centennial: It would have a population of 2,000,000, and the *Sun*'s circulation would be 500,000. (The population turned out to be 825,000; the *Sun,* morning and evening, to have a circulation of 300,000, with 200,000 on Sunday.) The paper, it went on, would be delivered by pneumatic tube within a radius of fifty miles, and by balloon beyond that. (For a while, the *Evening Sun* tried airplane delivery to Ocean City, Maryland.) It would have bureaus in Teheran and Timbuktu. (The *Sun* had them in Washington, New York, and London.)

On the anniversary, a paragraph atop the editorial column announced that A. S. Abell, the proprietor, had taken his three sons, Edwin F., George W., and Walter R., as co-partners. The middle son, George, 44, was running the paper, though in name his 81-year-old father was still editor and publisher. Edwin, 47, managed the large realty and securities holdings, and Walter, 38, was more interested in travel and books than journalism, though he did contribute prose and poetry to the paper.

After the Civil War, with George gradually assuming more responsibility, the Founder began to relax. He vacationed in the summer at Cape May and Atlantic City, and during the winter in Florida. He liked traveling and was off to California, Cuba, and Europe. He built an in-town mansion, standing yet at the northwest corner of Charles and Madison streets. He also had a country residence, Guilford, a 300-acre estate between York Road and Charles Street, extending from what is now University Parkway on the south to Cold Spring Lane on the north. This baronial domain was bought in 1872 for $475,000. Guilford itself, the mansion, a frame Italianate villa, had fifty-two rooms; twenty-five guests could be lodged overnight. The brick stable, with about twenty-five box stalls, had a marble fountain in its courtyard.

When Abell needed personal funds he did not go to a bank, but stopped at the *Sun*'s business counter and asked for whatever he needed, but he never gave a receipt. Later the clerk would get a written order, from Edwin Abell, for the amount. One day Abell asked Jimmy Myers, a new clerk, for $5 in quarters, thanked him, and walked out. The clerk, not knowing he was the Founder, jumped over the counter, shouting "That old man took my money," but he was stopped by laughing clerks before he could collar Abell on the sidewalk.

In his later years, tired and enfeebled, Abell still went to his office every day. And he still had time for old friends and admirers. At an early stage in the *Sun*'s history a reader who signed herself *Fair Eliza* had sent him a box of raisins packed in shavings as a joke. Many years later she wrote to remind him of her prank, saying she had heard he was of a "genial temperament and fond of a joke" so she decided to "crack a joke" with him. He replied editorially, "We have not forgotten the box of 'Fair Eliza,' packed with shavings and raisins, although all jokes have given place to business activities. But old friendships survive the flight of years and we not only enjoy a joke but the memory of one long past. Even the silver threads which time strews upon the hair are no indication of winter in the heart."

Even though he could afford a handsome carriage with coachmen, and even though his eyesight was failing, the Founder long rode a streetcar to work. He would arrive downtown regularly about ten o'clock in the morning. A policeman was on the lookout to help him cross through the carriage and dray traffic to the Iron Building. Abell's sight was so dim that more than once, when reaching for a pen to sign his name, he dipped his fingers in the inkwell. When he could no longer see well enough to read, a daughter read to him at home, and at work he had a clerk read the *Sun* and other papers.

Arunah Shepherdson Abell died on April 19, 1888, at his in-town mansion. He was 82. News of his death was posted on the bulletin boards of Baltimore newspapers and announced in a *Sun* extra. The flag at City Hall was flown at half-staff, an unusual honor for a private citizen. The long obituary reviewed his career and noted: "His self-reliance and independence were very remarkable, and well illustrated in late years, and even a short time before his death, by his objecting to ride in the streetcars because people would get up and insist on his taking their seats. For this reason his democratic habit of riding in the streetcars was somewhat restricted." The *Sun*'s lead editorial, thirteen inches long, said in part: "He was, in an exalted sense, a type of the American workingman, devoted to his business and never aspiring beyond it; for it was to him the means of doing good to others as well as to himself, and even in his later years . . . he looked after it with as much care and interest as he manifested in his early life when working at the case."

Singly and in groups, editors, reporters, telegraphers, printers, counting-room clerks, stereotypers, pressmen, mechanics, mailers, carriers, and job printers paid their respects at Abell's home. The only employee identified by name in the main story was Henry Shuck, "the venerable watchman . . . who for a long period has acted as general guardian of the *Sun* building." The Washington bureau sent a huge floral tribute representing a sunburst spanned by an arch with "Light for All" formed with small blooms. Fifty hacks carrying employees were in the funeral procession to Green Mount Cemetery, where 1,500 mourners gathered.

Abell's will was published on the front page. The paper and job printing business were left to the three sons. Abell was one of the largest property owners in Baltimore and the surrounding area. That property, real estate in Washington, D.C., and Florida, and stocks and bonds were divided among his five daughters and three sons. He bequeathed $10,000 to the Maryland Institute and $1,000 each to twelve charities. The editor of the *Sun*, Oakley P. Haines, was left $1,000, as were Norval E. Foard, the city editor; a bookkeeper, and three clerks. William B. Krout, a reporter, received $500; four people received $300 each: a pressman, two assistant engineers, and Henry Shuck, the venerable watchman.

FIVE

Sons of the Founder
1888–1906

Many subscribers visited the *Sun* Iron Building on May 17, 1888, to offer congratulations, the paper having completed its fifty-first year. An item in "Local Matters" recalled that the previous year the late A. S. Abell "received with a hearty grasp of the hand the many persons who called. . . . Yesterday his chair was vacant, but on his desk was a beautiful tribute of flowers. Nearby were the tokens of esteem which were given to him by employees last year, all of which were inspected by the visitors."

"Local Matters" still reflected the back-fence informality of small-town life. A housewife on Stricker Street "yesterday gave a colored man $5 in payment for some clams. The man left to have the money changed and did not return. . . . The work on frescoing the hallways of the Fifth Regiment Armory has been completed. . . . A Calvert Street lady sent to the *Sun* office an egg resembling a gourd."

The *Sun* described wagons filled with Polish and Bohemian families leaving the city for Anne Arundel County to work in the fields, "all of them accompanied by their children who were safely stowed on top of the bedding and household utensils." The reporter, probably ingrained with the Abells' conservative philosophy, added, "Besides the benefit to health of the change to country life these people, with frugality, return to the city at the end of the trucking season with substantial amounts of cash, which, with their winter employment, always keeps the wolf from the door."

On its fifty-first anniversary the *Sun* claimed it was being read by 250,000 people, was "The best advertising medium in the United States, . . . its prices . . . not one-fourth as much as leading New York dailies, with any of which the *Sun* favorably compares."

More and more, *Sun* correspondents were being sent on major assignments and identified by initials, as appended to their reports. In May, N.E.F. (Norval

E. Foard), the state editor who had joined the staff after covering the Civil War for Charleston, South Carolina, papers, was in New York reporting a Methodist conference. About the same time, F.A.R. (Francis A. Richardson) and W.H.D. (William H. Davis), who preceded Foard as chief of the Annapolis bureau when the legislature was in session, were covering the national convention of Prohibitionists in Indianapolis.

Richardson, unquestionably the *Sun*'s best writer, was adept at scene-setting. This is how he began his first dispatch:

When at a few minutes past 10 o'clock this morning the national prohibition convention was called to order, the scene presented was entirely different from the usual spectacle of a political convention. About 150 female delegates were sandwiched between those of the opposite sex, and of the spectators in the galleries fully one-third were women. While some of the female delegates were motherly, old-fashioned women, well advanced in years, a great many others were much younger, quite spruce in manner and attire. . . .

State delegations cheered each other vociferously, and every old and noted prohibitionist was saluted with acclamations. The female delegates did not join in the yells, but stood up on tiptoe and waved their handkerchiefs and fans just as long as the men shouted. . . . The galleries today were quite stoical in demeanor, and except for the occasional flutter of a handkerchief and a half-smothered cheer from some faint-hearted and isolated individual, it might have been supposed they were looking down upon religious services. The proceedings might indeed be said to partake of a semi-religious character of somewhat free-and-easy style. The doxology was sung at the beginning, not the end of the session. The national hymn of "America" and various prohibition ditties were also rendered at intervals, and helped very much to enliven the routine. The entire convention joined in the doxology and "America," making at least a thousand male voices and producing that wonderful effect which numbers give to vocalism.

Richardson and Davis also reported on the Democratic National Convention in St. Louis, at which Cleveland was nominated by acclamation for a second term. The *Sun* exulted:

In selecting Mr. Cleveland to lead them a second time, the democracy manifests its appreciation of the intelligence, honesty of purpose and success with which the federal administration has been conducted since March 4, 1885. . . . Sectional spite has vanished from the policy of the administration, the civil service has been vastly improved, economy has taken the place of extravagance, over 80,000,000 acres of land have been restored to the public domain, our finances have been put on a solid basis, and the attention of the nation has been called by the chief executive in a forcible manner to the grievous wrongs inflicted upon the people by the existing inequitable tariff taxes.

Commenting on its convention coverage, the *Sun* puffed:

The Baltimorean who stood in front of the *Sun* office yesterday and read the bulletins knew as much, if not more, than the citizen of St. Louis who was fortunate enough to push his way into the crowded Exposition Hall. The

Baltimorean could not hear the speeches, the deafening applause, the shouts, the martial airs of the bands. He could not see the faces of the prominent people there, the white hats of the delegates, the red bandanas, . . . but he could learn in detail the proceedings of the convention at the moment they occurred.

The paper had leased a special wire from the hall, "and each pulsation of the heart at the convention in St. Louis was felt in Baltimore . . . and . . . put in type by *Sun* printers and in incredibly short time were laid before the crowd in front of the *Sun* building." Richardson and Davis also filed comprehensive coverage from the Republican convention in Chicago, which nominated Benjamin Harrison. Sometimes they wrote more than five columns a day.

Not long after that convention, "Local Matters" mentioned that Mr. and Mrs. George W. Abell, their son Charles and daughter Jeannie [Jane], with two friends, had sailed for Liverpool to spend the summer in Europe. Later the *Sun* noted it had received complaints from travelers abroad—unnamed—who were not getting newspapers they had ordered. The *Sun* added parenthetically, "It happens that newspapers sent from places where they have an established business or valuable local interests may be more important to them than letters." George Abell, the publisher, obviously was not receiving his copies of the paper and he was upset.

Just before the November election Richardson was reporting from New York, a key state, and Foard was in Indianapolis at Harrison's headquarters. Foard described Harrison as "about 5 foot 6 inch height with a capon-lined rotundity which is covered by an ample breadth of waistcoat." Richardson, usually a perceptive and objective observer, let his, and perhaps the Abells' partisanship, show in his election-eve dispatch: "Your correspondent will say that he shall be disappointed if Cleveland does not have a majority in the electoral college, and shall not be surprised should it be greater than in 1884."

The *Sun,* again using couriers to forward election returns from all the counties, printed four updating editions. Its messenger left remote St. Inigoes at 8:45 P.M., and after traveling seventy-eight miles by horse had full returns from St. Marys County on the wire at Upper Marlboro at 1:13 A.M. To get returns from Solomons Island on the tip of Calvert County, the *Sun* engaged "Mr. Chaney, the expert rider of the county," who used a relay of seven horses to reach Upper Marlboro. Returns from all sections of Baltimore were reported on special telegraph wires, and these were posted on six bulletin boards. Crowds were so dense that streetcars had difficulty passing the Iron Building even though 200 policemen tried to hold the multitudes away from the tracks. Spectators responded to returns by sounding hurrahs with flute notes and "a rattle that resembled the tone of the old watchman's rattle."

But all these expectations—indeed, hopes—were dashed. Cleveland attained a popular majority, but the Electoral College vote turned the paper's hero out of office. Harrison got 233 electoral votes to Cleveland's 168, leaving the *Sun* to editorialize: "Four years hence there will be an opportunity for the defeated party to reverse the result of Tuesday's voting. . . . Bad economic ends, bad methods and bad leadership are almost sure within four years to produce a multitude of [Republican] party blunders, unpopularity and consequent disaster." Later, when summing up the year, the *Sun* offhandedly asserted that the Republicans had won "largely by the purchase of votes."

The paper had always been eager to expound its own achievements, but in this era it was more than ever boastful. In December 1888 the composing room, "unexcelled by any composing room in the United States," was moved from the fourth to the entire fifth floor. Referring to its new type, the *Sun* said it "can hardly be called a new dress, for years ago the *Sun* set the fashion hereabouts in newspaper clothing." The order for the type was the largest ever given in the state, it claimed, and the font three times as large as that of any other state newspaper. "Its weight is 20,000 pounds, or ten tons. As each pound averages 650 pieces, the total number of pieces is 13,000,000 and the type laid end-to-end would stretch 205 miles." The order was given to a local company "in pursuance of a policy of encouraging home manufacturers." The paper continued:

> The progress of the *Sun* has been so rapid and yet so steady that its career makes a notable chapter in the history of clean American journalism. . . . A remark of one of its own printers is enough to present a contrast between the present and the past. He said, "Thirty years ago, seventeen of us set up all the type used in issuing the paper and finished our labor by 10 o'clock at night. Now there are 80 of us and we get through at 3 A.M.!"
>
> The removal of the composing department necessitated the building of an automatic elevator carrying the tables with the heavy forms down to the stereotyping department, and making the round trip in fifteen seconds. All these improvements were made quietly from within doors. Tons of plaster and debris were taken out of the building and carted away, and tons of iron, lumber and stone were brought in with hardly any showing upon the street. No interruption to travel was caused to pedestrians on the sidewalks, as there was no desire to make an ostentatious display of what was going on.

Before Cleveland left office, the *Sun* pointed out that two of the biggest New York papers, the *Times* and the *Herald,* had followed its lead by interviewing him, adding, "The *Sun* is ahead of New York almost every day in the matter of important news and our metropolitan contemporaries have no doubt grown accustomed by this time to looking to the *Sun* for some striking piece of information."

In special dispatches from Samoa in 1886, the *Sun* had revealed efforts by Germany to secure control of the islands, but "was prevented by obstacles interposed by representatives of the United States." Germany, the United States, and Great Britain had trade agreements with that independent kingdom and the right to establish coaling stations there. In the spring of 1889, the *Sun* asserted that its dispatches were responsible "for setting the country right on the Samoan affair" and quoted Secretary of State Thomas F. Bayard as saying that it "contributed materially to the peaceful solution of the complication with Germany, which at one time threatened to be serious."

Commenting on the *Sun*'s coverage of Harrison's inauguration by its "able corps of writers at its Washington Bureau, assisted by the expert detachment from the staff," an editorial called it "the most graphic and interesting account . . . published by any paper in the Union. . . . The *Sun* is a Washington journal not less than a Baltimore journal as respects all points of news and today's issue illustrates the thoroughness of its treatment of incidents belonging strictly to the national capital."

Its coverage was comprehensive, detailed, and colorful, from the rain-soaked inauguration to the inauguration ball. Describing the effects of the downpour on the inauguration scene, the reporter wrote that water was on every seat and that although attendants tried to sponge the seats off, everyone stood, except the "Corean minister, who, rigged out in all his court regalia and resplendent silks, sat in a wet chair all during the ceremony." Three columns were devoted to the ball, including one naming the guests and what the women wore. A buffet supper was served from 8:00 P.M. to 3:00 A.M. It included 5,150 terrapin, 45,000 raw oysters, 20,000 steamed oysters, 7,000 chicken croquettes, 150 Virginia hams, 1,000 boned quail, 500 pounds of pâté de foie gras, 7,000 sandwiches, and ten barrels of fancy cakes and ice cream. A ticket to the dinner cost $1.

The *Sun* had solid and colorful reporting on the local scene too, and determined reporters. When the steamer *Johns Hopkins*, docked at the Fort McHenry wharf, was destroyed by fire, the paper's account also noted that its reporters were barred from the fort by "two sentries on watch with fixed bayonets which the sentries flourished with suggestive motives." But the reporters were not to be denied. They ran to a nearby pier and cut loose a rowboat. Having no oars, they broke a plank in half for blades, "the pulling of which for fully a quarter of a mile produced blistered hands; one hand had to be used as an oarlock." The reference to their resolve concluded on this triumphant note: "And Lieutenant Harrold's effort to keep out newspapermen was a failure."

Edward Paul Duffy was a *Sun* reporter who covered the waterfront, and as "Admiral" Duffy became a legend in the newsroom. His association with the paper began as a youth in 1873, when he became a carrier in Ellicott's Mills (now Ellicott City). Soon he was contributing news items to Foard, the state editor. When Duffy wrote to the publisher suggesting that he be paid, George W. Abell sent him a trunk full of books and $50. In 1879, Duffy enlisted in the Navy, and while on the frigate *Trenton* he obtained an admiral's permission to start a ship's newspaper, said to be the first newspaper ever published on a ship. During his travels he contributed articles to the *Sun*, often on naval matters that appeared in the paper before the Department of the Navy was informed. George Abell was impressed, offered him a job in January 1882, and sent him to John V. Hood, the city editor. Hood growled, "We have eight reporters now. I do not know where to place the ninth. Go out and get some news." Duffy began to canvass the docks around the Basin. At first he got little news, but gradually it increased in quantity and quality until, under the heading "Port Paragraphs," a new department was created. The column was crammed with local and international items packed with specific facts and figures: "Three vessels arrived from the Bahamas yesterday loaded with 16,220 dozen of pineapples"; "A seaman, boarding on South Broadway, while turning a somersault, fell and broke his right shoulder blade"; "Charters reported yesterday were: Schooner 'Ida Lawrence,' hence to Savannah, coal $1 per ton, oil 40¢ per barrel, lumber back at $5 per thousand . . . brig 'Rachel Coney,' general cargo to Berbice, $1,400; barkentine 'Joseph Baker,' lumber from Fernandina to Baltimore, $5, or option to Philadelphia $5.50 and free wharfage." In 1890 the *Sun* bought a launch and named it the *Sunbeam*. Duffy at the tiller cruised the harbor, stopping at piers or "pugnaciously sailing down upon some giant steamer just in from the sea." He carried a bundle of *Sunpapers* and, boarding a ship, he would throw the bundle on deck first, shouting, "*Sunpapers* coming on board." He got news from all over the world by giving ship captains envelopes with his name, asking them to send him news wherever they found something interesting. He was the only *Sun* employee to receive two gold watches from the company—when he completed twenty-five years on January 1, 1907, and again on January 1, 1932, for fifty years of service. He worked until a short time before his death on February 13, 1933, his seventy-eighth birthday. That day ships in the harbor, both American and foreign, lowered their flags to half-mast. The *Sun's* editorial on "Admiral" Duffy concluded: "His original appearance in the office more than a half century ago was beyond anyone's memory and his final disappearance was beyond anyone's belief."

Samuel C. Appleby started as a reporter in 1886, and according to a biographical sketch "the *Sun* used him largely in the fight for the reduction of the 17-hour workday of street car employees, for the abolition of horse cars and their replacement by rapid transit. He went to Boston, New York, Philadelphia, Chicago, St. Paul and Minneapolis to show how successfully the electric system worked." In his nineteen-year career he also was assistant city editor and "sporting editor."

Walter Poole started in the mail room around 1890 but before long became a receptionist-typist for the Abells, using the first and only typewriter in the building. Reporters wrote in longhand on special yellow copy paper. As a police reporter, he was the first one to ride a bicycle when covering his beat. He became the Towson correspondent before it was connected by telephone to Baltimore. At the end of the day he would ride his bicycle to Govans, telephoning in his stories from there. Covering a county barn fire late one night, the only way he could get the news to Baltimore in time was by awakening a telegrapher of the Maryland & Pennsylvania Railroad who dot-dashed it to the *Sun*. Toward the end of his career he was assigned to the city desk to answer phones. He originated an office custom of placing a lighted candle in a city-room window on New Year's Eve, and at midnight of moving ceremoniously from desk to desk with a tray of pickled herring, a good luck symbol for the new year. Poole retired in 1951 after more than sixty years of service.

Women also were responsible for the *Sun*'s breadth and depth of coverage. For seven years May Garrettson Evans, who joined the staff in 1888, wrote about the theater, concerts, lectures, churches, and fashion and did interviews and whatever the city editor assigned. In 1894, when interviewing Asger Hamerik, director of the Peabody Conservatory, she suggested that the Conservatory start a preparatory school (the suggestion was made because she was desperate for a news story). Hamerik liked the idea, but could not become involved at that point. She went back to the paper and wrote an article entitled "Preparatory Music School Talked Of." That fall, while still working as a reporter, she and her sister Marion opened such a school in two rented rooms. The school was an immediate success, and May regretfully left the *Sun* in 1895. Four years later the Peabody absorbed the school, and she served as its director until 1930, when she retired.

Gertrude B. Knipp, a graduate of Goucher College, was the second female reporter on the paper. She started in 1897 and recalled later that she "worked hard, tackling whatever was given me to do, regardless of how little I knew about it. Nobody said anything to me about a salary or pay for the work, but I was learning the game and let it go at that. The business office did not look me up and I didn't worry the cashier. I supposed this was the way newspapers were run . . . and hoped that day of financial reckoning would come to me, sometime." It finally did, after a month on the job. Her salary was $10 a week.

In her first interview with Cardinal Gibbons, Miss Knipp was assigned an escort by the city desk "who coached me all the way up to the Cardinal's residence to be sure I would say 'Your Eminence' and would conduct myself with due discretion." She scored a notable beat in 1901 on the resignation of Daniel Coit Gilman after twenty-five years as president of Johns Hopkins University. She attributed this to "sheer dumb luck" of having overheard a conversation on a streetcar. She was awarded a $10 gold piece for the story. Miss Knipp was on the *Sun* until 1905, when she resigned to join the *American*.

One woman who received more than a $10 gold piece was Annie Oakley. An entry in the Directors Book indicated that Miss Oakley—identified only as "the rifle shot"—had sued the paper for libel in April 1904. The *Sun* was one of more than fifty papers sued, and she won all but a few suits. The *Sun* case was settled in 1906 for $516.40.

Walter R. Abell, the youngest of the Founder's surviving sons, died on January 3, 1891, at the age of 42. Though he became one of three partners after the death of his father, he took little part in the paper's operation. The obituary editorial dwelt on "his nobility of heart and character." He left his share in the paper in trust to his son, Walter R. 2d, and his two daughters, with his two brothers as trustees.

The trust made it necessary to change the simple partnership. On August 9, 1892, the business was incorporated as the A. S. Abell Company with Edwin, George, Arunah S. 2d, Charles S. Abell, William H. Heindle, and George H. Karsner as incorporators. Arunah was the elder son of Edwin, Charles was the son of George, Heindle was the head bookkeeper, and Karsner was the cashier. Capital stock was fixed at $300,000 with 3,000 shares at a par value of $100. Each incorporator received a share, and the other 2,994 shares were exchanged for the interests in the partnership. As trustees, Edwin and George held 1,000 shares, and as individuals each had 997 shares. The incorporators, except for Charles, were elected directors, with George as president and general manager and Edwin as secretary and treasurer, each with a salary of $10,000.

The brothers had liked the informality of the partnership and on a sad note passed this resolution on August 10, 1892, the day after the new company began business:

As this is the last day of the existence of the time-honored partnership of A. S. Abell & Co., which owned and conducted for so many years the daily and *Weekly Sun*, established fifty-five years ago by the senior partner, Arunah S. Abell, and as this is also the anniversary of the birthday of the founder of these journals, and is the day of beginning of the corporation formed to carry on the business heretofore conducted by the said Arunah S. Abell and the said partnership composed of Edwin F. Abell, George W. Abell and the late Walter R. Abell, it is becoming to mark by some appropriate action the sense of this meeting of the stockholders of the new corporation, of the importance of the event today consummated, and of the responsibilities assumed.

Therefore be it resolved by the stockholders in meeting assembled, That, while regretting the necessity which led to a termination of the former partnership of A. S. Abell & Co., which for so many years conducted the business of daily and weekly *Sun* and The *Sun* Job Printing Office in Baltimore city, we hail with satisfaction the new organization which has sprung up in its place, and we pledge ourselves to exert our best ability to conduct the new enterprise on the same lines and on the same principles of honor and integrity which so eminently characterized the old management, in the hope and belief that the same success will attend our labors which crowned those of our predecessors.

In May 1893 the board was reduced to three members: Edwin, George, and Edwin's son, Arunah S. 2d. A dividend of 12 percent had been declared in December 1892, and another of 4 percent in April 1893. The next year, the regular 12 percent dividend was increased with an extra 6 percent, stockholders receiving $54,000 on the $300,000 investment. This was during a depression.

George, who had been directing the paper in his father's last years and was the editor and president after the death of his father in 1888, died on May 1,

1894, at the age of 52. He had studied law, was admitted to the bar in 1864, and had served as his father's attorney. He started in the paper's counting room but moved to the news and editorial departments. He was an able, aggressive journalist and was responsible for reinvigorating the paper after the near-moribund war years.

Edwin was then the only surviving son of the Founder. He was mild-mannered and retiring—different from his forceful brother—but he proved strong and determined when he led the *Sun* in its biggest political fight. Edwin was elected president on June 12, 1894, and at the same time his son Arunah was elected secretary and treasurer, and another son, Walter W., was elected a director. Charles became a member of the board when it was increased to four members in April 1898. In June 1901 the offices of secretary and treasurer were split. Arunah remained as treasurer, and Charles was elected secretary. Walter W. was also elected to the new office of vice president.

The Democratic machine had ruled Baltimore from the 1870s to 1895. Under A. S. Abell, the *Sun* was apathetic about the corruption and vulgarities of local politics and did not fight the machine except in 1882 in its campaign for a free judiciary. In 1885, as noted, the *Sun* ridiculed a reform movement and the Republicans for besmirching the reputation of Baltimore when they campaigned against the machine-controlled Democratic party. But the paper was gradually forced into a stronger political stand after Charles H. Grasty, who had made a quick reputation as a Kansas City newspaperman, bought the weak Baltimore *Evening News* in 1891 with the backing of four prominent Baltimoreans who wanted to elevate the tone of public life. Grasty, only 28 years old, was a crusader and an agitating editor and readily grasped the situation. He soon had the *News* revealing the inadequacies of city government, attacking the Consolidated Gas Company and the telephone monopoly for high rates and streetcar lines for their deficiencies, along with investigating slums, sweatshops and the Policy game, an illegal lottery played by the poor. The *Sun,* the established paper, which over the years had largely averted its glance from corrupt government and social injustices, was forced, as *News* circulation increased, to look below the surface of public life. Even so, as James Crooks points out in his *Politics and Progress,* a comprehensive and scholarly study of that period, "in comparison with the *News,* which was striving to awaken and direct public opinion, the *Sun* seemed more nearly [just] to mirror a gradually shifting public opinion."

The Baltimore Reform League, organized in 1885, became a powerful force in the 1895 election. Its core was elite—people of standing, particularly Charles J. Bonaparte, who was a great-grandson of William Patterson, one of Baltimore's earliest merchant-capitalists, and who was a grandson of Jerome Bonaparte, youngest brother of the French emperor. Grasty supported and encouraged the League, along with Republicans and reform Democrats, in combating the Rasin-Gorman machine. They crusaded for fair elections. The

Sun, even in the thick of its fight with the machine, never did much to promote the League's role.

For the *Sun* the issue was joined that August, at the Democratic state convention. Five prominent Marylanders had announced their candidacies for governor. But I. Freeman Rasin and Arthur Pue Gorman, who controlled the nominations, arbitrarily picked John E. Hurst, whose name had not been mentioned for the nomination. After Edwin Abell heard the details from Charles W. Dashiell, the city editor, and William H. Davis, the political reporter, who had covered the convention, he ordered an all-out attack. The next day, the *Sun* described "How the Deals Were Fixed," emphasized their significance, and editorially attacked the dictatorial nomination.

After Lloyd Lowndes, of Allegany County, was nominated for governor by the Republicans, the *Sun* pointedly noted that he was selected by votes, not bosses. It demanded that Rasin and Gorman be defeated: "The plank is out and they must be made to walk it. They have well-earned the fate of political pirates." Grasty must have been surprised but pleased. The *News* lauded its competitor for its "veritable broadsides." Gorman's men twitted the *Sun* for supporting Democrats in 1887, when some Democrats supported Republicans; the *Sun* replied that at least the candidates had been nominated by the party then. "This year the party nominated nobody. Its prerogatives and powers have been usurped by Mr. Gorman, an anti-Cleveland politician of Republican antecedents. . . . The revolt of that year was the revolt of a faction. This year it is the uprising of the people."

Though it had ignored or sometimes had been critical of Gorman during his long political career (Gorman had been a member of Maryland's General Assembly since 1881 and U.S. Senator), the *Sun* never sought to dethrone him or break up his organization until 1895. Gorman had practically run the 1884 convention that nominated Cleveland. During it, Gorman tried to ingratiate himself with the paper by giving Richardson a copy of the platform before it was adopted, enabling the *Sun* to score a national beat. When the Cleveland-Blaine election was so close that the outcome was in doubt for three days, Gorman telegraphed the paper as soon as he learned that Cleveland had enough electoral votes to win. The *Sun* even ran an editorial praising Gorman for his role in that victory. But during Cleveland's first term, Gorman, representing the sugar interests, led a group of fellow senators in adding 600 special amendments to Cleveland's low-tariff bill, effectively emasculating it; the President branded Gorman and his cohorts as traitors, "guilty of party perfidy and dishonor." After that the Abells turned away from Gorman. As noted, Cleveland was not only their hero but also their friend.

When George W. Abell was in charge at the *Sun,* he was often invited to the White House for private talks, and the President also kept in touch with personal notes. The President and Richardson were friends too. Richardson, the *Sun's* Washington correspondent, was on the committee in charge of the

1885 inauguration ceremonies and again in 1893. One day he received word that Cleveland wanted to see him. He hurried to the White House, thinking he was getting an exclusive interview. He was disappointed yet pleased; Cleveland wanted his advice.

The *Sun* seldom overlooked an opportunity to praise the President. After the Cleveland baby was born in July 1895, the paper, in a column-long editorial, "Great Presidents and Little Children," compared Cleveland's bliss (he was almost 50 when Esther was born) to that of Jefferson and Lincoln: "Thomas Jefferson was a babies' president. He was a confirmed baby-worshiper. Lincoln was as fond of his boys as Thomas Jefferson was of his girls. . . . It is a very common characteristic of men of exceptional power to be baby-lovers and child worshipers." A rare note of criticism was expressed when Cleveland appointed S. D. Warfield and William L. Marbury, Sr., to federal offices in Baltimore—both were bachelors. The *Sun* said marriage was a political and patriotic duty and cited Cleveland as an example of one who married as quickly as possible after his election. The *Sun* believed that the problem was the bachelor's "wild and ungoverned exuberance," which makes him "like an anarchist . . . fit for treason, stratagems and spoils, but not for civil service or any other genuine reform."

But its expressions of wonder and approbation never faltered. In fact, the *Sun* was so enraptured of Cleveland during his second term that it raised the possibility of a third: "Precedent Can Be Broken."

As the fight between Gorman and the *Sun* built up to a climax it became more personal. In a fiery speech, Gorman claimed that Lowndes was "nominated through a conspiracy between Edwin F. Abell of the Baltimore *Sun* and the B&O, who fear that their large exempted interests will be taxed. Mr. Lowndes is their friend, their banker, their attorney and would be their instrument as governor of Maryland." Gorman's men spread the word that the Abells had turned against him because they had failed to be awarded political appointments, including an ambassadorship. During the first Cleveland administration, George W. Abell had been offered the ambassadorship to the Court of St. James but had turned it down, wanting no part of politics. During Cleveland's second term, word reached the *Sun* that the President was considering offering Edwin F. Abell a cabinet post; Abell sent word that he was not interested.

The paper responded by labeling the alleged Lowndes connection "a falsehood," adding, "In a desperate but unavailing effort to break the force of the *Sun* and the people's warfare against the machine, the supporters of the bosses are ascribing all sorts of motives to the *Sun*'s opposition to Mr. Gorman, charging, for instance, that it has been influenced by the failure of individuals connected with it to get appointments as ministers to foreign countries. . . . The *Sun* pronounces it and all similar suggestions to be utterly false." The rumors were so widespread and persistent that they circulated long after 1895.

Someone signing himself "An Independent" wrote a letter to the paper, published as a "card," saying, "The *Sun* represents a few malcontents and its proprietor, and Mr. Gorman simply represents himself. In their personal squabbles neither of them represent the people nor yet the real and true Democrats of the state . . . and the sooner the *Sun* and Mr. Gorman realize this fact the better it will be for themselves, for the reason that the Democrats of Maryland will never recognize either a one-man or a one-paper dictatorship."

During this long and bitter campaign the *Sun* had an anti-Gorman editorial almost every day, sometimes two, three. One day it called him a "crawfish." The only light moment in the campaign happened when Mayor Ferdinand Latrobe traveled to Deer Park for a weekend, using the private car of a B&O vice president. Deer Park, in the Western Maryland mountains, was a popular resort for the ruling classes, particularly politicians, during the hot, humid days of late summer. In Washington, D.C., a young man boarded the private car and told the mayor the *Sun* had sent him for an interview. "What are your views on politics in Maryland?" he was asked. "I have nothing to say," the mayor replied. "Then," the young man said, "I must tell the *Sun* you have absolutely no opinion on Maryland politics." The mayor—hot, tired, upset at being disturbed while relaxing—shouted, "No! Yes! That is, oh well, you can write anything you d—— please, just so you get out of here and let me alone." At Deer Park the B&O vice president told the mayor it was a joke. He had induced the Washington stationmaster to impersonate a *Sun* reporter.

The mayor replied that he wouldn't have been fooled if the weather had not been so hot. The *Sun* obviously relished the mayor's concluding remarks, which were used to round out its story: "The methods of the *Sun* reporters," the mayor added, "are so entirely different from those assumed by my would-be interviewer that I ought to have known that he was not on the *Sun* staff."

The *Sun* was so agitated about the Gorman fight on election day that its editorial reached hyperbolic heights: "If honest citizens will do their duty today, the fifth of November, 1895 will take rank with the twelfth of September, 1814, and those who aid in the defeat of these modern enemies of Maryland will form a glorious army of New Defenders, not less worthy of honor and renown than the Old Defenders who repulsed the British attack upon this city."

Rowdyism was rampant. Violence in the Seventeenth Ward was as bad as it was in Plug-Ugly days, the *Sun* reported. Voters were kicked and a few were shot, though not seriously injured, it added. The Reform League had watchers at most polls, and a number were threatened and some assaulted. The president of the Good Government Club of the Twelfth Ward was hit in the eye and back. One Reform League watcher was jostled and then felt a gloved hand across his neck, which began to sting. Someone had rubbed it with "cow itch." No election bulletins were issued by the *Sun,* it explained, because in the past large crowds had spilled off the sidewalks and out over the car tracks, endangering lives.

Gorman's candidates were defeated, the Republicans electing the governor, the legislature, the mayor, and the City Council. Gorman even lost Howard, his own county. The *Sun* hailed the results as "a victory for democracy—not for republicanism—one of the greatest victories, in fact, that democracy has ever won in the whole course of its history." A few days later, as an afterthought, it praised the Reform League, calling it "a most influential factor," though it had said little editorially about the League during the campaign.

In the presidential campaign of 1896, the *Sun* campaigned vigorously for sound money. It seldom mentioned William McKinley, the Republican candidate, a sound-money man, but it continuously attacked William Jennings Bryan, champion of the free-silver forces and candidate of the Democrats, the Populists, and the National Silver party. After Bryan was nominated by the Democrats following his famed "Crown of thorns and cross of gold" speech, the paper proclaimed: "The triumph of the extremists in Chicago brings at least this benefit to the country, that it precipitates a pitched battle between the defenders of sound money and the champions of silver flatism, which must culminate next November in a victory that will be conclusive of the financial future of the country."

The *Sun*, traditionally a sound-money paper, predicted that if Bryan succeeded in making sixteen parts of silver equal to one part of gold, the nation would endure another financial panic. It enlisted women in its fight even though they had no vote. "The burden of the household finance rests upon them," it said, "and they are too practical to stand quietly by and see it increased." According to the *Sun*'s calculations, owners of $53,000,000 in silver bullion "by rushing it to the Treasury as soon as a free coinage law passed could get in exchange $100,000,000 in silver certificates which they would work off on people for a profit of $47,000,000." Later, on an almost hysterical note, it predicted that "each silver mine owner may be provided with a government mint of his own to coin for his own benefits the product of his own mine." Then, quoting Bryan as saying "Quantity, not quality is the essential thing," it added, "And so $1,000 may again be the price of a barrel of flour, or of a pair of boots, as in the days of Confederate money, unlimited in 'quantity,' but unfortunately sadly lacking in 'quality.' "

Bryan and McKinley waged different campaigns. McKinley conducted his from the front porch of his home in Canton, Ohio, making three or four speeches a day to visiting delegations. When crowds got so large that he could not be seen or heard from the porch, he mounted a bandstand erected on his lawn. Bryan traveled over 18,000 miles and made 600 speeches in twenty-seven states. He spoke twice in Baltimore, once before 20,000 persons. The *Sun* quoted his speeches in full, calling them "earnest, brilliant, though often illogical." A *Sun* reporter stood by as Bryan ate breakfast—oysters, fish, chicken, beefsteak, French-fried potatoes, and coffee, commenting, "He did it full justice."

Though the paper had no editorial mercy for Bryan, its news columns reported his campaign objectively; in fact, it claimed "its news columns have really contained more Bryan campaign literature than all the other candidates combined." Incidentally, two other candidates were Senator John M. Palmer, 79, and General Simon Bolivar Buckner, 73, Civil War generals who had been on opposite sides. They were nominated for president and vice president of the National Democratic Party, a secessionist band of conservative Democrats.

Following McKinley's victory, the *Sun*'s first two postelection editorials omitted the winner's name. One called it a victory for "sound money and sound morals"; the other praised the *Sun*'s old friend Cleveland: "The result of the election is much less an endorsement or a vindication of the principle or policy of the Republican party, apart from the sound money in its St. Louis platform, than it is a vindication of those principles and that policy for which Mr. Cleveland stood when the people chose him in preference to Mr. Harrison for President four years ago, and for which he has consistently stood through the whole of his administration."

For two generations, the *Sun* had been a loud and dependable Democratic organ. The earlier rejection of Gorman locally had cost it some advertising and circulation. In 1896, when the *Sun* deserted the party nationally, even more Marylanders were angered and there were still-greater advertising and circulation losses. The bitterness that developed was deep and long-lasting.

Unlike its stance in the Mexican War, when Arunah S. Abell asserted that a long conflict meant "the entire subjugation and annexation of Mexico will be unavoidable," the *Sun*, in the Spanish-American War of 1898, railed against imperialism, what President McKinley called "benevolent assimilation of the Philippines." After the U.S. battleship *Maine* was sunk in Havana's harbor in mysterious circumstances, the *Sun* cautioned, "There is no need for war." It termed William Randolph Hearst's *New York Journal* and Joseph Pulitzer's *World,* both clamoring for war, "jingo journals." But after the United States declared war against Spain, the *Sun* urged a "vigorous prosecution." Commenting on the 1899 treaty of peace, the *Sun* editorialized:

The only trouble in this gigantic scheme of philanthropy may be the fear on the part of the Filipinos that "benevolent assimilation" is synonymous with the surrender of all their aspirations for independence and self-government. . . . But the Filipinos, if their aspirations are properly understood, are not yearning for what the President tenders them any more than the Americans of the Revolutionary period longed for "assimilation" with their French allies, who helped them throw off the British yoke. . . . Benevolent assimilation may be an euphemistic synonym for imperialism and annexation. In fact, the majority of the Filipinos will probably take this view of it. . . . The Indians of North America have been under our influence for many years, but we have never been able to "assimilate" them and the problem is as far from solution now as it ever was. The negroes have been upon this continent almost as long as the whites and no one will say that we have satisfactorily "assimilated" them. How, then, can we expect to work a miracle in the Philippines?

After its assault on Bryan in 1896, the *Sun* flip-flopped, favoring him against McKinley in 1900 because it now perceived the Republicans as a force for trusts and imperialism (the McKinley administration was busily annexing Spain's biggest colonies). "Silver is not the vital issue," it said in its change of course. "The Republicans have made desperate efforts to frighten timid voters with the bugaboo of free coinage, but the practical common sense of the American people is proof against such flimsy attempts to deceive them." Though he also was defeated in 1900, Bryan had a role in framing the Democratic platform in 1904 when Judge Alton B. Parker was nominated as presidential candidate. The *Sun* supported Parker in his losing battle with Theodore Roosevelt. In 1908, when Bryan was for the third time the Democratic candidate, the *Sun* reverted to its original hostility—it was offended by Bryan's advocacy of public ownership for the railroads. William H. Taft, it felt, would better promote public welfare: "We support him from a sense of public duty."

Although the *Sun* was a leader in newspaper enterprise, it was slow to install the linotype, a machine that set type mechanically and quickly, a line at a time, replacing the centuries-old method of setting type by hand, letter-by-letter. The linotype was developed between 1877 and 1886 by Ottmar Mergenthaler in a Baltimore shop not far from the *Sun* Iron Building. Surely A. S. Abell must have heard about the machine, perhaps even seen it demonstrated. He might have had doubts about its practicality and also been concerned that it would displace many of his printers, a force that included a number who had been with him for years and were not only loyal employees but friends as well. The first paper to install the linotype was the *New York Tribune* in July 1886. Before the end of the year the *Tribune* was using a dozen machines, and soon many other newspapers had them. But it was not until November 1896, eight years after A. S. Abell's death, that the *Sun* bought four linotypes.

The *Sun* did not hesitate the following year when Simon Lake tested his Baltimore-built submarine, the *Argonaut,* in the depths of the nearby Patapsco River. A *Sun* reporter, assigned to accompany Lake on the test, was told, "If Lake succeeds he's worth a column. If not, write his obituary." In his autobiography, Lake told that story, and added that if he had not succeeded someone else would have written the obituary because the reporter would have been with him.

One exploit in *Sun* lore that promises to be still recalled when the political battles of that day have been forgotten occurred during the blizzard of 1899, when "Denny went to Towson." The *Sun* of February 14 described that blizzard as the worst in the city's history. More than fifteen inches of snow had fallen in one day, more than thirty-two inches in nine days. Most traffic was suspended. Mail could not be delivered. Business was at a standstill. Telephone and telegraph lines were down. "The unhappy pedestrian plodding along, battling with snow in his face," the paper reported, "would suddenly be brought to a stop by an unexpected plunge into a snow drift that would cover him almost to his waist. He would plunge and struggle to a more solid footing only to have his experience repeated."

Struggling against those conditions, Alexander J. Dennistone, a *Sun* carrier, known as Denny, who owned a route that began at North Avenue and extended eight miles to Towson, managed to deliver his papers. He started out from Baltimore and South streets at 1:30 A.M. with a subcarrier in a horse-drawn cart. Plowing through snowdrifts, sometimes pulling the horse and shoveling snow from under the cart, they made their way up York Road to Govans, about half the journey. Here the subcarrier and horse gave out. "Take the horse back to town," Denny ordered. "I'm going to Towson." Going was more difficult in the open country because no tracks had been broken. Denny waded in waist-deep snow and drifts up to his shoulders. Often he fell exhausted, but as he said many times later he kept telling himself, "I started for Towson. That's where I'm going!" He arrived there with his papers at 4:00 P.M., a struggle of nearly fifteen hours. When he was spotted, word was passed, and enough Towsonites managed to get to the courthouse to give him a rousing welcome. Still holding his papers, he was lifted on the shoulders of his greeters and paraded around the corridors as a hero. (Dennistone died in 1918; his widow managed the route until her retirement in 1939.)

His feat was, and is, more celebrated than any other exploit in *Sun* history. When the great blizzard of January 28, 1922, struck Baltimore with 26½ inches of snow, carriers that night were greeted with signs in the mail room saying "Remember When Denny Went to Towson." The *Sun* Route Owners Association stationery was illustrated with a sketch of Denny, papers under arm, wading through snowdrifts. The slogan is still a rallying cry in the circulation department when adversity threatens. And Denny is sometimes invoked in the news room when an emergency arises, even a minor one, but there the attitude can be derisive.

In 1901 the Abells began publishing a Sunday paper. (Their competitors, the *American* and the *Herald,* had been doing so for several years.) Entitled *The Sun,* it closely resembled the weekday paper and sold for the same two cents. In a front-page announcement the Abells said the "paper will be the *Sun* on Sunday as well as on every other day." They attempted to allay the fears of Sabbatarians by promising the paper would be "equal in moral tone" to the weekday issues and added, "There should be no day of the week in this era of quick communication upon which the quiet and orderly dissemination of intelligence should be banned." No advance notice was made to readers or advertisers. When the press agent for the Academy of Music heard about it from the gossip of reporters and printers, he telephoned the business office to ask if he could get an ad in the paper. "Yes," he was told, "if you send it down right away." Advertisers were not solicited because the Abells thought their newly available columns might be swamped with ads.

The first Sunday editor was O. P. Baldwin, who had been on the staff since 1882 as telegraph editor and editorial writer. He served as Sunday editor until 1906, when he was appointed managing editor of the *Sun*. That same year the board of directors authorized an increase in the size of the Sunday *Sun* "to any number of pages up to and including 24" (the first issue was fourteen pages). Later, a special board meeting was called to select a new Sunday editor. Walter W. Abell nominated H. L. Mencken but was not sure he could get him. Mencken, who had been hired by the rival *Herald* as a reporter at age 19, was soon made city editor, managing editor at age 24, and then, just before that paper went out of business, editor. He joined Grasty's *News*. Five weeks later came the offer from the Abells: Sunday editor at $40 a week. Mencken accepted, and July 30, 1906, was the beginning of his memorable association with the *Sun*.

The Great Fire of 1904

The fire broke out on Sunday morning, February 7, 1904, at 10:48 o'clock.

Insurance investigators later agreed that it had started when a lighted cigar or cigarette fell through a hole in a sidewalk "deadeye" into the basement of the John E. Hurst & Company dry-goods house at German Street and Hopkins Place, in the heart of the business district. A smoke explosion blew off the roof of the six-story building, shooting flames and firebrands across narrow German (now Redwood) Street into other buildings. Falling brands knocked out the first fire truck and steamer on the scene; it had been parked there as hostlers removed the horses to go back to the station house for more equipment. Within minutes, four buildings were burning fiercely and others were on fire. George W. Horton, chief engineer of the Fire Department, ordered the general alarm sounded, committing all equipment. Before noon a telegram notified the Washington Fire Department: "Desperate fire here. Must have help at once."

Only churchgoers were downtown at 11:00 A.M. But the clanging engines, the galloping fire horses, and the sight and smell of smoke soon drew many, who came running and shouting from all directions. Spectators stood ten to twenty deep across from the fires and felt a certain exhilaration. But moods darkened as the flames crackled and leaped. Women cried when flames ate into the places where they worked. Men, despite warnings from police and firemen, rushed into buildings in the path of destruction to retrieve records and money from safes. Bystanders bolted when the area was rocked by yet another explosion. It came from a hardware store's magazine, filled with gunpowder that had been stored on a sidewalk, according to fire regulations. Flames from that and other explosions were being driven by a twelve-mile-per-hour wind from the southwest. The swirling gusts sent sparks and firebrands as far as two or three blocks, igniting sheds, canvas awnings, and roofs. People climbed to rooftops to sweep off the showering embers, but they could not sweep fast enough.

Ordinarily, reporters took their time showing up for work on Sunday, a slow day. But this day, great clouds of smoke billowing over the downtown area, the multiple alarms, and the excitement had them scurrying to their offices, then to the onrushing edges of the flames which were soon out of control.

H. L. Mencken, 23-year-old city editor of the *Herald,* caught their excitement when he wrote in his reminiscences, "We had a story, I am here to tell you! There have been bigger ones, of course, and plenty of them, but when and where, between the Chicago fire of 1871 and the San Francisco earthquake of 1906, was there ever one that was fatter, juicier, or more exhilarating to the journalists on the actual ground?" All *Sun* reporters, even retired ones who rushed back to help, were gathering facts and impressions along the fire lines, running back to the *Sun* to write, then out again.

By early afternoon the fire had covered twelve blocks and was still surging east by gusting winds. Downtown Baltimore was a vista of burning warehouses, stores, offices, banks, and new (supposedly fireproof) skyscrapers. Despairing, the authorities decided to dynamite buildings. The dynamiting was done by a government demolition expert from Washington, D.C., and army sappers, but instead of creating a firebreak or nonflammable zone, early attempts just bored holes into the streetbeds. There was talk of trying cannon from Fort McHenry. One fireman, describing the force and fury of the fire, exclaimed, "A thousand fire companies couldn't stop it. Tonight fire is king." A spectator on the top floor of the Belvedere Hotel described the smoke and flames as looking like a fiery demon. The glow could be seen for fifty miles.

Because of illness, Edwin F. Abell, president of the A. S. Abell Company, was confined to the house he had taken for the winter at the northeast corner of Charles and Preston streets. His son Walter was managing the *Sun* and had been for some time. When it seemed likely that the fire might eventually reach the *Sun* building at Baltimore and South streets, Walter Abell and Edward Crummer, the business manager, ordered the removal of the subscriber mailing lists, books in the counting room, even bound files of the paper from 1837. They were hauled by wagon to safe storage. Other businessmen were also removing valuables from offices that appeared to be in the fire's path. They were carried away, as far as to Druid Hill Park, in wheelbarrows, on bicycles, even in market baskets. Wagons, drays, trucks, carts, and hacks—anything on wheels—were in urgent demand. The use of a wagon was bringing payments of as high as $25 and $30. Raucous entanglements of overloaded wagons, rearing horses, and shouting, cursing drivers blocked streets and alleys. Horses' manes and tails were singed by flying sparks. Wagons and drays, racing along streets laced with fire hose, cut the hose to ribbons.

As the fire edged closer, Walter Abell telegraphed the publishers of the *Washington Star,* arranging for the *Sun* to be printed there should his building burn. But work proceeded—reporters at their typewriters, editors copy-reading and writing heads, compositors tapping furiously at linotype machines. As soon as a page was locked up it was sent to stereotyping, then down to the press room. Press time for the first edition was advanced. The *American* building, across from the *Sun*'s, was dark. At 6:00 P.M. that paper's publisher decided it was no longer possible to get out a paper and ordered everyone out of the building. Meanwhile, sentinels had been stationed outside the *Sun* building and at upper-story windows to watch for fires and to sound an alarm if necessary. Toward 10:00 P.M., only two pages remained to be stereotyped, one page to be made up, and about a column of the lead fire story to be set in type. When that was done, the presses would roll.

Abell and his editors and supervisors felt confident they could start printing in a few minutes. But a printer at work on the fifth floor became frightened by showers of sparks on the composing room skylight. Accosting Abell, he blurted out, "It's dangerous to have all those men up in the composing room. If the building should catch fire we'd not have time to get out." Without hesitation Abell replied, "All right. Stop work. I'll order the building cleared."

Everyone was told to assemble at the Lexington Hotel, on Holliday Street, opposite City Hall. Printers crowded around Abell, cursing and protesting that the man who spoke did not represent them. They wanted to stay either until the type was set or until the building caught fire. Reporters, editors, and pressmen from the basement also exhorted Abell, insisting they wanted to get the paper out. Someone pointed out that the fire had spread only as far as Charles Street, three blocks away, and that it might be an hour before it reached them.

Abell was adamant. "We'll take no chances with men's lives," he said. "Much as I'd love to see us get out the last paper here, I'd never forgive myself if a single man should lose his life, or get seriously hurt, in order to do so." Grumbling, they left, taking with them the matrixes of the paper forms and the copy still to be set. Abell then walked through the building to make sure no one was left.

Harold E. West was sent to the B&O headquarters, at Calvert and Baltimore streets, to charter a train to Washington, D.C. The building seemed to have been abandoned. The roof was afire, and sparks were showering down the stairway and elevator shaft. But coming down, several steps at a time, was the very man West wanted: Arthur Hale, the general superintendent of transportation and the son of Edward Everett Hale, author of *The Man Without a Country.* West shouted that the *Sun* was abandoning its building and would get the paper printed in Washington, D.C. It needed a special train as soon as possible. They made their way back to Hale's office. Touching his telegraph key, Hale found the line still working. "That's luck," he exclaimed. Then he notified the stationmaster at Camden to ready a train with two coaches and the fastest locomotive available. When the *Sun* men were aboard, the special was to have a clear track to Washington. That was the last business transacted in the building. Fifteen minutes later, it was in flames.

Abell and a few employees stayed outside the *Sun* building, still hoping it might be saved. Doors and windows were shut to keep out sparks. Three times, burning embers came to rest against the wooden window frames, setting them on fire. Twice West went back into the building to put out fires on the second and fourth floors. By midnight the *American* building was burning; in a few more minutes, the Iron Building was in flames. Linotype machines crashed through the burning floors to the basement. At 12:30 A.M. the walls caved in. It was the end of a Baltimore landmark. Firemen estimated the heat in that area at about 2,500 degrees.

At 11:00 P.M. the *Sun* men left the Lexington Hotel, circling the still-spreading fire to reach Camden Station. The editorial staff was led by Allen S. Will, the telegraph editor, with West second in command. The "Flying Squadron" included the composing room force, the stereotypers, the mailing department, and counting-room clerks. Herbert A. Hallett, the city editor, stayed in Baltimore with the reporters. Frank R. Kent was still writing the lead story in longhand on the bar as the men filed out.

During the forty-five minute trip to Washington, Will made assignments so that everyone knew exactly what he was to do. The *Evening Star* men were waiting for the *Sun* contingent "with lights burning, steam up, and the telegraph wires ready for use." But before long the wires to Baltimore were down. Hallett then sent late news by messengers on scheduled trains. One difficulty in printing in a different shop was almost insurmountable. The *Star's* page was smaller than the *Sun's*. The page matrixes prepared in Baltimore would not fit in the *Star's* casting box. Scouts were rushed to other newspapers and finally, at the *Post,* an unused casting box that would work was found. Still, for other reasons, last-minute improvisations had to be devised to get the paper printed. A baggage car filled with papers was in Baltimore before 5:00 A.M. The eight-page paper had a four-column headline:

TWENTY-FOUR BLOCKS BURNED
IN HEART OF BALTIMORE
City's Most Valuable Buildings in Ruins
Loss Roughly Estimated at Fifty Million Dollars
Starting in John E. Hurst Building the Fire Sweeps South, to Lombard, East to Holliday and North to Lexington, Destroying Wholesale Business Houses, Banks, Trust Buildings, B. and O. Central and Other Prominent Structures

The lead was:

Fire, which started at 10:50 o'clock yesterday morning, devastated practically the entire central business district of Baltimore and at midnight the flames were still raging with as much fury as at the beginning.

To all appearances Baltimore's business section is doomed. Many of the principal banking institutions, all the leading trust companies, all the largest wholesale houses, all the newspaper offices, many of the principal retail stores and thousands of smaller establishments went up in flame, and in most cases the contents were completely destroyed.

What the loss will be in dollars no man can even estimate, but the sum will be so gigantic that it is hard for the average mind to grasp its magnitude. In addition to the pecuniary loss will be the immense amount of business lost by the necessary interruption to business while the many firms whose places are destroyed are making arrangements for resuming business.

There is little doubt that many men, formerly prosperous, will be ruined by the events of the last 24 hours. Many of them carry little or no insurance, and it is doubtful if many of the insurance companies will be able to pay their losses dollar for dollar, and those that do will probably require time in which to arrange payment.

All day and all night throngs crowded the streets, blocking every avenue to the fire district, and moving back out of danger only when forced to do so by the police on duty. Many of the spectators saw their all go up in flame before their eyes, and there were men with hopeless faces and despairing expression seen on every hand. In fact, the throng seemed stunned with the magnitude of the disaster and scarcely seemed to realize the extent of it.

They stood around usually in a dazed silence, and only occasionally would a word of despair be heard. That they were almost disheartened was apparent to the casual observer, and there is little wonder, for the crushing stroke fell with the suddenness of lightning from a cloudless sky.

For the most part the account stressed fact, with only some emotion and dramatics. It told how the fire started, how Chief Horton was disabled by a live trolley wire that fell on him, how the fire spread, and about the use of dynamite, the destruction of the Carrollton and Mullins hotels and other large buildings, and the arrival by train of Washington fire equipment. (Their hoses would not fit Baltimore hydrants, so they were wrapped to the plugs with pieces of canvas.)

A list of the largest dry-goods, clothing, and shoe stores, along with two banks, in the wholesale business district where the fire originated, was accompanied by a careful and conservative estimate of the loss at more than $15 million. "This estimate was made for the *Sun* last night by Mr. George E. Taylor, of the insurance firm of Jennis & Taylor, Holliday and Water streets. Mr. Taylor sat in his office dictating to a reporter of the *Sun* until it was stated that the fire was only a few doors away, when he found it necessary to remove the valuables and papers from his office. The estimate is for each building and its contents." The list was more than a column long.

Reporters produced many human interest sketches: A bank treasurer with a policeman went into the bank and recovered "two handsome rings belonging to him." The policeman kept the rings until the treasurer was identified by the deputy marshal. Earlier $20,000 in coins and bills had been removed from the bank for safekeeping. Later, bank officers—not knowing the money had been removed—opened the vault and found it empty. The *Sun* did not report their reaction. (Possibly that story was hearsay. Time locks on vaults had been set for Monday and could not be opened until then. Hysterical depositors rushed to some banks, pounding their fists against heavy doors, yelling "Give us our money!" Bankers, also alarmed about possible loss, could do nothing.)

Downtown telephone service continued until operators, in the Exchange Building on St. Paul Street, had to abandon their switchboards at 7:00 P.M. Patients were moved by ambulances from City Hospital on Calvert Street to four other hospitals. Those in critical condition were covered so they could not see the approaching flames. The *Sun* printed a list of patients moved. Governor Edwin Warfield somehow missed the special train to bring him and Annapolis fire equipment to Baltimore. He asked for and got another special, and was accompanied by a *Sun* reporter who quoted him as saying that he had been trying to reach the Fidelity Building since 5:00 P.M. by telephone and telegraph. "Naturally I felt anxious about the building," he said, "because not only my own securities but those of others are kept there." (He had been president of the Fidelity Deposit & Trust Company.) Many Washingtonians arrived on afternoon trains to witness the excitement.

In the rush and confusion of getting out the paper in two different cities, a "Gathered at Random" collection of seventeen paragraphs appeared on both page two and page three, along with three articles about the Fourth and Fifth regiments of the National Guard being called out (two of them identical), transposed lines of type, inconsistencies, and reports of four buildings destroyed that had not been burned (that was corrected a few days later). But these slips were insignificant compared to the painstaking, comprehensive— and perhaps heroic—report that was published. In addition to news on the fire, the *Sun* had news of events elsewhere that had been prepared earlier; among them was the beginning of the Russo-Japanese War.

The *Sun* even managed a second edition—labeled EXTRA—which was printed around 4:00 A.M. This contained an added line: "Blaze Still Spreading Eastward and Southward at 3 A.M." The headline bank was enlarged to include news that the *Sun,* Continental, Equitable, and Calvert buildings had been destroyed.

A page-one box announced that the paper was printed on the presses of the Washington *Star* and that a "a force of editors, reporters, compositors and stereotypers was sent to Washington and duplicate news facilities were installed in the *Star* office." The *Sun* did not say how many copies it printed, only that it was "circulated by ten thousands—even then, the demand was not satisfied." Later it claimed that no other morning paper could be obtained on Monday. That was not only wrong but also unfair. The *Morning Herald* managed to print an extra on Sunday night before the staff and crew had to abandon their building on Fayette Street at St. Paul, about where Court Square Plaza is today. Early Monday, the *Morning Herald* printed a four-page paper in Washington and had 20,000 copies in Baltimore by 8:45 A.M.—nearly four hours after the *Sun,* which had sold its papers to newsboys at the regular price. Although not authorized to charge more than one cent, they got ten to twenty-five cents a copy. Some collectors, aware of their future worth as souvenirs, paid as much as $1. The *Sun* had arranged for its carriers to pick up their bundles at Camden Station, and they were distributed near the normal time. The mail edition was sent from the Washington Post Office. As the *Sun* later observed, "All subscribers were supplied on Monday morning while the *Sun* office was a heap of scrap iron and the conflagration was not yet under control."

The front page of Tuesday's paper was all advertising. The George A. Fuller Company took almost half a page to announce it was prepared "to immediately commence construction of buildings in Baltimore in place of those destroyed by fire." Other ads told a story of determination. Wise Brothers Company stated: "*Everything* running as usual. Employees report as early as convenient." The B&O, its headquarters building a charred ruin, told employees to report to three different locations. The three-column headline on page two read:

DEVASTATING FIRE

IS STOPPED AT LAST

Declared Under Control at 5 P.M. After Raging 30 Hours

Leaps the Falls into East Baltimore

The Loss Now Estimated at from $75,000,000 to $150,000,000 — Sweep of Destruction Halted on Philpot Street — Business Heart of City a Scene of Desolation

The lead article bounded the fire zone: from Liberty Street north to Fayette Street, south to the harbor, and east to Jones Falls; listed the help supplied by fire equipment and police from New York, Philadelphia, Wilmington, and Chester, Pennsylvania; and reported that streetcars were moving again. They had stopped at 4:00 P.M. on Sunday, when current failed. Crews remained in the marooned cars. Wives, children, and concerned citizens brought them food and coffee. The news article was critical of how the fire had been fought and how the dynamiting was done. It claimed that too much time had been spent fighting fires in buildings already doomed and said the dynamiting was too little, too late, and in the wrong places. It called fireproofing a delusion and pointed out that the much-vaunted sixteen-story Continental Trust and the Equitable Building had burned just like other structures.

An editorial advocated "the importance of strengthening [the] Fire Department, and taking such other precautions as have not seemed to be essential in the past." (Not one fire station was located in the entire burned-out district.) But the thrust of the editorial was upbeat: "It is the duty of every Baltimorean, as it should be his pleasure, to devote his energies to the task of making Baltimore a greater city than it ever was before this colossal disaster. It can be done, and it should be done without delay." In referring to its own achievements, the paper was quick to cover itself with glory: "In thus immediately adapting itself to the emergency, the *Sun* has performed a task for its readers which will stand as another of its notable achievements in the field of American journalism.''

Brigadier General Lawrason Riggs of the National Guard was in charge of patrolling the burned-out area, which the paper described as ''practically under military control.'' To keep the curious out, the Guardsmen and the Baltimore police were assisted by police from Washington, Philadelphia, and Wilmington. When Riggs refused permission for businessmen to enter to inspect vaults and safes, and kept newspapermen out too, the *Sun* responded with a two-column boxed comment in its news columns, saying in part that news-gathering is ''quite important in its way, or even more so, than what General Riggs and the militia are performing. The community could get along without the militia better than they could without newspapers. . . . The militia is only for emergencies like the present; the newspapers are for this and all other times and any attempt to annoy or browbeat them will react upon those who attempt it.'' It said Riggs's attitude ''suggests the petty despot'' and that if he persisted with his ''popinjay'' ways he would have trouble.

The next day the paper announced with some satisfaction that Riggs, ''feeling the criticism of this arbitrary action,'' had summoned the publishers of newspapers to a conference. After keeping them waiting for twenty-five minutes, he told Felix Agnus of the *American*, Wesley M. Osler and Frank A. Peard of the *Herald*, Charles H. Grasty of the *News*, and a representative of the *Sun* that he ''would issue five passes to each paper.'' He said the publishers of the *Sun* had told him five were insufficient and had asked for thirty-five additional passes. Riggs rather flippantly referred to some newspaper reporters as ''beardless youth of 18!'' After discussion, the publishers present—but not the *Sun* representative—agreed on ten passes for each paper. The *Sun* protested that number and added that it did not employ ''beardless youth of 18'' as reporters. The next day the *Sun* headline read:

DOWN FROM HIS PERCH
The Mighty ''Laurie'' Riggs Not so Great After All

The four-word lead, ''The mighty has fallen,'' was followed with news that the president of the Police Board had ordered Riggs ''to immediately furnish the *Sun* and all other newspapers with as many passes as they might require or request, and Mr. Riggs gave immediate obedience to this command.''

In the days after the fire the paper was crowded with special advertising. On Thursday there were eleven pages of ads, plus several pages of classified advertising. From time to time the *Sun* would print an alphabetical list of advertisers in temporary locations, both as a service and undoubtedly as an incentive to advertise. On March 12 it printed a list of some 1,500 companies. Temporary offices were being opened in a church parish house and in homes, boardinghouses, saloons, livery stables, an unfinished attic, and a dilapidated building.

The day after the fire started, the *Sun* set up temporary offices in its Job Printing building on the southwest corner of Calvert and Saratoga streets, north of the fire zone. This alternate, emergency site had been built four years earlier at Edwin F. Abell's direction. He is said to have believed that Baltimore, like other cities, would one day have a great fire. (In 1873 the Clay Street fire, the most extensive up until 1904, destroyed 113 buildings in the downtown area and threatened the home of A. S. Abell, who was then living on Saratoga Street. On that occasion too Baltimore appealed to the Washington Fire Department for help.) The "job plant" served as a temporary advertising office, counting room, and news center. News was sent from there by telegraph and by messenger on the afternoon and evening trains to Washington, D.C., where editors and compositors remained for two months. A side effect was that the *Weekly Sun,* started April 14, 1838, was not published on February 6 and never reappeared.

During February and March the *Sun* pieced together a comprehensive account of the fire and its aftermath: The fire covered 139.9 acres, including 73 blocks or squares with 25 isolated sections around the waterfront; 1,343 buildings were destroyed, with more than 2,500 stores, warehouses, business firms, manufacturers, and individuals burned out. This included 20 banks, 9 newspapers, 9 transportation offices, 8 hotels, and one church. Some 35,000 persons were temporarily jobless. The value of the property destroyed was estimated at between $125 million and $150 million. This had been insured for $50 million, but insurance later paid out totaled only $32 million. (The Iron Building was not owned by the Abell Company, but by the estate of the Founder. Insurance on the printing equipment and other effects was $152,800.) The mayor declined all offers of financial assistance from the federal government and other sources. Not one fatality was confirmed. No looting occurred.

The *Sun* reported on the work of reconstruction through the Citizens Emergency Committee and the Burnt District Commission, which had authority to spend $8.5 million to make improvements in the fire area. This included widening twelve streets and improving the Pratt Street docks.

For two months Walter Abell also worked on plans to print the paper in the Job Printing building. Two quadruple presses raised from the basement of the Iron Building were reconditioned and moved to Calvert Street. Linotypes were purchased to supplement the few used in job work. New stereotyping equipment was installed.

On April 6 the *Sun* was able to resume printing in Baltimore. The next morning's editorial, "The *Star's* Great Service to the *Sun,*" was a heartfelt and grateful thank-you to the *Star's* management for its immediate and continued help. It ended with a grace note for its own employees: "The publishers of the *Sun* wish also to express their deep appreciation of the loyal services of its corps and staff in every department, who in an hour of need so earnestly and intelligently mastered the difficulties which none but newspapermen can properly estimate and which those not newspapermen could have seen as insurmountable obstacles.''

The *Herald* had arranged to print at the Washington *Post,* but it did not have the foresight, or perhaps the influence, the *Sun* had in chartering a train. The nucleus of its staff took an accommodation train, waiting an hour for it. Their improvised arrangements were tumultuous because the *Post* was also a morning paper and it was frantically filling its columns with news of the fire while the *Herald* tried to work in the same composing room. The *Herald* realized this was impractical, so it printed its Tuesday edition in the tiny plant of the afternoon *World,* the only Baltimore paper outside the devastated area. But there the physical plant was limited—the *World* had only four linotypes— and the *Herald's* crew had to resort to hand-set type. But that too was insufficient. More hand-set type was borrowed from a religious weekly; it was old, worn, and in different faces and sizes. This was so unsatisfactory and maddening that the *Herald* returned to the *Post* to print its Wednesday paper and thereafter, for the next five weeks, used the plant of the *Philadelphia Evening Telegraph.*

Mencken wrote a detailed account of the fire in the second volume of his reminiscences *Newspaper Days.* But many of his facts were exaggerated or wrong. For example, he wrote that the fire burned a square mile, 640 acres, out of the heart of Baltimore, but he had overstated by 500 acres. He recalled that after the fire one could see "the pathetic skeletons of no less than 20 overtaken and cremated fire engines," but only two pieces of equipment were lost. And he misremembered many facts involving the *Herald.*

The staff of the Baltimore *Evening News,* Grasty's paper, had to flee its building, at Baltimore and Grant streets, before 9:00 P.M. on Sunday. Dr. Frederick Taylor, the society editor, watching the flames gobble the structure, exclaimed, "Thank God the roaches and waterbugs are now dead!" Grasty started printing his paper at the *Washington Post.* Monday morning he telephoned his friend, Adolph Ochs, publisher of the *New York Times.* Ochs had recently bought the *Philadelphia Times* and merged it with another paper, so the *Times* equipment was idle. Grasty said, "I lost my plant in the fire and I need to buy another. How much will you take for the *Times?*" A deal was made. Within ten days the linotypes, stereotype equipment, and presses were moved to Baltimore by special train. Grasty took over the abandoned McShane Foundry at Holliday and Centre streets, a mere shell with an earth floor. Workmen swarmed in to lay a wooden floor and line the interior with temporary walls. Steam was needed for heat and power. Installing a boiler would have taken weeks, so Grasty bought an old locomotive, ran it on to a siding behind the foundry, removed the wheels, and soon had steam to run his presses. For a test run the paper was typeset in duplicate in Washington and Baltimore. Contrary to gloomy predictions by pressmen, everything ran smoothly. Grasty telegraphed to the staff working in Washington, "Tell Washington goodbye, and come home." The *News* and the *American* had a pact to help each other if a calamity struck. By February 28, 1904, both the *News* and the *American,* which had been coming off the presses of Munsey's *Washington Times,* were publishing in the converted foundry.

In June 1904, Grasty began work on new quarters at the southeast corner of Fayette and Calvert streets. On completion, this handsome seven-story structure had a large plate-glass window on the Calvert Street side. When the presses rolled, people waiting for streetcars could watch the show. Grasty installed an electrically lighted bulletin board for news flashes. The City Council renamed Calvert Street between Fayette and Baltimore streets "News Place."

Three weeks after the fire, on February 28, Edwin F. Abell died at his home. The oldest of the Founder's twelve children, he had been in poor health for some time. He had entered the *Sun's* counting room at age 16, but, as the obituary also noted, his primary interest had been in managing his father's estate until the death of his brother George in 1894, when he became president of the A. S. Abell Company. In the long obituary there was only one specific reference to his contributions to the paper: "He was the directing head of the paper's policies and views on national questions and local affairs."

Edwin Abell knew all the employees in the editorial, business, and mechanical departments—but as a friend, not as a boss. A cashier in those days said,

> He seemed to have not very much to do, but all day long a stream of people trickled into his office, and most of them came out with little pieces of blank paper about an inch-and-a-half long and two inches across, which Mr. Abell had torn off old envelopes. On these pieces of paper Mr. Abell would write "$5—E.F.A." or "$10—E.F.A." or "$15—E.F.A." or "$20—E.F.A.". That was all. But when those little pieces of paper were brought down to the cashier's window, we paid out the amount mentioned just the same as if they had been certified checks. We never knew the names of the people presenting them, but each piece of paper was put on a steel spike and at the end of the week we tallied them up and charged them to Mr. Abell. He must have had close to a hundred such friends who called more or less regularly during the year.

Other people received orders for supplies from various merchants. One was a former Union colonel. Abell had left orders with a grocer to give the colonel whatever he needed and to send a monthly bill to Abell. Glancing at the accumulated bills one day, Abell noticed that the colonel got a Smithfield ham each week for the same price of $4. He thought that strange because he knew hams varied in size, so he sent an office boy to the grocer to investigate. It turned out the weekly ham bill actually represented a gallon of rye whiskey. Abell chuckled at the trick, and he continued to be billed for a weekly ham and the colonel got his gallon of rye.

Abell, known to friends as Ned, weighed over 200 pounds, but he was mild-mannered and gentle, known for his modesty and dislike of prominence and for his charitable work. For days after his death the *Sun* printed columns of testimonials and messages of sympathy. Most were expressed in platitudes: a good and constant friend, a man of modesty, kindness, goodness of heart, charity, generosity, and private benefactions. John T. Morris, the police commissioner, was the only one to say that in a different way. "I can also say from personal knowledge," he wrote, "that Mr. Abell's sympathy and encouragement put the music of birds and the odor of flowers into many souls while his charity set a star in many a dark life."

An unusual and plaintive postscript to the fire turned up that summer in the minute book of the board of directors. A board member suggested that those handling company money be bonded. One of them, in a high position, admitted having stolen nearly $15,000 between 1888 and 1900 by falsifying bank deposits to save a relative from disgrace and, for himself, to live beyond his salary. Rather than risk dealing with the bonding company, he placed himself at the mercy of his employers "and hoped his service of 40 years would keep him from further disgrace." The minutes noted that Abell had ordered the employee to remove the records to a place of safety before the fire reached the *Sun* building. Abell was quoted in the minutes as saying, "It is my belief that books were purposefully left in the building to cover up all traces of irregularity."

———•———

SEVEN

Sun Square Days
1906–1910

On November 16, 1906, the *Sun*
moved from its temporary quarters in the *Sun* Job Shop to its new building
on the southwest corner of Charles and Baltimore streets, the geographical
center of Baltimore. The new home was twice as large as the *Sun* Iron Building.
The paper that day offered a description in the extravagant terms familiar to
that generation: "It is pronounced, by common consent, the most beautiful
building of original architectural design in Baltimore, as distinguished from
the Courthouse and a few other public buildings which follow established or
non-original lines. For the transaction of the newspaper business under the
most modern conditions it is unequaled in the world." The four-story building, in the style called French Renaissance, had 24 limestone columns adorning
it between the second and third stories. "These beautiful shafts," the report
continued, "lend the building a lightness and symmetry rarely found in any
structure save churches and libraries."

Large double copper doors on both the Baltimore and Charles Street corners
opened into a counting room, a vast, high chamber with a semi-circular marble
counter where public business was transacted. It was lighted with nine cut-
glass bulbs in the shape of a sunflower, radiating light "like the rays of the
sun, producing an effect in keeping with the symbolic designs found elsewhere
in the building." Next to the counter was a marble staircase ascending to the
mezzanine and the editorial offices on the second floor. William H. Love, one
of the first visitors, wrote a letter to the paper, saying, "As I passed from the
exquisite business office and placed my foot on the marble staircase leading
to the editorial rooms, I felt that I could see the arched instep of Queen Louise
descending, a queen on a queenly staircase."

The editorial department was described metaphorically as "like a great eye,
with rays of light reaching it from places near and far, which nothing that
is 'fit to print' escapes." Each reporter had a "desk and chair of unstained

quarter oak, the desk provided with a typewriter." "There is also ample and satisfactory provision for visitors who call to bring news items or to confer about other business. They will feel at home as soon as they enter and will be freed of all difficulty in the transaction of their business." Adjoining the newsroom was the library and record room. A "filing cabinet" contained an index system and "biographical sketches and data about public questions." Along the Charles Street side were the rooms of the editors. The officers of the company had offices overlooking Baltimore Street.

The composing room was on the third floor, with "24 of the latest models of typesetting machines, limited only by the rapidity of the operators' fingers." The basement contained the power plant, the stereotyping equipment, and the pressroom. The four quadruple presses each had the capacity to print 24,000 papers of twelve, fourteen, or sixteen pages or 48,000 papers of eight pages. The circulation and mailing departments were on the ground floor. Papers moved through eight slots for delivery to horse-drawn wagons that rushed mail sacks crammed with papers to railroad stations, and bundles to city dealers, carriers, and newsboys. Carriers who did not have their own wagons loaded their papers on the late-night streetcars for distribution to such outlying points as Highlandtown and Catonsville, throwing off the bundles at corners where subcarriers waited.

James W. Dove, who joined the paper on October 1, 1906, and subsequently became assistant business manager, kept a chronicle of the company's important dates, along with anecdotal remembrances. He recorded that the business office was to be kept open daily and Sunday, night and day. A self-appointed committee from the business office reasoned that the key to the front doors was therefore useless. On the night the new building opened, the committee, after frequent stops at prominent saloons on both sides of Baltimore Street, and on some cross streets, ceremoniously tossed the key into Jones Falls. Evidently concerned about how its hidebound subscribers might react to the new location, an editorial declared, "It has been said by a maker of proverbs that he who changes his habitation changes also his spirit. That applies only to fickle individuals. The *Sun* is an institution which will not be separated from the people, no matter in what part of Baltimore it might be located."

The location was but a few minutes walk from the financial, wholesale, and retail districts. When referring to the last-named, the *Sun* added "and so . . . is convenient to the advertisers from the department stores." Eight car lines passed the intersection, and within a block or two there were four more. "It is within three squares of the northern end of the Light Street wharves, from any steamer that comes into the harbor one can reach the *Sun* by a walk of three minutes." Summing up, the paper said, "The *Sun* is not only now in the funnel, as it were, of the whirlpool of the city's life and activity, but will remain in this advantageous position for untold years to come."

Across Baltimore Street was "the superb new skyscraper of the Baltimore

& Ohio building . . . by long odds the finest office building south of New York.'' Across Charles Street was the uncompleted marble pile of the Savings Bank of Baltimore, modeled after an Athenian temple. Mr. Love, the letter-writer enchanted with the *Sun*'s marble staircase, was also rapturous in his reference to that building, calling it ''the temple of Erechtheus [one of the finest examples of classical architecture]; its western wall will face the eastern wall of 'The Temple of *The Sun*,' beautiful and chaste as if dedicated to the Vestal Virgins of old Rome.''

The *Sun* building stood on land purchased partly from the estate of Edwin F. Abell, partly from other owners. The design was by Baldwin & Pennington, an old Baltimore firm; construction was by Edward Brady & Son. The building itself cost $289,206. The total outlay for land, building, and equipment was $600,000. Because the A. S. Abell Company had a surplus in its treasury of nearly $575,000 financing required the borrowing of a mere $25,000. Two weeks after the building was occupied, the president was authorized by the board of directors to borrow $50,000 to settle a few outstanding debts, but he never borrowed more than $25,000, and this was quickly repaid. By a city ordinance on December 12, 1906, the crossing of Charles and Baltimore streets was named *Sun* Square, and it subsequently became a gathering place for major events.

The formal opening of the *Sun* building was on Thursday, January 17, 1907. Thousands of engraved invitations were mailed, and through announcements in the paper the public was invited—''Ladies, as always, will be particularly welcome''—to inspect the premises between 11:00 A.M. and 5:00 P.M. Though 4¹/₂ inches of snow and sleet covered the streets from a Wednesday snowstorm (50 loads of rough cinders had been scattered on the slippery wooden block pavements) and sleet continued until Thursday afternoon, more than 5,000 visitors came. Governor Edwin Warfield, Mayor E. Clay Timanus, and James Cardinal Gibbons were among the prominent guests. After his tour the Cardinal gazed out the window, scanning the snow-covered sidewalks, and remarked that it was so warm, so cheerful, and so full of light inside that it made a sharp contrast to the scene outdoors. It reminded him of Shakespeare's lines, which he quoted with his own revision:

Now is the winter of our discontent
Made glorious summer by this *Sun* of Abell.

Special guests were escorted to the fourth floor, later to be occupied by The *Sun* Job Shop, which had been turned into a dining area. At tables seventy feet long a buffet luncheon was served:

Spiced Oysters   Fried Oysters
Olives   Celery   Radishes   Pickles   Salted Nuts
Chicken Salad à la Club Hotel
Cold Beef   Saratoga Potatoes

Assorted Sandwiches
Fancy Ices   Fancy Cakes   Assorted Fruit
Apollinaris   White Rock
Edam Cheese   Fancy Crackers   Café Noir

The centerpiece was a reproduction of the building created with vegetables and pastry. The account of the reception pointedly noted, "No alcoholic drinks were included among the refreshments." The next day the paper printed the names of more than 1,200 visitors, leading with the name of Cardinal Gibbons and other clergy.

The two-page description of the building emphasized its various facilities, especially the ventilation, which was mentioned three times in one article. This system was hailed as "perfect" and "thorough and up-to-date." "It is highly advisable that the lighting, heating, ventilation, and sanitary arrangements be of the best, and in these points the new building of the *Sun* shall be unexcelled." At once, however, the work force discovered shortcomings. There was no passenger elevator. The editorial staff on the second floor had no hot water, though the printers and pressmen had an oversupply. Sometimes the pressroom caught fire. On summer days its temperature shot above 100 degrees, and wagons of ice had to be brought in and fans placed behind it to give relief to the pressmen. After the Savings Bank of Baltimore was built, the afternoon sun reflected off its marble walls with a blinding glare and intense heat. "This glare and heat pretty well cooked the city editor, telegraph editor, state editor, Sunday editor and other such functionaries, all of whom had offices along the east wall," Mencken recalled in *The Sunpapers of Baltimore*, published on the *Sun*'s centennial in 1937. The architects' massive columns prevented the installing of remedial awnings. The glare and heat were so oppressive that after women reporters had left the city room, men would strip down to their trousers. (In the 1940s, when air conditioning was proposed, "a reactionary rump" nonetheless made such an outcry that by one account the question of whether to cool the city room was put to a vote.)

Attired in his customary all-white suit, Samuel L. Clemens, who had been a guest of Governor Warfield, toured the building on May 11, 1907. Although a reporter dogged his steps throughout, the only lively comment he could get had to do with the editorial writers' cubicles: "This is a sanctuary, not a sanctum. Beautiful! Fine! I even believe I could write something good in here myself." The strictly enforced no-smoking rule of the Abells was suspended for Mark Twain, and he produced a long cigar, blowing smoke as he went.

Even before the 1904 fire a new building had been under consideration. An editorial noted, "The fire hastened to a slight degree a change which would have been made in any event." When company officers were discussing plans, they told stockholders they wanted "to erect a building that will for all time meet the requirements of the company." Yet before long the building had to be extensively revised, and in the 1930s and 1940s two adjoining structures were purchased for additional space. Even so, the publishing process kept requiring more and more space—one department after another complained of overcrowding.

The site at Charles and Baltimore streets had been chosen by Walter W. Abell, who was named president of the company in 1904 at the age of 32. He was the second son of Edwin F. Abell, the eldest of the Founder's twelve children. After attending Georgetown University, Walter worked with the National Marine Bank, in which his father had an interest. In the early 1890s he joined the *Sun,* first in the counting room but later working as a reporter. Soon he had a more prominent role. His father, who was not interested in journalism, left much of the active management to his sons, Arunah S. 2d and Walter. Arunah preferred the business side, Walter the editorial side and the news. Walter was also asked to succeed his father as trustee of the estate of his uncle Walter R. Abell, but believed he could not give that task the time it required. Charles J. Bonaparte was appointed trustee instead, but inasmuch as he was a Republican and engaged in politics, the Abells felt that a role for him in *Sun* affairs could be embarrassing, and he agreed. Bonaparte was succeeded by John J. Nelligan, of the Safe Deposit & Trust Company, and later by the company itself, with Nelligan as its representative.

During his five years as president, Walter W. Abell introduced methods that were considered revolutionary, by both the staff and the subscribers. One of his most radical changes was to appoint Harry Martin Leitch, after much debate and apparently some misgivings, "rate demonstrator"—the *Sun'*s first advertising man. Until then, as noted, the *Sun* had boasted in print that it did not solicit advertising; advertisers, even the biggest advertisers, had to deliver their ads and pay in advance. Leitch, who had been hired on July 10, 1905, at $25 a week after working twenty-two years on the *Herald,* was instructed to confine his activities to "explaining the rates." But evidently he did not take these instructions literally. He was a supersalesman, selling ads to stores and companies that had never advertised before, in the *Sun* or elsewhere. He described his job this way: "I want the advertiser to feel that, in advising him on advertising, I am as careful with his money as I am of my own. High-pressure salesmanship? I want none of that." He worked until he died at age 75 on December 19, 1935. One customer of his, before long a steady and successful advertiser, was the Stieff Company. Upon Leitch's death the directors passed a resolution describing him as "one of our most valuable and loyal friends, associates and advisers for nearly 30 years." Another firm hung his picture in its office and declared him "its advertising counselor," although he dealt with that firm only as the *Sun'*s representative. Leitch, "the man who knew everybody," brought in so much advertising that a year later advertising solicitors—not "rate demonstrators"—were hired. About the same time the paper engaged a representative for foreign advertising.

Advertising rates were based on an archaic "square" system dating back to the paper's beginning in 1837. Then a square was sixteen lines or less, but over the years the square shrank to six lines, then four. All advertising appeared under classified headings—department stores under "Dry Goods"—all display ads were handled on the same basis and charged the same rate as classified ads. This was $6 a square, daily for a month. When the *Sunday Sun* appeared, the rate was $7 a square, daily and Sunday. This made the rate less than 6 cents a line for running advertisements. An additional 5 cents a line was charged if there were copy changes, effectively pushing up the store rate to 11 cents a line as most large stores listed different wares daily. Until 1907 even national advertising was billed at the same rate as classified ads.

In 1906 the board of directors reduced the rates for classified ads, including "Situations Wanted," to 10 cents a line, with a minimum of 20 cents. Although other classified rates tripled over the years as circulation increased, the low rate for Situations Wanted held fast until and during the Great Depression. On January 1, 1908, the first rate card was introduced. This gave rates based on total lineage instead of monthly insertions. The old rates—about 11 cents a line—remained optional, but only the smaller advertiser used them; the large advertiser could buy space at 10 cents a line.

James W. Dove recorded a story about Walter R. Abell, Jr., who worked for a time as a clerk at the lobby counter. One day, when Abell was still new at the job and unfamiliar with rates, a merchant came in to place an ad in the Personal column, "Highest prices paid for old clothes." The Personal rate was complicated and difficult to memorize, and what was worse, young Abell could not find a rate card. Finally he asked, "Did you ever put this ad in before?" When the answer was yes, he replied, "Well, it'll cost not a cent more this time!"

Dove also remembered that "In Memoriam" verses were popular in the advertising obituary column. Much of the doggerel was clipped from a counter scrapbook and rewritten to fit individual cases. "But sometimes," he wrote, "a critical widow, gifted with literary taste and flush with insurance money, would object to the usual dreary stuff and demand something special. Then a clerk handy with his rhymes would retire to the seclusion of a corner of the mail room to woo the muse, and using a tin-top table caked with mailing paste as a desk, write some lines to suit the customer, all metered and rhymed as became a young man with poetic gifts."

For years no typographical display could be used in advertisements. Then, in the early 1900s, advertisers were permitted to attract attention, not with large type but by forming large letters composed of small letters, known as logotypes. Column rules could not be broken, so in ads spanning several columns the rules might jut through the synthetic large letters. On February 26, 1908, the board of directors, as part of the modernization, resolved "That black type not over 72 points in height, the style to be determined upon by the board of directors, be used in advertisements in the *Sun,* daily and Sunday, excepting on the first and last pages and besides editorials and death notices." Then, on April 4, came another big step: "Resolved, That black cuts not exceeding 72 points in height and 150 in width may be used in the *Sun* in advertisements at the discretion of the business manager, all black cuts exceeding this height and width to the stippled, tooled or Bendayed." Mencken told this story in the 1937 *Sun* history:

> The revolution had got underway slowly, but once it was in progress it moved very fast. It came to a dramatic climax in 1909, when a Baltimore corsetiere sent in copy for an advertisement including a half-tone showing a lovely female creature stripped to her whalebones to exhibit the efficiency of a dollar reducer model. It was passed by Business Manager Unduch only after hours of doubt and soul-searching, and the staff of the advertising department came to the office the next morning expecting to find indignant subscribers canceling their subscriptions by the hundreds, and the Abells in a great state of perturbation. But nothing was heard from the subscribers, and nothing from the Abells. The *Sun* was on its way.

Edward Crummer, who had been business manager for 25 years, thought it "immoral and unthinkable for a great public journal to broadcast its circulation." He believed the ultimate test "was not the number of copies a newspaper sold, but what news it printed in every copy, and the test for the advertiser was not the number of potential buyers reached but the number of actual buyers brought into his store." During this time the *Sun* never revealed its exact circulation, except once, though it often boasted that it had a larger circulation than all local dailies, or had the greatest circulation of any paper south of Philadelphia. The exception was copy that Crummer furnished *Printers' Ink,* the advertisers' organ, in 1898: "Only once during the history of the *Sun* have the publishers made known its circulation, and that was in December 1894, when they stated to the American Newspaper Directory that the smallest edition during that year had not been less than 66,432."

One day in 1906, when Mencken was Sunday editor, he asked Walter W. Abell about Sunday circulation figures and Abell replied that it was the invariable and immemorial rule of the paper not to reveal its circulation. Mencken added, "That rule, it appeared, applied even to responsible members of its own editorial staff. Indeed, it was the general view in the editorial rooms in those days that prying into such matters was not quite sporting. The first duty of a good *Sun* man was to assume as a cardinal article of faith that the circulation of the paper touched the extreme limits of the desirable, and that there was not a single literate white person in all Maryland who did not read it."

In May 1905 the board of directors appropriated $2,000 to promote circulation outside Baltimore, and later that year it approved other administrative improvements: having a public accountant examine the books twice a year, and engaging an accounting firm to set up a new system of accounts in the business department. In October "the president was authorized to increase the number of pages of the *Sun* to fourteen on days during the week on which business and news demanded it."

Crummer died in September 1906 and was succeeded by William L.

Unduch, who suggested another revolutionary change in the company's staid ways. The minutes of the board of directors for January 29, 1908, read: "Upon the statement of the business manager, Mr. Unduch, that he believed the telling of the circulation of the *Sun* to advertisers would result in more revenue for the paper, [the board resolved] that the circulation . . . may be told to advertisers in the discretion of the manager."

Changes were also taking place in the news and editorial departments. Over the years, competitors liked to mock and tease the *Sun* for its conservative and stodgy ways. Back in December 1891, when a hole was dug outside the Iron Building so a new press could be installed, the editor of the *Herald* wrote that what the *Sun* really needed was "to dig a hole in the roof and put some brains upstairs." The *Sun* ignored that thrust, but in Walter W. Abell's day it enjoyed replying to a laudatory editorial, "*The Sun* Hires a Poet," which appeared in the *Herald* on the *Sun*'s sixty-ninth birthday. It read in part: "The older it grows the more chipper and vigorous it seems to become. In its middle age it was solemn and perhaps a bit ponderous. Today it is showing daily evidence that its corpuscles are bright red and its eye clear. It is printing a big paper, full of pictures and good humor; its editorial policy is positive and free spoken; it has hired a staff poet. . . ." The *Sun* replied, in part:

> One expression which our contemporary uses causes us some pain. It says "The *Sun* has hired a staff poet." Poets cannot be hired. Their minds are far above sublunary things. The fragrance of a lily, the modest beauty of the primrose and the buttercup; the field daisy; the gushing fountain under the spreading tree, the song of the birds which he terms the flowers of the air, the twinkling star—it is these things which fill the mind of our poet. And if perchance the weakness of the flesh should call him down to earth for food, it is such airy nothings as pie and mint julep alone that can satisfy the poetry of his soul. Hire a poet! Perish the expression *Poeta nascitur,* not hired. You might as well talk of hiring a zephyr.

The poet was Folger McKinsey, who had started newspapering in Ocean Beach, New Jersey, where he came to know Walt Whitman. McKinsey worked successively for the *Frederick* (Maryland) *Daily News,* the *Washington Post,* and the Baltimore *News,* becoming its managing editor. He was hired by the *Sun* as exchange editor on April 19, 1906, and began contributing a daily column of verse and prose to the editorial page, entitled "Maryland Musings." McKinsey was the *Sun*'s first columnist. His work, long association with the paper, and popularity with his readers will be described later.

The weekday *Sun* often contained the maximum number of pages, fourteen, and was crammed with advertisements, news, and features. International and national news was provided by the *Sun*'s Washington and New York bureaus, the Associated Press, and the *New York Herald.* (A surprising number of datelines from such places as Terre Haute, Indiana, and Westerly, Rhode Island, were "Special Dispatches to The *Sun* .") But the emphasis was on local, county, state, and regional news. In addition to special correspondents throughout Maryland, the *Sun* had correspondents in Virginia, West Virginia, North Carolina, Pennsylvania, and Delaware. Much of the news was in short items, and only for unusual or spectacular articles were the headlines more than one column wide. (On one such occasion, Samuel Spencer, president of the Southern Railway, and seven other people were killed when a train crashed into Spencer's private car. The three-column headline on page one read: "Sam'l Spencer Killed On His Own Railroad.")

Considerable space was devoted to cultural affairs. When the Metropolitan Opera season opened in New York, it was front-page news. In addition to detailed coverage of the Baltimore theater and musical events, the paper printed four columns of book reviews once a week, along with a column of literature prepared with the help of faculty members from 50 colleges and universities.

Long after the new building opened, the main local news page carried a feature, "From the *Sun*'s Friends" (later "The *Sun*'s Friends Call"), listing the previous day's visitors and letters of praise. One George P. Gardiner wrote: "Since 1900 I have visited the leading newspaper offices in London, Paris, Peking, St. Petersburg and other cities abroad, and I declare the best I've seen no more compare with the *Sun* office building in Baltimore than a wheelbarrow to an automobile. But then it is only *Sun* like, and may it endure and shine long enough to shed a ray on the decayed ruins of the Sphinx."

Under Mencken's editorship, the second section of the *Sunday Sun* was a lively mix of features. It serialized the work of popular authors, such as George Ade's revised history; Finley Peter Dunne's "Mr. Dooley's" pieces, "the national guide, philosopher and comedian," were played up. But the section was most noteworthy for pieces capturing the spirit and customs of contemporary and old Baltimore. That time and place were recalled with such articles as those entitled "When Baltimore Society Received on New Year's Day" and "Baltimore Surnames, Their Origin and Meaning." The street cries of the early 1900s were portrayed in a scholarly account with musical notations. One article explained why divorce was difficult in conventional Baltimore; another portrayed the neighborhood mayors of Highlandtown, Little Bohemia, Chinatown, the Ghetto, Grasshopper Hill, and Bottle Hill (the latter had local option, and beer could be sold there only in bottles). Cardinal Gibbons, as always, got special attention; a column was devoted to his Christmas letters.

One feature, "Why I Dislike Baltimore"—in which a New Yorker "put forward certain alleged facts to support his attack"—carried the vague byline "By a New Yorker," but it bore touches of what appeared to be Mencken's developing style. The writer's unnamed hostess—"A Southern beauty, gracious but narrow"—"seemed to have no comprehension of any question that could not be solved by the ordinary rules of law, order and the church."

In addition to Mencken, the Sunday staff consisted of J. S. M. Hammond, who was to write many books, and Helen Forman Kerchner, later married to J. Fred Essary (who became the Washington Bureau chief in 1912). Emily

Emerson Lantz, a reporter on the *Sun,* was assigned to the *Sunday Sun* on two different occasions. The first was several years before World War I. When the news staff was depleted during the war, Lantz returned to reporting on the *Sun.* After the war she returned to the Sunday paper, writing features and art criticism. Her collection of articles on Maryland's twenty-three counties in 1930 was published in a book entitled *The Spirit of Maryland* and dedicated "To the *Sun* of Baltimore." Despite failing eyesight, she finished the Maryland sketches, but she was forced to retire from regular work soon after. She continued to write at home, dictating to her sister. She died on April 22, 1931. A *Sun* editorial described her as "a brave one who bore illness and distress and her greatest cross, a rapidly approaching blindness, with a fortitude and defiant gayety."

Mencken termed the early 1900s "a day of revolution in journalism," but he said:

Life in the *Sun* office in the era of the Abells was comfortable and leisurely, and I once described the atmosphere as that of a good club. There was a stately courtesy that is uncommon in the dens of journalism, and indeed in any other working place of busy men. All hands save the office boys were mistered by the proprietors, and even by most of their superiors, and no one was ever upbraided for a dereliction of duty, however inconvenient. The worst a culprit ever encountered was a mild expostulation, usually couched in very general terms.

I recall with blushes a day when my own carelessness admitted to the *Sunday Sun* an unhappy sentence which made the issue a collector's item in the barrooms of Baltimore the next day, with the price approaching $1. When I got to the office Monday morning a note was on my desk saying that Walter Abell wanted to see me. There was no defense imaginable, so I entered his office as jauntily as possible, saying "I am not here for trial, but for sentence." But there was no sentence nor even any trial. Mr. Abell, in fact, referred to the matter in hand only obliquely, and with great politeness. All his talk was about the paramount necessity, on a paper as ancient and honorable as the *Sun,* for the utmost care in copyreading. He discoursed on that theme at length, but always in broad philosophical terms. Finding his argument unanswerable, I offered no caveat, and withdrew quietly at the first chance.

After the death of Edwin F. Abell in 1904, differences developed between his two sons, Walter W. and Arunah S. 2d, and Charles S., the son of George W. When the Safe Deposit & Trust Company succeeded Edwin as trustee of the Walter R. Abell interests, it held the balance of power when the Abells differed—Charles repeatedly dissenting from what the others proposed. Nelligan, the trust company representative on the board, usually sided with Walter W. Abell when he was president. The board minutes for those years record the disagreements in short, nonemotional words. The board minutes for April 19, 1905 note: "Election of officers: J. J. Nelligan nominated W. W. Abell for president, seconded by A. S. Abell. C. S. Abell nominated himself. Vote for W. W. Abell, J. J. Nelligan, and A. S. Abell; C. S. Abell voted for himself. W. W. Abell nominated A. S. Abell for treasurer. C. S. Abell nominated himself. A. S. Abell elected. J. J. Nelligan nominated C. S. Abell for secretary. He was elected.'' At a special meeting of the board that year, C. S. Abell asked why the *Sun* had favored the sewer loan without the consent of the board, as required by the bylaws. The president said he had forgotten to mention it. The board then decided the paper would continue to support it. When the board approved the hiring of employees, promotions, and salary increases, C. S. Abell usually had counterproposals and voted against the majority. When the president was authorized to send a reporter to "Chicago or any Midwestern city" to compare that city's commercial standing with Baltimore, C. S. Abell voted against the trip. That was the pattern—the conflict—for five years.

In April 1909, Walter W. Abell announced he would decline reelection by the stockholders as a director, and by the directors as president. Charles S. Abell was elected vice president, the presidency remaining vacant, but he was also to function as general manager. Since there was no president, the bylaws giving that officer authority to set *Sun* policy was superseded by the following section: "There shall be a committee of three members of the board of directors, to be known as the executive committee; said committee shall meet daily and shall have control of the policy of the paper, and no measure shall be advocated or opposed in the publications of the company, unless the same shall first have been approved by said committee, or a majority thereof." But it must have been inconvenient for the executive committee to meet daily, and committee rule must have been unwieldy for policy-making. In any event, Charles S. Abell had a mind of his own. The following month that section was repealed and the previous bylaw was reinstated: "He shall direct, subject to the approval of the board of directors, the measures and policies advocated or opposed in the publications of the company." The "he" in this case referred to the chief executive, Charles S. Abell. He had dropped out of Harvard to help at the paper after the death of his father (who had been elected president and general manager of the company when it was incorporated). Charles said he too had "printer's ink in his blood," and he is remembered as having a deep love for the paper and its traditions. Strong in self-confidence, he regarded his own election as general manager "as an opportunity to do it my way." He particularly liked working with the news and editorial departments, and enjoyed entertaining editors at Ridge, the Abell country estate on Joppa Road, built by his father. Behind the 30-room mansion was a recreation hall with a billiard room and bowling alley, where *Sun* men relaxed before taking the train back to the city. Charles Abell's city residence was Marble Hall on Woodbourne Avenue, once the home of his father, who purchased it from the Enoch Pratt estate.

In February 1908, Charles H. Grasty had sold his Baltimore *News* for $1.5 million to Frank A. Munsey, a New York capitalist who made millions as a magazine publisher, and the operator of a grocery chain, hotels, and banks;

Munsey also acquired newspapers. Grasty sold him the *News* (an afternoon paper but a strong competitor of the *Sun*) after Munsey's candidate for governor, Republican George R. Gaither, who was the *News*'s counsel and a personal friend, ran for governor in 1907 and lost. The winner was Austin L. Crothers, the *Sun*'s candidate. During the campaign, Grasty heard rumors that reflected on Crothers's character, and after investigating his background had a five-column exposé prepared. The *News* evidently planned to hold this as a bombshell until just before the election. Someone on its staff sold proof sheets of the article for $50 to two politicians, who in turn gave them to Frank R. Kent, the *Sun*'s political reporter. He showed them to Crothers, a county judge in Elkton, listened to his explanations, made an independent inquiry, and found the charges to be based only on hearsay. When Grasty printed what he thought were devastating revelations, the *Sun* was ready with a column counterblast, effectively negating what it called Grasty's "baseless slander." Long afterward, Kent sent this note to Mencken: "Grasty told me that our story broke his heart. He said he would have never sold the *News* to Munsey but for that. . . . He had set his heart on beating the *Sun* in that campaign and was certain he could elect Gaither. In all the years he had been in Baltimore he had never had a victory. Here, when the thing was in his grasp, he lost because one of his own troops shot him in the back. I think he got very drunk."

After selling the *News,* Grasty was named general manager of Munsey's papers. But the eccentric Munsey proved hard to get along with, and a month later Grasty resigned. In late 1908, Grasty bought an interest in the *St. Paul* (Minnesota) *Dispatch* and later acquired the *Pioneer Press* and combined it with the *Dispatch.* He improved them but was unhappy in St. Paul, and late in 1909 he sold his interests and went to Europe. Somehow he learned of the disagreements among the Abells and returned to Baltimore determined to buy the *Sun.* Grasty talked to Nelligan and made an offer for the paper. He told him he had four wealthy, prominent Baltimoreans as his backers: H. Crawford Black, R. Brent Keyser, Robert Garrett, and John Campbell White.

Black was born in Cumberland, Maryland, on May 14, 1845, and as a 17-year-old schoolboy enlisted in the seventeenth Virginia Cavalry of the Confederate army. After the war, he worked in Mexico on the construction of the Imperial Mexican Railroad and later in Oklahoma and Nebraska. Returning to Maryland in the late 1860s, he got a job as a clerk in a coal mine. On his own, he located an area he believed was rich in coal deposits. With two friends he formed a company, and its mines became the second largest producer of bituminous coal in Maryland. With a senator from West Virginia, Black purchased the Consolidated Coal Company, which became one of the largest producers in the United States. Meanwhile, Black moved to Baltimore to manage the business side of his enterprises and became a director of the B&O Railroad, banks, and various corporations. He was one of the founders of the Fidelity & Deposit Company, the first of the large national bonding companies.

Robert Garrett was a partner in the banking firm of Robert Garrett & Sons, which had its beginnings in 1840. He was a track-and-field star at Princeton University, but his fame as an athlete was assured in the first modern Olympic Games, held in Athens in 1896 after they had been suspended for some 1,500 years. Without competitive experience in the event, Garrett entered the discus throw and won, becoming the first American to win an Olympic gold medal. He also won the shot put, placed second in the broad jump, and tied for second in the high jump. Active in civic and cultural affairs, he was also a member of the syndicate that purchased Guilford, the A. S. Abell estate, in 1907, with plans to develop it into a residential area of fine houses.

R. Brent Keyser, a descendant of Maryland's first settlers, was president of the Baltimore Copper Smelting & Rolling Company and in 1910 negotiated its sale to the Guggenheims. He was also involved with other enterprises, but was primarily interested in the *Sun,* the B&O, and Johns Hopkins University. During the fight for political reform in the 1890s, Keyser's father had been president of the Baltimore Reform League.

John Campbell White was the son of Henry White, U.S. ambassador at Rome and Paris. His uncle, Julian LeRoy White, had been one of Grasty's backers at the *News* in 1891. After graduating from Harvard, young White joined the *St. Paul Pioneer Press* and was there when Grasty bought it.

Nelligan was amenable to Grasty's offer. He was upset about the disagreements among the Abells and convinced that Grasty was determined to get back into Baltimore newspapering by buying back the *News* from Munsey, by buying the *World* or the *Star,* or by introducing a new paper. As agent of the Walter R. Abell estate, Nelligan decided the offer should be accepted. He cabled Walter W. Abell, who was then in Egypt on a trip around the world, urging him as a trustee of the Edwin F. Abell estate to agree. The Charles Abells believed that "Walter W. Abell did not have to be hit on the head to sell. He took Nelligan's word for what might happen. His willingness to sell didn't show any depth of feeling for the paper, or the family's part in it."

When the directors met on January 28, 1910, Charles Abell asked, "Is there any new business?" Nelligan, who had a reputation among the Abells "as somewhat of a dictator," replied, "Yes. The Sun has been sold to Charles H. Grasty." Charles Abell resigned as vice president and as a director. While he had been in charge, the reorganization and improvement of the paper had continued, along with increases in circulation and advertising. He had served for just nine months. When Grasty took over, Charles was the only Abell to retain all his stock, and although no longer connected with management or on the board, Abell still wanted to be involved. He stayed for months to help with the transition. Grasty invited Abell to join the new board, and he served until October 1911.

Charles Abell's post-*Sun* career is so unusual it is worth recording. He bought the Norfolk Landmark Publishing Company and announced, "The *Landmark*'s policy shall be that of the Baltimore *Sun* as declared in the editorial in the first edition of that paper," and he reprinted that policy. He also switched the *Landmark*'s local news to the back page, for years the hallmark of the *Sun*. He developed his paper into a worthy competitor of the established *Virginian-Pilot,* and later the two papers were combined, with Abell having a substantial but minority interest. Wanting to learn more about circulation, he studied it at the *Philadelphia Public Ledger,* selecting it because it was aggressive, but even more because it was a paper his grandfather helped found in 1836.

After officers' training school in World War I, Abell worked for Bernard M. Baruch, chairman of the War Industries Board. When the war ended, he returned to the Norfolk papers as an officer without portfolio. After the colorful but erratic Edward Beale "Ned" McLean took over the *Washington Post* from his father, John R. McLean, the paper developed problems, and Charles Abell was hired as business manager. "Ned" McLean had a reputation for temporizing. After much pressing, Abell finally got him to make a major move. Pleased, Abell got on an elevator carrying another executive and exulted that he had gotten action from McLean. The executive shook his head and responded "I talked to him ten minutes ago and he gave me an answer exactly opposite to what he gave you."

Abell's most unusual odyssey was outside newspapering. He had always been fascinated by trains and often talked about working for a railroad in the Midwest. The Chicago, Burlington & Quincy Railroad (CB&Q) had its headquarters in Detroit, and Abell was offered an administrative post there (and later did accept one), but then he said he wanted to live in the *real* Midwest and he chose Iowa. He joined the CB&Q freight department in Ottumwa. His son, William, who was born there, said his mother would pack his father's lunch pail and his father would ride a freight train to work and return on one in the evening. William observed, "My father, for no other reason than his own desire, went from one of the leaders of Baltimore to a workingman's job in Ottumwa."

Charles Abell died in 1953 at the age of 76. In a resolution, the A. S. Abell board remembered him as "a man of great personal charm, innate kindliness and genuine humility. Soft of voice, gentle in manner, generous in disposition, he nevertheless possessed a firm character and real ability."

EIGHT

Charles H. Grasty's Paper
1910–1914

On January 28, 1910, under the heading

Mr. Grasty Comes to the Sun
Joins Present Owners and Becomes President of the A. S. Abell Co.

the following eleven-line news item appeared on the *Sun*'s back page: "Judge Niles, in the Circuit Court yesterday, ratified the sale to Mr. Charles H. Grasty of a portion of the interest in the *Sun* held by the Walter W. Abell estate. The action of the court completes a transaction by which Mr. Grasty becomes president of the A. S. Abell Company, publishers of the *Sun*, and executive head of the paper. All of the present owners retain large interests. No changes are contemplated."

One can imagine how the principals and apprehensive editors struggled over the wording. It is clear that efforts were made to say as little as possible. Curiously, no mention was made of Grasty's newspaper background and his prominent involvement with the Baltimore *News*. And the last sentence was not true. Although Grasty had told no one, he contemplated a drastic change.

Grasty took charge immediately, but it took almost two months to arrange the actual sale. The directors of the liquidating company did not meet until March 24 to determine the sale or exchange of the property and assets "for bonds, preferred stock and common stock of the purchasing company and cash . . . or for some other considerations." To facilitate the transfer, Grasty resigned as president and director, and Charles S. Abell was reelected to the board and to his former post as vice president. Nelligan, the prime mover of the sale, presented a draft of the contract between the old and the new companies, and on his motion it was unanimously accepted. Then in a special meeting the stockholders ratified the agreement. This was the capital structure of the new company, with stock at a par value of $100:

3,000 shares of Class A common stock	$ 300,000
2,000 shares of Class B common stock	$ 200,000
1,000 shares of Class C common stock	$ 100,000
6,000 shares of 5% cumulative preferred stock	$ 600,000
$1 million of 1st mortgage 5% bonds due 1965	$1,000,000
	$2,200,000

The bonds, $2,000 in cash, and all the stock except twenty shares of Class B common stock were turned over to the old company for the property, assets, trademarks, membership in the Associated Press, and goodwill. But in supplemental agreements the old company sold back to Grasty, acting for himself and his associates, most of the preferred stock and substantial blocks of the Class B and Class C common stock. The remainder of the preferred stock and part of the Class B common stock were sold to Charles S. Abell. The old company divided what it received among its shareholders. The A. S. Abell Company of Baltimore ended after twenty-eight years. Later the *New York Times* described the *Sun* as one of the most valuable newspaper properties in the United States for its size.

The new company, The A. S. Abell Company, was incorporated the same day, March 24, 1910. The directors were Grasty, Charles S. Abell, and Arunah S. Abell 2d. Grasty was elected president, Charles S. Abell vice president, and Arunah S. Abell 2d secretary. Grasty's salary was $15,000 a year. For working capital the company sold its preferred stock in varying amounts and for $500,000 cash to H. Crawford Black, Robert Garrett, John Campbell White, and Grasty, the latter acting partly for himself and partly for R. Brent Keyser. Each share of Class A stock had one vote without any qualifications, and all of it was held by the Abells. Class B stock was restricted. Except for small blocks owned by Grasty and Charles S. Abell, it was held by Black, Garrett, White, and Keyser. As long as any Class C stock was outstanding, Class B stockholders could not vote for the amendment or repeal of any bylaws providing for the election of the president by the stockholders, for the election of the president, or for his removal. But Class C stockholders could vote on these questions, and as long as the vote was cast as a whole those 1,000 shares would count as much as the combined votes of the Class A and Class B stocks. Since Grasty held all the Class C stock, this gave him control of the company. He could not be removed as president without his consent, nor could any changes be made in the bylaws regarding his duties and prerogatives. These were set forth as follows:

> The president shall have full managerial and editorial control of the company. He shall have the right to determine the policy of the company's papers or publications on all matters, to employ and discharge editors, reporters and employees, to determine the contents of the publications, and to enter into any contracts not imposing an obligation in excess of $100,000 for the purchase of presses, machinery, equipment and paper. The board of directors shall have no power to direct, control

or reverse any action of the president in the exercise of the powers or discharge of the duties conferred by this section.

Grasty's two fellow board members, the Abells, were both professional newspapermen. In 1911, when the board was increased to five, Grasty added two of his backers, White and Harry C. Black, son of H. Crawford Black. White had been working on the *St. Paul Pioneer Press* when Grasty bought it. While a director, he now became a member of the *Sun* editorial staff, later an associate editor, and, in January 1913, a vice president of the company. But in 1913 White left the company to join the diplomatic service, retiring in 1945 after serving as U.S. ambassador to Peru. Harry Black was a newspaperman at heart. A perceptive observer during Grasty's regime, he later became an enthusiastic shaper of policy and tone. The other backers, as nonprofessionals who admittedly lacked newspaper instincts, were not only kept off the board but never informed of major decisions. Though it seems improbable, Grasty undoubtedly was able to do this to these financiers, who were accustomed to a voice in management, because of his success with other papers, his reputation as a strong personal editor in the mold of Greeley and Bennett, and his personality. "Not many men had as great personal charm as had Mr. Grasty," an admirer wrote. "He never lost the appearance of youth. There was always something buoyantly boyish about him, and his laugh, his wit, his philosophy and knowledge, his strength and his weakness, his energy and indomitable courage made him a most engaging and unusual personality." The late Douglas H. Gordon had known Grasty, his namesake father having been one of Grasty's backers at the *News* in the 1890s. The younger Gordon recalled Grasty "as not slender, not fat, with a rubicund face and a bristly mustache. He had a charming manner, a great way with women, dominated dinner parties with his conversation, had an understanding of people, and was a wonderfully interesting man." Grasty was also quick, bright, and precocious. He entered the University of Missouri when he was 13, but was unable to finish for lack of money. At age 16 he was teaching Latin in a Missouri school. At 20 he was managing editor of the *Kansas City Times,* probably the youngest such editor in the United States. During his meteoric career and despite his charm, Grasty also had enemies, especially among politicians. And, it was said, he too knew how to hate.

Within two weeks after the new Abell company was formed, Grasty paid $63,000 in cash, without telling his board, for the 20-year-old Baltimore *Evening World,* which was in receivership. There were two other bidders: General Felix Agnus, proprietor of the *American* and the *Evening Star;* and a man who spread the impression that he was an agent of William Randolph Hearst, who was then building a national newspaper chain. But in actuality the man represented the *World's* owners and this purpose was to inflate the bidding. When Agnus opened at $15,000, the undercover *World* agent jumped at once to $40,000 and pushed the bidding to $63,000, then dropped out. This dubious bargain consisted of four old linotypes, two ancient gasoline-operated presses, and woebegone stereotyping equipment. Grasty, who had been offered the paper for $25,000 when he returned to Baltimore but then was not in a position to buy, said afterward he had paid so dearly because of the rumors that Hearst was scheming to enter the Baltimore market—and Hearst had to be kept out because Grasty was starting an evening paper.

In that matter also, the impetuous Grasty had not so much as notified his backers and board, let alone consult them. A few days after the sale of the *World,* he announced in the *Sun* of April 6 that the new paper would appear on April 18. But not until April 9 were the directors formally told of the purchase and asked for their approval. The stockholders first heard of the new paper when, like the public, they read about it in the paper; their official notice came only at a special meeting on April 27. Evidently to show their displeasure, most refused to attend. The meeting, adjourned three more times, finally took place on May 2, when Grasty and the two Abells appeared; Black, Garrett, White, Keyser, and the Walter R. Abell estate were represented by proxy. If there were questions and complaints they were not recorded, the minutes merely stating that the agreement to buy the *World* was ratified. In the meantime— only twenty-five days after the new company's formation—the new evening daily was presented to Baltimore. That story will be told in the next chapter.

The new paper created financial pressures and problems for Grasty and the company. At a special meeting of stockholders in June, Grasty said it was necessary to sell $200,000 of Class B stock, which in April had been increased from 2,000 to 6,000 shares. This was subscribed to by stockholders, although Charles S. Abell relinquished his right. He also resigned as vice president and was succeeded by Louis M. Duvall, who had been business manager of the *News.* Duvall also became a director in February 1912 and served until his death in December of that year.

In November, seven months after the evening paper first appeared, the board authorized a larger Sunday paper. (The year before Grasty took charge, the *Sunday Sun,* on June 10, 1909, began reproducing, in a one-page art supplement on special paper, a color print of famous paintings, such as Stuart's portrait of Washington and Turner's *Grand Canal of Venice.* These ran most weeks until June 1910, when Grasty ordered them stopped.) The enlarged paper was to include "a comic section, magazine section and other features that go to make up the general Sunday paper." Grasty contracted for four pages of comics from Hearst's International News Service at $200 a week, including the Katzenjammer Kids, Happy Hooligan, Jimmy, and In the Land of Wonderful Dreams by Winsor McKay. Old subscribers were shocked to find their staid *Sun* containing these so-called "funnies," and a number called at the *Sun* office to complain, shaking their heads and speculating that old Mr. Abell was spinning in his grave. Presently, the *Sunday Sun* added splashy illustrations and other features. "The Adventures of Kitty Cobb," a half-page drawing by James Montgomery Flagg, portrayer of beautiful young women, was serialized. A page was devoted to children, asking them such questions as "What was the greatest emergency in your life?" and "Who was the most famous person you ever met?" Women's features were emphasized, and much attention was paid to society news. The column headed "Society" had an underline: "Events of the polite world, present and to come."

The cost of enlarging and improving the Sunday paper was $120,000, but readership increased. In 1911 average paid circulation was 61,882; in 1912 it was 72,454. And Grasty enlarged the staff of the morning paper. Two of the new-hires were Virginia Dashiell, daughter of Charles W. Dashiell, city editor for fifteen years until his death in 1898, and Edwin L. James. When she applied to be a reporter, Grasty replied, "Your name is enough! It would disgrace me forever if the news got out that a daughter of Charles Dashiell had wanted to come on the *Sun,* and I had not found a place for her." She turned out to be a fine reporter. In 1918 she married John W. Owens, then political reporter on the *Sun.* James, likewise beginning work in 1910, was only 20 years old. Stumbling onto a murder one day, James telephoned his city editor, Allen S. Will. Because James was a novice, Will indicated he would send an experienced reporter to take over. "The hell you will," James replied. "This is my story and I can handle it." He did too, drawing compliments from Will. But two years later Will fired him, and James went to the *Pittsburgh Dispatch* as news editor. James later joined the *New York Times,* becoming a war correspondent, chief European correspondent, and, in 1932, managing editor. He succeeded Carr V. Van Anda, a legendary figure who had been night editor of the *Sun* from 1886 to 1888.

The minutes recorded a continual need for more money. In 1911 stockholders were asked to subscribe to the remaining Class B stock. Harry C. Black offered a resolution for the company to borrow money when needed. Immediately the company borrowed $25,000 from the Fidelity Trust Company, in which the Blacks were involved. A special meeting was called in November to provide even more funds. It was agreed to issue four-year notes at 6 percent, not to exceed $500,000. By January 1912, eighteen $5,000 notes had been sold. The minutes for that meeting also noted that Charles S. Abell had resigned as a director. Grasty was doing things his way, and he ignored Abell's questions and advice. The minutes quoted this note from Abell, written from the *Landmark* office in Norfolk: "About a week ago I wrote you a letter in which I resigned as a member of the board of directors of the A. S. Abell Company. Having received no reply and presuming the letter was lost I hereby resign as a member of the above-mentioned board."

Though A. S. Abell 2d was still on the board, the Abell imprint and traditions had been eliminated or were fading. When the Abells were in charge they preferred an anonymous role, but not Grasty. He added his name to the masthead as president and general manager. Oswald Garrison Villard, in an article in the April 1922 issue of *The Nation* entitled "*The Baltimore Suns—A Notable Journalistic Resurrection,*" wrote: "For generations the '*Sun-paper*' . . . was synonymous, under its previous ownership by the Abell family, with stodgy, ultraconservatism; its rate of intellectual progress was that of the Maryland Club, which in turn regarded '*Sun-paper*' much as it did the United States Treasury, or the sanctity of private property, or the Supreme Court, though the latter could not be quite as infallible as the *Sun*. . . . If you ask a present member of the *Sun*'s staff as to just when the new *Sun* was born the answer invariably is: 'Under Grasty.'"

On May 17, 1912, a significant date, no mention was made that it was the *Sun*'s silver jubilee. And, ironically, on the same day, Grasty's *Sun* carried a lengthy story under the headline "Guilford Work to Begin," which began, "After a long period of dignified isolation as a family country estate, Guilford, in the northern suburbs . . . is soon to give up its individuality to the demands of the fast-growing city." There was not one reference to the fact that this 300-acre estate was once the country home of A. S. Abell. Belatedly, on May 18, a short editorial acknowledged the anniversary, but there was no mention of the founder, A. S. Abell, or of the paper's achievements under the Abells. Emphasis was on the present: "The *Sun* is now at the summit of its career. . . . Never before was it stronger in the confidence of the people than it is at this day; never have the people been more content to rely upon its news and upon its advice." That same day another editorial suggested, "The son of Lincoln might be a dark horse worth considering by the Republicans this year, if, as Colonel Roosevelt says, a Lincolnesque man must be nominated." During the Civil War, the *Sun* had derided Lincoln and once termed him a "bar-room Phunny-Phellow."

After the March 1912 meeting, when the cost of the *World* was charged off to goodwill, the next six board meetings were recorded with the words "Minutes read and approved for previous meeting. There being no further business, the meeting was adjourned." After two postponements, the October meeting authorized the president to call for the fourth $50,000 installment of Class B stock, which had been sanctioned in April 1910. The *Sun* Book and Job Printing Shop was sold in December 1912 for $44,000, the board approving except for Arunah S. Abell 2d. The board meetings were changed from the second to the fourth Monday of the month so the board could study the financial statement from the previous month.

With Grasty in absolute charge, the company was losing money. The evening paper lost $143,188 in 1910, offsetting the *Sun*'s net profit of $43,842. In 1911 the *Sun* and the *Sunday Sun* had deficits of $89,661; the evening paper had deficits of $212,248. In 1912 the deficits of the *Sun* and the *Sunday Sun* were $69,066 and, for the evening paper, $195,911. In 1913 the *Sun* and the *Sunday Sun* had a profit of $17,839, but the evening paper lost $178,916. The total deficit for those years was more than $800,000.

During those stressful times, Grasty gave less time to the business side than he did to the news and editorial departments and to politics. In the mayoral election in May 1911, the *Sunpapers* campaigned against James H. Preston, a wealthy lawyer who had been speaker of the Maryland House of Delegates and at one time a police commissioner of Baltimore. He was a member of what remained of the old Gorman-Rasin machine, which Grasty's *News* had attacked for years. The machine fought back rallying to its support enemies Grasty had made. Preston won, defeating his Republican opponent, E. Clay Timanus, by only 699 votes. But Preston's strength grew, and he won reelection eight years later as mayor and bought whole columns of advertising space in the *News* to denounce the *Sunpapers* and Grasty. Preston even impugned Grasty's private character, claiming he had left Kansas City for questionable reasons. In the gubernatorial election of November 1911, the *Sunpapers,* reverting to Democratic habit, supported Arthur Pue Gorman, Jr., son of the old Maryland Democratic boss but a less blatantly political animal. However, Grasty rejected most of the other names on the party ticket. To him they were agents of the old organization in which Preston was now a leader. When Gorman lost (to Phillips Lee Goldsborough), Grasty blamed it on the unpopularity of the Preston city administration. Two days later, Preston took out a two-column ad in the *News* which began: "This advertisement, in answer to Grasty's statement that the defeat of state Senator Gorman was due to the unpopularity of the Democratic City Administration, was refused by the *Sun.* This is Grasty's idea of fair journalism." Preston attributed the defeat of Gorman and part of the local and legislative ticket to the fact "that Grasty was conspicuous in the campaign on behalf of the state ticket." Preston stormed, "The Democrats of Maryland do not intend to permit Grasty to become the political dictator of the state or of the Democratic party in this city. He will always injure any cause he espouses." The feud continued. In a May 31, 1912, editorial the *Sun* charged:

> Mayor Preston is accusing the *Sun* of "forgery" and moral obliquity in general for declining to open its columns to abusive personal allusions to the editors of the *Sun* and other papers that are treating the Baltimore public fairly as against the Preston administration.
>
> The simple fact is that the *Sun* dealt very generously with the Mayor—much more than he deserves—and he is behaving very badly and ungratefully. In the case complained of, the *Sun* gave him something like a half-column of its valuable space for matter that it knew to be disingenuous and misleading. It cut out the personal, irrelevant and abusive parts, but printed every word he had to say in reference to his official duties. . . .

The suggestion that the Democratic National Convention of 1912 meet in Baltimore is said to have originated with O. P. Baldwin, managing editor of the *Sun,* but it is more likely that McKee Barclay had a direct hand in it. Barclay began his newspaper career in Kentucky, once owning a weekly paper, which he sold when he moved to Baltimore in 1891, for a $19 profit. He worked for the *World,* the *Herald,* and the *News* before joining the *Sun* in 1908, the same day his younger brother, Thomas Pollard Barclay, was hired. McKee Barclay was a cartoonist for most of his career, but in his early *Sun* days he was a political writer; he became chief of the Washington Bureau on December 11, 1912, relieving Frank R. Kent, and served for about a year. McKee Barclay was the only newspaperman to accompany Woodrow Wilson and Frank Parker Stockbridge, a reporter hired as Wilson's publicity agent, on a cross-country tour before the convention. He died in 1947, and his obituary in the *Sun* credited him with being largely responsible for bringing the Democratic National Convention to Baltimore.

Long before the convention began on June 25, the *Sun* was filled with stories about it, and the Republican convention to be held in Chicago earlier in June. The *Sun* engaged Samuel G. Blythe, former chief of the Washington bureau of the *New York Herald* and, "one of the most noted political writers in the country," to write about both conventions. Along with politics the front pages had stories about Harry K. Thaw and the Floradora Girls, the dispatch of marines to Guantánamo and eight battleships to Key West because of an insurrection in Cuba, and the suspension of Ty Cobb, "the greatest baseball player in the world," after he jumped into a grandstand and attacked a handicapped person who Cobb claimed had insulted him. The new automobiles and the many accidents involving them were being reported in detail. In many cases the cars were owned by prominent, wealthy citizens. For example, one accident involved a car driven by a chauffeur for Daniel Willard, president of B&O; another, "driven by a well-known capitalist"; a third, the chauffeured touring car of the vice president of Hutzler's.

The new head of the *Sun*'s Washington bureau, J. Fred Essary, was in Chicago a week before 1912's first convention began, filing stories initialed J.F.E. President William Howard Taft's forces gained control of the convention machinery, and former President Theodore Roosevelt's delegates were voted out. Roosevelt rushed to Chicago, and Essary's story began: "Excitement bordering on frenzy has seized the convention city. Theodore Roosevelt has come and the thousands here have been swept away with enthusiasm. Delegates are meeting in the streets with flags and banners. Bands are playing in hotel lobbies—all this three days before the convention meets." The *Sun* termed Roosevelt's appearance "a startling move, audacious in its conception and staggering in its execution." After Taft was nominated on the first ballot, the *Sun* published an extra with a four-column headline quoting Roosevelt as declaring "I'm Through" and asking his forces to bolt. Essary had predicted that Roosevelt would form a third party, the Progressives, known informally as the Bull Moose Party.

Officials began arriving in Baltimore nearly two weeks before the Democratic convention began. The site would be the Fifth Regiment Armory, which could seat 12,000 with standing room for another 4,000. The *Sun* termed it "the Pride of Baltimore," "the greatest convention center in the world." An editorial crowed, "When we remember the lukewarmness with which the *Sun*'s suggestion for holding this convention in Baltimore was first received. . . ." Hotels said they had rooms for 3,000, and twice that many persons could be accommodated, the *Sun* reported, in boardinghouses, in parked Pullmans, and in private homes. The *New York Times* had an ad in the *Sun* to announce that it was running a special train to Baltimore to deliver late editions of its paper by 8:00 A.M. The *Sun* reported a Police Board ruling that on the Sabbath delegates would not be allowed to parade on the streets headed by bands playing either martial strains or Sabbath music. They could parade, "but they must do so quietly and not create any loud noises." Mayor Preston controlled the Democratic state convention and he recommended that the Maryland delegation to the convention "use every honorable effort" to have him nominated as vice president. The *Sun* was sarcastic: "This year the Mayor of Baltimore, an official who has rarely attended national conventions as a delegate, will be in the spotlight."

As early as March, Grasty and his *Sun* were favoring Woodrow Wilson for the Democratic presidential nomination. The two men were old friends and had a common Virginia heritage. Wilson, a graduate of Princeton, had studied at Johns Hopkins in the 1880s, earning a Ph.D. in government. He returned to Baltimore almost every year between 1887 and 1898 to deliver special lectures at Hopkins on political science. Grasty probably got to know him at that time. Wilson also addressed a rally at the Lyric Theatre, probably at Grasty's request, for the Reform movement when it was fighting the senior senator, Gorman. Wilson was elected president of Princeton University in 1902, and when he resigned in 1910 in a fight over the democratization of the university, Grasty offered him the editorship of the *Sun*. He declined, and that fall was nominated for governor of New Jersey. Grasty wrote to Wilson, promising him the support of the *Sunpapers.* Victorious, Wilson soon became a national political figure. Although by 1912 Grasty and the *Sun* were eager to see Wilson bear the Democratic standard, the *Sun* was not supporting Wilson openly as the convention began, only indirectly. On June 4 it reprinted a lengthy *New York World* editorial entitled "For President—Woodrow Wilson," remarking that "it has attracted wide attention and is reproduced here at the request of a number of well-known Democrats." The next day the *Sun* reprinted an editorial by Henry Watterson of the *Louisville Courier-Journal,* which strongly argued for Champ Clark of Missouri as the Democratic nominee and criticized Wilson as untrustworthy and merely a "mild-mannered Roosevelt."

William Jennings Bryan, a three-time loser in previous presidential campaigning, announced that he would not accept the nomination, but when he arrived in Baltimore he was met by an immense cheering crowd. Champ Clark, who was Speaker of the House, was the preconvention favorite. The *Sun* reported that the fight was between Clark and Wilson, with Mayor William J. Gaynor of New York a dark horse. Bryan charged that New York financiers August Belmont and Thomas Fortune Ryan, and Charles F. Murphy of Tammany Hall, were conspiring to control the convention and forestall a progressive platform and candidate. When Ryan, a power in railroad and financial circles and a head of a tobacco trust, arrived in Baltimore, the *Sun* announced that he had "slipped into town quietly in his private car." It printed his picture in three columns on page one, and the story under it began "For the first time one of the great money kings of America has appeared in person at a national political convention to carry on the fight for the money interests." Ryan replied that he was there as a delegate from Virginia, his legal residence, but the *Sun* continued to fume that he and his cohorts were there to dominate and control the convention. Breathlessly, it told where Ryan was hiding out after reserving quarters at another place, and how he had a private telephone line to keep in touch with his lieutenants. Printing Ryan's picture on the front page was said to signify to the delegates that something sensational was in the making. Later several historical references claimed the picture had special impact because it was the first time the *Sun* had ever appeared with a picture on its front page. And in retrospect, this was termed "the most effective piece of newspaper work in the fight." Undoubtedly the tactic was effective, but it was not the *Sun*'s first front-page photograph. The day before, it had printed a three-column picture of Mr. and Mrs. Bryan.

The *Sun* covered the proceedings in overwhelming detail; sometimes 8 or 10 pages were devoted to the convention. Yet the paper was not prescient. On opening day it reported, "So definitely is the situation drifting to Bryan that Wilson's name is already being considered as the vice presidential nominee with the Commoner." The next day it reported that the nomination "hung in the balance last night among Champ Clark, Woodrow Wilson, and a dark horse, with the chances favoring Clark."

Editorially, the *Sun* still did not come out directly for Wilson, but was doing so by implication. "The convention must nominate a real progressive on a progressive platform, not a spurious one or an imitation, if it desires to inspire public confidence and support." None of the other candidates was remotely progressive; they were allied with conservatives or party machines.

On Wednesday, Wilson's supporters staged a 33-minute demonstration, and the next morning the *Sun*'s lead story began "A swift and sudden change in the Baltimore convention occurred yesterday and at midnight the drift toward Woodrow Wilson was so strong, so enthusiastic and so plain that the conservative and financial and political combinations opposing him were badly frightened."

By the end of the first day of voting, ballots had been cast ten times. Clark had a majority, but two-thirds was necessary for nomination. Baltimore was experiencing a hot, humid June and the hall, filled to capacity, grew more and more oppressive. At first the delegates removed their coats and then their wilted collars; the women took off their hats and, the *Sun* reported, "decorated the railing with them, hanging the exquisite creations among the bunting and making the whole thing look like a floral scheme." From time to time many a delegate ducked out—the women for ice-cream cones, the men retreating to nearby saloons. The balloting continued through Thursday and Friday, with

Clark still ahead but Wilson gaining, and Oscar W. Underwood of Alabama, Governor Simeon E. Baldwin of Connecticut, and Governor Judson Harmon of Ohio trailing. The Friday session adjourned at 3:05 Saturday morning and met again that afternoon. Bryan startled the delegates by bolting Clark on the fourteenth ballot and coming out for Wilson. On the twenty-sixth and last ballot Saturday night, Clark had 463$^{1}/_{2}$ votes, and Wilson, still gaining, had 407$^{1}/_{2}$. For nomination, 731 of the 1,096 votes were needed. The heat had intensified; many of the perspiring delegates were on the verge of prostration from heat and lack of rest. Delegates had expected the convention to end Friday; by Saturday, many had run out of money and hundreds wired home for more. Some missed Bryan's bolting speech because they were waiting at the telegraph office.

The *Sun*'s editorial tone grew more hortatory, but the name Wilson was still omitted. Only on Monday, as the exhausted delegates reconvened (a number had gone home, leaving their places to alternates), did the *Sun* finally endorse Wilson. A two-column editorial in larger-than-usual type proclaimed: "With Wilson for its candidate, the Democratic party will face the impending contest with courage and confidence. . . . It will have for a leader a man of the highest qualifications for the presidential office, a man who, by his character and career, has won the confidence of the country." That same day, July 1, Grasty wrote to Wilson: "The *Sun* has tried to be wary as well as loyal, and to avoid anything that might produce reaction. We sent the paper to all delegates for four weeks before they came to Baltimore and when they came they kept on reading it. We gave all candidates a fair show and this kept the minds of delegates open to our 'poison.' Our support has warmed up crescendo fashion, our editorial this morning striking the top key up to date." The *Sun* made sure that the delegates, and everyone else, knew how it stood. During the long balloting, extras were hammered out and rushed to the hall within minutes. The *Sun* even ran a story on how much money its newsboys made; some sold more than 1,200 papers in a few days, hawking the two-cent paper for five cents.

In the balloting on Monday, Wilson gained about 100 votes, reaching 494 on the forty-second ballot. But he still needed nearly 240 more votes for the necessary two-thirds. The *Sun* caught the atmosphere of the hall in one paragraph: "Weary, bedraggled, peevish aggregations of delegates and alternates drifted into the convention hall. Police were warned to exert extraordinary vigilance. Police were forced to remove offenders who became involved in quarrels. Every shifting of vote, every demand for a poll of a delegation awakened the bitterness that lay beneath the proceedings. Hisses, jeers, half-hearted cheers greeted the few changes on each ballot."

The *Sun*'s editorial on Tuesday said flatly, "The country will be satisfied with nothing less than Woodrow Wilson." Finally, at 3:22 that afternoon, on the forty-sixth ballot, Wilson was nominated. It was not the longest balloting in convention history to that point. Fifty-seven ballots were cast in

Charleston in 1860, and 49 in Baltimore in 1852, when Franklin Pierce was nominated.

Mayor Preston was still bent on having his name presented as vice presidential nominee. His chances as a Clark man were remote. The *Sun,* which had been pointedly ignoring Preston's candidacy, reported what happened this way:

> The Preston boom for the vice presidency collapsed last night about 11 o'clock. By the time it was formally presented to the convention by Mr. Alonzo L. Miles, of the Maryland delegation, it had shriveled to microscopic proportions, and when Mr. Miles concluded his speech it was entirely invisible to the naked eye. Not that Mr. Miles did not make a good speech, because he did. He told the great gathering that Baltimore had erected the first monument to Columbus, and that it was in this city the first message over a telegraph wire had [been] received. He said the city was the home of Democracy and that Mayor Preston had a strong intellect and a good address and that neither prince, potentate, power, hostile press nor political enemies could swerve him once he set his face toward duty. Mr. Miles said a lot of other things too, but the crowd for some reason or other did not appreciate them.

The *Sun* also reported that when the nominator mentioned Columbus a hoarse voice from the gallery shouted, "Well, then I nominate Christopher." That brought such shouting from the floor that proceedings were suspended for five minutes. The speaker became "so confused" that he was unable to conclude "with the eloquence which marked the beginning of his address." Mencken, a reporter at the convention, later wrote that the speaker had imbibed too freely before making his speech. After the first ballot, with Preston receiving fifty-eight votes, friends withdrew his name. Governor Thomas R. Marshall of Indiana was nominated for vice president. The convention finally adjourned at 1:55 A.M. on Wednesday, July 3. It had been in session since Tuesday, June 25.

The following day the *Sun* reproduced a telegram it had received from Woodrow Wilson: "I want you to know how warmly and deeply I have appreciated the splendid support of the *Sun.*" It also reproduced a letter from William F. McCombs: "As manager of the Wilson campaign I want to thank the *Sun* for its loyal and enthusiastic support of Governor Wilson. It has been one of the most effective agencies in bringing about his nomination for the presidency. . . ."

That praise was not enough for Grasty. The *Sun* solicited the opinion of delegates and others and published two columns of praise for its coverage, many people claiming they were converted to the Wilson candidacy "largely through the clear, truthful editorials of the Baltimore *Sun.*"

Nearly six months after the convention, on December 19, 1912, the *American* printed a dispatch from its Washington bureau which began, "A report current among Democratic politicians and President-elect Wilson's intimate friends is that Charles H. Grasty, president of the A. S. Abell Company, of

Baltimore, will seek the appointment of Ambassador to France under the incoming Democratic administration. . . . According to a report here, Mr. Grasty will go direct to President Wilson in seeking the honor. It is known in the Wilson circles here that the President-elect is anxious to recognize in some manner Mr. Grasty's effort in behalf of his nomination and election as President. . . ."

The next day, under the heading "The *Sun* Will Send No Bill to Governor Wilson for Services Rendered," Grasty replied. He reprinted the *American* article and a letter he had written six weeks earlier to James M. Thomson, proprietor of the *New Orleans Item,* who had mentioned Grasty for a cabinet post or ambassadorship. In the letter he wrote in part, "I do not think there is any office that you, or I, or any other earnest and intelligent editor can afford to accept. This is particularly and preeminently true in a case where an editor has been useful to a cause and his acceptance of an office would put him and his paper in the position of making a sordid swap of his support in return for office." He gave his reasons for supporting Wilson: "The *Sun* began its support of Woodrow Wilson in March, 1910. It gave this support in the most efficient way it knew how up to the time of his nomination and election. But none of this did we do for Woodrow Wilson the man, or Woodrow Wilson the friend. We thought that Mr. Wilson would be the best nominee to elect and the best President after he was elected. Mr. Wilson is, therefore, under no obligation whatever to the *Sun* or to me. Our purpose was an entirely selfish one, I confess. The only reward for a newspaper that is substantial and enduring is public confidence. . . ."

NINE

The *Evening Sun* and Grasty
1910–1914

Grasty at first rejected the name *Evening Sun* because he felt the competition and wisecrackers would refer to it as the *Setting Sun*; he would call it the *Press*. But at the last moment he submitted to logic and accepted the family name that is now well known.

On April 6, 1910, two weeks after the new company was incorporated, this announcement appeared at the top of the first column on the *Sun*'s back page:

A NEW SUN WILL RISE
Evening Edition of This Paper to
Appear April 18
13 Issues, 10 Cents a Week
Morning and Evening Editions to be
Delivered to All Subscribers
in City and Suburbs

The Sun will begin the publication of an evening edition on Monday, April 18.

The morning, evening and Sunday editions will be delivered to subscribers of *The Sun* in the city and suburbs, all 13 papers for 10 cents a week.

The Evening Sun will be similar in make-up to the morning paper. It will be orderly and plain in its presentation of the news, without thrills or frills.

The Sun has acquired, through the purchase of the *World,* the news franchise of the United Press, which will be supplemented by the service of the *Sun*'s special correspondents in New York, Washington and elsewhere.

Grasty's training, experience, and success had been on evening papers. He liked their immediacy, compared with morning papers, which dealt with news of the previous day. He believed that with competitive, improving press associations providing fast-breaking national and international news throughout the day, the evening paper was the paper of the future, not only for information, but for circulation and advertising as well.

His first issue was late. According to the amateurishly drawn horoscope on the editorial page, "At the moment of the first issue . . . the celestial configurations are generally auspicious." It added that the paper was to appear at 3:00 P.M. But Dove wrote in his journal: "Couriers came down from the composing room every few minutes during the afternoon to report progress, 'Another page locked up. We'll have her out soon.' Until, finally, at a few minutes after four the presses started to grind."

It was a twelve-page paper with twenty-three stories and four columns of advertising on page one. The lead story reported the ocean liner *Minnehaha* running aground in a fog off the coast of England, adding that the sixty-four passengers had been rescued. The longest story, $17\frac{1}{2}$ inches, was about suffragists—"Joyous Body of Women Move On / Congress With Monster Petition." Short items mentioned that Mark Twain was ill and growing weaker and that between 300 and 400 applicants were undergoing "mental" examinations for the Naval Academy.

Headlines were only one-column wide, but the body type was slightly larger than that in rival papers. Readers were told: "The extent to which the *Evening Sun* uses large print is an experiment, and an interesting one, in metropolitan journalism. The combination of modest headlines with book type is a reversal of the prevalent fashion, which apparently assumes that only headlines are read in a newspaper. Whatever may be the case in other cities, the *Sun* has reason to know that Baltimore people read the right kind of newspaper through and through." A few days later the *Evening Sun* quoted the *Charlotte Chronicle* as raving, "Typographically the *Evening Sun* is a beauty." Later, the first editor recollected: "Among the problems that much perplexed early editors of the *Evening Sun* was that of makeup. To have the appearance of the paper reflect the character which its makers hoped to give it, as the facade of a well-designed building suggests its purpose and use, required much more thought and experimentation than the casual reader is apt to imagine." But on the paper's seventy-fifth anniversary, in April 1985, an *Evening Sun* anniversary magazine described the first issue as looking "pretty much as if the type were set with a sieve" and said the front-page stories "were stacked up like soup cans in a grocery." It ridiculed the "large" type, claiming it was "about as easy to read as an endorsement to an airline insurance policy."

In the first issue of the *Evening Sun,* the lead editorial announced:

Good Evening! *The Evening Sun* makes its bow today. It is a new paper only in the sense that it enables the *Sun* to present its news and views in the afternoon as well as the morning. The public, therefore, will need no elaborate explanation or forecast of its method and policies.

The evening edition, like the morning, will be orderly in form and reliable in substance. It will be a home paper. It seeks to be interesting to the family circle and to gain the confidence of the public, in whose interest it will always be on duty.

The editorial page had a column from the *World,* which the *Evening Sun* had absorbed. It was from that paper's last issue, Saturday, April 16, and began "The end of the *World.*" Also on the editorial page were several short features, such as "Barks and Bites" by McKee Barclay, and "Finnigan in Ag'in" by Strickland Gillilan, the author of "Off Again, on Again, Gone Again Finnigan," who was making his appearance "after several years absence from the Baltimore newspaper field." A well-traveled newspaperman, Gillilan had previously worked on the *American* and was popular for his Irish dialect verses and lyceum recitals. At the bottom of the page was a short piece entitled "We're Happy, Anyhow." It read in part: "Let us confess it to one another, Baltimore is a good old town. The cobblestones are rough—but they might be tin cans. The tax rate might be high—but out of every dollar collected fully 95 cents is spent honestly and fully 40 cents intelligently." The writer congratulated the citizens, saying they were a good bunch and lived in a good town. "Let us be glad that we are Baltimoreans," the author concluded. "Just suppose an unkind fate made us Pittsburghers." The tone, as well as the single appended initial, "M," identify all this as the work of Henry L. Mencken.

The main local news was on the back page, along with a cartoon titled "Good Evening" by Tom Bee, the pen name of Thomas Barclay, McKee's brother. In the drawing, a boy was wearing a paper hat fashioned from the *Sun*'s front page and carrying a sign that read "Another *Sun* presented at a new time. That's all!" The issue also contained three columns of financial and shipping news, and a page for sports with an enumerating standing streamer, "Baseball–Bowling–Racing–Lacrosse–Track Athletics–Boxing," but not all were covered. Features got the most attention. A serial, "Lord Loveland Discovers America," was to appear alternately in the *Sun,* and "Answers" was an advice column "designed to help all those who need information on any subject which it is in the province of a newspaper to give. . . . Thus, young girls who are bothered about their love affairs, or some question of etiquette; women who wish a formula for hair tonic, a dinner menu, suggestions about dressmaking, or information concerning the ancient Egyptians; men who wish to be enlightened on matters, however erudite, are all welcome to the fold of correspondence." The first question was "Does the United Railway Company sell ticket books?" and the answer was "Yes." Another question, in the treacherous shoals of amatory behavior, was "Is there any place where I can get a complete flirtation code?" which gave "Answers" pause. He or she replied evasively, "Flirtation is in a state of evolution, it is never completed." A local column, "Dolly and I," which was to become popular because of its wit and descriptive powers, was written by the Woman's Page editor and later sometimes signed with the initials L.C.C., for Lillian Craigen Coyle, a widow who had begun her newspaper career in 1899 when hired by Grasty to write women's features for the *News.* After joining the *Evening Sun,* she married its editor, John Haslup Adams, and later wrote a Monday-Wednesday-Friday column for the editorial page of the *Sun,* signed L.C.A.

To satisfy the curious, the press run for the first issue was announced as 71,420. Evidently many copies went unsold or undelivered. A back-page box in the second issue revealed that "some difficulties were encountered in the suburbs and outlying sections of the city due to the heavy rains that interfered with the speedy delivery by motorcycle and automobile and also to troubles inherent in the inauguration of a service involving more than 500 carriers. In certain suburban sections the circulation will not be in good shape until the beginning of next week, although solicitors will continue to take orders."

On the second day the press run dropped to 60,830. Advertising was a fraction of that of the previous day. The Society heading appeared as "Soceity." The back page had a column headed "The *Evening Sun* Welcomed" in which politicians were asked their opinion of the new paper. (Telephoning people who like to see their names in print and who will give predictable replies is a hoary newspaper practice that is still resorted to. When telephone calls cost five cents, those names and numbers were known as "the nickel list." In making such an assignment, the city desk would furnish a reporter the question and he or she would pick up "the nickel list.") Those polled included Governor Austin L. Crothers (who said he had read the first issue cover-to-cover), Mayor J. Barry Mahool, the city comptroller, and assorted officeholders. All replies were congratulatory, not to say enthusiastic. A deputy state's attorney, Eugene O'Dunne, outdid them all: "The rays of the *Evening Sun* cast a genial warmth over the city of Baltimore. Modest in dress, solid and substantial in manner, lofty in aspirations and determined in purpose; these qualities when found in an individual bring, in a life, all that is worthwhile." O'Dunne later became a judge on the Supreme Bench of Baltimore and was esteemed for the literary flourishes in his decisions. He was sometimes also an adversary of the *Sunpapers.*

The first editor of the *Evening Sun* was John Haslup Adams. Born in 1871, he left grammar school to become an office boy for the B&O Railroad. He became interested in art, not as an artist but as an aspiring cognoscente, and in his early twenties he went to Paris. He stayed nine months and became familiar enough with the Louvre to serve as an occasional guide for American tourists. When he returned to Baltimore he began to write about painting. In 1899 he entered a short-story contest sponsored by the *News.* Though he only won second prize, his writing so impressed Folger McKinsey, then the managing editor, that he recommended him to Grasty. Adams was hired as a reporter and by 1904 had been promoted to managing editor. Two years later he turned to writing editorials. He stayed with the *News* until it was bought by Frank A. Munsey in February 1908. Adams was the first person hired after Grasty became president of the A. S. Abell Company. Adams wrote the *Evening Sun*'s lead editorial and usually one or two other editorials. Adams was described by Mencken, whose title was associate editor but who preferred "minister without portfolio," "as an old-fashioned Liberal" and one who "had all the virtues of the Puritan—and, at their best, what virtues they are! . . . He saw a great modern newspaper as largely, if not mainly, an engine for rectifying injustice." In addition to writing editorials, Mencken said he "had many other duties including the daily concoction of an editorial page article which sometimes ran to 2,000 words."

The evening news staff was drawn from the *Sun,* the *American,* the *News,* the *Star,* and the *World.* Munsey later accused Grasty of luring away many of his best people, but such principals as Adams and McKee Barclay had left before the *Evening Sun* began. More came from the *World:* Edward Green, who became the first telegraph editor; E. A. Fitzpatrick, later city editor and then assistant managing editor; William F. Schmick, who had become business manager of the *World* at age 20; Charles O. Reville in advertising; and Edward McCleavy as the first foreman of the composing room. C. M. Purdy, one of the organizers of the *World* and later its editor, came from the *American* and became city editor. John E. Cullen, who joined the *Sun* in 1907 after working for the *World,* the *Herald,* and the *American,* was named city editor in 1913. In a note to Mencken, Cullen claimed to have been the first editor to use women on rewrite: Charlotte Mann "was my first one and she did a good job." Cullen was soon made managing editor and was succeeded as city editor by Philip B. Perlman, who had been the court reporter. Perlman, previously on the staff of the *American* and the *Star,* seems to have been the first Jewish person hired by Baltimore dailies in the twentieth century. After studying law on the side, Perlman changed careers in 1917. Subsequently, he was Maryland secretary of state, Baltimore city solicitor and United States Solicitor General.

Paul Patterson, only 33 years old but with twelve years of varied newspaper experience, joined the *Evening Sun* on April 11, 1911. He succeeded Robert B. Vale as managing editor; Vale was appointed assistant business manager and then business manager. Grasty often transferred men from the news side to the business department. In 1913, Robert B. Ennis, a political reporter, was made advertising manager (he later became a prominent political figure in Maryland), and Henry Edward Warner was switched from staff poet to circulation manager. In 1914, Cullen became a special assistant in the advertising department. ("Frank Kent thought I was looney.") When Vale left in the fall of 1913, Patterson succeeded him as business manager. Patterson later was elected president, and he was succeeded by Schmick. Their careers will be detailed in later chapters.

The *Evening Sun* had stiff competition from Munsey's *News.* When Grasty was in control the *News* gained in circulation—during his last month its circulation was 82,661 higher than that of the *Sun*—and had revenues of about $800,000. But Munsey did better still. Despite competition also from the *American's* afternoon version, the *Star,* revenues of the *News* passed $1 million in 1910 and more than $2 million in 1912. Munsey, who at one time owned eighteen newspapers, boasted that the Baltimore *News* "was the best-paying paper I ever owned." Munsey, successful but idiosyncratic, became agitated when, on a tour of his chain, he happened to spot fat men, old employees, smoking, and sloppiness. Word would be passed when he visited his papers.

In his biography, *Forty Years—Forty Million: The Career of Frank A. Munsey,* George Britt wrote, "Frank A's coming was an alarm cry producing immediate results . . . staff frozen into expressionless tension . . . coats on . . . cigarettes and pipes out . . . the fat and the old out of sight . . . paper off the floor . . . broken chairs to the cellar." Munsey had a roving eye for the minute detail ("How was ink spilled on that desk?").

After the purchase of the *News,* Britt quoted Munsey as saying, "I adopted the home-rule policy. After I selected Mr. [Stuart] Olivier as general manager and found he made good, I left the *News* entirely in his hands and in the hands of his associates. While I was still owner, I did not interfere with its policy or its management except in a general way." Olivier, a talented and colorful man who had a close relationship with Munsey and the Baltimore newspaper scene, will be chronicled later. But at first Munsey dealt with the *News* in more than "a general way."

During the 1911 state election campaign, the *Evening Sun,* supporting the Democratic ticket (as did the *Sun*), denounced Munsey as a "stand-pat Republican in disguise." Munsey replied on November 6, 1911, with a signed editorial that covered four columns on his front page. The first third was a rebuttal on the political charges, "Grasty tells you that I am a 'stand-patter!' Yes, I am a stand-patter in the matter of old-fashioned honesty and in square dealing man-to-man." The other two-thirds was his version of buying the *News,* claiming that when Grasty returned to Baltimore he "started to destroy the property which he had sold me a short time before. . . . However bad a newspaperman Grasty is, he is a good enough newspaperman to know that three evening papers cannot live in Baltimore and be self-supporting, honest, worthwhile newspapers. He knew perfectly well that if he made a success of his evening paper it would be made at the expense of the *News,* and that the success of his paper meant the death of mine." He concluded:

For more than ten years Grasty preached independence in Baltimore and defiantly assailed and assaulted the *Baltimore Sun* in its support of the Democratic ring. But, no longer with the *News* and now in control of the *Sun* whose chief asset is and has been for half a century its party grip, Grasty suddenly becomes the apostle of all he had for more than ten years denounced and vilified. If Grasty was still in control of the *News* it is a practical certainty that he would have lined up against the Democratic ring and its reactionary candidates in the present campaign.

The next day Grasty printed a four-column reply entitled "Mr. Munsey's Statements Corrected" with his byline but referred to himself in the third person. He assailed Munsey for converting the *News* from an independent paper "to the organ of the Republican party" and said that Munsey had revolutionized the paper, "making of it the typical yellow journal in both typographical appearance and contents." But the thrust of his retort was that he had not violated a tacit agreement by returning to Baltimore, purchasing the *Sun* and the *World,* and starting the *Evening Sun.* He claimed he had made no agreement, and if Munsey did not want him to return he should have paid him to stay away—"Mr. Grasty was willing to sell the fruit of his past labor, but saw no reason for mortgaging his future to a millionaire publisher without a cent of consideration." Grasty concluded by maintaining that Baltimore could support two morning and three evening papers, and that "no other city of Baltimore's size had so few papers." He paid to have his reply printed in the *News*.

The *News* got most of the advertising placed in evening papers. Advertising in the *Evening Sun* had dropped to such an extent that many readers remarked that they liked the paper more because its reading matter was not encumbered with ads. Grasty made little effort to woo advertisers. In fact, he was known for his clashes with them, believing they wanted to intrude on his fierce editorial independence. When he was still on the *News*, a number of leading advertisers had organized a boycott in 1905 to withdraw all advertising for one year. Grasty claimed it was because of an increase of one cent a line in their rates, but his treatment of advertisers was a factor. On January 6, 1905, Grasty wrote an editorial about the boycott. He said that the moment a newspaper "acknowledges the dependence [on advertisers] as one which may be permitted to control its conduct, it ceases to be what it ought to be—a public institution as well as a commercial enterprise. . . . From submission to such coercion, or to the threat of such coercion, the step is not a long one to the loss of all genuine newspaper independence." For years Grasty referred to that editorial as his declaration of independence.

Evening Sun circulation also fell precipitously in a short time. Grasty had introduced the new paper by forcing it on subscribers to the *Sun*. The price of that paper had been reduced to one cent since 1902. The *Sunday Sun* had been three cents since 1908. Delivered by carrier, both cost nine cents a week. The day before the evening paper appeared, the price of the Sunday paper was dropped to two cents and the *Sun* was raised to two cents. The next day, the combination rate for the two, plus the *Evening Sun,* was ten cents a week, just one cent more for the new paper. But subscribers to the *Sun* were also forced to take the new paper. Grasty thought this was an astute move to start the new paper with the same home delivery circulation as the established morning paper. But many subscribers to the *Sun* were used to taking the *News* in the evening. They objected so strongly to Grasty's high-handed selling that a month after the *Evening Sun* appeared Grasty was forced to make the evening paper optional. Circulation plunged in contrast to the first day's press run of 71,420; daily sales for the first year averaged only 29,028. To make the distribution of carrier bundles as economical as possible, the company supplemented its own vehicles and the throw-off service of streetcars by hiring horse-drawn wagons. One sent from a livery stable was an ancient, dilapidated hearse. When circulation supervisors spotted it backed up to the *Sun* office, they thought subscribers might take it as an omen of impending last rites and ordered it out of service.

As a promotion stunt, Grasty had Hubert Latham, a French aviator called "the greatest in the world," fly over Baltimore in the first airplane ever to do so. Flights over cities were unusual then, owing to the dearth of emergency-landing space. Citizens called Latham's flight-plan suicidal, but on November 7, 1910, he went ahead with it during an aviation meet at a farmer's field in Halethorpe. As Latham flew over Baltimore in his fifty-horsepower machine named *Antoinette,* the whole town turned out. The musicians' union had asked that the flight take place before 1:00 P.M. so members who played at matinees could watch. Students were let out of class. The *Sun* had offered Latham $5,000. Ross R. Winans, a bedridden wealthy Baltimorean, paid Latham an additional $500 to fly past his window. The *Sun* and the *Evening Sun* stationed reporters at ten locations, including the dome of City Hall and Winans's mansion, at 1217 St. Paul Street, to report reaction. The flight was the talk of Baltimore for days.

On May 10, 1911, the *Evening Sun* invited Baltimoreans to become acquainted with East Baltimore in what it called "Broadway Visiting Day." The crowds were so great that the street railway had to switch its cars off South Broadway. The paper tried to duplicate that success by promoting West Baltimore Visiting Day at the end of May, but it rained and the crowd was slim.

Strickland Gillilan's column was dropped in October 1910, and he was succeeded by Henry Edward Warner, whose column "Sidelights" continued until April 1913. In addition to his editorial duties, Warner also arranged tours of the *Sun* building for schoolchildren. At Mencken's suggestion, Professor Alexander Geddes was engaged to write a daily poem "as a bit of comedy for the magazine page at an honorarium of $1 a poem," but one day when Mencken was away, the editors dropped the feature.

After signing his first pieces "M," Mencken began using his full initials as a signature. He wrote on a range of topics—whiskers, Indians, psychotherapy, a Negro state—but mainly about books and authors: *Huckleberry Finn,* Mark Twain, Joseph Conrad, and the death of the Norwegian poet and novelist Bjornstjerne Bjornson.

Meanwhile, Harry C. Black had returned after working in the London office of the Fidelity & Deposit Company of Maryland and in February 1911 became a member of the A. S. Abell Company board. While in London he read the *John Bull* columnist Horatio Bottomley, and he told Grasty that such a column would help set the tone of the new paper. Grasty agreed, and Black said he knew just the man for the job, the one who signed his pieces "H.L.M." Grasty's instructions to Mencken for the column were "Write about anything you please, anything at all," adding, "as long as it remains irresponsible and readable." The column, titled "The Free Lance," began March 8, 1911. William Manchester, Mencken's biographer, wrote in *Disturber of the Peace*:

> He opposed everything respectable, mocked everything sacred, inveighed against everything popular opinion supported. He defended prostitution, vivisection, Sun-

day sports, alcohol and war. He attacked democracy, Christian Science, osteopathy, the direct primary, the single tax, and every civic improvement boosted by the city fathers. He openly advocated armed resistance against the prohibitionists, the supporters of the Blue Laws. . . . His aim was "to combat, chiefly by ridicule, American piety, stupidity, tin-pot morality, cheap chauvinism in all their forms"; his chief target was the civic leader or, as he preferred to call him, the Honorary Pallbearer. . . . The Honorary Pallbearers were organized into a baseball team and their achievements recorded in box score form, with hits scored for support of the Anti-Saloon League, Lord's Day Alliance, Society to Protect Children, Board of United Railways, the Reform League, Drip-Coffee Chautauqua, S.P.C.A., Goucher College Board, Penitentiary Board, and Society for the Suppression of Vice. Each player's batting average was listed daily.

Some subscribers enjoyed Mencken's savage sarcasm, but others took him literally and were outraged, and many wrote to complain and rebut. Their letters were gleefully printed in a column entitled "Editorials by the People." But Grasty, Manchester wrote, became nervous at "the floodtide of indignation." Some of Mencken's most telling paragraphs were killed. Grasty told Mencken not to attack the Christian church, but when Baltimore clergymen joined the boosters and politicians in censuring Mencken, Grasty reversed himself. When the war broke out in Europe, Mencken was outspokenly pro-German; in Manchester's words, he was "an arrogant and offensive spokesman at that." Ultimately, subscribers—and the *Sunpapers*—would no longer put up with it. The Free Lance column was halted abruptly on October 23, 1915, but then for more than a year Mencken contributed pieces to the editorial page, sometimes ridiculing America's preparation for war, "the professional Anglo-Saxons," and proclaiming himself a "volunteer attorney for *kultur*." At the *Sun*'s urging in late 1916 he went to Germany as a war correspondent. In its promotion ads the *Sun* pointed out, "Mencken is not neutral—He is pro-German," and implied this would help him get the inside story. In his first dispatch, which the *Sun* termed a "letter," he said the Germans were united in their "fight for freedom." He wrote some twelve pieces and left Germany when the United States broke off diplomatic relations in March 1917.

Before the war monopolized page one, there was the day (April 15, 1912) when the White Star liner *Titanic* crashed into an iceberg in the North Atlantic on its maiden voyage. The *Evening Sun,* relying on wire-service reports, was wrong. Although 1,517 of the 2,000 passengers drowned, the *Evening Sun*'s banner headline was "All Titanic Passengers Are Safe." In the 1970s the paper reproduced a series of famous-event front pages, including the page with the wrong headline.

To reduce expenses and cut losses, in the spring of 1912 Grasty made Adams editor of both the *Sun* and the *Evening Sun,* and Frank R. Kent, managing editor of the *Sun,* also the managing editor of the evening paper. The evening staff, never large, shrank to an overworked few. On May 1, editorials, down to one a day, were moved to the back page, occasionally to page one. The editorial page was filled with articles contributed by local personages and editorials from other papers. That page, and the paper itself, was dull. In November, editorials—short and lifeless—were returned to the editorial page. The *Evening Sun* was no match for the sprightly *News* in appearance, coverage, or content. The *News* had the valuable Associated Press franchise, then limited to one Baltimore afternoon paper; the *Evening Sun* had to be content with the inferior United Press service (it did not get AP until 1928, then only after a long fight). Grasty became disenchanted with his dream for a dynamic new paper when it did not achieve instant success. He lost interest in it and turned his efforts to the established morning paper.

In May 1914 the stockholders met to discuss the deteriorating situation. Some wanted to turn the property back to the Abells under the mortgage covering the $1 million bond issue. They also talked about asking for the appointment of receivers. Then Edwin G. Baetjer, their senior counsel, suggested that Grasty's role be restricted to editorial director and that a stockholder assume charge of the business operation. An obvious choice was H. Crawford Black, the largest stockholder and an experienced businessman. But he was 69 years old and disinclined to assume so challenging a task. He asked his son, Van-Lear, then 39 and a successful financier. The younger Black instantly agreed.

Under the terms arranged when he came to the paper, Grasty could not be removed without his consent. The beset stockholders, however, could cut off the supply of money, and that they did. On June 30, 1914, Grasty was asked to give up control of the business side and be replaced by Van-Lear Black. His options limited, Grasty made the best of the situation and agreed. The bylaws were changed to restrict his power to spend money without consent of the board. The special rights of Class C stock, his alone, were abolished. All three classes of stock now had the same rights, with one vote for each share.

A new board was elected. It consisted of Van-Lear Black, Harry C. Black, Robert Garrett, R. Brent Keyser, John J. Nelligan, James C. Fenhagen (a banker and also a partner in Robert Garrett & Sons), and Grasty. For the first time no Abells were on the board. Charles S. Abell had resigned in 1911, and Arunah S. Abell 2d, who had also been secretary and treasurer, was ill. He died at the age of 49 on July 28, 1914. The eldest son of Edwin F. Abell, he had been associated with the *Sun* since 1892.

In addition to retaining his autonomy as editor, Grasty was still president of the company. But obviously disillusioned, if not offended, Grasty sailed for Europe as soon as the agreement was signed. With the outbreak of war in Europe, he was not able to return until late summer. For a week or so he resumed his editorial duties, but then he asked to be relieved of his responsibilities. The next day, September 12, a four-sentence notice appeared on the *Sun*'s back page under this headline:

MR. GRASTY RETIRES FROM
THE MANAGEMENT OF SUN

It announced: "Charles H. Grasty, who for four and a half years has been president and general manager of The A. S. Abell Company, has withdrawn from active connection with the *Sun*. Mr. Grasty retains his stock in the Abell Company and will continue to be a member of the board of directors." Then it listed the other board members and their chairman, Van-Lear Black.

On November 30, Grasty resigned as a director. He was succeeded by Charles McHenry Howard, of the law firm of Venable, Baetjer & Howard, counsel to the A. S. Abell Company. Grasty held his stock until September 29, 1919, when he sold it to the Blacks, Keyser, and Walter W. Abell.

Meanwhile, Grasty had gone back to reporting, having found a job as war correspondent for the *Kansas City Star* and the Associated Press. But in 1916 he underwent one more career change, returning from overseas to become treasurer of the *New York Times*. An interval of desk work was sufficient to revive the old restlessness. Back to Europe he went, as a roving correspondent for the *Times*. As the *Times* later remarked, he had "a remarkable facility in making friends who trusted him." He became friendly with and won the confidence of General John J. Pershing, leader of the American Expeditionary Force, David Lloyd George, Great Britain's wartime prime minister, Marshals Joseph Joffre and Ferdinand Foch of the French army, Take Jonescu, war premier of Rumania, and King Constantine of Greece, getting interviews with them all. Foch, who had given no interviews, talked to Grasty. The *Times* published Grasty's beat and then distributed it worldwide. Many of these dispatches were also printed in the *Sun*. During the years of Wilson's presidency, Grasty remained a friend and confidant. While Grasty was still at the *Sun*, an acquaintance remembered, he telephoned Wilson at the White House as often and as casually as a *Sun* reporter would call the mayor of Baltimore. While representing the *Times* at the Versailles peace conference, Grasty was taken ill. When Wilson heard this he had Grasty moved to his presidential quarters until he recovered. After the war, Grasty settled in London. When he became seriously ill with hardening of the arteries, Raymond S. Tompkins, a *Sun* correspondent then in London, was asked for a report on his condition. Tompkins cabled that the physician said Grasty could not recover. Nonetheless, Grasty was still reading the British newspapers, which accordingly did not publish news of his condition.

Charles Henry Grasty died on January 19, 1924, at the age of 60. The obituaries described him as "the best informed American journalist in Europe, and none had a higher standing and reputation." Fabian Franklin, a former Johns Hopkins professor who had worked with him as an editor for thirteen years, termed him "the ablest all-around newspaperman in America." The *Sunpaper* obituaries and comments were long and laudatory. The *Sun* editorial included this tribute: "His monument belongs in Baltimore, not in New York or in London, where he served the *Times* so long. He left an indelible mark upon journalism here, and he left a no less indelible mark upon municipal history. He changed our newspapers and he changed our politics, and both changes were for the better."

TEN

—————•—————

Van-Lear Black Takes Charge
1914–1919

When Charles H. Grasty abruptly re-
signed as president and editorial director in September 1914, Van-Lear Black
and his board were dumbfounded. They were financiers-businessmen, with
no aptitude or experience with regard to the news and editorial side of a
newspaper. Unwilling to take time to search for a dynamic new editor—and
beset with burgeoning pressures to limit expenditures and increase revenues—
they opted to function temporarily without a president and editor-in-chief.
Grasty's cost-paring but unwieldy system of double executive workloads was
continued: John H. Adams remained as editor of both morning and evening
papers, writing editorials for both, and Frank R. Kent remained managing
editor of two lean, overworked staffs.

As chairman of the board, Black had the responsibility of saving the papers.
His experience was limited, and this was the first time he assumed command.
After private schooling in Baltimore and nearly four years at the Belmont
School in Boston, Black had begun his career in 1895 as a clerk in the family's
Fidelity Trust & Deposit Company, later serving as a teller in the banking
department. In 1900 he was elected assistant secretary and treasurer, but after
a few months he resigned to become secretary and treasurer of the Black,
Sheridan, Wilson Company, coal operators, of which firm his father was
president. In 1902 he became a director of the Fidelity Trust & Deposit
Company. When the banking business was separated from the bonding company and organized as the Fidelity Trust Company, he was elected a vice
president. While in that capacity, Black became chairman of the board of the
A. S. Abell Company.

His son Gary long afterward recalled a story that William F. Schmick, Sr.,
used to tell: "This handsome young man [Van-Lear Black], wearing a derby,
walked around the *Sun* plant for a day or two and then introduced himself
to [Paul] Patterson, the business manager, and Schmick, the advertising man-

ager, saying, 'I was sent here by my father to straighten things out. You have one year to show a black line on the ledger.' " And they did, though Gary Black said it was less than $20.

Van-Lear Black was handsome, athletic, and gregarious, but also "soft-spoken and full of quiet humor" and altogether the opposite of the public's image of Wall Street financiers. To the end of his life, friends and colleagues referred to his boyishness. He would leave board meetings, even climactic ones, at the sound of a fire engine. Circuses were still more compelling; he befriended circus performers, flavored his speech with circus jargon, and engaged circus acts to entertain guests at his estate, Folly Quarter, in Howard County. After buying a one-ring circus, Black invited *Sun* staff members to join him on a two-week tour throughout Maryland.

Although his title was chairman of the board, Black in effect was also general manager. He was confronted with two crucial situations. First, po-litically and economically the time was bad for rejuvenation; fighting was growing fiercer in the Great War in Europe, and the United States faced uncertainties because of that war. Second, but more immediate, Baltimore's business community was buzzing about the Abell Company. In June, when Grasty lost control of the business operations, rumors flew that the company was bankrupt and might suspend publication. Competing papers whispered to advertisers that the *Evening Sun* was to be dropped, that the *Sun* was to be sold to the *Chicago Tribune* or the *Philadelphia Ledger.* Munsey's *Evening News* printed a cartoon showing the *Sun*'s owners pouring money down a rat hole. Confronted with all this, potential advertisers hesitated to give their business to the *Sunpapers.* On August 3, 1914, the Abell board met and asked its counsel, Edwin G. Baetjer, to take whatever legal action was necessary against the calumnies.

Black would not wait for the projected workings of the law. His mind turned to ways of making a sudden, favorable impression. Black had seen the hit Broadway comedy *It Pays to Advertise,* and he sent John E. Cullen, then in the business office, to talk to the producers about bringing the show to Baltimore and putting on a special performance for advertisers. The producers thought the costs would be prohibitive, with innumerable complications, but after much cajoling they agreed to do it "as a lark." After the October 12 evening performance in New York, the cast of twelve, the support crew, the producers, and others involved, along with drama critics from six New York papers (the stunt attracted considerable attention in New York) came to Bal-timore in two sleepers, arriving at 6:00 A.M. After breakfast at the Belvedere Hotel, the cast put on its show at the Academy of Music on Howard Street at 10:00 A.M. to a packed house of invited advertisers, potential advertisers, and their employees. They not only saw a Broadway hit, free, but they were exposed to the show's theme: it pays to advertise. And the audience must have realized that no company on the verge of going out of business would have gone to such trouble and expense. Immediately afterward the troupe took a train back to New York, arriving in time for its regular evening performance. The next day the *Sun* had a long story about its rousing promotion and a four-column cartoon showing a baseball player labeled "Newspaper Advertiser" at home plate, marked "Business Success," tagging out a man sliding home identified as "Old Fogy." The umpire, designated "The Public," shouted "You're Out!" Gossip around town was that the tour de force had cost the *Sun* between $10,000 and $12,000. The appropriation by the board was $2,500.

Other, less spectacular promotions followed, drawing attention to the papers and, more important, letting everyone know that the *Sunpapers* were alive and robust, not expiring or even enfeebled. At the same time, Black was indefatigable in calling on advertisers, current and potential, and cutting operating costs. He told Patterson and Schmick, "An endowed newspaper cannot be made to succeed. We shall never get anywhere until the public, and particularly the advertisers, understand the *Sunpapers* are standing on their own feet." For a year or more, Black's salesmen labored under a contractual disadvantage imposed by Grasty in 1910. To encourage advertising in his new *Evening Sun,* he offered space in both papers for only two cents a line more than it cost in the *Sun.* When that did not attract the volume he anticipated, he desperately cut the rate difference to one cent. Some advertisers, including a department store, jumped at that bargain and signed up for five years. The contract proved even better than they expected because circulation was increasing. Grasty's enticing rate cost the company dearly in that fifth contract year, because it could not impose the rate raises justified by greater circulation.

In November 1914 the circulation department was reorganized and vitalized. In 1914, Grasty's last year, the *Sun* had a net average daily sale of 91,652 copies. In 1915 this rose to 94,715, and in 1916 to 102,404. The *Evening Sun's* net average daily sale, 42,978 in 1914, was up to 50,543 in 1915 and to 60,805 in 1916. The *Sunday Sun's* circulation for 1914 was 81,999, 87,932 in 1915, and 96,212 in 1916.

From May 19, 1910, when the *Sun* returned to one cent a copy, the three papers were delivered by carrier in combination for ten cents a week—promoted as "Thirteen for Ten." On January 29, 1917, the rate was increased to thirteen cents a week—"Thirteen for Thirteen"—or two weeks for a quarter. Then came wartime inflation, and three combination-rate increases in 1918: Fifteen cents a week on January 1, twenty cents a week on June 10, and twenty-five cents on September 1. On February 4, 1917, the *Sunday Sun* was raised from three cents to five cents.

That same month a subscriber in Pittsfield, Massachusetts, wrote the paper, "Send me the *Sunpaper* forever." He enclosed a signed check with the amount line left blank, to be filled in by the subscription department. The *Sun* featured the letter in a promotion ad, commenting that it was the longest subscription order ever received, but would be difficult to fill because "The *Sun's* distribution does not extend beyond this planet." It added, "Here is a subscriber who will expire before his subscription does."

The increased circulation, together with imaginative promotion and vigorous salesmanship, produced more and more advertising, from both old and new advertisers.

In the fall of 1914, though money was still tight, Black realized it was necessary to enlarge the Charles Street plant, built eight years earlier to accommodate one newspaper but now producing two papers and a large Sunday paper. The five presses were replaced with three large decuples. While the new ones were installed, the old presses had to be kept operating, and this created logistical problems for months. To recapture space, the steam engines and generators that produced the plant's electricity were removed and replaced by public power.

This brouhaha took place in a news room that was ever more preoccupied with the expanding war in Europe. The manager of the new Hippodrome Theater complained that his vaudeville acts did not get the same attention other theaters did. Editors ignored his grumbling, believing that the Hippodrome offered second-class shows. The custom was for a police reporter to stop by at the Hippodrome on Monday, pick up a new show's program, and write a few lines from it for Tuesday's paper, but the theater manager thought the reporter should instead view the show and write an extended review of his dancers, comedians, and jugglers. To expose this negligence, the manager included in the program an act not on the bill, so that when the reporter wrote his paragraph from the program it would prove he did not get his information first-hand, as *Sun* reporters had a reputation for doing. After the short appeared with the bogus listing, the manager confronted Frank R. Kent, the managing editor. Kent told him his cheap show was not worth the time of a *Sun* reporter, and added that the *Sun* would print no further Hippodrome notices, wanting nothing more to do with its tricky manager. The theater owners were distraught and offered to fire the manager if the *Sun* would relent. The matter was resolved through the conciliatory efforts of Schmick. The manager apologized, kept his job, and the reporter continued to use the program for the paragraph he wrote.

The United States declared war on Germany on April 6, 1917, and when Maryland men went to camp the *Sun* had reporters cover the training. Vincent de P. Fitzpatrick was assigned to Camp George G. Meade near Baltimore, and J. M. Daiger wrote a series on the Maryland naval reservists at Norfolk. The Maryland National Guard, subsequently organized as part of the Twenty-ninth Division, was sent to Camp McClellan, a raw camp hurriedly built on sandy cottonfields surrounded by the hills of northeastern Alabama. Raymond S. Tompkins, a 27-year-old reporter who had joined the paper in 1915, covered its odyssey and the fighting in Europe until the men returned home in May 1919.

Tompkins wrote with warmth, compassion, and style. His dispatches were carried in both the *Sun* and the *Evening Sun* and were copyrighted by the A. S. Abell Company, probably the first time that had been done. In his three-column story about the first two men in the Twenty-ninth Division to be awarded the Distinguished Service Cross, the *Sun* prefaced it with "This is one of the finest of the stories that have come from Mr. Tompkins." He told how Sergeant John H. E. Hoppe of Baltimore and Private First Class Andy Youngbar of Fairfield had repulsed a German raiding party. During the action, Hoppe lost part of his hand and was shot in the foot; Youngbar suffered thirty-two wounds from an exploding German grenade. Tompkins pictured their battalion drawn up on long company front lines in a meadow for the presentation, the two heroes arriving in the general's limousine, which had fresh pink flowers in the vase decorating the passenger compartment. The judge advocate, a Baltimore lawyer, read the account of their exploits in a tone "that had swayed juries successfully and mayoralty campaigns not so successfully." The only spectators were two girls from the Y.M.C.A. who had entertained the night before at regimental headquarters with songs and a harp—"they were pretty girls, real American girls, and until Hoppe and Youngbar arrived, the greatest curiosities in the sector." When the awards were made, Tompkins wrote, "it was the first time I ever saw tears start in the eyes of an American Army division commander." Later, with the Twenty-ninth Division at Mountfaucon, Tompkins's story began:

> Those Germans, who were lucky enough to get away from the Baltimore wrecking crew that stormed the heights of Montfaucon, were led back to prison pens by wounded Marylanders. Surgeons put their bullet-torn arms in slings or bandaged their wounded legs, and our heroes became commanding officers of platoons of captives.
>
> From a captain in a Baltimore company, who saw the thing, I heard how one wounded private in the Baltimore regiment rode back to the hospital on a stretcher borne by four Germans, two of them officers. The private lay smoking a cigarette and bawling out the officers, and the officers bawled out the German privates.

In addition to the wire-service budgets, the *Sun* and the *Evening Sun* reprinted *New York Times* articles, including the dispatches of its former reporter, Edwin L. James, the chief correspondent of the *Times* with the American army, and Walter Duranty, a rising star as a foreign correspondent, along with the analysis of foreign military experts and such British writers as Hilaire Belloc.

Black was one of the driving forces—perhaps the dominant force—of the Liberty Loan campaigns in Maryland, though his position was merely that of chairman of the publicity committee. Because the first loan was hastily organized and its machinery creaked, the *Sun* opened a Liberty Bond bureau in its business office and detached a force of clerks from their regular duties to sell bonds. A loan information desk was set up to answer questions about the loans. The first bonds were not available when the campaign opened, so Black had certificates of purchase engraved, and the *Sunpapers* paid interest on all purchases made through the *Sun* bureau between purchase and when the bonds themselves began to draw interest.

During the loan campaigns the *Sunpapers* were veritable promotional papers for selling bonds. Most days, the papers carried overlines above the front-page logotype—"Germany Will Surrender Only If You Do Your Duty—Buy Bonds!," "Buy Your Bond Today And Help Seal Prussia's Doom!" The back page sometimes had three or four articles about the campaign—details of sales, promotional boxes, and lists of those who bought bonds. The articles were not news accounts but promotional pieces: "Don't be afraid of overworking the *Sun*'s bond bureau. It can't be done!" Four days after Tompkins's piece on Hoppe and Youngbar appeared, Black ordered a full-page advertisement on their heroics and urged the people of Maryland to show their pride in the two doughboys by buying bonds.

In the spring of 1918 the *Sunpapers* presented an "Over There" exposition at the Fifth Regiment Armory for four weeks to stimulate the sale of the Third Liberty Loan Bonds and of War Saving Stamps and to increase interest in war activities. More than 300,000 people attended and inspected the imitation trenches and other war exhibits constructed to give those at home an idea of conditions at the front. By May 1919 this sustained patriotic effort had brought about the purchase of $4,190,750 worth of bonds, sold over the *Sun*'s counter to 28,499 persons. The *Sunpapers* also sold $254,933 in Thrift and War Saving Stamps to 3,000 adults and children. After a bank near Camp Meade failed in February 1918, the *Sunpapers* proposed to their readers that a guarantee fund of $40,000 be raised to meet the claims of the soldier depositors, many of whom were about to leave for France and wanted their money right away. Nearly $80,000 was contributed, including $10,000 from the *Sunpapers*. The bank examiner supplied the names of soldier depositors to the *Sunpapers*, and each soldier received the money due him. When the bank was reorganized, all claims were paid and contributors to the *Sunpapers'* fund were refunded their money.

A catastrophic home-front event in the fall of 1918 was the influenza epidemic. Several thousand Baltimoreans died of flu, as did many people in the armed forces at nearby camps and bases. So many were flu victims that Baltimore schools and colleges were closed in October, along with theaters and the Laurel race track; stores and saloons were open only from 9:30 A.M. to 4:30 P.M. The *Sun* often ran nearly a page of obituary notices. To help bury the dead, the city had to appeal to the military at Camp Meade for 500 coffins, and Mayor James H. Preston appealed to Baltimoreans not to have elaborate funerals.

From April 18 to December 11, 1918, the *Sunpapers* published an overseas edition of the *Sun,* known affectionately as the *"Baby Sunpaper."* This was an eight-page paper, one-quarter the size of the regular paper, containing local news in brief and sent by first-class mail each week to 8,000 Maryland soldiers and sailors in camps and hospitals abroad and in the United States. It was edited by Gustafus Warfield Hobbs, the Sunday editor, and those who received it called it "a weekly letter from home."

The *Evening Sun* of November 7 and the *Sun* of November 8 printed premature reports of an armistice-signing, as did other papers across the nation. Their source was a United Press dispatch based on erroneous information from the commander of American naval forces in French waters. On November 9 the *Sun* apologized editorially: "To any habitual reader of this paper it is needless to say that the *Sun* regrets, more than profoundly, that it should have been the instrument for the circulation of an untrue statement." When the end of the war was officially announced on November 11, some faithful readers still thought the first report was true; they believed the *Sunpaper* enterprise had simply received the news before it was officially announced.

On the night of November 11, Black had Ernestine Schumann-Heink, a grand opera diva who had sons fighting on both sides in the war, rushed from New York to sing the "Star-Spangled Banner" and other songs in *Sun* Square. When she arrived, she wanted to know who her accompanist would be and the make of the piano. The *Sunpapers* had arranged for a band, but not a piano or accompanist. Schumann-Heink refused to sing without either. Patterson telephoned the manager of the Knabe Piano Company, who made a piano available, and a circulation truck took it to *Sun* Square about the same time an out-of-breath accompanist arrived, just before the program began. All was well—except that, after two songs, the crowd that packed *Sun* Square became so boisterous that Schumann-Heink gave up. The entertainment was brought to an abrupt end with the words "Good Night!" flashed on the *Sun* screen.

When Maryland troops returned from Europe in May 1919, the contingents were met at Newport News, Virginia, by *Sunpaper* members who established a *Sun* bureau at Camp Stuart, the debarkation point. Black arranged that the soldiers' first meal ashore would be in the "Maryland Home Kitchen" where they dined on Maryland fried chicken, soft crabs, crab flakes, asparagus, fresh strawberries, and pastries. The cost of feeding some 7,000 men was $40,000. Gertrude Leimbach, one of the women reporters hired during the war, was among the reporters assigned to interview the returning men. One day she had three byline stories from Camp Stuart.

When Brigadier General Nicholson, whose command had included Baltimore's 313th Infantry Regiment, arrived in New York, a *Sun* correspondent was sent to ask him how the Baltimoreans, whom he had trained at Camp Meade, had fought. He replied, "I wish I could meet every mother and father in Baltimore who had a son in France and tell them how their sons covered themselves with glory." After reading that, Black invited the general to Baltimore. Nicholson accepted, and Black rented the Lyric Theatre, so those parents could hear the general praise their sons.

In June, Black gave a dinner for *Sun* men who had served in the war. (Two had been killed in action and one died from the flu at Fort McHenry.) The evening concluded with Black pinning a medal on each serviceman. The medal, suitably inscribed, was made of zinc from the engraving room.

Amid the euphoria of victory and the approach of armistice, the *Sunpapers* were concerned with the censoring of dispatches from Europe. Kent, detached from his managing editor's duties, went abroad in late October with other American editors as guests of the British War Mission to America. As soon as he got back he wrote a series of page-one articles. He led off on November 28 with a bombshell five columns long under the headline "Paris Seethes with International Jealousy and Suspicion." An editor's note said: "This article is the first uncensored account of actual conditions in Paris to be printed in this country or abroad. The writer was in Paris at the time the terms of the Armistice were determined upon, and returned to this country on the first ship that left England after it had been signed. It was not possible to have gotten this article by either mail or cable."

A storm of acrimony and disbelief followed because other U.S. newspapers had been portraying the Allies as working together and the United States as beloved by all. Kent's revelation was an international coup. He wrote, in part:

> For weeks past, under the surface, Paris has been simply seething with international jealousies, friction and feeling, and between us and our noble allies at this time there is a tension and a strain that does not appear on the top, but that is very real none the less. . . . The truth is, and everybody in Paris knows it, that in governmental and political circles they do not love us at all over there, neither the English nor the French. . . .
>
> As to the French, there is believed to be a disposition on their part to reach out for more territory than is exactly just. There is talk of extending France to the Rhine and to the Alps—God's boundary lines, as they call them there—and to look to the acquisition of certain German colonial possessions. . . . We are expected to sit still, look pleasant, and agree to this programme like a good nation. Some of our representatives over there say emphatically they'll be damned if we do.
>
> You hear, too, in Paris, what will be news in America, of the serious mutiny in the French Army in 1917, and of the difficulty in suppressing it. In this direction the advent of America into the war seems to have saved the situation. Neither England nor France have any use for Italy. They tell you that the Italian troops were a bitter disappointment, that they fight all right when things are going their way, but they cannot be depended upon when they are not, and have to be stiffened by support whenever a real fight is due. And that they were eternally demanding men and money and refusing to carry on unless they got them.

Today such a piece, offering not one named source, would if printed on page one perhaps carry the qualifying label "Analysis."

Two days after the publication of this first installment of a three-week series, Black gave a lavish dinner for Kent and his co-workers at the Rennert Hotel. Kent's twenty-one articles were reprinted in a deluxe brochure of seventy-five pages entitled "A Little Souvenir of That Remarkable Trip." Later, in a memo on copy paper summarizing this career, Kent wrote this about his exposé:

We went to both the French and British fronts, but could not get up to the American fronts where the real fighting was being done. Later in Paris, from Blythe, Grasty, Martin Eagan and others, I got the story they all wanted to write but couldn't. I came back on the first unconvoyed boat—after the Armistice—and my story, printed in the *Sun* on Thanksgiving, was the first uncensored story from the other side in four years. It was reprinted in the *Times* and other papers the next day. It did raise hell. I thought for a while it would destroy me. Some of the stuff I wrote was of an incident that had taken place between Pershing and Foch. Nearly every newspaper denounced me and there was a demand on Pershing to deny it. But the Old Boy wouldn't do it. The denunciation lasted a week, but in about three weeks the facts began to substantiate the story. What really made it sensational was because it came on the eve of Wilson's leaving for the Peace Conference. . . . I took an awful lacing. Van Black stood by me in a way I never forgot—and so did Adams. Otto Kahn, Rabbi Wise and others flooded Black with telegrams demanding my life. And a Portuguese lieutenant named Gonzales announced in New York he was taking the next train to Baltimore to shoot me on sight. Stephen Lausanne, Pertinax and others roasted me. The British grieved.

In November, Marguerite Harrison, 38, newly widowed and impecunious, approached her old friend Black to ask for a job on the *Sun*. She came from a prominent Baltimore family; her father, Bernard N. Baker, had owned the Atlantic Transport Line, which developed into the United States Lines. And she was well connected: Albert Ritchie, soon to be governor of Maryland, had married her sister. Mrs. Harrison, visiting England, sat in the royal enclosure at Ascot.

Because Mrs. Harrison had no professional writing experience—she didn't even know how to type—Kent had her write society items for the *Sun*. (One of the first things she noticed was that reporters wrote on yellow copy paper, evidently the same type of special paper reporters used back in the days of the *Sun* Iron Building.) She was inquisitive, smart, a good reporter—and she could write. After a stint as reviewer of concerts and plays, she was assigned to the war effort. During the winter of 1917–18 she worked for a few days as an unskilled laborer at Bethlehem Steel's Sparrows Point shipyards and as a streetcar conductor, writing about her experiences. Her salary was increased to $28 a week.

But, she wrote later in her autobiography, *There's Always Tomorrow*, she became restless, and in the summer of 1918 wanted to find out what was going on in Germany. She recounted, "There was only one way to do this—by entering the Intelligence Service. I was willing to become a spy." A relative was a friend of General Marlborough Churchill, chief of the U.S. Military Intelligence Department, and after a casual interview with one of his staff in a Baltimore hotel lobby she was engaged to go to Germany to collect social and economic data. She would receive a captain's pay and expenses. "Mr.

Kent," she wrote, "was in sympathy with our scheme and suggested that the *Sun* might send me to France on a special assignment." The *Sunpapers* had just finished a 15,000-foot motion picture on fifteen reels for showing to Maryland soldiers waiting to come back from overseas. The movie, titled *Miles of Smiles,* had been filmed in Baltimore and in the principal towns of Maryland; the movie-making was promoted in advance, and the day pictures were to be taken mothers, wives, sweethearts, as well as fathers, brothers, and in-laws, paraded in front of the camera, smiling, waving and carrying pets and signs with personal messages.

Mrs. Harrison took the movie and equipment abroad and exhibited *Miles of Smiles* in division areas with large units of Maryland men. It was not an easy assignment. Sometimes the movie was shown in the open in heavy rain with the men standing ankle-deep in mud. At Seugneulles, where the 313th Infantry was based, electricity was not available and the batteries of the projection machine failed. To operate it, soldiers harnessed it to the motor of a German plane that had been shot down. But the voltage was too high, and the operator had to stop the projector every few minutes to allow hot wires to cool.

As soon as that *Sun* mission was completed, Mrs. Harrison hurried on to Berlin to report on Germany's postwar internal affairs for Military Intelligence—the status of morale, and whether pacifist and revolutionary activities were weakening the army and the government. In her autobiography she said she smiled when she compared her life to that of the beautiful spies of fiction and the movies who stole secret documents from drunken diplomats after champagne suppers, but she did write that she sat in one apartment in some jeopardy to gather information, "night after night, emptying my wine into a jardiniere behind me." Along with intelligence data, sent by courier to Paris, she wrote "stories for my paper." "They had to be entertaining, they had to be informative, and I had to edit them carefully to avoid revealing anything which it was unadvisable at the moment to make public."

In September 1919, Mrs. Harrison was back at the *Sun,* again doing reviews and interviews. But she soon became restless, and she told General Churchill she wanted to go to Russia as a newspaper correspondent and at the same time work for Military Intelligence. She spoke German, French, and Italian fluently. She mastered Russian and a smattering of Polish, later Turkish, Persian, Japanese, and Arabic. She said a gift of tongues was her only outstanding talent. Churchill agreed to her request. Marguerite Harrison was taken off the *Sun* payroll on October 12, 1919, but Kent gave her press credentials, and she arranged to write for the *New York Evening Post* and also became a temporary correspondent of the Associated Press. The Bolsheviks had learned of her work as an American agent and refused her permission to enter Russia. She spent six weeks in Poland and then, crossing the border illegally, made her way to Moscow by sleigh. The War Department had wanted her to stay only six weeks, but her visit stretched to more than a year. More curious and more aggressive than ever, she had a rare opportunity to examine most aspects of revolutionary life. Once she managed to walk into the restricted Kremlin, where she chanced upon Leon Trotsky, the Minister of War, whom she interviewed. She filed stories for the Associated Press almost daily. But the Cheka, the Bolshevik commission charged with preventing counterrevolutionary activities, obtained proof of her intelligence work through an informer in Churchill's department. Arrested, Mrs. Harrison was released on the proviso that she furnish the Cheka with weekly reports on the colony of foreigners. She accepted this double-agent role, promising herself to supply only partial or misleading information. The Cheka, sensing some or all of this, then imprisoned her for ten months. In July 1920, Jacob France, U.S. Senator from Maryland, appeared at her prison. He had been asked to go to Russia to secure her release, she later wrote, by "my loyal friend, Van-Lear Black." France had been in Russia for weeks and had interceded with Chicherin, head of the Foreign Office, Litvinov, and Lenin on Mrs. Harrison's behalf without much prospect for success. In the meantime, Herbert Hoover, on behalf of the American Relief Association, offered to send food supplies and personnel to Russia to combat the growing famine, but it was stipulated that all Americans detained in Russia be released. The authorities in Russia accepted Hoover's offer but let Senator France believe they were releasing Mrs. Harrison as a favor to him.

Mark S. Watson, who had recently joined the *Sun* as assistant managing editor, accompanied Senator France on his mission but had to stay in Riga when authorities refused him permission to travel to Moscow. His first story was headlined with two streamers across the front page:

MRS. HARRISON OUT OF RUSSIA
REACHES RIGA WITH SENATOR FRANCE

The Bolsheviks, expelling Harrison on the condition that she never return, called her "a self-confessed spy." The State Department denied she was a secret agent. The *Sun* described her as a *Sun* correspondent, though she was not on its payroll (while in Russia she had sent back stories, which the *Sun* published). She was met in New York by Black and sailed to Baltimore on his yacht *Sabalo*, receiving a heroine's welcome. General Churchill, she wrote, told her she "had given Military Intelligence more information about Russia than any other agent."

Kent ("who worked untiringly to get me out of Russia") asked her to rejoin the staff, and she did, in December 1921, evidently on a part-time basis because personnel records indicated her salary was reduced to $20 a week. She wrote a book, *Marooned in Moscow*, and spent much of the year on the lecture circuit. But again impelled by a restless spirit, and craving more adventure, she arranged with *Cosmopolitan* magazine to write on the Far East and was off to Japan, Korea, Mongolia, and Manchuria, traveling much of the time on her own, and then to Siberia. Why did she violate the expulsion order? She wrote afterward that she naively supposed she would be welcome because of her understanding of Soviet aims. But she was arrested again, jailed, then released and expelled.

Subsequently she made a movie with the Hollywood producer-director Merian C. Cooper, with whom she had danced in Warsaw and whom she had aided when he was a prisoner in Moscow. Called *Grass,* the movie, made in Persia, pictured a nomad tribe, the Bakhtiaris, on their age-old seasonal migration through remote mountain regions. Released in 1925, it ran for four months in New York and attained something of the status of a classic. Mrs. Harrison married Arthur M. Blake and went on to live in France and French Morocco, and finally returned to Baltimore. She died there in 1966 at the age of 88.

One more story should be told about Mrs. Harrison. In 1905 she prevailed upon her father to turn over a vacant farmhouse on the family property near Catonsville, and after she had it refurbished it became the Ingleside Convalescent Home, a summer center for a small group of handicapped children. After three years it moved to larger quarters and became more of a hospital. Mrs. Harrison persuaded doctors and nurses to volunteer their time. Later the hospital moved to Green Spring Avenue in Baltimore and, with Harrison raising funds, was incorporated and enlarged. In 1975 the institution installed a plaque: "In Memory of and to Honor Marguerite Harrison, Founder of Children's Hospital."

Another World War I female staff member was Eleanor Purcell, who joined the *Sun* in 1916 and was Frank R. Kent's secretary. In the early 1920s she began submitting recipes to the paper, and they appeared daily and Sunday as "Aunt Priscilla's Recipes." So explicit were the directions that Miss Purcell must have had inexperienced cooks in mind. The recipes were for Southern cooking and were illustrated with a drawing of a stout, smiling black woman with a bandanna around her head. The writing was an imitation of dialect; for instance, the recipe for broiled reedbirds began, "Pick de birds carefully, den open an' clean 'em washi' 'em out good. Dey should be split down de back instead of on de breast side. Lay 'em between the folds of a clean cloth an' mash de bones flat wid a rollin' pin." In 1929 her wintertime recipes were published in a book titled *Aunt Priscilla in the Kitchen.* With the success of the Aunt Priscilla feature, Miss Purcell began writing an "Aunt Ada" column for the *Evening Sun,* "giving advice to persons seeking solutions to personal problems." It was illustrated with a little old lady knitting in a comfortable chair. (To honor her, a constant reader named his racehorse "Aunt Ada.")

Throughout, Frank A. Munsey's *Evening News* remained a strong competitor. In 1908, Munsey got the novel idea of bringing out a Sunday afternoon paper. He had Paul Patterson, his young managing editor at the *Washington Times,* develop one on two weeks' notice. Then he started one at the Philadelphia outlet in his chain, and soon afterward the Sunday afternoon Baltimore *News* appeared on December 20, 1908. It was popular and profitable, though no threat to the *Sunday Sun,* and it lasted until William Randolph Hearst acquired Munsey's Baltimore properties in 1923. With the *News* prospering, Munsey, capricious in many decisions, thought that its building, erected by Grasty on the southeast corner of Calvert and Fayette streets, looked like a club and ordered it torn down, though it was only five years old. It was replaced with the nineteen-story Munsey Building, which still bears his name. During construction, Munsey, in New York, was sent samples of the material, down to the smallest tile and fixture; he scrutinized each one. On seeing the new building for the first time in 1910, Munsey pointed to the marble wainscoting in the lobby. Not the same as the sample he had seen, he remarked. The architect insisted it was the identical marble, although the grains in the larger slab might seem slightly different. Munsey told him to rip it out and replace it with the right marble. The architect said he would have no legal action against the contractor. Munsey replied that he wasn't interested in suing, he just wanted the marble he ordered. The bill for the replacement was $96,000.

Munsey kept the spacious ground floor open, hoping to attract a bank, but he could not get any bank interested. "It looks like we aren't going to get a bank," Stuart Olivier, his general manager, told Munsey, "unless we start one ourselves." "All right," Munsey said, "go ahead and start it." The Munsey Trust Company opened in December 1912, with Munsey putting up $500,000, half the capital. He sold the bank in February 1915, and it became the Equitable Trust Company.

On August 28, 1915, Munsey, who bought and sold or killed many newspapers (thereby becoming the most hated man in the newspaper business), sold the *News* to Olivier, who became publisher. Olivier's life included quite enough improbabilities to read like fiction. He was a friend of William C. Durant, a founder of General Motors, and an associate of his in the stock market. With J. S. Cosden, who had worked on the *Sun* in 1905 for $15 a week and was soon fired, Olivier made a fortune in the Oklahoma oil fields. On his 360-acre estate, now the Baltimore Country Club's Five Farms Golf Course, Olivier built a mansion and had a special basement excavated to hold his huge collection of whiskies and the fine wines he collected on European expeditions. During Prohibition the wine cellars of several of his friends were hijacked, so he had two steel towers built near his house, equipped with searchlights and machine guns manned by World War veterans. His place was not disturbed. At some of his lavish parties he entertained as many as several hundred guests. Often, when invited to dinner, he insisted on bringing the wine and the food and doing the cooking himself. In addition to his Baltimore County estate, Olivier had a mansion in Baltimore, a ranch in Montana (he hunted with Hemingway), a cabin in the Canadian wilderness, and a castle in Vienna. He wrote three plays, which were produced.

Olivier operated the *News* less than two years; then Munsey bought it back. Munsey was not through buying. In 1920 he bought the Baltimore *American* and the *Star,* from General Felix Agnus. This is the way George Britt, Munsey's biographer, described the purchase:

Negotiations had been finished off for him by Charles M. Harwood, editor of the Baltimore *Evening News.* Everything was settled. The price was $1,250,000. General Agnus and Harwood together came to New York for the formality of signing the contract, meeting Munsey in his apartment on Sunday morning. The purchaser was dapper and gay, wearing one of his emphatic checked suits, moving about the room with long bounding strides, excited as a youth. The seller, a wily and alert octogenarian, sensed the mood and made it his opportunity. He began talking about the insignificance of the sum agreed upon. He must have $250,000 more. Munsey interrupted hurriedly,

"General, are your papers worth that much money?"

"Why, yes indeed, Mr. Munsey. They're a bargain at that."

"Very well, sir. We'll pay it."

Then he flashed grandly to his employee, "See, Harwood! That's the way we buy a newspaper."

The *American* he kept as a morning edition of his Baltimore *News,* but the *Star* was dropped in its tracks with dispatch. That was the way he bought newspapers.

Olivier stayed as general manager of the *News* until Munsey sold it and the *American* to William Randolph Hearst on April 1, 1923. The price was about $4 million. John E. Cullen, former managing editor of the *Evening Sun,* who had gone over to the Hearst organization in 1922, became publisher of both papers.

Olivier died in January 1973 at the age of 92.

ELEVEN

The Beginning of the Modern Era
1919–1930

The appointment of Paul Patterson as president of the A. S. Abell Company on November 11, 1919, marked the beginning of the modern era of the *Sunpapers* and recognition of the *Sun* as one of the nation's important newspapers.

After functioning without a president since Grasty's abrupt departure in September 1914, Van-Lear and Harry C. Black concluded that it was necessary to reinvigorate the news and editorial departments. They began a discreet search around the nation for a dynamic executive and considered several newspapermen with established reputations, but they finally agreed that the best man available was Patterson, their business manager.

Though not quite 41 (he was born in Jacksonville, Illinois, on November 18, 1878), Paul Patterson was a man of wide experience on both the news and the business sides. After finishing high school, he wanted to try newspapering but, unable to get such a job, went to work for Marshall Field & Company in Chicago, starting as a messenger and rising to salesman in three years. In the summer of 1899 he became a free-lance sports reporter for the *Chicago Tribune*. That fall, the role of campus correspondent for the *Tribune* at the University of Chicago enabled him to study English and history there. The following year, Patterson was offered a job as a reporter on the *Chicago Journal*. In three years, he was its city editor. He then became night city editor of the *Chicago Inter-Ocean* and later city editor of Hearst's *Examiner*. When the *Washington Herald* was started in 1906, Patterson joined its staff as Capitol and White House correspondent, later becoming city editor. He left to join Munsey's *Washington Times* and was successively city editor, managing editor, and general manager. Unable to get along with Munsey, he resigned in 1911.

On the recommendation of Frank A. Noyes, president of the *Washington Star* and also of the Associated Press, Patterson was hired by Grasty in May of that year as managing editor of the year-old Baltimore *Evening Sun*. He succeeded Robert B. Vale, who was made assistant general manager and later business manager. When Vale left in 1913, Patterson again replaced him. In 1914, Patterson was named assistant secretary and treasurer of the company and, after Arunah S. Abell 2d's death in July of that year, became secretary-treasurer.

In September 1919 the Blacks told Patterson that they had selected him as president, two months before he was formally appointed. The advance notice was to give him time to study the potentials of the papers and establish a plan for their growth and influence. Patterson sought the advice of Harry Black and H. L. Mencken. Black had long been fascinated by the editorial and news operation, and he had a philosophic turn of mind. Patterson and Mencken had been friends from the days when they sat at adjoining desks in the *Evening Sun;* Patterson was impressed by Mencken's mastery of newspaper techniques and his perceptive and pungent judgments.

Patterson and Black began meeting at Black's home on Warrenton Road in the evening, joined by Mencken when he was in town. (Mencken and George Jean Nathan were editing the *Smart Set,* and part of Mencken's time was spent in New York.) The thrust of the discussions, and the arguments, was the role and future of the *Sunpapers* and how to attain the lofty goals they envisioned. The three agreed that no one man should dominate the papers in direction and tone as Grasty had done, but that the papers should be molded by a group of editors who "must examine all ideas offered." They met on and off for several months, even after Patterson became president.

One night Harry Black handed them copies of a document entitled "An Editorial Memorandum." Its twenty-three triple-spaced typewritten pages began with a statement that the *Sun* had come to lack character (adding parenthetically, "after July 1914"—when Grasty left). Character was defined as "that which causes the institution noticeably, notably, and nationally to stand out from its fellows. . . . To make the *Sun* a nationally distinctive newspaper and a newspaper of national distinction, just as were the *New York Sun* and the *London Times,* is the goal I have in mind for us to reach. Not to make the *Sun,* mark you, like the old *New York Sun* or *London Times,* but to make it equal to them in degree but not in mind."

Because the *Sun* was "now in good, and probably secure, financial position" and was in "a peculiarly favourable position editorially, both locally and nationally," it could become a paper of national distinction in two ways. First it could gain a national reputation by more diligent, studious, and careful coverage of national news: "No matter how much circulation and influence the *Sun* obtains in Maryland, it will always remain a local newspaper. But if, by presenting the full news of the day earlier than any New York paper can do it, and better than any Washington paper can do it, it can compel every important man in Washington to read it daily, then it will attain to national importance and exert an influence upon national affairs out of all proportion to its size and the nature of its principal circulation." Second:

It must have a consistent and vigorous policy to attain any such influence, and that policy must be free from any suspicion of loyalty to private interest or to rigid formulae. The *Sun* must convince by means of sound information, unquestionable honesty and unshakable common sense. It must be alert to new ideas and hospitable to them. It must be absolutely free. . . . All this at once bars out any steady fidelity to either of the great political parties as such. It may, at times, support the policies of either one of them with all of its resources, but the *Sun* cannot allow itself to be forced to accept policies ready-made, or to vacillate over them as the two great political parties often vacillate. . . .

As a necessary function of its independence it should be free to make its own mistakes. More important still, it should generally resist this tendency to convert the old conflict of ideas into a conflict of mere men, for the governmental theory of the United States rests firmly upon the doctrine that the latter is undesirable and evil, and that theory has been amply borne out by experience. What is needed primarily is a careful and unsentimental separation of genuine national issues from all merely superficial and transient issues. What is needed secondarily is a prompt and vigorous statement of preferences and a support of them that goes beyond eloquence and enthusiasm—a support which is securely grounded upon complete information, absolute independence of judgement and a persistent and intelligent concern for the national welfare. To political parties the national welfare must always be less important than the party welfare and to great popular leaders it must always be less important than their own success. But to a great national newspaper it must be the object of first and sole concern, above and beyond all questions of party personality. To such a newspaper its loyalties are its greatest weaknesses. It must get rid of them in order to acquire something infinitely more valuable and useful and that is its reputation for having special and early information, for presenting it honestly and fairly and for interpreting it with the utmost independence that is humanly possible.

The latter part of the lengthy memorandum dealt with "Fundamental American Ideals" and the independence of the American people. In discussing that, it underscored the role the American people should play in "the new international politics."

The foreign news that comes to the United States is still coloured in the interests of this nation or that. . . . The Associated Press and the United Press still depend quite largely for their European news upon the exchange arrangements with the great European agencies, and all these agencies are controlled by foreign governments. . . . To get fair and accurate news is by no means as difficult an enterprise as they [the press associations] pretend. The Associated Press, in particular, is open to grave criticism, both in the domestic field and in the foreign field. . . . If, as has been argued, its management is worn out and incompetent, then our influence should be used to bring about a change.

(Black was critical of the Associated Press all his life. His favorite expression was "It always tells you everything except what you want to know.")

The memorandum did not suggest that the *Sun* develop its own foreign news sources; it limited its suggestion to a broad "finding news sources of its own." (Two years later Patterson arranged for a number of prominent foreign journalists to write for the *Sun,* a strong and influential beginning for the later development of the *Sun*'s foreign bureaus.)

In summing up, the memorandum declared that a newspaper cannot hope to establish the issue of fairness, justice, and freedom by mere argument and expostulation. That issue "must be put in dramatic form."

> It [the first-rank newspaper] must show the people what is going on and not infrequently what is going on is going on in secret. It must devote itself to news gathering in new fields and against new difficulties. It must oppose to the last drop of its ink every effort to colour the news. It must see clearly that the evil of injustice lies not in the importance of the victim, but lies in the lethargy of the spectators— that when a Mooney case passes without indignant challenge the damage to all that is essentially American, to all justice and honesty and fair dealing among free men, is as great as the damage that would arise if a foreign invasion went unchallenged. And, demanding fairness to all men, it must itself be unquestionably fair. It cannot protest when striking steel workers are deprived of the right of free assemblage and remain quiet when violent legislation impairs the inviolability of contract. It cannot denounce one man for robbing the government and stand silent when another man is robbed by the government.

The *Evening Sun* was dealt with in a one-paragraph postscript: "The *Evening Sun* has not been mentioned, but it does not lie outside this inquiry. It cannot enter Washington on terms as favourable as those which confront the morning edition, and hence it will not have the same chance to exert an influence upon national affairs. But in its narrower field it faces an opportunity almost as fine. There is injustice in Baltimore as well as in the steelworks of Pennsylvania. . . ."

In discussing the differences between the Democratic and Republican parties in Maryland, the memorandum got into the question of race and reflected attitudes then prevailing:

> Here we have an important and a living issue in the question of the Negro and his part in politics, and the two parties are still clearly separated upon it. On this question the *Sun* can take but one position. As between the black man and the white man, it must be in favor of the white man. Thus the *Sun* will find itself in the Democratic camp so long as the Democrats view this issue as they do now. In the course of time, needless to say, the Negro question may leap the gap between the two parties as Prohibition has already leapt it, but, in my judgment, that time will not be soon.

The memorandum became known in the *Sun* office as the "White Paper." Most editorial and newsmen and newswomen, even comparatively new members of the staff, have heard of it though it is likely that few have read it.

An editor who joined the *Sunpapers* in the 1930s believed the memorandum was written by more than one person because of "the distinct changes in style." Part of one paragraph does read like Mencken in both content and style:

All sorts of utopian ideas, economical, political and ethical, are precipitated into statutes without sensible consideration and efforts are made to enforce them against the will and against the consciences of a large number of people. As a logical and natural consequence, the land is overrun with stupid and often dishonest police, uniformed and ununiformed, and there is much persecution. Assuredly no well-disposed American can comfortably contemplate the fact that scores of his fellow citizens are in prison today as the victims of bureaucratic stupidity and malignancy and that thousands are habitually deprived of their rights of free speech, free assemblage and even free suffrage. This sinister thing rolls up like an evil snowball. One crime makes another. As they gain in power, the bureaucrats gain in enterprise and daring. No man of active, original and courageous mind, unless he be rich or of established position, is any too safe in the United States today. The desire for draconian laws has passed beyond the state of interference with private acts; it now seeks to challenge even secret thoughts. And this enterprise, instead of being checked by a judiciary jealous of the common rights of man is actually fostered by a judiciary that seems to have forgotten the elemental principles of justice and rules of law.

But "I" and "me" are used throughout, and British spelling is used for such words as "favourable" and "colour." Such affectation was not characteristic of Patterson or Mencken, who had been schooled in the city rooms of Chicago and Baltimore. Obviously all three contributed their thoughts, aspirations, and particular points of view, and notes were undoubtedly made of specific attitudes and phraseology, but credit for the structure, content, tone, and writing belongs to Harry Black.

After those weeks of lengthy and lofty deliberations on substance, policy, and goals, the first change was a practical one: to reduce the number and size of the advertisements on page one. Since 1837, ads had occupied a prominent space on that page, as they did in most U.S. papers. Often they filled three columns, sometimes more. But by the 1920s most metropolitan papers had cleared their front pages for news. Schmick, the former advertising manager who had succeeded Patterson as business manager, and Joseph A. Blondell, the treasurer, were concerned about possible loss of revenue if the front page were entirely cleared. As a compromise, advertising was confined to the lower left-hand corner of both papers. With this beginning, the papers had a more contemporary look. Before long all advertising was removed from page one.

The *Sun*'s first step in becoming an important chronicler of national news was demonstrated with Patterson's comprehensive coverage of the Republican and Democratic presidential nominating conventions in 1920. (In the past, excepting its home-city exertions for the Democratic convention in 1912, the *Sun* had sent one or two men from the Washington bureau along with a staff political writer to report on the Maryland delegation.) Patterson, as self-appointed coordinating editor, led a team of eight: Adams and Kent, J. Fred Essary (chief of the bureau), John W. Owens (the chief political reporter), Stephen Bonsal (who knew politics and had been a foreign correspondent for the *New York Herald* and the *New York Times*), Stanley M. Reynolds (Washington correspondent of the *Evening Sun*), Mencken, and Henry M. Hyde, who had joined the *Evening Sun* in 1920 after being a star reporter for the *Chicago Tribune* and later its London correspondent.

It was not a congenial group at the start. Mencken had just written a bitter piece describing President Wilson as "a congenital liar." Woodrow Wilson had been an idealistic hero to the *Sun*'s editorial writers ever since his first inauguration, in 1913. Adams and Owens were so upset and angry at Mencken's diatribe that they threatened to resign unless Mencken were dropped from the convention team. Mencken offered to step aside, but Patterson would not agree to it. To soothe hurt feelings, Patterson packed a case of 100-proof whiskey for the trip (Prohibition had become the law the preceding January). It worked. Everyone was talking—and singing—when the train reached Chicago, the site of the first convention.

In September the board approved Patterson's request to reorganize the papers. His first objective was to separate the management of the *Sun* and the *Evening Sun*. Adams, though he had been in poor health since 1915, remained as editor of the *Sun,* and Kent remained as its managing editor, but they were relieved of their responsibilities for the evening paper. Reynolds came from Washington to become acting editor of the *Evening Sun*. He had worked for the Baltimore *News,* the *Washington Times,* three New York papers (the *Tribune,* the *Press,* and the *Sun*), and the International News Service, chiefly in Washington, D.C. At the same time, in October, J. Edwin Murphy was named managing editor of the *Evening Sun*. Murphy, who was to become a legendary figure, began his career on the Baltimore *News* in 1894 and in his early days was its bicycle editor. With the exception of three years on the Baltimore *Herald* and six months on the Baltimore *Star,* he was with the *News* until 1912, the last two years as its managing editor. In 1913 he was appointed managing editor of the *New York Press* and in 1915 managing editor of the *Washington Times.* He joined the *Evening Sun* in March 1917 as its news editor.

Patterson's reorganization was announced at two "divorce dinners" held at the Merchants Club. John T. Ward, who had just joined the *Sun,* recalled that they were "more formal than informal," with a member of the board of directors seated at each table. Patterson explained that each paper would have a complete and independent staff, from editor and managing editor to copy boys, and encouraged the staff to develop a friendly rivalry. He emphasized that no one would be fired. Kent in his talk made a comment that Ward said he has never forgotten: "The heart of Maryland beats in the *Sun* office." When the "divorce dinner" was held for the *Sun* staff, the *Evening Sun* crew temporarily took over their duties. Pranksters sent notes to the Merchants Club by copy boys bragging how they had improved stories by rewriting them and feigned a report of a spectacular, gory murder in City Hall. To undergird the separateness of the two papers, on November 22, 1920, the board authorized the improvement of morning, evening, and Sunday papers. That was done by increasing the staffs and broadening news coverage.

When the major powers agreed to confer on naval disarmament in Washington, D.C., in the fall of 1921, Adams said the *Sun* could attract national attention by covering the conference with a thoroughness never before attempted by an American paper. Patterson agreed, but he added a dimension by wanting to engage foreign journalists, who would know the principals and the stated and unstated objectives of the participants, the United States, Great Britain, France, and Japan. Patterson believed that in addition to giving *Sun* readers, particularly Washington officialdom, a comprehensive picture, the foreign viewpoints would be enlightening to the American delegates and also of interest to the foreign delegates, who would see what their countrymen were reading about the conference.

To that end, Patterson and Adams went abroad in the summer of 1921 to talk to government officials and newspaper editors in London and Paris. They signed up the best available journalists: Hector B. Bywater, the author of *Sea Power in the Pacific* and the foremost British naval expert; H. N. Brailsford, a spokesman of radical British opinion; J. St. Loe Strachey, editor of the *London Spectator* and an exponent of conservative ideas; H. W. Nevison, a veteran correspondent; H. W. Massingham, of the *London Nation;* Wilson Harris, diplomatic correspondent of the *London Daily News;* George Lechartier, of the *Journal des Débats;* Jean Longuet, the French Socialist leader; Adachi Konnosuki, K. Ishikawa, and Midori Komatsu, of the Japanese press; and Jabin Hsu and P. K. Chu, special correspondents of the *Chinese Daily News* in Shanghai. These were supplemented by American specialists: John Dewey, of Columbia University; John H. Latane, professor of American history and head of the Department of History at the Johns Hopkins University, and Rear Admiral Walter McLean, U.S.N. retired, Patterson's father-in-law.

In addition to their reports, the *Sun* printed the dispatches of the *New York Times,* the *New York World,* and the *Chicago Tribune.* Boardman Robinson, an outstanding artist, was engaged to do cartoons during the conference. His powerful drawings, in the style of Daumier's lithographs, were sometimes spread over four or five columns on the front page. They carried a copyright line but could be reprinted if credit were given to the *Sun.* The *Sun* staff included Owens (who wrote many of the main stories with knowledge and clarity), Essary, Reynolds, Theodore Tiller (a new man in the bureau), and Raymond S. Tompkins from the local staff. More than 300 correspondents, including four women, reported the conference for papers around the world.

The Naval Disarmament Conference began on November 12, 1921, and continued into December. Many days the *Sun* had eight or more articles. Often reaction articles were printed from London, Paris, Berlin, and other world capitals, along with a lengthy interpretive thesis on the editorial page by an international authority. During the conference, Van-Lear Black entertained 150 correspondents on a Sunday afternoon at his estate, Folly Quarter, in

Howard County, with an American barbecue. While they lunched on an ox that had been roasted whole over a log fire, young men and women working in fields nearby slowly gathered at the party's edge and began singing Negro spirituals. The guests were astonished at the diversity of the songs and the quality of the blending voices. What they did not know was that this had been carefully staged by Black. The singers were not "field hands" but members of the famed Hampton Institute Glee Club. After lunch the guests were welcomed by Indian chiefs of the Crow and Sioux tribes from Montana. Then they watched, from a temporary grandstand, rodeo rough-riding and steer-chasing by Chester Byers, the world's champion rope-twirler, "Cyclone" Kiser, "and a brave company of plainsmen and plainswomen, including Ken Maynard." The enraptured guests included H. G. Wells (whose dispatches appeared in the *Evening Sun*) and H. A. Tokugawa, son of Prince Tokugawa, head of the Japanese delegation.

In retrospect, the *Sunpapers* greatly overplayed the Washington Naval Conference, which accomplished little of permanent value, but the papers were honored for their effort, nationally and internationally. The breadth and depth of *Sunpaper* coverage began bringing it what the White Paper just two years earlier had set forth as a goal: recognition "as a newspaper of national distinction."

Two other developments strengthened the *Sun*'s international coverage and brightened its growing luster. While Patterson and Adams were abroad on their talent search, they had met many editors and correspondents, and connections and friendships were developed during the conference. Thus they could with confidence choose and hire the best and most knowledgeable foreign journalists. Patterson arranged for an influx of articles and commentary for the *Sun*. Bywater, Nevison, Brailsford, and Lechartier continued as contributors; they were reinforced by André Géraud, chief political writer of *L'Echo* in Paris, whose pen name was Pertinax; S. Miles Bouton, in Germany; Wilbur Burton in Shanghai; C. R. Bradish, in Australia; Louis Fisher, in Moscow; Paula Arnold, first in Vienna and later in Israel; and J. A. Stevenson in Canada.

The *Sun*, in cooperation with the *New York World*, which had American rights for *Manchester Guardian* material, had been using *Guardian* dispatches from European capitals and during the conference had printed articles by C. P. Scott, editor of the *Guardian*. When the *World* dropped its arrangement in 1924, James Bone, the *Guardian*'s London editor and a friend of Hamilton Owens, the newly appointed editor of the *Evening Sun*, cabled Owens suggesting that the *Sun* replace the *World*. Patterson readily agreed, and a close bond developed between the papers, with Bone becoming a special friend of Patterson and his editors. The depth and warmth of that relationship will be described later.

In 1922, Patterson replaced Kent as managing editor of the *Sun* with Reynolds, who was succeeded by Hamilton Owens as editorial-page editor of the *Evening Sun*. Patterson and others complained that Kent had been filling the paper with too much politics and had waged too many tiresome battles with Baltimore mayors. (Years later, when an *Evening Sun* managing editor was fired, Kent wrote him a warm note wishing him well and pointing out, "About 25 years ago some such thing happened to me. In my case it turned out to be the best thing that ever happened to me.") Before becoming managing editor, Kent had been an astute political reporter of Maryland and national politics. At this point Patterson offered Kent a new role—daily columnist, on page one—writing on his pet subject. This has been called the first daily newspaper column devoted entirely to practical politics and politicians. Soon the column was carrying a never-varied headline, "The Great Game of Politics."

Adams, who had labored heroically and well as editor of the *Sun* and the *Evening Sun* from 1910 to 1920, was handicapped by a physical disability. In 1915 he was given a year's medical leave but insisted on returning before it ended. In his last years, beset by arthritis in his arms and legs, he was often in the hospital or confined to his home in Ruxton, where he had a direct telephone line to his office. A year before he died, Adams improved enough to get to his desk almost daily, hobbling along in pain on crutches. He was described as frail of body but strong of mind. Kent, who had been a tough managing editor while Adams was in charge of the editorial pages, wrote afterward in a memo to Mencken, "I liked and respected him, though I was greatly afraid of him."

Adams died on October 12, 1927. In an editorial page tribute, Mencken wrote:

> Of all the journalists I have known, the late John Haslup Adams, who died yesterday, was the only one who never made a visible compromise with his convictions. Such compromises are very common in the profession. . . . He saw a great modern newspaper largely, if not mainly, as an engine for rectifying injustice. If it simply printed the news that came in, from anywhere and everywhere, it failed in a prime duty. That duty, he believed, obliged it to get behind the news to find out whence the news had come and by whom it had been set afloat, to detect and expose any falsity that was in it, or any self-interest. To this business he addressed his chief energies all his life.

Because of his poor health there had been talk of asking Adams to step aside as editor in 1920. Van-Lear Black had been impressed with Herbert Hoover's work in famine relief and suggested that Patterson talk to him when he returned from Europe to sound him out for the position of editorial page editor of the *Sun*. Patterson did, but he was convinced that Hoover would not make a good editor, so the matter was dropped.

Adams was succeeded by John Owens, who had become his assistant in 1926. The editorial staff included Charles McHenry Harwood, who had been editor of Munsey's Baltimore *News;* H. K. Fleming, for a short period; and

Felix Morley, brother of Christopher Morley, who joined the paper as an editorial writer in 1922. Morley also had overseas assignments, in the Far East in 1925 and in Geneva in 1928. He resigned the next year, complaining about what he called the "excessive influence" Mencken had on editorial policy.

In 1928, Patterson asked Mencken to comment on the *Sun*'s editorial page after it had typographical improvements. Mencken responded with a six-and-a-half page letter critiquing not only the typography but also its cartoons, letters to the editor, "Down the Spillway" column, and the editorials. As an old columnist himself, whose forte was brashness, Mencken thought the Spillway "badly executed": What "the stuff mirrors is somewhat feeble and obvious; it suggests . . . a rather self-conscious young college professor—the sort of fellow who admires Christopher Morley and dreams of getting a whimsical essay into the *Atlantic Monthly*."

Predictably, Mencken thought editorials were "too cautious in tone," "too judicial." He wanted more invective. "When a scoundrel is on the block he ought to be denounced in plain terms, and without any judicial tenderness. So with fools. So with fool ideas." He also wanted more conviction: "In order to carry conviction it is needful to *have* conviction. It is also needful to remember that most men are convinced, not by appeals to their reason, but by appeals to their emotions and prejudices. . . . One of the chief purposes of the *Sun*, as I understand it, is to stir up such useful hatreds."

Patterson passed the letter to John Owens, who replied with a five-page-plus memo. He did not think the Spillway was "badly executed," but he did believe it could be improved. Its shortcoming was that "one man has done most of the work, in addition to a very great deal of other work. The consequence is too much of one flavor and too great haste." The signature appended to the Spillway was "John O'Ren"—the initials representing (John) Owens, (Stanley) Reynolds, (A. D.) Emmart, and (Frederic) Nelson (Owens was referring to himself). On editorials Owens responded:

> The essential thing in this criticism is attitude. On that I am in flat disagreement with Mr. Mencken. There can be no argument about the need of vigor. But I want a vigor that proceeds from mastery of facts.
>
> That has been the end in view in all the charges that have been made. It was the reason for the grant of leave to Morley to go to Geneva. The purpose was to build up a body of solid information, not alone about the operation of the League of Nations but about European affairs in general, in addition to the information he had acquired in the trip to China. The same end dictated the search for and the employment of Dexter Keezer. In a country in which business largely dominates public affairs, I wanted a man who knew how to get the facts. Again, the same end dictated the effort to develop Emmart, and to train him so that his extraordinary knowledge of literature and the arts in general could be effectively used. Every move that has been made was directed to the purpose of developing vigor based on facts. Mr. Mencken wants the kind of vigor which proceeds from single-minded partisanship.

This paper has set itself up as liberal, and I take it that the discussion assumes the continuance of that policy. If Liberalism means anything, it means that kind of intellectual honesty which opens the door to all facts. It is true, of course, that liberalism in politics and in journalism is identified with the advocacy of certain causes and policies. But if liberalism is anything more than pretense, such advocacy results from a fair survey of all that is pertinent, and the striking of a balance in favor of a given course. That course may be advocated with passionate vigor, but all the factors must be kept in mind and must not be concealed from those to whom arguments are addressed.

After calling Mencken "incomparably the most brilliant man engaged in journalism in America," Owens proceeded to deny that his approach was effective. He pointed out that for eighteen years Mencken had addressed the people of Baltimore, and to a lesser extent those of the entire state, on two principal themes, the prohibitionists and the evangelicals, and "always he has used precisely the method he proposes for the *Sun.*" These two targets, Owens pointed out, had no defenders in the daily press—nothing "to deflect or break the force of this fire on the drys and evangelicals from the ablest exponent and practitioner of the art of no-quarter polemics." Then the big *but:* "In this very community where Mr. Mencken's theory has had a test without parallel in duration and intensity, when the pitched battle came Governor Smith [Alfred E. Smith, the Democratic presidential candidate in 1928] suffered his worst defeat north of the Potomac River."

Owens assumed that Mencken was not concerned, in his criticism, with results in Maryland, but "that he is concerned with the *Sun's* acquiring a national leadership." Owens continued:

> I *am* concerned with the *Sun's* power and prestige at home. It is a continuing institution, nearly a century old, and I wish it to be a continuing institution, and I doubt that it will be so if it should neglect the salient nature of its own constituency. Even from the exclusive standpoint of a large, enduring national prestige, this home prestige is essential. It is the foundation. Again, I see no reason to suppose that a policy which fails, in its violence, to command strength at home will succeed in commanding strength in the more sophisticated and discerning audience to which we appeal in Washington and other centers.

He concluded, "And so, God bless us everyone."

There is no record of a Patterson decision or comment. He showed both viewpoints to Harry Black, who commented in a handwritten note, "God knows there is vigour here. In the meantime the H.L.M.–J.W.O. debate strikes me as really a debate as to the display of our wares. Actually what M. feels (even if he doesn't realize it) is that our wares should be displayed loudly and with brighter lights, whereas O. feels that the shop window ought not to have too gaudy colours in it." Mencken and Owens not only differed philosophically and politically, but evidently, below the surface, did not like one another. In his waning years, Mencken became vicious and personal in his attacks, even after Owens stepped aside as editor-in-chief.

Under the Blacks and Patterson, the 1920s were invigorating and profitable years. The *Evening Sun*, limited to thirty-two pages because of press capacity, often had to drop up to 150 columns of advertising (some national advertising could be switched to another day, but much retail sale advertising could not). An ad for the Wiessner Brewing Company attracted unusual attention. During Prohibition the word "beer" was not permitted in advertising. Wiessner made near beer, which was permitted, and the *Sun* persuaded the company to advertise it. The paper's promotion department circumvented the ban on the word "beer" with a three-column ad in large type: "Wiessner's Superlative Beverage." The word "beverage" was set with the first, second, fourth, and fifth letters in boldface and the other letters in outline type, something like "Wiessner's Superlative BEvERage." The ad attracted attention but did not sell much near beer.

In those days the *Sunday Sun*, with a number of sections, was printing 100 pages or more. When the blizzard of January 28, 1922, prevented traffic, even streetcars, from moving, circulation bosses hung a large sign in the carriers' room: "Remember When Denny Went to Towson!" One carrier looked at it and grumbled, "Hell, Denny just had a ten-page morning paper. The gazette we got is around 100 pages!"

The *Sunday Sun* had been enlarged when a sepia photogravure section was added on January 28, 1917. It created so much interest that the day's paper was sold out by 9:00 A.M. Gustafus Warfield Hobbs had been hired as Sunday editor to start it. While an editor of the *Philadelphia Inquirer*, Hobbs had introduced the first photogravure section in the nation. On March 23, 1923, he started a literary section. That fall he resigned to enter the Protestant Episcopal ministry. Mark S. Watson, assistant managing editor of the *Sun*, assumed responsibilities for the Sunday sections and later was named editor of the *Sunday Sun*. Watson had worked for the *Pittsburgh Press* and the *Chicago Tribune*. During the war he served abroad, and as a major was officer-in-charge of the soldiers' newspaper, the *Stars* and *Stripes*, whose working staff of enlisted men included Harold Ross, later the founding editor of *The New Yorker*, and Alexander Woollcott. After the war, Watson was managing editor of the *Ladies' Home Journal* before joining the *Sun*. On March 8, 1925, Watson changed the literary section to a handsome tabloid letterpress magazine written by staff members and writers of national reputation. Reflecting these improvements, the newsstand price of the *Sunday Sun* was raised from three cents to five cents on February 4, 1917; in September 1938 it went to ten cents.

The 1920s were a turbulent era for Baltimore newspapers. On November 20, 1920, as related in Chapter 10, Munsey bought General Felix Agnus's *American* and *Star*, the circulation of which had plummeted between 1914 and 1919. The *Times*, a one-cent tabloid, appeared on October 30, 1922, but lingered only until March 20, 1923. The Scripps-Howard newspaper chain entered Baltimore, inaugurating the *Post*, an afternoon penny tabloid, on November 20, 1920; it was welcomed with a friendly editorial in the *Evening*

Sun. Baltimoreans so inclined could buy three papers—the two-cent *Evening Sun* and *News* and the penny *Post* for a nickel. Harold Duane Jacobs, a former United Press editor, became editor of the *Post.* For the first six months it did not take advertising. It was increased to 2 cents a copy on January 31, 1927, and two years later went to a standard-size paper.

When William Randolph Hearst was 60 years old he bought his way into the Baltimore market on April 1, 1923, by taking over the *News* and the *American* from Munsey for an estimated $4 million. The *News* was then making more than $3 million a year and had a larger circulation than the *Evening Sun.* John E. Cullen, former managing editor of the *Evening Sun,* was named publisher of both the *News* and the *American.* In 1923, Hearst also started the tabloid *New York Mirror.* He then owned twenty-two daily papers with a claimed circulation of 3,028,437 and fifteen Sunday papers with a claimed circulation of 3,587,871. "But," W. A. Swanberg noted in his biography *Citizen Hearst,* "Hearst at 60 had lost most of his public following because he so often compromised his own ideals for expediency."

Munsey's *News* was conventional in design; few photographs were used, and headlines did not shout. As soon as Hearst took over, headlines and photographs were splashed across the front page. Three ace reporters covered crime stories in depth and detail. A "pink" edition appeared on pinkish paper. Sports and features were emphasized and a page of fiction was added. Later a news-tip contest was introduced, paying $50 for the best weekly news tip, preferably about a crime. The *Evening Sun* did not attempt to compete with Hearst's flamboyance; it really ignored it and went its measured way, gradually increasing in circulation.

The *American* fared poorly, and on January 28, 1928, it was changed to tabloid form. When that did not revitalize it, Baltimore's oldest surviving daily paper was merged with the *News* on April 2, 1928; a separate *Sunday American* was created. The *Post,* with falling circulation and advertising, was put up for sale, and purchased by Hearst and merged with the *News* on March 24, 1934. The consolidated paper carried the cumbersome name "Baltimore *News* and Baltimore *Post*" until January 13, 1936, when the name was changed to the Baltimore *News-Post.*

When Cardinal Gibbons died on March 21, 1921, the *Sunpapers* printed 20,000 copies of an illustrated brochure for free distribution. The brochure was so popular that it had to be reprinted twice. And so many requests were made for extra copies of the *Sun's* and the *Evening Sun's* stories on the burial of America's Unknown Soldier on November 11, 1921, that they were reprinted in a copyrighted booklet on calendar paper. The *Sun's* five-column story was addressed "To His Mother, Whoever and Wherever She May Be: They buried your soldier son in Arlington today."

The papers had grown and more space was needed. To accommodate new presses, the Armstrong-Cator Building, at 9–11 West Baltimore Street, was purchased in May 1922, and the pressroom was enlarged by extending it into those basements. In June 1924 the abutting Redwood Street property was acquired. Later the additions were rebuilt and incorporated into the *Sun* building to provide a new boardroom and additional space for all departments.

In addition to directing expansion and renovation plans, Patterson was confronted with an irksome libel suit. In February 1922 the *Sun* began an account of a women's meeting: "Intermarriage between white women and Japanese, Negroes, Hindus or members of any other race is justifiable, providing the union is founded on love," said Mrs. Donald H. Hooker, speaking yesterday at a meeting of the Just Government League. Mrs. Hooker's statement followed an address by Theodore Gould on the Japanese and was made in response to a question asked by one of the members of the club." The one-column head on the seven-paragraph story was

FAVORS WHITE WOMEN
WEDDING OTHER RACES
Mrs. Donald H. Hooker Justifies Such Unions
Provided They Are Founded On Love
Includes Negroes On List

Public reaction was swift and furious. The next day the *Sun* printed two stories. One was headed:

LEGISLATORS STIRRED TO WRATH BY SPEECH OF MRS. HOOKER
Her Stand On Interracial Marriages Denounced
On Floor Of Senate
Women Lobbyists Quail Before Tide Of Indignation

The other headline read:

WOMEN RESENT REPORTED VIEWS
OF MRS. HOOKER ON MARRIAGE
Report That She Advocated Abolishing Color Lines Raises Indignation —
Speaker Flatly Denies Remarks Credited To Her

Three days later Mrs. Hooker sued the *Sun* for $100,000, alleging libelous misquotation of her statement. The trial in March 1923 lasted for nine days and was covered in detail, the stories being prominently displayed on the back page. Mrs. Hooker, described by her attorneys "as a leading advocate of equal suffrage and the emancipation of women from unjust restrictions," testified that the quotation the *Sun* used was the exact opposite of her views. She was on the stand for several days, during which her book, *The Law of Sex,* was attacked, defended, and explained. Twelve witnesses testified that she had not made the statements attributed to her; a *Sun* attorney pointed out that one of those came late to the meeting, sat in the last row, and was hard of hearing. The vice president of the Just Government League testified that she was the one who asked the question that resulted in the disputed quotation. She said the *Sun* reported it accurately but she thought part of the headline misleading. Patterson, copy-desk men, reporters, assistant editors, and

Reynolds, the managing editor, were on the stand. Under cross-examination, Reynolds said there was "no animus" in the *Sun* office toward Mrs. Hooker and that there had been no instructions to ban her name from the paper (after the suit was filed). The jury awarded Mrs. Hooker one cent in damages.

Before she filed suit, the *Sun* had printed many stories about her: adopting a baby; criticizing Kipling's poem "The Female of the Species" as a slur on women; talking about Leap Year equality; and joining the Bull Moose Party. But according to office lore, there was a policy of ignoring Mrs. Hooker after the trial. There is nothing in her file in the *Sun* library from the time of the trial until 1949, some twenty-six years. Then her name appeared once more, in her obituary.

H. K. Fleming, who was born in England and first worked on papers there, joined the *Sun* in October 1924 and was a reporter, part-time critic, editorial writer, New York correspondent, city editor, assistant managing editor, and managing editor. In a letter and in a draft of his autobiography, he drew a nostalgic and romantic picture of his early days:

> My first day aboard, I was shown the washroom which looked like it had been torn apart. Actually it had. I was told the perpetrator was James M. Cain, later the author of "The Postman Always Rings Twice" and other successful novels. He was a reporter who had either quit or just been fired.
>
> The city room was hot as hell in summer. The streetcars made a thundering roar; the room was always in an uproar—phones ringing (no acoustical treatment in those days) and the floor was littered with newspapers and discarded cigarettes. Cigarette fires were frequent and they caused no comment. Keep in mind that the 1920s were the era of "The Front Page." Reporters were a tough breed and looked it. The copy desk men were a breed unto themselves and I have to confess they would scare anyone seeing them for the first time. Asa Biggs was as gruff as ever, his face half-hidden behind the bowl of a huge curving pipe, and while working he always bore a battered hat. Bob Murray, never without a cigarette, wore a dirty handkerchief around his head. He looked like a character out of the Beggar's Opera, and usually one night a week would be forced to leap out of his chair and stamp out fires on scattered chunks of newspaper caused by his cigarette ashes. Another copy reader whose name escapes me [Thomas Dorsey] wore a high old-fashioned collar, looked like a church warden, and carefully pulled paper cuffs over his sleeves. Newton Parke looked like a prize fighter.

Fleming continued to recreate those days this way:

> Old Admiral Duffy is a stocky, taciturn little man with a bold, blue seaman's eye. He talks little and goes his own way. Folger McKinsey is not so old but he knew Walt Whitman in his Camden days. As the Bentztown Bard he can write verse faster on his typewriter than he can write prose. A delightful fellow who deserves a better fate than to be the idol of the women's clubs. Oliver Perry Baldwin, associate editor, is 75. Burwell Snyder [head of the copy desk and later news editor] sits toying with the editorial scissors. An unruly lock of hair hangs over his eye. He is from West Virginia and at one time was a Methodist minister although never

actually ordained. The Civil War may be over but the soul of Burwell Snyder is still marching with Robert E. Lee and Stonewall Jackson. Kenneth Dole, who has come to us from Harvard, has a habit of stripping for action when he writes. He takes off his coat, his tie, unbuttons his shirt. Next he takes off his shoes.

Young Zemurray, son of Sam Zemurray, tsar of giant United Fruit, is in the sports department. He is big, somewhere around six foot six or seven, friendly and popular. Sometimes Zemurray nods in his chair around midnight and we put an alarm clock underneath him. The alarm goes off. He comes crashing down with a noise that shakes the office. One day he buys a ready-made suit for $40 and starts to write a check.

"Sorry," says the salesman. "No checks unless you have an account here."

Young Zemurray, who is shy and never pushes himself forward, doesn't know what to say. Finally he explains, "But I'm a reporter on the *Sun*."

"Oh, that's different," says the salesman.

Since Zemurray's check was backed by one of the great fortunes in America we felt complimented that his rating as a $35-a-week *Sun* reporter should outrate $20,000,000.

The edition has been put to bed and the well-worn deck of cards is coming out of the copy desk. The cleaning women disturb the room and disappear. At 5 A.M. we are still playing. Then—in spring and summer—follows not bed but golf. We tee off in semi-darkness, sometimes with the aid of flashlamps. A bottle of beer placed in a stream at the third hole helps us on our way. Sleep for awhile. Breakfast sometime early in the afternoon at Childs' on Charles Street. More office.

At 24 South Charles Street, Lloyd B. Councill operated a tavern and grill in the 1930s and 1940s that was a hangout for *Sun* employees. Councill had a Jimmy Cagney bearing, a clipped way of speech while jerking a shoulder for emphasis and a bluster that could not hide a big heart. As a convenience for his clients, the wall clock facing the bar had numerals and hands in reverse position so it could be read by those at the bar simply by glancing at the bar mirror. Every morning Councill had his handyman scatter fresh sawdust on the sidewalk in front of the tavern, then, to entice passersby to stop in for a cool one on the way to work, sprinkle the sawdust lightly with beer.

The *Sun* opened New York and Chicago bureaus in the late 1920s, and Fleming was assigned to New York. The *Sun* office was in the *Herald Tribune* building and linked to Baltimore by a leased wire. When the wire was turned on at 6:00 P.M. Fleming would ask "What's new in Baltimore?" But, he recalled, he seldom heard any of the gossip he wanted. The copy boy at the other end moved exclusively in copy-boy circles. The answer almost always was "Nothing." Once in a while the machine might jerkily report something like "Ike got canned today." "Who is Ike?" Fleming would ask. "A copy boy," came the reply, and that would end the conversation except for office messages—"Want 1,000 words on vice hearings" or "Send 400 on Grover Whalen."

Others on the staff in Fleming's early days were Ed Flynn, who later became city editor of the New York *Post* and then executive editor of *Post* enterprises, and Ernest von Hartz, who moved on to become managing editor of the *Chicago Sun-Times* and later an editor of the *New York Times*. Hanson Baldwin, a graduate of the Naval Academy, was a reporter who later became the military correspondent and analyst of the *New York Times*. Anne Schumacher, another reporter, became "the founder and queen of radio soap operas."

Turner Catledge joined the *Sun* in the summer of 1927 and stayed until 1929, when he went with the *New York Times,* subsequently becoming its executive editor. In his autobiography, *My Life and the "Times,"* he wrote:

> I was in Baltimore only two years and I'm afraid the *Sun* did more for me than I did for the *Sun*. . . . The *Sun*'s city editor was a gentle and meticulous man named Charles P. ("Peck") Trussell, who later joined the *New York Times*. Trussell knew good writing and he knew how to get it. . . . I introduced the previously unknown art of picture-snatching to Baltimore, with lamentable results. The picture that I snatched and that we printed as the likeness of a dead railroad president, turned out to be his brother, who was very much alive. At that, I gave up picture-snatching. Fortunately, I found, mistakes on whether a man is dead or alive usually don't cause a great complaint. If you say a man is dead and he is alive, he's too relieved to sue you. If you say he's alive and he's dead, he can't sue you.

Catledge had his first experience as a Washington correspondent during the presidential campaign of 1928. He wrote:

> The *Sun* had four men in its bureau, and three were out following the campaign. The fourth was an outstanding newspaperman who unfortunately let his drinking get the better of him. In 1922 [it was 1921] he had written a feature about the burial of the Unknown Soldier, which became famous and won prizes. His inspiration had been to write the article in the form of a letter to the Unknown Soldier's mother. It was a moving piece of writing and deserved all the acclaim it received. But now he drank too much to do his job and I had been sent to Washington not only to replace him but to tell him he was fired. It was a bad thing for the *Sun* editors to do, to the other reporter and to me, but they lacked courage to break the news themselves. The reporter took my news graciously; he said he had been expecting it. But later that day his wife rushed into the office, gave me a terrible tongue-lashing and threw down on my desk a copy of his Unknown Soldier article, which had been reprinted in pamphlet form.
>
> "You'll never see the day when you can write a story like that," she shouted. I kept quiet and all her husband said, trying to calm her, was "Now, mama. Now, mama."

When David Gibson was city editor of the *Sun* in the early 1920s, he gave his reporters cards with their names and telephone numbers to be handed out to potential news sources as a reminder to call if they saw or heard anything out of the ordinary. George C. Dorsch, who joined the staff in 1921, in the late 1920s left one of those cards at a delicatessen he patronized, and months later the counterman called to report that Jack Hart, a notorious criminal serving a long prison sentence, had just walked down the street. Dorsch followed up on the tip and discovered that Hart, famous for his jailbreaks, had indeed escaped a few hours earlier. Robert F. Sisk, a fellow reporter who in the 1930s became a producer of some of Hollywood's most successful films, also got surprising results from his cards. After he left the *Sun* and went to New York to write a column about Broadway, which the paper carried, he was still getting tips from Baltimore.

Dorsch, a versatile reporter who could cover a murder in the afternoon and an opera in the evening, was named society editor of the *Sun* in 1955. In 1960 the paper sent him to Monaco to cover the wedding of movie star Grace Kelly and Prince Rainier. (The *Sun*'s society column bordered on the austere, for years limited to those who were listed in the Social Register or eligible for the Bachelors Cotillon and the Baltimore Assembly, composed of about 700 members of old Baltimore society. The *Evening Sun*'s society items were more eclectic, ranging widely. This, for example, was an item in a 1960 column: "Mr. & Mrs. Hugo R. Hoffmann are back in their Goodwood Gardens home after a West Coast stay and a world cruise, via plane. Adding to the excitement of their trip was their strategic arrival for the tidal wave in Honolulu, the student uprising in Japan, and the typhoon in Hong Kong, all of which make interesting dinner table chit-chat.")

Hendrik Willem van Loon, author of a number of best-sellers, including *The Story of Mankind,* joined the *Sun* as a columnist in May 1922. The column, titled "H.V.L.," was frequently illustrated by the author and ranged widely in subject matter. His restatement of Charles Darwin's ideas startled Baltimore fundamentalists, causing van Loon to style himself "the man who introduced the theory of evolution to Baltimore." He remained on the *Sun* for about a year.

When John Thomas Scopes, a schoolteacher, was tried for violating Tennessee's antievolution law in the spring of 1925, the *Sunpapers* sent Kent, Hyde, Edmund Duffy (editorial page cartoonist), and Mencken. After William Jennings Bryan offered his services to the state, Mencken got Clarence Darrow to defend Scopes. The *Evening Sun* put up Scopes's bond and when he was found guilty paid his $100 fine. (The money was later returned because the trial judge had set the fine above the amount fixed by statute.) Fifty out-of-town newspapermen wrote thousands of words about "the monkey trial" in Dayton, but it was Mencken's account that attracted attention. According to William Manchester, his biographer, Mencken's stories "came closer to syndication than any other reportorial mission of his career; managing editors from all over the country . . . had besieged the *Sun* with requests to buy his correspondence."

Kent and Hyde reported in meticulous, objective detail, but Mencken, writing with fire and passion, termed Dayton "the new Jerusalem" and, speaking of jury selection, said that to the people of Dayton "an Episcopalian or Northern Methodist is virtually an atheist." When the trial opened he wrote, in part:

The real trial, in truth, will not begin until Scopes is convicted and ordered to the hulks. Then the prisoner will be the Legislature of Tennessee, and the jury will be that great, fair, unimpassioned body of enlightened men which has already decided that a horse hair put into a bottle will turn into a snake and that the Kaiser started the late war. What goes on here is simply a sort of preliminary hearing with music by the village choir. For it will be no more possible in this Christian valley to get a jury unprejudiced against a Bolshevik.

I speak of prejudice in the philosophical sense. As I wrote yesterday, there is an almost complete absence of bitterness in these pious hills, of the ordinary and familiar malignancy of Christian men. If the Rev. Dr. Crabbe [a Maryland prohibitionist] ever spoke of the bootleggers as humanely and affectionately as the town's theologians speak of Scopes, and even Darrow and Malone [Dudley Field Malone, a defense lawyer], his employers would pelt him with their spyglasses and sit on him until the ambulance came from Mount Hope. There is absolutely no bitterness on tap. But neither is there any doubt.

Mencken also wrote a long piece about a camp-meeting revival. Back in Baltimore, Murphy tacked it on to the *Evening Sun*'s bulletin board with the comment "That's reporting." (In 1945, Jerome Lawrence and Robert E. Lee wrote a highly successful play, *Inherit the Wind,* which was a fictionalized account of the trial. For legal reasons all the names were changed; the character who portrayed Mencken was named E. K. Hornbeck.)

Shortly after the trial, while still in Dayton, Bryan died of a cerebral hemorrhage. Mencken devoted his *Evening Sun* editorial page column to an obituary of Bryan. His harsh and unforgiving words were heavily edited, but it was still a violent hate-piece. To balance it, Gerald W. Johnson, an editorial writer, was told to write a sober, dignified account of Bryan's life. Johnson's piece caused no comment, but Mencken's diatribe drew many letters denouncing its bad taste and demanding that in the future he be censored.

A popular *Sunpaper* service in the 1920s and 1930s was the World Series scoreboard, erected on the side of the building overlooking *Sun* Square, which lured large crowds. This was before the day of the ubiquitous portable radio. A telegraph operator at the game would send a play-by-play account to the *Sun;* the announcer, Johnny Neun, an International League manager, popular Baltimorean, and later a part-time *Evening Sun* sportswriter, would call balls and strikes and comment on the game and the players. A pantograph moved a white ball suspended on a fishing line over the giant green baseball diamond to show where it had been hit. A man on base was indicated by a white light. When, for example, the batter hit into a double play, the pantograph would move the ball from pitcher to batter, to shortstop, second base, and first base beating out the moving white dots representing the baserunner. Behind the scoreboard was a bell that was struck once for a single, twice for a double, three times for a triple, and four times for a home run. Automobiles were kept out of *Sun* Square during the games because crowds filled the area, but trolley cars were permitted to inch their way through it. Sometimes, nervous or mischievous motormen would clang their bell, which sounded like the scoreboard bell, three or four times. That would bring men running out of nearby shops or offices thinking the game had reached an exciting moment.

One of the biggest sporting crowds to gather in *Sun* Square was in 1928— not for the World Series, but to listen to a description of a horse race in England. Baltimore, a horse-loving town, was excited because one of the forty-two entries in the Grand National at Aintree was Billy Barton, a temperamental and colorful horse owned by a Baltimorean. Billy Barton had been a winning handicap thoroughbred until he was ruled off Maryland tracks as unmanageable. After being ridden in eighty-one fox hunts he became a steeplechase racer and won seven of the eight races he entered. Because the town was agog over his chances in the Grand National, the world's most demanding steeplechase, Van-Lear Black arranged for a description of the race to be transmitted from a *Sun* man at Aintree by phone to London, then by radio across the Atlantic to Baltimore.

The telephone company said it was the first time transatlantic equipment had been used this way. Graham McNamee, the best-known radio announcer, was inveigled into broadcasting the race by loudspeaker to the crowd in *Sun* Square. Two jumps from the finish, Billy Barton was leading; all but two others had fallen or quit. At the last jump Billy Barton stumbled, throwing his rider. The rider scrambled to his feet, caught the horse, remounted, and pounded to the finish line, only to lose by a nose to the one other horse finishing.

Before the decade closed, the *Sun* had a new managing editor. William E. Moore, a Missourian, had worked on Chicago papers (when he was city editor of the *Inter-Ocean* Paul Patterson had been his night editor) and the *New York Herald* and the *New York Tribune*, becoming managing editor there in 1917. During the war, as an army captain, Moore was at General Pershing's headquarters. He joined the *Sun* in 1922 as the assistant managing editor. When Reynolds became ill, Moore replaced him as managing editor, just before the Wall Street crash of 1929. Moore's post was taken in turn by Paul J. Banker, an Ohio newspaperman, who had joined the *Evening Sun* as its assistant managing editor in 1927. H. K. Fleming remembered Moore this way:

> He looked like a Western cavalryman, small and wiry. Sometimes as I watched him at this desk I thought "there is Jackson standing like a stone wall." The man, and the wall, were immovable. Or, to put it another way, immune. The appearance of immunity and of remoteness was with him during the 20-odd years he and I were on the *Sun*.
>
> We came to look on Moore as a wall that stood off the pressures from above and below that are well known to newspapermen, and in that security was a great sense of freedom. He had no favorites. We were never called upon to twist a story. When there was a choice between the right thing and the slick thing, we didn't have to look for an answer. . . .
>
> An executive from a distillery came into the office one evening, an important

man in the community, and his advertising account with the *Sun* was large indeed. He was interested in a story that mentioned his brand of whiskey. The argument began politely enough, then our visitor made the mistake of mentioning his advertising.

"Who let you in?" Moore growled. "Get the hell out of here."

The visitor fled.

Moore was lame. This was due to an attack of infantile paralysis; it was not a marked infirmity. Two hours after midnight he would rise from his desk, steady himself with his hand for a moment and limp slowly half the length of the room for his coat. It was a matter of pride with him to show his independence. Only rarely on this part of the trip did he use his cane.

Van-Lear Black never had an office at the *Sun*. This custom was followed by his brother Harry and Van-Lear's son Gary, as later chairmen of the board. (Van-Lear Black's father, H. Crawford Black, seldom visited the *Sun,* and it was said that he went above the first floor only once.)

A test of Van-Lear Black's willingness not to interfere came early in the 1920s, when warfare broke out in the West Virginia coal district between the United Mine Workers (UMW) and the operators and a state of martial law was proclaimed. The *Sun* sent W. Jett Lauck, an economist for the railroad brotherhood, and James M. Cain, one of its best reporters, to investigate. Each was to write a separate report. Black, a major stockholder in West Virginia mines, was offhandedly told of the arrangements: "Whom are you sending from the staff to check Lauck?" he asked. When told, he chuckled, "Well, Cain will write a report more radical than Lauck's." That was all.

The two reports did not differ markedly as to facts or tone. The UMW had both sets of dispatches printed and circulated in support of their demands. For their part, the operators demanded that the *Sun* fire Cain, claiming that his stories were biased. Reynolds's response, as managing editor, was to send another reporter, John W. Owens, to the coalfields; Owens's findings only underscored Cain's proving them to have been incisive and honest. "We can't have operators telling us who to fire," Reynolds fumed, and he kept Cain in West Virginia for six more weeks. Cain's work attracted national attention, encouraging Cain to propose a piece for the *Atlantic Monthly.* Ellery Sedgwick, the editor, replied, "The attitude of the Baltimore *Sun* regarding the West Virginia mining situation long ago attracted my attention, and I consider its treatment of a difficult and dangerous situation as a public service of a high order," and told him to submit the article. Cain was on the way to making a name for himself.

While Van-Lear Black was chairman of the Abell Company board, he also was active elsewhere. In January 1920 he was elected president of the Fidelity Trust Company, and about the same time was elected chairman of the board of the Fidelity & Deposit Company, which had taken over the bonding business of the old Fidelity Trust & Deposit Company. He also bought into a variety of enterprises, including banks, a sugar corporation, and a shipbuilding yard. Somehow, in the early 1920s or before, Black and Franklin Delano Roosevelt became friends. While Roosevelt was practicing law in New York in February 1921, Black offered him a vice presidency of the Fidelity & Deposit Company, to direct its New York office. Roosevelt agreed, and Black paid him $25,000 a year, five times the salary Roosevelt had received during World War I as assistant secretary of the navy. As Nathan Miller told it in his *F.D.R.: An Intimate History*, that August he and Black sailed to Campobello on Black's yacht *Sabalo*. On a warm day they went cod-fishing in the *Sabalo*'s motor tender. Roosevelt insisted on baiting the hooks and doing the strenuous work, and soon he was soaked in sweat. Suddenly he tumbled overboard. Years later he still remembered the shock: "I've never felt anything so cold as that water . . . the water was so cold it seemed paralyzing." That evening, Roosevelt, who was 39, became ill and had to crawl on his hands and knees to reach the bathroom. A few days later severe pain had spread through his back and legs and he was unable to move the muscles below his chest. Two weeks later a specialist diagnosed his condition as poliomyelitis.

In addition to yachting, Black reveled in other sports. As a young man he owned and drove prize-winning tandem teams. He loved horseback riding and was a powerful swimmer. He helped foster Chesapeake Bay workboat races and wanted international racing on the bay. When he was in England in 1926 and 1927, he was impressed with barge-racing on the Thames and the seamanship involved. He offered to take the winning barge and its crew at his expense to Maryland to race bay boats. Such a contest, he held, would do more to promote Anglo-American friendship than America's Cup races. But the barge captain turned him down, saying, "We ain't no bloody showboat." Instead of showing irritation at this rebuff, Black laughed and observed, "Well, I have seen John Bull at last."

While in England, Black engaged Rene MacColl, a young Oxford man, as a secretary. MacColl, who was with him for two-and-a-half years and even worked a few months as a police reporter in Baltimore for the *Sun*, afterward published *A Flying Start: A Memory of the 1920s*. The book revealed a lot about Van-Lear Black, a man whose "fancy was always taken by the unexpected or unusual, both in people and things." Black was of medium height, "but when he entered a room you knew it, and people would look back at him on the street. . . . He had quizzical eyes, deeply lined face, determined chin, an air of alertness and force. . . . In appearance he was not unlike Lewis Stone, the film actor, for whom he was sometimes taken." He loved to entertain in a grand fashion and insisted on perfection in every detail—the invitations, the menu, the flowers, and the miniature flags for the table decorations.

When John Owens came to the end of his two years as London correspondent and J. Fred Essary of the Washington bureau arrived as his replacement, Black gave a "hail and farewell" dinner for between 200 and 300 guests.

The bill for the party was £1,046, and Black was amazed that it could be done so "moderately" (the pound was then worth about $5). MacColl never got over Black's generosity in tipping. At one casual restaurant dinner, Black handed a £10 note to each of five waiters. Another time, he gave the leader of a night club marimba band £150. When Black returned to the States, he had the lamplighters and dustmen on his street tipped, and the staff of the house he rented got a year's wages as a parting gift.

Shortly after the Wright brothers made their first successful flights in 1903, Black wanted to buy a plane and build a landing field on his farm, but his father discouraged him, reminding him that aviation was still in an experimental stage. In 1927 Black at last felt free to indulge his passion for flying by chartering a Fokker monoplane from Royal Dutch Airways, K.L.M., and by engaging two of the airline's pilots, Gerrit J. Geysendorffer and Johann B. Scholte, to take him on an aerial tour of Europe. Black expressed the pleasure the experience gave him in the way he knew best—investing £10,000 in K.L.M. stock. Later he purchased his own Fokker, had it specially equipped, and named it the *Maryland Free State*. With the two pilots now in his personal employ, Black flew from London to Cairo, and later from Amsterdam to the Dutch East Indies by way of India, making the 20,000-mile round trip in 183½ flying hours. The Dutch acclaimed Black as an aviation pioneer, and he was decorated by Queen Wilhelmina. The next year, 1928, he planned to fly from London to Cape Town but was forced down in the desert near Khartoum; later he started anew and completed the flight, again being treated as a hero. In 1929 he flew from London to Calcutta, where his plane was destroyed in a storm. The following year he bought another Fokker, and with his two pilots started from London around the world. They flew to Tokyo, boarded a ship for San Francisco, then flew across country to Baltimore. With these flights Black became the best-known and most-traveled airship passenger in the world. He wrote about his experiences in three articles for the *Sun* in the spring of 1930, pointing out that these flights demonstrated that the airplane would soon be a means of regular international travel and communication. The final aircraft, also called the *Maryland Free State*, was later included in the K.L.M. Museum in Amsterdam.

In August, Black was in New York. After entertaining Roosevelt, then governor of New York, for a few days aboard his yacht, and later Rear-Admiral Richard E. Byrd, another friend, whose attempt to reach the North Pole by air he had encouraged, Black flew to Newport, Rhode Island. There he visited his daughter, Ida Perry (Mrs. Alfred J. Bolton), who had just given birth to twins. When he returned to New York, friends commented on his excitement and happiness over the birth of grandchildren. That evening, August 18, he set sail on the *Sabalo,* bound for Baltimore after a stop at his lodge near the mouth of the Chesapeake. Following dinner he went aft alone and, as he often did, sat nonchalantly, sailor-fashion, on the taffrail with his feet caught in a lower guard rail and his hand on the stanchion. Black had been warned by his captain that this was a dangerous practice when the ship was under way. That night the ship was rolling "in rather heavy seas."

About 10:00 P.M. his valet reported that Black was missing. A quick check was made of the 140-foot yacht, then the captain reversed course and, with searchlights scanning the water, went back and forth across the area, which was about twelve miles south of Scotland Light off the Jersey shore. A nearby Coast Guard vessel asked what the *Sabalo* was doing, and several steamers were offshore, but none joined the search. At dawn, the *Sabalo* returned to New York harbor.

Announcement that Black was missing was delayed until midday, "owing to the hope that somehow he had escaped." Aircraft manned by volunteers who knew Black swept the area. They were joined by four Coast Guard boats and the naval dirigible *Los Angeles,* about to start a practice cruise from its Lakehurst, New Jersey, base. Governor Roosevelt urged that everything be done to expedite the search.

Word reached the *Sunpapers* in the early afternoon. The Six Star Wall Street Close edition carried a streamer, "VAN LEAR BLACK MISSING OFF YACHT." The account was written by Murphy, the managing editor. As a staff member recalled, "It was too important a story to entrust to a rewriteman." For several days the search was front-page news, but the only clue was a yachting cap, found by fishermen, which was identified as Black's. The morning and evening papers printed his name differently—the *Sun* hyphenating Van-Lear, the *Evening Sun* not hyphenating it. The *Sun*'s obituary editorial praised Black's service, character, and "the justice of the man," but said nothing of his connection with the paper. The English press treated the story as a noteworthy event, recalling Black's "sensational" flights and journalistic enterprise.

Black's will was probated on September 3, and the *Sun* printed it in full. He had requested that if he died in the United States he be buried at sea and "there shall not be any outward expression of mourning." Documents estimated his estate at $3,270,000. He bequeathed his Abell Company stock to his brother Harry. In addition to leaving the bulk of his estate to his widow and children, he left $100,000 each to his confidential secretaries, one in Baltimore and one in London, and $25,000 to Geysendorffer and $15,000 to Scholte, his pilots. He also left $100,000 to a friend, a widow who was with him on the yacht. Though this was the restrained 1930s, when such friendships were whispered, not mentioned in print, the *Sun,* to be objective and thorough, used her name in its accounts of his disappearance and in printing his will. It offered no special treatment for one of its own, even if he was the chairman of the board and principal stockholder and his brother succeeded him.

There are two postscripts to the Van-Lear Black story, each contradictory of the other. Days after he disappeared, authorities reported a corpse washed up on the New Jersey coast. Charles W. Maxson, the *Sunpaper* medical director, was sent to identify it if possible. The clothing—Black wore British suits with a distinctive cut—could have been Black's, Dr. Maxson felt, but he told the authorities that he wasn't sure. He thought it would be agonizing to the family for the body to be returned to Baltimore; also on his mind was Black's wish that there be no public mourning. Consequently, the body was buried in a potter's field, ground reserved as a burial place for strangers and the friendless poor. Black was 54.

According to the other story Black had told friends on different occasions that he would like to start life over without the responsibilities that great wealth entails. In her autobiography, Marguerite Harrison, who knew Black, recalled being amazed by the confidence of "a well-known business man who had never overcome a secret desire to run away and go to sea." Louis J. O'Donnell, a political reporter on the *Sun* from 1929 to 1946 and a man not given to loose or fanciful talk and meticulous in his reporting, said he had heard Black fantasize about starting another life. In the 1930s O'Donnell was in Hartford, Connecticut, on an assignment. Walking down the street he saw a man approaching who bore a striking resemblance to Van-Lear Black. O'Donnell was so startled by the similarity that he impulsively stopped and extended his hand. But the man, he said, sidestepped him, winking as he did, walked hurriedly on, and was soon lost in the crowd.

Arunah S. Abell, founder of the *Sun,* and his partners, Azariah H. Simmons, *left,* and William M. Swain, *right.* This was taken in 1836 when they established the *Philadelphia Public Ledger.* Their capital was $1,033.37.

Arunah S. Abell, once a printer, was the highly successful publisher of the *Sun* when this portrait was painted in 1866. Bound volumes of the *Sun* are on his desk. He died in 1888 at the age of 81.

The *Sun* Iron Building, erected in 1851, was the first iron office building in the United States. For years it was the most famous commercial structure in Baltimore.

The *Sun* Iron Building, *top,* on the southeast corner of Baltimore and South streets, was one of 1,343 downtown buildings destroyed in the great fire of 1904. After the fire the *Sun* was printed in Washington for two months. The *Sun* building, *bottom,* at the southwest corner of Baltimore and Charles streets, the geographical center of Baltimore, was built in 1906 and functioned as the *Sun*'s headquarters until 1950. The intersection was known as *Sun* Square.

From 1896 to 1975 type was set on linotype machines. The *Sun* used more than fifty of them. Operators sat at a keyboard much like a typewriter and produced one line of type at a time.

Opposite page

Top: the news room in 1908. Some editors and reporters wore wing collars. Every desk had a wastebasket (two of them upside down), and one a spittoon. *Bottom:* type set on linotype machines is placed in page forms in the composing room under the direction of makeup editors (wearing jackets). The *Sun* employed several hundred printers.

THE SUN.

VOL. I.—NO. 1]   BALTIMORE, WEDNESDAY, MAY 17, 1837   [PRICE ONE CENT.

THE SUN.

VOL. IV.—NO. 145]   BALTIMORE, MONDAY, MAY 6, 1839.   [PRICE ONE CENT.

THE SUN.

VOL. VII.—NO. 1   BALTIMORE, MONDAY MORNING, MAY 18, 1840.   [PRICE ONE CENT.

THE SUN.

VOL. XXI.—NO. 133]   BALTIMORE, FRIDAY MORNING, OCTOBER 22, 1847.   [PRICE ONE CENT.

THE SUN.

VOL. XXV.—NO. 86]   BALTIMORE, MONDAY MORNING, AUGUST 27, 1849.   [PRICE ONE CENT.

THE SUN.

VOL. XXX.—NO. 94]   BALTIMORE, MONDAY MORNING, MARCH 8, 1852.   [PRICE ONE CENT

THE SUN.

VOL. LXIII.—NO. 120]   BALTIMORE, MONDAY MORNING, OCTOBER 5, 1868.   [PRICE TWO CENTS.

THE SUN.

VOL. LXXXV.—NO. 2   BALTIMORE, MONDAY MORNING, MAY 19, 1879.   PRICE TWO CENTS.

THE SUN.

VOLUME CIV.—NO. 29.   BALTIMORE, MONDAY MORNING, DECEMBER 17, 1888.   TWELVE CENTS A WEEK.

THE SUN

VOL. CLXVI.—NO. 8.   BALTIMORE, TUESDAY MORNING, NOVEMBER 25, 1919.   22 PAGES   TWO CENTS

THE SUN

VOL. 182 D   BALTIMORE, FRIDAY, JANUARY 13, 1928.   24 PAGES   2 CENTS

LIGHT • FOR • ALL

THE BALTIMORE SUN

Charles H. Grasty, *top left,* became president of the A. S. Abell Company in 1910. He was a superb journalist but a poor businessman. He resigned in 1914 after the company incurred large deficits. John Haslup Adams, *top right,* was the first editor of the *Evening Sun.* From 1912 to 1920 he was editor of both the *Sun* and the *Evening Sun.* Subsequently he was editor of the *Sun* until his death in 1927. John W. Owens, *bottom left,* was editor of the *Sun* from 1927 to 1938 and from 1938 to 1943 was the first editor-in-chief of the *Sunpapers.* He won a Pulitzer Prize in 1936 for editorial writing on national politics. Neil H. Swanson, *bottom right,* was executive editor of the *Sunpapers* from 1941 to 1954—the only person to hold that position. While he was editor, the *Sun* won more Pulitzer Prizes than any other paper except the *New York Times.*

Left: the nameplate of the *Sun* since 1837. A railroad train and a ship have been part of the vignette since the first issue. In 1983 the vignette was redesigned to project stronger images.

Van-Lear Black, *top*, was the dynamic chairman of the Abell board from 1914 to 1930. In the early days of commercial aviation, Black became the best known and most traveled airship passenger. Harry C. Black, *bottom left*, succeeded his brother Van-Lear as chairman and served until his own death in 1956. He was a newspaperman at heart and visited the news room every day to absorb the atmosphere. The appointment of Paul Patterson, *bottom right*, as president of the A. S. Abell Company in 1919 marked the beginning of the modern era at the *Sunpapers*. He was president until his retirement in January 1951.

Editors, company executives, and board members at a luncheon in the boardroom in 1951.
Harry C. Black, chairman of the board, is at the head of the table.

Henry L. Mencken, *top left,* joined the *Sun* in 1906 as Sunday editor. He was associated with the *Sunpapers* as a noted columnist and correspondent, and as an adviser on policy, until the 1950s. Hamilton Owens, *top right,* was editor of the *Evening Sun* from 1922 to 1938, editor of the *Sun* from 1938 to 1943, and editor-in-chief of the *Sunpapers* from 1943 to 1956. Gerald W. Johnson, *bottom left,* author and historian, was an *Evening Sun* editorial page columnist. He, Frank Kent, H. L. Mencken, and Hamilton Owens wrote the history *The Sunpapers of Baltimore,* published in 1937. Frank R. Kent, *bottom right,* was managing editor of both the *Sun* and the *Evening Sun.* From 1923 to 1958 he wrote "The Great Game of Politics," a nationally syndicated column that for years appeared on the *Sun*'s front page.

J. Edwin Murphy, *top left*, was managing editor of the *Evening Sun* from 1920 to 1939. A demanding editor and inexhaustible idea man he "ruled the premises with thunder and lightning." William E. Moore, *top right*, the *Sun*'s managing editor from 1929 to 1941, was remembered by a co-worker as a "wall that stood off pressures from above and below that are well known to newspapermen." Mark S. Watson, *bottom left*, was Sunday editor, then the *Sun*'s military correspondent from 1942 until his death in 1966 at age 78. In 1945 he won a Pulitzer Prize for his war reporting. Lee McCardell, *bottom right*, joined the *Evening Sun* in 1925. During his 38-year career he was an outstanding reporter, war correspondent, chief of the *Sun*'s London and Rome bureaus, and an editor.

THE "OUTSTRETCHED HAND"

Edmund Duffy, *top left,* was a prize-winning editorial cartoonist at the *Sun* from 1924 to 1948. His "Old Struggle Still Going On," *bottom left,* published in the *Sun* in 1930, won the Pulitzer Prize as the best editorial cartoon of that year. His third Pulitzer was won in 1939 by the cartoon, *above,* depicting a ruthless Hitler crushing minorities after his conquest of Poland. He sometimes took a more liberal position than the editorial page. Later he was cartoonist for the *Saturday Evening Post.*

Richard Q. Yardley, known as "Moco," was editorial cartoonist for the *Sun* from 1949 to 1972. His style, exemplified *top right,* was described as "early Ming, middle comic strip, late Picasso, and all Yardley."

Tom Flannery joined the *Evening Sun* as cartoonist in 1957 and succeeded Yardley on the *Sun* in 1972. He says, "I like to present a viewpoint—my viewpoint—rather than illustrate an issue."

Mike Lane and Flannery were both auditors before becoming cartoonists. Lane has been the *Evening Sun* cartoonist since 1972. He believes "ninety percent is the idea, not the drawing."

Baltimore old gas lamps

"Of course I won't forget you
—you'll always be my first love."

Space shuttle *Challenger*

Paul A. Banker, *top left,* began his *Sun* career in 1942 as a reporter. He was city editor from 1954 to 1966. From 1966 to 1982 he was the *Sun*'s managing editor. Philip S. Heisler, *top right,* who started as a reporter in 1939, was managing editor of the *Evening Sun* from 1949 to 1979. Charles H. Dorsey, Jr., *above,* joined the *Evening Sun* in 1931. He was the *Sun*'s managing editor from 1947 through 1966. Price Day, *left,* was editor-in-chief of the *Sunpapers* from 1960 until his retirement in 1975.

Left: William F. Schmick, Sr., was president of the A. S. Abell Company from 1951 to 1960. His son, William F. Schmick, Jr., succeeded him and was president until he retired in 1978. Gary Black, *below left,* succeeded his uncle, Harry C. Black, as chairman of the board in 1956 and served until 1984 when he became chairman emeritus. Donald H. Patterson, *below right,* son of Paul Patterson, joined the *Sunpapers* in 1946. He served in many capacities, including publisher and president of the A. S. Abell Company. He retired in 1982.

To house the new $35,000,000 offset presses and auxiliary equipment, a $16,000,000 annex, *top,* was added to the south side of the Calvert Street building and completed in 1981. The news room, *bottom,* was completely renovated in 1986 and a new computer system installed. After a news room renovation in the 1970s, the editor-in-chief observed, "It looks like the accounting department of a bankrupt Italian airline."

Printers, *left,* paste up sixty or more pages with columns of type before an edition goes to press. The modern composing room is far different from that of the day when printers worked with hot rather than cold type.

Four nine-unit Goss Metroliner presses, *below,* were built for the *Sun* in 1981 as part of "a total systems approach to manufacturing"—from the automated handling of newsprint rolls to a counting and distribution system in the mail room.

James I. Houck, *top,* became managing editor of the *Sun* in 1982. He has said, "The well-written paragraph is not always the most effective means of communication." Joseph R. L. Sterne, *above left,* succeeded Gerald Griffin as editor of the *Sun*'s editorial page in 1972. He has been a reporter, assistant chief of the Washington bureau, and a foreign correspondent. Ray Jenkins, *above right,* became editor of the *Evening Sun* editorial page in 1981. While on another paper he was on a reporting team that won the 1955 Pulitzer Prize for Meritorious Public Service. In 1985 he won the Ernie Pyle Award. John M. Lemmon, *left,* worked on the *Star* and the *Post* in Washington before joining the *Evening Sun* as managing editor in 1979. The paper concentrates on news of the Baltimore metropolitan area.

Reg Murphy, *top,* who had been editor of the *Atlanta Constitution* and editor and publisher of the *San Francisco Examiner,* became president and publisher of the Abell Publishing Company in 1982.

Bottom: the last meeting of the A. S. Abell Company board was in October 1986. *Seated; from left to right:* W. Shepherdson Abell, Chairman William E. McGuirk, Jr., Gary Black, Jr.; *standing, from left to right:* Osborn Elliott, Robert Garrett, and Reg Murphy. George L. Bunting, Jr., and Donald H. Patterson are not pictured.

The Great Fire of February 1904—the worst disaster to strike Baltimore—destroyed much of the downtown area. In this historic photograph streams of water attack the flaming and smoking Hurst building where the fire started.

Top: a flag-waving, celebrating mass of Baltimoreans jam *Sun* Square, Baltimore and Charles streets, in August 1945 after Japan surrendered to end World War II. *Bottom:* Mayor Howard W. Jackson welcomes the Duke and Duchess of Windsor on their visit to Baltimore in October 1941.

Spiro T. Agnew is surrounded by reporters and photographers after announcing his resignation as vice president of the United States in October 1973. (*Sun* photo by Clarence B. Garrett.)

The photograph of Ethiopian children, *below*, in the Tigre region was part of a 1983 *Sun* series depicting the problems of local, national, and global hunger which won a $10,000 national media award. (*Sun* photo by Robert K. Hamilton.)

Top: Brooks Robinson (5) and winning pitcher Dave McNally (19) after the Orioles won the 1966 World Series. (*Sun* photograph by Paul Hutchins.) *Bottom:* the Baltimore Colts won the National Football League title in 1958 when Alan "the Horse" Ameche scored the touchdown to beat the New York Giants, 23-17, in sudden-death overtime.

Choptank Oyster Dredgers —

A. Aubrey

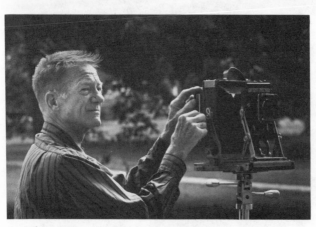

A. Aubrey Bodine (Photograph by C. B. Sittle)

From 1929 to 1970, A. Aubrey Bodine was a *Sunday Sun* photographer whose pictures won innumerable international awards. This study of Choptank River oyster dredgers in 1948 won a $5,000 first prize in a national contest attracting more than 50,000 entries.

TWELVE

The *Evening Sun:*
The "Rollicking Son," 1922–1938

The personality of the *Evening Sun* in
the 1920s and 1930s was expressed through its editorial page—at once ram-
bunctious, breezy, imaginative, visionary, mocking, whimsical, mischievous,
saucy, and sometimes irreverent. It liked to think of itself as the rollicking son
of the staid old lady, the morning *Sun.* Next to hurling brickbats, it reveled
in dodging them. It cheerfully admitted that it lost most of its battles. It was
attuned to its time and place, and above all it was readable.

In its first days, Mencken's "Free Lance" column and later his Monday
column, started in February 1920, set the tone of the editorial page. So did
Stanley M. Reynolds, when he was in charge from 1920 to 1922. A high-
spirited man, Reynolds had fun whacking away at the buffoons of his day,
both self-appointed and elected. After he went to the *Sun* as managing editor,
for a few months J. Edwin Murphy served as both managing editor and editor.
The man Murphy believed would make the ideal editor was Hamilton Owens,
who had been with him on two different papers and was then in London
working for a bank. On Murphy's recommendation, Patterson hired the
34-year-old Owens.

Owens was born in Baltimore in 1888 and graduated from Johns Hopkins
University in 1909. That fall he was hired as a reporter by Murphy, city editor
of the Baltimore *Evening News.* After Murphy went to the *New York Press* in
1913 as its managing editor, he sent for Owens to be his Sunday editor and
assistant drama critic. During the war, Owens was managing editor of the
Foreign Press Bureau of the Committee on Public Information, a propaganda
agency formed by President Wilson. With peace, Owens joined the Guaranty
Trust Company, handling public relations and advertising for a year in its New
York office and later for two years in London.

Owens became editor of the *Evening Sun* on February 1, 1922, and for the
next sixteen years asserted and burnished its personality. In an interview

recorded in 1958 for the Oral History Research Office of Columbia University, Owens recalled, "In those days, in the Roaring '20s, the chief issue of the country was of course Prohibition. Most newspapers had abandoned the fight. I can remember when I came to the *Sun,* I was told the fight was a lost cause, that it no longer was a political issue. I said, 'Well, if I come on the paper it is going to be a political issue all right. I'm going to make it one.' . . . Mencken and Harry Black joined hands on the thing, and we concocted every day at least one editorial denouncing Prohibition. We never referred to Prohibition agents, we always said 'spies, snoopers and *agents provocateur.*'"

Maryland had not passed an antialcohol law, and Governor Albert C. Ritchie would not let Maryland police make arrests under the Eighteenth Amendment and the Volstead Act. The *Evening Sun* supported him and, even more, made fun of the Anti-Saloon League, the Women's Christian Temperance Union, and any dry who cleared his throat in Congress or the Maryland legislature.

When Owens wanted to write what he termed "loud stuff" and did not want to dignify it with an editorial, he used it in articles he signed "G.A.D." One such piece was printed during a hot Prohibition debate. William D. Upshaw, a congressman from Georgia and a leading dry, denounced Maryland as traitorous to the Union because Ritchie would not sponsor or sign a state enforcement act. Using his nom de plume initials, Owens solemnly proposed that Maryland secede from the Union and go it alone as the Maryland Free State. The name, echoing the Irish Free State of that period, appeared a day or two later as a title for an editorial; then Owens began using it often, seldom referring to Maryland except as the Maryland Free State. Before long the term was in conversational and commercial usage and could almost pass for the state's motto. (In the late 1950s Governor Theodore R. McKeldin gave a speech telling how Maryland got to be known as the Free State; he mistakenly traced it back to colonial times.)

In 1922 the *Evening Sun* offered a $100 prize for a model platform plank "which would seem like a wet plank to the wets and a dry plank to the drys." The winning entry began: "On the subject of law enforcement, we desire to make our position perfectly clear." The next four sentences were political clichés and obfuscations. After Congress announced plans to recruit 10,000 men to enforce Prohibition on land, as the Coast Guard did on water, the corps became known as the "Dry Marines." The paper offered a $100 prize for a Dry Marine hymn in the same meter as the Marines' stirring "From the Halls of Montezuma." The winning lyrics:

> From Vancouver's foaming waters
> To Old Fundy's mighty tide
> From the dives of Tia Juana
> To the Rio, rolling wide
> We're on guard with sabers flashing
> 'Mid the boundary's varied scenes

For the honor, or what have you
Of the U.S. Dry Marines.

Owens founded the *Evening Sun* Bloc, "an involuntary association of public men who have, in one way or another, supported the *Evening Sun*'s concept of the good, the true or the beautiful." Its Grand Master was George Washington. It included the state forester, for suggesting that trees be planted along the highways to hide billboards; Hoover's secretary of agriculture, for saying that "the only way the farmer can be helped is for him to help himself"; and Congressman Otis Wingo of Arkansas, for advocating the repeal of 40,000 laws. In 1924, Owens instituted a "More Laws Association"—"Any politician is entitled to life, active or associate membership according to his zeal in proposing new laws." Eminent statesmen and politicians of both parties, reformers, and visionaries swelled its rolls. A regular feature of the page, "Tidbits from the National Pork Barrel," listed names of congressmen introducing bills to provide federal buildings, monuments, and so on, for the small towns in their districts.

On its birthday in 1923 and again on July 28, 1936, the *Evening Sun* printed an editorial, titled "Articles of Faith," which read in part:

The most important things in this country are the men who make it up. Experience has taught—the Founding Fathers knew it better than we know it today—that men grow best when they are treated as men and not as children. The important thing for the conservative is to conserve the opportunity for men to grow to their full stature. Hence the *Evening Sun* opposes all those measures, all those organizations, all those movements which seek to encroach upon the right of men to be men.

Of all the evils threatening this country today, the greatest is the constant inflation of government. We Americans have more government to start with than most peoples. We have our local governments, our state governments and on top of them the federal government. This last is the most dangerous because it is the furthest removed from the people over whom it rules.

And it is swelling enormously. Nearly every law which Congress passes clips a little off the edge of the citizen's independence. And the same law takes a little more out of his earnings. The lawmakers get us coming and going. If they keep on, we shall soon have little of either left. The *Evening Sun* proposes to try to conserve that liberty which we still have and get as much back of what we have lost as it is possible to get.

In addition to this vastly bloated legal government, there are a whole host of extra-legal governments which are striving with might and main to do their bit toward taking away from the citizen his few remaining rights. The Anti-Saloon League is the arch example of this kind of extra-legal government. The Ku Klux Klan is one of its absurder manifestations. One is run by shrewd fanatics, the other by avaricious clowns. But the spirit which animates both of them, and all the other leagues and associations of those who want to make the other fellow do it their way, is precisely the same. Consistent with our "live-and-let-live" policy, we are against the lot of them.

If we have a rule about these things, it is this—let them talk. That goes also for the Bolsheviki, the Babbitts, the uplifters-in-general. When they talk, they are fulfulling their God-given right. When they strive to do more, they are to be scotched.

The *Evening Sun,* finally, is a firm believer in old-fashioned economics. It has an abiding faith in the law of supply and demand, and it resents any interference by the Government with that law.

Herein, we believe, are contained the most important of the articles of faith to which this paper has subscribed.

They are so old-fashioned, so out of date, as to read almost like an eighteenth century manifesto. Indeed that is exactly the time from which they are taken. All of them, in fact, come out of the Declaration of Independence, the Constitution of the United States—as it was—and the Bill of Rights.

Owens enjoyed noting the paper's birthday disparagingly. He would point out that two other events shared the anniversary: On April 18, 1739, Dick Turpin, the English highwayman, was hanged; and on April 18, 1775, Paul Revere rode through the night to spread the alarm that the British were coming. Using the pseudonym Thucydides, Jr., Owens would recite the defeats and disappointments the *Evening Sun* had suffered in its endorsements and recommendations. In 1923 he invited its enemies to have their say and printed their missiles under the heading "A Bundle of Birthday Bricks." The president of the Anti-Saloon League wrote: "Too many editorials smack of lawlessness encouragement. They appear to favor evil-minded men and discount those who are fighting the stubborn, contested battles of reform. Too much beer emphasis. Not enough of rich milk and pure Adam's ale for us mortals. . . . But with all your faults, I love you still. Once in a while, you allow me to write for you an editorial—in this you are eminently fair."

Arthur Machen, Jr., acting chairman of the Association Against the Prohibition Amendment, wrote: "Your editorials are too short and jerky and often undignified. An appearance of flippancy is a high price to pay for brevity. You would command more weight if your editorials were sometimes sustained arguments appealing to the intelligence of your readers." And James H. Preston, mayor of Baltimore from 1911 to 1919 and often under attack by the *Sunpapers,* wrote:

What I dislike most about the *Evening Sun* is its congenital insincerity—an inborn defect of character which is unfortunately inherited from its morning progenitor. As a modern newspaper from the standpoint of publishing the news, the *Evening Sun,* like the morning *Sun,* leaves little to be desired. Editorially, however, I think that even you will agree that the force and power with which the *Sun* was endowed by the Abells is now but the fine tradition of an earlier day in Baltimore journalism. What I dislike about the *Evening Sun,* also, is its lack of independent thought—its easy submission to the hypocrisy and cant and humbug of the disgruntled and defeated political editors of the morning *Sun.* Why don't you try to write editorials that will "animate the conduct and mold the destiny" of Baltimore?

When Owens became editor he had only one editorial writer, Clark S. Hobbs. A Baltimorean who had worked on the Baltimore *American* and the *Evening News,* Hobbs joined the *Evening Sun* as a reporter in 1919 and the editorial staff in 1921. In addition to those duties, he wrote a column that appeared on page one, called "Good Evening." It consisted of light comment and "Sun Square Doin's, or the Diary of a Traffic Cop." Later it was moved to the feature page and appeared there until September 7, 1935. In his Oral History interview, Owens said he often wrote the entire page except for the Letters to the Editor and the excerpts from other newspapers, used as column-fillers. In 1922, he hired a second editorial writer, Gilbert Kanour, a Virginian who had worked as a draftsman and as a designer of cranes before writing for a small Virginia paper, where his clever pieces attracted the attention of Owens.

The editorial page printed two columns of letters. Many disagreed violently with the editorials. L. G. Penney put it this way: "Why do you find it necessary to flavor so many of your editorials with vinegar? . . . Why irritate your readers the way you do? Why'n hell don't you go fishing and give somebody a rest?" Letters had to be signed as an evidence of good faith, but in that era the writer's name did not have to be printed. Consequently many pen names were used: Obscure Proletarian, Wage Earner, Spinoza, Just a Baltimore Girl, Paratus, Give Me Liberty, A Negro Reader, An American for Better or Worse, A Modern She-Wife (answering a Modern He-Husband on why she worked), and, the most controversial and celebrated of them all, An American Mother.

Letters from An American Mother first appeared in the early 1920s and continued for nearly twenty years. They were deadpan spoofs so deftly done that the hasty or careless reader, taking them literally, noticed only the intentional errors and fired off sputtering rebuttals. "An American Mother" became a Baltimore institution. In a magazine article, Eric Lund wrote:

> Mother was an unyielding moralist, a militant Prohibitionist, a staunch defender of the Sunday blue laws, and a devoted churchgoer opposed to the theory of evolution, to Italian opera and to nude statues. She had the knack of taking something that nearly everyone regarded as fairly innocent (an opera, for instance) and discovering that it was immoral (she objected to *Tristan and Isolde* because it "condoned free love"). Frequently she offended someone or some group, always perfectly naturally but in a way that demanded response. Almost invariably she committed some blunder in stating her argument, an error of fact or logic that called for correction. In 1925, during the Scopes trial over the legality of teaching evolution, one of her letters began, "Sir: I think that trial of religious liberty down in Dayton is the most wonderful thing since Martin Luther stood up before the Cardinals and said, 'Give me liberty or give me death!'"
>
> On the positive side, she proposed a Get-Baptized Week, prayer meetings on streetcars for young people on their way to work, and enforcement of the Ten Commandments by the police.

Many readers believed she was real; some, of course, recognized and savored the lampooning (one reader wrote, "I strongly suspect 'she' wears trousers and wields a razor.") The cognoscenti were positive it was Mencken. But An American Mother was Holger A. Koppel, born in Copenhagen, who was the Danish consul in Baltimore. His identity as the letter-writer, a well-kept secret, was not revealed until his death in 1941.

Although the *Sun* and the *Evening Sun* differed typographically and the editorial pages were poles apart in style (the evening paper's ridicule contrasting with the morning paper's earnestness), people found it difficult to separate the two papers. This happened not only with readers as they saw a news article or editorial in one and attributed it to the other, but with other newspapers as well. When a newspaper reprinted an *Evening Sun* piece and credited it to the *Sun,* J. Edwin Murphy, the evening paper's managing editor, would dash off a letter of protest and explanation, pointing out that the *Evening Sun* was independent of its sister and had not only its own staff but also its own policies and way of doing things, often adding, "The *Evening Sun* is incomparably the greater." *Sun* staffers, imbued with their paper's seniority and regarding the evening paper as a pipsqueak offspring, would refer to it as "our caboose." When Murphy heard that, he would snarl, "As I see it, the caboose is pulling the train." There was merit in his reply. Once it gained momentum, the *Evening Sun* was producing more revenue than the *Sun.* In 1920 its March circulation was 82,667. In 1921 it had risen to 101,246, and by 1922 circulation had shot up to 127,759. Those gains resulted in a sharp rise in advertising.

When Murphy took charge the news department was woefully inadequate. He had no assistant managing editor, an undermanned copy desk, few reporters, no one responsible for features, and no society editor. Business and financial news was handled incidentally; the sports department, except for baseball, racing, and college football, covered sports by telephone. His ranking assistant was the news editor, Clark Keefer. His first city editor was Edwin A. Fitzpatrick, who had worked for the *World* and the *Sun* before joining the first staff of the *Evening Sun;* Fitzpatrick became Murphy's first assistant managing editor. When the *Sun* library files began to overflow, Fitzpatrick ordered clippings on the world war discarded because "there no longer was a need for them." In his last years he was made promotion manager. Henry Hyde was the top reporter, writing a page-one column and often covering national stories. John Carson was the Washington correspondent in the early 1920s.

The most influential writer on the staff was John Oldmixon Lambdin, a critic without a byline, only the appended initials "J.O.L." After reporting for the *Philadelphia Public Ledger* and writing drama criticism for New York magazines, he joined the *Sun* in 1911 as a reporter. Lambdin soon became a critic for the *Sun* and the *Evening Sun,* but most of his career was spent writing "The Three Arts" column for the latter, reviewing the theater, music, and the fine arts. His judgments had impact; a great many Baltimoreans regarded him as their guide and mentor. Though known publicly only as J.O.L., a *Sun* editorial described Lambdin as "almost as closely identified with the *Sunpapers* as the front page itself." His theater reviews carried weight outside Baltimore too, and a number of New York producers, especially the noted impresario David Belasco, opened their plays in Baltimore because they wanted Lambdin's opinion. His obituary, in 1923, described Lambdin as occupying "a position in dramatic criticism which was almost unique in the America of today." Gilbert Kanour was then named to review plays, and movies as well.

On September 1, 1920, the *Evening Sun* became the first paper in the nation to have its own airplane for news-gathering. An announcement said this new technique would be experimental, "for the purpose of gathering news at points difficult of access by railroad, auto or steamer travel" and "would bring back pictures and stories for afternoon editions previously unattainable because of time limitations." The public was reminded that "so many agencies of modern life had started in Baltimore that it seems only fitting that a beginning of this sort should be made here." The aircraft was a Canadian Curtiss biplane; "under ideal conditions, it can exceed 75 miles per hour." It was flown by W. D. Tipton, a fighter pilot in the world war who was also a special writer on aeronautics. The plane was used to cover such stories as railroad wrecks, flooding, fires, a disabled submarine off the Delaware capes, even a bishop's consecration in Easton, Maryland, and at various times to deliver papers to the Eastern Shore. It was used until 1927, when commercial aviation overshadowed the novelty of such enterprise.

Murphy was described by respectful staff members as "a short, stage Irishman with a pug nose and an abrupt manner—but quite a guy," "the ugliest Irishman I've ever seen," who "always looked like the unhappiest human around." One who worked in the comparatively safe distance of the editorial department said that he "ruled the premises with thunder and lightning." Everyone agreed that Murphy was an exceedingly able newspaperman, an inexhaustible idea man, and an editor who demanded that reporting be accurate, fair, and complete. Most of his day was spent in his glass box in the city room, "his head bowed over his desk, scanning the paper, edition after edition. He puffed incessant clouds of cigarette smoke as he pored over the pages, and sometimes he puffed fire and brimstone when he discovered something that had gone awry." He was inordinately weather-conscious and insisted—no, ordered—that windows be open, even on cool or cold days. Believing everyone to be as interested in the weather as he was, on most days Murphy commanded a weather story. Often the weather was just weather—not cold, hot, humid, rainy, or even overcast—but once Murphy had ordered a weather story it was up to some rewriteman to produce a readable one, which was usually done with imagination and wit.

Fitzpatrick was succeeded as city editor by his assistant, Bruce Earnest, who had worked on Pennsylvania papers before joining the *Evening Sun* in 1920.

Murphy had a cannon voice that could blast fissures in the ceiling. When he yelled *"Bruce!!"* Earnest seemed to eject from his chair, and he had taken two long steps toward the glass box before his name had stopped reverberating through the city room. Earnest was amiable and endearing, with a sense of humor flavored with whimsy. His chief asset as a city editor was the devotion of his staff, but his competence was encumbered by certain personality traits. He lived in an orbit of acute apprehension, sensing that something, anything, was about to go wrong; no matter how close a deadline was, he had time to listen to a tip on a race; and he was superstitious, in uncounted ways. Earnest chewed, rather than smoked, long cigars and never failed to twist their cellophane wrappers the same number of times before tossing them over his left shoulder. He insisted on leaving the building the same way he had entered, no matter the ruse or obstacle concocted by his staff. One time they nailed the door shut. Earnest, not an impetuous man, broke the glass and, with a sigh of relief, walked through the door. After betting on a horse that lost, he would give away his tie. After betting a parlay he would become disconsolate if a clerk named Esther, a nonstop talker whom he regarded as a hex, spoke to him. "I'll never win now," he would lament.

Earnest's police headquarters man was Donald K. Miller, who telephoned facts to rewritemen. He had colorful expressions, for example, fornication became fornification, and heretofore became heretobefore. When he reported assaults and accidents, he was brief and to the point, but if he had something he thought would startle the jaded city desk, he would include every detail and save the significant fact for a dramatic ending. One busy morning he called Earnest with an account that went something like this: "At 1:35 A.M., a 1936 four-door Plymouth, license number 179-628, going south on St. Paul Street at an excessive speed and in what must have been an erratic manner, rammed a streetlight and three parked cars on the west side of the street. When police arrived they found the driver asleep behind the wheel and arrested him for drunken driving. The driver, white, 42, of such-and-such an address, was"— then after a long pause came his punch line, the name of the driver, a *Sun* reporter.

On Friday afternoons Miller came to the office for his pay envelope and to stop in the city room to relate his week's supply of macabre and dirty stories he had heard at police headquarters. One day Earnest told him, "Donald, from now on I want you to write up these Friday stories, every Friday so everyone on the staff can enjoy them." And Miller did, faithfully, in detail, and in Millerese. This was the only writing that Miller did in some forty-five years on the paper.

The senior reporter was Harry S. Sherwood, who drew the difficult assignments. When the wife of the Rev. Dr. Arthur B. Kinsolving, rector of St. Paul's Episcopal Church and a figure revered throughout the city, was said to have converted to Catholicism, Sherwood had the task of calling him for confirmation, detail, and comment. Kinsolving, as usual, was gracious and candid. Later, when Kinsolving's daughter married a member of the Jewish faith, his philosophical deduction was that God intended him to be a connecting link between the Pope and Abraham.

Because Sherwood was hard of hearing, he compensated by shouting on the phone. For example, when he called the governor, which was often, he might shout, "Wait a minute, Harry [this was Governor Nice], I'm just trying to find out what fence you're straddling this time." Activity in the city room would stop and the staff, especially neophytes, sat mesmerized by a hardened pro in action. Sherwood knew everyone and seemed impressed with no one. A colleague said he was a reporter who would call God by his first name. He typed with two overlapping fingers for additional force, and he banged the typewriter so hard that the *c*'s, *e*'s, and *o*'s became holes in the paper, forcing the copy desk to puzzle over words. Stories were written on copy books then, with three carbons: the original and one carbon for the city desk, one for the AP and one for the reporter. When copy boys picked up Sherwood's copy, they'd flip the books in the air and the punched out vowels would cascade like confetti as the copy boys wended their way to the city desk.

The staff admired and respected Murphy, but were cowed by him. Out of his sight and hearing, even in gripe sessions, his staff referred to him as Mr. Murphy. Reporters joked that one reporter was Murphy's match—Gertrude Leimbach, a robust woman with a commanding presence. Joke or not, it was a fact that in the early 1920s she was the only city staff reporter to get a byline. She covered "men's stories" in that era when women worked only on the women's page.

Bylines were scarce; reporters had to be content with seeing their names scrawled in thick pencil over their stories on the ponderous file of back issues kept up by the city desk in the event of inquiries or complaints. Unlike today, a reporter never lobbied for a byline, let alone start a story by writing his or her name. A byline was a special reward authorized by the managing editor, sometimes by Patterson. Only the top two men in the Washington bureau were given them, and senior reporters received them only on major out-of-town assignments. A regular byline was so unusual that the recipient would be given a byline party. Gilbert Kanour did not get a byline until he had been a critic for three or four years. At Kanour's party, as a souvenir, he was presented his byline cast in 72-point Bodoni bold type, almost eight columns wide. At the same party, Harry Black told him to go to a tailor to be measured for a new dinner jacket. Theater critics wore black tie to opening nights, and the music critic covering opening night when the Metropolitan Opera came to town wore white tie and tails.

Sportswriters were regarded as roughnecks, and their office was separated from the news and editorial departments on the fourth floor. They had a cubbyhole on the second floor, behind the outdoor scoreboard erected for the World Series. They didn't have desks, but used typewriters on a long shelf. At night the machines were secured by putting locks around the space bars.

Fred Turbyville, "a hard-driving man," was the sports editor and often wrote two columns a day. The other byline writers—in sports they were more common than in news—were Leo Doyle, the racing writer; Randall Cassell, who covered high school, then college, sports; "Colonel Bogey," a pseudonym for Carl Waller, a news reporter who wrote about golf for an extra dollar or so a week; and Margaret Haesecker, the first woman in evening sports—but she didn't get her full name, just "By Margaret."

In those days reporters and photographers were often promoted from the ranks of the curb school copy boys. One, Bill Thomas, had risen as far as assistant city editor. Copy-boy stories are part of the lore of the *Sunpapers*. Many a copy boy was addressed not by name but by some incidental attribute. One who had injured his hand by slapping copy too vigorously on a city desk spike was thereafter called "Spike." Another arrived wearing a pink shirt, and Murphy, calling it undignified, told the boy not to wear it again; from then on the boy was "Pinky." (Murphy ruled that his staff had to wear business suits in the office, even in the hot, humid summer, and this was before air conditioning. After the first edition, if it was a slow day, he got everyone away from their desks for group exercises.)

The most oft-repeated story concerned Harry Black when he was chairman of the board. He visited the *Evening Sun* city room every day to inhale the atmosphere, and his arrival was an event: He was dapper and debonair, sported a straw boater at a jaunty angle and a boutonniere that never looked wilted, and twirled a malacca cane as he moved slowly but elegantly with a splayed gait past the city desk. A new copy boy, Paul Dorsey, asked, "Who's that guy? He walks around like he owns the place." The answer, of course, was "He does." Black enjoyed the story so much that he gave Dorsey, who later became a reporter, five dollars.

One copy boy, who did not rise to photographer or reporter, was sent by a rewriteman to a department store for several pairs of stockings for his wife. His instructions were specific: "sheer chiffon, size nine or nine-and-a-half." The copy boy was gone for an hour and finally reported by telephone. "Mr. C.," he said, "I'm over here at Hutzler's and they say they don't have any stocking like that except for women."

Michael Lhotsky, who became make-up editor of the *Sunday Sun*, started as a copy boy in the *Evening Sun* editorial department. One of his tasks was to open the letters to the editor. A letter from Werner Janssen mentioned that he was resigning as conductor of the Baltimore Symphony Orchestra. Lhotsky had seen nothing in the paper about this, so he took the letter to the editorial-page editor, who immediately took it to Murphy. Lhotsky's enterprise so pleased Murphy that he wrote out a $20 pay chit. When Lhotsky presented it to Joseph Janushek, the chief of payroll, who disbursed the company's money as if it were his own, Janushek double-checked with Murphy in disbelief—the $20 bonus was so much greater than Lhotsky's $12-a-week salary.

At that time—and until December 1963—employees were paid in cash.

Often a wife who wanted her household money before it went to a bookmaker would wait for her husband at the payroll window. A pastime for bachelors standing in line was to count the cluster of waiting wives.

By the mid 1920s and early 1930s Murphy had assembled a staff that came up even to his standards. Many of his reporters and desk men were college-educated and had worked for smaller papers. Some on the news side are better reporters than writers, some are better writers than reporters. It is a rare person who has both skills to a high degree. Reporters who excelled at both were Lee McCardell and Thomas M. O'Neill, who joined the paper in the mid-1920s. McCardell did everything superbly—rewrite, covering fast-breaking spot stories, writing a memorable feature. (Most features, like fashions, are soon dated, but not those McCardell wrote. A person chancing on one in the *Sun* library is likely to be amazed at the story's freshness.) McCardell became a distinguished war and foreign correspondent for the morning and evening papers; O'Neill, one of the most polished *Sunpaper* writers (there were and are many), became a noted political-page columnist. He never resorted to newspaper files for reference, using what he had ferreted out that day and, if background were needed, depending on his phenomenal memory. His one idiosyncrasy, like "Listerine" Bensinger of the *Tribune* in *The Front Page,* was fear of disease-producing microorganisms. Before he sat at his desk, O'Neill would wipe it clean with a dustcloth, flick the cloth over the typewriter keyboard, wipe the mouthpiece and receiver of his telephone, wash his hands, then go to work.

From time to time the talented rewrite battery included McCardell, Allen Will Harris, James P. Connolly, and W. Fenwick Keyser. Connolly had the most imagination and the lightest touch. With just the report of an open fire-hydrant on a humid day he could contrive a bright weather story, or with a few facts about a vice-squad raid he could turn out a humorous feature that was more Connolly than vice squad. Keyser also had a quick, light touch, but he is more remembered for his antics. A Yale man and a grandson of R. Brent Keyser, an Abell stockholder from Grasty's time, the winsome Keyser probably made only one reference to his wealth. Police reporters' travel was paid for in streetcar tokens, not more than ten a day, the equivalent of about $1 (and this continued until the early 1940s). Earnest sent Keyser, as a new reporter on an assignment, offering him some car tokens. "That's all right," Keyser said. "I don't need them. My Packard's right out front."

Harry Black, ever eager to provide story ideas, mentioned in one of his daily visits to the managing editor that he seldom saw workmen wearing painter's caps anymore and wondered if that might be worth looking into. Keyser got the assignment. But rather than pursue the story suggestion of the chairman of the board, Keyser bought several dozen such caps. Next day, when Black came in everyone in the office was wearing one. Black enjoyed not only the joke but also its subtle connotation, for the news staff was trying to organize an American Newspaper Guild local, and newspeople regarded themselves as workmen, not professionals.

Covering a vaudeville act about a trick horse, Keyser convinced the trainer that he would get a better story, and probably a picture, if he took the horse to the paper and had him perform for the city editor. Keyser got the willing trainer but not-so-willing horse up to the news room in a freight elevator. The staff claimed it was the closest Earnest had ever been to a horse. One of Keyser's hobbies was toy trains, and he kept his desk drawers filled with miniature sets. Between editions he would take them out to play with them on his desktop.

Others prominent on the staff were A. K. Darby, the financial editor, succeeded in 1930 by Rodney Crowther; John Conley, who also covered business and finance; Stephen E. Fitzgerald, a prize scholar at Johns Hopkins University who in 1939 became the first *Sunpaper* reporter to be awarded a Nieman Fellowship at Harvard; and Frances Shattuck Nyburg, the women's page editor who wrote a sophisticated column, "Getting Around," and was succeeded as editor by Sally Wilson.

Roger S. Williamson was the painstaking City Hall reporter. At the end of the day he would dictate "overnights"—stories for the next day's paper—to a city desk clerk, never using a typescript and seldom using notes. Often he would get partway through an interminable story—say on a sewer loan—and he would ask the clerk to keep the phone line open while he went to check a few facts. When confronted with a complex subject that might require several subordinate clauses in each paragraph, Williamson would lie down on the couch in the City Hall pressroom to sort out his thoughts, leaving the clerk to wait and wait. This drove clerks wild, but it was tolerated though not appreciated by the city desk. Sent to Detroit to do a series on blacktop street-paving costs, Williamson called the city desk to dictate his first story. He was twenty minutes into it when the city editor left for lunch. On his return, the city editor asked the clerk why she was wearing the telephone headpiece while reading a novel. He should have anticipated her reply, "I'm waiting for Williamson to finish."

From the start in 1910 on, the *Evening Sun* had been subscribing to United Press news and sports wires. The *Sun* was a member of the Associated Press, the largest, most thorough, and most prestigious of national news-gathering organizations. Charles H. Grasty attempted to get an AP membership for the *Evening Sun* in 1914 but was turned down. The rule then was that any new franchise had to be approved by the existing AP members of the city in question. While Felix Agnus, publisher of the *American* and the *Star*, was agreeable, Munsey, publisher of the *Evening News*, a better paper than the *Evening Sun*, would not yield his competitive advantage. Paul Patterson made another try in 1924, invoking an AP bylaw under which a local veto could be overridden by a four-fifths vote of the entire membership. This too failed, because of the voting strength of the Hearst chain, which by then owned the Baltimore *Evening News*. Four years later, with Mencken pressing the *Sunpaper* case, Hearst waived his veto, and on March 31, 1928, the *Evening Sun* finally obtained an AP franchise. An agreement contained a clause that the two papers would not be competitive on late-breaking stories. When one would replate or issue an extra, the other had to be notified as soon as a decision was made, but did not have to say why it was being done. The agreement was in effect until extras and most replates were outmoded.

In the pre-television age newspapers printed a series of afternoon editions. Hearst's *Evening News* and the *Evening Sun* competed for street sales by implying that they had the latest news. When the *Evening Sun* decided to call its noontime edition the Five Star, Hearst countered by calling the comparable edition of the *Evening News* the Six Star. When the *Evening Sun* responded with a Seven Star, Hearst made its competing edition an Eight Star. The *Evening Sun*'s Nine Star was topped by Hearst's Ten Star. But the *Evening Sun* had the last word with an All Star, still its final edition.

When a big story broke after the final edition, Baltimore papers would produce extras with hand-set, end-of-the-world headlines. Youths, hastily rounded up by circulation hustlers, would hawk the extras, shouting, "Extra! Extra!! Read all about it!" In slow periods some extras were based on fires that screaming headlines—and shouting newsboys—turned into holocausts.

Over the years, the *Evening Sun* has sponsored an infinite number of contests and promotions. By 1911 it joined the Women's Civic League in giving prizes for the best gardens in Baltimore and environs. In October 1913, Henry Edward Warner, who had moved from the editorial department to become circulation manager, formed a walking club called the Wanderlusters. In 1922 the paper began a black-and-white sketch contest that became an annual event. Prize-winning entries were hung in the corridor of the *Evening Sun* editorial offices, known as "Brain Alley." Harry Black, acting anonymously in 1925, offered through a letter to the editor a gold medal—not to architects or builders but to the owner of the most pleasing building erected in Baltimore that year. The first medal went to the Pittsburgh Plate Glass Company; later winners included St. Casimir's Church in Canton; City College; St. John's Episcopal Church in Mount Washington; an apartment house; the Scottish Rite Temple; and a filling station.

In 1924 the paper awarded a $100 prize to the reader furnishing the best answer to the question "What is the difference between a Republican and a Democrat?" The winning answer was: "A Republican is a person who thinks a Democratic administration is bad for business. A Democrat is a person who thinks a Republican administration is bad for business. Both are right."

The Evening Sun has offered medals, cups, and trophies for workboat racing on the bay and for such sports as model-yacht racing, quoit-pitching, tennis, basketball, football, swimming and bowling. Every year until the late 1960s its bowling tournament attracted thousands of bowlers. It also held contests to choose the bravest policemen and firemen, the most polite streetcar conductor, the best fiddler, the best caddy, the best recipes, a name for the zoo's first elephant (Mary Ann), and the most meritorious mutt and alley cat.

Another promotion was the *Evening Sun* Newsboys' Band, organized in May 1922. Originally limited to actual newsboys, the band later included other youths. It traveled around Maryland, Virginia, West Virginia and Pennsylvania, and the paper logged every appearance: "*Evening Sun* Band Marches in Parade," "City-Wide Concert Tour Staged by Newsboys' Band," "Newsboys Will Camp with National Guard." The band never played where an admission fee was charged. (When a big advertiser, the Bernheimer-Leader Store—"A City in Itself"—asked the band to play in its bargain basement, the request was turned down.) Twice a year the band toured Maryland, and every year it played at the Chesapeake Bay workboat races. On July 4, 1924, the boys were returning from that event on the excursion steamer *Three Rivers* when the boat caught fire. The fifty-nine members of the band acted heroically, awakening sleeping passengers and helping elderly women don life jackets. Five boys were among the ten passengers who lost their lives. Although shattered by the tragedy, the band continued until 1932. The five heroes were buried in Loudon Park Cemetery and a bronze plaque was installed bearing their names, the circumstances of their deaths, and the quotation "They have 'moved a little nearer to the master of all music.'" For a long time the *Sunpapers* placed a wreath on the plot on the Fourth of July and on Christmas. A few years ago a visitor found the plaque discolored and called the *Sun*. Nancy Oppel, of the paper's public relations staff, took it upon herself to scour the plaque with lye and baking soda.

Hamilton Owens gradually added other editorial writers to his two-man staff of Hobbs and Kanour. Francis F. Beirne, a Virginian and a Rhodes Scholar who had worked on the *Sun* as a reporter before the war, was hired in 1923. Gerald W. Johnson, a North Carolina newspaperman whose critical articles on Southern culture and politics attracted the attention of Owens and Mencken, joined in 1926. R. P. Harriss, another North Carolinian and just out of Duke University, was hired for the news staff in 1927 but spent part of his time writing editorials. He resigned in 1930 to go abroad, where he worked for the *Paris Herald Tribune*. In 1934, Harriss returned as an editorial writer. Philip M. Wagner was employed by General Electric but was being published in the *New Republic, Harper's,* and the *Atlantic* when he came to the paper. Before he was hired, Wagner was invited to have lunch in the boardroom with Black, Patterson, Owens, Murphy, and Mencken. It was customary to use such an occasion to size up a candidate for an important position.

The daily editorial meeting began at 8:00 A.M. By 8:05, Owens had received telephone calls from Patterson, Black, and Murphy. Patterson might say, "Look on page fourteen of the *Sun*. So-and-so is shooting off his mouth again. What about hitting him again?" Black's ideas might be preposterous, but sometimes they were preposterously successful. When his ideas were passed over he did not complain, or even ask why they were not used. Murphy, as noted, was an idea man, and his suggestions carried weight. (He was a powerful man in the company; in 1932 he was elected a vice president.) When

Owens became editor, Murphy told him he was going to "keep a sharp eye" on him, and he did. Lhotsky, hired as a copy boy in 1927 (five years after Owens became editor), said his orders were to show all editorials to Murphy, who gave them a quick once-over, before Lhotsky sent them down the tube to the composing room.

One day when Harriss was in charge while Owens was away, he wrote an editorial taking a strong stand on a subject. After the first edition, an executive in the business office telephoned Harriss saying, "We're going to lose thousands of dollars in advertising because of that damned editorial." Harriss, unsure and nervous as acting editor for a day, killed the editorial for the next edition. Murphy was immediately on the telephone: "What happened to that editorial?" Told, he blew up. "Put it back with a chaser [changing the page while the edition is still being printed]. And then call the business department and tell them you thought it over and decided to run the editorial, no matter the consequences." Harriss did and Murphy later confided, "I can see why they complained. But that's their problem. If you ever let the business office run you they'll keep running you forever."

The page had seven or eight editorials. Most were only two or three paragraphs and had been written in a matter of minutes in the morning. Wagner, who later became editor, said that Johnson, a prose stylist, was the fastest writer, "His editorial was done before anyone else had finished. And it was perfectly typed. Not an x or a strikeover. In the meetings he would agree on what he would write, but his editorial had nothing to do with what we had discussed." Owens, in his Columbia Oral History interview, described Johnson as "a wheelhorse on the paper . . . a beautiful writer of course, although one so addicted to paradox that it was sometimes hard to follow his reasoning. . . . Another characteristic of Gerald's—and I have said this to him many times—is, he is allergic to facts. Or, in his own words, 'Get as few facts as possible and you can distort them to suit your pattern.'"

After the first edition appeared, Bill, the copy boy, brought a tray of coffee and buns, and the writers relaxed and read what they had wrought. Harriss recalled, "If it had something utterly outrageous to insure a flood of letters, we felt the day had gotten off to a good start."

Wagner said they liked to use catchphrases. "During Prohibition one of the phrases went something like this, 'A high tax for liquor, but a low tax for beer and wine.' It would be worked into every editorial on the subject." He said the quick time-frame in writing precluded philosophizing and, he added, "Sometimes there wasn't much thinking behind the editorials. There were all sorts of inconsistencies in our policy, but it was fun." Owens said the page gained a reputation for "being, at worst, smart-alecky and, at its best, witty and pungent. Most of it was due to Mencken."

Beginning on February 9, 1920, Mencken began writing a Monday column, long and considered, unlike the old "Free Lance" and printed in the form of an editorial-page article. He wrote some 800 columns, lambasting most subjects except the old Baltimore of his youth, which he recalled nostalgically. Mencken was at the height of his fame in the 1920s and 1930s. Walter Lippmann called him "the most powerful personal influence of this whole generation of educated people."

During Prohibition, from its ratification in January 1919 to its repeal in December 1933, the evening editorial page—along with the *New York World*— had become famous for its biting and scoffing attacks and was widely quoted. Many readers were known to turn first to the editorial page which was showcased as the first page of the second section, before reading the front page or the back page, where the local news was showcased. But the end of Prohibition deprived the editors of a continuing and varied source of crazy events to lampoon, and the page lost the edge of its gustiness.

As far back as 1922, Owens and Mencken had set out to include reporting and opinion from various sections of the nation by recruiting a corps of well-known writers, including Edmund Wilson, to write exclusively for the *Evening Sun*. At first some were identified not by name but by locality or subject—"Our Great Plains Correspondent," "Our Sporting Life Correspondent"—but later they were named. Many were from the south: Grover C. Hall, of Montgomery, Alabama, and R. Charlton Wright, formerly of Columbia, South Carolina, both Pulitzer Prize winners; Louis Graves, a respected author; and Virginius Dabney, editor of the *Richmond Times-Dispatch*, who became a well-known historian. Others were David Warren Ryder of San Francisco, Duncan Aiken and Wayne Gard of Texas, and Malcolm B. Ronald of South Dakota. Mencken was an indefatigable talent scout, recommending writers who had been published by the *American Mercury* and *Smart Set*. In 1922 he suggested Robert Duffus and Lewis Mumford, soon to be well-known names. When Hilton Butler lost his job on another paper as a result of an article he had written for the *Mercury*, Mencken told Owens that Butler wrote well, had a civilized point of view, and was young.

One free-lance correspondent, a former Baltimorean, worked for a midwestern paper that sent him around the nation on assignments, and he often contributed to the *Evening Sun*. He contributed so much from so many different places that the *Evening Sun* editors were amazed that he could travel so far and do so much so fast. When his pieces began to be submitted in different styles, they worried that he might be plagiarizing them. And he was—first reworking good articles from small papers he read on his trips, and later brazenly putting his name on them. The denouement came when he submitted something in his name that was the work of a popular syndicated columnist, Westbrook Pegler.

One unexpected success was a brief, bottom-of-the-page filler headlined "Gob Humor." In 1924 the USS *Tennessee* invited newspaper editors on an inspection trip, and the jokes in the ship's newspaper caught the eye of the *Evening Sun*'s representative. The first Gob Humor appeared on November 6, 1924, and beginning in late 1925 it became a "must" filler for many years, with the jokes drawn from 181 fleet and station newspapers. Readers thought some of the jokes were too raw for a family newspaper, and individuals and groups, such as the Holy Name Society, would complain. When Newton Aiken became editor in 1943, he wanted to drop it but was told it was the best-read item on the page. He never understood some of the jokes selected by whoever was Gob Humor editor that month, and he would try them out on a subordinate. Invariably the answer was "It's okay, Newt. That'll get by. It's a tame one." But now and then after the first edition was rolling, some printer would alert Aiken that he had a dirty joke on his editorial page, and it would be yanked for an innocuous one. In-office collectors of *Sunpaper* misprints, miscalculations, and blunders prize numerous Gob Humors that lasted only one edition, and some that never got beyond the page proof. Finally, Gob Humor was dropped when the navy replaced the fleet and station newspapers with a servicewide journal lacking salty jokes.

A feature that appeared irregularly was written by Harriss but carried no byline. Reading French or French-Canadian papers, Harriss would search out a feature or crime-story—he thought the French papers had marvelous descriptions of crime—and translate the story literally; if a word had two meanings he would use the inappropriate one. The pieces would begin "The estimable Monsieur Pom Frit [Fried Potatoes], who occasionally translates for us, renders the following. . . ."

Still another staple was a one-or-two line letter composed by an editorial writer but signed "Oswald," usually addressed to a politician who was involved in or embarrassed by a news event, great or small. The best Oswald letter was not written by a member of the staff but amiably contributed by Louis Azrael, a columnist on the rival *News-Post.* When Cyprus was beset by one more Greek-Turk conflict, John Marshall Butler, a U.S. senator from Maryland, demanded that the United States invade the island. His press release spelled it "Cypress." Oswald's letter to Butler asked "Dear John, When you talk about Cypress you aren't barking up the wrong tree, are you?"

In February 1938, responsibility for the page was reordered (to be dealt with later), Hamilton Owens having been promoted to the editorship of the *Sun.* When Owens told his staff that he was leaving, he had a difficult time stifling tears. Stunned and apprehensive, some believed that this was done "to bring the *Evening Sun* into line, to heel." At a farewell luncheon, Owens was presented with a silk tophat because on the older, more sedate paper "he should be high-hatting us." In his Oral History interview, Owens said:

> "I recommended [as his successor] my right-hand man, Philip Wagner. . . . But Mencken wasn't sure that Wagner was mature enough. There was a long argument about it, and finally, much to my surprise, Mencken said, "I will take over the editorship of the *Evening Sun* for not longer than three months. By that time I will know the capacity of the various men on the editorial staff, and will be able to judge whether Wagner or some other member of that staff is the proper man to be editor." . . .

Mencken took the job over in his usual vigorous, not to say, violent, fashion. What transpired was that Mencken had all but forgotten the necessary disciplines of a daily newspaper. . . . Mencken did not feel, as I had felt, that a great part of the strength of the *Evening Sun* arose from the fact that the editorials in the evening paper were based on the news in the morning paper, so he began to give his men overnight assignments. That is to say, on Tuesday they were supposed to be writing editorials for Wednesday's paper. Also, his standards of thoroughness and precision, and his determination to have these, were so great that frequently the assignments he gave could not be done overnight, indeed might take a week, so that when morning came and the paper had to be made up, the material to fill the page simply wasn't there.

Fortunately, Phil Wagner, . . . a highly competent and disciplined man, saw the situation and pitched in, so that whether or not the editorials that appeared were precisely the kind that Mencken would have liked, the fact is that there *were* printable, publishable editorials, and the page did come out.

Mencken was in his glory. Patterson had ordered a massive desk, a junior version of a dictator's escritoire. Mencken installed a brass spittoon for his Uncle Willie stogy stubs and a target for chewing-tobacco. When setting out for the composing room, Mencken would don a Princeton beer jacket. But most of his exhilaration came from scotching what he considered the radical tone of the page and expressing instead a savage, unrelieved hostility toward Franklin Delano Roosevelt and the New Deal. In a memo to Patterson in 1937, Mencken had warned, "At the time the *Sunpapers* were rehabilitated many of the persons chosen to man them, especially on the side of the foreign service, were of Liberal politics. Some of these persons have since become radicals." The relatively liberal editorial writers viewed Mencken's editorship with misgiving and alarm, and with good reason. Day after day the paper passed over local concerns to attack Roosevelt, then in his second term. When an editorial written by one of his staff struck Mencken as hesitant or weak-voiced, he would heavily edit or rewrite altogether. The tactic of switching a writer from one impracticable, uncompleted assignment to another appeared to have an ulterior motive in Gerald Johnson's case. Johnson, a Roosevelt admirer, was often kept out of the paper. It had become almost a one-man page.

Two stunts of Mencken's attracted more attention than any previous editorial-page high jinks. On February 10, 1938, he printed what became known as "The Page of Dots." The editorial, titled "Object Lesson," began:

In the six adjoining columns the *Evening Sun* today presents a graphic representation of the Federal Government's immense corps of jobholders. Each dot stands for one jobholder, and there are 1,000,000-odd of them. The actual enrollment, at 10 o'clock this morning, was reported to be 999,264 head, but additions were being made at the rate of more than one hundred an hour, so the million mark will no doubt be passed before the last edition of the *Evening Sun* is on the streets. This is the first time in human history, so far as can be ascertained, that a million dots have ever been printed on one page of a daily newspaper. . . .

"The Page of Dots," alleviated only by a short editorial on the Japanese beetle and a three-line Gob Humor, caused much talk and some perplexity. Readers with impaired eyesight could not see the fine-screen dots made by the Benday photoengraving. They called the paper to say something like, "I hear you got a funny editorial page today but something went wrong with my paper—most of the page is just gray. Can I get another paper?"

On March 4, Mencken filled the entire page with one editorial, "Five Years of the New Deal," which went after not only Roosevelt but also those who would benefit from his adminstration's programs. But Mencken believed that the other side should be heard, and he invited Johnson to write a rebuttal, though not a full-page one. Johnson's article, "On the Profit Side: A Reply to That Huge Editorial," concluded:

> Now at last, we have a government that has turned away from dreams and fantasies and ghosts and is dealing with stern, hard facts. It has made plenty of blunders and perhaps has committed some crimes, but at least it is living in the Twentieth Century; at least it is not guided by a dead hand, whether that of George III, of Patrick Henry or of Adam Smith; at least it has striven to bring some intelligence to bear on the problem of ruling. If it had cost twice as much, it would still be the most profitable investment the American people have made since the Louisiana Purchase.

Wagner and Harriss tried to pull off a stunt of their own, but Mencken strenuously opposed them, shouting, "No. No. No. I won't let you pull a Katzenjammer trick on me." Harriss recalled the incident as a shouting match, but added that one couldn't stay angry with Mencken and that he never held a grudge. At the end of the day, even one filled with discord, Mencken usually made a funny remark and his associates left on relatively good terms.

Beirne had been writing a light column, "The Rolling Road," under the pseudonym Christopher Billopp since July 1931. It was a miscellany of comment, contributions, and a short essay of observations on such commonplace subjects as neckties, garage doors, and library books. Mencken told Beirne to drop everything except the essay, and Beirne grieved. To cheer him up, Mencken said the essay was as viable in Cincinnati and Tuscaloosa as it was in Baltimore and therefore could be syndicated. Beirne pointed out the company policy against syndication (except for Kent's "Great Game of Politics"). "Gammon and spinach," Mencken replied, using a favorite expression. "I'll have you syndicate before the horseflies appear." Mencken got Frank Markey, a syndicate salesman, interested in the feature, then persuaded Patterson to assent. Beirne got the additional income, marveling at Mencken's thoughtfulness.

Harriss and other editorial writers felt that, apart from the two stunts, Mencken's page was not up to the professional level of any three months in previous years. Harriss described the temporary editorship as "interesting, exciting, but wearing." When the interim ended, everyone was exhausted, even Mencken. He went to Johns Hopkins Hospital for a few days and then off on a vacation; the staff went back to work putting out a page.

Before leaving, Mencken announced, "There's only one man to be editor of the paper, and that's Philip Wagner." Patterson celebrated the appointment with a dinner at the Maryland Club for his top editors and the board of directors. Wagner's page was not as reactionary or conservative as Mencken's, but it was more conservative than it had been under Owens. It was still lively, innovative, and readable.

THIRTEEN

The Paul Patterson Years
1930–1952

In the 1920s and 1930s the Abell board
had a number of changes. After the death of R. Brent Keyser in 1927 and the
resignation of Robert Garrett in 1930, it was reduced to five members. In 1934
it was again increased to seven: In addition to Harry C. Black (the chairman),
Paul Patterson, J. J. Nelligan, and James C. Fenhagen, it consisted of John
E. Semmes, elected in 1932, and the two newest members, H. L. Mencken
(a close Patterson friend from many years back) and Edwin F. Abell Morgan,
a great-grandson of the Founder (his mother, Mary, was the only daughter
of Edwin F. Abell). In 1936, George C. Cutler succeeded Nelligan, who died
in 1935. As in the past, the board had the strength, and parochialness, of an
all-Baltimore membership.

Despite the grinding Depression, the board, sometimes grudgingly, gave
Patterson the resources he argued were essential if the papers were to continue
improving. The physical plant was expanded, staffs were enlarged and up-
graded, and international conferences were reported in depth.

In 1928, along with John W. Owens, Reynolds, and Mencken, Patterson
had attended the Pan American Conference in Havana. Two years later
Patterson had Owens, Mencken, Drew Pearson (the new diplomatic correspondent), and André Géraud (Pertinax) and Hector C. Bywater, two of the
Sun's special correspondents, reinforce Dewey L. Fleming, of the London
Bureau, in covering the second naval conference in London. For the 1933
London Economic Conference, the Sun sent Dexter M. Keezer, a former
professor of economics at Dartmouth who became an editorial writer in 1929,
and again had Géraud give the French viewpoint.

More recognition—and honors—came with the quality of the Sun's reporting and the vigor of its editorial page. In 1931 the University of Missouri
School of Journalism awarded its medal of honor "for distinguished service

in journalism to the *Sun*," and in 1935 *Time* magazine chose the *Sun* as one of the fifteen best papers in the United States.

In less than a decade the *Sun* won four Pulitzer Prizes: three by Edmund Duffy, the editorial cartoonist, and one, in 1937, by John W. Owens for distinguished editorial writing. Duffy's first, in 1931, was for "An Old Struggle Still Going On," showing a Russian soldier trying to wrest a cross from a Russian church. The second, in 1934, "California Points with Pride," depicted a double lynching. The third, in 1940, was for distinguished service as a cartoonist, as exemplified by "The Outstretched Hand"—Hitler offering a bloody hand and broken promises to prostrate minorities. Later in the Patterson era the *Sun* won five more Pulitzers.

Duffy worked with a grease pencil, drawing large images and, in the manner of the times, a series of familiar symbols. Critic Richard H. Levine wrote that, by World War II, Duffy was producing illustrations rather than cartoons and was relying on realism and draftsmanship more than on caricature and wit. He characterized Duffy as a political realist with a romantic's eye, a liberal "always to the left, in spirit and occasionally in print, of the *Sun's* own positions."

Duffy had studied at the Art Students League of New York with Boardman Robinson (a contributing cartoonist to the *Sun* in 1921–22), then spent two years abroad, and later worked for New York papers and magazines before joining the *Sun* in 1924. An unusually fast worker, he often got his idea and had the cartoon finished in minutes. Duffy dressed elegantly—his clothes were custom-made in London—and his hobbies also included horse-racing and the theater. He backed Broadway plays, and it was said that he made more money with some hits than he did as a cartoonist. He resigned in 1948 to become the editorial cartoonist for the *Saturday Evening Post* and after becoming bored there went with *Newsday.* Some 3,000 of his cartoons were given to the Milton S. Eisenhower Library of the Johns Hopkins University.

The *Sun* was the first paper to underwrite the plan of the Associated Press to send pictures by wire. That was in May 1934, even before the system was named Wirephoto. Patterson, a member of the AP's board for many years, wanted to be first for symbolic reasons, because the *Sun* had been first in other innovations. Until the first Wirephoto was transmitted on January 1, 1935, news pictures had been sent by mail, and important ones from Washington, D.C., by motorcycle.

In February 1935, *This Week,* a new nationally syndicated magazine, was added to the *Sunday Sun* and twenty other metropolitan papers, and two years later the Sunday paper dropped its letterpress magazine. In 1939 the price of the daily papers rose to three cents. To accommodate the expanding papers, two buildings that adjoined the *Sun* plant, 12–14 and 16–18 West Redwood Street, were acquired. After the Baltimore *Post's* plant burned on January 1, 1931, it accepted Patterson's offer to assemble and print its paper in the *Sun* plant for thirty-three days.

During the 1930s, amid the cheerlessness of hard times and ideological turmoil, ill-feelings festered. Patterson had to contend with a series of boycotts. These grew out of the papers' coverage and comment on lynchings, Ignatius Loyola, and bread prices, and also out of rate increases for movie advertising.

The *Sunpapers* described the 1931 lynching of a black man on the courthouse grounds in Salisbury, which followed the failure of local authorities to act against a mob. In his column, Mencken castigated the Eastern Shore's "boozing-day politicians" for staging a "public obscenity worthy of cannibals" and assailed Salisbury as "the Alsatia of morons." Subscriptions were canceled, and stores that sold the *Sunpapers* were forced to stop doing so on threat of a boycott. Representatives of eighteen Shore firms voted not to do business with Baltimore until the *Sun* and Mencken apologized. Telegrams to Patterson threatened harm to any reporter who ventured on the Shore. Two circulation trucks were ambushed, their papers thrown away and their drivers beaten. A second lynching occurred in Princess Anne in 1933, and the National Guard was called out to protect witnesses identifying members of that mob. Again the story prompted large headlines on page one, and again the Shore took umbrage at big-city newspapers with threats made and subscriptions canceled. Animosity toward the *Sun* lingered for years.

An extensive boycott by Roman Catholics resulted from a dispatch on June 18, 1934, written by S. Miles Bouton, a special correspondent of the *Sun* for thirteen years who had just been expelled from Germany for his unadmiring accounts of the Nazi regime. Writing about Hitler, he declared: "It has seemed to me at times that there is a kinship between him and Ignatius Loyola [the founder in 1534 of the Society of Jesus]. One finds in both men the same complete faith in their mission, the same readiness and determination to exercise their power with utter ruthlessness and brutality to carry out that mission. No consideration of personal profit or glory ever entered Loyola's mind and I believe that the same can be said for Hitler."

Letters from irate Jesuits were printed. Patterson, replying to a personal letter from the president of Loyola College, regretted the reference, and John W. Owens called on Archbishop Michael J. Curley to smooth matters over. But the archbishop, who had feuded with the *Sun* in the past, demanded a "complete" printed apology. On June 29 the *Catholic Review*, the weekly paper of the archdiocese, printed an open letter from the archbishop that filled three columns of its front page. The archbishop denounced Bouton's report as "a gratuitous insult, not only to the Jesuit fathers . . . but also to every Catholic priest and every Catholic lay member. . . . For twelve years and more, the *Sun* has seen fit to offend Catholics by their editorials and news stories. . . . We have stood enough of the insults of the *Sun*. We are now through. We ask no favors of the *Sun*. We demand justice. The organized Catholics of the archdiocese know exactly how to act."

When the *Sun* refused these terms, the archbishop called for a boycott. In an even longer letter in the *Review* of July 6, he "defied" the *Sun*. The analogy between Ignatius Loyola and Hitler "was not as Mr. Owens, the editor of the morning *Sun,* would have us believe, a mere lapse, a mere slip, something for which they are sorry and which should have never been published. No! No!"

> I call for action and now direct myself to the Knights of Columbus, to our organized groups of women, to our 80,000 Holy Name men of the Archdiocese, to our Polish, Bohemian, Lithuanian and Italian organizations to tell the *Sun*, not by words, but by deeds that they resent the insult of the *Sun*, a common ordinary insult, a plain, unvarnished lie for which the *Sun* refuses to apologize, simply because it might hurt this "brave exiled" correspondent from Berlin.

Catholics responded by ceasing to buy the paper, and some advertising was dropped. The *Review,* which claimed that large numbers of Protestants and Jews had expressed support, kept attacking. Across the bottom of its pages for the next few weeks it printed eight-column darts—"The memory of James Cardinal Gibbons has been insulted by the *Sun,*" "Washington and other out-of-town papers can be delivered to your home every morning."

Before sailing off to Ireland to visit his mother, the archbishop ordered his auxiliary and vicar-general, Bishop John M. McNamara, and the chancery staff to carry on the fight. They were, however, less vociferous, and Patterson sensed an atmosphere propitious for resolving the dispute. Patterson, Owens and Mencken lunched with Bishop McNamara. Mencken noted in his account:

> It would be impossible for the *Sun* to draw up a statement which would present its own case fairly and yet be in such terms that any priest of the archdiocese could formally approve it in advance of publication. From the *Sun's* point of view, it would have to embody some criticism of the archbishop and no priest could afford to associate himself with that.
>
> The bishop agreed that this was a serious difficulty and that the best way out would be for the *Sun* to make the most conciliatory statement it could and then let the clergy take it or leave it.

In a long statement on July 19, the *Sun* reviewed the controversy and admitted that the words "ruthlessness" and "brutality" "were badly chosen and are not in accord with the prevailing historical opinion." It added that Bouton's "error should have been detected by the sub-editor who prepared the article for publication, but again there was a lapse and the words got into the paper. That inadvertence was and is regretted by the *Sun.*" The statement, written by John W. Owens, concluded, "It bears no ill will for the temper that has been shown by some in the discussion of certain aspects of the present case. . . . But the *Sun* does not grant the truth of the allegations made against it in the *Catholic Review,* nor can it accede to demands which violate its general policy."

The *Review* printed the statement on its front page, titling it "The *Sun* Apologizes" (which it had not done). The *Sunpapers* had lost about 1,000 lines of advertising and about 4,000 subscriptions, which the circulation department claimed were quickly regained.

In a later story about Archbishop Curley there was one unintentional slip. Polish Catholics held a convention with the archbishop as guest of honor, and the *Sun* included his picture in a layout. The name of a Polish dignitary did not end on one linotype slug and the last four letters ran over to a second line. Inadvertently that "widow" line got placed next to the name of the archbishop, a sensitive man who was ever proud of his Irish heritage. He was identified as Michael J. Curleyiski. The moment the typographical blunder was spotted, the presses were stopped. The managing editor himself ordered all papers retrieved and destroyed, not only from the press and mail room but from the city room as well, lest some prankster send one to the archbishop.

The same year as the Catholic boycott, the *Sunpapers* had two others to cope with, though of far less bitterness and impact. For two months, three grocery chains boycotted the papers in a dispute over the positioning of their ads; for five months, Baltimore bakeries withdrew their advertising. The latter had increased the loaf price of bread three times in three months, and in protest the Baltimore Housewives Alliance and the Baltimore Housewives League urged housewives to bake their own bread. While the *Sun* was publishing this message, the rival *News* pussyfooted. One bakery that had advertised exclusively in the *Sun* switched $10,000 worth of advertising to the *News*.

In January 1937 the *Sunpapers* faced more pressure from advertisers. Downtown movie houses limited their ads to fourteen lines after rates had been raised ten cents a line, and they withdrew all national movie ads. They threatened to show screen trailers attacking the *Sunpapers*. James W. Dove, the assistant business manager, noted in his date book, "It was thought advisable to give them [exhibitors] a kick or two in the pants to demonstrate the paper was still under *Sun* management and not likely to permit Loew-MGM to take control of advertising rates." Because Loew's local manager was the protest's organizer, the papers dropped his listings from their movie guides and for a time refused his advertising. Ad boycotts continued until March 1938. Then the *Sunpapers* added another charge of ten cents a line when requested to position ads on the movie page or the page opposite.

In April 1932, as the business slump continued, Patterson cut wages 10 percent, except for employees in the lowest brackets. This was the only pay cut made during the Depression, though other Baltimore papers made two or three, some totaling 25 percent. During the presidentially ordered national bank holiday in March 1933, competitors, lacking cash, paid employees in scrip redeemable at chain stores for food, but the *Sunpapers* managed to pay in cash. The wage cuts were partly restored in 1933 and 1934, and by January 1935 salaries were back where they began.

During the Depression, Harry Black continued, though not every year, the tradition of *Sun* family parties started by Van-Lear Black in 1926. The 1931 party, "Light for All," was held at the Lyric with more than 100 employees taking part in a stage show backed by a twenty-four-piece orchestra. A star was James Farmer. Wearing a boater, twirling a cane, and looking as if he owned the place, Farmer strutted across the stage between acts doing a silent impersonation of Harry Black. In the grand finale the company, led by Black, sang this song:

> After the news is gathered,
> After the presses roar,
> After the carrier's leaving,
> After the *Sun*'s at your door,
> Many a home will be reading
> *Sunpapers*, three in all,
> Let's give three cheers for our paper,
> Real "Light for All."

Black was so pleased with the show that he gave a costume party for the cast.

In September 1935 the *Sun* family party was held at Bay Shore Park with crabs, beer, and dancing. During the afternoon, Black "testified" over the loudspeaker that the printers seldom made typographical errors. This was greeted by cheers—from the printers. Mencken led one of the bands, and the festivities ended with Patterson organizing a parade of employees and their families marching around the park behind a German band. The last family party was held at the Alcazar in January 1937. No reason was given for ending the parties, but perhaps the family (upward of 1,000 people) was simply too large.

Meanwhile, the papers under Patterson had lost none of their old absorption with national party politics. To review, back in 1908 the *Sun* favored a Republican, William Howard Taft, against Bryan. Then it endorsed the Democratic presidential nominee six straight times: Wilson (like Grover Cleveland, always a *Sun* favorite), whose opponents were Taft and Theodore R. Roosevelt in 1912 and Charles E. Hughes in 1916; James M. Cox over Warren G. Harding in 1920; James W. Davis over Calvin Coolidge in 1924; Alfred E. Smith (ardently) over Herbert Hoover in 1928; and Franklin D. Roosevelt when Hoover ran again in 1932. The *Sun* termed Hoover, as a statesman, "one of the most calamitous failures of our history." It praised Roosevelt for "an enlightened conception of the realities of such issues as tariffs, debts, railroads, power companies, agriculture, and economic matters in general, although he has not been as frank as he should have been on those issues having foreign phases. And he speaks so all can understand on national prohibition." It concluded, "The *Sun* is not in the business of underwriting miracle men. But we can say that Governor Roosevelt is the candidate of a new deal and of hope. Mr. Hoover is the candidate of old, calamitous error, stubbornly upheld."

But in the spring of 1933, after Roosevelt persuaded Congress to enact the National Recovery Administration's plan for economic rehabilitation, the *Sun* began its break with him—a break that grew into a chasm when he turned away from what the paper considered the spirit and letter of the Democratic platform—and the New Deal unfolded. The paper registered growing dissents to price-fixing, production controls, subsidies, the plowing under of crops, the "extravagance" of relief, and such programs as that of the Works Progress Administration. Later it would say, "The *Sun* stands for competitive capitalism. It is the system which most effectively uproots the unfit, the unworthy, the lazy. It is the system which gives place to the vigorous, the competent, the purposeful."

While the *Sun*'s editorial page under John Owens was consistently attacking Roosevelt and his "vaguely formed and superficially considered ideas of planned economy," the *Evening Sun* under Hamilton Owens sometimes found positive points in the Roosevelt program. Then its editorial writers bragged among themselves that they were saying "The hell with the old lady [the *Sun*]."

These differences in philosophy, style, and tone between the two editorial pages caused comment and questions, inside and outside the office. Letters to the editor mocked the *Sunpapers* for seeming to be of two minds. Patterson found this untenable. On September 10, 1936, he summoned the editorial staffs of the two papers to a luncheon in the boardroom. In his journal, R. P. Harriss of the *Evening Sun* wrote:

> We knew a statement on the political situation was forthcoming, but we didn't have an inkling of what it would be until we sat down. At each place was a galley proof of an editorial. It was a solemn group of hired hands who exchanged knowing looks. Patterson said you have copies of the editorial I want to read to you. He was so nervous his hands were shaking. He probably felt someone might jump up and object in strenuous terms, or even resign. It was a long editorial (about 1,500 words).

The editorial had been written by John W. Owens. The first paragraph declared: "The *Sun* now states that in this campaign it is unable to advocate the reelection of President Roosevelt." The editorial then reviewed what it considered Roosevelt's failing and examined what his opponent, Alfred M. Landon, stood for, though raising more questions than answers. It concluded: "If Governor Landon speaks in clear and bold terms, facing specific problems and taking his stand unequivocally on the side of true economic liberalism, the *Sun* will support him, no matter what his prospects might be. If he does not speak in clear terms, the *Sun* intends to continue to fight for ideas that it believes to be sound and in the interest of the people, and will make the best of a situation in which it cannot advocate the election of either candidate."

After Patterson finished reading, he said he hoped for "general and useful acceptance." "First there was silence," Harriss noted.

> Then Gerald Johnson got up and said he realized that this was a fait accompli but he added that he thought it was the wrong decision and that he was for Roosevelt's reelection. It was a careful, reasoned statement, done in a quiet way. Then I stood

up and said I associated myself with Gerald's view. No one else said a word in rebuttal, but most looked sort of sheepish. Everyone felt that Gerald had acted beautifully. Nothing dramatic, but he made a reasoned case for the papers to support Roosevelt. Hamilton stayed to suggest some mechanical changes in the editorial. The rest of us went back to our desks, trying to do routine work, but felt like we had been kicked in the ass.

The papers were in effect ordered to reject the New Deal from then on in full and in chorus, throughout that autumn's election.

In 1972, in a personal letter to a *Sun* editor, Johnson wrote: "In 1936, the *Sun* made the most ghastly mistake, journalistically of which I have knowledge. . . . A newspaper that would have come to his aid, even half-heartedly, would have been for the next twelve years *the* authoritative paper in American journalism. Ed Murphy and Ham Owens knew it and Paul Patterson saw the point, but Frank Kent and John Owens were rabidly opposed to Roosevelt, and they carried the day."

The day after the boardroom meeting, the editorial was printed on page one of the Friday *Sun* and the *Evening Sun*. Mencken maintained that Johnson should have his say as soon as possible and gave up his space in the *Evening Sun* on Monday and took Johnson's on Thursday. "So I wrote the article," Johnson continued, "and in the blast that followed it tempered the wind to the *Sun,* not because it was particularly good, but because printing it proved the papers' disposition to be fair." The editorial drew a cascade of letters, most criticizing the *Sun's* stand. One asserted, "The *Sun* has gone Benedict Arnold"; another noted, "I have been told that a private poll of your own employees shows a trend for President Roosevelt of four to one over the Kansas candidate."

After the election, Mencken entertained Alfred M. Landon at a dinner in Baltimore. The menu included Chesapeake Bay oysters, terrapin à la Maryland, Maryland beaten biscuits, fried chicken à la Maryland, cream sauce, grilled bacon, corn fritters, potato croquettes, Maryland ham, Maryland hearts of lettuce, Maryland water ice. Maryland rye whiskey was used in the cocktails. The book *Maryland: A Guide to the Old Line State,* referred to the menu in its chapter on cookery and added, "It is Maryland's belief that Mr. Landon was somewhat consoled for the loss of the election."

The following spring, on May 17, 1937, in a front-page announcement of about 100 words, the *Sun* took note of its centennial:

One hundred years ago this morning A. S. Abell published the first issue of the *Sun.* Since that day, this newspaper has met varying fortunes and, with the rest of the community, has enjoyed and endured a variety of experiences. During all this time of war and peace, prosperity and depression, the *Sun's* successes and failures, its championship of truth or consortings with error, have been weighed and judged by successive generations of Maryland people. To that continuing jury the *Sun* cheerfully submits confident that during the next hundred years, its critics will be as generous as they have been over the century just ended.

The highpoint of the celebration was the publication of a history, *The Sunpapers of Baltimore.* It was the work of four men: Gerald Johnson, writing the first six chapters, up to the death of the Founder in 1888; Frank R. Kent, chapters 7–10, dealing with the *Sun's* political battles in the 1880s and 1890s; Mencken, the next eight chapters, up to the election of Patterson as president; and Hamilton Owens the last three chapters. Opposite the title page was a photograph of A. S. Abell flanked by his two partners. Unfortunately the namelines for Abell's partners were reversed: Azariah H. Simmons is actually on the left, William M. Swain is on the right. Mencken was the supervising editor of the history. Some 6,000 copies were printed; a special edition for employees contained an appendix with their names.

In February 1938, Patterson nullified the autonomy of the two editorial-page staffs by appointing John W. Owens editor-in-chief. This was a new position, with "full responsibility for the direction of the editorial pages of both papers." Hamilton Owens became editor of the morning page, and three months later Philip M. Wagner was appointed editor of the evening page.

John W. Owens considered himself a classic liberal and saw his task as the dominant editor to emphasize what the *Sunpapers* had traditionally stood for— free enterprise, states' rights, economy in government. Coincident with the change, the editorial staffs were handed a statement of policy that stressed three points: democracy, liberty, and the capitalist system. Newton Aiken, then an editorial writer on the *Sun,* wrote in his unpublished autobiography:

I don't think any of us had any difficulty with these principles, but the change in personalities posed problems. . . . John Owens edited copy with careful attention to all detail, rewriting when necessary and blue-penciling with a free hand. He was, however, an easy boss who rarely ordered anyone to do a thing and who never, as far as I can recall, chided a subordinate. His disposition and method can perhaps be indicated by mentioning the fact that he once hired an editorial writer who did not fulfill expectations but who remained on the staff trying for six months without ever having a single piece he wrote printed. . . . At first, Hamilton Owens told everyone [on the morning page] what to write. . . . I imagine it was just as hard for Hamilton as it was for us. In a sense he had been deprived of some of the independence he had formerly enjoyed.

John W. Owens was a courtly man with a solemn mien—some of his associates thought him pompous, and one described him "as pontificating as he strode along the corridor of Brain Alley." Wagner recalled that when he was editor of the *Evening Sun* Owens would call Wagner in "for one-on-one sessions. He would question the depth of my understanding on issues: 'What do you think of our agricultural policy? What are the long-range implications of NRA?' " And Wagner remembered Mencken observing, "Hell. The trouble with John is he's a reasonable man. Ready to reason things out. That's why I can't get along with him."

In January 1943, when diagnosis showed a cerebral tumor, Owens requested to step down to the role of contributing editor; he would write when he was able. Hamilton Owens succeeded him as editor-in-chief. Mencken, his cantankerousness only heightened by the nation's new war against Germany, got along with Hamilton Owens on the surface but often was uncomplimentary to them both, new top man and old. Mencken believed that John Owens's editorials, "two times out of three, were full of sound and fury, signifying nothing and that he was the perfect specimen of the Methodist evangelist turned publicist."

Johnson (who had described Patterson as "diplomatic, but refractory as basalt") became increasingly restless under the ever more conservative editorial policies. He and Wagner had not hit it off, and in 1939 Wagner made a trade with Hamilton Owens, getting Frederic Nelson from the morning *Sun* for Johnson. Johnson continued to write his *Evening Sun* Thursday column in his trenchant style, but he felt constrained in writing political editorials. Feeling "very gloomy," he took a trip and told friends, "When I get back it will be the beginning of the end. I'll go free-lancing." He resigned in November 1943, a month before Wagner became editor of the *Sun*. But, at once displaying a new prolificness as author of many acclaimed books on public affairs and history, Johnson continued to contribute articles and letters to the editor to both papers, almost to his death in 1980 at the age of 89.

From the time of the "divorce dinners," Patterson had encouraged—nay, intensified—the rivalry between his news departments. "He would get Bill Moore aroused," Fleming recalled, "by singing the praises of the P.M. paper, and I'm sure it worked in reverse on the other side with Murphy. This went on for years. No wonder there were bad feelings. Both papers would word a news story to indicate that the other paper should have had it, but didn't." (For example, if a prominent Baltimorean died in the morning and the evening paper did not report it that afternoon, next morning the *Sun* would give the exact time, say 6:18 A.M. yesterday, in the lead of its obituary.) Fleming added, "When Patterson noticed that one paper had made a slip, he would sarcastically mention this at his daily conference with his editors."

The conference was also attended by Mencken, and often by Black. After the Friday conference Black would invariably say, "I've listened to enough horseshit for one week. I'm going home." Mencken, commenting on such a conference, which he termed a council when it convened to discuss policy, wrote: "A council is quite competent, perhaps, to run a missionary society, a savings bank or a country club. But it must always be a curse and a handicap to a battleship, a city and a newspaper."

On September 3, 1939, minutes after England and France declared war on Germany, an extra edition of the *Sunday Sun* was on the streets. It continued to be printed until the Sunday supplements were exhausted. Then a four-page extra appeared, and then an eight-page paper. By 1:30 P.M. that historic day, six more extras had been published. In all, 75,000 extras were sold.

With the outbreak of war, Patterson centralized the news departments under one editor, as he had the editorial departments the year before. Moore, while retaining his title as managing editor, was made news editor of both papers. But Moore's health was failing. Fleming remarked in his autobiography: "The grimness was going out of his voice. He was talking more and more about the West, especially his own Pike County, Missouri. When he was supposed to be scanning the latest edition, it was obvious his mind was far away, and sometimes he appeared to be dozing. One night, in the course of his trip without his cane, he stumbled and fell. The sight of Moore floundering on the floor was catastrophic." Not long after that, on December 27, 1941, Moore died at the age of 63. Fleming, the assistant managing editor, became acting managing editor.

On January 4, 1942, Patterson named Neil H. Swanson, managing editor of the *Evening Sun* and assistant news editor under Moore, as executive editor of the *Sunpapers,* a new position. On his first night as executive editor, Swanson strode into the city room of the *Sun* around 11 o'clock with his wife and another couple. They were in evening clothes and were preceded by two Great Danes straining on a leash held tightly in both hands by Mrs. Swanson, a striking brunette. They disappeared into the editor's office, and Swanson reappeared with his dinner jacket off. Dramatically he pulled off his bow tie, unbuttoned his collar, rolled up his sleeves, and proclaimed "Now we'll start to get out a *newspaper!*" Editors, reporters, and copy-desk men looked at one another as much as to say "What have we been doing all these years?" But aware of how Swanson had been running the *Evening Sun* and cracking the whip over its staff, they realized that life at the *Sun* was about to change.

Swanson was born on a Minnesota farm in 1896. He attended the University of Minnesota for two years until his money gave out, and then went to work on the *Minneapolis Journal,* in 1915. Paid $8 a week, he tried, in his words, "sleeping on the office floor to save room rent." During World War I, Swanson served overseas as an army officer and was detached for duty with the Chasseurs à Pied, the French Blue Devils. (Years after, he had his portrait painted wearing their colorful uniform and invited his editors to his home for the unveiling.) Returning to the *Journal,* Swanson worked his way upward and became managing editor in 1928. In 1930 he was managing editor of the *Pittsburgh Press,* but he left there the next year to become assistant managing editor of the *Evening Sun.* Reporters nicknamed Swanson the "Iron Duke" after watching him burst into the city room wearing a military trench coat with an officer's swagger stick under his arm. He was hard-driving, and even more of an idea man than Murphy had been. (When Murphy retired because of poor health in 1939, Swanson succeeded him.)

Swanson believed he was the first newspaper editor to introduce the packaging of news, that is, assembling related items in one place instead of scattering them through the paper, in the accepted practice. However logical— and by now common—news-packaging was a radical development then, attempted only by newsweeklies. Swanson liked to explain what the news meant in "News Behind the News" articles, and sometimes he even ran a "News Ahead of the News" feature. He drove reporters to look for and stress the "common denominator in stories," using "those elements in the news in which readers can see themselves." Swanson possessed a keen news sense and was masterful in directing a far-flung staff on fast-breaking major stories. He made assignments, laid out the main pages, and wrote the headlines. With a talent for typography, he redesigned the *Evening Sun* and introduced an ultra-modern look with upper- and lower-case headlines, flush left to make them easier to write and to read. Headline banks and overlines on pictures were eliminated, giving the paper a clean, fresh appearance. Swanson regarded this new typography as one of his notable achievements. It was widely imitated.

He had his political reporters select one hundred Baltimore precincts that had consistently reflected voting trends in municipal, state, and national elections. On election night, fifty checkers—reporters, supplemented with men and women from advertising and circulation—fanned out all over the city, each responsible for two specific precincts. As soon as the polls closed and officials unlocked the voting machines, the checkers telephoned these results in to a battery of news room typists. Thus the *Sunpapers* had an almost instantaneous and foolproof projection of how the city had voted.

Even though he was a demanding boss, Swanson would overlook the traditional *Evening Sun* high-jinks—to a point. The staff had placed their horse-track bets with outside bookies until "Sunny Jim" Callanan wangled a part-time job as a handicapper for the racing page. It was rumored that he took it for $5 a week; what he wanted was the lucrative illegal bookmaking he could do from his desk in the sports department. His business boomed to such an extent that he was busier than the city desk. Swanson posted a notice: forthwith, anyone placing or taking a bet would be summarily dismissed. It had the desired effect until William F. Schmick, Sr., the executive vice president, and Emmett P. Kavanaugh, the business manager, unaware of the edict, appeared to put down their daily $2 show bets. Before Callanan could hide under his desk, each executive handed him money and named a horse. All eyes turned toward Swanson: What would he do? He did nothing—until the office emptied that evening. Then he removed the notice. Pittance or no pittance as paycheck, Callanan became well-to-do.

Before the United States entered the war, the *Evening Sun* simulated air raids between editions. Joseph Jean Shaner, a reporter, imitated the drone of approaching bombers. Reporters and copy-desk editors bombarded each other with rolled up copy paper. The one closest to the wall map, wound tightly on its spring, would release it with a jerk so it snapped shut with a resounding bang, quickly repeating the process during the attack. Sometimes "guerrillas" from the composing room would sneak up the stairway to toss paper "grenades" from behind filing cabinets. Harry Black and Swanson enjoyed the horseplay, but when the bombing of England began, Swanson announced, "That's not funny anymore."

Lee McCardell of the *Evening Sun,* who had won an honorable mention in the 1933 Pulitzer Prize competition for his reporting of the Bonus Army's march on Washington, was the first of many *Sunpaper* war correspondents. In 1941, he was sent to Iceland to cover the arrival of U.S. forces there.

Before Pearl Harbor, Swanson moved Mark S. Watson, a staff officer at A.E.F. General Headquarters in World War I, from editor of the *Sunday Sun* to Washington to look into the nation's military readiness. Watson's ensuing series was said to have irritated President Roosevelt. After Pearl Harbor, Watson wrote discerning analyses, ranging from General Douglas MacArthur's retreat in the Philippines to General Rommel's escape from the British pincers in Libya.

In the fall of 1943 Watson went abroad, first covering the fighting in Sicily, then reporting on the war as it moved up the Italian peninsula. On important dispatches from army headquarters his byline carried the underline "Representing the Combined American Press." As a former staff officer, he was adept at interpreting army communiqués that were often befogged in military terminology, and explaining what they meant in terms and from a perspective the lay reader could grasp. Later, when his name became well known to readers, his analysis of battles was carried on the *Sun's* front page under a two-column headline, "Watson—Tactics."

McCardell was in Italy too, out among the shell holes. His words seemed three-dimensional, conveying now the fury of an awesome battle, now the casual heroism of medics as they broke off from a card game to rescue enemy wounded during a barrage. Back home, Grace Darin, who edited McCardell's stories, observed, "Lee never lost his capacity to be hurt. His sensitivity was such that every hungry child, every injured soldier was a personal affront and he conveyed this in his stories." He wrote Christmas letters to his daughters describing the children he saw in his travels and what they could expect in their Christmases. These moving letters were published on the front page of the *Evening Sun.*

When England was threatened with the possibility of invasion, proprietors of the *Manchester Guardian* worried that the Germans might seize control of their paper—the *Guardian's* historian termed this "careful concern for the niceties of copyright in a revolutionary situation." They appointed Patterson, an old friend, a trustee and sent him the trust deed in an ordinary envelope. Patterson visited England in 1941, 1942, and 1943, reporting on what he saw, and returned to Baltimore with other valuable *Guardian* documents for safekeeping. Later, while touring the Pacific, Patterson inquired after Marylanders and collected their names to print in the *Sunpapers.*

Price Day, who had studied architecture at Princeton, written fiction for magazines, and worked on Florida newspapers, became a rewrite man on the *Evening Sun* in 1942. Late the following year he went abroad as a correspondent with the Eighth Air Force. Early in 1944 he was in Italy covering the bloody Anzio beachhead landing, and in June he accompanied Allied troops into

Rome. (Howard Norton, the first *Sunpaper* correspondent in the Pacific, was injured on Guam but was able to cover the closing months of the war in Italy.)

Norton and three other American correspondents were in a press camp in Verona, Italy, in the spring of 1945 when they heard a rumor that Partisans had captured the fleeing Italian dictator, Benito Mussolini, and his mistress, Clara Petacci, sentenced them in a summary court-martial, shot and killed them, and were exhibiting the bodies in the mud of Milan's public square. The four rushed to Milan, saw the bodies, interviewed the Partisans, then drew straws to see in what order they would file leads with their exclusive news of Mussolini's death. Norton, drawing the longest straw, said he had to file last. The other three, including a *New York Times* man, first sent four-word flashes, "Mussolini killed by Partisans." Norton's lead was 800 words long, crammed with pertinent detail. As soon as it was filed, sunspots temporarily disrupted further wireless communication from Europe. Later the *Sun* informed Norton that it was his dispatch that had been distributed by the Associated Press and other wire services, scoring a world beat.

McCardell was one of four U.S. correspondents who described the D-Day landings in Normandy from the air. Holbrook Bradley, the *Sunpaper* reporter assigned to the D-Day armada, could not get ashore until the second day, and then his stories were delayed. Louis Azrael of the Baltimore *News-Post* was one of the few correspondents, picked by lot, to land with the Twenty-ninth Division, which was composed in great part of personnel from Maryland, Virginia, and Pennsylvania. Consequently, the first word that appeared in the *Sunpapers* about Marylanders taking part in the invasion was under the byline of a *News-Post* correspondent, who was representing the combined American press.

McCardell, Day, and Bradley were with American forces as they fought their way across France. Watson was with the American First Army and literally led a column of its troops into Paris. In its suburbs, Watson was frequently called to the head of the line to translate the excited directions of French civilians. "I was called forward so often to interpret," he wrote in his dispatch, "that the affair wound up with me being placed in a French civilian's car to lead the way for our particular column. This is the sort of thing a newspaper correspondent dreams of, but usually encounters only in the movies."

To reduce costs, correspondents sent their copy in cablese, running together two or more words. Reporters would help with the decoding if the copy desk was rushed. A reporter decoding a story that read something to the effect that a general lessening of resistance had been noted decoded it to read "General Lessening, of Resistance. . . ." Stories were also sent by mail on onionskin paper. Censors would cut words, sentences, often paragraphs, of seemingly innocuous dispatches. Sometimes a third of a page or more would be scissored out, making much of what remained incomprehensible.

Bradley specialized in getting names of soldiers from the Maryland area, appending them to his stories. A long list of Twenty-ninth Division soldiers was introduced with the line "Among those encountered were—" but through a typographical error it appeared as "Among those wounded were—" As soon as this was discovered, the staff was mobilized to call the families of those involved, offering good news to the grieving, then attempting to placate those who were outraged by the mistake.

Bradley, who married Patterson's only daughter, Polly, was believed to be covering the Battle of the Bulge. But day after day no word came. Everyone was concerned for his well-being. Finally a letter arrived from Bradley. He had been in London for a week or more, to see a dentist. It later turned out that he had been in a fistfight with a Frenchman, who had knocked out his front teeth. The war correspondent had been in London having them replaced.

After Day had covered the invasion of Southern France and the winter campaign in the Rhone Valley, he and Watson were assigned to Supreme Headquarters of the Allied Expeditionary Force (SHAEF). In May, Day later wrote:

> The correspondents were attending a routine press briefing at SHAEF in Paris, when, very quietly, the men from various services were invited outside. One of those was a British reporter who was doing double duty and he asked if I would cover for him. I left the briefing and joined others outside who were boarding a special bus. Just as we pulled away, the uninvited correspondents, suspecting something unusual, swarmed around demanding to be taken along. It was too late. Our destination—unknown to us—was Rheims. The date was May 7, 1945. The next day we were to report eyewitness accounts of the unconditional surrender of Germany. I was the only correspondent representing an individual paper. After filing for my British friend, I filed for the Sun.

In addition to the correspondents in Europe, Swanson had at his command, variously, Thomas M. O'Neill and Frank R. Kent, Jr., in the London bureau, reporters crisscrossing the United States to report on the home front, and the Washington bureau working long days. When dealing with military or strategic matters, the bureau had to call the censor's office and read sensitive passages aloud to determine whether they could be printed. Swanson directed his far-flung staff with the verve of a field marshal, moving colored pins back and forth on his wall map to locate his correspondents, when he knew where they were. He was a tall man with an imperial bearing, and his characteristic stance was in the middle of the city room with coat off, sleeves rolled up, hard blue eyes squinting through (at that time) pince-nez and curling cigarette smoke. World in crisis but in control.

Swanson had six correspondents in the Pacific: Watson in the Philippines after Germany surrendered; Philip Potter, who had been city editor of the Sun, Thomas J. O'Donnell; and three from the Evening Sun: Norton, Robert B. Cochrane, and Philip S. Heisler. Potter, assigned to the China-Burma-India theater, was for a time with the Soviet army in Manchuria. Cochrane arrived in the Pacific shortly before the war ended. Heisler had worked on a Pennsylvania paper before coming to the *Evening Sun* in 1939. In one of his first stories he used a Pennsylvania Dutch expression, "Firemen outen the fire," contending to a laughing copy-desk that it was acceptable English where he came from. Heisler had studied psychology in college and learned hypnosis. He occasionally used it in the city room if things were dull. In the Pacific he was assigned to amphibious landings and aircraft carriers. He entertained crews by hypnotizing volunteers, having them sing, stand on one foot, and so forth. Once, when he had the skipper of a dive-bomber squadron in a hypnotic trance, the pilots asked Heisler to order him to call for a "happy hour." Heisler did; the skipper complied. That night the happy pilots drank up a month's supply of medicinal liquor. A *Chicago Tribune* correspondent on board wrote about it without mentioning Heisler's name. The *Evening Sun* picked up the story for its front page, adding a sidebar: "Sounds Like Our Man Heisler." Near the end of the battle for Iwo Jima, Heisler was on a command ship offshore. Through his binoculars he saw an American flag being raised over Mount Suribachi. He started writing, the censor had no objection, and Heisler's story was an exceptional beat, picked up by wire services and radio, because it implied that the Marines had finally wrestled control of that strategic island. Correspondents ashore, from foxholes, had watched the Marines beat back the Japanese but were unable to get to a communications ship to file the momentous news.

When the war ended, the Japanese surrender ceremonies aboard the battleship *Missouri* in Tokyo Bay on September 2, 1945, were reported from the scene by three *Sunpaper* correspondents: O'Donnell, Potter, and Cochrane. Cochrane's sixty-seven-paragraph account was later included in the book *Masterpieces of War Reporting*. (After the war Cochrane was named program director and assistant general manager of the *Sunpaper* television station WMAR and served in that capacity until he retired in 1975.) Day reported on the Potsdam Conference and the Nuremberg trials in 1945–46. Watson, back in Washington, wrote about demobilization, the sale of surplus war materials, and the congressional investigation of the attack on Pearl Harbor.

What should be accepted as the first scientific description of the atomic-fission bomb to appear in an American newspaper was printed in the *Evening Sun* on September 12, 1939, six years before the original nuclear bombs were dropped on Hiroshima and Nagasaki. The two-column editorial-page article, a detailed account of the development of atom-splitting and its military potentialities (detonation "a million times more violent than dynamite"), was based on material from *Discovery*, a scientific journal of Cambridge University, published before Great Britain declared war. The article attracted no comment, let alone response. Not until years later did the editors realize the uniqueness of their piece. A *New Yorker* magazine profile of William L. Laurence in August 1946 declared the news of the atomic bomb "was presented to the general public for the first time by Laurence, on Page 1 of the [New York]

Times of May 5, 1940." Harriss, who wrote the *Evening Sun* article, sent it to the *New Yorker* and, in its Department of Correction and Amplification, printed his account of the *Evening Sun* article.

Eight years later, as the British mandate in Palestine ended, the *Evening Sun* scored a world beat on the formation of the new Jewish state. Julius Goodman, Jr., a copy editor and a friend of a world Zionist official living in Baltimore, obtained from this official comprehensive insight into the new state's territory, the officers of its provisional government, and an outline of its proposed constitution. Goodman's two-column exclusive was the lead story of the paper under an eight-column headline. It appeared on May 12, 1948, two days before the formal announcement. Goodman had just one fact wrong: He wrote that the proposed name, *Eretz Israel,* Land of Israel, had been found to be inappropriate and that the new state would be called "Judea" or "New Judea."

During the war, as they lost much of their male staff to the services, the *Sunpapers* hired older men, usually drifters, and for the most part young women just graduated from the Columbia School of Journalism. One of the first hired was Grace Darin (she remained on the copy desk until 1978), whose professors told her she was making a mistake because the *Sunpapers* had a reputation as an antiwoman's organization. (She said she thought they were antifeminist after the war because they seldom hired women for general staff work.) In addition to Darin, the Columbia contingent included Sara (Sally) Wilson, Betty Jo Poe, Jane Bedell, Lena Lou Dickenson, Betty Jean Lee, Lois Felder, Virginia Paty, Hope Pantell, Julia Edwards, Claire Cox, Anne Hutchison, and, from other schools, Margaret Dempsey, Henrietta and Elizabeth Leith, Margaret Ellington, Susanna Ingalls, Betty Cate, Helen Delich, Carol Wharton, Eleanore Sybert, Barbara Woollcott, Stella Dernoga, Maureen Brooks, Margaret Jackson, Marjorie Mathis, Mary Cutler, Irene Brown, Odette Scrivanish, Margarethe Jespersen, and Lila Thomsen, who worked in Washington. Two who had long been on the staff were Amelia Muller and Banny Near.

Hope Pantell was successively a reporter, a copy reader, a picture editor, and for years music, drama, and television critic. Sally Wilson was the women's page editor. Virginia Paty became one of the paper's stars and was regarded as one of its best writers. She went to England on a Columbia Pulitzer scholarship, worked briefly in the London bureau, and later reported from Scandinavia. Margaret Dempsey made her mark writing features under deadline pressure. Carol Wharton covered state offices and the state general assembly for the *Evening Sun* until her death in 1958. Anne Hutchison had the same beat for the *Sun* and later became an acting assistant city editor, the first woman in that position. Betty Cate, though married, continued to use her maiden name as a byline. When her husband returned on a troop ship she wrote a dramatic story of the reunion, identifying her husband as Sergeant Berbig. After the first edition, the *Evening Sun,* conscientious and undoubtedly prudish, changed the byline to conform to her husband's name.

Early in the war the evening paper published seven editions: a Home, two Five Stars, two Seven Stars, and two All Stars. War stories would have six or more new leads. On busy days the entire newshole of the last edition bore little resemblance to the first edition. Replates were common, as were extras. After the All Stars were printed, page-one type was kept in the form, except for the streamers and space, for a two-column flash. If important news broke after the last edition and before the *Sun*'s bulldog edition, the foresight expedited printing an extra. Owing to time difference in Europe, many war stories broke during *Evening Sun* hours. Radio was first with the news, but apparently listeners wanted confirmation and details they could read. Street sales were large, and the circulation department would take bundles of all editions to sell at the gates of war plants.

Unconfirmed announcements raised false hopes. One day the AP teletype erupted with an urgent signal as it tapped out this flash: "Allied forces today landed in Normandy." Within seconds the machine clattered an advisory: The AP was double-checking. In a few minutes the AP offered this embarrassing explanation—a clerk in the London office was learning to use the teleprinter but did not realize it was open for trans-Atlantic transmission.

The *Evening Sun* staff had office pools on the World Series, the Derby, the Preakness, the Indianapolis 500, and even a "ghoul pool"—when the first person would jump off the new Chesapeake Bay Bridge. (That pool in 1952 was won by Gary Black, who was in Europe when his twenty-five-cent chance paid off. The *Evening Sun* notified him of his winnings by cable, which cost more than the $8 he won.) In the summer of 1945, with American forces on Okinawa poised to invade Japan, the copy desk started a VJ pool. Some picked dates in 1946 or 1947. McCardell, with first-hand experience on how the war had dragged on in Europe, put down 1949. The managing editor, who had just attended a confidential meeting in Washington, D.C., picked August 1, 1945; the assistant managing editor picked August 31. Studying the pool sheet, head copy-boy Andy Kelly noticed the dates chosen by the two most important editors. He split the difference, picked August 15—and won the pool.

Another copy boy story is about Swanson when he lived on Gibson Island. A neighbor, a retired army colonel who was beside himself with boredom, asked Swanson about a job, saying he would take anything just to have something to do. Swanson hired him as head copy-boy for the *Evening Sun,* convinced he was just the one to instill discipline in the six or seven teenagers who had become even more listless if not lazier during the tenure of the easily intimidated Andy Kelly, just retired. Although the colonel addressed his charges as men and strove for a sense of army order, they paid little attention to the old man until several beribboned officers visited the *Evening Sun.* During the war, these officers had crossed paths with the colonel, who was evidently a heroic figure. As soon as they spotted him they saluted. From then on the head copy-boy was treated by his charges with respect, if not awe, often saluting after he issued an order.

The war caused cutbacks in circulation and advertising. In November 1942, pursuant to government delivery regulations, 1,000 street-sales racks throughout Baltimore were withdrawn, and 80 percent of roadside-tube circulation in rural areas was halted by the rationing of tires and gasoline. Four horse-drawn wagons and buckboards supplemented delivery to newsstands. (Harry Black experimented with a horse-drawn chauffeur-driven trap for his daily journey from Guilford to the office and home again.) Route owners, without gasoline for their cars, resorted to bicycles. Paper deliveries beyond the city were sent by train, bus, or common-carrier trucks.

To conserve newsprint, which was rationed, two editions of the morning and evening papers were discontinued. Space for local news was cut, and the editorial page was reduced to four columns. Classified advertising was eliminated, except for death notices, in out-of-town editions. Retail and national advertising space was rationed, and in late 1944 that advertising was omitted outside the Baltimore retail market. This brought howls from subscribers who maintained that advertising was as important to them as news. Even with the war over, newsprint was scarce. Sometimes the *Sunpapers* would have only a two-day supply. Patterson sent George T. Bertsch, the business manager, to Canada on a foraging expedition. Bertsch, working not with the mills' sales departments but by wheedling the dispatchers, kept a trickle of newsprint moving to Baltimore.

In peace as in war, Swanson thought big—not just stories that could be played on page one, but also comprehensive series that could be republished as booklets for free distribution to readers, schools, and libraries. While other newspapers were recalling their correspondents after the war, Swanson had his fan out for a worldwide examination of the postwar scene. That coverage will be described in Chapter 16.

Swanson also ordered many in-depth series on national and local affairs, ranging from taxes and Social Security to a critical study of Baltimore hospitals, titled "Our Hospitals Are Sick." The thinking behind such projects is shown in an announcement he wrote for one series:

News is not necessarily something that happened in the last five minutes, or today, or even yesterday. Sometimes it is a situation half-concealed beneath the surface of events, hinted at, perhaps, in day-to-day dispatches, but developing so slowly that its importance to the world cannot be clearly seen. Sometimes the significance of such a situation is not understood until after its accumulating consequences have made great and lasting changes in the lives of ordinary people—generations later, thousands of miles distant. Then it is no longer news. It has become history. The *Sun* believes it has a duty to report and to illuminate such situations while they are developing, even though they do not make dramatic headlines.

In response to a reader's request in 1942 for the names of the ten greatest newspapers in the world, *Time* magazine picked only nine and placed the *Sun* fifth. And during Swanson's editorship the *Sun* won five Pulitzer Prizes in six years:

- Dewey L. Fleming in 1944 for distinguished national reporting. (The unusual way he won it will be told in Chapter 14, on the Washington bureau.)

- Mark S. Watson in 1945 for "his distinguished reporting during the year 1944 from Washington, London and the fronts in Sicily, Italy and France."

- The *Sun* in 1947 for "meritorious public service for a series by Howard Norton dealing with the administration of unemployment compensation in Maryland." The eighteen articles, published in June and July 1946, were a detailed analysis of the Unemployment Compensation system, examining the effectiveness and adequacy of management services, including personnel, internal budgeting, accounting, and practices that made it possible for many to obtain unemployment benefits improperly. As a result of the series, the Maryland General Assembly enacted eighteen major changes in the law to close loopholes. The number of recipients dropped from 60,000 to less than 10,000. Weekly payments were increased from $20 to $25. Following a Grand Jury investigation of irregularities, ninety-three people pled guilty or were convicted in criminal court.

- Paul W. Ward in 1948 for his series on "Life in the Soviet Union."

- Price Day in 1949 for international reporting with his series of twelve articles, "Experiment in Freedom: India and Its First Year of Independence."

In January 1946, Swanson killed the sepia photogravure section of the *Sunday Sun,* known to its readers as "the Brown Section." To replace it he planned something larger and grander—a picture-and-story magazine that would be distinctive. Again he composed his own compelling promotion for "a magazine with an idea—Maryland is a fascinating place to live, a place filled with interesting people and chock-full of untold stories." After naming Heisler, one of his principal assistants, as its editor, Swanson remained so engrossed that he furnished many of the story ideas, selected the covers, wrote many of the headlines, and often rewrote the leads just before an issue went to press. He even had his wife on the cover, modeling a gown borrowed from the Maryland Historical Society that had been worn by a Baltimore belle who married Napoleon's younger brother.

Long after he left the *Sun,* Swanson was asked what his major contributions were. He typed out a short list: "Typography, complete with new dress for the *Evening Sun;* election coverage, a foolproof projection of results; the Magazine; significance of news events; integration of news stories; novelist's tools applied to news; the McCarthy days; the first photo of a black man on the back page." No mention of the outstanding war and foreign coverage that he directed, of the Washington bureau, or even the five Pulitzer Prizes.

Miles H. Wolff, head of the Associated Press bureau in Baltimore, was hired by Patterson in August 1934 as his assistant, a new position. (Wolff later noted that, with no responsibility, "it was complete boredom.") When Swanson became managing editor, Wolff was named his assistant. After Swanson's promotion to executive editor, Patterson named H. K. Fleming managing editor of the *Sun* and Wolff managing editor of the evening paper. In his unpublished autobiography, Wolff wrote that Swanson had never liked him. "There were," he recounted, "periodic outbursts when he became almost violent and abusive." Following Patterson's appointments, Wolff wrote, "There was a nagging feeling that Swanson did not want me; that if it had been his choice he would have selected someone else. . . . I doubt that Swanson's displeasure was due entirely to my appointment. I believe he did not like Fleming any more than he did me. Fleming had been Bill Moore's man and there was no love lost between Moore and Swanson. I am sure Swanson would not have selected Fleming."

Fleming was not managing editor for long. Shortly after being appointed, on January 5, 1942, he asked to be transferred to the Washington bureau, but Swanson ignored the request. Fleming noted in his unpublished autobiography that he had tired of the *Sun*'s editorial attacks on Roosevelt, especially Kent's vituperative columns: "It was difficult to believe that Senator Byrd, as it was implied, was the greatest statesman since Jefferson, or that so many businessmen were strangely noble while almost all labor leaders were ignoble. And it was also difficult to believe that with a little tinkering, or after a little sleep, we could return to Cleveland or Adam Smith." Following a Kent column ripping into Vice President Wallace for urging distribution of food to children in distressed countries, Fleming wrote to Wallace saying he thoroughly disagreed with Kent. Wallace invited Fleming to lunch and offered him a position on the Board of Economic Warfare, and Fleming accepted.

In September Swanson named Patterson's oldest son, Maclean, who had become assistant managing editor when he returned from the London bureau, as managing editor to succeed Fleming. (A close friend of Mencken for years, Maclean Patterson, who preferred to work without a desk in his office, collaborated with Mencken in producing a new *Sun* style book.) With the appointment of Patterson, Swanson also announced eight other changes: Bruce Earnest was made his assistant; Charles H. Dorsey, Jr., assistant city editor of the evening paper, was promoted to assistant managing editor of the *Sun;* William H. Y. Knighton, Jr., from assistant managing editor to the Washington bureau; Edwin P. Young, Jr., assistant city editor of the *Sun,* became city editor of the evening paper; and Robert B. Cochrane, the music critic, became his assistant; Philip Potter was transferred from the evening copy desk to the morning *Sun* as city editor; Harold S. Goodwin also moved over from the evening paper to become day city editor of the *Sun;* and William J.

Wells, Jr., left sports to become night assistant city editor. Such major reshuffling occurred often under Swanson. It was not uncommon for editors to learn that they had been shifted to another position on the other paper—or even to find that they had been replaced, not transferred—by first seeing it on a posted notice.

Paul Patterson read the paper thoroughly. The news department assumed he started on page one, column one, and did not stop until he got to column eight on the back page. He seldom missed anything. He would call an editor and, without identifying himself (he expected his voice to be instantly recognized), ask, "What's this fellow Brown up to?" If the editor didn't recognize the reference, Patterson would growl, "What's the matter? Don't you read your paper?" He might be referring to an AP short on page 28 and thought it was worth pursuing.

Patterson had two telephones in his home with a direct line to the *Sunpapers.* He also had a fire alarm signal, as did the *Sun* city rooms, connected with the Baltimore City Fire Department system. These sounded when alarms were activated in fire stations. By checking the number of rings, say 8-1-2-6, in the Fire Department's code book, the city desk (or Patterson) knew where the fire was.

Saturday afternoons were often slow at the *Evening Sun.* To pass the time the staff played high-stakes blackjack. One such afternoon Patterson telephoned and demanded to know what was going on. He got the news editor, who grabbed the AP news budget and nervously began reading it. "I'm not interested in that," Patterson gruffed. The telephone was passed to Earnest, the city editor, who said it was one of those quiet days with nothing happening. Unable to contain himself, Patterson bellowed, "I want to know about the fire down there!" The staff, absorbed in its game, had not checked the alarm when, moments before, it sounded the *Sun's* location for a small fire in the press room.

Patterson was a man of many prejudices. "Assault" once had to be used instead of "rape." Even a minor vulgarity such as "belch" was forbidden. "Damn"? Never. No "kids" or "tots" appeared in his newspaper, only children. He despised the word "hike" as a verb to mean increase. At least once he ordered the presses stopped and the front page replated to delete "hike" in a headline. He objected to nicknames in the news columns. When Betty Jean Lee got a page-one byline, Patterson telephoned the copy desk; "Make it Elizabeth," he ordered. But Betty was her legal name, and she refused to let the copy desk change it. Patterson grumbled, "If that's her name, that's her name, but it's a silly one for a grown woman."

The possibility that some firm or product might get free advertising infuriated Patterson. At one point radio was deemed a competitor; therefore program listings were not printed. The very word "radio" was not mentioned unless it appeared in a police report of stolen items. The make of an automobile was never given, even when it was a pertinent description in a police story.

The department store Hochschild Kohn sponsored a Thanksgiving Day parade, but in the *Sun*'s report the sponsor was "a downtown department store." And if the *Sun* had a picture of a fire on a street that included the marquees of nearby stores, even those of large advertisers, their names had to be airbrushed out before the picture could be used.

Editors and copy editors kept bulging files of Patterson ukases. Morning *Sun* editors resolved slips that got into the edition normally delivered to Patterson's home in Guilford by correcting the mistakes in the following edition. An editor on his way home at four or five o'clock in the morning would quietly substitute the later edition for the one that would have brought down Patterson's wrath.

Patterson did not speak, and especially did not wish to be spoken to, on a *Sun* elevator. The most one would get would be a blank stare. If he did not feel like staring he would face a back corner of the elevator. At a party at his home in honor of James Bone, London editor of the *Manchester Guardian,* Patterson got the group singing. He was so pleased with the rendition of one of his editors that he put his hand on the editor's shoulder and told him what a great fellow he was. The next morning the two were on the same elevator. On the basis of the fellowship expressed a few hours earlier, the editor gave Patterson a hearty greeting. He didn't even get a "Harumph!"

Patterson loved to play the host at home, while traveling, in the boardroom. The boardroom had choice paneling (not included when the *Sun* Square property was sold) and a library at one end with books written by *Sunpaper* people. Patterson had found its rough-hewn antique table while traveling in England. Dignitaries were often invited for lunch, and Patterson especially liked to entertain well-known actors and actresses in town for a play. Gertrude Lawrence and Noel Coward were favorites.

Reed Sarratt, an editorial writer from 1946 to 1952, contributed the following anecdote of a boardroom fiasco for the *Evening Sun*'s seventy-fifth anniversary booklet. Hamilton Owens decided that editorial writers should be better acquainted with Patterson, and he arranged a luncheon in the boardroom. Owens ordered his favorite dish, shad roe and bacon. As it was served, one of the editors accidentally knocked the tray out of the waiter's hand, sending the contents flying. Sarratt wrote:

> Everyone looked at Mr. Patterson for a cue. Should we laugh? Mr. Patterson didn't smile. He said to the waiter, "Go get some more." The waiter said, "There isn't any more." Mr. Patterson replied, "Go get some more."
>
> All of us sat awkwardly for what seemed an interminable time. Eventually the waiter returned with another tray of shad roe and bacon. When Mr. Patterson was served he took two pieces of shad roe. When the tray arrived at Mr. Owens's place he said, "I don't care for shad roe." He had counted and there was exactly one piece for each person. This was the last, as well as the first, such effort to enable the editorial writers to become acquainted with Mr. Patterson.

In 1935, Paul Patterson's salary and bonus amounted to $81,304. (The President of the United States received $75,000.) When the Treasury Department made public its report to Congress listing salaries and bonuses of those who made more than $15,000 that year, the *Sunpapers* published columns of the list, including the names of its executives and editors. In addition to Patterson, they were William F. Schmick, executive vice president, $33,579; Frank R. Kent, columnist, $34,864; John W. Owens, editor of the *Sun*, $20,212; J. Edwin Murphy, managing editor of the *Evening Sun*, $20,157; and William E. Moore, managing editor of the *Sun*, $16,082. Harry C. Black, chairman of the board, received $24,211.

Every spring, Harry Black liked to give a "Beer-Among-the-Daffodils" party as thousands of daffodils bloomed in the three-acre garden behind his home on Warrenton Road. Conversation was always light, but one subject not to be discussed was any television program that appeared after 9:00 P.M. Black, a TV fan, went to bed at 9:00 and did not know—or wouldn't care—about any program after that hour. Each year the newest guest was chosen to sit at Black's right. When Edgar L. Jones was in that chair, he mentioned that he had heard Jacob Blaustein was the richest man in Baltimore. Black corrected him: "No, Mr. Jones, the second richest." Black told Jones that a young man had recently asked him about a job on the *Sun*, and added that he was "the most unlikely prospect. All he wanted to know about were the health benefits and the retirement plan." Black's view of newspapermen inclined to the romantic. He felt that, like artists, they were free spirits and preferred a Bohemian life. He believed that they lived quite well because they got passes to everything, were entertained royally by politicians, and forever feasted at press parties on rich food and the best liquor.

Black was more superstitious than Bruce Earnest. He would not sit at a table with thirteen. Gary Black, his nephew, was told "to dress decently" and to stand by in case thirteen showed up for the Daffodils party. When unexpected guests appeared to make it thirteen for a boardroom luncheon, an editor would be called at the last minute to put Black at ease. Black closed his office on Friday the thirteenth and telephoned his two male secretaries at their homes to make sure they stayed in the house that day. For good luck he kept a horse chestnut in his pocket—a new one each season. Because he would not carry matches, a silver bowl of kitchen strikers was kept on the board table for him.

Fastidious in dress, Harry Black affected a five-button sleeve. The artist included this detail in the portrait that hung in the boardroom until 1986. Black imported French or Belgian automobiles, but preferred to travel in a two-door Plymouth or Chevrolet convertible; he rode in the front seat beside his chauffeur with the top down even in the coldest weather. He visited the *Sun* office every day at the same time and would walk into Patterson's office and sit down no matter who was there. Bald, Black never took his hat off except at home. After he and Patterson had a falling out over the new building,

Black spent that time in the office of the managing editor of the *Evening Sun,* arriving at precisely the same time every day. He was intensely interested in everything, often minutiae: Why are martini olives bigger this year than last year?

When Black was honored by the Sun Route Owners Association for his forty-four years of contributions to the *Sunpapers,* the *Evening Sun* of January 18, 1955, inexplicably reported in a back-page story, "Harry C. Clark, chairman of the board of the A. S. Abell Company, was awarded a special honor. . . ." And the former chairman of the board was misidentified in the *Evening Sun* gravure magazine commemorating its seventy-fifth anniversary in April 1985: The captions for the color portraits of Van-Lear Black and Harry C. Black were reversed.

For more than forty years, Folger McKinsey was a *Sunpaper* luminary. As the Bentztown Bard, he began writing a *Sun* column in April 1906, and it appeared daily until May 6, 1948, when he was incapacitated by illness. Then, because of its popularity, columns were reprinted for a year. The column included his verse, a quotation from Scripture, small-town doings culled from county papers, a comforting reflection on the weather or time of year (the smell of the season's first hay crop), and doings at his imaginary Pilduzer Park, with such characters as the Honorable Freezer Fry, Aunt Petunia, Effie Unglebower, Joey the Jail Poet, the Ladies Talk About Each Other Club, the Park Pinochle and Heavy Hammer Throwers Union, and the Mint Julep committee. One Pilduzer Park social note read: "Aunt Hettie Dewbiddle gave a cheese sandwich reception the other day in honor of the arrival of spring." In later years the column, titled "Good Morning," opened with Carlotta Perry's lines

> It was only a glad "Good Morning,"
> As she passed along the way,
> But it spread the morning's glory
> Over the livelong day.

The well-known quatrain was dropped in a space-saving cut during the war, but so many indignant readers protested its disappearance that it was quickly restored. In addition to his column verse (done on the typewriter), the Bard— as McKinsey was known—wrote a poem every day for the *Evening Sun,* beginning with its first edition in 1910, an estimated 40,000 to 50,00 verses about Maryland.

McKinsey traveled throughout the state, writing rambling series about its towns and villages which were printed only in the county edition. Wherever he went he was treated as a celebrity, honored at luncheons and dinners and sometimes with a parade. He considered the lima bean the king of vegetables and annually greeted its arrival with a feast for friends, including Mencken, who arrived by boat and marched up to his front door on the Magothy River playing musical instruments, mostly drums. McKinsey died in 1950 at the age of 83.

Two well-known reporters were Ernest V. Baugh, later a *Sun* editorial writer, and Carroll E. Williams. Baugh covered politics and the Maryland legislature in the days when correspondents rented a house in Annapolis with servants, entertained at dinner, and had the convenience of filing their stories from the house on a direct telegraph line to the city room.

Carroll Williams began writing for all three *Sunpapers* as a free-lancer in 1913 at the age of 16. He was known as a "liner" because he was paid two cents a line, $4 a column. At the end of the month he pasted his stories together for payment. Walter Poole, then the office "stringer," using a piece of string one-column long, measured Williams's output. The pasteup, unrolled, often stretched from one end of the city room to the other and out into the hall. For this Williams would be paid about $80, more than some reporters made in a month. He started full-time at the *Sun* in 1936 at $35 a week, giving up a job with the *Manufacturer's Record,* where his salary had been $75 but during the Depression had been cut six times to $31.50. He started covering northern Anne Arundel County, gathering five or six stories every day. He soon learned that he could get even more news by covering the port and switched to that beat. Mary Helen (Bebe) Cadwalader was appointed his assistant. Overly excited on one of her assignments, she stepped off a Curtis Bay pier. Alexander Malashuk, a *Sun* photographer, snapped her picture floundering in the water. Hung in the city room, it was captioned, "Bebe covers the waterfront, and the water covers Bebe."

Williams scored many outstanding beats through hard work, ingenuity, and knowing more people than other reporters. To cite just one example, in the spring of 1941, before Congress passed the Lend-Lease Act, the nation debated how far the United States should go in helping Great Britain. On a Sunday night, Rome radio reported that a British destroyer, damaged by a German submarine, was heading for an American port to be repaired. The AP quoted the British Embassy's naval attaché as doubting that such help was planned. The city desk telephoned Williams at home, asking for sources it could call. He said he preferred to work the story and asked how much time he had until the next edition. Told twenty minutes, he said he would call back in fifteen—and he did, with the complete story. His front-page byline piece began:

> A British warship, first British fighting unit to be ordered into an American yard for repairs, headed last night toward the Virginia Capes.
> Authoritative sources here reported that the craft, a heavy cruiser, would put into the Norfolk Navy Yard, which has plans in readiness to speed such repairs by working 24 hours a day.

The story ran for a column and a half. As it was being copy-read, the Associated Press speeded bulletins over its newspaper and radio wires, attributing this significant news to the *Sun.* Patterson heard the radio flash, called to find out how the *Sun* got the story, and ordered a bonus for Williams—one of many he received during his career.

After the United States entered the war, Williams would return to the office from his beats—he covered at least two—summarizing for the city editor what he had gleaned. The city editor then assigned a relay of two or more reporters to interview Williams, each writing one or two stories so they could be included in the morning paper.

In addition to his newspaper work, Williams acquired and managed eighty-five apartment units and other properties. After the war, Williams suggested that the *Sunday Sun* include news and features on real estate. In time, his three weekly stories grew to an inside section and finally to a separate section, with Williams as real estate editor in addition to his other reporting. In 1962, on his 65th birthday, he retired from the *Sun* but kept busy with other interests, calling newspapering "the best career in the world—meeting people, learning new things, educating the public, never sitting still."

In the days when Williams joined the paper, its society editor was Mrs. Banny McLean Near, a descendant of old Maryland stock; a grandfather owned coffee ships, and an uncle was master of the Green Spring Valley Hunt Club hounds. She made her debut the same year as Wallis Warfield (later married to the Duke of Windsor, the former Edward VIII of England), whom she often described as "smart, witty and full of badinage." Mrs. Near was known around the office as "the *Sun's* own orphan of the storm, society-style." She was not fashionable, or even careful, in her attire, wearing sagging cotton stockings. For important events she wore a shawl that might once have been a lace curtain. One night, while gossiping in the city room before attending the opera, she leaned close to the pneumatic tube that shot copy down to the composing room. Accidentally or intentionally, a copy boy held the tube flap open long enough to suck the shawl off Mrs. Near's shoulders. "Don't worry, Banny," a copy editor consoled her. "It'll be back up in the next edition."

Her title was receptionist, but Miss "Bernie" Moorman, whose desk was a few feet from the front elevator of the *Sun* Square building, believed her ultimate duty was to keep as many people as possible from reaching the upper floors, even though they might claim to be new employees, visitors with legitimate errands, or, in one memorable case, a prominent businessman who said he was coming to attend his first meeting as a member of the A. S. Abell Company board of directors.

But once beyond this formidable, not-to-be-swayed guardian, employees and visitors were greeted by the warming smile of Bernard E. Barney, always addressed by the single name Barney in the mistaken belief that it was his first name. (He addressed employees by their correct name.) Barney operated the front elevator from 1925 until the Calvert Street building opened in 1950. Whenever Paul Patterson boarded the elevator, Barney would take him non-stop to his destination. Other passengers, no matter their rank or mission, had to wait until the return trip before Barney would stop at their floor.

Barney was also a middleman for transfers. The *Sun* Square intersection of Charles and Baltimore streets was a major streetcar transfer point. Many employees rode to and from work on streetcars. They gave their unused transfers to Barney, and he in turn dispensed them to other employees, who used them for a free ride. His thoughtfulness must have cost the Baltimore Transit Company at least $20 a week, even though fares were only eight cents. In the Calvert Street building, where the elevators are automatic, Barney would still man an elevator for executives or special guests. He also served as a greeter and guide and had time to tend the plants in the lobby. He worked for the *Sunpapers* for forty-five years. When he died in 1971, an *Evening Sun* editorial said of him, "He was one of the always too few people who give personality to a utilitarian building and humanity to a corporate enterprise."

With the papers growing in size and circulation, crowding became a continuing vexation at the Baltimore Street plant. For lack of space, newsprint had to be brought in every day from warehouses. During snowstorms deliveries were late, sometimes arriving just before press time. The mail room was so crowded that Sunday advance sections were stored in the advertising department. During the war and postwar years, Sunday papers were delivered on chartered streetcars to drop-off points. The idea was a good one: streetcars operated citywide, and in snowstorms the lines were kept plowed.

Because the worn presses often broke down, three new ones were ordered in February 1946. Architects said walls would have to be torn out to accommodate them, probably weakening the building, and the presses would rise way above street level, squeezing the first floor into a half floor. Patterson and Schmick Sr. were in favor of completely renovating the plant, a feat that would have to be performed without interrupting the almost 24-hour-a-day, seven-day-week operation. One official who vehemently opposed this said it would be comparable to lengthening a ship while crossing the ocean. Schmick was concerned that moving to another site would inconvenience advertisers; most classified advertising came in the front door, and the department stores were within walking distance.

But after much discussion and wrangling, the board decided a move would have to be made. Mencken advocated building "a barn" for the presses and keeping everything else at the existing location. Sites were considered on West Pratt Street, but the site chosen was a five-acre plot on the northeast corner of Calvert and Centre streets, occupied by the historic Calvert Street Station and adjacent to rail lines for delivery of newsprint.

The architectural firm of Palmer, Fisher, Williams & Nes drew up plans for a four-story building with a feature especially desired by Patterson, a ten-story tower. In addition to the presses, other worn heavy equipment would be replaced. In postwar days it was difficult to get a fixed price for construction; much work was on a cost-plus basis. A board meeting discussed this. Harry C. Black, as chairman, seldom gave his own opinion. He asked the board, in order of seniority, what it thought and if there was consensus that action be taken. But this time, after Patterson, who was determined to build, urged moving ahead without a fixed price, Black said, "Unless there are objections, we'll do that." William S. Abell, who had recently joined the board, said, "I'd like to be recorded as 'No.' " Then Gary Black, an even newer member, added, "And I want to be recorded as 'No.' " Abell and Gary Black both remember that the faces of Harry Black and Patterson turned purple. A long silence followed. Al Miller, superintendent of the pressroom, was called up to the boardroom. He was questioned about the deteriorating presses. For $40,000 to $50,000, he said, they might be patched to run a few more years.

After the meeting, Black asked his nephew and Abell to ride out to his house. The trip was made in silence. Black went upstairs, leaving the two young men fidgeting in the drawing room. They agreed that their short tenure on the board was soon to end, or had ended. After an interminable time the butler said, "Mr. Black, your uncle will see you now." Later he came back and got Abell. On the way up, Abell thought "Now I'm going to be fired," but Harry Black, rubbing his hands together, announced, "Young Black, Mr. Abell. That was the best goddamned board meeting we've had since I've been chairman. I want to thank you both." As Harry Black began having second thoughts about spending so much money, a coolness developed between him and Patterson. Black stopped going to Patterson's office, angering Patterson by writing him notes in longhand rather than communicating in person. Some board members felt, meanwhile, that Patterson had become autocratic, taking altogether too much into his own hands. Animosities festered.

The board had stop-orders issued on the new building and its equipment. Because spare parts for the old presses were not available, they had to be manufactured, which was expensive. Then a fire broke out in the pressroom. The assistant to the president for plant remodeling, Donald H. Patterson, in a memo to his father, emphasized that the future of the paper was jeopardized by the cramped space and antiquated equipment; he was convinced the company was in danger of not being able to print the paper. Paul Patterson went back to the board with those assessments and won. The board voted for a new building, though without the tower. Mencken had fretted about "enormous costs." (It was estimated that building and presses would cost $4 million, which, he noted, "will make a serious hole in our surplus." His old friendship with the publisher notwithstanding, Mencken grumbled, "Patterson is in a state of exaltation and seems to pay little heed to the cost of these things. He is eager to build himself a monument and doesn't seem to remember that it may be a monument to the loss of solvency of the *Sun*."

The architects wanted Franklin Street closed between Calvert Street and Guilford Avenue so it would not intersect the new *Sun* property, extending two whole blocks from Centre Street to Bath Street. If and when the city government sanctioned this, Patterson said nothing was to be printed until he or Swanson had seen the story. After street and building permits were approved, the City Hall reporter telephoned the news to the *Evening Sun*. As was customary with all company-related stories, the managing editor was immediately consulted. Wolff could not reach Patterson or Swanson and ordered the story printed in the next edition. Anyway, Wolff remarked, he recalled Patterson's saying the news should get routine treatment, "which we're doing." The city editor shook his head in disbelief. A friend, meeting Patterson at the Maryland Club that afternoon, congratulated him on starting a new building. "How do you know about that?" an incredulous Patterson asked. "Why, I just read it in your paper," was the reply. Patterson's reaction must have been volcanic.

Wolff, in his unpublished autobiography, wrote that Swanson telephoned him that night "and delivered a most abusive castigation. The recurring question was why had I printed the story about the new building? I had, it seemed, committed an unpardonable sin." Patterson left for Europe. After he returned, Wolff, who had been hired by Patterson and had been close to him socially, found him "cool and aloof": "The luncheons in the boardroom were canceled permanently, and he did not ask me to play golf with him any more. The ensuing period was a nightmare." Swanson handed Wolff a memo saying that he was to take no part in handling the news but was to spend all his time in the composing room to see if he couldn't finally get editions printed on time. Wolff was convinced that he would be fired, and he soon was. When he asked why, Swanson replied, "Let's just say you are not capable of handling a metropolitan paper."

Gary Black described his uncle as generous with friends and causes: "If Princeton called about a need, a check went right off, but he was tight when it came to bricks and mortar. He preferred to put off spending such money." Worrying about costs, and not wanting to borrow money, the board ordered the new building reduced to a mechanical production plant, with the news departments squeezed into what had been planned for the circulation department and future growth. The advertising, circulation, and business departments were to remain in the old building. Patterson had his son Donald prepare a report on a split-plant operation; the verdict was that it would be inefficient and costly. The senior Patterson asked the board for money for a fifth floor to provide space for a unified operation. The contractor was set to roof the four-story building on a Friday; if a fifth floor were to be added, he said, he had to know by Monday. The board met on Monday and agreed to a fifth floor at 4:00 P.M.

Economy was still the primary consideration. Instead of four presses, only three eight-unit Hoes were bought. Equipment that had been ordered, including newsprint conveyors from the unloading dock to the storage area, was canceled. The design called for only four passenger elevators, two each at front and back; one of these two front and back shafts was sealed off after Harry Black discovered this would save more than $100,000. On a tour of the building before it was completed, he pointed to exposed ducts and wiring in the ceilings and asked when they would be covered. Because of severe cost-cutting, he was told, finished ceilings had been eliminated. "We can't have that," Black exclaimed, overruling himself.

Among the dignitaries invited to the cornerstone-laying was Mayor Thomas J. D'Alesandro, Jr., who had suggested that a copy of a city brochure extolling his administration be included in the cornerstone box. Patterson turned him down. After the sealed copper box had been placed in the aperture, Patterson and his guests turned away. Then Thomas J. O'Donnell, who had left the *Sun* to become the mayor's press secretary, slipped the brochure atop the box just before the cornerstone was mortared into place. Later, City Hall let word of what O'Donnell had done seep back to the *Sunpapers*. Patterson was furious, and even more furious when he discovered what it would cost to extract the unwanted brochure.

Calvert Street was one-way southbound when the site was chosen. Architects took that fact into their planning when they designed the red-brick, limestone-trimmed building with its huge, eye-catching glass windows so passersby could watch the presses roll. The structure was best seen from the north, but then the one-way street was reversed from south to north.

The move to the new building was made in 1950 on Christmas Eve. In addition to office furniture, forty-four Linotype machines, weighing up to 4,800 pounds each, and two matrix rollers for stereotyping, weighing 11,000 pounds each, were included. (That same evening, photographers went through the old building collecting cockroaches and released a pair on each floor of the new building for old times' sake.)

The aftermath to nickel-nursing was often painful but sometimes hilarious. Stereotype mats got stuck in the chute to the pressroom. To dislodge them, a chunk of lead from a stereotype pot, tied to a rope, had to be lowered into the chute several times a day. With high humidity, bundles of papers from the mail room would jam up in the chutes to the loading platform. To prevent this, dancehall-floor powder was sprinkled in the chutes. Then bundles would zoom out as if shot from a gun, banging on the platform or, more often, overshooting it and landing on the pavement. To economize, ducts from electrical and telephone lines on office floors had been placed six feet apart. Desks had to be placed near a duct, which resulted in odd arrangements of furniture. No venetian blinds or shades were provided. In bright sunshine on the east and south sides of the building it was almost impossible to work, or to see. For these and other necessary changes and additions, management had to go back to the board.

A single elevator (quite capable of breaking down) was at once the source of seemingly endless waits and frayed nerves, so the board approved a second elevator, front and back. And it agreed to the installation of a fourth press. The mechanical department had predicted that if one of the three presses went down it would not be able to print the full run of the three papers.

The *Sun* Square building served a variety of tenants, notably WMAR-TV and the Air Force, until its demolition in 1964. The *Sunpapers* retained a ground-floor business office in the old building until July 14, 1961. Just before the wreckers took over, office sentimentalists appropriated mementos: a door handle, a piece of marble from the business counter, a hunk of molding from Brain Alley. James Hartzell, an artist who drew the Oriole bird used on the *Sun*'s front page for many seasons, took the frame from the front of the building that held the daily copy of page one. A. Aubrey Bodine went to the rest room he had used and pried off the button marked "Press." Today, the *Sun* Square site is home to the Morris Mechanic Theatre.

When operations moved to Calvert Street, Donald H. Patterson started the tradition of having a gigantic Christmas tree adorn the front of the building during the holiday season. The trees come from tree farms when they have become too big to be transplanted, or are offered by individuals who want to have an overgrown evergreen removed from their property. Because the trees are so huge, outsize ornaments are necessary for this beacon of cheer to the traffic flowing out of downtown Baltimore.

When Sam Abt, a newly hired *Sun* copy reader, left the building late one December night he noticed that wind had blown a number of ornaments off the tree. Conscientiously, he picked up each and every one scattered on the steps and along the sidewalk and placed them in the lobby for safekeeping. The following Christmas, Abt noticed that the midnight wind had again scattered ornaments in front of the building. That year the American Newspaper Guild was negotiating a new contract with the company, and Abt, a resolute member of the Guild and gloomy over the months of bargaining, this time just muttered something and left the ornaments where they lay. A year or two later the Guild was again in protracted negotiations on a contract. That year, passing a dozen or more ornaments that had blown off the tree, Abt took time to kick each one into the street.

During the board's disagreements over the new building and its costs, the company applied for a license to operate a radio station, and the board debated, often heatedly, the advisability of applying for a television station license. Patterson and Schmick Sr. were in favor of both, Patterson claiming that television was a natural adjunct for the transmission of news. Mencken, who had been against a radio venture (though he owned stock in a local station), was stridently opposed to television, calling it "Madness": "It's a boobs and tubes business. It's Hollywood." Patterson and Schmick won out. WMAR-TV went on the air on October 31, 1947, broadcasting from the tallest building downtown—today's Maryland National Bank building. Assigned Channel 2 in the commercial range, WMAR was Maryland's first television station and one of the nation's earliest. The company also entered FM radio, with less success; its station went on the air with but a single advertiser and a lone commercial. The company came near venturing into Transit Radio, a project for the broadcast of advertising in streetcars and busses. Patterson, Schmick, and Swanson, none of whom rode public transit, thought it was an imaginative idea and a technique that would reinforce newspaper advertising. Women taking public transportation downtown to shop would be reminded of department store sales that had been advertised in the *Sunpapers*. Mencken, an old-time straphanger, said that "the proposition was staggeringly insane." The *Sunpapers* spent $7,000 on a survey. While response was favorable, letters to the editor foretold ill-will as Transit Radio badgered its captive audience. The notion was abandoned.

In the mid-1940s Mencken, growing old, became a grump. He harassed Patterson about the editorial pages and fumed because Patterson did nothing. He charged that the editors "at their best were banal; at their worst, almost idiotic," and that the editorial writers were "all quacks." He felt the result was a decay in prestige: "The two papers have lost all their old character and are no longer taken seriously outside Baltimore." In one outburst Mencken accused Patterson of being afraid to tackle the two Owenses. His diary noted that he had told Patterson "if he didn't undertake a reform of those editorial pages himself, . . . I was prepared to launch one of my own. This annoyed him greatly and for two or three minutes he was quite silent." The issue of Mencken's querulousness settled itself on November 22, 1948, with the cerebral hemorrhage that ended his career as writer and critic. He died in 1956.

The day after the move to North Calvert Street, Patterson handed in his resignation to the board. He remained as president for one more month, until January 31, 1951, to preside over a series of luncheons and tours of the fine new $4 million building, twice the size of the outmoded *Sun* Square plant. Patterson, almost single-handedly, had brought the new building into being.

For many years he sat on the board of directors of the Associated Press. Patterson was also a charter member of the American Society of Newspaper Editors, and president for two terms of the American Newspaper Publishers Association. In later life his hobby was long airplane trips, particularly those establishing new overseas routes. (He was a close friend of Juan Trippe, president of Pan American Airways.) His death in April 1952, at the age of 73, followed an infection he developed on a trip to Africa. A New York *Times* editorial assessed his contributions:

> To Patterson belongs the lion's share of the credit for solidly establishing the international reputation the Baltimore *Sun* has earned as one of the great newspapers of the country. Patterson's unswerving belief in freedom of the press carried with it the corollary of freedom for his editors. He was tough, but he was fair. He built up a superb staff, and we on this newspaper are proud to count among our own colleagues a number of outstanding men who worked hard and learned much under Paul Patterson.

Two small plaques were placed in the lobby of the Calvert Street building in memory of Patterson and Mencken. Patterson's reads:

In Honor
of
Paul C. Patterson
1878–1952
by employees of A. S. Abell Co.
President of A. S. Abell Co. (the *Sunpapers*)
from November 11, 1919, to January 31, 1951

Mencken's contains the epitaph he wrote for himself:

Henry Louis Mencken
1880–1956
Newspaperman
Author   Critic
Editor   Philologist
If after I depart this vale,
you ever remember me and have
thought to please my ghost,
forgive some sinner and wink
your eye at some homely girl.
H. L. M.
Placed Sept. 12, 1957
by Sigma Delta Chi
National Professional Journalist Fraternity

FOURTEEN

The Washington Bureau
1837–1987

The *Sun*'s first correspondent in Washington, D.C., was James Lawrenson, a Post Office clerk with a flair for news commentary. He began sending letters to the paper a few weeks after the start of publishing in 1837, and he wrote about once a week for some twenty-five years. Lawrenson was the first of many part-time correspondents who also wrote for other papers. Two other early contributors were W. W. Warden and O. K. Harris; but nothing is known of their background. They and Lawrenson wrote anonymously. The first three contributors to be identified with pseudonyms were Elias Kingman, who signed his dispatches "Ion," Francis J. Grund, who used "X," and A. G. Allen, who used "Aga."

In the early nineteenth century the few newspapers that had their own Washington correspondents kept them there only when Congress was in session; there wasn't much to write about at other times. John T. Crow, an assistant *Sun* editor, was the paper's Washington correspondent for about two years until 1864, when he was appointed managing editor following the death of Thomas J. Beach. His part-time successor was Francis Asbury Richardson, who had joined the *Sun* after the war and became the full-time correspondent in 1866.

Richardson soon achieved a national reputation and was the first *Sun* man to be directly identified in the paper, his initials, F.A.R., were appended to his articles. Richardson, named for a celebrated early Methodist bishop, Francis Asbury, was nicknamed "Bishop." In recalling the early Washington scene, he said that only twenty-six correspondents were accredited to Washington in the 1860s. Most wrote for six or more papers, and many were also congressional clerks and wrote speeches for senators and congressmen. Their income, he said, ranged from $10,000 to $20,000 a year, then an astounding amount.

In the late nineteenth century, Washingtonians depended on Baltimore newspapers for their news. Correspondents took little if any account of the Washington papers—"mostly party rags," Richardson claimed, "edited to be sure with distinguished ability, but paying only indifferent attention to the news." In postwar days high-ranking public officials often visited newspaper offices. "In old Newspaper Row, as it used to exist," Richardson continued, "there might be found any evening senators, representatives, Cabinet members, now and then the Vice President, foreign ministers, prominent officials from the large cities, governors of states, etc. In the phrase then common among Washington correspondents, every one of them had his own senator, representative or Cabinet member who came to his office and told him the news." According to Richardson, interviewing originated with J. B. McCullagh of the *Cincinnati Commercial:*

> I well remember the hubbub created when President Andrew Johnson, early in the period of his stern and bitter contest with Congress, talked in the first person through Mr. McCullagh in the newspapers. It is true claims have been made for others as being entitled to credit for authorship of interviewing, but Mr. McCullagh unquestionably antedates them all. The example set by the President of the United States excited not only sensation but strong criticism. [But Johnson said, "Everybody seems to read my interviews and nobody seems to read my messages."] It was not long, however, before this example was rapidly and widely followed, and interviewing became what it is today [1902]. President Grant also gave interviews and one correspondent, R. De B. Keim, of the *New York Herald,* could always get him to talk and for the eight years of Grant's presidency made quite a bit of money from the interviews. After Grant, no other nineteenth century President favored interviews.

Benjamin F. Butler, who was elected to Congress after the war, "was the author of interviewing one's self," Richardson said. "He was never willing for a newspaperman to take down what he said. When applied to, if agreeable, he would say, 'I will send you something prepared just as I wish it.' . . . He was among the most brilliant and clever men who have ever shone in American politics, and incapable of any expression devoid of spice and meat. The interviewer was delighted that he preferred to write out his own opinions." When a former Speaker of the House found that congressional views had a monetary value, he began interviewing himself and averaged $100 a week selling what he had to say.

In 1872, Richardson became chief of the small bureau at 1418 F Street, N.W. In 1885 the *Sun* began construction on a building of its own, the first out-of-town newspaper building in the nation's capital. An eight-story Victorian Gothic structure at 1317 F Street, N.W., it was designed by nationally known architect Alfred B. Mullett. On completion, it was the most expensive private building in the capital and its first skyscraper, the *Sun* claimed. The 116-foot tower was a downtown landmark. A decorative sun and sunflower were repeated on the exterior and the interior. The first floor contained the *Sun*'s counting room, offices, and library; the upper floors were rented out.

When it became necessary to distribute the assets of the Abell estate, the building was sold in 1907 for less than the $500,000 it had cost to build.

Richardson retired in 1901 and was succeeded by John Pierce Miller, the chief political reporter of the *Washington Star,* who served until 1910 and was followed, for one year, by Frank R. Kent, and for a short time by McKee Barclay, the *Sun's* cartoonist and an experienced political reporter. J. Fred Essary was bureau chief from 1912 to November 1941, except for a year when he was the London correspondent.

Essary began his long career on papers in Norfolk, Virginia. One day in 1903 he got a tip on a great story from a friend on the Outer Banks of North Carolina. Two brothers named Wright, inventors, had managed to rise off the ground in their motor-driven biplane, an unheard-of feat. Essary, a stringer for the *Sun* and the *New York Herald,* filed the story to both papers, enabling them to later boast of beating other newspapers on one of the century's great news stories. Essary had one important fact wrong. He said the plane flew three miles, but went only 120 feet. Later Essary came to Baltimore as financial editor of the *Star,* then went to Washington as correspondent for the Baltimore *News.* He joined the *Sun* in 1912. He looked the part of the old-school correspondent, wearing a homburg and swinging a walking stick while making his daily rounds of the capital.

During his twenty-nine-year tenure, the bureau grew from a three-man staff, business manager, and office boy, to one rivaling the bureaus maintained by the *New York Times* and *New York Herald Tribune.* The *Sun* was a voice to reckon with in Washington, because only the *Star,* one of four local dailies, attempted to cover the national government and, editorially stodgy, its impact was limited. The *Times-Herald* and the *Daily News* aimed at a popular audience and had little influence in government. The *Washington Post* had not yet become a force locally, let alone on the national scene.

In his *Covering Washington,* Essary recounted some of his experiences. In 1913, soon after Woodrow Wilson became President, Essary heard that Wilson was about to shake up the Civil Service Commission, firing two commissioners, promoting the chief examiner to one vacancy and a woman to the other. He wrote:

> I had all the names and all other essential details, which I promptly worked into one of the best beats of my Washington career. A week passed after the story had been printed and nothing happened. Then a month, then a year. In time my colleagues stopped badgering me for confirmation of a story which had been so prominently featured. . . . Six years later, however, almost to a day, Woodrow Wilson announced from the White House an order shaking up the Civil Service Commission, firing two of the commissioners, promoting the chief examiner, and appointing the woman—all of it just as I had predicted. That was one time, I might now confess, when I did not have the courage to write into my new story the fact that the President's action had been exclusively forecast in the *Sun* six years before or even call the attention of my editors to my belated triumph.

One Essary exclusive attracting national attention was his account of Wilson's illness. The President had suffered a mild stroke while traveling in the West, and a more debilitating one after he returned to Washington. It was feared that a third might be fatal. The White House released only cryptic bulletins, resulting in wild, disturbing rumors. The Wilson family then realized the importance of giving the public reliable information, but it did not want to make a formal announcement. Essary, as one of the best-known correspondents, was chosen to write the first authentic account. He did it by quoting in detail Dr. Hugh H. Young, a Baltimorean who was one of the consulting specialists. Other papers had to use the *Sun's* report.

In 1939, Essary was offered one of the biggest stories of the year, but he passed up an exclusive, believing that it should be shared with his colleagues. After President Franklin D. Roosevelt appointed Hugo L. Black, a senator from Alabama, to the Supreme Court, Black went to London on vacation. While he was there, the news broke that years before he had been a member of the Ku Klux Klan. The British press, in hot pursuit of the story, laid siege to the Blacks in their hotel. Black appealed for help from Paul W. Ward, the *Sun's* London correspondent, whom he had befriended in Washington. Ward surreptitiously got them out of the hotel and to an American-bound ship just ahead of the pursuing newsmen. When the Blacks arrived in Norfolk they were met by a fusillade of reporters. Mrs. Black spotted Essary and invited him to their cabin, where Black told him about his involvement with the Klan and asked advice. Essary urged him to give the full story to the clamoring reporters. Black then answered their questions, but saved his full explanation for a national radio broadcast.

It was customary for the *Sun* and other large bureaus to "black-sheet" their stories—pass their carbons—to friends working for smaller papers outside their orbit. When Paul Patterson heard about this, he ordered it stopped. He said it was costing $75,000 a year to operate the bureau and he wasn't going to spend that to help other papers cover Washington. (Essary told about a *Detroit News* reporter who turned up an offbeat political-party convention feature. A friend on the *Washington Star* asked for a "black-sheet." Then a *Washington Times* man did, and later so did his associate. It was filed without change to the *Star,* and the two *Times* reporters, each unaware of what the other had done, wired it under their respective bylines. The *Times* news editor received the same story twice from his reporters, then read it again in the *Star.*)

Patterson wanted his bureau "to show the flag"—have the *Sun* concentrate on the major stories of the day, in effect duplicate the wire services but do it better and more thoroughly. That was the policy from Essary's day until recent years. Most stories ran more than 1,000 words, some frequently to 1,500, and they were seldom cut. In fact, editors liked long pieces. One might telephone a correspondent, "Write enough to turn a column"—enough to jump to an inside page. Patterson glowed when the front and inside pages were filled with bureau reporting.

William E. Moore, the managing editor, would call Essary at 1:00 P.M. to find out what was going on and to issue orders. Gerald Griffin said, "He kept close watch on assignments and how they were fulfilled. He was a tyrant in a way. He could be abrupt, but never as fierce in his actions as he was in his words. He wanted the staff to know that it was his paper."

As was the Washington custom, the bureau chief wrote the lead story, and it carried his byline. In the early 1930s the *Sun* initiated the practice—now universal—of awarding bylines to bureau staff members. Among the first to merit one was Drew Pearson, the diplomatic correspondent.

In 1931, Pearson and Robert Allen, bureau chief on the *Christian Science Monitor,* anonymously wrote *Washington Merry-Go-Round,* a gossipy book about inside Washington. In it Pearson praised the *Sun,* Essary, and himself. The *Sun,* he wrote, is an example of "that now practically extinct spectacle in American journalism of honest and independent reporters working for honorable and brilliant newspapers." Essary was described as "a staunch and loyal defender of his reporters." Pearson immodestly extolled himself: "The *Sun*'s expert on foreign affairs had the reputation of knowing more about the State Department than most of the people who run it, and to a considerable extent this is true. He is the State Department's severest critic, yet because its members either fear him or value his opinion, he is taken into their confidence on many important international moves." (What he did not include— or tell the *Sun*—was the five-year secret contract he had signed in 1930 as western hemisphere director of the Irish Hospitals Sweepstake, at $30,000 a year, with a chauffeur-driven Lincoln Continental and legal and other expenses paid. If friends asked about the impressive car and uniformed chauffeur, he blithely replied that he was doing public relations work of a confidential nature.)

Washington Merry-Go-Round was an immediate sensation. More than 180,000 copies were sold. But soon the Justice Department discovered who the authors were. President Hoover sent his press secretary to the *Monitor* and the *Sun* to ask if they took responsibility for the foul things their reporters had been writing about the President of the United States. The *Monitor* fired Allen, but Essary proved that he was "a staunch and loyal defender of his reporters" by retaining Pearson. Since few Washington insiders knew who wrote the book, Pearson's and Allen's anonymity was secure when they published a sequel, *More Washington Merry-Go-Round.* In that Pearson related the intimate lifestyle of his mother-in-law, Mrs. Eleanor (Cissy) Patterson, editor of the Washington *Herald.* This and other scurrilous gossip was too much for Moore. He told Pearson, "the *Sun* is not a keyhole paper," and gave him the choice of resigning or being fired. Pearson quit. Later Pearson wrote a syndicated column, first with Allen, then by himself. It was the most widely syndicated Washington column.

Essary, as the senior correspondent in Washington, was admired by his fellow newspapermen. He was chairman of the National Press Building's tenant committee (the *Sun* got the choicest suite, on the twelfth floor, facing the White House) and was the first correspondent to be elected president of both the National Press Club and the Gridiron Club, then limited to fifty members. As president of the Gridiron Club, it was his privilege to invite the President of the United States to the club's annual white-tie dinner. Once, while President Coolidge was listening to Essary's invitation, he reached into a box of expensive cigars and lit one. Then he pulled out a box of inexpensive cigars and offered it to Essary, who said, "Don't mind if I do, Mr. President," as he reached across the President's desk and helped himself to an imported cigar.

The Gridiron dinner is famous for the President's off-the-record remarks and for satirical skits performed by members. Costumes are rented from a Baltimore theatrical costumer. Ever since Essary's time it has been traditional for the *Sun* to entertain the club's officers and its music committee at a terrapin luncheon at the Maryland Club when they come to select the costumes. After toasts are exchanged, the music committee sings selections from the show. The *Sun* has been represented in the Gridiron Club almost from its founding in 1885; current members are Ernest B. Furgurson, the bureau chief, and Jack W. Germond, a political columnist for the *Evening Sun* and a past president.

Because of poor health, Essary was forced to retire in November 1941, but he continued to visit the bureau almost daily and died there the following March. He was succeeded by Dewey L. Fleming, who had worked for the United Press and for a year with the Baltimore *American* before joining the *Sun*'s city staff in 1923. The scrapbooks Fleming kept provide a running view of American history, from the Hall-Mills murder trial in 1926 and the Chicago Valentine's Day gangland massacre of 1929, through the Depression, the New Deal, and World War II, to the postwar years.

Fleming was chief of the *Sun*'s New York bureau in 1927–28 and of the Chicago bureau in 1928–29. He captured the violence of a Chicago election with one lead: "A candidate killed by machine-gunners, two workers wounded seriously with gun shots, scores of voters beaten, clubbed and slugged into insensibility, a half-dozen ward leaders kidnapped, wholesale intimidation of voters and a few scattered reports of ballot box stuffing. This was Chicago's record in today's primary election. . . . Almost no one would admit that violence had been unusual." He first went to Washington in 1926, returned after two years in the London bureau, 1929–31, and remained there except for a second tour in London nearly twenty years after his first one. During the 1937 battle over President Roosevelt's request for six additional Supreme Court justices, he covered the Senate. Patterson, opposed to the plan, was so delighted when it was defeated that he gave a party for the bureau staff, inviting Harry C. Black, John W. Owens, and Mencken to join the celebration. The party began with mint juleps, and champagne flowed during the dinner. Patterson gave a speech praising the bureau for its reporting. Mencken jumped up, proposing that Patterson give everyone a raise. Griffin, who was there, remembered that Patterson was euphoric, but not to that extent.

Fleming was a painstaking reporter and meticulous writer. He and Gerald Johnson were the two cleanest typists. No xx's or pencil revisions marred their copy. If Fleming wanted to change a sentence or paragraph, or even a word, he would scissor it out and paste in the corrected portion. The only three who saw his typing were the bureau desk man and the two punchers who sent the copy to Baltimore. (They could send about seventy words a minute, but when they had been drinking it took both to file a story: one could read but not punch accurately; the other could punch intuitively, but not see well enough to read.)

Fleming could capture an issue succinctly and with imagination. This is how he described a political uproar over a swimming pool built for Governor A. B. "Happy" Chandler: "Kentucky's most famous swimming pool isn't so very big, but it splashes from the Ohio River to the Cumberland, from the Mississippi Valley to the coal fields over against West Virginia." He relished political reporting and won the Pulitzer Prize in 1944 for national reporting, then known as "Telegraph Reporting (National)." He got the prize in an unusual way. After examining the entries, the advisory board agreed that none was worthy of the award. Kent, a member of the board, asked it to delay its decision until the next day. He telephoned Moore, the managing editor, suggesting that he send Fleming's clippings to New York by messenger. In most cases, entries are submitted in attractive presentations, but Moore only had time to send the clips as they were kept in the *Sun* library, folded, dog-eared, and worn from use. Kent passed them around to his fellow judges, and they decided—even though the entry was made after the deadline—that Fleming deserved the prize.

The Pulitzer selection process was criticized in the *American Mercury* of April 1948 by Carroll Binder, editorial editor of the *Minneapolis Tribune*. "Frank Kent," it began, "scorned the vanity and ingratitude of a younger colleague on the Baltimore *Sun* before a group of Washington correspondents recently. 'I got that fellow a Pulitzer Prize and he never even thanked me for it,' Kent observed. 'I suppose he thinks he won the prize all by himself.'" The article charged that "the frequency of Pulitzer awards to organizations represented on the board . . . gives rise to the charges of log-rolling. Last year the board scored an all-time high in awards within the family. Seven of the nine prizes in journalism awarded in 1947 went to organizations represented on the board. The prize for meritorious service in journalism went to the Baltimore *Sun*, represented on the board by Frank Kent."

After recounting the number of awards won by the *Times*, the Associated Press, and the two Pulitzer papers, the *New York World* and the *St. Louis Post-Dispatch*—all represented on the board—Binder again mentioned Kent: "The *Sun* papers in Baltimore also have some very able writers and cartoonists on their staff and thus provide vice president Kent, who had been on the Pulitzer Advisory Board since 1932 [really from 1928 to 1953], with good material for promoting Pulitzer awards to *Sun* men." (In that span the *Sun* won nine Pulitzers. After Kent left the board a quarter century went by with no prizes awarded to the *Sun*.) Kent wrote Binder that he was distressed by the article and personal reference. In his reply, Binder wrote in part,

> Your remark about Dewey Fleming's prize was so widely quoted about the Press Club after you made it that I thought it would do no harm to put it into print. I softened the phrasing attributed to you and omitted Fleming's name so as to spare him embarrassment. The way the story was told, you were reported as saying that the entries for that category of reporting were not very good and that you had taken the trouble to assemble and submit examples of Fleming's work which neither he nor his immediate chief had taken the trouble to enter.

As executive editor, Swanson pushed Fleming hard, wanting not only major stories, but side, background, analytical, and investigative pieces as well. Fleming covered the White House and the State Department. Mark S. Watson, the military authority, commuted from Baltimore, carrying his papers in what resembled a doctor's satchel. Watson had the distinction of having one of his analysis pieces printed twice on the front page within two days. The second time it carried this introduction: "The following article by Mr. Watson was printed in last Saturday's paper. The adjoining article from Moscow seems to give it a relevance which, when first published, was not altogether apparent." Unlike Fleming's clean copy, Watson's was ornate with changes and additions in a minute hand, not only between the lines but round and round the four margins of the page. (Essary never used copy paper. He felt comfortable only when writing on Western Union or Postal Telegraph blanks.)

William H. Y. Knighton, Jr., who had been assistant managing editor, covered the House of Representatives and later the Eisenhower White House; Howard Norton covered labor and the war agencies along with Griffin; and Rodney Crowther covered the Treasury and economics. Crowther had been financial editor of the *Evening Sun* for eight years during the Depression before he was transferred to Washington, first writing for the *Evening Sun*. He became a series specialist, some subjects running to twenty installments. Even experts recognized him as a financial authority, and prior to federal budget hearings he would give informal seminars for colleagues and friends on other papers. After he and Paul W. Ward covered the United Nations Monetary and Financial Conference at Bretton Woods, New Hampshire, Crowther rhapsodized, "That was one of the biggest events of my life."

In addition to Crowther, the *Evening Sun* bureau included for a time Lila H. Thomsen, Ben H. Miller, Nathaniel T. Kenney, and Frank R. Kent, Jr. Thomsen was the first woman assigned by the *Sunpapers* to Washington shortly before Pearl Harbor. Miller was killed in a Kansas plane crash during a tour of defense industries. His death "in action" was commemorated in 1942 with the launching of the Liberty ship SS *Miller.* (Later the paper wanted to know where the ship had been during the war. A search turned up nothing. Finally, it was discovered that the name of the ship had been changed to honor someone else.) For several summers Kenney was detached from the bureau to be the yachting editor for morning *Sun* sports.

A semi-professional baseball player in his youth, Paul Ward, slight and dapper, joined the *Sun* in 1930 as a business writer and two years later was transferred to Washington to cover economic news. After covering the Senate, he became the diplomatic correspondent and held that post for nearly thirty years. Ward wrote about and gained the confidence of eight presidents, nine secretaries of state, and hundreds of diplomats here and abroad. He became a well-known figure not only in Washington but also at major international conferences. Often he would file several thousand words not only on important conferences but on day-to-day activities at the State Department or the United Nations, which he covered from its beginning. After getting his fourteenth or fifteenth add, an editor might plead with him "to knock it off," or, arbitrarily, the bureau desk man might not send the last few takes; but often his full report was printed. Secretaries of state, and Ward's competition, were said to read the *Sun* not only to find out what was happening in the far reaches of the department, but also to see how Ward was assessing developments. A *Sun* editorial said of him:

> Scholars attempting to write a definitive history of the United Nations' first quarter-century will be compelled, if they are meticulous in their research, to turn to the files of the *Sun*. For it was in the pages of this newspaper that Paul W. Ward chronicled in detail the growing pains of the world organization—its rhetoric, its hypocrisy, its maneuverings and its achievements. All these were present in Mr. Ward's dispatches, which were required reading at the U.N. and, we would guess, in foreign ministries around the world. As diplomatic correspondent of the *Sun,* Mr. Ward went at a story with a tenacity rivaled only by his stunningly ency-clopedic knowledge of our times. Rather than merely report the specific events of an upheaval in Jordan during the 1950s, for example, he would use the occasion to provide a backgrounding on the rise of the Hashemite monarchy and its place in the Middle East.

In 1970, at the age of 65, and when editors were insisting on shorter stories, Ward volunteered to become the news editor, usually the entry position for a bureau job, and went on working until his death six years later. He was as conscientious as he had been as a correspondent and, among other created duties, continued to index the daily Foreign Broadcast Information Bulletin, as he had for years. He never seemed to throw away a government press release, and they would be stacked high on his desk until they tumbled to the floor under their own weight.

Ward was a pretelevision journalist, a writer who conveyed detail that became redundant when television's omnipresent cameras provided even more intimate pictures. To illustrate that point, Furgurson read an excerpt from a Ward piece at the memorial service for Ward. Ward had interviewed Alfred Landon in Topeka after his nomination in 1936 as the Republican presidential candidate, and his story in effect introduced the little-known governor of Kansas to the readers of the *Sun:*

At a luncheon in the cafeteria, Landon merged with that background of farmers and small-town businessmen . . . and became almost as indistinguishable as a wren among old leaves. Like most of them he wore a suit of drab gray stuff, comfortable-looking old black shoes and a colored shirt. In his case the shirt was dark blue and the dark-figured tie he wore sagged loosely away from the collar. Despite the heat he wore a vest, and little beads of perspiration wetted his lip just under his nose. His steel-gray hair was rumpled, though close cut, and the straw sailor, which the Independence delegation had given him, was balanced most of the time on the back of his round skull.

Thomas M. O'Neill covered Alger Hiss's two trials, and his graphic portrayal of courtroom drama was widely praised. Alistair Cooke, in the preface to his *Generation on Trial,* termed O'Neill's reporting "incomparable." Beginning in 1953, O'Neill wrote a national political column, "Politics and People," first for the *Evening Sun,* then for the *Sun.* John W. Owens, once a political reporter, said that O'Neill had a gift for illuminating corners one didn't even know were there.

Joseph H. Short, Jr., was an Associated Press reporter until moving to the *Sun* in 1943. He was assigned to the White House and was not only a friend of Truman when he was Vice President and President, but also one of Truman's poker-playing buddies. Stakes in the game were high, and if Short lost several hundred dollars, the *Sun* reimbursed him, believing that such a friendship was invaluable. Short left the paper in 1950 to become President Truman's press secretary.

Fleming died in 1955 and was succeeded by Gerald Griffin, a Nebraskan, who started on the *Sunday Sun* in 1930 and moved to the bureau in 1934 as its news editor before covering the New Deal agencies, war boards, and Congress. The biggest war story that he and a friend from the *Star* dug into could not be printed. They discovered that huge work forces were being hired for construction work at Oak Ridge, Tennessee, and Pasco, Washington, involving a new explosive. They kept asking questions until they reached a member of the Cabinet, who told them succinctly but confidentially, "They'll try to split the atom. Whoever [the United States or Germany] does it first will win the war." In a biographical sketch Griffin wrote for the *Sun* library, he noted that he had "never even mentioned this to his Baltimore editors."

Griffin was in the Washington bureau except for naval service during World War II, and from 1947 to 1949, when he was in the London bureau. He specialized in politics and accompanied President Eisenhower and later Vice President Johnson on their world travels. When President Kennedy was assassinated in 1963, Griffin was appalled to learn that the bureau had no prepared obituary. Joseph R. L. Sterne started writing one around 3:00 P.M. and kept writing until midnight, using references but for the most part writing from memory. Set in type, Sterne's account filled more than a page, the longest story, he said, he ever wrote.

Ever since Richardson's day, the *Sun* had comprehensive reporting on the national conventions, conventions of the Prohibitionists, the Bull Moose Party, the Socialist Party, the Farmer-Labor Party, Father Coughlin's National Union for Social Justice, and Henry Wallace's Progressive Party. The core of this coverage was the Washington bureau's responsibility, but it had help from Mencken, editors, cityside political reporters, cartoonists, desk men, and support personnel. At major-party conventions the task force numbers fifteen to twenty men.

Patterson relished both directing the coverage and the partying that went on late at night in the *Sun* suite. Mencken was a star of the report until World War II years, when he stopped writing. Patterson urged him to attend the 1948 conventions, but Mencken, in failing health, was reluctant. He finally agreed. "Oh, well," he sighed, "it's a heroic death." He got what he called a whangdoodle of a story when the Southern Democrats bolted over states' rights, but Lee McCardell got an even better one. As the delegates marched out of the hall to the music of "The Stars and Bars" and into the night, McCardell, without a word, vaulted over the railing of the press platform and followed them. His next dispatch was datelined Birmingham, where the bolters were preparing to hold a Dixiecrat convention and nominate their own candidates.

The 1948 Progressive Party convention was Mencken's last. It was in Philadelphia, and Mencken, after writing about the outrageous heat "and lazy puffs of gummy wind from the mangrove swamps surrounding the city," lambasted the Wallaceites. They in turn drew up a resolution censuring Mencken's "contemptible ranting." William Manchester, his biographer, assessed the Mencken reporting "as among the best he has ever done." After work, Mencken joined Patterson and the others in the *Sun* suite, singing the catchy Wallace songs. This attracted a Wallace crowd, who asked Patterson, "Who are you?" Patterson replied, "We are representatives of the capitalist press." He invited them in, and they added their voices to "Hen-ry Wall-ace, Friend-ly Hen-ry Wallace," in chorus after chorus, ending the songfest with a beery rendition of "Maryland, My Maryland."

After Patterson retired, Neil H. Swanson announced, "I'll run the bloody show," and he did for the 1952 Chicago conventions. He demanded a flood of copy for both papers. For the first time he had *Sun* men writing overnights for the evening paper. Griffin remembers one night, after filing his *Sun* story, pounding out three overnights for the *Evening Sun.* In addition to scrutinizing

Sun copy, Swanson watched the AP wire and would announce, "Keep pushing. We beat the AP by six minutes on that development." Long after the *New York Times* staff had settled down to its nightly poker game, Swanson had his staff prowling hotel corridors during the Democratic convention, catching, before the other media, the drift to Adlai Stevenson as the presidential candidate and hitting that angle hard.

Frank R. Kent attended political conventions from 1900 to 1952, except when he was managing editor. In 1922, after returning from a year as a correspondent in France and Germany, he began writing a daily article emphasizing the human elements of politics under a news head. On February 23, 1923, the reports became a column, "The Great Game of Politics." Franklin D. Roosevelt urged Van-Lear Black to syndicate it—an ironic suggestion, because during Roosevelt's presidency Kent excoriated him. In 1923 the company's policy was against syndication, but eleven years later, with many papers requesting permission to reprint columns, it was syndicated beginning on October 30, 1934, and soon was in 140 papers. Arthur Krock, of the New York *Times,* noted: "Historically it is probable that Kent was the first American reporter to write, on a fixed and continuing schedule of publication, articles of news review and comment that dealt wholly with politics and politicians, and were nationally distributed."

In 1925 the *New Republic* asked Kent to write, anonymously, a political column. Bruce Bliven, the editor, was still searching for a pseudonym when riding the subway to a printer with the first column. According to an oft-told story, he noticed a placard saying "BRT" (Brooklyn Rapid Transit). He reversed the initials and signed the column "TRB." Though later many prominent newspapermen wrote the column, it has always been signed "TRB."

In the 1920s, Kent was a fighting liberal, condemning Prohibition and castigating Coolidge. But he liked Hoover, and for the rest of his life Kent supported Republicans. Once the Democrats of Franklin D. Roosevelt were in office, Kent, believing that big government was intrinsically bad, was continually on the attack. For a long while his column was based on hard-nosed reporting, usually by phone. He said he had learned that "when three politicians talk political business privately, you will always be able to find out what they were talking about if your questions—put to each of them singly—are adroit enough." His style was forceful and lucid, written in pencil on copy paper in a large hand with seldom a word changed. An admirer of Woodrow Wilson, Kent saw himself as a traditionalist, with faith in the old order of social, cultural, economic, and political life. He believed that Wilson's big-government, regulatory-agency policies were evolutionary but that Roosevelt's were revolutionary. The column could infuriate those with a different viewpoint. The *Washington Post-Times-Herald* noted: "He became, like his old friend and associate, H. L. Mencken, less and less the satirical analyst and more and more the apologist for a political point of view." Kent's negativism grew so predictable, so hostile and vitriolic, that in February 1937 Patterson moved "The Great Game of Politics" from its favored position on the front page, where it had appeared four or five times a week, to the page opposite the editorials.

During Truman's administration, Kent was even more abusive of the President and his Fair Deal than he had been toward the New Deal. After one column critical of the Truman family's financial affairs, Truman, according to Kent's old friend Krock, "wrote Kent an agonized letter, in which he went into the most utter detail":

> How much his laundry bill was, how much the cook got, and that sort of thing. It was such a revealing letter, and it was written in such personal terms that Kent, being as high-minded as he was, . . . returned the letter by hand to the White House and simply said, "I think the President would rather have this back." Truman wrote him a letter of thanks that was simply heart-warming.

In addition to his newspaper work, Kent wrote six books. One, entitled *The Great Game of Politics* became a standard college text on practical politics.

Kent continued writing several columns a week until 1947, when at the age of 70 he cut back to one a week. He was a frequent visitor to Washington, lunching with the bureau staff, but he lived and did his writing in Baltimore. He arrived at the *Sun* in a chauffeur-driven automobile. In the Calvert Street building he had no private office, just a desk in the Sunday department, where he enjoyed the company of reporters young enough to be his grandchildren. His last column appeared on January 5, 1958. He died a few months later at the age of 80, after fifty-eight years with the *Sun* as a reporter, editor, foreign correspondent, columnist, and, from 1921, a vice president of the company.

A colorful bureau character in the Kent years was George Washington Combs, a native of Kentucky who was addressed by his honorary title, Colonel. He joined the bureau in 1908 when it still sold advertising and subscriptions, and he worked in the business department until that was closed, in 1924. Then he handled staff expenses, doling out streetcar tokens for local assignments and reluctantly paying the fare when a correspondent took a taxi. He became a part-time reporter, covering the Maryland delegation, which regarded his visits more as social occasions than as professional. He was not a good writer. A former bureau chief said his copy had to be decoded, and another claimed that Combs knew less about newspapering than any reporter he had ever met. Combs was a good friend of Fred M. Vinson, also a Kentuckian, who held important posts, including that of Secretary of the Treasury, before becoming Chief Justice of the United States. Through Vinson, Combs met many movers and shakers. Sitting in the bureau reading an exclusive in the *Washington Star* or the *Times-Herald,* he would disparage the story, asserting, "That's not news. I heard that at a dinner party two weeks ago." After the bureau chief overheard a number of such comments, he began quizzing the colonel, asking where he had been the night before. If it involved a party of Washington insiders, the colonel would be debriefed so a colleague could follow up as leads table talk which the colonel did not realize was more than that.

Philip Potter, a bony, lanky Minnesotan with a cavernous voice, described by Muriel Dobbin, a colleague, as looking like "a remarkable cross between an elongated Gandhi and a superannuated pixie," was assigned to the bureau in December 1946 and for the next eight years was in and out on foreign assignments. The capital press corps rated Potter as a driven, indefatigable reporter, one of the best in digging out hard-to-get facts. At the 1960 Democratic convention in Los Angeles, Henry W. "Hank" Trewhitt, the *Sun* reporter assigned to Lyndon B. Johnson, went to the Johnson suite early in the morning to get the jump on other reporters. Arriving, he met Potter, who was leaving after having breakfast with the Johnsons. A Johnson aide did not think this unusual. "A lot of newsmen," he remarked, "have gotten up early to see someone and met Potter coming out." (For a reporter to intrude on a colleague's beat, as Potter would do when on the trail of a good story, was known as "big-footing.")

Potter's habitual attitude toward politicians was skepticism. He himself phrased this colloquially: "The son of a bitch is lying to us." Potter wrote long, detailed stories, and after they were filed he might telephone the copy desk to make sure his inserts were made, the spelling of an unusual name was not mistakenly standardized, and, if the copy editor was patient, even improve the phrasing of a clause in the fifteenth add. To someone of Potter's temperament, detachment was no virtue; he was emotionally involved in the stories he worked. A friend observed, "If he covered a fire, he'd feel the burns." Many topics and individuals ignited his wrath. They were, in descending order, communism, columnists, hypocrisy, injustice, "the goddamned, phoney, sophisticated Washington press corps," and "people who think war is unnecessary." He relaxed in the National Press Club bar by erupting with intense personal opinions on whatever subject he had just been covering. During the Vietnam War, Potter was a fiery hawk, and because of such outbursts the *Sun* bureau got the reputation of being hawkish. Yet Potter kept his feelings and opinions out of his dispatches.

In the 1950s, when a Senate committee held hearings into Senator Joseph R. McCarthy's accusation that the State Department was sheltering Communists, and later when McCarthy impugned the loyalty of General George C. Marshall and the Army, Potter did some of his best reporting. Price Day, editor-in-chief of the *Sun*, said afterward, "As much as any reporter, Potter was responsible for the destruction of Joe McCarthy." Through exclusive tips from congressional sources, Potter had a role in getting G. David Shine, a brash, controversial McCarthy aide, belatedly drafted into the Army. Then, with confidential information from Robert Kennedy, Potter revealed the favored treatment being given Shine in the Army at the behest of the McCarthy staff. These labors helped bring about the ultimate senatorial censure of

McCarthy and his eventual disappearance as a national figure. In the course of this coverage, Potter, along with Griffin and Knighton, wrote some of the longest stories ever printed in the *Sun.*

The name of Owen Lattimore, a Johns Hopkins University professor and an adviser to the government on Asian affairs, also surfaced during the 1950 hearings. In a closed session, McCarthy first termed him "an espionage agent," later changing the accusation to "the chief architect of our Far Eastern policy—and a policy risk." Lattimore was in Afghanistan and on his way back to testify to his innocence he stopped in London. In his book *Ordeal by Slander,* Lattimore wrote:

> Among the group at London airport was Hamilton Owens, editor of the Baltimore *Sun.* The fact that he had come all the way to London to meet me was like getting a signal in a code to which I had the key. I knew that the Baltimore *Sun,* as my home-town paper, would be exposed to the full pressure of unreasoning emotion as soon as the McCarthy charges against me came out. I also knew that the editorial page of the paper had a tendency to be flabby. I had therefore guessed that as soon as the sensational McCarthy charges had come out into the open, the *Sun* had played the news on its front page with the biggest headlines that the printing room could provide, while hesitating, on its editorial page, to point out that in my own university and own community my loyalty has never been doubted. . . . I could therefore see right away that at least one of the reasons why Hamilton Owens had come all the way to London was that he was looking for a safe way to write a friendly story about me. This he did, and I was very grateful to him for it.

For the next few years, Lattimore was in the news. In 1952 and 1954 he was indicted for perjury before a congressional committee, but the charges were dismissed. The *Sun* reported this in detail, while its editorial page was restrained in its comment. The *Sun* struggled to sum up the long-drawn-out Lattimore case in a June 1955 editorial: "Most of the years through which the Lattimore affair dragged on were years of confusion and high emotion. We are calmer now largely because we know where we stand and what is demanded of us. The final disposition of the case reflects the change for the better."

Potter covered many political campaigns. On a trip with Richard Nixon he had noted how mechanical Nixon was becoming in his role. Nixon's party landed at a deserted airport to change planes. Deep in thought, Nixon strode to the second plane, mounted the steps, and on reaching the doorway, in a reflex action, turned, waved, and flashed his smile at the nonexistent crowd. On another Nixon campaign, Potter suffered a shredded disc but refused to give up. He was relatively comfortable only when lying in the aisle on the plane. Unable to type, he dictated his stories to Nixon's personal secretary, Rose Mary Woods. After the election he took time to have an operation. Potter's spunk was also evident in 1968 after the assassination of Martin Luther King, Jr., as looting and burning broke out in Washington. The National Press Club was kept open into the early morning hours to accommodate reporters.

Waiters nervously wondered how they would get home; a curfew had been imposed, and no taxis were operating. Potter crowded six of the help into his car and drove them to their homes in areas where rioters were still active.

In 1964, Potter became bureau chief when Griffin was transferred to Baltimore to be editorial-page editor of the *Sun*. Under Griffin the bureau had functioned in a sedate, orderly fashion. One member said approvingly that it had the atmosphere of a gentleman's club. Griffin himself perhaps best revealed its style in the biographical sketch he left in the *Sun* library as he retired. It concluded:

> Another close friend was Mark Watson, who had come to the Washington bureau as the newspaper's military correspondent early in World War II. Mr. Watson, who had first hired Griffin for his Sunday staff, and who had interceded for him when there was a Washington bureau vacancy, gravely pretended to be working under Griffin's direction in Washington. This was a little joke between the two, for they both knew that Griffin was sensible enough to see that Mr. Watson had the freest possible hand to work as he chose.

(In 1963 President Kennedy awarded Watson the Presidential Medal of Freedom. He was the first newspaperman to receive the medal, "the highest civilian honor the President can confer for service in peacetime." Watson was still the *Sun*'s military correspondent when he died in 1966 at the age of 78. The Pentagon press room is named in his honor.)

Under Potter the bureau was different from Griffin's day. Because of his bursting presence it was disorganized—even chaotic at times—but an exciting place to work. Because of Potter's unwillingness to administer, Paul A. Banker, the managing editor, created the post of assistant bureau chief, naming Sterne. But Sterne later said that because of the confusion "it was an empty title." Sterne happily spent his time covering the Senate. Sterne added that the only one able to bring the slightest sense of order was James MacNees, the desk man, who somehow kept track of the daily outpouring of copy.

Potter called only one staff meeting. Assembling, the staff braced itself for cataclysmic news. Potter, glancing about, announced: "I want to bring up something I know nothing about. I need your advice because I'm thinking of buying a car." During those turbulent years, correspondents on other papers sometimes referred to the *Sun* as "Potter's paper."

Potter's friendship with Lyndon B. Johnson began when Johnson was Senate majority leader. Potter wrote a stinging story comparing the senator's arrogant attitude toward his staff to that of a feudal baron. When Johnson protested, Potter only laughed, saying he knew his story had induced the senator to send his overworked press secretary, George Reedy, on an all-expense-paid vacation to Acapulco. After Johnson became President he would invite Potter to the White House for private chats over a bottle of Chivas Regal. When fellow correspondents complained about such favoritism, Douglas Kiker, an NBC correspondent, remarked, "Potter might be somebody's favorite, but he's nobody's pet." Johnson once ordered Potter out of the White House after Potter offered him unsolicited advice on how to run the country, then called him back to continue the argument. Once Johnson was driving Vice President Hubert Humphrey and Potter around on his Texas ranch for moonlight deer-watching when his Cadillac became mired in an unseen mudhole. Potter gibed, "How can you run the country if you can't find your way around on your own ranch?" Johnson ordered, "Get out and push!" Potter did, and the President chortled as the car was freed by his mud-splattered critic.

(A few weeks after Johnson became President, William F. Schmick, Jr., then president of the A. S. Abell Company, was entertaining the board, editors, executives, and their wives at a Christmas party in his home. The telephone rang, and the message brought a pause to conversation. The White House was calling. The President wished to speak to Mr. Dorsey, the managing editor. After Dorsey returned to the gathering, again there was a hush as all waited to hear what had been said. Dorsey was still glowing, but he tried to be nonchalant as he explained, "The President wanted to wish you all a happy holiday. He said the *Sun* was the top paper on his desk every morning, that he read it faithfully and learned more from it than any other." Sedate cheering and clinking of glasses followed. Later it was learned that same week the President had called a number of other papers around the nation and told their editors much the same thing.)

In 1972, at the age of 65, Potter stepped down as bureau chief, then spent the next one-and-a-half years as London bureau chief until he retired. The *Sun* library had more than 200 bulging packets of his stories.

His successor was Peter J. Kumpa. Originally a Bostonian, Kumpa had been first hired in 1947 as part-time bureau switchboard operator while attending Georgetown University. In 1951 he moved to Baltimore for three years on the local staff, and then returned to the bureau as its desk man. Later Kumpa covered the White House when correspondents could quote President Eisenhower only after his press secretary had reworked the garbled syntax into comprehensible sentences. (Thomas M. O'Neill became so frustrated from covering Eisenhower that once while attending a party at Dorsey's home he jumped up on the sofa, after a drink or two, and announced, "As of right now I quit covering the White House." Russell Baker, having left the *Sun* for the *New York Times,* was presently assigned to the Eisenhower White House. Asked if it was exciting, he replied, "It's like covering the Tomb of the Unknown Soldier.")

Before becoming bureau chief, Kumpa had been a Nieman Fellow at Harvard and a foreign correspondent in the Middle East, the Far East, and the Soviet Union. Five of his staff had been assigned to Moscow: Ernest B. Furgurson, Jr., Adam Clymer, Stephen E. Nordlinger, Bruce Winters, and Dean Mills. Furgurson, as noted, wrote a political column; Clymer covered politics and the White House; Nordlinger and Winters covered Congress;

Mills covered the Supreme Court. James S. Keat was assigned to the White House and State Department, Charles W. Corddry had the Pentagon, Walter Gordon had the courts and investigative reporting, and Gilbert A. Lewthwaite, John S. Carroll, and Frederic B. Hill were assigned general reporting. From 1962 to 1972, Albert Sehlstedt, Jr., covered the nation's manned space flights and for the next three years was assigned to Congress and the White House. In 1975 he became the paper's national science writer, working from Baltimore.

Starting toward the end of 1972 and on into 1973 and 1974, the *Washington Post,* through its resourceful reporters Bob Woodward and Carl Bernstein, pursued the Watergate investigations involving the Nixon White House. The *Columbia Journalism Review* reported at one point that fewer than fifteen of the more than 400 Washington correspondents were assigned full-time to Watergate; two were from the *Sun,* Walter Gordon and later Muriel Dobbin. (Dobbin had been a Scottish correspondent for London papers before joining the *Sunday Sun* in 1958 and was transferred to Washington in 1962 to help cover the Kennedy White House. She was the first woman in the *Sun* bureau except for Lila H. Thomsen, who wrote for the *Evening Sun* in the 1940s. In 1977, Dobbin succeeded Bruce Winters, the *Sun's* first West Coast correspondent, and was based there until 1985.) Nevertheless, Banker insisted on handling the Watergate story gingerly. With such a watch-and-wait approach, the *Sun* trailed other papers. *Sun* coverage became thorough and decisive only when the matter aroused Congress, the courts, and the whole nation.

During two other history-making newsbreaks of that time, the *Sun* again cautiously held back on its own reporting, largely relying on wire-service reports. It published none of the so-called Pentagon Papers, which the *New York Times* and the *Washington Post* printed to expose Pentagon deception and mendacity during the Vietnam War. And when Spiro T. Agnew, the only Baltimorean or Marylander to win election to the vice presidency, was forced out of office by revelations of financial misdeeds, it was the *Wall Street Journal* that was first with the story.

The Watergate denouement and the attending acclaim for the *Post*—including the movie *All the President's Men,* which made the paper known far beyond its reach—enhanced the *Post's* reputation and helped project it into a paper of national importance. Although the *Sun,* with its solid, informed reporting, continued in the 1970s and onward to be read by members of the federal power structure, the paper no longer had the influence in Washington that it had enjoyed before the *Post*—absorbing the *Times-Herald* in 1954 and then racing ahead of the fading *Washington Star*—became the capital's dominant newspaper.

In his book *The Washington Reporters,* published by the Brookings Institution in 1981, Stephen Hess propounded that capital newsgathering was divided into three rings: inner, middle, and outer. His inner ring consisted of the three national networks, the two wire services, the three weekly newsmagazines, the *Washington Post*, the *New York Times*, the *Washington Star*, and the *Wall Street Journal*. He contended that newsmakers regularly leak information to these organizations, less often to others, "because through them [the government] learns what the country is learning about what it is doing."

The *Sun* was listed second in the middle ring, behind the *Los Angeles Times* and ahead of the *Boston Globe*, the *Christian Science Monitor*, the *Chicago Tribune*, Knight-Ridder newspapers, the *Journal of Commerce*, the *New York Daily News*, and the Cox newspapers. Hess listed four criteria in establishing the standing of a news organization: (1) scope, or national orientation; (2) resources, number of reporters and the amount they travel; (3) audience, the characteristics of readers or listeners—is the audience important either in number or as elites? (4) purpose—seriousness of function: "being educational is mandatory to gain high standing; only then is it acceptable to be profitable or entertaining." On these criteria, the *Sun* ranked high. "Its bureau," Hess wrote, "has twelve reporters, twice the minimum requirement for middle-ring eligibility. Its coverage is heavily national (only one reporter is assigned to regional news) and it rarely runs a Washington wire service story on page one. It is read by Washington journalists and high government officials." He also pointed out that with its weekday circulation (then 180,000) it had the highest ratio of Washington reporters to readers of any major news organization.

Furgurson began writing a national affairs column for the editorial page in 1969, and he continued to write it after he became bureau chief in 1975. (The column now appears on news pages and on Sundays in the Perspective section.) Not content to stay in Washington and pontificate, he roamed far and wide—from Lodge Pole, California, to write about the commercial exploitation of a remote valley in the Sierra Nevada mountains, to Solola, Guatemala, to describe the feast of Corpus Christi and the plight of the Indians. In 1981 the column, which was syndicated, was titled "U.S.A." It covered not only politics and national affairs, but also anything that drew Furgurson's attention—spring arriving in the Great Smokies at Trillium Gap, Tennessee, the MX missile silos in Wyoming—all written in a fresh, graceful style.

From its early days the bureau operated almost with a free hand in deciding what it would write and at what length. Covering the top stories of the day, it knew these reports would be displayed on the front page and appear almost word-for-word as written, no matter what their length. If Baltimore editors occasionally thought an Associated Press story should be on the front page, the bureau expected, as a matter of courtesy, to be advised so it then could produce its own version to be used instead of the wire story. The bureau regarded the front page as its domain, to be shared, reluctantly, only with the *Sun*'s foreign correspondents.

That unquestioned, traditional priority disappeared when recommendations of the News Room Task Force were adopted in the summer of 1979.

The managing editor, who in the words of a line editor "had been running the news operation from his hip pocket," delegated substantial authority through his assistant managing editors to the line editors—a radical change from the way national and foreign news had been edited. Well into the late 1960s the managing editor and an assistant managing editor selected the page-one stories; the news editor, besides supervising the copy desk, was responsible for the rest of the foreign and national news going in the main news section, and he drew up the page layouts for this "telegraph" news. Even when the news editor's title was changed to national editor in 1979, the job had limited authority and the editor had no voice in, or even knowledge of, the department's fiscal budget.

After authority was decentralized, the bureau had to work closely with the national editor, who had responsibility not only for what went into the paper but also for preparing and supervising the fiscal budget for his operations.

Under this restructuring, Paul A. Banker, the managing editor, wanted the best stories for page one, no matter where they might originate. An aggressive metropolitan desk, also operating with more authority, pushed and fought to get its best local stories on the front page. (When Dorsey was managing editor, a local story seldom made page one.) Initiative as to what went into the paper, where it appeared, and at what length had passed from Washington to Baltimore. For the first time the bureau had to compete for page-one space.

In July 1979, Frank C. Starr succeeded Charles G. Whiteford as national editor. Before coming to the *Sun,* Starr had been the *Chicago Tribune*'s Moscow correspondent for four years, chief of its Washington bureau for four years, and national columnist for two years. The national desk—Edward T. Jones is assistant national editor—keeps in close touch with the bureau. It gets a rundown of possible stories by 10:30 A.M., an early budget at noon, a complete budget at 3:00 P.M., and advisories whenever necessary. Although the stories are read by the deputy bureau chief and edited by the bureau's news editor, they are also edited by the national desk. Occasional disagreement between reporter and editor in story assessments has been going on since newspapering began, and such differences of opinion sometimes occur between the bureau and Baltimore editors. Also reporting to the national editor are John Schidlovsky, national reporter, and Douglas W. Struck, West Coast correspondent, one of a hundred semi-finalists (among 1,703 applicants) in NASA's competition to select a journalist to ride the space shuttle.

After James I. Houck succeeded Banker as managing editor early in 1982, he appointed Edwin W. Goodpaster, who had more than thirty years of newspaper experience, much of it in Washington, as deputy bureau chief to relieve Furgurson, the bureau chief, of day-to-day assignments, giving Furgurson more time for his column. (Goodpaster and the bureau write "Memo from Washington," a lively column of tidbits for the Sunday Perspective section.) Houck also codified and expanded the operating guidelines for the bureau and the national desk. Instead of using resources to duplicate what the wire and news services do well, emphasis was placed on enterprise reporting and in-depth series. Exceptions are made when the bureau can do a better, more thorough job, if a story has a strong Baltimore or Maryland angle, or if the story is of such magnitude that it demands the *Sun*'s own treatment.

In addition to Furgurson, Goodpaster, and Sheila M. Dresser, the news editor, the bureau includes Robert R. Timberg, who covers the White House; W. Stephens Broening, Jr., diplomatic correspondent; Vernon A. Guidry, Jr., covering the Pentagon; Lyle W. Denniston, covering the Supreme Court and the Justice Department; Nancy J. Schwerzler covering Congress; Paul West on politics; Stephen E. Nordlinger on economics; Julie Ann Johnson doing government-business, trade, and lobbying; Mark H. Matthews on general assignment; and Douglas M. Birch, assigned to the Baltimore metropolitan desk but the beat person covering Maryland's congressional delegation and stories dealing with Maryland. Charles W. Corddry is on part-time special assignment.

Timberg won the White House Correspondents' Association Aldo Beckman Award for his reporting on President Reagan's trips overseas in 1985—the U.S.-Soviet summit, the economic summit, and the President's V-E Day visit to West Germany's Bitburg military cemetery. Timberg was cited for his "insightful reports taking readers behind the scenes with careful reporting and lively writing."

The *Evening Sun* has its own Washington correspondents. Timberg became its Washington correspondent in 1980. When he was transferred to the *Sun*'s bureau, he was succeeded by Richard L. Berke and later by John H. Fairhall. After the Washington *Star* stopped publishing in August 1981, Jack W. Germond and Jules Witcover, the *Star*'s widely syndicated political columnists, made the *Evening Sun* their home base for the four columns they write weekly.

Since 1982 the *Sun*'s bureau has been located at 1627 K Street, N.W., a glass-walled office building in Washington's new downtown, two blocks from the White House. The bureau had been in the National Press building for fifty-five years, but it moved when the building was being renovated. For sentimental and historic reasons, the *Sun* considered returning to the restored *Sun* building on F Street, N.W. with its twelve-foot ceilings, chandeliers, and marble fireplaces, but it did not meet the special needs of a modern newspaper office.

FIFTEEN

Two Generations of Leadership
1960–1983

Van-Lear Black, Paul Patterson, and William F. Schmick, Sr., were a compatible, dynamic team that reorganized the *Sunpapers* after World War I. Patterson admired Schmick's acumen, work ethic, and newspaper-business knowledge, and as soon as he was elected president he promoted Schmick from advertising director to business manager; then, in 1924, he promoted him to vice president, and in 1934 to executive vice president. But when the board proposed Schmick as Patterson's successor, Patterson was skeptical. He believed that the president of a newspaper should have a news background. But the board disagreed, and on February 1, 1951, it named Schmick, then 67 years old with fifty-two years of experience, president of the A. S. Abell Company.

Schmick had joined the Baltimore *World* when he was 16, at a salary of $5 a week. On a small paper—and the *World* was the smallest in town—a neophyte might work in a different department every day. Schmick started in the mail room, moved to the mechanical department, where he lost the tip of a finger in a press, and was one of five reporters when the managing editor himself made $12 a week. While working in circulation and advertising, Schmick and others were asked by the publisher to write a letter suggesting what could be done to save the sinking paper. Schmick's ideas were the best, and he was appointed business manager. He was 20 years old. Seven years later, Charles H. Grasty bought the *World* for $63,000. Afterward, Grasty admitted that the paper had little value, but said the high price was justified if for no other reason than that it brought Schmick to the *Sun*.

Schmick started work in circulation but soon switched to classified advertising, building that section almost from scratch. He positioned the paid death notices just ahead of classified advertising, reasoning that many readers, having turned there in search of familiar names, would then scan the ads that followed.

When he assumed the presidency, advertisers were still being given tours of the new building. If they were major-account advertisers, their guide had orders to include the president's office for a personal greeting. Jack Neeley, of the advertising staff, recalls that four or five times when he stopped by with a group Schmick began his welcome by saying, "This office is too big and ornate. It wasn't my idea. It was planned and furnished by my predecessor." The explanation was characteristic of the man.

Schmick's first order as president to his managing editors was "You're the editors. I want you to keep on running the paper as you have been." A managing editor at the time said that Schmick never interfered with the news operation but, laughing, added, "I would hear from him, when there was a typo on the stock tables." The news side liked to believe that Schmick, coming from the business department, did not grasp how reporters functioned. They told these stories: When a reporter's name came up for, say, a merit increase, the president was said to have asked, "How many columns a week does he write?" And shortly after becoming president, he walked through the city room between editions and noticed many a person seemingly at ease, reading the newspaper or conversing. Schmick asked the managing editor, "Why aren't these men typing?" He lived across from the Loyola College athletic field on Milbrook Road, where the houses are large. When the house next door was sold, he was startled to learn that the purchaser was one of his reporters, Carroll E. Williams. He called Williams into his office, asking, "Did you really buy 4603, next to me?" Williams said he had, and Schmick commented, "How can you afford it?" Williams replied, "Mr. Schmick, I can't on the salary you pay me. But I have other income." (He owned some fifty apartment units.)

The tradition of son following father at the *Sunpapers,* begun by the Abells (and repeating under Patterson), was continued when William F. Schmick, Jr., after graduating from Princeton and spending a year at the *Dallas Morning News,* joined the *Sunpapers* in 1937. Following various jobs on the business side, he was promoted to advertising manager in 1943. At that time the *Evening Sun,* with a larger circulation than the *Sun,* carried the bulk of advertising, and Hearst's *News-Post,* with the largest circulation in Baltimore, had as much retail advertising as the *Evening Sun.* "Young Bill," as he was known, believed the morning paper had been neglected as an advertising medium—it was so thin that it was a one-section paper with international and national news on the front page, local news on the back page, and everything else sandwiched in between. He had his salesmen push advertising for the morning paper, though his father thought this was a mistake. But the plan worked, and advertising began to flow into the morning paper. On March 1, 1948, it was split into two sections on a regular basis.

"Young Bill" was named assistant business manager in 1948, assistant to the president in 1952, and executive vice president in 1953, and was elected to the board in 1956. In 1953, Thomas M. O'Neill, a reporter of pronounced anti-Eisenhower administration feelings, was being considered as a political columnist for the *Evening Sun*. Schmick, Sr., wondered if such a man would agree with the editorial position of the paper. His son interjected, "I don't think that's a proper question," and his father agreed.

The son described his father this way, "The paper and his family were his life. He was up at 6, read the paper and was off to the office. He was punctual. Meticulous. Straightforward. Dedicated. Every evening he reviewed what he had done and how it could have been done better. I, and many others who worked with him, learned to do the same thing." The senior Schmick relaxed by going to the racetrack with John E. Semmes, a member of the board, and Gaylord Clark, a stockholder. He kept a running tab of his $2 bets on his desk calendar, and many who noticed it supposed it was a complicated record of advertising, circulation, or both. He seldom took a full-length vacation. When taking off briefly to visit Harry Black at the board chairman's winter home at Boynton Beach, Florida, Schmick would say to his son and Gary Black, "You young fellows keep an eye on things while we're away." They put a lock on the executive washroom. When Schmick returned he wanted to know what had happened and was told they had thought it best to put everything under lock and key. He couldn't use the washroom until a handyman had removed the lock.

The senior Schmick's special aptitudes and interests were for organization, administration, and financial management. His philosophy—and a board imperative since the post-Grasty era—was to keep the company financially independent. He and the board did not approve of borrowing from banks. His administration was tightly run, economical, with a controlled circulation. The *Sun* had only one foreign bureau, London, for thirty-one years, except for a small one in Paris, started by Patterson in 1950, which operated for only eighteen months. Schmick approved the opening of three more in two-and-a-half years: Bonn in 1955, Moscow in 1956, and Rome in 1957.

Paul Patterson had warned Schmick that there would be problems in controlling Swanson, who had been difficult to keep in line. (Patterson once told his son Maclean that the biggest mistake he had made was appointing Swanson executive editor.) Harry Black had been dealing directly with Swanson on news matters and this, Patterson discovered, made Swanson believe he was free to operate independently of the publisher. Swanson had also sought to succeed Patterson.

In January 1954, for accumulating reasons, Schmick told Swanson that he had decided it was no longer necessary to have an executive editor, and Swanson quietly resigned from the *Sunpapers*.

The memories he left behind had already assumed the proportions of legend. A man of seemingly inexhaustible energy, Swanson wrote nine books, doing much of the writing between 3:00 A.M. and 6:00 A.M. A 1948 historical novel about the Pontiac Indian uprising, titled *Unconquered*, was produced as a movie by Cecil B. deMille, starring Gary Cooper and Paulette Goddard. Until recent years it was one of Hollywood's biggest box office successes. Swanson signed a lifetime contract with his publisher to write thirty historical novels, "the series to constitute a continuous narrative of the advance of the American frontier, dealing with a central group of characters, minor ones in one book becoming central figures in succeeding novels." His publisher hailed him as "the American Dumas." In *The Perilous Fight,* a history of the War of 1812, he made the forgotten General Sam Smith, commander of the land forces defending Baltimore, into what he hoped would be a national hero. *Sun* tradition has been for its editors to remain out of the public eye, but Swanson sought it and became not only well known but also influential in city affairs. He persuaded the city to create a park in honor of Smith at Light and Pratt streets (now obliterated by the Inner Harbor complex) and had Smith's statue moved from upper Charles Street to the park. He was president of the Star-Spangled Banner Flag House Association, was ever available to give a speech on the flag or American history, and was chairman of the Constellation Commission, which fought the Navy's plan to dismantle the frigate *Constellation,* rotting in a New England navy yard, and had it returned to Baltimore, where it had been built and commissioned. Swanson broke ground for its new berth with his penknife when someone forgot the ceremonial shovel.

After leaving the *Sun,* Swanson was hired as national affairs editor and columnist for the rival *News-Post* and the *Sunday American.* Later, when it started a section intended for teenagers, he was put in charge and worked as hard and as enthusiastically editing it as he had when he was executive editor at the *Sunpapers.* He retired in 1973 and resumed work on his projected historical series, plotting and writing three at one time. (The series were never completed.) He died in 1983 at the age of 86.

The *Sunpapers* recalled Swanson's career and contributions in long obituaries. A *Sun* editorial hailed him as "an innovator extraordinaire," remarking that few individuals have dominated an entire era in the 146-year history of the *Sun* as Swanson did. The *Evening Sun* editorial ended,

> When Swanson loomed in the doorway of the newsroom, there was a fellow who would begin visibly trembling. Another *Sunpapers* writer, not in Swanson's domain, told of gaining eventual recognition; when they passed in the corridor, no sound emerged but Swanson's cigarette would briefly glow. In the city room, it was agreed ultimately no one would write the book about the executive editor— the anecdotes would exceed outsiders' credulity. As they said, in the more or less good old days, it must be wonderful to be a newspaperman because you meet such interesting people. Sure, the other people working there, and, high among them, Neil H. Swanson.

Schmick retired in March 1960, in his 77th year, and was succeeded by his son. Three months later the new president revived the office of the editor-in-chief as a means of coordinating editorial policy. He appointed Price Day, a *Sun* editorial writer and former war correspondent, to the post. The two promotions were a big step forward, portending a fresh viewpoint in both editorial and business conduct.

In the era of John and Hamilton Owens, editorials had the grace, tone, and length of essays. The two editors and their staffs wrote from an intellectual point of view. Editorials were grounded in extensive reading and a lively set of preconceived abstractions. Often these editorials showed more interest in the theory of government than in its practical applications. The guiding principle was: state the specific situation, explain how it came about, expound the precedents or tenets by which it might be corrected—a rational public would understand and concur. Thundering (except for Mencken) was abhorrent. In retrospect, one former editorial writer likened this method to "drips of water on stone," a slow but continual wearing away of what the editors thought should be changed.

Both Owenses consciously adhered to traditional *Sun* values and objectives of nineteenth-century liberalism. Free trade had been the watchword of their institutional ancestors. Free trade would be the *Sun*'s cry still. They prized consistency and they dominated their pages, often telling their editorial writers what to say. Hamilton Owens and Wagner, particularly, were civil libertarians, an area distinct from civil rights. They flared up when First Amendment freedoms were infringed, their viewpoint still colored by the paper's loud battle against Prohibition, their perspective unfortunately also overlooking the accompanying rise in public disrespect toward law enforcement. Editorials often reflected the philosophy of British liberalism and the *Manchester Guardian*. A letter-writer taking note of that in 1958 complained, "Today one cannot pick up the *Sun* without finding most of the editorial page full of news and editorials concerning Britain, particularly on Sunday. One wonders what country the *Sunpapers* owes allegiance to."

Hamilton Owens and Wagner lunched at the 14 West Hamilton Street Club, and some of their staff thought that they were impressed, if not influenced, by opinions voiced there. Its members included a large number of senior Hopkins men, mainly from the medical institution, federal and state judges, partners from the prestigious law firms, architects, newspapermen, and a smattering of businessmen. Letters to the editor referred to *Sun* editors as part of a "Guilford–Homeland–Roland Park axis," influenced by the thinking of the upper middle class.

On taking over the morning editorial page in 1943, Wagner veered from abstract considerations toward the practicalities of public life. He began examining government more closely, especially state and municipal government. For years the editorial page had functioned as an ivory tower, the staff seldom venturing out to see for themselves how government bureaus and agencies work and to do their own information-gathering. Wagner had his staff look into agriculture, oyster conservation, urban sprawl, mass transit, zoning, and the Baltimore "lung block," which was said to have the highest incidence of tuberculosis in the nation. Tasks were assigned to each writer. Edgar L. Jones, who joined the paper in December 1946 from the *Atlantic Monthly*, was told that his job was "to make Baltimore a better place in which to live." Janetta Somerset Ridgely was assigned to the Third World, "whole, entire, complete." To give the page a wider perspective, Wagner, in 1956, had invited Ridgely to leave the city staff where she had worked for three years to become the first female editorial writer on the *Sunpapers;* she served for nine years. At the daily conference, she soon found, some senior writers would "talk out, argue a point, but it was Wagner's page." Wagner, incidentally, dictated his editorials to his secretary and then edited the typed copy.

Intellectually and politically, he still considered himself a classic liberal in the mold of John W. Owens: "Not liberal as it is understood today. People of my group held to their underlying philosophical position while the world moved away. We didn't change. We carried on." The interesting thing was that, after World War II, John Owens, his health stabilized, resumed writing occasional signed pieces for the morning paper. And his point of view had changed—many aspects of the New Deal, he now conceded, were wisely taken.

Others on the staff were similarly moving with the times, and that led to differences. Wagner asserted that classic liberal tradition was violated when government became involved in the everyday life of its citizens. In May 1954 the Supreme Court ruled unanimously that segregation by race in public schools was unconstitutional. The *Sunpapers* (Hamilton Owens was still presiding) editorially endorsed it. The Supreme Court, they reminded readers, has the final say as to what is the law of the land, and it is the duty of citizens to obey the law. In the weeks that followed, however, Wagner's page seemed to be in no hurry about the "all deliberate speed" of the Court's order for actual desegregation. Some of Wagner's staff felt that he was not abreast of the times on social issues and programs.

From *Evening Sun* days, Wagner had doubts about the space and attention that editorial cartoons received, though on the *Evening Sun* he had used three free-lancers briefly—Bertha Kelley, a caricaturist, in 1929; Jack Lambert, a sculptor who fashioned cartoons with clay figures, in the 1930s; and Aaron Sopher, a well-known pen-and-ink artist. Later Wagner tried photographs, mostly of slum housing, as "visual editorials." He had always objected to giving the most conspicuous spot on the page to a cartoonist when the latter's viewpoint differed markedly from that of the editor. Richard Q. Yardley had succeeded Duffy as *Sun* cartoonist. If, for policy reasons, Wagner rejected one of his cartoons, Yardley would sometimes show it to his friend Charles H. Dorsey, Jr., the managing editor, and Dorsey was likely to use it in the news section. In addition to causing hard feelings, this sidestepping underscored the widening differences on editorial policy.

Within the paper, dissatisfaction with the paper's conservatism, entrenched for more than thirty years, was widespread. The younger Schmick, and those he consulted—principally Dorsey—wanted a new direction, an editorial page more in tune with the nation's political, economic, and social progress. In the normal course of events, Wagner, as senior editor, would have become Hamilton Owens's successor as editor-in-chief, and C. P. Ives, his senior associate editor, would have become editor of the *Sun* when Owens retired in 1956. But the two promotions did not take place. The position of chief editor remained open for four years until Schmick Jr. decided that a new policy could be achieved—and signaled—only by getting someone with a different, more contemporary viewpoint. Price Day was his choice.

There was a touch of irony in Day's appointment, which Wagner said was made while Wagner was on a fact-finding trip to the Soviet Union. After Day had finished the articles on India that brought him a Pulitzer Prize, Wagner thought that Day seemed at loose ends in the news department. He suggested to Hamilton Owens that Day be invited to become an editorial writer. Owens, Wagner said, was dubious, but he agreed, and Day joined Wagner's staff in 1952. In 1956, Wagner promoted him to associate editor.

After Hamilton Owens retired, Day took charge of the editorial-page column, "Down the Spillway," which still carried the name John O'Ren, the "floating pseudonym" for all who contributed. But the column became so much the work of Day that on October 15, 1957, with the title changing to "The Spillway," Day's name replaced that of O'Ren. An editorial explained:

> John O'Ren, through these years, had displayed a chameleon like quality of personality and style. He has recalled a dozen different childhoods. His other biographical references, if collated, would reveal him as being at once the most widely traveled and most sedentary of men, an introvert and an extrovert, a *bon vivant* and an ascetic. At times he has seemed mainly interested in the trivia of politics, at other times in the familiar essay, at other times in odds and ends of unfamiliar learning that he liked to call Useless Information. Sometimes he preferred to preside over a column written mainly by contributors. . . . During the war, when space was at a premium, he took a long vacation—then, always the good soldier, emerged from retirement when the paper shortage passed and there was room again for him.

Day's "Spillway" ranged widely in its low-voiced, reflecting, wry way. From time to time he wrote about a "small piece of swamp" on his property in North Baltimore. Here he is trying to turn it into a decorative pool:

> Water lilies would accent its otherwise immaculate surface. On its clipped and verdant verge little groups of well-bred, well-groomed people would gather in the summer twilight to sip their pale drinks, converse dulcetly, and now and again pat the head of a well-bred, well-groomed dog couchant at their feet: A tableau. It has not turned out that way. The lilies bloom each year, and are lovely. The dog is well-bred enough, to all appearances, though he has yet to come forward with his papers. But the dog goes into the pool and tracks slime all over the house, and the lilies blossom amid a rankness of cattails, underwater growth, coarse and errant watercress, decayed sycamore leaves, and disintegrating fruit from an over-hanging apple tree. The edges are a mess of mud and immoderate grass. It is, in fact, no

pool at all. It is a pond. What's more, it is a frog pond. The tadpoles are as many as the lamps of the firmament, and a good deal more lively. In summer the grown frogs, like massed tubas, make the night loud. Sometimes a green heron comes to stalk and catch a frog. Smaller birds, with their desperate metabolism, try for dragonflies. This man has not made a pool. He has created the conditions for the rise of a wild little world, full of wonders, teeming and violent and primitive, not a bit well-bred.

A colleague commented, "In the years that Day wrote 'The Spillway' it was the most consistently creative, amusing and thoughtful writing in the paper— perhaps in any newspaper. Even on the most humdrum subject you could find an unexpected turn of phrase, a wry bit of understatement." Day enjoyed writing the column and added, "I feel it was some of my best writing." That said a great deal. His news stories, ranging from the rewrite desk to his foreign reporting, were regarded by fellow workers as some of the best writing in the *Sunpapers*.

About the time the new "Spillway" appeared, Thomas M. O'Neill's column, "Politics and People," was moved from the *Evening Sun* to the *Sun*. Kent's column, "The Great Game of Politics," continued until a few months before his death in April 1958.

After Day took over "The Spillway," a "Notes and Comment" was added for contributions by the editorial writers. But when Day became editor-in-chief, he abandoned "The Spillway" and wrote "Notes and Comment" with occasional help from Theo Lippman, Jr., a Georgian with Washington experience, who became an editorial writer in 1965. Ten years later it became Lippman's column on Day's retirement, and in March 1984 it was retitled simply "Theo Lippman, Jr." Two years earlier Lippman had won the American Society of Newspaper Editors distinguished writing award for commentary. Alternating with his column also is the twice-a-week "Gallimaufry"— a "confused medley, a hodgepodge"—of editorial writers' thoughts, reports, and explanations.

Day considered himself a moderate rather than a liberal. An *Evening Sun* editorial after his death commented, "Gently, as was his way, he inched the *Sunpapers* from an increasingly rigid posture on the right to a rather moveable location somewhere near the philosophic middle." The *Sun* editorial noted:

> The *Sunpapers* had gone through a long period of what we might call push-button conservatism when Price Day took over. He preserved the best of that doctrine, with its high regard for the principles of the Constitution and its distrust of intrusive government power. But he broadened the papers' outlook by giving positive support to the civil rights movements of the Sixties, by perceiving the needs of less developed nations and questioning, with increasing intensity, the wisdom of American involvement in Vietnam.

In Day's thinking, "up with this" and "down with that" editorials fail their purpose to enlighten or persuade. He objected to the word "should" in editorials, holding that the modern reader welcomes guidance but resists a shove. And he was concerned about how editorials were written, often tightly editing them or even rewriting them—not to stress a point of view but to polish the phrasing.

It has been the practice at the *Sunpapers,* as it has been at many other papers, for the president/publisher to make the final decision when the paper endorses a candidate. A *Sun* "Letter from the Editor" explained the procedure for state and municipal elections:

> After the filing deadline for political office has passed, the *Sunpapers* send letters to all candidates in Baltimore city and in Anne Arundel, Baltimore, Carroll, Harford and Howard counties. Their biographies and their political views are sought, and if any candidate requests a personal interview an effort is made to accommodate. Similar letters are sent to candidates for statewide and congressional office.
>
> Members of the editorial staff are then assigned to specific races, and it is their responsibility to gather information on all candidates who can be reached. Then, as election day approaches, the editorial staffs of the *Sun* and the *Evening Sun* meet to make preliminary decisions.
>
> Such meetings have a special flavor, because they mark the only times the two staffs meet jointly. In commenting on day-to-day issues, there is complete separation between the *Sun* and the *Evening Sun* and differences of opinion come often. But in making endorsements, a common stand is taken to avoid any temptation to hedge or play games with the public (as some double-header newspapers have been known to do).
>
> Once the editorial staffs have discussed the various candidates with the judgment of the staffer assigned to a specific contest usually prevailing, their conclusions are reported to the publisher by the editorial page editors of the *Sun* and the *Evening Sun.* The publisher has final say. This is his right and his responsibility. Most of the time (but not always) there is agreement between the two editors, and the publisher usually concurs.

In recent years four local columnists, Roger Simon and Michael Olesker of the *Sun* and Dan Rodricks and Wiley A. Hall 3d of the *Evening Sun,* have supplemented editorial opinion with divergent comment on controversial issues, including political endorsements. In the 1986 gubernatorial primary, Rodricks took strong exception to the papers' endorsement of William Donald Schaefer, the mayor of Baltimore, as the Democratic candidate because he is "good for business." In a column titled "So why'd they back Schaefer?" Rodricks wrote:

> Nowhere in either the *Sun* or the *Evening Sun* endorsements this week did we read details of Schaefer's past achievements and future ambitions in public education, in the preservation of the Maryland environment, in the pursuit of a better quality of life for the state's poor and homeless. . . . If Schaefer made his positions on these issues clear, the editorial writers of the *Sun* and the *Evening Sun* did not seem overly inspired by them. They were not detailed in the endorsing editorials, anyway.

Though readers frequently reject the *Sunpaper* candidate endorsements, they are likely to follow the papers' recommendations or rejections on bond issues, charter changes, or state legislative referendums. A common sight at polling places is lines of voters clutching a boxed summary of voting recommendations, clipped or torn from a *Sunpaper* editorial page.

In presidential-election years the endorsement meeting was attended by senior editors, who presented their views pro and con on the principal candidates. Day preferred not to speak then. Later he would confer with Schmick, then relay the decision to his staff. Until recent years the opinions of editorial writers were not solicited. Gerald Griffin, who became editor of the *Sun* in 1964, believes he was the first one to poll them and make their views known in the meeting.

If the high command's choice for president was different from that of the editorial writers—which was often the case—in minor and subtle ways "they would still chew away at their own beliefs and prejudices" (as one editorial writer noted), communicating why they believed their candidate would make a better President.

In the 1960 campaign between John F. Kennedy and Richard Nixon, Day assigned Wagner to write the editorial endorsing Nixon. It began apologetically, "It has not been an easy decision to make," and though it went on at great length the reason was summed up in thirty-three words, "The *Sun* believes that the doubts about Mr. Kennedy's domestic policies, in particular since internal soundness is one of the foundations of foreign policy and international prestige, outweigh the doubts about Mr. Nixon." A letter to the editor complained: "Shame on the *Sun* for such a wishy-washy endorsement of a candidate for the presidency of the United States of America. It read like a forced statement by a writer with a Colt .45 at his temple. I doubt very much that the editorial even convinced the author that the *Sun* made the right decision."

Wagner left the paper on early retirement in August 1963 to write a syndicated political column and to devote more time to his Boordy vineyard and nursery. The author of books on wine-making that have gone through many editions and printings, he is internationally known for introducing and popularizing French hybrid grapes that have been the basis for the phenomenal spread of vineyards in the United States.

Ives, the senior associate editor, might logically have replaced Wagner. He had been on the staff since 1939 and was an authority on Edmund Burke, the eighteenth-century British political philosopher whose conservative views Ives championed in editorials and in a column, "Monday Morning Views," which he wrote until the early 1960s. But Day judged Ives to be too far to the right for the *Sun*'s new direction, and Wagner's position was left open, Day also functioning as editor of the page. The practice had been (and still is) for the editorial-page editor to hold a daily meeting with his staff to discuss events and assign topics. Day, reserved in manner, rarely held a meeting, preferring to talk to the editorial writers on an individual basis.

In the fall of 1964, Day invited Griffin, head of the Washington bureau, to become editor. He accepted on the understanding that the paper's posture on human and civil rights would grow even sturdier. That had been developing slowly but surely.

In 1946 the Sidney Hollander Foundation, established by Hollander's family in honor of his work for civil rights, gave its first award "for an outstanding contribution toward achievement of equal rights and opportunities for Negroes in Maryland" to the *Sunpapers*. The award cited editorial support for Morgan State College, efforts to repeal vestigial Jim Crow transportation laws in Maryland, impartial reporting of Negro contributions as part of the total community life in Baltimore, and the decision to abandon racial designations in headlines where they tend to make an unfavorable impression.

At that time the only public places whites and blacks could eat together were Penn Station and the Y.W.C.A. Blacks had to sit in the second balcony at Ford's Theatre, they could not attend downtown and most neighborhood movies, department stores were indecisive and nervous about accommodating black shoppers (they could not try on clothing), and there were instances in those stores when black children were asked not to gather around the white Santa Claus. Up until the early 1950s the Baltimore Police Department did not allow black officers to operate squad cars.

In 1961 the *Sunpapers* dropped racial identification in crime stories, except for such felonies as murder and rape. For several years before that, reporters and rewrite persons, on their own, had omitted such designations in many minor crime stories with the tacit knowledge of editors. An apocryphal anecdote relates that, during that time, a front office executive mentioned to an editor that he had noticed a big drop in racial crime.

The *Sunpapers* had never been characterized as segregationist or antiblack, but for many years they made only minimal effort to cover the black community, on the grounds that blacks did not read the paper. Even after the *Sunpapers* began concerted moves to do so, some readers thought them insufficient. In September 1967 the *Sun* printed this letter to the editor:

> Since moving to Baltimore recently we have relied on the *Sunpapers* to learn more about the community. The profile of the Baltimore Negro as projected by the city's leading newspapers: He never gets married; he is the white man's tax burden, so are his children; he is a fine athlete; he is a member of the Supreme Court, or a sloth; he could riot, but he doesn't, because someone finds him a job; he seldom dies, except in Vietnam.

In 1964 the editorial pages strongly supported the Civil Rights Act of that year, strongly opposed the segregationist George Wallace, governor of Alabama, running as a third-party candidate for President, and enthusiastically supported Lyndon B. Johnson over Barry M. Goldwater, the Republican candidate, "for compelling reasons of the national interest . . . a man supremely qualified to be continued in office . . . a President of extraordinary force, wisdom and vision." Goldwater was easily dismissed: "Space does not permit a recital of all of Mr. Goldwater's disqualifications." No mention was made that this was the first time the *Sunpapers,* identifying themselves as independent newspapers, had supported a Democratic presidential candidate since 1932. Following its refusal to make an endorsement in 1936, the *Sunpapers* backed the Republican candidate in six straight presidential campaigns: Wendell Willkie in 1940, Thomas E. Dewey in 1944 and 1948, Dwight D. Eisenhower in 1952 and 1956, and Richard Nixon in 1960.

In the 1966 gubernatorial campaign, the *Sunpapers* rejected the Democratic nominee, George P. Mahoney, whose appeal to bigots included the segregated-housing slogan "Your home is your castle." Instead they supported Spiro T. Agnew, the Republican county executive of Baltimore County, and Agnew, then regarded a moderate on race relations, won. For a year, relations between the governor and the *Sunpapers* were harmonious, both championing the new, modernized state constitution that a special convention was framing (but which the voters subsequently rejected). In the black ghettos of Baltimore and Cambridge, Maryland, however, economic and social resentments were rising. In April 1968 the assassination of Martin Luther King, Jr., in Memphis resulted in a firestorm of burning and looting in Washington, D.C., and then in Baltimore. The National Guard was ordered in, and for the first time since the B&O riots of 1877, the Army, to pacify the city. When the calm returned, Governor Agnew, who had stayed in Annapolis, summoned a number of black leaders to his Baltimore office to charge them with failure of leadership and with letting themselves be intimidated by radicals. Price Day wrote an editorial, entitled "No, Governor," that commended the leaders for their courage in preventing the radicals from taking over and suggested to the governor that he seek reconciliation. But Agnew was veering more and more toward a conservative political posture, and he drew the attention of Richard Nixon. By 1968, to national amazement, Nixon chose the governor of Maryland as his running mate, and after the election Agnew was Vice President of the United States.

In those years Richard Q. Yardley, who had succeeded Edmund Duffy, was the *Sun's* editorial cartoonist. He had joined the *Evening Sun* in 1923, first retouching photographs and executing such lowly chores as diagraming sewer locations in new developments. After a year or two he was permitted to do "dingbats," tiny drawings for features, and in the early 1930s he did a Sunday cartoon and cartoons for the *Sun's* back page. "Everything," a marveling fellow artist remarked, "houses, trees, water, animals, people—had a vitality all their own. The girls were corn-fed, lovely, nubile and nifty. Villains were mean, ambitions raw, politicians crafty, embarrassments keen." Above all, Yardley captured—stressed—the liveliness and good times of his day and place.

Duffy had zeroed in on one idea and could bludgeon it with his pen.

Yardley's style was often whimsical, and his editorial cartoons were jammed with detail, jokes, and sometimes, if the editor had not examined them minutely, with suggestive graffiti and sly anatomical detail.

His style was described as "Early Ming, middle comic strip, late Picasso, all Yardley." He was so eclectic that he did cartoons in the style of a Bayeux tapestry, a Persian rug, a comic strip, prehistoric cave figures, almanac woodcuts, as the English artist Hogarth might have rendered a modern American political campaign, and, his favorite, old-style maps depicting a nostalgic Baltimore, home of the ten-cent crabcake.

Though Yardley achieved a national reputation, he was best known for his local cartoons, where political bosses wore derbies labeled "boss" and bosslets ones with "1/6 boss." In such cartoons he had first depicted himself as a tiny figure with a patch on his pants, wearing a beret and a flowing tie, often with "Ye Editor" standing by with a lash. His sidekick was a cat. The two became his hallmark. Yardley explained their symbolism this way: During the Depression he had to do extra cartoons without extra pay. The patch signified extreme poverty, his diminutive size that he was abused by a great and powerful editor. His landlady ordered him to get rid of his cat or get out. He left, but he drew the cat thumbing his nose at her, and the cynical cat became a fixture. Yardley, called "Moco" by associates, cabdrivers, and bartenders, was far different from his cartoon character. He was six feet, three inches tall, with a Falstaffian figure, a gargantuan appetite for food and drink, and a zest for life and joyful company in every walk of life. He retired in June 1972. That day he went home and told his wife, "Peggy, the little cat died today."

Griffin had long lobbied for a modern op-ed page. (For years, obituaries had appeared on the page opposite. That was also done at the *New York Times,* and its news room cynics claimed they were put there to make the editorial page look brighter.) But Day was not enthusiastic about such a page because he did not think the editorial staff was large enough to handle those additional duties. In 1970 an op-ed page was started, with syndicated opinion columns selected by Griffin and the managing editor, but it was controlled by the news department. The bottom part carried ads.

Griffin was described by associates as "having a sense of government, of what was politically right, and always a rock of good sense." He retired at the end of 1972, recommending—as did Day—Joseph R. L. Sterne as his successor. Day retired three years later, in January 1975. After his death in December 1978, Edgar L. Jones, an editorial writer and friend of Day, wrote a piece for the *Evening Sun* editorial page titled "Some Loving Words as We Lose Price Day," saying: "As an editorial writer he had some difficulty initially in writing as though convinced that an editorial might change the course of events. Detachment dies hard. His convictions were strong enough, but expressing an opinion as though some good might come of it, or evil be lessened by it, took time." Before the piece was printed, he showed it to Day's son, Anthony, editor of the *Los Angeles Times* editorial page. His comment was,

"That's quite true." Jones also wrote: "His own editorials came to full strength, in my mind, as the Nixon era took hold. He early saw through the pretensions of noble ideals. He wanted to stop the abuses of power, and wrote from a strong sense of outrage, controlled and dispassionate but no less biting. And when, soon after Nixon was deposed, he first slacked off on writing, and then retired . . ." the position of editor-in-chief was not filled.

Newton Aiken, who became a *Sun* editorial writer in 1936 after working in the Washington and London bureaus, succeeded Wagner as editor of the evening editorial page in 1943. He regarded the page as a team production with himself as the captain, and confessed that he "had a rather plain, unrhetorical mode of expressing my ideas." He did not approve of flair in writing. Rueful colleagues averred that Aiken, editing, had an instinct for the telling word and the apt phrase and would delete them. He was especially knowledgeable about governmental budgets and politics in the South, and according to those who worked with him he "brought to his work a political liberalism as firm as the generosity with which he defended it. Wilson, Cordell Hull and several but not all aspects of Franklin Roosevelt were his guides." He looked hard to the logic or lack of it in his page. Despite having once been a reporter, he was wary of the newsroom. If an editorial writer suggested an editorial based on a solid news story, he might demur, saying, "I don't think you can trust these reporters. You'd better look into the facts yourself." He felt the same way about the Associated Press, claiming, "It always exaggerates." On December 7, 1941, when the Japanese attacked Pearl Harbor, Aiken commented, "I'd feel better about this if the announcement had come from somewhere other than the White House." In his unpublished autobiography, he wrote that he had been "very anti-Roosevelt" but that when he was in the London bureau in the mid 1930s he got a new perspective on the New Deal and favored a second term. He added, "I was to find myself at variance with the policy the *Sun* later followed." Although he considered himself conservative, colleagues said he became more liberal as he aged. He rode the No. 8 streetcar and joked that he would keep working until the No. 8 line stopped running. He retired at the age of 71 on November 1, 1963, after twenty years as editor, and coincidentally the line was converted to buses almost at the same time.

While Aiken was editor, William F. Schmick, Jr., suggested that he hire a cartoonist. After a year-long search, Thomas Flannery was engaged in March 1957. He had been an auditor for hotels and had taken a night course in drawing at Brooklyn's Pratt Institute. During the war he became a cartoonist for the army magazine *Yank,* and after the war at the *Lowell* (Mass.) *Sun* for nine years. When Yardley retired in 1972, Flannery succeeded him as cartoonist for the morning *Sun.* His deftly drawn pen-and-ink sketches range from the local scene ("I live here") to barbed comment on front-page news and combine subtle humor with apt and clever captions. He said his role was "to criticize." "I like to present a viewpoint, my viewpoint, rather than illustrate an issue. I'm prejudiced as to what I think is right. I'm not always right, obviously, but that is the way I see my job."

Mike Lane, who succeeded Flannery, was also an auditor before he became a cartoonist. He had worked for the General Electric Credit Corporation, rising through seven management positions, but he wanted to be a cartoonist—though he never had gone to art school—and after work for a year-and-a-half he practiced drawing cartoons. He tried a number of papers, then sent samples to Day, who was looking for a replacement for Yardley, whose health was failing. Lane was hired in September 1971. His first six months were on the *Sun,* getting a cartoon printed only when Yardley was sick and Day could not find a syndicated cartoon he liked as a substitute. But when Yardley retired, Flannery was switched to the *Sun* and Lane to the evening paper. Day's explanation was: "The morning paper is the senior paper, and also the morning paper publishes on Sunday, and you want your senior cartoonist out front."

An editor of the evening paper at first found Lane's cartoons "inexplicable," but added that Lane soon emerged with a style all his own. James H. Bready, an editorial writer, described Lane's interpretation of newsmakers as "uglification." "I draw as exaggeratedly as I can," Lane says, "to slam home my point." And he adds, "Ninety percent is the idea, not the drawing." In 1985 Lane was first-place winner for editorial cartooning in the national Sigma Delta Chi Distinguished Service Awards Competition.

Aiken's successor was A. D. Emmart, who had been with the *Sunpapers* since 1924, first as a copy reader on the *Sun,* then as an editorial writer, London bureau correspondent, and, after 1942, editorial writer for the *Evening Sun* and editor of its daily book review. At two different times Emmart was the art critic of the *Sunday Sun.* A native Baltimorean and a Phi Beta Kappa graduate of Johns Hopkins University, where he majored in biology (later returning annually to lecture on T. S. Eliot), he was acknowledged by colleagues as the most erudite man on the editorial staff. Known as "Dol" (a double contraction of his first name, Adolphus), he worked in shirt-sleeves, with collar unbuttoned, and always wore an all-blue patternless knit tie (buying them six at a time).

Ives recalled that when World War II began, John Owens asked Emmart to write "an instant piece on the historical, diplomatic, ideological, and military background of this new cataclysm. Emmart sat down at his typewriter and in an hour or perhaps somewhat more composed four columns of immaculate syntax, terse, communicative, with names, dates, topographies, logistic reckonings, all without opening a book or flipping a note. A new boy on the staff briefly contemplated catching the next train back to New England, where mere competence had been all that was required."

In later years, associates found Emmart super-cautious in his editorial comment. One pointed out that the *Evening Sun* refrained from commenting on the 1968 rioting in Baltimore. Another recalled, "Dol would put qualifier inside qualifier, sometimes a qualifier inside that." An associate said Emmart had no knowledge or interest in local politics and no strong convictions on economics or national politics. He was editor for five years and in 1968, at the age of 65, became an associate editor of the *Sun,* and continued writing editorials until he retired in 1971. It was estimated that he had written some 22,500 editorials, totaling more than 9 million words (at 400 words an editorial), all published without a byline but many recognizable as his because of their learned nature. In 1973, after his death, his friends established the annual A. D. Emmart Memorial Award "for a distinguished example of journalism in the field of the humanities, written by a Marylander and published in a newspaper or magazine in Baltimore or its vicinity." In 1978 the first prize was raised to $300, and three $50 honorable mentions were included in the awards.

Emmart was succeeded by Bradford Jacobs, also a Baltimorean, who had graduated from Princeton University and then served in military intelligence. He joined the paper as reporter and rewriteman in 1946. After five years as the *Evening Sun*'s political reporter, he became an editorial writer from 1953 to 1954 and then London correspondent, then worked in the Washington bureau and returned to the editorial page in 1957. In 1962 he began writing an editorial column "which turned a less formalized light on politicians and government than that of news stories, less advisory than editorials, but warmer and more illuminating than both."

Jacobs liked to get out to see for himself. He attended the presidential nominating conventions, writing a daily editorial and column, and sometimes the Maryland General Assembly. During the 1968 rioting he toured Baltimore at night in a police squad car, and was interviewing rioters during racial disturbances in Cambridge, Maryland, when they were gassed by the Maryland National Guard.

In March 1979, Jacobs changed and expanded the op-ed page, titling it "Other Voices," with a focus primarily on metropolitan Baltimore. As its first editor, he hired Gwinn Owens, son of Hamilton Owens, who made it innovative, brash, and a forum for Baltimore free-lancers. Owens edited the page until 1986, when he switched to editorial writing. He was succeeded by Mike Bowler, who started as education reporter for the *Sun,* then became an *Evening Sun* editorial writer, returned to the *Sun* as higher education reporter, and came back to evening editorial as editor of "Other Voices." Associates characterized Jacobs's editorial page as "strong and prickly, stamped with his personality and philosophy."

Jacobs was responsible for a *Sun* endorsement that influenced a gubernatorial election. The four candidates in the Democratic primary of 1978 were Blair Lee, acting governor after Governor Marvin Mandel was indicted on corruption charges; Walter S. Orlinsky, president of the Baltimore City Council; Theodore Venetoulis, chief executive of Baltimore County; and Harry Hughes, former state transportation secretary, running last in the *Sun*'s election polling. Jacobs said to Joseph R. L. Sterne, editor of the morning editorial page, "I think the best of the four is Hughes and we should go for him early." Sterne agreed. They held a joint editorial conference, a rare occurrence, and it was almost unanimous that the *Sun* should endorse Hughes. That night Jacobs and Sterne drove down to see Donald H. Patterson, the publisher, at his home near Annapolis, telling him how they and their staffs felt and urging an early endorsement. They also pointed out that the papers could be the laughingstock by backing a candidate who could finish last in the voting. A prominent politician had characterized Hughes as "a lost ball in high grass." Patterson replied, "If that's your decision, go ahead and do it." The editors scheduled the endorsement editorial to run two weeks earlier than endorsements were usually made. After an endorsement editorial was written, it was customary to give a proof to the managing editor and one to the city desk, so they could catch any factual mistakes. When the city-desk hands read the proof, they laughed hard and long and told the editorial people, "You guys are off your rocker."

But after the endorsement appeared, Hughes quickly rose in the polls and won both the primary and the general elections. Politicians agreed that the early and strong endorsement elected Hughes. Orlinsky declared, "The *Sunpapers* are now the biggest political boss in Maryland." Wiseacres termed Hughes "Son of *Sun*."

Jacobs took a leave of absence in late 1979 to write *Thimbleriggers*, a book about Maryland politics and the downfall of former Governor Mandel. In 1985, Jacobs formally retired. He was succeeded in 1979 by Dudley P. Digges, a graduate of the Virginia Military Institute. Following service in World War II, Digges had been assistant U.S. secretary of the Four Powers Control Council in Berlin. Germany was the focal point of attention in 1948 when he went job-hunting, and because of his special knowledge Digges was hired as an editorial writer. Aside from a year as general European correspondent of the *Sun* in 1953, Digges was an editorial writer and versifier until he became editor.

From 1969 to 1980, Edgar L. Jones, a morning *Sun* editorial writer, also wrote a gracefully crafted Friday column for the evening editorial page about the men and women who make urban life work—inspired teachers, workers at sewage disposal plants, neighborhood activists, foremen in the water department, unsung policemen and firemen. In his last column, Jones described this task as "seeking ways to grasp the essence of Baltimore's being and thus attain the wisdom of an urban authority. That he fell short was implicit in reports that in his latter years, when arranging to meet strangers at a crisis center or dump site, he described himself as an aging male with glasses, wearing an expression of compassionate bewilderment."

Two libel suits were filed for material that appeared on editorial pages. In 1959 a policeman, suspended from the force for allegedly planting fake evidence in a numbers raid, sued for $100,000 because a *Sun* editorial called him "infamous." He was awarded $45,000. In 1957 a city official sued for $972 million, objecting to being depicted in an *Evening Sun* editorial cartoon with his hand above a church poor box. The suit was dismissed because the plaintiff had not shown that the cartoon was in reckless disregard of the truth.

Joseph R. L. Sterne took over from Gerald Griffin as editor of the morning editorial page in 1972. A Philadelphian, Sterne had worked for the *Salt Lake Telegram*, the *Wall Street Journal*, and the *Dallas Morning News* before joining the *Sun*. He was on the *Sun*'s city staff from 1953 to 1957, in the London bureau from 1957 to 1960, in the Washington bureau from 1960 to 1969 (the last five years as assistant bureau chief); he traveled extensively in Africa in 1960, 1962, and 1967; and he was the Bonn bureau chief from 1969 until he became editor.

With twenty-five years of experience as a reporter, Sterne defines himself as "a fairly pragmatic, nonideological person" and thinks of his page as "interested in what works—and what works well for Baltimore, Maryland, and the country." Sterne made the editorial page more timely and aggressive in commenting on news developments, and he increased the local focus, supplementing editorials with op-ed columns dealing with state and local subjects. The *Sun* takes a strong stand on human and all civil rights. In that broad area it considers itself a liberal newspaper. As for national economic policy, its stance is old-fashioned conservatism. Since Day's retirement, *Sun* policy has undergone a marginal shift to the right on foreign affairs with a less-conciliatory attitude. It does not label itself Democratic or Republican.

In the 1984 Ronald Reagan–Walter Mondale presidential campaign, Sterne advocated a nonendorsement policy, and the publisher agreed. The reasoning was explained in a long editorial shortly before the election. "Our reasons have little to do with the policies or personal capabilities (of the candidates)," Sterne wrote. "They have a lot to do with the nature of this newspaper." The editorial reviewed the *Sun*'s political stance—"mildly Democratic" from its beginnings, denying its endorsement to Roosevelt or Landon in 1936, then endorsing Republican presidential candidates in every election except 1964 and 1980 when it endorsed Lyndon B. Johnson and Jimmy Carter. The editorial continued:

In the late 1950s the *Sun* took a more liberal path, especially on civil and human rights and in its attitude toward government assistance for the needy. Yet this shift was not reflected in our three endorsements for Richard Nixon. It was an awkward time for the paper, which chafed at being identified as being pro-Nixon when, in fact, it frequently criticized him.

During the past decade we have made a conscious effort to avoid dogmatism, to sidestep any ideological mold. We welcomed President Reagan's unapologetic readiness to have the United States play the role as a superpower, even while we deplored his indifference to civil rights and the disadvantaged. We challenged Walter Mondale's embrace of protectionism even while we applauded his views on separation of church and state. Presidential endorsements have not come easily under such circumstances. . . .

Do our endorsements mock our day-to-day policy positions or inhibit our commentary? Is the paper's image twisted through identification with a presidential candidate or party? Do endorsements harm the credibility of our news columns?

The mere posing of such questions helps explain why we are embarking on a course that we hope will be reassuring to our readers and persuasive to future publishers and editors. Except in extraordinary circumstances, we do not plan as a general rule to endorse in presidential elections. . . .

Many writers of letters to the editor denounced the nonendorsement policy. One labeled it "a lamentable lapse of courage," another cried "Shame!" and a third described the *Sun* "as a wimp newspaper."

Barry C. Rascovar is the deputy editor of the editorial page and specializes in Maryland government and economic affairs. Daniel Berger writes about Baltimore, Jerome G. Kelly has the counties (Sterne was the first editor to assign an editorial writer to concentrate on the counties), Garland Thompson has science, Theo Lippman, Jr., covers the judiciary and politics in addition to his column, and Sterne does Congress, the executive branch, and foreign affairs. Jerelyn Eddings, who joined the staff in 1982, writing on national government and finance, was a Nieman Fellow at Harvard in 1984–85. Upon her return to the staff, she began writing a twice-a-week column. Sterne hired the *Sunpapers'* first black editorial writers. The first, in 1979, was Denton L. Watson. Later public relations director for the NAACP, Watson is writing a biography of the late Clarence M. Mitchell, Jr., director of the Washington bureau of the NAACP for twenty-nine years. Two now on the staff of seven are Eddings and Thompson. Though the staff has special duties, Sterne notes, "The seven have to be agile enough to cover the universe."

On September 19, 1977, the editorial department started a new op-ed page, called "Opinion—Commentary," which replaced the half-page, supervised by the news department, consisting of syndicated columns. Sterne appointed Stephens Broening, who had served more than a decade as an Associated Press correspondent in Moscow, Paris, and Lisbon, as editor. Broening designed the page as a forum for topical "points of view which might not get published elsewhere in the paper." In addition to original pieces and columns, the page from time to time includes translations from Soviet, French, and German newspapers; texts of speeches, declarations, and treaties; and question-and-answer interviews with newsmakers. In 1986, Broening became the *Sun's* diplomatic correspondent in the Washington bureau and was succeeded by Hal Piper, who had been the London bureau correspondent.

W. Maclean Patterson, who had been managing editor of the *Sun* since 1942, was given a new title—general managing editor—and made an officer of the company in August 1947. Charles H. Dorsey, Jr., the assistant managing editor, then became managing editor. Patterson resigned in 1952 to join the Rouse Company.

Dorsey, a Baltimorean, was a graduate of Johns Hopkins University and a philosophy instructor in its teachers college until he joined the *Evening Sun* in 1933 as a reporter and rewriteman. He became an assistant city editor in 1942 and nine months later was advanced to assistant managing editor of the morning paper, an unheard-of promotion. A tall man of patrician mien, known to all as "Buck," he could be tough or benign, gruff or charming. He was rated variously as "a super gentleman" and "a terror as a managing editor." He could be counted on to stand behind his staff. His was the old-fashioned news judgment, strong on breaking news and on individual and collective news integrity. Dorsey was reluctant to yield space for graphics and for personal commentaries; otherwise, the *Sun* in his day was a reporter's paper. He had confidence in the ability of his reporters, and consequently they got little or no instruction on assignments. What they wrote, no matter the length, usually got printed. But pity the reporter who made a stupid mistake. In those days correction boxes were not as forthcoming as they are in the 1980s. If possible, errors were rectified with a "skinback," a short news item that made the matter right without admitting a mistake. But if a correction were demanded for a flagrant error, Dorsey, five or six times, ordered the perpetrator's name included with the apology. One mistake that fortunately escaped Dorsey's attention was made by a new reporter. He wrote an obituary that had the wrong time for the funeral. Even worse, the chairman of the Abell Company board of directors was one of the pallbearers. He appeared an hour early for the service.

Dorsey worked a six-day week, but a short day. He came in at 2:00 P.M., made fast work of administrative details, conferred with his editors and the Washington bureau, scheduled or approved the page-one schedule for the first edition, and left promptly at 5:30. If a decision needed his attention in the evening, he could be reached by direct telephone to his home. His bulletin board announcements reflected his style, for example: "Word has gone forth from Caesar Augustus that all space shall be cut. You are therefore requested to eliminate all nonessentials to the best of your ability—nonessential stories, nonessential paragraphs, nonessential words. Reasonable cooperation will spare me the necessity of eliminating nonessential people."

Dorsey, like his staff, like morning *Sun* people before and since, smugly believed that the *Sun* was far superior to the *Evening Sun*. Passing Grace Darin, an *Evening Sun* copy reader, in the hall, Dorsey would say, "Any time you want to go to work for a good paper, let me know." He seldom suggested story ideas and did not claim to be an idea man, in the way that Swanson and Murphy were. He said he could remember only two of his ideas that amounted to anything: the Sunday op-ed page in the 1950s with news letters from his foreign correspondents, and the Thursday food page featuring correspondents writing about foreign restaurants with accompanying recipes (an Inner

Mongolian restaurant provided three recipes for camel hump). Readers were told of the best dining in Soho, in the suburbs of Leningrad, in the Italian boot, and along the Amazon, but nothing about Baltimore restaurants. *Sun* policy at that time was not to write about local restaurants because it would be free advertising.

Dorsey saw the *Sun* as a national newspaper and strove to address that audience. "My greatest problem," he added, "is to walk the knife edge between what is significant and what is readable." *Time* magazine believed that he did a good job. In 1964 it picked the *Sun* as one of the top ten newspapers in the United States. "The *Sun* demands a high order of intelligence from its readers," *Time* noted. "Stories are written not to entertain, but to inform; text is never displaced for purely cosmetic considerations—by a picture, say, to break up a formidable looking front page. If Baltimoreans do not know what is going on everywhere, their ignorance is not the *Sun*'s fault. It staffs bureaus all over the world, keeps 14 men in Washington. Upon being asked if the *Sun* was a crusading newspaper, managing editor Charles H. Dorsey, Jr. answered with feeling, 'Good God, I hope we never become one.' "

Local news focused on Baltimore, and the city desk tried "to cover it like a blanket." If neighborhoods, age and interest groups, and ethnic committees were largely overlooked, this was before they systematically clamored for attention. Little notice was paid to the far reaches of the state, or even to Baltimore and Anne Arundel counties; for a long time the *Sunpapers* were content with one reporter in each county for both papers.

Hewing to a hard-news approach, Dorsey would not countenance what he called "boosterism," to the dismay, grumbling—and pressure—of City Hall and the Baltimore Association of Commerce. In its 1964 report, *Time* also noted: "The *Sun* is the unbending patriarch of Baltimore, and acutely conscious of the dignity and the responsibilities of venerable old age. . . . The paper remains aloof, aristocratic, old-fashioned, proud and something of a snob—just the way Baltimoreans like it."

The city editor was Edwin P. Young, Jr., who had joined the paper as a reporter in 1935, but for most of his career he was a city editor—of the *Sun* in 1942, of the *Evening Sun* from 1942 to 1949, and of the *Sun* again from 1949 to 1954. An admirer imagined that if F. Scott Fitzgerald had created a city editor he would have come up with someone like Ed Young. Of his generation, without question, he was the most beloved city editor, an adjective not normally associated with that position. He had unerring instincts as an editor, but most of all, even though he was the boss, he conveyed to those working for him that he was on their side. An amiable man, he encased himself in tight-fitting vests and jackets, handed down from a lesser-size brother-in-law who had died intestate some years earlier. The tight clothing, never unbuttoned, intensified the ruddiness of his cheeks and made him appear momentarily about to explode. At staff parties—or any party for that matter—

it was not long into the evening, or early morning, before Young, glass in hand, was singing his alma mater's song, "Far Above Cayuga's Waters," with staff, friends, and sometimes police joining in for chorus after chorus. If there were no party, or postmortems at the Press Club, he wended his way home at 2:00 A.M. by No. 8 streetcar, in cold weather bundled in a raccoon coat from college days, a pint of gin nestled inside it, which he sipped through a straw, not wishing to make fellow passengers envious by swigging ostentatiously from the bottle.

His two assistants on the *Sun* were Paul A. Banker, who succeeded him and later succeeded Dorsey as managing editor, and Clarence Caulfield, who looked like a red-haired leprechaun and held new reporters spellbound, often on deadline, with implausible tales of his carefree days as a hay-and-feed traveling salesman.

Young and Dorsey were adept at picking talent. Dorsey seldom hired graduates of journalism schools, preferring men and women with diverse backgrounds—philosophy majors, like himself, applicants who had studied economics or anthropology, even a Harvard man who had majored in Chinese poetry, Matt Seiden, who became a foreign correspondent in the Far East and later a *Sun* columnist.

In 1947 Dorsey hired Russell Baker, who recalled that experience with wry humor in the last pages of his book *Growing Up*. Baker later related how he finally got a chance to shine after working a year or more in the police districts and then, after being brought into the office, writing shorts about Hadassah meetings and Y.M.C.A. shindigs. He told how an editor had walked back to his desk in the far corner of the room, asking his name and whether he could type. Replying that he could "type a little," Baker was invited to fill in on an undermanned rewrite desk. Before that feverish night ended, he had written close to 5,000 words, "almost the entire content of the local news pages." He did not include one detail, which is part of office lore: Young had noticed him in the back room busily typing. Asked what he was doing, a sheepish Baker replied that as a personal challenge he was trying to condense Paul Ward's latest 3,000-word analysis of State Department intrigue into 300 words. Curious, Young read the exercise and was amazed to find it succinctly and lucidly done. From then on, Baker was often on rewrite and before long was recommended for a raise. The recommendation read: "Present salary $61. Reports of his work are excellent. He is described by his managing editor as 'the most brilliant man hired' since Dorsey has been on the *Sun*. For merit, and to bring him into line with others doing comparable work, I recommend an increase of $9 to $70 a week." In 1952, Baker was awarded the *Sun*'s golden apple—assignment to its London bureau. There his coverage of Queen Elizabeth II's coronation was admired as far away as New York—at the *Times*, which later lured Baker into joining its Washington staff. But he disliked Washington, and Dorsey invited him to return to the *Sun* as a columnist, to write whatever he pleased. To retain Baker, the *Times* in turn offered him a column, the first nonpolitical column to appear on its editorial page, and he accepted. Baker has won two Pulitzer Prizes, one for his "Observer" column in 1979 and one for his memoir of a partly Baltimore childhood, *Growing Up.*

Helen Delich from Nevada joined the staff in 1945, and after doing general reporting she began covering the port and doing it more thoroughly than Admiral Duffy had done. Through her stories and her television program, "The Port That Built a City," she dramatized the port's economic importance to Baltimore and the state. A hard-boiled, salty woman, she not only covered the port, but also dominated it whenever she could. While she was on vacation, a substitute was sent to check on a union matter. Questioning an official, he was told, "Miss Helen said we're not to talk to any other reporter. We can't tell you anything until we check with her." Delich pushed her way aboard naval vessels where, by tradition, women were unwelcome. She was given the title maritime editor in 1948 and soon broadened her beat to include Washington, the East and West coasts and, before long, the world. She scored international beats, including the return of Bay of Pigs prisoners by Fidel Castro, learning about it through a ship in Baltimore that was being prepared to carry ransom goods to Cuba. In 1969 she resigned from the *Sun* to become chairman of the Federal Maritime Commission, the first woman to hold that post or to be appointed chairman of a federal regulatory agency. In 1984 she was elected to Congress from Maryland.

Others on the staff, before, during, or around that time, were John C. A. Watkins, the aviation beat man who became president, publisher, and chairman of the board of the *Providence Journal* and in 1954 hired Young as his general manager and assistant publisher; E. T. Baker, who was deft at rewrite and features and later a senior Newspaper Guild official; Edward C. Burks, a news reporter imaginatively reassigned to Oriole coverage in 1954 when Baltimore was readmitted to baseball's major leagues; James M. Cannon, later an editor of *Newsweek,* an aide to Governor Nelson Rockefeller, and secretary of the Cabinet during a Nixon administration; J. Anthony Lukas, who went on to win two Pulitzer Prizes, one while he was a reporter for the New York *Times* and one in 1986 for his book, *Common Ground: A Turbulent Decade in the Lives of Three American Families;* Peter Kumpa, Joseph R. L. Sterne, and Ernest B. Furgurson, Jr., who won promotion to the Washington bureau and foreign assignments; Jesse Glasgow, who became financial news editor and columnist; Carleton Jones, whose specialties were the historical past and the culinary present; Patrick S. Catling, a mercurial and talented personality, who later worked for the *Manchester Guardian* and *Punch* before becoming a novelist; and Charles G. Whiteford, who trained a generation of *Sun* political reporters.

Whiteford, a man of rumpled attire whose face in repose called to mind an off-duty bloodhound, worked for the Associated Press before joining the *Sun* in 1951. A colleague remembered, "Few reporters could match Charlie's ability to clump up onto the rostrum while the House of Delegates or State

Senate was in full sonorous session, settle onto a chair, and unceremoniously tug the presiding officer down by his coattails to respond to a question." In addition to state politics, which he covered with Odell Smith, Whiteford was sent out on presidential campaigns and conventions and the civil rights confrontations in the South. He knew Baltimore and its newsmakers so well that even when out of town on assignment he was frequently called upon to provide background on a story or write an obituary, doing it quickly from memory. During his last years he was national editor.

Furgurson, one of those trained by Whiteford, nostalgically remembers when Obrycki's Crab House would sell reporters the crabs that were left over for half price: "Sometimes they were paper shells [crabs with little meat because they had recently shed old shells for new], and sometimes it was a half bushel or more of No. 1 Jimmies [jumbo males]. We'd take them over to the Press Club down near the harbor and feast." On Thursday night—the night before payday—Furgurson and colleagues would drift down to the Calvert bar, just below the *Sun* building, throw what money they had left on the bar and drink until closing. Then, with what beer that was still due them, they would sit on the curb under the Orleans Street viaduct, between the bar and the *Sun,* philosophizing until the bottles were empty.

One woman copy reader was called "the witch" for these superficial reasons: she dressed in black, including witchlike hats, came from Salem, Massachusetts, and was never seen in daylight (her fair skin was sensitive to sunlight). She walked wherever she went and had no raingear, but was never wet coming into the office when it rained. Edwin Young was convinced that she tiptoed between raindrops.

Donald Kirkley was movie and dramatic critic for twenty-five years, then became the *Sun*'s first television critic, holding that chair for seventeen years. R. H. Gardner, one of a feature-writing clique that strove to outshine one another on the back page, succeeded Kirkley as movie and dramatic critic, reviewing for thirty-three years and retiring in 1984. The 23-year-old Judy Bachrach followed Kirkley as television critic. Her savage attacks on every aspect of television had bloodthirsty readers turning to her column before glancing at the front page. Bill Carter switched from assistant foreign editor to television in 1975. He reports on national and local television as well as being the critic.

Weldon Wallace became music critic in 1940, and later chief of the Rome bureau. His successors as music critic included Elliott Galkin, later director of the Peabody Conservatory, Stephen Cera, Karen Munson, and since 1986, Stephen Wigler. Emmart was followed as art critic by Kenneth Sawyer, in 1955 winner of a national award as the best art critic for newspapers and magazines, Barbara Gold, Elisabeth Stevens, and now John Dorsey.

The copy desk too had talent and personalities. From 1944 to 1955, the head of the copy desk was Robert B. Murray, as meticulous in editing as he was unkempt in dress. (A bachelor, he sometimes would go for three or four weeks without opening his weekly pay envelope—employees were paid then in cash—and kept them for safekeeping in the ball pocket of his golf bag.) Charles F. Young was a lively octogenarian, a newspaperman for sixty-two years, and the last one around who had covered The Fire of 1904. He delighted in taking newcomers on a tour of downtown as it was in his youth. That meant pointing out the sites of vanished landmarks, such as the *Sun* Iron Building, the Carrollton Hotel, and the Rennert. The only building on his tour still there was City Hall, built in 1875. The trudge was affectionately known as "Charlie's Ghost Tour."

Colleagues rated Hervey Brackbill the fastest and fiercest of copy readers, first as chief of the *Evening Sun* copy desk and later as an assistant editor of the *Sunday Sun.* A birdwatcher, really a respected ornithologist, Brackbill wrote polished pieces on that subject for the evening editorial page and for scholarly journals. He had first worked as a telegraph operator when newspaper stories were sent by wire with Morse code, the operator rapidly tapping out each letter on an instrument with dots and dashes. Those days were recalled as he edited a story, the fingers of one hand impulsively beating out a swift tattoo on the desk top, as if he were sending a message by wire. Ralph Reppert, who wrote features and a humor column for the *Sunday Sun,* claimed to have learned the Morse code just so he could discover what Brackbill, a perfectionist, really thought of his stories.

Albert Hammond, who taught philosophy during the day at Johns Hopkins, wore the back of his sweater over his head because of a cold neck. Greg Greene had sensitive hearing. Any loud noise upset him. He resigned because Joseph Ridgely chewed Lifesavers and crunched them when writing heads. Greene moved to a remote western state where, he bragged, "the loudest noise was falling snowflakes." Ridgely, who had just received his Ph.D. from Johns Hopkins University, and Janetta Somerset, daughter of Lord and Lady Raglan, a reporter who wrote crisply and with British flair, chose a Sunday night to reveal their engagement to the staff (usually little stirred in city rooms on Sunday nights). Before the announcing could be started, a municipal transit strike began, H. L. Mencken died, a raging inferno-like fire swept a crowded hall killing ten and injuring 230, and the annual Maryland Kennel Club show had to be covered. Long afterward, in a memoir about her "newspaper marriage," Janetta Ridgely added a further touch: The day after all that deadline turmoil, a woman telephoned the city desk to complain that the wrong name had been given for second place in the Weimaraner bitch class. The city editor apologized, but mentioned that it had been a busy Sunday night. "Why?" she asked. "What else was going on?"

At Murray's death Pierce Fenhagen became chief of copy desk; Fenhagen, in turn, was succeeded by John H. Plunkett. When Plunkett became an assistant to Paul A. Banker, the managing editor, in 1966, Edward Ballantyne became copy chief. He was followed by Hal Piper and then Robert Grover in 1970. Grover was replaced by the present chief of the copy desk, Andrew Faith, in 1985.

Philip S. Heisler, the Pacific correspondent of wartime, was managing editor of the *Evening Sun* from 1949 to 1979. Thirty years remains the *Sunpaper* tenure record at that level. His threefold objectives were to attract the most talented men and women to the staff, to progressively increase local coverage, and to strive for a complete paper. To this end, he increased Maryland coverage, opened an Eastern Shore bureau, and expanded sports, women's, and financial news while reorganizing and expanding the paper. In the late 1950s circulation passed 200,000. His assistant managing editors included Harold Lutz, William J. Perkinson, Lee McCardell, Paul Broderick, Philip Evans, and Ernest M. Imhoff. Most had advanced from city or news desks. (News editors included George Trisik, Vernon Sherwin, Philip Lee and Paul White.) Robert Keller was the first metropolitan editor, and he was succeeded by William E. N. Hawkins.

Heisler, like Dorsey, assembled a talented staff: Perkinson started as a copy boy and after the war became the *Evening Sun*'s prize-winning science writer, covering the Berlin airlift, atomic bomb tests, Antarctica, Chesapeake Bay pollution, and the Apollo moon mission. He was the only copy boy to rise as far as assistant managing editor. James McManus, who married a versatile fellow reporter, Margaret Dempsey, was transferred in 1947 from the news department to the company's new television station because of his experience—as a public-address announcer for basketball games at Loyola College. Friends counseled against the move, positive that newspapering offered more possibilities. But, known on the air as Jim McKay, he became the anchor of ABC's "Wide World of Sports," winning nine Emmies for his sports coverage and one, as he put it, "for tragedy." That came for his steadying on-air reporting, hour after hour, during the 1972 Olympics while Palestinian terrorists seized, then slaughtered, eleven Israeli athletes. Other reporters who left for television included Louis R. Rukeyser, star of public television's "Wall Street Week," David Culhane, a CBS correspondent, and Tom Fenton (he was on the *Sun*), chief European correspondent of CBS. Spencer L. Davidson and Ray Cave joined *Time,* Davidson becoming a senior writer, and Cave, after eight years as its managing editor, becoming corporate editor of *Time, Inc.*

William Manchester came to Baltimore in 1947 to write a biography of Mencken and on Mencken's recommendation was hired as a reporter at $55 a week. Heisler, his managing editor, described Manchester "as an excellent reporter and writer for a morning paper—terrible for an evening paper. He would come back with a daily story, type his notes, cut them apart and arrange them in the order he would use them, then start to write. Thoroughly reported, beautifully written, but it was often the 7 Star, and usually the All Star, before his story got in the paper." But he was a prolific writer, as a cityside reporter and later on assignment in India. After leaving the *Sunpapers,* Manchester became a prolific author; among his books are *The Death of a*

President; The Arms of Krupp; biographies of Mencken, John F. Kennedy, the Rockefellers, MacArthur, and Churchill; three novels; and *Goodbye, Darkness,* an account of World War II service as a combat marine.

Burke Davis was a fast and descriptive writer, never better than when filing a running account of some melodramatic trial for an afternoon paper, a pressure job. He too, going it on his own, turned out books in a stream—histories and biographies, but also fiction that once saluted his former colleagues by using their names for Revolutionary War deserters who were shot. Richard K. Tucker was a reporter who did everything well, including cheering up servicemen. For extra pay he wrote the *Sunday Sun* Service Edition mailed to Marylanders in the armed forces during the Korean War. This included his chatty "Letter from Home" signed "Anne." Lonely servicemen wrote to Anne, probably imagining her to be the girl of their dreams, and asked for her picture. The last Service *Sun* included "Anne's" picture: Tucker at his typewriter in the city room, hat tilted on the back of his head, chewing a cigar stub.

Lawrence Efford projected a different image. A courtly old-timer from Virginia, he was long stationed in Towson—a quiet, almost remote county seat in those years. A new reporter, being shown around by Efford, marveled that even on a crowded schedule he had time to lavish his Southern charm on strangers, knew the name of everyone they passed, and when they got to the courthouse steps could even identify by name the dogs sleeping in the sun.

One of the most colorful writers was Jacob Hay. With his Grenadier Guards mustache, trenchcoat, tweed jackets, deerstalker, and clipped accent, Hay may still be the truest-blue Britisher ever to have grown up in York, Pennsylvania. His specialty was features with a comic touch, which he dashed off seemingly faster than a determined stenographer could type. Sometimes Hay contrived a fictitious story that would get by a permissive or nodding city desk. Two that got through were about a British waiter at the Belvedere Hotel who was returning to England in despair because of the atrocious table manners of Baltimoreans, and about a foreign munitions manufacturer who was flying to Baltimore to inspect the nineteenth-century Shot Tower as a possible subsidiary operation. Jake Hay originated the *Evening Sun*'s local column "Mr. Peep's Diary," and when he left for a career as publicist and novelist he turned it over to his friend John F. Goodspeed.

On a slow day in December 1952, a morning *Sun* writer, commanded to rewrite as many club and sisterhood handouts as possible to fill empty columns, concocted a story about an imaginary society, the Greater Baltimore and Maryland Citizens Moral Improvement Council, and Sherman Chase Brown, its imaginary president. Brown, it seemed, had just denounced holiday drinking as godless: "It is extremely doubtful whether the Pilgrim Fathers admitted any refreshments except milk, and possibly root beer, to their Yuletide gatherings, and we may be sure that any rum which found its way on board the *Ark* and the *Dove* was purely medicinal in character." The story, printed, unexpectedly drew the attention of temperance groups seeking speakers; they telephoned the city desk, asking for particulars. The sweating hoaxer had a friend send in a fabricated paid obituary notice stating that Sherman Chase Brown had been killed in an automobile accident in a remote section of the Deep South.

Robert Moyer started a Baltimore custom with pennies. *The Sea Urchin,* a bronze of a naked child, decorates a sculptured shell in Washington Place. After it lost part of an arm and a leg, Moyer, a reporter, proposed that the *Evening Sun* attempt to create a new image for it. "How?" asked Young the city editor. "I'll show you," replied Moyer. He lived nearby, and when passing the *Urchin* he would toss pennies into its pool. Soon passersby were adding their own change. Moyer interviewed some for a story, recording the wishes they had made. A year after he flipped in his first penny, Moyer, deeming his mission accomplished, submitted an expense account for $2.56 for "Creating a Baltimore custom."

John Stees, a member of the evening art staff from 1936, started a Sunday cartoon in 1954 about the oddities and humor of everyday life that was soon syndicated in more than 100 papers. He used simple line drawings, without shadings or cross-hatching; a squiggle became a fat man's paunch or a frisky puppy. He also drew cartoons for the evening op-ed page, continuing "Baltimore Glimpses" after he retired in 1979.

Heisler and a number of colleagues pooled money to form an Un Stable of racehorses. Its first investment was named Running Story. One of the incorporators was Bill Burton, the outdoor editor, who referred to a furlong pole as a "fathom marker." Heisler also started the *Evening Sun*'s Ugly Tie contest. This was inspired by the *Evening Sun* reporter whose 1981 obituary began "Horace C. Ayres, Jr., a gruff, dogged, hard-living, hard-working reporter whose ties rarely matched his shirt, died yesterday as he lived most of his life—working on a newspaper story." The obituary, written by Carl A. Schoettler, described by an editor "as a reporter-writer who captures and reflects the flavor of the *Evening Sun,*" also said of Ayres, "He even occasionally affected a floral tropic shirt in the city room, which he often wore with a skinny tie that seemed to have been salvaged from a trunk packed in 1958. He dressed with a nice sense of the absurd. He was vastly amused and inordinately proud of having won a couple of early editions of the office's annual Ugly Tie contest. He was banned from later contests on the grounds that his taste in ugly ties made him a professional." Winners of the contest have their names inscribed on the strange trophy, a brass spittoon, kept on display in the *Evening Sun* which is festooned with past winning ties.

Jesse Linthicum was the *Sun*'s sports editor for thirty-two years and never carried a typewriter on assignments; he wrote his column from press boxes in longhand. Rodger Pippen was the sports editor of the *News-Post*. Linthicum and Pippen sniped at each other in their columns. Pippen could be teased, or ignited, by mention of his penchant for collecting stray dogs and running notices about them in his column and throughout the sports pages; Linthicum, by a sneer at his department's cold-sober prose. The two elderly battlers nicknamed each other's paper "the evening hot towel" and "the morning wet blanket." After World War II, Paul Patterson ordered Linthicum to start coverage of Chesapeake Bay racing. Louis Hatter returned from service that day, and Linthicum asked if he knew anything about boats. Hatter said he had learned the difference between port and starboard while on a hospital ship for a few days. "Great!" Linthicum rejoiced. "You're our new boating editor!" Patterson's yacht, the *Elda,* was entered in many races but seldom won. One day it did. Hatter had been ordered to skip that regatta to save expenses. Linthicum was frantic when handed an AP wire mentioning *Elda's* victory. He told Hatter to call race officials for facts. Hatter did. Then Linthicum wanted detail, color, the cheers of the spectators. Hatter made more calls and obliged. Still Linthicum stewed. With sudden inspiration he ordered, "Put a dateline and your byline on the story so Mr. Patterson will know we were there on the job!"

Charles H. Dorsey, Jr., the *Sun's* managing editor, kept his eye on the paper's racing news. One of his notes to the sports editor read: "The read-out on the racing story in column one of your first page referred to the horse, Fat Cat, as a 'longshot.' He was a little better than 5 to 1. Whatever our racing people, our copy readers, or anyone else under heaven might think to the contrary, no horse in the columns of the *Sun* is a 'longshot' unless he is 10 to 1 or better. Will you see to it, please."

A. Paul Menton was sports editor of the *Evening Sun* from 1925 to 1966. A nationally recognized sports authority, he preferred to think of himself as a businessman. In fact, his ambition always had been to work in the *Sun's* business department. On the side, at a time when conflict of interest was a cry yet unborn, he was part-owner of a Philadelphia black cemetery, the Victory Horseshoe Company, and a paste-manufacturing plant that kept the *Sunpaper* paste pots filled. (Before electronic journalism, gallons of paste were used daily. Stories were written in copybook takes, and these were pasted together by the copy desk in strips a yard or more long before being sent by pneumatic tube to the composing room—only to be scissored up there for distribution among linotype operators and simultaneous typesetting.)

Menton was also commissioner of the Maryland Scholastic Conference, responsible for assigning officials. Incessantly pressed as sports editor and businessman, Menton made use of every free moment. During half-time while covering the Army-Navy football game in Philadelphia, for example, he would pick up a press-box telephone and make assignments for high school games the following week in Maryland.

In his day, sports editors were showered with passes and were pestered for them by cadgers from all over the *Sun* building. If Menton did not want to be bothered by whoever got through to his desk—he had arranged the furniture in his department as a barricade in front of him—without looking up he would hand the supplicant a printed card. It consisted of Bible verses containing the word "pass" and was titled "There Were No Passes Even Then." The long list included, "The wicked shall no more pass, *Nahum I,15*" and "Though they roar, yet they cannot pass, *Jeremiah I,22.*" The climax was "SO HE PAID THE PRICE AND WENT, *Jonah I,3.*"

Gruff as he was, and a man who smiled once or less a week, Menton treated his staff as his sons and daughters. Behind his back they called him "Father" and cringed at the thought of Menton learning his nickname. But when Jim Ellis, who covered the Orioles for the *Evening Sun,* was dying of cancer, Menton wrote him and signed the affectionate note "Father."

As part of his training, Gary Black, the only son of Van-Lear Black to have a newspaper-business career, worked for Morgan & Company in Paris, the West Coast office of the Fidelity & Deposit Company, and the Milwaukee *Journal.* His short apprenticeship as a reporter on the *Journal* was recorded in a four-page paper, "The Setting Sun," produced by the *Journal* staff when he left in 1939 to get married and in the 1981 history of the paper, *The Milwaukee Journal,* an informal chronicle of its first 100 years. The history noted, "When he'd been sent to Milwaukee for seasoning, Black had rented an apartment at the Cudahy Tower for himself and his valet, then reported to Murray Reed. The city editor told him he'd been picked for a responsible job: 'Whenever anybody dies in Milwaukee—unless, of course, he's somebody important— you get to write his obit.' "

Black had trouble typing—"No matter how hard I hit the keys, none of the letters came out capitals"—until the shift key was explained to him. His city editor later commented, "When he came he couldn't type his name without five errors. Now he can get all the way through it without a single mistake."

Before leaving Milwaukee, the popular Black (his friends nicknamed him Schwartz, the German word for black) gave a roast guinea hen and champagne dinner for the staff, complete with German band, a jazz pianist, and dancing girls. The history described it as "what may be the most discussed farewell party in *Journal* history":

> "The air was filled with broken glass," a reporter wrote in fond remembrance of the evening, "and the shrieks of the dead and dying." The glass shards were supplied by another reporter. In the spirit of the evening, he demonstrated his ability to drop-kick a champagne glass. Somone protested that Gary would have to pay for it. Black grandly waved the protest aside. He picked up the phone, "Send up several cases of champagne goblets, please." The host placed the glasses in front of Sam, one at a time. And one by one he kicked them.

In 1940 Black enlisted with the 110th Field Artillery of the Twenty-ninth Division. During the war he rose from private to captain and was awarded the Bronze Star for meritorious service in the Battle of Lorient. At the age of 32 he joined the *Sunpapers,* and underwent a training course under the tutelage of William F. Schmick, Sr., then the executive vice president. He started as a solicitor in classified advertising and was told by his mentor that every solicitor wore a hat. (Black said he might have worn a borrowed one the first day, but the only headpiece he ever wore was a hunting cap.) He was to report to Schmick every morning and was asked, "What did you do yesterday [in selling]? In recalling the story, Black laughed and added, "He already knew what I had done"—and laughing harder—"or had not done." Black was told that he could not regard himself as a salesman or a newspaperman until he sold his first ad. More than forty years later he still remembers the sale of his first classified—"Newago Collie Kennels in Ellicott City"—adding with a touch of pride, "It was a two-liner that ran for about a month." Black said he learned more about newspapering from "William Frederick Schmick, Sr."—he always respectfully referred to him that way—"than anyone else."

In circulation he worked for Joseph Coolidge, street sales director. Black owned several racehorses, and when they ran at Pimlico he and Herbert B. Reynolds, circulation director, would sneak off to watch them, sitting on a bench in the backstretch so they wouldn't be observed by Emmett P. Kavanaugh, the business manager, who was also stealing out to the track when *he* could. One day Kavanaugh, from his box seat, spotted the truants with his binoculars. It was a day when one of Black's horses won, at long odds. Black remembers that Kavanaugh was annoyed at his subordinates for ducking out of work, but more upset at not having bet on Black's horse.

Black became a member of the board in October 1947, seven months after another young man, William S. Abell, age 33 and a Chevy Chase lawyer and great-grandson of Arunah S. Abell, had been added—the first director with the name Abell since his father, Charles, had resigned in 1910. After William S. Abell's discharge from the World War II Navy as a commander, he asked his father, "Why not have someone represent the Abell stock on the board?" His father and his aunt, Jane Homer, "had clung to every stick of *Sun* stock, even when it wasn't worth much." William Abell had been on the board of Landmark Publishing Company of Norfolk, Virginia, chairman of its planning committee; the newspaper business fascinated and challenged him. But he learned that Harry C. Black was skeptical about having an Abell—he had disliked Walter W. Abell—and considered "the Abells bad news." After meeting William Abell, Black changed his mind and welcomed him as a member. Gary Black said he had never met William Abell until October 1947. "We just happened to hit if off from the beginning," he recalled. "He had the highest integrity, a sense of humor—everything. The biggest and best thing that ever happened to me—that came out of my association with the paper—was my friendship with Bill Abell."

Before board meetings convened, there was luncheon in the boardroom. Gary Black said that at his first meeting he saw his uncle and William F. Schmick, Sr., each put down a ten-cent tip. He put a quarter next to his place.

His uncle, seeing this, shook his head, made change for the quarter, replaced it with a dime and give his nephew the fifteen cents, with an admonishing glance.

Gary Black was 16 years old when his uncle, Harry C. Black, succeeded his father as chairman of the board, and the relationship that developed was close and mutually admiring. "He was one of the fairest men I've ever known," Gary Black said, "always willing to hear the other side." A formal man, Harry Black addressed men he saw every day as "Mr." but referred to his nephew as "Young Black" until his return from service, then "Black," and, after he was named vice chairman of the board in 1950, as "Vice Chairman, with the emphasis on the former."

Harry C. Black died in November 1956 at his winter home in Boynton Beach, Florida. Editorially, the *Sun* called him "a true newspaperman" and recalled the "infectious enjoyment he had in everything that interested him . . . from recollections of the popular songs of other years and some forms of jazz through books, architecture, flowers and all the happenings of the moment to the intricacies of such matters as British budgets." His will included bequests to his alma mater Princeton University, and to Johns Hopkins University, the Enoch Pratt Free Library, and the Peabody Institute. Not publicly known until Black's death were his earlier gifts financing a replanting and landscaping of the four squares around Baltimore's Washington Monument; providing spring tulips and fall chrysanthemums, which were his idea, for Preston Gardens; and restoring St. Paul's Cemetery and the gravestones of many a great name in Maryland history. He left 3,000 shares of Abell stock to his nephew and the remaining stock in the company to a charitable foundation, to be known not by the Black name but as the A. S. Abell Company Foundation.

Gary Black succeeded his uncle as chairman. Like his uncle, he enjoyed his associations and friendships with newspaper people. Through the annual *Sun* golf tournament, which he started in 1951, Gary Black got to know employees in all departments. Even those, say, in stereotyping and the pressroom, seeing him in the hall or elevator, would greet him as "Gary," and he returned the greeting by hailing them by name or nickname. He said that the only direct order he ever gave to a managing editor was "If I'm ever caught shooting across bait, I want it in the paper on the back page," which was the main page for local news.

In the 1960s and 1970s, under Gary Black and William Schmick, Jr. the *Sunpapers* were modernized and expanded. A sixth floor was added in 1961, at a cost of more than $3 million, almost as much as the original building. (With the growth of the papers, the building had become so overcrowded that advance *Sunday Sun* sections overflowed the third floor mail room and had to be stored in the hallways leading to the cafeteria.) Four foreign bureaus were opened: New Delhi in 1961, Rio de Janeiro in 1962, Hong Kong in 1966, and Paris in 1968.

In the 1960s Schmick authorized new sections for the *Sunday Sun,* including a *TV WEEK* magazine. Circulation rose from 320,877 in 1960 to 365,894 in 1979 (when Schmick retired), while the rival *News American*'s circulation dropped from 317,430 to 231,225. When the *Sunday Sun* was introduced in 1901, it had one editor and two reporters, one male and one female. By the 1970s the number had grown to more than thirty. At various times the multitalented staff included Hervey Brackbill, James D. Dilts, Brian Hayes, Frank Henry and later his widow Helen Henry, Paul H. Hutchins, Martha Jablow, Lydia Jeffers, Patricia Kavanaugh, Judith K. Keys, William Klender, Henry Knoch, Floyd Knox, Michael Lhotsky, Edward J. McKee, Ellis Malashuk, Deborah Morrison, Thomas Oliver, Ralph Reppert, Mark Reutter, Celina Richardson, Richard Stacks, John Stubel, William Stump, James F. Waesche, Frederick A. Weisheit, Jr., plus a number who are still on the staff of the *Sun* and *Sunday Sun* feature department (to be named in Chapter 17). The most honored member was A. Aubrey Bodine, the *Sunday Sun* photographer. Throughout his forty-three year career, Bodine recorded the look of his native Maryland—its earth, water, and sky, its people and buildings—and with his stunning pictures won international salon competitions and published books of photographic studies. In the years after Mencken, Bodine's was unquestionably the most widely recognizable of *Sunpaper* names.

In April 1965 a strike forced the *Sunpapers* to suspend publication for the first time in its history. The story of the strike goes back to 1939, when the American Newspaper Guild was organized at the *Sun* after it won a representational election. But then it failed to get a contract. Mencken, one of the company's negotiators, believed that reporters needed a means to achieve better pay, secure tenure, and "protect their general impudence." But he also had reservations, including the forty-hour week, introduced by the the New Deal. "You can no more have a forty-hour week for a reporter," he declared, "than you can have a forty-hour week for an archbishop." Union-organizing resumed after World War II, particularly at newspapers adhering to the tradition of low pay and high job turnover. At that time Neil H. Swanson, the executive editor, represented the company. The Guild sought better wages, improved working conditions, and a pension system. The company policy and tradition had been to deal with employees in a paternalistic way in sickness and old age. Pensions were granted by the board on an individual basis "in accordance with the needs in each case."

In 1949, Swanson wrote a letter to employees, urging them to vote against the Guild, claiming, "We believe that a change . . . to the stiff and formal relationship of a union contract would introduce rigidities." The letter backfired, and the Guild won a new election—and a contract. Starting salary for reporters, copy readers, and photographers was set at $40 a week, $87.50 after four years. "Its pay scale and other terms, however, equated with those in force at Nashville and Grand Rapids, rather than at Boston or St. Louis," Richard K. Tucker, an *Evening Sun* reporter, recalled. "We went on asking how people deemed so unmeritorious nevertheless put out a paper ranked among the nation's greatest." A factor in Baltimore was that editorial employees at the *News-Post,* organized only in a company union, consistently worked for still less money than the *Sunpapers* were paying.

Every few years, one contract followed another, more or less matching the gradual rise in consumer prices but not affecting the basic relationship. Tucker added, "The unwritten attitude often was for you to be working here will look good on your resume—you should think of the paper as doing you a favor. If some other paper were to offer you $10 a week more, goodbye. Just don't come back and expect the *Sun* to rehire you." In February 1965 the Guild's national headquarters merged its weak Baltimore and strong Washington units. Gerard Borstel, chairman of the Baltimore local, said:

> The union had little muscle and sometimes people unhappy working at the *Sunpapers* blamed the union for its own ineffectiveness. When time came for a new contract, management would drag out negotiations. A year or more past the expiration date, still with no settlement, management could use retroactivity as a factor. A raise retroactive to the previous contract's expiration date would form a lump sum—no matter if the raise itself were tiny—and visions of sugar plums would dance in employees' heads.
>
> Other things rankled. The paper wouldn't even deduct Blue Cross premiums from our pay. There was no contractual pension plan or sick leave system.

On April 15, 1965, when the Guild contract expired, and negotiations were at an impasse, the Guild went on strike. Publication was suspended two days later, after other unions honored the Guild's picket lines. To supply Baltimore with interim newspapers, Johns Hopkins University students started the *New Baltimore Morning Herald,* and the Guild published a tabloid, the Baltimore *Banner.* Grace Darin, who was on the *Banner* staff, recalled:

> It was a crazy operation. Stuart Smith was publisher. He began wearing three-piece suits to work, sat at a desk weighing matters. Janetta Ridgely thought he began to look more like Mr. Schmick every day. George Cook, a photographer, was business manager. He leased enough telephones to man the *New York Times.* Don Bremner was the city editor and resisted efforts to make the paper a propaganda organ for the strikers. Horace Ayres was our labor reporter. He would call up Mr. Patterson [the general manager of the *Sunpapers*], "This is Horace Ayres of the Baltimore *Banner,* Mr. Patterson. Did any printers return to work today?" He was quite serious and he would get serious answers from Mr. Patterson.

The forty-seven-day strike ended on June 4. Wages and union security were settled by arbitration. Reporters salaries were raised. Seven out of ten new employees were required to join the Guild (a later contract raised this to eight), and dues checkoffs began.

Five years later, on January 2, 1970, the Web Pressmen's Union, Local 31, called a strike, basically over scheduling of the work week. The strike shut the *Sunpapers* down for seventy-four days, ending on March 17. Settlement resulted in wage increases for the pressmen and two other craft unions, the International Typographers and the Baltimore Stereotypers.

After its contract expired in June 1978, the Guild began a three-day strike, but the *Sunpapers* continued to publish scaled-down papers. The ensuing three-year contract raised salaries of reporters with five years of experience to $485 a week by 1981, an increase of $40 a week from the previous contract. The 1981 agreement called for a top minimum of $620 by 1984, and the 1984 contract called for $700 a week by December 1986.

Irksome as these conflicts had been, and at times bitter, they could nevertheless be seen as educating all parties. Personnel in editorial and business departments, long used to ignoring one another, conceded that the other was a set of people. The company increased fringe benefits; pensions were standardized; a scholarship program for employees' children was started in 1967; the company paid for Blue Cross and Blue Shield; and awards were made for long service to the company.

The company's principal labor negotiator from 1963 until his death in 1976—during two of the strikes—was J. Stephen Becker, business manager and senior vice president. *Sun* editorials praised him as an "executive who realized that employees provide 'the breath and pulse of a newspaper,' " but the most significant tribute came from Brian Flores, administrative officer of the Washington-Baltimore Newspaper Guild, whose eulogy of Becker in a Guild bulletin said in part, "Steve Becker appeared to fight each change [in the contract] with a vigor which seemed to indicate that each concession to the union was coming directly from his pocket or his hide. I say 'appeared' because many of the changes are changes which he wanted to see and which he believed would make the relationship between the *Sun* and its employees a more workable and efficient one. . . . I believe he was good for the Guild and good for the *Sunpapers*."

Dorsey had asked to be relieved of his responsibilities as managing editor in May 1966 and was named associate editor (to act in an advisory capacity) and continued as a vice president of the company. Upon his death in 1973, a *Sun* editorial spoke of his taste and integrity, adding, "Buck Dorsey hated flash. He hated sham and show. He strove always for an honesty that reflected not only journalistic zeal but also the kind of judgment that should be expected from educated and reasonable men."

He was succeeded by Paul A. Banker, who had joined the paper as a reporter in 1942, was named city editor in 1954, served in the Rome bureau from 1962 to 1964, then returned as city editor. He is the son of Paul J. Banker, who had been an assistant managing editor on both papers until his death in 1938, when he drowned in a boat accident while fishing with his 17-year-old son, who tried unsuccessfully to rescue him. The *Sunpapers* provided a scholarship for Paul at Yale, from which his father had also graduated.

Banker instituted a number of changes. Dorsey's front page invariably had streamers, a standard format, and seldom a local story. Banker varied the makeup and included major local stories. He engaged Edmund C. Arnold, a nationally known typographer, to restyle the paper's headlines. As noted, he started a daily op-ed page and in 1968 created Perspective, a Sunday commentary section, with James S. Keat as editor. (Succeeding editors of that section were Charles Flowers, Davison White, Leo Coughlin, and M. William Salganik.) In one of the first moves to change the *Sun* from a reporter's paper to an editor's paper, national and foreign editors were appointed to supervise and edit that coverage. A West Coast bureau was opened in 1971, with Bruce Winters as its first chief. To supplement county news and improve circulation, two zoned sections were introduced, *Arundel Living* in 1977 and *Howard Living* in 1979 (later named the *County Suns*).

The assistant managing editors, under Dorsey or Banker, were Daniel J. Meara, Harold S. Goodwin, John H. Plunkett, Hal Piper, Keat, and Harold A. Williams, who had been Sunday editor. The city editors—later known as metropolitan editors—were Scott Sullivan, William F. Schmick 3d, John E. Woodruff, Gilbert L. Watson 3d, Steven M. Luxenberg, and, since 1984, Thomas Linthicum, Jr.

On April 8, 1974, a historic date, local news that had been on the back page of the *Sun* and the *Evening Sun*—with stories jumping toward the front of the paper—was moved to the front of a third section. The drastic change stunned readers, many of whom during their lifetime flipped the paper to the back page before reading the front page.

To prepare for a production system with cold type and a computer-operated composing room, in 1971 Schmick hired Louis J. Franconeri, a technological expert with the American Newspaper Publishers Association, to study obstacles and propose solutions in the manufacturing area. Before a new electronic writing and editing system could be installed, the partition separating morning and evening news rooms was removed, the floor of that half-acre area was raised to cover wires and cable, and the worn linoleum was replaced with a blue-green carpet. Gray furniture gave way to buff-colored desks with orange swivel chairs. Price Day, walking through the refurbished room for the first time, commented, "It looks like the accounting department of a bankrupt Italian airline."

Early in 1975 the composing room switched from hot metal (one linotype was kept as a museum piece) to cold type. In May 1975, some seventy-six Harris 1500 video display terminals began to hum in the news room, and the era of clattering typewriters, copy paper, pencils, and paste pots ended. At that early point in the twentieth century's single most revolutionary change in newspaper production, the nation's most elaborate example of computer printing was the three-paper operation at the Baltimore *Sun*. Soon tour groups were a daily feature of office life; representatives from 139 other newspapers, some from as far away as New Zealand and South Africa, came to study the comprehensive operation. In 1976 in accord with a nationwide trend toward fewer, wider, more flexible columns of print, the *Sunpapers* switched from eight to six columns in its standard page format.

While the *Sunpapers* changed in these ways, in the perception of some it had not changed at all. Michael Olesker, a popular columnist with the *News American,* moved over to the *Sun* in February 1979. In his first column he wrote about the change. He quoted his friend Eddie as saying the *Sunpapers* looks down its nose at people, is not considered lovable, and "tells you everything about South Africa and misses every nuance about South Baltimore." He quoted a man from Little Italy as saying, "They're cut off from people like us. They only like people in their own establishment." Olesker commented:

> This is not exactly isolated talk. People who work in this building have heard it for years, and wonder about it. They seem like normal human beings here, but somehow the paper comes out every morning with all the warmth of bank vaults. On other newspapers, things are different. This is the era of trendy features instead of hard news coverage; editors on other papers have learned how to make their papers more cuddly. This is not a cuddly newspaper. . . . They tell me here that the *Sun* is changing, too. It's still a hard-news paper; when it laughs dust still comes out of its mouth. But they want to humanize it, they tell me. They want to loosen things up.

One way the company tried to "humanize" the papers was with a film titled *First Edition.* Unlike the usual newspaper promotional movie showing every aspect of newspaper production, this was a dramatic mosaic of a day in the news and editorial departments, without narration. The only voices were those of the staff and the people they encountered in gathering the news. In 1977 the thirty-minute documentary, produced by Dewitt L. Sage and directed by Helen Whitney, award-winning moviemakers, was nominated for a Motion Picture Academy Oscar in the short-subject category. The film was also distributed nationally by the Newspaper Readership Council.

During this period of change, and even longer, from January 1970 through 1986, one mission remained constant: Rudolph J. Handel stood at a tip of *Sunpaper* property on the corner of Calvert and Centre streets, swiveling a sign that read, "SUN LIES" on one side and "SUN ERRS" on the other. Handel, a retired sheet-metal mechanic for the U.S. Coast Guard, started picketing in 1967 in front of a store that he claimed had sold him a defective television set. After many hours of picketing, the store replaced the set and the *Sun* wrote an article about it titled "A Veteran Picket Cashes His Gripes at the Counter." But Handel claimed the article lied when it said it was a new set—he maintained it was second hand—and he felt that follow-up sympathetic features about him contained errors. So he started standing at Calvert and Centre streets with his sign. He also had picketed a shoe store because of shoes that were too tight, a door company for an undersized door, and his dentist for a set of false teeth that didn't fit.

At his weekday afternoon spot on Calvert Street he became one of the more familiar figures in town, a living landmark, and automobile commuters on their way home honked and waved as they passed by; Handel responded with a nod and a smile. For the curious who stopped to inquire, he handed them a typed photocopy sheet headed "I Walk on Principle Only," which gave the background on all his picketing. On the last line he updated in pen the number of hours he had walked. At the *Sun* it was more than 4,000 hours. Handel was a pleasant, peaceful, nonemotional man. The relationship between him and the *Sunpapers* was not acrimonious, perhaps even affectionate, certainly on the part of *Sun* people. The *Evening Sun* invited him to be its guest at its seventy-fifth anniversary banquet in 1985, with or without his sign, but he politely declined. Handel died in the fall of 1986, and the *Sun,* in announcing his death, put his picture on the front page.

During William F. Schmick, Jr.'s eighteen years as head of the *Sunpapers,* he also served a two-year term as president of the American Newspaper Publishers Association, using that forum to protest increasing government interference in the newspaper business. After forty-two years with the company, he retired on December 31, 1978, as president of the A. S. Abell Company and was succeeded by Donald H. Patterson.

After graduating from Princeton and serving as a naval officer in World War II, Donald H. Patterson joined the company in February 1946, working in the plant maintenance department, then as assistant to the president and as coordinator during the construction of the Calvert Street plant. He became maintenance manager in 1948, production manager in 1950, assistant to the president in 1961, vice president in 1963, secretary and general manager in 1966, senior vice president in 1976, publisher and member of the board in 1977, and, succeeding Schmick as chief executive officer, president as well as publisher January 1, 1979.

In Schmick's last year, Organization Resources Counselors (ORC), a New York consultant group, was engaged to examine the *Sunpaper* management system. Working with Patterson and a committee composed of department heads, the ORC directed a study of the decision-making process, personnel, and ways to enable senior editors and advertising, marketing, and circulation chiefs to participate more fully in the total operation of the company. After receiving the ORC's extensive report, Patterson put much of it into practice, while still "keeping the machinery running."

The well-worn Hoe presses were giving out. The Hoe Company had gone out of business, and spare parts were not to be had. The options were few: Goss was the only press manufacturer in the United States. TKS of Japan was beginning to test the American market, but it had never produced a press folder as large as the *Sunpapers* would need. A contract with Goss was signed in 1978, with specifications for more color compatibility and automation in presses then being contemplated. Engineering consultants spent nearly two years in studies on where to place the new presses. The old ones, of course, had to be kept running while the new ones were being built and installed. Some executives favored building a satellite plant outside Baltimore, but Patterson decided that the best solution, based on costs and logistics, was to construct a second new Calvert Street building adjoining the 1950 plant.

Work on the annex—to cost $16 million and to house another $35 million worth of presses and auxiliary equipment—began in 1979. Four nine-unit Goss Metroliner offset presses were installed as part of "a total systems approach to manufacturing," from the automated handling of rolls of newsprint to a counting and bundling distribution system in the mail room.

With its new presses, Goss provided training manuals, but Franconeri (named vice president of operations in 1976), stressing human factors as much as technological ones, devised a training program in cooperation with the Rochester Institute of Technology, with a classroom set up off the pressroom. The program, unique and effective, was copyrighted by the *Sunpapers* and sold to other newspapers, including foreign ones, that were installing similar equipment. Offset printing replaced letterpress in 1981, with full color capability following soon after.

In Donald H. Patterson's four years as publisher and president, he decentralized the management system, oversaw plant expansion and a modernization of technology, financed the $51 million capital-spending program during double-digit interest rates, and controlled budgets during an inflationary period when the price of newsprint reached record levels.

Until 1981 the A. S. Abell Company embraced the *Sunpapers,* WMAR-TV, and a subsidiary in Salisbury, Maryland, consisting of a television station, two radio stations, and an industrial park. In 1982 the company established two subdivisions, A. S. Abell Publishing and Abell Communications. Patterson continued as president of the parent company while relinquishing executive responsibilities for the publishing division. He retired in January 1983.

A four-page in-house paper was prepared saluting his career. Joseph R. L. Sterne wrote in part: "The spectacle of Mr. Patterson presiding over a meeting of the planning and operating committee, or over a lunch for Ronald Reagan or Harry Hughes, or over a seance for citizens outraged by morning *Sun* editorials, was memorable. To each occasion, he managed to impart an aura of disbelief. What bugged him about the planning and operating committee was the length of meetings and the size of club sandwiches. What left him unimpressed by the utterances of high muckamucks was their utter inanity. What turned him to wonderment, in meetings with the irate public, was how his editorial writers could write such dumb stuff. He managed to go along with all the pecksniffery of office without ever really condoning it."

SIXTEEN

The *Sun* Abroad
1887–1987

Francis A. Richardson, the *Sun*'s star reporter in Washington, D.C., was the paper's first foreign correspondent. In the early fall of 1887 he made a tour of Europe, writing long descriptive letters of his impressions. In Belgium he commented on our "shabby diplomatic service"; in Vienna he wrote about the emperor's 3,000 horses and Austria's "broken-down but exclusive aristocracy"; in Switzerland's resorts he saw Bourbon princesses who were "fat, homely, and loud." In Ireland he visited the Baltimore of County Cork and praised its industrial fishing school. Only in Paris did Richardson concentrate on politics. He found the French weak and the Germans ready for war.

In 1888, John T. Morris, later the city editor, was sent to Italy to cover the Papal Jubilee of Pope Leo XIII's fiftieth anniversary as a priest. This was undoubtedly done because Baltimore had a large Roman Catholic population and James Cardinal Gibbons was one of its most prominent citizens. The *Sun* noted that it was the only American newspaper to have sent a correspondent to Rome; the Pope, via Morris, complimented the *Sun* on the energy and range of its quest for news. Morris had the honor of presenting President Cleveland's gift to the Pope, a copy of the United States Constitution.

Thirty years later, Raymond S. Tompkins, a star of the city staff, accompanied Maryland troops abroad in World War I and remained with the army of occupation. Joined by J. Fred Essary, of the Washington bureau, Tompkins covered the Versailles Peace Treaty in Paris. Frank R. Kent, as noted in Chapters 10 and 11, was in England and France in 1918, and he returned to England in the fall of 1921 to report on British reaction to the course of the Washington Naval Disarmament Conference. (Kent later recalled that the hour-and-a-quarter private talk he had with Lloyd George, the British prime minister, was "one of the most unforgettable interviews I ever had with a public man. He talked with a freedom, force, and fearlessness I have never known matched. He said things that made my hair stand on end. And I was never able to print a single word.'')

In the summer of 1923, Paul Patterson sent Tompkins back to Germany to report on that country's exploding inflation and kept him in Europe until March 1924 to cover the Rhineland uprising, the Munich beer-hall putsch organized by Hitler, the election of Ramsay MacDonald as British prime minister, and turbulent events in Ireland. Patterson, determined to enhance his paper's growing reputation for attentiveness to international news, went to England in September 1924 and obtained exclusive U.S. rights for the news service of the *Manchester Guardian,* one of England's most influential newspapers. He also seized upon that occasion to expand the *Sun*'s own foreign reporting by opening a London bureau.

That was the beginning of a *Sun* presence around the world which added immeasurably to its stature and influence. By the 1960s the *Sun* had opened bureaus in Bonn, Moscow, Rome, New Delhi, Rio de Janeiro, Hong Kong, and Paris—one of the largest number ever established by a U.S. newspaper for its own readership. And its innovative practice of awarding these coveted assignments to its own young, promising reporters attracted outstanding talent from around the nation and sometimes abroad to the *Sun* and *Evening Sun* local staffs, eager to compete for the opportunity to become a *Sun* foreign correspondent.

The first London bureau chief was John W. Owens, the *Sun*'s chief political writer, who was not quite 40 years old. The 1937 history of the *Sunpapers* named Kent as the *Sun*'s first London correspondent, but in a later chapter it attributed that honor to Owens. Kent was the first correspondent to be based in London for some months, but Owens was the first bureau chief.

When Owens opened the bureau in December 1924 it was "in two top rooms in Fleet Street near St. Paul's Cathedral." But the bureau soon moved to quarters at 40 Fleet Street, adjoining the *Manchester Guardian*'s office, where a succession of *Sun* correspondents came under the benevolent influence of James Bone, the *Guardian*'s London editor.

Bone noted that Owens "interpreted and diagnosed serious British opinion." Owens was more commentator than reporter, and so were his early successors. They were more likely to be smoking a pipe with their feet propped up on the bureau desk, not dashing around England covering a hard-news story. In December 1925, Owens began writing a column, "From a Window in Fleet Street." In an early column he observed that while reading British newspapers and magazines he had become fascinated by the loquacity of the English in writing about the reticence of the English. The column was an "adjustable window"—"a viewpoint which all of Britain, or bits of it, may be seen, an optical device of variable telescopic and X-ray functions, specially intended for looking past the big news of the day to see some of the incidental oddities, the peculiar minutiae that make England such a baffling and enchanting place in which to live." The column became a *Sun* fixture until the early 1970s, when it and essay-style columns written in other bureaus were dropped in favor of news-related feature stories.

For some while, Paul Patterson himself, not his managing editor, chose the bureau correspondents. He insisted on a rotation system of one or two years, to give as many members of the staff as possible foreign experience and to prevent them from losing an American viewpoint.

Owens was succeeded in 1926 by J. Fred Essary, chief of the Washington bureau, and he in turn was succeeded by others from the bureau: M. Farmer Murphy, W. A. S. Douglas, and Dewey L. Fleming. Each served one year, except Fleming, who stayed two years. They were followed by four editorial writers: Frederic C. Nelson (he had arrived in April 1931 when Great Britain went off the gold standard, "thereby upping the Life of Riley to the Life of Lucullus, for I was paid in dollars"), A. D. Emmart, Newton Aiken, and Philip M. Wagner. Wagner recalled that his instructions from William E. Moore, the managing editor, were: "You are one man. If you try to compete with the Associated Press on the lead story each day you can come right home. And you're not going to be a diplomat, either. Write about England."

In reminiscences a number fondly recalled Bone, "their mentor and guide." Owens remembered his "watching over an American as over an infant," later getting Owens a seat in the gallery for the opening of Parliament, and most of all remembering "the wonders of London as set forth by Bone in midnight walks, rain or no rain." Emmart pictured "James Bone's office at 1 A.M. where I sat nightly and tried to store up in my mind the phrases he turned and the stories he told; the rambling walks we took while he illuminated the magnificences of a great city and its hobgoblin places." In his unpublished autobiography, Aiken wrote, "Among my most cherished memories were those of late afternoon meetings with Bone's group at the Red Lion and midnight visits to the Cafe Royale." Bone was a friend and tutor to *Sun* men for more than twenty years, and a number of times was Patterson's guest in Baltimore. When he retired in 1946 at the age of 90, colleagues from both the *Sun* and the *Guardian* toasted him "as the adopted son of Baltimore." (The *Sun-Guardian* relationship ended in the mid-1950s, when Alastair Hetherington, a *Guardian* editor, dropped the *Sun* in favor of the *Washington Post*.)

Because of Moore's edict, *Sun* correspondents, until World War II was imminent, limited their main-event coverage to the opening of Parliament, an election, a coronation, or the like, and on such occasions they took a special angle. These stories were cabled, but most of what they wrote was sent by ship's mail (this was before transatlantic air service). Mailers had to be still usable six or seven days after they were posted. Correspondents developed frugal ways. To save postage, one correspondent ran his words together, cable fashion; another, writing a long series, typed the stories single-spaced. Although the *New York Times* and other papers sent their correspondents daily cable frontings to indicate where their stories had appeared in the paper, the

Sun home office thought it sufficient to send the bureau tear sheets by ship's mail (later they were sent airmail). It was a correspondent's only way to know how much of what he filed then made the paper, and on what page.

Correspondents got little or no direction from their editors; in fact, they seldom heard from Baltimore. One said, "We felt very much alone, and on our own." Another wrote a friend on the staff, "Have you heard any whispers who might be coming this way? If past history means anything, I'll be the last to be notified when a successor is picked." The correspondents were conscientious and hardworking; the practice was to take just one Sunday off every two weeks.

Philip M. Wagner was in London in the mid-1930s, when Edward VIII was about to give up his crown to marry "the woman I love," the twice-divorced Wallis Warfield Simpson of Baltimore. During the rising furor, Simpson fled to France. Wagner, who happened to be there, asked to see her, saying he could tell her what the *Sun* and other American papers were writing about her (the British papers were still circumspect). She agreed, even though the British Foreign Office had cautioned her not to give interviews. After they had met, Wagner left a carbon of his story at the gate of the country chateau where Simpson was staying, pointing out that it was not an interview but an account of a visit. He added that he would not send it to the *Sun* unless she agreed. Within an hour she sent a note to the inn where he was staying: "You may use it. It is perfectly lovely. Just make one correction. You wrote my hair is black; it is, rather, dark brown."

Wagner did not have enough money to cable the story to the *Sun.* He called Bone in London, saying that if Bone would permit him to send it collect to the *Guardian,* and if the *Guardian* would forward the story to the *Sun,* Bone was free to use it as an exclusive in England. Bone agreed. Wagner felt that Bone had done him a big favor and that he had done Bone an even bigger one. But the *Guardian,* evidently cautious about a still-delicate situation in England, placed the story at the bottom of a page deep inside. The *Sun* used the story on its front page.

Wagner recalled that when he was stationed in London the American press colony numbered only about a dozen correspondents, not all of them Americans. However, the number increased dramatically as war threatened in Europe. In 1937, Wagner was followed by Paul W. Ward from the Washington bureau. When Prime Minister Neville Chamberlain set off to meet Hitler at the time of the Munich crisis, Ward cabled from London that Chamberlain was "going with a plan and, if the plan works, the result may be worse than war." He forecast in detail what indeed happened at Munich when Chamberlain capitulated to Hitler's demand that Germany immediately occupy the Sudetenland. (His source for that report was Chamberlain himself.) Following the Munich crisis, Ward predicted that Hitler would next seize the rest of Czechoslovakia—which duly happened the following spring. Ward's forecast was so accurate that the *Manchester Guardian* chided the British Secret

Service for not having inside information as good as Ward's. Still later, Ward filed an accurate forecast of Mussolini's preparations to invade Albania.

After the Nazi invasion of Poland in September 1939 and the Anglo-French declaration of war on Germany, Ward spent much of his time in France. As rumors and mystery persisted about what was happening along France's Maginot Line—little or no fighting took place in the winter of 1939—Ward summoned a taxi and drove to the front. His report was called "a story that stood out."

Ward returned to Washington in 1940, and his wartime successors were Frank R. Kent, Jr., Maclean Patterson, Lee McCardell, and Thomas O'Neill, who reported on the Allied war efforts and the attempts of Germany to bomb England into submission. The cast-iron letters of the Baltimore *Sun* sign— the *Sun* was the only American newspaper to display its name on Fleet Street— attracted many homesick Maryland servicemen who passed through London. By this time the role of the *Sun* correspondent had gradually changed from that of the contemplative observer of John W. Owens's day to vigorous news coverage. O'Neill's superb reporting of breaking stories added a dimension that successors in the London bureau strove to match.

Rodney Crowther, as part of a *Sun* contingent headed by Paul Patterson, was in San Francisco in the summer of 1945 for the formation of the United Nations Conference. One day Neil H. Swanson, the executive editor, telephoned him: "I don't know whether I'll send you to China or London. I'll let you know tomorrow." It turned out to be London, where the new Labor government of Clement Attlee was undertaking to nationalize basic industries and to socialize medicine.

During the war years, Lord Winster (Reginald T. H. Fletcher), a member of the Labor party, was a contributing writer for the *Sun,* and he continued until 1961, except when he was a cabinet minister in the first postwar Labor government and the governor-general of Cyprus. His pieces were described as "a sort of diary of the life and politics of Britain, full of pungent commentary and peppered occasionally with personal quirks and foibles. He could irritate as easily as amuse, and the corpus of the correspondence is rich in footnotes to the history of two decades of drastic change in Britain's place in the world." He was the kind of man who could draw confidences even from queens. He recalled the time he met the Queen Mother, soon after the death of her husband, King George VI. He studiously avoided any reference to the king's death, but she brought it up: "You know, Lord Winster, the thing you miss most is having someone to come home to giggle with over the day's doings."

Swanson visualized large concepts. After the war, other papers deemphasized foreign coverage, but Swanson dispatched a number of correspondents, known about the office as "the household cavalry," to fan out worldwide for an inspection of the crumbling British Empire. To put it in Swanson's more dramatic terms, "The *Sun* began one of the most extensive news enterprises ever undertaken by an individual paper." The findings were published as series of articles; the first, captioned "Crisis in South Africa," was by Price Day. The second, "Retreat from the Desert," a study of Great Britain's changed position in the Mediterranean, East Africa, and the Middle East, was by Potter; the third, "Experiment in Freedom," was the result of two studies by Price Day, a year apart, to assess the consequences of India's first year of independence. The fourth was a study of England, the heart of the Commonwealth and Empire, also by Day, with contributions by Lee McCardell.

When Griffin succeeded Crowther in 1947, England, which had realized few material gains from winning the war, still had rationing and wage-price controls. The life of a correspondent had changed since the "Lucullan" days of Nelson. Austerity applied to correspondents and their families too. Gas in the bureau's office grate flowed weakly and irregularly. Griffin reported on the Labor government's continuing economic and social changes. Working with Lewis Douglas, the U.S. ambassador to England, who had a leading role in reorganizing and stabilizing West Germany's barter-based living standards, Griffin was able to report also on that country's economic recovery.

In 1949, with the French government in turmoil and the North Atlantic Treaty Organization under way, Patterson wanted a "presence" in Paris, and Janetta Somerset was asked to open a bureau there. A graduate of Oxford, she had been hired by McCardell in late 1946 as London bureau manager—"to do all the things I was really bad at"—but, enriched with other talent, she was soon writing "From a Window in Fleet Street" and filing news stories.

Somerset operated the Paris bureau from a Left Bank apartment built by the Duc de Sully, premier of Henry IV, "and," as she noted, "scarcely improved thereafter." She did not have an AP teleprinter to follow developments, but had to rely on telephone calls from friends in the AP bureau when there were fast-breaking news stories. When Somerset resigned to return to her home in England, the bureau was closed in March 1951. (In 1952 she joined the *Sun* staff in Baltimore, working as a reporter and later as an editorial writer.)

While Somerset was in Paris and the London bureau was functioning as usual—manned by Dewey L. Fleming (for a second tour) and then Howard Norton—Swanson extended the *Sun*'s European coverage to Germany. William J. Perkinson described the tense Berlin airlift in 1948–49 after the Soviets had withdrawn as one of the four occupying powers and cut off supplies for West Berlin. Harold A. Williams covered the formations of the West and East German governments in 1949–50. In 1953, Dudley P. Digges, an *Evening Sun* editorial writer, was named general European correspondent. He was there for elections in Austria, Germany, and Italy, for land reform in Southern Italy, and for Yugoslavia's role after it broke with the Soviet Union. As part of a comprehensive series conceived by Swanson, labeled "Keys to Your Future," Digges wrote a fourteen-part report on the resurgence of West Germany.

Meanwhile, the *Sun* was printing a sixteen-part survey by William Manchester of Southeast Asia's heartland—Indochina, Thailand, and Burma.

In 1950, when President Truman committed U.S. forces in support of South Korea after its sudden invasion by North Korea, Swanson made sure that the *Sun* would carry eyewitness accounts of the fighting. First to reach the scene was Philip Potter, who had been a correspondent in the China-Burma-India theater in World War II, the civil war in Greece in 1947, and the Arab-Israeli war in Palestine in 1947 and 1948. Soon after he arrived in Korea, Potter was returning from the front with other correspondents when they were ambushed by guerrillas. Potter was hit in the leg by a submachine-gun bullet. Taken to a field hospital, he insisted on writing his story before being treated. He was in an army hospital in Tokyo to have the bullet removed when he got word of the planned landing at Inchon and signed himself out. Potter duly went ashore with the Marines and reported the battle of the beachhead. Only after an infection developed did he return to the hospital to have the bullet removed.

A few days later, William D. Blair, Jr., a 23-year-old *Sun* correspondent, was covering a U.S. Marines attack along the Han River when he was shot by a North Korean sniper, but he was not seriously wounded. Other *Sun* correspondents, before the war's end in 1953, were John T. Ward, Richard K. Tucker, Patrick Skene Catling, and James M. Cannon. Cannon, a flamboyant reporter, carried a small bar with him on his rounds to help sources relax before he interviewed them. He was in Tokyo with its tantalizing attractions trying to write a series on the Far East, but was too distracted to get the pieces to crystallize. A train buff, he decided he needed a more relaxing setting, so he traveled around Japan on its remarkable trains, writing comfortably and easily until the series was completed.

From the early 1950s, Swanson, and after he left the paper, Charles H. Dorsey, Jr., the managing editor, began staffing the London bureau with talented young *Sun* men: Russell Baker, Bradford Jacobs, Catling, Joseph R. L. Sterne, Louis Rukeyser, and David Culhane, who had the first four-year assignment. Catling, in *Better Than Working*, a memoir of his carefree days as a *Sun* reporter, wrote:

> If anyone were to ask me what newspaper assignment to work for, I would recommend, without hesitation, the post of London correspondent of the Baltimore *Sun*. I would add a warning that the job is such a gratifying one that it leads almost inevitably to subsequent anticlimax. This was the job I was assigned in February, 1956. . . . The *Sun*'s London correspondent is given the resounding title of chief of the London bureau; but his administrative responsibilities are not exhausting. The bureau consists of two small rooms in the Reuter Building at 85 Fleet Street. The staff consists of himself and a woman who orders the sherry, opens the mail, confects the monthly accounts, and writes occasional articles, usually about fashion shows and the affairs of the royal family.

(Catling demeans the role of the bureau assistant, who not only manages the office but also writes on a variety of subjects. Janetta Somerset was followed by Anne Walker for two years, then by Joan Graham, who was assistant to fifteen bureau chiefs in thirty years. In 1952 Graham ran the bureau for four months between the departure of Rodney Crowther in July and the arrival of Russell Baker in October. Judy Anderson has been bureau assistant since 1986.)

Catling mentioned that he had decorated the office with burgundy-red wall-to-wall carpeting. It was a tradition for the new bureau chief to select his own decor. One added scarlet draperies made from the same cloth used for the greatcoats of the Grenadier Guards (they hung for years without sign of wear). McCardell brought photographs of Maryland taken by A. Aubrey Bodine, the *Sunday Sun*'s famed photographer, and Robert F. Kniesche, who was director of the *Sunpapers* photographic staff. On Maryland Day, March 25, McCardell would hang a Maryland flag out the *Sun*'s window to the bewilderment of other Fleet Street newspaper offices, which telephoned to ask "What kind of flag is that?" Crowther, who was nicknamed the Grandfather Moses of Fleet Street, filled the walls with his own bold watercolors of London scenes ("his blues were bluer, his greens greener, his purples more regal and his reds more revolutionary than life itself"). His joy was to go to the office at dawn and paint happily until Graham arrived. In 1972, Daniel Berger moved the bureau to its present location, Gough Square, just off Fleet Street.

While Dorsey was managing editor and during the presidencies of William F. Schmick Sr. and Jr., the *Sun* opened six overseas bureaus, the first three in as many years: Bonn in February 1955; Moscow in January 1956, and Rome in July 1957. The New Delhi bureau was opened in 1961, a South American bureau in 1962, and one in Hong Kong in 1966. During the Vietnam War a Saigon office was also established.

Bonn was selected because a resurgent West Germany had a central role in Europe and its capital was a strategic post from which to cover new developments in the Soviet-bloc countries. The first bureau chief was Edward C. Burks. A later correspondent, Gene Oishi, became nationally known after he returned to the United States. A member of the press corps accompanying Spiro T. Agnew in the vice presidential campaign of 1968, Oishi was referred to by Agnew as "the fat Jap." The incident touched off an indignant public reaction, particularly from Asian-Americans. After the Bonn bureau was closed in 1983 and its chief, Hal Piper, went to London, the continent was covered from the Paris bureau.

Howard Norton, the *Sun*'s first Moscow correspondent, arrived there in 1956, the year the Soviets bloodily suppressed a revolt in Hungary. The only other Moscow bureaus were operated by the *New York Times*, the *New York Herald Tribune*, McGraw-Hill publications, and the wire services. Norton's assignment "was to do a better, more thorough job than the AP." He broadened his news coverage by writing a Sunday column, "Under a Moscow Dateline," describing facets of Soviet life. The column was the basis of a Norton book, *Only in Russia*, published in 1961. Moscow was an expensive post to maintain. The *Sun* had to import an automobile (with spare parts and tires) and replace it every three years. The correspondent required a chauffeur and an interpreter. Cable charges were high.

Norton was followed by Peter Kumpa, who covered the "kitchen debate" between Vice President Richard Nixon and Premier Nikita S. Khrushchev in 1959 when they argued ideology in a model of an American kitchen at a Moscow exhibition. Despite the crowds, Kumpa managed to squeeze next to the principals. He wrote a fourteen-page account of the famous confrontation. Because transmission of correspondents' copy from Moscow was erratic, Kumpa filed his story to go through three different relay points. But it never got beyond the cable office—it had been censored by the Soviets. Kumpa was accredited as a foreign correspondent, thus subject to censorship. Through a mix-up he was not also accredited to the Nixon party, whose accompanying correspondents were not censored.

Kumpa, his wife, and three children lived in a small Soviet-assigned apartment that also had to serve as the *Sun*'s bureau, where Kumpa and his secretary/translator worked. Leonid Ofslov, the chauffeur, was a well-known man-about-town. According to his Soviet contract, the *Sun* had to provide his clothing. Ofslov spent his spare time in the *Sun* apartment/bureau choosing clothing from back issues of *Esquire* and French fashion magazines.

While Kumpa was still in Moscow, Ernest B. "Pat" Furgurson, Jr. arrived to help cover the twenty-second Party ("deStalinization") Congress and the beginning of the split between the Soviets and the Chinese. Furgurson then had three busy years: the heyday of the unpredictable Khrushchev, Soviet space achievements, the Cuban missile crisis, the widening of the Soviet-China split and the test-ban treaty of 1963. After many delays and much negotiation, Furgurson obtained a second apartment, across from the first one, which became the *Sun* office.

Adam Clymer succeeded Furgurson. In February 1965, while covering a demonstration of 1,500 Chinese and Vietnamese who stoned the U.S. Embassy protesting American air raids in North Vietnam, Clymer was beaten by demonstrators. When he tried to reach the embassy, shouting in Russian that he needed a doctor, he was barred by a Soviet militiaman. Accused of slapping the soldier, Clymer, who had been in the Soviet Union less than a year, was subsequently expelled from the country.

Furgurson returned as interim correspondent until Stephen E. Nordlinger was ready to replace him. Nordlinger was followed by Bruce Winters, Dean Mills, Hal Piper, and Anthony Barbieri, Jr.

In the spring of 1978, Piper, who became the senior American correspondent during his four-year tour, was detained by Soviet border guards who seized his notes and research material on his return from a reporting trip to Poland and Yugoslavia. That summer he and Craig R. Whitney of the *New York Times* were found guilty in a civil suit of defaming the State Radio and Television Administration by quoting dissidents who alleged that Soviet television had fabricated a confession by a Georgian nationalist. The U.S. Senate condemned the Soviet action, and the federal government threatened retaliatory moves against Soviet journalists in the United States. The Soviet court imposed court costs of $1,675 on each correspondent and ordered them to retract their stories. Court costs were paid, but retractions were refused. Both correspondents, who were on vacation outside the Soviet Union during the trial, were permitted to return to their posts after each had paid a fine of $73 for failure to publish retractions.

Barbieri also spent four years as Moscow correspondent. During that time he reported extensively from Poland during the rise of the Solidarity movement, and from other Eastern European countries, as well as Afghanistan following the Soviet invasion in 1979. Antero Pietila, who came to the *Sun* from Finland in 1969, became Moscow bureau chief in 1983 and will finish his tour in September 1987.

In the summer of 1957, Rome was selected as the site of a Mideast bureau. It was not only a world capital with unmatched amenities, but also a strategic base to reach what the bureau was to encompass—the Mediterranean region and Africa, an area, as one correspondent described it, larger than the domain of Alexander the Great. Lee McCardell, then an assistant managing editor of the *Evening Sun,* was the first bureau chief. A major assignment was covering the revolt of the Algerian nationalists against the French, who had controlled that country, three times the size of Texas, since 1830. In a ten-part series that attracted wide attention because of the quality of the reporting and writing, McCardell described how the Algerian Nationalist Army lived and fought:

> The troop to which I had been assigned was encamped on a flat mountain crest covered with cedars [he wrote in his characteristic unadorned style]. The forest floor, a thick mat of brown needles and cones, might have been that of any Maryland or Virginia pine woods.
>
> But as far as I could see in any direction there were no roads, no telephone poles, no villages, no houses, no fields, no flocks, nothing but mountains. Not too far away there were children. Faintly from a vale to one side of our mountain camp came their shrill voices, and occasionally the distant barking of a dog, but I could see no one. . . .
>
> I was impressed by the personal cleanliness of everyone in camp. The latrine was simply a designated area of scrub cedar on the mountain slope, and from what I later saw of the cooking they paid little attention to camp hygiene. But personally the soldiers washed every morning, shaved each other, brushed their teeth with their fingers and combed their hair. . . .
>
> That morning the captain, whom we came to know as Mustapha, inspected his troops. In a fairly open area among the trees, they were drawn up in close formation, 50 or 60 riflemen in line, three files deep. They were uniformed very much as I was except for their caps. They wore visored campaign caps and French leather cartridge belts.
>
> They ran through the manual of arms with snap and precision. They wheeled and passed in review. They presented arms while a small Algerian flag (red star

and crescent on a green-and-white panel) about the size of a yacht ensign was lowered solemnly from a tree stripped of its branches to form a flagpole. An officer folded the flag carefully and took it away. It was the first and last Algerian flag I saw in the field.

In 1960, McCardell was succeeded by Paul A. Banker, city editor of the *Sun,* who was being trained to succeed Dorsey as managing editor. Banker was followed in 1962 by Weldon Wallace, the *Sun*'s music critic and its first medical reporter. During Wallace's four years in Rome, he spent much of his time covering the Ecumenical Council of the Roman Catholic Church and was the only correspondent writing in English for the secular press to report day in and day out on the four sessions, which lasted until 1965. Altogether, Wallace missed one day—he had to rush off to northern Italy, where there was a disastrous flood.

While traveling in the Belgian Congo in 1963, Wallace and two other correspondents were arrested by drunken Katanganese troops who accused them of being spies for the United Nations. At gun point they were taken to an outpost in the bush. As they were ordered to strip off their clothing— the correspondents believed this was a prelude to being executed—an army major arrived and ordered them to be released unharmed. (In 1983, Timothy Phelps and Helen Winternitz, two *Sun* reporters on assignment to write about the Congo River, were arrested by security police in Zaire, had their notes and film confiscated, and were questioned and detained for eight days.)

When Wallace returned to Baltimore he became the paper's first religion editor and covered the subject on an international basis. He was succeeded in Rome by Thomas Fenton, later chief European correspondent of CBS, William F. Schmick 3d (in 1980 he was a member of a three-man team for Gannett News Service, which won a Pulitzer Prize), and Oswald L. Johnston, Jr. Because of growing tensions and fighting in the eastern Mediterranean, the Mideast bureau was moved in June 1972 to Beirut, with Stephen J. Lynton as chief. (Kay Withers, an assistant in the bureau for many years, remained in Rome as "correspondent in residence." In the 1980s she went to Warsaw as a free-lance correspondent and on a special basis to represent the *Sun* in Poland.)

In 1973, Lynton was succeeded by G. Jefferson Price 3d. He covered the Yom Kippur War and the subsequent prolonged disengagements. After civil war broke out in Lebanon in 1975, the Mideast bureau was moved to Cairo by Michael Parks, who took over from Price. Parks's successor, Douglas Watson, moved the bureau to Jerusalem. After writing editorials for the *Evening Sun,* Price returned to Jerusalem as Mideast correspondent in 1983.

Philip Potter was in Hyannisport, Massachusetts, the night after John F. Kennedy's election as President, when Dorsey telephoned to ask if he would open a bureau in New Delhi, which Potter did in January 1961. Potter, who stands six feet, three inches tall, received a cable from the White House announcing that President Kennedy was sending a man Potter could look up to—Ambassador Kenneth Galbraith, six feet, eight inches. Later Potter said of Galbraith, "I don't think he quite performed as adequately as I like to see a diplomat perform." Then, admitting his manner of dominating the give-and-take of Galbraith's informal meetings with the press, Potter added, "I felt he was not adequately informed about certain things and I proceeded to inform him." Potter's stories made Krishna Menon, minister of defense, so angry that Menon publicly berated Potter in his press conferences and finally stopped talking to him.

Potter covered India's invasion of the Portuguese enclave of Goa and India's border-fighting with China. Dorsey thought Potter's dispatches so outstanding—this from an editor not given to praise—that he submitted them for a Pulitzer Prize. When Potter did not win, Dorsey complained that the Pulitzer jury obviously could not recognize superlative work and announced that never again would he submit, or permit to be submitted, any *Sun* material to the Pulitzer committee.

After Potter returned to Washington he was at the White House one day when Galbraith arrived to see the President. "Well, Phil," he observed, "after running India I see you're now running the United States."

James S. Keat was sent to India in 1962 to work with Potter for several months. Louis Rukeyser moved from the London bureau in 1963 to replace Potter, then Keat returned to New Delhi in 1965 as bureau chief. During Keat's two years, India and Pakistan fought in Kashmir, tension continued between India and China, and India had to cope with domestic turmoil and famine. When Keat returned to Baltimore to become the first editor of the new *Sunday Sun* Perspective section, he was succeeded by Adam Clymer.

A South American bureau was opened in September 1962 by Nathan Miller, who had been the *Sun*'s first labor reporter. Dorsey wanted to locate the bureau in Sao Paulo, the commercial and industrial center of Brazil. William S. Abell, a member of the A. S. Abell board who was interested in news and editorial matters, thought this was a mistake. He invited Miller to lunch with a knowledgeable friend who had lived in Brazil. The friend maintained that locating the bureau in Sao Paulo would be comparable to a South American paper basing its only United States correspondent in Pittsburgh. Miller got the bureau placed in Rio de Janeiro. In the four years Miller was in South America—he and his successors were responsible for twenty-two countries—he covered revolutions in Brazil, Bolivia, and Argentina. By chance he arrived in Haiti as an attempt was made to overthrow the dictatorship of François Duvalier, and as the only visiting correspondent he was arrested until the attempted coup was squashed. Miller was followed by Arnold Isaacs in 1966, Robert Erlandson in 1969, and Richard P. O'Mara from 1973 to 1975, when the bureau was closed as a cost-saving measure. Ironically, O'Mara pointed out, while he was in Brazil an American advertising agency flew in a planeload of actors and technicians to film a Super Bowl beer commercial on the Amazon.

The minute-and-a-half commercial, he said, cost more than it cost to operate the *Sun* South American bureau for a year and a half.

While Dorsey was managing editor, it was his practice to give his correspondents an unbelievably free hand. They were sent off with only the broadest guidelines after a martini launching luncheon or dinner at the Maryland Club. Before Kumpa went to the Middle East in 1956 on his first foreign assignment, he asked Dorsey what he should cover. Dorsey replied, "If I didn't think you were a good reporter who would find out what to cover, I wouldn't send you abroad." When Kumpa asked what country he should go to first, Dorsey said, "I'm the editor. You're the reporter. You find out where the news is."

Dorsey seldom communicated with his correspondents. Only a few recalled specific orders. Furgurson said that although he was in Moscow for three years he could remember only several questioning cables: "Why didn't you cover such and such? Wires did. Love, Dorsey." After Dorsey started using stories about foreign restaurants on the food pages, busy correspondents sometimes got an ominous cable: "Send food stories. Or else. Love, Dorsey."

Sometimes correspondents would go months without word from Dorsey. The first nine months Bradford Jacobs was in London he heard nothing from the managing editor or anyone else. Before the 1955 Geneva summit meeting of the leaders of the United States, Great Britain, France, and the Soviet Union, Jacobs cabled Dorsey that he felt it imperative that he should be there. The reply was, "Oh, well. Okay. Love, Dorsey." Edward C. Burks, in Bonn, sent much the same message and received the same casual approval. Paul W. Ward, the *Sun*'s diplomatic correspondent, was in Geneva and regarded all aspects of the summit as his prerogative. Jacobs said he and Burks had to entreat Ward to get small pieces of it.

When Joseph R. L. Sterne was the London correspondent in the early 1960s, he became interested in the African independence movement. On an extended trip to Africa he had written a number of stories and had heard nothing from the *Sun*. From Bamako in Mali he wrote Dorsey asking what he thought of the pieces and if he had suggestions for future ones. Several weeks later he received this reply: "Your material from Africa is satisfactory, as I knew it would be or I would not have sent you. Now please stop asking me to write letters. Love, Dorsey."

Before leaving for his first assignment abroad, Kumpa sought practical advice from Thomas M. O'Neill. O'Neill's advice was, "After you cross the Susquehanna River, start traveling first class." (Kumpa found this enlightening and reassuring because the city desk had fussed with him for $3 cab fares.) When Kumpa was the Hong Kong bureau chief in the late 1960s, he got word that William F. Schmick, Jr., president of the A. S. Abell Company, his wife, Betty, and their friends, Robert Taylor, publisher of the *Philadelphia Bulletin,* and his wife, would be touring the Far East. Their itinerary for Japan, Hong Kong, and Thailand was attached. Feeling duty-bound to escort them throughout, Kumpa booked passage on the same flights the visitors would be taking. When they boarded their first flight, Kumpa discovered that they were flying economy class while he had booked first-class passage. In telling the story, Kumpa said, smiling, that he had become instilled in Asian ways and thought he might "lose face" if he switched to economy, so he traveled first class while the president and the publisher and their wives flew economy. Concerned about their comfort, Kumpa added that from time to time he would pop back to where they were sitting to ask, "Is there anything I can do for you?" James S. Keat, who had been in India twice and abroad on other assignments, said it was his theory that Dorsey wanted his men to go first class because Dorsey believed all travel was a hardship, and that included the drive from his home in North Baltimore to the Laurel Race Track. Keat added that Dorsey never objected to luxuries included on expense accounts but sometimes grumbled over what correspondents considered necessities. When Keat wanted to replace an ancient Telex machine, a hand-me-down from the Associated Press, Dorsey groused, "No, sir! I'm too old for such new-fangled contraptions."

In 1965, after the United States increased its military support of South Vietnam in counteraction to the invasion from North Vietnam, Dorsey began sending a succession of correspondents to cover the war. The first was Albert Sehlstedt, Jr., who was there for only a few weeks. Almost as soon as he arrived, the *Sun* shut down because of the American Newspaper Guild strike. Since it was pointless to cover and file spot news, and fearing that feature stories would become dated in a long strike (it lasted for seven weeks), Sehlstedt went home. After the strike ended, Peter Kumpa opened a Saigon office (considered temporary, it was not termed a bureau). Dorsey wanted stories for the front page on the top news of the day, but Kumpa preferred to write about the men fighting the war, so his stories "were cut and buried." After Kumpa came Ernest Furgurson (who made a second trip to Vietnam while writing *Westmoreland: The Inevitable General,* a biography of General William C. Westmoreland, commander of U.S. forces in Vietnam), and, among eight others, Robert A. Erlandson. Erlandson, who was slightly wounded by a North Vietnam booby trap, said he was more frightened covering the bloody street demonstrations protesting the Vietnam War during the 1968 Democratic National Convention in Chicago than he was in Vietnam.

Correspondents believed that a three-to-six-month tour in Vietnam was not long enough to become knowledgeable about the war or the country. When Paul A. Banker succeeded Dorsey as managing editor in 1966, he extended the tour, starting with Erlandson, to about a year. After assigning several correspondents, Banker felt that the war was winding down and he would tell the next replacement, "I'm sure you're the last one." Matthew J. Seiden, the last correspondent sent to Saigon, was told he could expect to be in the

Far East for a short time. He engaged a house-sitter for a few months and left with two suitcases. After six months in Vietnam, he was named bureau chief in Tokyo. His expected short stay stretched to four-and-a-half years. After he returned to Baltimore in 1978, his assignment was to write a local column.

During the Vietnam War the *Sun* opened two Far Eastern bureaus, Hong Kong in 1966 and Tokyo in 1968. Before long the paper was forced to relocate those bureaus as news developments shifted in unpredictable ways. At the same time, it jumped correspondents from place to place like chessmen. Peter Kumpa was the first Hong Kong bureau chief, with responsibilities for covering much of Asia. He was succeeded by John E. Woodruff in 1970 and Arnold Isaacs in 1973. When Seiden was transferred from Vietnam to Tokyo in 1974, Isaacs went back to Vietnam to cover the unraveling of the South Vietnamese army and government and the withdrawal of American forces. Isaacs was among those evacuated from the Saigon airport on April 29, 1975, the day the United States pulled its last military personnel out of Vietnam. He returned from Hong Kong in 1978 to become an editor in the *Sunday Sun* department, and in 1981 resigned to write *Without Honor: Defeat in Vietnam and Cambodia,* a critically acclaimed book.

His successor in Hong Kong was Michael Parks, who covered the opening in 1978 of diplomatic relations between the United States and China. After China invited American media to open bureaus, Parks established one for the *Sun* in Peking in October 1979. (The first *Sun* correspondent in China was Felix Morley, who was there for a short time in 1925 while traveling in the Far East. Morley later was a Pulitzer Prize winning editor of the *Washington Post* and then president of Haverford College.)

The Tokyo bureau, staffed by Thomas M. Pepper, Seiden, and then Bradley K. Martin, was closed in 1980 when Martin reopened the New Delhi bureau because of the Soviet invasion of Afghanistan, the execution of Pakistan's Prime Minister Zulfikar Ali Bhutto, the burning of the U.S. Embassy there, and Indira Gandhi's second term as prime minister of India. Martin was in India only a short time before he was transferred to Peking to succeed Parks. He in turn was followed by John E. Woodruff in 1983.

John Schidlovsky was sent from Baltimore to fill the New Delhi post. Although India and Pakistan did not continue as international news areas, Schidlovsky spent two years writing about the Indian states open to foreigners and reporting from twenty-two Southeast Asia countries, including Vietnam and the Philippines. When he returned to the states in 1983, the Far East bureau was moved to Tokyo because of Japan's economic resurgence and the impact it was having on the United States and other nations. Tony Barbieri was transferred from Moscow to Tokyo and, in addition to writing about Japan, covered the downfall of the Ferdinand E. Marcos government in the Philippines and the new administration of Corazon C. Aquino.

The Paris bureau, opened in 1968 to provide coverage of the French role in European, Asian, and African affairs, has been manned by five correspondents on an irregular basis. Thomas Fenton, the first bureau chief, was followed by Scott Sullivan, later the chief European correspondent of *Newsweek,* Gilbert A. Lewthwaite, Frederic B. Hill, and Robert Ruby. It was shut down after Lewthwaite's tour and reopened by Hill in 1976 for three years. After Bonn's bureau was phased out in 1983, the *Sun* moved its continental bureau to Paris because France was generating more news on a wider front, including the arts and fashion, and was more widely recognized as a cosmopolitan capital than Bonn.

During the years that the *Sun* opened, closed, and moved bureaus around the world, the London assignment remained constant and perhaps the most prestigious. The responsibilities of the London bureau broadened over the years and were enlarged when Banker became managing editor. For example, when Charles V. Flowers succeeded David Culhane in January 1967, his coverage included the Scandinavian countries, NATO meetings in Brussels, Franco's dwindling role in Spain, the six-day war in the Middle East, Romania's show of independence against the Soviet Union, and the civil war in Nigeria.

After Flowers came Daniel Berger, from the *Evening Sun* editorial staff, Philip Potter, for a year-and-a-half until he retired, and Frederic B. Hill, who also reported from South Africa and Spain and for much of 1974 and 1975 from Portugal, covering the revolution that ended the Salazar/Caetano dictatorship.

Peter Kumpa moved from chief of the Washington bureau to London in 1976 with the title of chief European correspondent, a new position. During his tour the *Sun* purchased a house for its London correspondent. Located in Kensington Court, a site used for movie locations, the terrace (town) house is several hundred years old. After moving twenty-two times during his career, Kumpa returned to Baltimore in 1979 as a columnist for the *Evening Sun,* writing about politics and Maryland history.

Kumpa's successor was Robert A. Erlandson, who in his four years covered the assassination of Lord Mountbatten, the Irish hunger strikes and accompanying violence, the marriage of Prince Charles and Princess Diana, the birth of their first son, and, from London, the war in the Falkland Islands. Erlandson was followed by Hal Piper for two-and-a-half years and by Gilbert A. Lewthwaite in February 1986.

In 1980 a South African bureau was opened in Johannesburg for three-and-a-half years to cover the apartheid regime, with Antero Pietila as bureau chief. He also made extensive tours of West and East Africa.

The *Sun*'s foreign bureaus had expanded to four by 1957 and were supplemented by correspondents on special assignment, but their flow of copy still passed over the desk of the news editor, Burwell C. Snyder, who also handled national news and supervised the copy desk. (When the flow was particularly heavy, two assistant managing editors—Daniel J. Meara and Harold S. Goodwin—helped evaluate the copy.) A colleague wrote of Snyder:

Each day he would come to work with his gray hair neatly plastered down. Each night he would leave for home with his hair mussed like a Hottentot's. Not only did he read the reams of wire-service copy, the heavy volume of correspondence from far-flung staffers and the grist of the local news-gathering mill, he also commented on it as it came in. And frequently those comments could be heard in the far reaches of the city room. He even demanded to see all the sports copy that came over the wires—copy that ordinarily would not come his way. At times on election nights, he would let his interests get the better of him. He more than once was so anxious to find out how his Democratic party was faring that he would yell for copy before it was written.

Snyder retired in 1957 at the age of 75. (His son, Cameron, was a *Sun* sports reporter for forty years, and Cameron's son, Dudley, works in the *Evening Sun*'s business-news department. By 1988 the three Snyders will have worked for the *Sun* for 100 years, though not consecutively.) Burwell Snyder was succeeded by Robert P. Anderson, the telegraph editor, one of the last old-time copy readers to wear a green eyeshade.

When Anderson retired in 1966 at the age of 76, Banker appointed Sam Abt as foreign and national editor, with two assistants, Hal Piper and Davison D. White. That dual role still proved unwieldy. In 1969, Banker named James S. Keat as foreign editor, Leo Coughlin as his assistant, and Stephen E. Nordlinger as national editor with White as his assistant. In 1972, Coughlin became foreign editor, serving in that capacity until 1979; Charles G. Whiteford succeeded Nordlinger as national editor, and Gilbert Watson 3d was named news editor.

In 1979 an extensive reorganization took place following the recommendations of the News Room Task Force which Banker had formed in the fall of 1978 to analyze all departments of the *Sun* and the *Sunday Sun*. In dealing with the foreign desk, the report quoted "one of the *Sun*'s most experienced foreign correspondents" as saying that an overseas reporter for the *Sun* "does what he believes is necessary. . . . He decides what he covers, when he does it, how long, etc. In this regard we are a most peculiar paper. No other news organization permits its men in the field such leeway." The report continued:

> The foreign editor has sought to improve communications with the foreign staff recently with a weekly memo. However, the editor and his staff "lack any continuing substantive dialogue on news coverage," as one *Sun* correspondent put it.
>
> Given the importance, the expense, the unfulfilled potential of its foreign news operation, it is essential for the *Sun* to strengthen the role of the foreign editor.
>
> The effectiveness of the foreign editor is currently undermined because he has little say in appointing correspondents. Correspondents tend to regard the managing editor as the actual chief of foreign operations. The foreign editor today is primarily a news clerk, obliged to spend his time scanning stories on the terminal and then fetching, transferring, chaining and copying reports to prepare each day's foreign pages. One editor calls it a "mindless, numbing" job. The uncertain authority of the foreign editor, coupled with a traditional "hands off" approach to the management of foreign bureaus, has hampered decision-making in Baltimore

on several instances when editors were faced with major international breaking stories. The *Sun* did not cover the Jonestown [Guyana] massacre last month. It did not cover the abduction of Aldo Moro [the former premier of Italy who was abducted and killed by the Red Brigade in 1978]. It barely got its correspondents to the scene to cover the 1973 Middle East War.

As an outgrowth of the report, Banker appointed Richard P. O'Mara, who had been Perspective editor for three years and an *Evening Sun* editorial writer for six years before becoming the South American correspondent, as foreign editor and Myron Beckenstein as his assistant. O'Mara was given broad autonomy in directing the foreign staff, in preparing its fiscal budget, and in selecting correspondents.

The task force had quoted a correspondent as noting that the foreign editor "lacks any continuing substantive dialogue on news coverage." O'Mara recalled that in the two-and-a-half years he had been in South America he had never gotten one telephone call from the *Sun* office. In the three years he had been in Hong Kong, Woodruff said he had telephoned the *Sun* just once—to dictate a story on the release of James E. Walsh, a Catholic bishop from Cumberland, Maryland, who had been imprisoned by Chinese Communists for twelve years.

Unlike the Swanson era, when a correspondent was dispatched overseas with little or no preparation—sometimes with only a day or two notice—a systematic plan for selecting and rotating correspondents was introduced by James I. Houck after he became managing editor of the *Sun* in 1982. Correspondents are usually posted for four years, and ideally two posts are rotated each year.

O'Mara made communication an integral part of the operation. Shortly after he became foreign editor he telephoned Erlandson in England. Erlandson, never expecting a call from Baltimore, asked incredulously, "What are you doing in London?" Instead of waiting for correspondents to file, O'Mara began telephoning them to ask what was developing in their areas, to suggest stories, and to keep them informed on home-office planning and what the Washington bureau and the other foreign correspondents had under way. The foreign desk's overseas telephone bill averages $1,500 a month. Periodically O'Mara goes abroad to confer with correspondents and, when conditions warrant, to scout new bureau locations.

Because of turmoil in Central America, particularly in San Salvador and Nicaragua, and Mexico's problematic economic and social relationships with the United States, a bureau was opened in Mexico City in 1983. James Bock, who had lived in Latin America and covered the Falkland Islands war for the *Sun*, was named the first bureau chief.

O'Mara prepares a rotation schedule for each bureau, showing bureau openings for the next three years. The schedule indicates when applicants can apply for a post, when the correspondent will be selected, and the posting date.

For most bureaus, the correspondent has five months between selection and placement, time used to prepare for the assignment and study a foreign language if that is necessary. Those assigned to Peking or Moscow were given a year's leave to study the language at a university or language institute. Correspondents selected for those two posts are now sent abroad for two weeks of indoctrination and to get a taste of that life before they begin language training.

Houck introduced a home-leave policy, every two years, and a "repatriation plan," so correspondents know in advance what their next assignment will be. In recent times, some correspondents have been transferred from one bureau to another. After his Moscow assignment, Hal Piper attended Stanford University for a year as a National Endowment for the Humanities Fellow, then was assigned to the Bonn bureau and from there to the London bureau. When he returned from England he succeeded Stephens Broening as Opinion-Commentary editor for the *Sun*'s op-ed page. Antero Pietila moved from the Johannesburg bureau in South Africa in 1983 to the Moscow bureau. Anthony Barbieri was transferred from Moscow to Tokyo late that year. His tour ends in February 1988, and the 1986 rotation schedule noted, "For this job there is a preferred candidate."

SEVENTEEN

Reaching 150 Years
1981–1987

For sixty-two years, from 1919 to 1981, the *Sunpapers* were directed by two sets of fathers and sons: Paul Patterson, William F. Schmick, Sr., William F. Schmick, Jr., and Donald H. Patterson. That dynastic control ended on July 1, 1981, when at age 47 John R. (Reg) Murphy became publisher of the *Sunpapers*, the first person to be brought in from outside and put in charge since Charles H. Grasty became president, editor, and general manager of a reorganized company in 1910.

In selecting Murphy, the Abell board broke with tradition for three weighty reasons: No one within the company seemed a likely prospect; it was believed that someone with a more diversified background could instill an invigorating perspective; and Organization Resources Counselors, the New York consulting group studying the management system, had recommended that the new chief executive have a strong orientation toward modern business management. A board member commented, "We did not know of anyone of that disposition and background, and perhaps it was unreasonable to expect us to find one. Solving the problem in the *Sun* family environment was psychologically impossible. A dispassionate study was needed." The board appointed a three-member search committee: Gary Black, chairman, William S. Abell, and William E. McGuirk, Jr. They sought a chief executive officer for both the company's newspapers and its radio and television stations. A New York "headhunter" was engaged, but the search was unsatisfactory and ended when the "headhunter" was killed in an automobile accident. The board then engaged Hague & Company, an Illinois firm specializing in recruiting talented executives. The firm produced five candidates, and after the choice had been narrowed to three the board unanimously picked Murphy. When the company formed two divisions, the A. S. Abell Publishing Company and Abell Communications, Murphy was named president and chief executive officer as well as publisher of the publishing division. (Stephen D. Seymour, who was president of WMAR-TV, continued as chief executive officer of Abell Communications.) When Donald H. Patterson relinquished executive responsibilities for the publishing division, in January 1982 he became president of the A. S. Abell Company, the parent organization.

Murphy was born in Gainesville, Georgia, on January 7, 1934. He worked his way through Mercer University as a sports reporter on the morning *Macon Telegraph*. His ambition was to attend medical school but, lacking funds, he stayed with the paper after college and became chief of its Atlanta bureau. In 1959–60 he was a Nieman Fellow at Harvard. He was political reporter and political editor of the *Atlanta Constitution* from 1961 to 1965, when he left the paper to become a management consultant and to free-lance for magazines. In 1968 he was invited to return to the *Constitution* as editor and daily columnist. He co-authored a book on politics, *The Southern Strategy*.

On February 20, 1974, a man appeared at Murphy's home, asking for advice on how to give 100,000 gallons of heating oil to charity. When that ruse got Murphy outdoors, the man, who identified himself as a member of a revolutionary army, pulled out a pistol and said he was kidnapping Murphy, because "I'm going to straighten out the lying, leftist liberal press in America." Murphy's feet were tied, his hands bound behind him and his eyes taped. Then he was pushed into the trunk of the kidnapper's car and for two days he was held prisoner in a house. Murphy was finally set free when the *Constitution* paid $700,000 in ransom. Hours later the kidnapper, one William A. H. Williams, was arrested and the money was recovered. Williams served a nine-year prison term.

Because of the headline value of the kidnapping and Murphy's own graphic account of the ordeal, Murphy became a national figure. (That spring Murphy was playing in a pro-am golf tournament; one of the foursome was "Sonny" Jurgensen, a quarterback for the Washington Redskins. Upon approaching every green, Murphy would be met with applause. Finishing the hole, he would be asked for his autograph. After this happened at five or six holes, Jurgensen, who rightly believed that *he* was the celebrity of the foursome, turned to Murphy and asked, "Who the hell are you anyway?")

Murphy's kidnapping occurred two weeks after Patty Hearst, daughter of Randolph A. Hearst, publisher of the *San Francisco Examiner*, was abducted from her apartment by members of the Symbionese Liberation Army, who demanded that her father give millions to the poor. About a year later, Randolph Hearst, who had become interested in Murphy's career after his kidnapping, invited him to become editor-publisher of the *Examiner*. The original Hearst newspaper, the *Examiner*, had come to be the Hearst chain's flagship.

At first resistant to the offer, Murphy joined the *Examiner* in September 1975. Eighteen days later, the FBI arrested Patty Hearst, who had joined the Symbionese Liberation Army, participated in a bank robbery, and been an "armed, dangerous fugitive" for more than a year and a half. Murphy had told his reporters to cover the story as if Patty were the daughter of the owner of the *New York Times*. It was reported that Randolph Hearst did not interfere with that detailed coverage but sometimes complained afterward.

In the early 1970s the *Examiner*, an afternoon paper, and the larger *San Francisco Chronicle*, a morning paper, began producing their papers from the same plant, to reduce costs. Each retained its own news and editorial staffs and a skeletal business staff, but a formula was instituted for apportioning gross revenues between the two papers.

When Murphy took over the *Examiner*, in its heyday the "Monarch" of the Hearst dailies, it was specializing in murder and mayhem. He set out to modernize the paper, retiring more than fifteen employees over the age of 65, reorganizing the staff, hiring a new managing editor, improving the business and sports sections, placing more national news and in-depth pieces on the front page, and redesigning the paper.

The announcement of Murphy's appointment as publisher of the A. S. Abell Publishing Company disconcerted many in the *Sunpaper* family. How could an outsider know and accept the tried-and-true ways of the *Sunpapers*? And he was coming not from the *New York Times* but from a *Hearst* paper, the name Hearst conjuring up memories of old-time sensationalism. Would the *Sun*'s staid presentation of news give way to yellow journalism? And would heads roll? *Sunpaper* employees were settled in their jobs and had not worried about job security. Beyond the paper, how would Murphy adapt to Baltimore, and Baltimore respond to his ways? The town was provincial compared with cosmopolitan San Francisco.

When Murphy arrived in the summer of 1981 he saw "the *Sun* as a great paper, but one that had fallen behind the times," overshadowed by such papers as the *Boston Globe*, the *Philadelphia Inquirer*, and the *Miami Herald*, which were leaders at new-idea testing and adopting. He believed that the *Sun* had not come to terms with its inherent contradictions. It stressed national and international coverage, but its readers regarded it as a Maryland newspaper. It could not become a national paper in scope or influence because, having long since lost out in its White Paper designs on Washington, it did not have national distribution or a national audience.

He found that the papers had a healthy circulation system but lacked aggressiveness. The new $36 million four-color Goss Metroliner offset presses were state-of-the-art, but had not been committed to full-color capacity. He felt that "virtually nothing" had been done in data-processing, which he foresaw as a prime expansion area in newspaper operations.

Murphy walks through the building almost every day, stopping to chat, ask questions, and receive suggestions. His manner is informal, relaxed. If addressed as "Mr. Murphy" he invariably responds, "Call me Reg." Of medium height with the trimness and casual posture of an athlete (he played semi-pro baseball in Georgia and is a handicap golfer who plays in the pro-am event of major tournaments), he runs 2¹/₂ to 3 miles most days, starting at 5:45 A.M. from his home in Murray Hill. He works in shirt sleeves, not bothering to put on a coat when his picture is taken. The coat is draped on an office doorknob.

Murphy introduced annual publisher's assemblies with employees. These took the form of an hour-long session, repeated throughout a day and an evening so that employees on different shifts could participate. Unfazed by seven or eight consecutive sessions, Murphy would talk of company plans and answer questions: What are the possibilities of layoffs? Will the *Evening Sun* be dropped? Why weren't the Library, Ad Service, Checking, Bookkeeping, and Billing included in the promotion department's new slide-presentation show? Such communication was supplemented with a "Publisher's Memo" in *Between Editions,* the employee paper.

Murphy's management philosophy is based on goals—goals that have shared values—and communication. Shortly after taking charge, Murphy developed a five-year plan for growth and change:

Expand the *Sun*'s network of foreign bureaus. (A Mexico City bureau was opened in 1983 to cover Latin America.)

Broaden *Evening Sun*'s news coverage, improve the quality of its writing, and strengthen its role as "the voice" of the metropolitan area.

Reorganize some sections of the *Sunday Sun.*

Focus more attention on working women, two-income families, and readers who stay home.

Strengthen circulation within the five-county region, particularly among minorities not buying the *Sunpapers,* and boost circulation at an annual rate exceeding the growth of households in the metropolitan area.

Increase advertising lineage at a pace greater than the annual cost-of-living index.

Explore expansion of the A. S. Abell Publishing division into such areas as regional magazines or acquiring weeklies or small dailies.

The planned retirement of Dudley P. Digges, editor of the *Evening Sun* editorial page, in August 1981 provided the first look at what Murphy had in mind by way of new management. Digges was succeeded by Ray Jenkins, age 55. A native of Sylvester, Georgia, Jenkins began his career as a reporter with the *Columbus* (Georgia) *Ledger* and was a member of the team that won the 1955 Pulitzer Prize for its exposé of political corruption in Phenix City, Alabama. In 1959, Jenkins became city editor of the *Alabama Journal* in Montgomery and then managing editor and editor of its editorial page. From 1976 to 1978 he was editorial-page editor of the *Montgomery Advertiser* and then was named editor and vice president of the *Montgomery Advertiser* and the *Alabama Journal.* He was a Nieman Fellow at Harvard in 1964–65 and has a law degree. In 1979 he became a special assistant to President Jimmy Carter. Before joining the *Evening Sun,* he was publisher of the *Clearwater Sun* in Florida. Jenkins quickly made his mark in Baltimore, winning the national Ernie Pyle Award for human interest reporting, for a collection of editorial-page columns written after joining the *Evening Sun.*

Jenkins hired as his deputy Sara Engram, editorial-page editor of the Baltimore *News American.* Engram, a native of Alabama, has a master's degree from the Yale Divinity School. An editorial introducing Engram to the readers noted, "We trust she will exert a somewhat restraining influence on occasional irreverent lapses." The staff includes Gwinn F. Owens, Mike Bowler (editor of the Other Voices page), and Glenn McNatt, who had been with Time-Life Books, writing for their history series, and before that had taught at Wellesley. (Daniel Berger, of the *Sun* editorial staff, contributes pithy comments on the news, called "Italicisms," which appear under the editorials.)

McNatt's predecessor was James H. Bready, who joined the *Evening Sun* news staff in 1945 and was an editorial writer from 1952 to 1985, earning the accolade "Dean of Baltimore editorialists." His column, "Books and Authors," which started in the *Sunday Sun* in October 1954 and still continues, makes Bready the longest-running columnist on the three papers. Bready is the author of *The Home Team,* a history of Baltimore baseball, published in 1958. The longest running nonstaff column is "Baltimore Glimpses," reminiscences of people and places by free-lancer Gilbert Sandler, which has appeared on the Other Voices page since 1975.

Murphy began making management changes early in 1982. After Paul A. Banker, managing editor of the *Sun* for sixteen years, turned down the position of senior editor and retired, Murphy hired as his successor James I. Houck, the 40-year-old associate managing editor of the *Dallas Morning News.* Houck had been news editor of the *San Francisco Examiner* for six years under Murphy before going to Dallas in 1981, shortly before Murphy came to Baltimore. A Californian, Houck graduated from the University of California at Berkeley, where he was managing editor of the *Daily Californian.* In 1963 he joined the *Examiner* as a copy editor and was promoted to telegraph editor, then to news editor.

Robert H. Kavanaugh retired in March 1982 after thirty-three years with the company, almost half of that time spent in senior management. A month earlier he had been promoted by Murphy to senior vice president responsible for the Abell Publishing Company's properties and new ventures. Before that he was vice president, secretary, and general manager. His father, Emmett P. Kavanaugh, had been vice president, secretary, and business manager.

Richard M. Basoco was promoted three times in three years by Murphy. In 1982 he moved from director of human resources to director of administrative services, in 1983 to senior vice president for administration, and in 1984 he was given the additional responsibilities of general manager in charge of advertising, circulation, and production. A favorite Murphy story is that Basoco received these promotions while engaged in labor negotiations that lasted eighteen months. The Murphy punch line: "The guessing around the building was that if the negotiations had gone on for another month he would have had my job." Basoco joined the *Sun* in 1966 as a reporter and later became maritime editor. He was chairman of the Baltimore Newspaper Guild from 1970 to 1973, and was president of the Washington-Baltimore Newspaper Guild from 1973 to 1974. Later he became assistant sports editor. In 1975 he switched to the business side of the papers as training and development manager, and in 1978 he became director of human resources. He was succeeded by Sandra H. Gill.

Peter L. Stegner, age 44, who had been director of advertising for the *Rochester Democrat and Chronicle* and the *Rochester Times-Union*, Gannett Company newspapers in New York, became advertising director in October 1982, succeeding Robert E. Trainor, who retired. The following spring, Diana M. Zinda was promoted to national advertising manager, Gerald V. Smolinski to manager of public affairs, and John Patinella from assistant circulation director to circulation director. The former director, Edward L. Bennett, was named a senior consultant.

Murphy's management committee has fifteen members: John J. Banach, Jr., vice president/labor relations; Richard M. Basoco, senior vice president and general manager; Louis J. Franconeri, vice president/operations; Ann T. Gallant, marketing and communications director; Sandra H. Gill, director of human resources; Jean Halle, director of task forces; James I. Houck, managing editor of the *Sun;* Ray Jenkins, editor of the *Evening Sun* editorial page; John M. Lemmon, managing editor of the *Evening Sun;* James P. McCrystal, director of computer services; John F. Patinella, circulation director; James D. Shaw, director of finance; Diana M. Zinda, advertising director; Joseph R. L. Sterne, editor of the *Sun*'s editorial page; Donald W. Thurlow, publisher for the suburban editions.

Gary Black, Jr., began working for the *Sunpapers* in the circulation department in 1969 and four years later was elected a member of the board of directors. While on the board he also was assistant to the president, then marketing services manager, director of marketing and communications, and sales and marketing director, responsible for advertising and circulation sales and the distribution and marketing of the newspapers. Murphy thought it unusual for a member of his management group also to be on the board that passed judgment on management. He promoted Black to vice president of the parent organization, the A. S. Abell Company, in charge of development for company-wide diversification into new market areas and to operate the acquired property.

In 1982 the Abell Publishing Company acquired the monthly *Mid-Atlantic Country* magazine, whose themes are the Middle Atlantic states and travel. It has a circulation of about 102,000. In 1984 the company purchased *Ski Racing International,* a monthly published from September through May and distributed nationally to some 26,000 subscribers. Gary Black, Jr., became publisher of that magazine, which has its headquarters in Waitsfield, Vermont.

Three weeks after Murphy arrived, he began making changes and improvements in the papers. The first change in the *Sun* was to move Sports to the front of a new section that also contained Business. (Sports had been buried in the local news section, and Business, with the financial tables, was in the main news section.)

As he had in San Francisco, Murphy strengthened those two sections. Beginning in October 1982, special Business sections were printed on Wednesday in the *Sun* and the *Evening Sun,* and in the spring of 1983 Business became a special section in the *Sunday Sun,* with expanded news and financial tables. Philip T. Moeller, who had written about business and finance for the *Louisville Courier-Journal* and the *Chicago Sun-Times,* was named business editor of the *Sun* and director of its financial news department. A New York bureau was opened in September 1985 to cover national business and financial news. Patricia Fanning was appointed financial news editor of the *Evening Sun.*

Substantial changes were made in Sports, both morning and evening. Marty Kaiser, who had been the executive sports editor of the *Chicago Sun-Times,* was appointed to that position on the *Sun.* For years *Sunpaper* sports coverage had been parochial, limited to local teams except for such national standbys as the World Series, the Super Bowl, and the Kentucky Derby. Now the papers began covering the All-England tennis tournament at Wimbledon, golf's British Open, the quadrennial World Cup soccer elimination, and other important contests across the United States. New writers hired from other papers around the nation added a new dimension to the reporting and the quality of the writing. Four years in a row the Associated Press Sports Editors Association selected the *Evening Sun* Sports section as one of the top ten sports sections in the nation. *Sunday Sun* Sports consisted of two thick sections, one of the largest sports sections of a metropolitan paper.

Four months after Murphy took charge, he made changes in the *Sunday Sun.* Maryland Kitchen, a food section, was created; the Trend section became Maryland Living, emphasizing the home and interior decorating; and Society—for years possibly the only feature section of a metropolitan paper with a full-page ad for its front page—turned into People. (Planning for this predated Murphy's arrival.)

For some fifty years, Society had led off with two full pages of weddings and engagements. The first page, with two- and three-column studio photographs, was restricted to young women who made their debut at the Bachelors Cotillon or whose parents were listed in the Social Register or the Society Visiting List (the so-called Blue Book) or, depending on available space, who were from a prominent family (e.g., the father might be a bank or corporation president). The second page, with smaller pictures, was peopled by brides and fiancées from the better neighborhoods or colleges. Announcements from ordinary Baltimoreans were relegated to the back of the section with brief text and one-column pictures. Now and then a blue blood whose daughter's picture had not been published with the prominence or the page position the family considered its due would telephone to berate the society editor, Sally D. Goodhue, who succeeded George Dorsch.

The People section was instead a democratic assortment of personalities, picture layouts of receptions and parties, and a variety of columns. Wedding and engagement announcements were placed as far back as they could go. Pictures were one-column wide, and the accompanying details were uniform in length. The disappearance of Society gave rise to the shrillest complaints the *Sunpapers* had received in years. A commercial photographer who specialized in the wedding and engagement pictures that had appeared on the first page told Murphy his business was ruined.

In telling that story, Murphy added, shaking his head, "And I knew nothing about the Bachelors Cotillon." About forty (at one time as many as seventy) teenage girls from old Baltimore families are invited to make their debut at this exclusive annual ball. Once the Cotillon's prestige was so great that Baltimore acknowledged as debutantes only those who were presented. Stories were told that some girls believed their lives were socially ruined because they were not invited to make their debut. An oddity of the ball is that a mother of a deb is invited as a chaperone, but if the father is not a subscriber to the Cotillon he is not invited. Preceding the Cotillon the Society section would carry four pages of pictures of the debutantes and descriptions of what they would wear and the flowers they would carry, although the Board of Governors would not permit newspapers to cover the event itself. After the Society section gave way to People, the pre-Cotillon elaborate coverage was no longer printed. Many mothers and fathers of debutantes were outraged and vented their resentment on Murphy in letters and in person. "For the first year-and-a-half I was here," he recalled, "at social gatherings I was a pariah." But he could point out that readership surveys showed Society as low as 17 percent among Sunday subscribers, while the new People section soon had a 54 percent readership.

The Sunday Perspective commentary section, edited by M. William Salganik, was reorganized to include reports on science, technology, education, and the environment, a summary of Maryland news, Ernest B. Furgurson's USA column, and Memo from Washington by various members of the Washington bureau. Display and classified real estate advertising, which had been in two different parts of the Sunday paper, were integrated in the two Real Estate sections. The *Sun Magazine,* under the editorship of Susan Baer, was redesigned and given a broader, more contemporary focus. The *Sun*'s feature section, which had a different theme each day, was restyled as the Today section, covering entertainment, lifestyle, consumer and spectator information, and merchandising news. The tabloid *Maryland Live,* an entertainment guide to Baltimore and Maryland, was added to the Friday *Sun* in February 1987. A four-page fashion feature became part of the Thursday Today section in March 1987.

For years the *Sun* was Baltimore-city-oriented in its local reporting, concentrating on the city's government, institutions, politics, and police news. Under James I. Houck, the managing editor, coverage has broadened and intensified in the four metropolitan counties, and to a growing extent in the state as well. The local section is titled "Maryland," but major local stories go on the front page. With this extended coverage, the *Sun* has become less a paper of record. Until recent times it printed a list of all bills introduced in the Maryland legislature, a list of all bills passed, and then a list of those signed by the governor. Now the lists are pared to the most important legislation. And the *Sun,* for example, no longer prints the agendas of the City Council and municipal boards. Space limitations preclude doing that for the city and the metropolitan counties. The paper has deemphasized reporting announcements and formal procedures of government and institutions. Thomas Linthicum, Jr., the metropolitan editor, said, "In today's complicated world we have to be selective in what we print. We think we best serve the reader by taking the most significant actions of government, explaining and backgrounding them—and showing how they affect the public." Fewer reporters are assigned to the Baltimore police districts and to the courts. "At one time," Linthicum said, "there was more emphasis on crime and punishment in this paper than there is now. Today we believe the reader is interested in community and lifestyle stories."

To broaden county news coverage, two new zoned sections were introduced: the *Harford County Sun* in 1984 and the *Carroll County Sun* in 1985. The *Sun* then had zoned sections in all four metropolitan counties. (Zoned sections had been started in Anne Arundel and Howard counties in the late 1970s). The four tabloids, originally published on a weekday, now are included in the *Sunday Sun.* In the fall of 1986, the *Anne Arundel County Sun* also became a weekday-zoned section. In 1983 the *Sun* added an Ocean City bureau for the vacation season, and in 1986 it introduced Ocean City, a zoned supplement in the *Sunday Sun* distributed all summer the length of the Maryland-Delaware resort coast.

John M. Lemmon succeeded Philip S. Heisler as managing editor of the *Evening Sun* in October 1979. A native of Illinois, he attended the United States Naval Academy before graduating from the University of Illinois with a degree in journalism. During the Korean War he served in the Navy and taught English at the Naval Academy before joining the *Washington Star* in 1956, becoming chief of the copy desk. Lemmon taught at Ohio State University for two years before joining the Washington *Post* in 1966. He served as chief of the metropolitan copy desk, news editor, and night managing editor, then headed the task force that directed the technological changes at the *Post.*

The *Evening Sun* has become a strongly oriented community newspaper for the Baltimore metropolitan area. To supplement its bureau in Towson, the county seat of Baltimore county, Lemmon opened bureaus in Dundalk and Pikesville, in the southeast and northwest corners of the county which wraps around Baltimore City. Often the paper's front page is all local news and features. When the paper was redesigned, emphasis was placed on bold, eye-catching graphics—color photographs and drawings, maps and charts, with indexes and boxes as guideposts for the reader. The *Evening Sun* prints four editions, and its final, the All Star, designed for street sale, has a remade front page with a different color bar atop the page, many times with a color photograph of a late morning news event. William E. N. Hawkins, assistant managing editor in charge of the metropolitan staff of some forty reporters, said, "We are not a formula paper—we like to experiment in the way stories are written. Reporters are given a great deal of leeway in writing." In hiring he looks for "bright people with a range of interests and rounded background who can write." These have included an architectural student from Yale and a chemistry major. Many, like *Sun* staff members, have master's degrees in nonjournalism subjects. The *Evening Sun* illuminates local news with investigative series on municipal government, urban social issues, the ramifications of crime, and other subjects that affect readers everywhere.

A December 1983 series, "Home Without Fathers: The Poverty Cycle," on black, single-parent families, was denounced by representatives of the Baltimore branch of the National Association for the Advancement of Colored People (NAACP) as "biased" and "grossly insensitive." Although the *Evening Sun* pointed out that the articles themselves were in line with what the national NAACP and the National Urban League had found, local NAACP members saw the series as an example of the way newspapers cover the negative impact of racial discrimination rather than its causes. They called for increased hiring of black reporters, correspondents, editors, and managers, more positive coverage of Baltimore's black community, and establishment of a foreign bureau in Africa. (The *Sun* had a bureau in Johannesburg, South Africa, from 1980 to March 1983, when it was closed as part of a reorganization of its foreign bureaus.) In February 1984, in an effort to get the papers to meet its demands, the NAACP picketed the newspaper's offices and called for a circulation boycott. The boycott and sporadic picketing ended in early April when an agreement was reached with the *Baltimore Sun* over the company's hiring policies and coverage of the black community.

In a prepared statement published in the *Sun* on April 6, 1984, the Abell Publishing Company said it was "committed to continued recruiting and promotion of members of the minority community, to balanced, comprehensive and fair coverage of all communities in Maryland, to expression of opinion from all constituencies, and to continued quality coverage of all parts of the world." The company said it also would continue to "vigorously pursue its proposal for a suitable memorial for Clarence M. Mitchell, Jr.," which the *Sun* had suggested in an editorial shortly after the noted Baltimore civil rights activist died in March 1984. The following March, the Baltimore city courthouse was named in his honor, and in conjunction with its dedication the *Sun* and the *Evening Sun* published a special magazine, "A Vision of Justice, A Legacy of Humanity," about Mitchell and his achievements, which contained a number of the 253 columns he had written for the *Sunday Sun* op-ed page between his retirement in 1979 and his death.

When the NAACP held its national convention in Baltimore in 1986, the same year it moved its national headquarters to Baltimore from New York, the *Sun* and the *Evening Sun* published a special convention magazine, "Building for Equality." James B. Parks, the weekend metropolitan editor of the *Sun* who edited the magazine, noted in a "Letter from the Editor" that "the *Sun* has a black editor overseeing this special publication as well as both black and white reporters covering the NAACP's 77th annual convention. And I am not the only black here. On both the *Sun* and *Evening Sun,* three of 48 news officials including editors and directors and three of 15 editorial writers are black. Over one-eighth of our newsroom staff of 338 is black."

Since 1980 the A. S. Abell Publishing Company has offered an all-expense journalism scholarship for minority students to attend the University of Maryland's College of Journalism. The scholarship includes a paid summer internship and qualifies every winner for full-time employment after graduation.

In 1983, for the first time in their history, the *Sun* and the *Evening Sun* became a combined paper, the *Holiday Sun,* with morning delivery on July 4, Labor Day, Christmas, and New Year's Day. This was done for reasons of production and economy. In subsequent years the *Holiday Sun* also appeared on Thanksgiving Day and Memorial Day. Beginning in March 1984 a combined paper was printed for morning delivery on Saturday with four sections: News, Sports, Home & Garden and Saturday. Murphy said this was done to meet the "special weekend needs of readers." The *Sun* produced news, sports, the editorial page and Home & Garden. The section titled Saturday was put together by the *Evening Sun.* Before the combined paper appeared, the *Sun*'s Saturday circulation was about 161,000, some 20,000 less than its weekday circulation, and the *Evening Sun*'s circulation was 133,000, some 30,000 below its weekday sales. The combined *Sun* is now 376,000.

The *Evening Sun* staff and the American Newspaper Guild, representing 600 company employees, questioned whether the combining of the two papers was not the first step toward a possible merger and the disappearance of the *Evening Sun.* (More concern was voiced in May 1986 after the Baltimore *News American* stopped publishing.) On a number of occasions Murphy declared that no merger was contemplated.

Color photographs and illustrations were used tentatively, and never on the front page of the *Sun* before Murphy arrived. When Gary Black was chairman of the board, he opposed using color on the front page because he believed it would detract from the character of the paper. (For years Black and Charles H. Dorsey, Jr., the *Sun*'s managing editor, would not permit advertisements using color to run in the main news section.) Murphy made a presentation to the board showing that fourteen of the nation's twenty leading newspapers had begun using color, without page restrictions. Black changed his mind, and color began appearing on the *Sun*'s front page and on section fronts for both papers, not only for feature material but for spot news and sports pictures as well.

Because of the extensive use of color, and with more emphasis on photography in general, the Photographic department was reorganized and strengthened. (A longtime practice on the morning paper had been to throw out photographs to make space for stories. Up until the mid-1960s, the *Sun*'s front page sometimes had only a one-column picture, and often no pictures at all.) K. Kenneth Paik was named director of photography. A native of Korea, he had been director of news illustrations for the *Florida Times-Union* and the *Jacksonville Journal* and had held the same position with the *Kansas City Star and Times*. (In 1986, Paik became an assistant managing editor of the *Evening Sun*. David M. Lewis succeeded him as director of photography.) The new breed of photographers, using ultra-sophisticated color film and lighting, were professionally trained. Their predecessors, often promoted from the ranks of copy boys, had picked up their training on the job. Some, not long retired, could remember when illumination was obtained by igniting flash powder with a match. All used the bulky Speed Graphic camera with glaring flashbulb to snap everything from spot news and action sports to portraits.

The new management found the papers' appearance forbidding and sought to make them more attractive and readable. Emphasis was placed on graphics— charts, graphs, maps. In commenting on the new graphic look, James I. Houck, the *Sun*'s managing editor, remarked, "The well-written paragraph is not always the most effective means of communication."

The *Sunpapers* were once known as a reporter's paper because the experienced reporter was given free rein (one foreign correspondent called it "a long leash"), and their stories, usually long, were seldom cut. Today Murphy refers to the *Sun* and the *Evening Sun* as "writers'/photographers'/designers'/editors' papers." "And that," he adds, "makes them a reader's paper."

The *Sun*'s front page is far different from what it was, with more color (Murphy believes a color picture "gets more the smell of the street" than a black-and-white print) and more local news, often as the lead story. "If you are to be Maryland's newspaper," Murphy points out, "news that impacts locally has to be given prominence."

News stories were shortened to get more news into the paper. A news story longer than forty inches (about two columns) must be approved by an assistant managing editor. Editors supervising copy were told to exercise more control in the preparation and editing of stories. Well aware of the competition from television, they strive not only to cover breaking news faster but also to give news fuller meaning by analyzing causes and effects.

Not all readers and staff members agreed with what was done. Some believed that in remaking the *Sun* to give it a broader, more contemporary appeal its distinctive personality, based on a long tradition, was blurred if not lost. But many felt that the papers had fallen behind other major newspapers. In a letter to Between Editions, a member of the editorial staff declared, "The management of these newspapers has given them a shaking up that is distressing to some, less so to others, but arguably, in the long run, essential for their survival."

In 1985, as if in confirmation of these new directions, Alice Steinbach, a *Sun* feature reporter, won the Pulitzer Prize for feature-writing, and Jon D. Franklin, an *Evening Sun* special reporter, won his second Pulitzer. (It is unusual for one organization to win two Pulitzers, the most prestigious award in journalism, in one year.) Steinbach's story described the world of a blind fourth-grade student. It appeared in the *Sun Magazine* and was illustrated with photographs by David W. Harp. It was the tenth Pulitzer for the *Sun,* but its first in thirty-six years. Franklin's award, in a new category of "explanatory journalism," was for "The Mind Fixers," a seven-part series on research on the frontiers of brain chemistry and psychiatry. It was the second Pulitzer for the *Evening Sun* in six years. In 1979, Franklin won the award in feature-writing for "Tales from the Gray Frontier," a two-part story about an astonishing brain operation. Franklin left the *Evening Sun* in 1985 to teach journalism at the University of Maryland, his alma mater.

In recent years the papers have encouraged staff members to enter contests, and they have won a number of national and regional awards for news and sports reporting, commentary, photography, and graphic design.

The *Sun* has a staff of 254, including its bureaus, the features and sports department, and support personnel. Houck's three assistant managing editors are James S. Keat, news (national, foreign, and metropolitan) and Library; John H. Plunkett, Photographic, Business, Sports, copy desk, and news technology; and Gilbert L. Watson, 3d, features, daily and Sunday. John B. O'Donnell, Jr., is night editor, Richard C. D'Agostino is design director, and Donna L. Albano is design editor.

Thomas Linthicum, Jr., the metropolitan editor, has a metropolitan desk composed of Rebecca L. Corbett, city editor; Suzanne W. Wooton, state editor; Stephen Proctor, counties editor; Carol M. Frey, regional affairs editor; Peter C. Meredith, weekend metropolitan editor; Peter Wetmore is weekend editor, Sam Fulwood, night metro editor, and Edwin H. Brandt, Jr., is special sections editor. The metropolitan desk directs a staff of about forty rewrite persons and reporters. Veteran staff members include Rafael M. Alvarez, Sandra A. Banisky, Jerry Bembry, DeWitt Bliss, Michael Burns, Eileen M. Canzian, Michael J. Clark, Will Englund, Robert A. Erlandson, David Michael Ettlin, Jesse Glasgow, Edna Goldberg, Deborah Greene, Karen A. Hosler, Mary A. Knudson, Kathy Lally, Laura S. Lyons, Joel S. McCord, Albert Sehlstedt, Jr., Theodore F. Shelsby, Richard H. P. Sia, C. Fraser Smith, Frank P. L. Somerville, Louis Roger Twigg, Sr., and Karen M. Warmkessel.

The copy desk includes Andrew D. Faith, chief of copy desk; and Jerry M. Bayne, Judith E. Burke, Michael T. Dresser, Carol L. Gesser, Bruce G.

Guthrie, Leslie V. Hall, Terry Jones, Jeffrey M. Landaw, Michael R. Levene, Clay C. Perry, Scott D. Ponemone, Harold S. Roberts, David P. Thomas, John D. Tullier, and Frederick S. Vondy.

Sun columnists are Róger Simon, a nationally syndicated columnist with the *Chicago Sun-Times* who joined the staff in November 1984 and has twice won the American Society of Newspaper Editors award for distinguished commentary; Michael Olesker, a Baltimorean who joined the paper in 1979; Rob Kasper, the "Happy Eater" columnist for the food sections; and Laura Charles, who writes about people and parties.

The critics are Stephen C. Hunter, film; Stephen Wigler, music; John Dorsey, art; J. Wynn Rousuck, drama; and William C. Carter, television. Carleton Jones is restaurant reviewer for the *Sun,* Janice Baker for the *Sun Magazine.*

The three feature editors are Elizabeth Large, home and food; Eric Siegel, arts and entertainment; and Jan Warrington, lifestyle. Veterans on the feature staff include Malcolm M. Allen 2d, Alison Chaplin, Charles H. Devaud, Ann R. Feild, Sally Goodhue, Charles R. Hazard, Randi M. Henderson, William Hyder, John Kelly, Connie Knox, Gerri A. Kobren, Patrick McGuire, Barbara J. Maiolatesi, Linda Morris, Andrea Pawlyna, John E. Raschka, Jr., Isaac B. Rehert, Henry Scarupa, Alice Steinbach, Davison D. White, Lynn Williams, and Luther Young, Jr.

Sports columnists are Bob Maisel, the sports editor, who has been writing a column since 1959, Alan Goldstein and Mike Littwin; Bernard V. (Lefty) Kreh is outdoors editor. In addition to fishing and hunting, Kreh writes about such nature subjects as songbirds and wildflowers. The sports staff includes Dale Austin, Sam Davis, William Free, James Jackson, Susan Reimer, and John Stewart. Seymour Smith and Peter Baker are assistant sports editors.

The *Evening Sun* has a staff of more than 130. John M. Lemmon's five assistant managing editors are Ernest Imhoff, administration; K. Kenneth Paik, news: William E. N. Hawkins, metropolitan news; Michael Hirten, features; and George Rodgers, projects and planning. James Day is executive news editor, and Charles A. Lankford, Jr., is art director. C. Wayne Hardin, deputy metropolitan editor, has five assistant metropolitan editors: Sharon Dickman, Patrick Joyce, Michael Shultz, Michael Wheatley, and Norman Wilson.

Veteran staff members include Larry Carson, Michael Fletcher, Kelwin Gilbert, Ellen Hawks, Patrick Gilbert, Ross Hetrick, Joan Jacobson, Mary Maushard, Sue Miller, Frank Roylance, Carl Schoettler, Michelle Singletary, Linell Smith, William Talbott, Kevin Thomas, Winifred Walsh, and Michael Wentzel. The copy desk includes David F. Cohn, chief of copy desk, D. Robert Greenwood, news editor, Daniel Donahue, Jr., George H. Hanst, and Wallace Reid.

Columnists are Dan Rodricks, who won the Newspaper Guild's 1983 Heywood Broun Award for outstanding journalistic achievement; Jack Germond and Jules Witcover, who write a widely syndicated Washington column; Peter Kumpa, whose topics are politics and Maryland history; and Wiley Hall, the papers' first minorities columnist. Elise T. Chisolm, Stephen McKerrow, Stephanie Shapiro, and Suzanne Kelly write for Accent, the evening features section.

The critics are Louis R. Cedrone, who became television critic in 1961 and film and drama critic in 1963. Michael Hill succeeded Cedrone as television critic in 1978. Hill describes himself as a "newspaperman, not a personality or entertainment writer." Scott Duncan is music critic. Joseph G. D'Adamo is the restaurant reviewer.

Sports columnists are G. William Tanton, Jr., the sports editor since 1967, who has been writing a column since 1961, W. Kevin Cowherd, Philip Jackman, and Jack Mann, Jr. Bill Burton is the outdoors editor; he also writes a column for the Food section, "Catchin' & Cookin'." John Gibbons is executive sports editor, and veterans on his staff include Doug Brown, Larry Harris, Sandra McKee, Ross Peddicord, and John Sears.

Weyman D. Swagger, Jr., is picture editor, and veterans on the photographic staff, which serves the three papers, include Lew Bush, J. Pat Carter, George H. Cook, William G. Hotz, Sr., Paul H. Hutchins, Jr., Edward J. Kirschbaum, Jr., Walter M. McCardell, Jr., William H. Mortimer, G. Lloyd Pearson, and Irving H. Phillips, Jr.

Charles E. Tait is director of news technology, and Peter Wetmore was systems editor for the *Sun*. Michael Himowitz is systems editor for the *Evening Sun*. Ramon Baier is chief of the wire room.

Carolyn Hardnett is chief librarian with a staff of eighteen. She succeeded Clement G. Vitek, who was chief librarian for more than thirty-five years. In 1984 Vitek received the national Joseph F. Kwapil Award given for major achievement in the field of newspaper librarianship.

Since the late 1970s the *Baltimore Sun* has syndicated its news and feature material. In May 1984 it formed its own news service, which is sold and distributed by the New York Times Syndication Sales Corporation. The *Sun* News Service has more than fifty clients, ranging from the *Daily Times* of Primof, Pennsylvania, to the *Chicago Sun-Times*, the *San Francisco Examiner*, and the *Cleveland Plain Dealer*.

In November 1984, Gary Black retired as chairman of the board of the A. S. Abell Company, upon reaching the mandatory retirement age of 70. He had joined the board in 1947 and became vice chairman in 1950 and chairman in 1956, serving twenty-eight years—longer than any of his predecessors. When he retired, it was the first time in seventy years that a Black had not been chairman. His father, Van-Lear Black, had been chairman from 1914 to 1930 and was succeeded by Harry C. Black, who served until his death in 1956.

Gary Black, who became chairman emeritus, was succeeded by William E. McGuirk, Jr., age 66, a member of the board from 1966 and since January 1983 president of the A. S. Abell Company. From 1970 to 1984 he had been chairman of the board of Mercantile Bankshares Corporation, and before that chairman of the board of Mercantile Safe Deposit & Trust Company, which was a trustee for much of the Abell stock. Originally a New Yorker, McGuirk is a graduate of the United States Naval Academy.

Emblem and nomenclature underwent modification in November 1983, to enhance consistency and clarity in the company's internal and external image. The term *"Sunpapers"* had been coined in the Paul Patterson era to encompass the *Sun,* the *Evening Sun,* and the *Sunday Sun*—readers were urged to ask for a *Sunpaper,* not a newspaper. Now it was replaced by *The Baltimore Sun.* A research committee, working for more than a year, considered it important to include the word "Baltimore," the home city, which had never been part of the name. And, the committee reported, *"Sun"* was the best name to serve as a collective noun representing the three papers. "Some *Evening Sun* staff members took offense," Gwinn Owens wrote to *Between Editions.* "Scuttling of the term '*Sunpapers*' defies logic and convenience. . . . We of the *Evening Sun* can have no identity as *The Baltimore Sun.* That name means, regardless of the management's intention, the morning *Sun* and always will. . . . The people of Baltimore will never stop using the term '*Sunpapers.*' "

Simultaneously, the vignette in the *Sun*'s logotype was redesigned to project stronger images. The motto "Light for All," which was first used May 18, 1840, and had been in a rainbow shape, became the base of the design. The lighthouse is gone and the 1930s vintage steam engine and ship have been replaced by a locomotive and ship of an earlier era. The new vignette is "a reflection of Maryland's history and economic strength. A shield of 13 stars and stripes proclaims Maryland's place as one of the original colonies. A bold eagle faces the Western frontier. An anchor symbolizes shipbuilding and the sail-steam cargo ship links the port of Baltimore with international commerce. A sheaf of wheat depicts the bounty of the state's agriculture and a beehive represents Maryland's industrious workers. Themis, the traditional goddess of justice, holds a sword and the scales of justice." The new vignette was introduced in November 1983. It was the twelfth revision since the first vignette, adorning Vol. I, No. 1, on May 17, 1837. A bronze casting of the vignette and the name "The Baltimore Sun" were affixed to the Calvert Street entrance of the building in 1985.

Within living memory, the *Sun,* the *Evening Sun,* and the *Sunday Sun* have sponsored projects and programs benefiting their readers and the community— from paying to have their first airplane fly over Baltimore in 1910, to promoting Hands Across America (for the hungry and homeless) in 1986. Thousands in number by now, these occasions have included garden and photographic contests, events at the Aquarium and the Zoo, Chesapeake Bay Appreciation Days, an inner-city basketball league, a city basketball tournament with profits going to a Fuel Fund, and the Maryland marathon. (Only one contest was unproductive from an entry standpoint. In 1958 the *Evening Sun* promoted safety for elementary school children by having "Sunny," a performing wonderdog, show the right and wrong ways to cross the street.

The child who submitted the best scrapbook of the paper's multitudinous stories and pictures on "Sunny" and the participants would win a pedigree wire-haired fox terrier. The winner was the only child to submit a scrapbook.)

For years the *Sun* has sponsored and been involved with "Newspapers in Education," a reading and writing program in which every Maryland school system participates. Since 1959 the *Evening Sun* has made Police Officer of Year awards of $1,000 to recognize achievements in law-enforcement and community service, and since 1955 the paper has honored high school male and female athletes of the year.

In 1980 the *Sun* established the annual H. L. Mencken Writing Award as a highlight of centennial observances honoring its famous columnist, correspondent and editor for nearly fifty years. This national prize of $2,500 goes "to the newspaper journalist whose columns stir the spirit as Mencken's did." The award is made in September, the month of Mencken's birth, at the National Press Club in Washington, D.C., and the winner's name is inscribed on a permanent plaque at the club.

Since the late 1970s the *Sun* and the *Evening Sun* have held "Meet the Editors" meetings throughout the metropolitan area. The miscellaneous public, and specific groups such as businessmen, church groups, and professional organizations, are invited to voice comments and ask questions. Another innovation was the company's speakers bureau, which annually provides a thousand or more speakers, drawn mainly from the news and editorial departments, for civic, community, and social groups.

When Murphy was in Atlanta and then San Francisco, he believed that as an editor and publisher it was important to be actively involved in civic life. In Baltimore he began speaking to business, fraternal, ethnic, neighborhood, and church groups about the *Baltimore Sun* and answering questions on how and why the papers were changing. He noted: "I believe we have to lead this organization out into the community to a much greater extent than had been done before." He added, "Someone once said that a great newspaper shows a community talking to itself. The *Sun* had not always been doing that effectively." He tells the story of one of his first days in Baltimore, when he was in the downtown tower office of William McGuirk. Looking out the window, Murphy admired what he called Baltimore's new look. Murphy quoted McGuirk as replying, "And done without any help from the Baltimore *Sun.*"

Murphy is chairman of the board of visitors of the College of Journalism of the University of Maryland, a member of the board of trustees of Johns Hopkins Hospital, Loyola College, and the Baltimore Museum of Art, a member of the board of directors of the Enoch Pratt Free Library, and on the executive board of the Baltimore Urban League.

On May 27, 1986, the Baltimore *News American,* under the streamer "So Long, Baltimore," announced it was ceasing publication. Despite a prolonged search, its owner, the Hearst Corporation, could find no buyer for the paper, which traced its history, with twists and a lapse, to 1773. The closing was not unexpected. In December 1985 the Hearst Corporation announced it was looking for a buyer so "this second editorial voice can be preserved in Baltimore," but bidders could not produce sufficient capital.

Up until 1976 the News American had a larger circulation than the Evening Sun and the Sun, but then its blue-collar audience began to disappear, and so did its advertising income. In 1978 the paper changed its image, to identify with the new Baltimore, but it was too late. Circulation slipped from 160,000 to 142,000 and finally to 100,000 or less, against the Evening Sun's 150,000.

The News American was a feisty paper, as typically Baltimorean as white marble steps and Formstone rowhouses. One former editor remembered the glory days when "we were Baltimore's paper, written for the real Baltimore, the working people, and the Sun was the fussiest thing ever created by man. One time in 1978 the Sun was running a three-part series on avalanches in Switzerland and, my God, there were murders in Dundalk, breweries closing, high school drug scandals—a hundred good stories a day right here in town. And that's what we were covering." A Sun editorial declared:

> We will miss our energetic competitor . . . which for 213 years chronicled the story of this community, contributed to its lore and reflected its special character. . . . In its Hearstian heyday, it was Baltimore's biggest daily, truly a beer-and-crabcakes paper for a beer-and-crabcakes town. That source of strength proved an eventual weakness. . . . Baltimore was the last American market of its size and larger to have competing afternoon papers, competing Sunday newspapers, competing publishers and three daily newspapers.

The day the News American closed, Murphy called a meeting of his fourteen-member management committee to discuss the contingency plans that had been prepared: the circulation campaign (an increased press run for News American readers not already subscribers to the three Sun papers), what News American features would be acquired, and who would be hired. (Among those subsequently added to the Evening Sun staff were John Steadman, the sports editor and columnist for some thirty years, Jacques Kelly, chronicler of Baltimore's neighborhoods, and Sylvia Badger, conductor of a what-people-are-up-to column.)

Later, in a press conference, Murphy noted that the Hearst Corporation had approached him about a joint plant-operation agreement with the News American and that he had rejected it. Asked about rumors floating along Wall Street that either the Gannett Company or the Los Angeles Times Mirror organization was interested in acquiring the Sun properties, Murphy answered obliquely, "I would bet money they are, but it's difficult to pin down."

Another meeting of the management committee to deal with the News American's closing was scheduled for 4:15 P.M. the next day. Murphy, accompanied by three men, arrived at 4:25 P.M. He interrupted the meeting, which was discussing circulation sampling, by saying, "I have an announcement of great importance. The A. S. Abell Company has been purchased by the Times Mirror Company of Los Angeles for $600 million in cash. It is the end of one dream; the beginning of another." A member of the committee recalled, "I was stunned. I looked around and everyone looked stunned too. It was obvious that some were disappointed."

Murphy introduced the three who had accompanied him, David Laventhol, president-elect of the Times Mirror Company, W. Thomas Johnson, publisher of the *Los Angeles Times* and Times Mirror senior vice president, and William J. McCarthy, an A. S. Abell Company attorney. Laventhol said, "The key to this is we think the people in Baltimore should run the Baltimore *Sun*." Murphy noted that the announcement of the sale would be on the wires after the stock market closed at 4:30 P.M. and urged the men and women of the committee to go back to their departments to announce the news.

The news room had already heard about it. Bill Carter, the *Sun*'s television critic, had a telephone call from a friend who covers media business for the *Chicago Sun-Times*. "Hey," the friend said breathlessly, "you guys have just been sold to the L.A. Times Mirror." Carter dropped the telephone and shouted to everyone around him in the feature department, "We've been sold!" Then he rushed to the news room with the news. It was greeted with disbelief. "Are you sure?" he was asked. "Is someone pulling your leg?" Since there was nothing on the news wire, Carter, now doubtful, replied, "No. I'm not sure." A minute or two later, as the news was coming over the wire, Murphy, accompanied by Laventhol and Johnson, announced the news of the $600 million sale and answered questions in the jumbled, construction-littered news room, which was being renovated and reorganized. Later Murphy went to departments throughout the building to answer questions from the still-shocked employees.

Six months earlier, in November 1985, the *City Paper*'s Phyllis Orrick had written in her column, "Pressing Matters," "In spite of word that an un-named stockholder in the A. S. Abell Company has approached the Times Mirror Company about possibly purchasing the *Sunpapers*, which Abell publishes, a survey of representative board members and stockholders produced repeated denials that such a sale was being considered." William S. Abell, Jr., termed the sales talk "kind of surprising." "There's a pretty strong sentiment among the people I know who own the paper that the paper serves a public interest by being a privately held company with relatively local owners. Someone could be shopping around," he added, "but I think I'd hear about it." William McGuirk, chairman of the Abell board, was quoted as saying that such a sale "is about as likely as a July snow in Baltimore." Donald H. Patterson, the retired publisher, observed, "There's always a lot of rumors."

In 1958, *Time* magazine reported that Samuel I. Newhouse, who had acquired an empire of thirteen newspapers in thirty-six years "was chasing one of the brightest properties in the nation: the Baltimore *Sunpapers*." "Newhouse has offered to buy between 51% and 70% of the stock of the

A. S. Abell Company, which owns the three papers plus the *Sun*'s TV station WMAR. Estimated price for 51% control: $20 million. So eager is Publisher Newhouse to get the prestigious *Sunpapers* that he might be willing to plunk down more than $40 million for the whole outfit." (Testimony in a federal court case on another matter revealed that Newhouse had offered $355 a share for some 110,000 shares.) *Time* added that if Newhouse bought the *Sunpapers* "the deal will be by far the largest in the U.S. newspaper history."

In a letter to the editor of the *Sun*, a subscriber wrote, "just say that he [Newhouse] 'ain't got' the slightest chance in the world of getting the *Sunpapers*. For a number of generations we folk down here on the Eastern Shore of Virginia have been 'fotched up' on the *Sunpapers* and we don't want to 'get away from our raising.' " An editor's note declared, "The *Sunpapers* are not for sale and have never been for sale." It was the only public notice the A. S. Abell Company took of the Newhouse offer.

Because of that offer, Mrs. Jessie Black Blakiston, daughter of Van-Lear Black, brought suit in federal court in Baltimore over the evaluation made on 3,300 shares of A. S. Abell Company stock that had been placed in trust for her in 1932 by her uncle, Harry C. Black, in settlement of her father's estate. After the uncle's death in 1956, the trust deed and his will called for the company to repurchase the 3,300 shares. The Mercantile Safe Deposit & Trust Company had appraised the stock at $138 a share. That valuation was set after 4.35 percent was determined as the proper yield for the $6 annual dividend. The valuation listed company revenues of nearly $28 million in 1956, with net earnings of $2,217,760. Reserves totaled $5 million. Mrs. Blakiston claimed the $138 paid for the repurchase of her stock did not represent a fair market value, which she thought should be about $350 a share. She asked the court to review the appraisal. Despite the much higher rate per share that Samuel I. Newhouse had been willing to pay, the court dismissed the case in 1960, ruling that the $138 was within the fair market value. A similar suit filed by Van-Lear Black 3d, son of Van-Lear Black, Jr., who died in 1956, was also dismissed.

By 1986 such large newspaper chains as Knight-Ridder, the Gannett Company (which owned more than ninety newspapers), and the Times Mirror Company had begun an ardent effort to buy up the remaining independent dailies, particularly those in a monopoly market, because they were considered excellent investments. Nine days before the announcement of the A. S. Abell Company sale, the Gannett Company agreed to buy the *Louisville Courier Journal* and the *Louisville Times* from the Bingham family, which had owned the papers for about seventy years for $300 million. The price was almost three times the 1985 revenues of $103 million. That same year the Abell Company's revenues were $204.8 million, including $172.5 million in publishing revenue.

The *Sun* announced the sale of the Abell Company to the Times Mirror as its lead story on May 29 and devoted two inside pages to details and background. (The sale was front-page news in the *New York Times*, the

Washington Post, and other papers.) The *Sun* pointed out that the $600 million price was among the largest ever agreed to for the sale of a newspaper company. In addition to the three newspapers, the deal included the NBC-affiliated WMAR-TV station in Baltimore and the independent WRLH-TV in Richmond, Virginia, as well as the magazines *Mid-Atlantic Country* and *Ski Racing International.*

A second story on the *Sun*'s front page was headed "Surprise, concern, praise voiced over sale of *Sun.*" A University of Maryland journalism professor was quoted as saying, "I think everybody would prefer local ownership for the qualities of localness, intimacy, and connectedness that connotes." A publisher of metropolitan weeklies commented, "I think that they [the Times Mirror] will come in with their own style and will shake the media market up in our town, in many ways, as all new owners do . . . an old institution like the *Sun* tends to get laid back. I don't think this company will be." He added, "It will probably break up some institutional relationships that have a lot of clout in town," noting that the boards of the Mercantile Safe Deposit & Trust Company and the A. S. Abell Company had shared members in the past. The chairman of the board of the Baltimore Gas & Electric Company said, "I don't think it is good news for Baltimore. My experience with other corporations with headquarters elsewhere . . . [is that] the causes of the city are not high priorities with outsiders whether you're talking about the symphony or whatnot."

But most of those interviewed were optimistic, pointing out that the Times Mirror had an excellent reputation for first-rate journalism and preferred to let local management run the papers comprising its chain. Commenting editorially on the sale, the *Sun* began, "What we were yesterday, we are today and will be tomorrow." It declared:

> Our readers are entitled to know the reasons for this change in the ownership of their hometown newspapers. The publishing world is changing dramatically, not only because of the financial consolidation seen in other industries but because technological change is a driving force in this information age. Independently owned newspapers are becoming an anachronism facing an uncertain future. Rather than risk our present strength, which is considerable, we have decided to build on it by associating with newspapers we respect. . . .
>
> Yes, there is sadness in the loss of corporate independence. One member of our board bears the name of our founder, Arunah Shepherdson Abell, thus representing a continuity through five generations that few companies in any field can boast. But what matters to our readers is what they get in the way of news, features, attractive presentation and service. And what they will get will be in the great tradition of *The Baltimore Sun.*

Since its founding in 1884, the Times Mirror Company has become one of the nation's foremost media companies, with coast-to-coast operations. Its flagship, the *Los Angeles Times,* which has a daily circulation of 1,088,000 and is the bulkiest paper in the United States, is so dominant and lucrative that investment analysts nicknamed it "the cash cow." Since 1970 the Times Mirror Company has acquired the Long Island daily tabloid-size *Newsday;* the *Denver Post;* the *Dallas Times-Herald* (sold in June 1986 for $110 million); the *Hartford* (Connecticut) *Courant;* the *Morning Call* in Allentown, Pennsylvania; and the *Stamford Advocate* and *Greenwich Time,* both in Connecticut; a number of nonnewspaper publications, including such magazines as the *Sporting News, Golf, Ski, Outdoor Life,* and *Popular Science;* Times Mirror Press; broadcast and cable television; and newsprint and forest products. In 1981, Times Mirror sales were $2.1 billion, and by 1985 they had risen to nearly $3 billion, while its net income had risen from $150.3 million to $237 million.

Murphy said that the first contact with the Times Mirror Company was in April 1986, when he was attending a meeting of the American Society of Newspaper Editors in Washington. W. Thomas Johnson, publisher of the *Los Angeles Times* and Times Mirror senior vice president, approached him, saying, "When will you guys stop trying to buy newspapers and sell yours?" Murphy and Johnson are old colleagues, both having started about the same time on the *Macon Telegraph.*

Murphy said Times Mirror executives continued to approach him, and later, Robert F. Erburu, chairman, president, and chief executive officer of Times Mirror, telephoned William McGuirk, the Abell board chairman, and said he would like to come to Baltimore to meet with him and Murphy. On May 13 he and Philip L. Williams, the executive vice president of Times Mirror, met with Murphy and McGuirk in the Abell Company boardroom and offered $550 million in cash for the Abell properties. The size of the offer surprised them. It was substantially higher than the evaluation made that month for the Abell Company by an independent appraiser. Ten days later Murphy and McGuirk flew to Los Angeles to resume discussions and to ask for $50 million more. On May 24 the Times Mirror agreed. On May 28 the Abell board, entitled to vote about 24 percent of the company's privately held stock, voted to recommend to the stockholders that they sell the company. Directors pointed out that, once the Times Mirror offer had been made, their options were limited. By law the board had an obligation to the stockholders to consider bids almost entirely in terms of money involved. "There is a fiduciary responsibility under which a director has to consider the best interests of the stockholder," one pointed out.

A special meeting of stockholders was held on June 12, 1986, with about twenty attending. The meeting was formal and routine, ballots representing 101,164 of the company's 104,400 shares, some 96.9 percent, had been cast by mail in favor of the sale. The only informal note was a comment from the floor by Gary Black, emeritus chairman of the board, who mentioned the long association the Abells and Blacks had with the *Sun* and praised McGuirk for his contributions as chairman of the board. At the end of the twenty-minute meeting, two women sitting in the first row applauded.

The 104,400 shares were owned by 135 shareholders. With the sale each share was worth $5,741.18—an astounding increase in value. In 1966 the book value of the A. S. Abell stock was $183 a share; in 1980 it was $446; in 1981 it was $519.50; in 1982 it was $525.69; in 1983 it was $550.00; in 1984 it was $623.88; in 1985 it was $785.19; and in March 1986 it was $803.21. The board, which had given Murphy more authority than it had to previous presidents, credited the increased profitability to Murphy. Murphy was aided by falling interest rates, the leveling off of the cost of newsprint, and the growth of retail business.

The circulation of the three papers, primarily distributed in the Baltimore metropolitan market area, which has about 800,000 households and a population of 2.2 million, has increased since 1981. In September 1986 the *Sun* had a circulation of 222,000; the *Evening Sun*'s circulation was 175,000 and the *Sunday Sun*'s was 465,000.

Because of "rising costs of newsprint and distribution," the price of the *Sunday Sun* was raised from $1.00 to $1.25 on February 1, 1987. When the Sunday paper was introduced in October 1901, it sold for two cents. The price was increased to three cents in April 1908, but reverted to two cents when the *Evening Sun* was introduced in April 1910. In January 1911 the *Sunday Sun* again sold for three cents. The price increased to five cents in 1917, ten cents in 1938, fifteen cents in 1951, twenty cents in 1957, twenty-five cents in 1965, thirty cents in 1969, thirty-five cents in 1970, forty cents in January 1974, fifty cents in September 1974, sixty cents in 1978, seventy-five cents in 1980, and $1.00 in 1982.

The *Sun,* the first penny paper in Baltimore, raised its price to two cents in December 1864 but later reverted to one cent in 1902. The price was raised to two cents in 1910 when the *Evening Sun* was introduced. The *Sun* and *Evening Sun* sold for two cents until 1939, when the price was increased to three cents. In 1946 the price rose to five cents, seven cents in 1960, ten cents in 1964, fifteen cents in 1975, twenty cents in 1981, and twenty-five cents in 1983.

Advertising has increased substantially since 1981, primarily as a result of the growth of retail sales and classified advertising. In 1981, total advertising lineage for the three papers was 75,572,814. In 1986 it was 82,482,957 lines. The volume of advertising is now recorded in inches rather than lines. In 1986 it was 4,664,686 inches.

The A. S. Abell Foundation, formed in 1954 by Harry and Gary Black, held 19 percent of the Abell Company stock and was the largest individual stockholder. The Times Mirror purchase transformed it. The foundation's share of the proceeds, some $98 million, made it suddenly more than twice as rich as the next-largest foundation in Maryland. The Abell Foundation allots most of its grants to educational, medical, and cultural institutions. Gary Black is chairman of the foundation and Donald H. Patterson is president.

The principal individual beneficiaries were descendants of Arunah S. Abell or of H. Crawford Black, Robert Garrett, and John Campbell White—three of the four wealthy Baltimoreans who invested in the company in 1910. Those four families together controlled more than 56 percent of the Abell stock. The Black descendants received about $93 million, the Abells $91 million, the Garretts $82 million, and the Whites $69 million. Gary Black received the most as an individual, almost $48 million. Murphy owned 2,500 shares, worth about $14.5 million. McGuirk who was not a stockholder, received $500,000 in recognition of his services.

Because Federal Communications Commission regulations prohibit companies from acquiring newspapers and television stations in the same market, Times Mirror sold WMAR-TV and the UHF station in Richmond to Gillet, a privately held media group owned by George Gillet of Nashville, Tennessee. The price was more than $208 million, considerably greater than the $165 million the stations were expected to bring.

The last meeting of the board of directors of the A. S. Abell Company, the parent organization, and its two subsidiary companies, A. S. Abell Publishing and Abell Communications, took place in the staid, blue-toned boardroom on the fifth floor of the Calvert Street building on Monday, October 20, 1986. Six of the eight board members were present: W. Shepherdson Abell, the great-great-grandson of Arunah S. Abell, founder of the *Sun;* Gary Black, Jr., the grandson of H. Crawford Black, a prime mover in reviving the floundering paper in 1914; Robert Garrett, a grandson of Robert Garrett (an associate of H. Crawford Black and his son Van-Lear Black); Osborn Elliott, dean of Columbia University's Graduate School of Journalism, who joined the board in 1982; Reg Murphy; and William E. McGuirk, Jr., chairman of the board. The two directors unable to attend were Donald H. Patterson and George L. Bunting, president and chief executive officer of the Noxell Corporation, who also had joined the board in 1982. Also present at the hour-and-a-half meeting were Arnold J. Kleiner, president of Abell Communications; Jean Halle, vice president of finance of Abell Communications; and Richard M. Basoco, senior vice president and general manager of A. S. Abell Publishing.

When the directors signed their resignation papers, Murphy noted that this act was an anticlimax. The excitement and emotion generated by the unexpected announcement of the proposed sale in May, Murphy said, "had washed away."

A catered lunch was served. Dessert was ice cream and swan-shaped cookies. "I made them that way," the caterer explained, "because this is a swan song." At the luncheon, "Shep" Abell spoke informally about the great traditions of the *Sun,* the role the five generations of Abells had played in the *Sun*'s history, and the mixed feelings he and his father had that day. He praised Murphy for his contributions in enhancing the papers and making them profitable, and McGuirk for his role as a board member since 1966 and chairman since November 1984. He concluded by saying that the *Sun* was passing into an organization that respected the quality and integrity of its newspapers. Pictures were taken of the historic occasion. It was the first time that McGuirk, vehemently camera-shy, permitted his picture to be taken in fifteen years.

As a memento, the directors and those attending the meeting received a large framed embossed design of the Baltimore *Sun* vignette with the words "The Abell Company," created by Joanne Isaac, a Quakertown, Pennsylvania, etcher. The memento was also presented to four retired directors: William S. Abell, Gary Black, Harrison Garrett, and William F. Schmick, Jr., known around the executive office as "the gray beards."

Before the luncheon the three portraits that had adorned the boardroom for more than thirty years were removed because the room was being re-decorated. The portrait of A. S. Abell will be returned if the new directors want it; if not it will go to the Abell family. The Black family presented the portraits of Van-Lear Black and his brother Harry to the Maryland Historical Society.

Late Monday morning, October 27, 1986, the A. S. Abell Company was merged with TMAC, Inc., a subsidiary formed by the Times Mirror Company. The legal requirements took place in the conference room of Venable, Baetjer & Howard, the Baltimore law firm representing the A. S. Abell Company. Murphy was present along with a number of lawyers. The financial transaction was completed in routine fashion with a telephone call followed by the transfer of funds by wire from the Morgan Bank in New York to the Mercantile–Safe Deposit & Trust Company in Baltimore, representing the 135 shareholders of the A. S. Abell Company. Although the amount had always been stated as $600 million, the money that changed hands, because of transfer charges, was $599,999,933.37.

The A. S. Abell Company, which had its beginnings as a penny paper 149 years earlier, was no more. *The Baltimore Sun* was now a Times Mirror Newspaper.

Epilogue:
The Anniversary and After

Commemoration of *The Baltimore Sun*'s 150th anniversary began in January 1987 when the *Sun* was designated "a historic site in journalism" by Sigma Delta Chi, the Society of Professional Journalists.

Beginning in February, *The Baltimore Sun* sponsored free concerts in communities throughout Maryland, and, beginning in March, offered free admissions to some forty Maryland tourist attractions.

The main celebrations were held in May, the anniversary month. On May 16 an anniversary eve gala was held at Baltimore's Inner Harbor, featuring free concerts by Chuck Mangione, the Preservation Hall Jazz Band, local entertainers, and a display of fireworks. The company entertained some 2,000 guests at a party in the Maryland Science Center, which introduced a new laser show, "Light for All," underwritten by *The Baltimore Sun*. Sunday evening, May 17, another party was held in the Maryland Science Center for some 3,000 employees and retired employees of the *Sun*.

The *Sun* of May 17, 1837, contained four pages, was typeset by hand, and cost a penny. The *Sunday Sun* anniversary issue of May 17, 1987, was printed on computerized presses, weighed 6.1 pounds, comprised twenty-four sections, consisted of 1,090 pages, and cost $1.25. It included a special magazine, "150 People Who Shaped the Way We Live," which was so popular that extra copies had to be printed to meet the demand. This was the biggest issue ever printed by the *Sun*. Circulation reached an all-time high of 596,694 Sunday papers sold. In 1986 average Sunday circulation was 465,000.

Maryland Public Television produced an hour-long documentary, "*The Baltimore Sun*, 150 Years." "Light for All, a History of *The Baltimore Sun*," an exhibit of historic front pages, photographs, equipment, and memorabilia was assembled by the staff of the Albin O. Kuhn Library and Gallery of the University of Maryland, Baltimore County. After its display at the UMBC Catonsville campus, the "Light for All" exhibit traveled to five other Maryland colleges. An exhibition of the photography of A. Aubrey Bodine, who achieved an international reputation with his *Sunday Sun* photographs, was held at the Baltimore Museum of Art and was later shown at museums and galleries in various cities in the United States.

Altogether, the company's outlay for sesquicentennial celebrations was about $1 million.

On May 27, 1987, the *Sun* published this letter from Ronald Reagan, President of the United States:

> Editor: I am happy to be able to contribute a few words to *The Baltimore Sun* and to congratulate the readers and staff of this historic newspaper as you celebrate your 150th anniversary.
>
> The world has changed a great deal in the century and a half since Arunah Shepherdson Abell founded your newspaper and charged a penny per copy, and since the *Sun* used relay horsemen and the railroad to scoop other papers. But some things do not change, and today the *Sun* continues its tradition of journalistic excellence long maintained by H. L. Mencken, Gerald Johnson, William Manchester and so many others over the years. That is good news indeed, for Baltimore and for all of us.
>
> Again, congratulations on your Sesquicentennial. You and your readers have my best wishes for many more years of success. God bless you.
>
> Ronald Reagan, Washington.

Staff and executive changes made since the *Sun* history was set in type include the following:

Ernest B. Furgurson, Jr., chief of the Washington bureau since 1975, in June 1987 was appointed an associate editor of the *Sun*. His column, which had appeared in the news section, was moved to the *Sun*'s opinion-commentary page. Frank C. Starr, national editor of the *Sun* since 1979, succeeded Furgurson as bureau chief. Edwin W. Goodpaster, deputy Washington bureau chief since 1982, was named national editor.

Diana Henry, of the *Evening Sun*, succeeded Robert Ruby as chief of the Paris bureau. Ruby succeeded G. Jefferson Price as chief of the Mideast bureau in Jerusalem. Price returned to Baltimore as an editor on the *Sun*'s metro desk. John M. McClintock succeeded James K. Bock as chief of the Mexico City bureau. Bock was named a University of Michigan Journalism Fellow for the 1987–88 academic year to study modern history and public policy. John Schidlovsky succeeded John E. Woodruff as chief of bureau in Beijing, China. Woodruff, after a year of study and teaching at the University of Michigan, is scheduled to become chief of the Tokyo bureau in 1988.

Ellen Uzelac of the *Sun* staff, succeeded Doug Struck as West Coast correspondent. Struck was named national correspondent. Tom Horton, the *Sun*'s environmental reporter and columnist, took a leave of absence and moved to Smith Island in the Chesapeake Bay to conduct environment tours for the

Chesapeake Bay Foundation. His book, *Bay Country*, was published by the Johns Hopkins University Press in 1987.

Martin Kaiser, executive sports editor of the *Sun*, was also appointed an assistant managing editor. John Eisenberg, a feature writer for the *Sun*'s sports section, was appointed a sports columnist. Bob Maisel, a reporter, columnist, and sports editor at the *Sun* for thirty-seven years, retired in May 1987 after writing some 7,000 columns but continued to contribute a Sunday column.

J. D. Considine was appointed *Sun* pop music critic. Catherine Cook was appointed *Sun* fashion editor.

On the *Evening Sun*, Michael Davis replaced Michael K. Hirten as an assistant managing editor. Kevin Cowherd switched from *Evening Sun* sports columnist to the *Evening Sun* accent section.

Diana M. Zinda, display advertising manager and former national advertising manager of *The Baltimore Sun*, was appointed advertising director, overseeing more than 150 sales and support employees. John W. Wittman was named associate advertising director.

Robert C. Embry, Jr., former president of the Baltimore City school board and from 1977 to 1981 assistant secretary of the federal Department of Housing and Urban Development, was appointed head of the Abell Foundation. The foundation grew from about $14 million to some $112 million with the sale of the A. S. Abell Company to Times Mirror. Before the sale it was known as the A. S. Abell Foundation.

The 650 members of Local 35 of the Washington-Baltimore Newspaper Guild went on strike June 11, 1987, after their three-year contract expired. The strike involved wages, health benefits, and the two-tier pay scale through which employees of the suburban editions are paid less than their counterparts on the daily papers. Engravers, printers, pressmen, teamsters, and mail room employees refused to cross the guild's picket lines, but the company continued to publish the *Sun*, *Evening Sun* and *Sunday Sun* using employees not in the guild's jurisdiction. The papers were smaller than usual. The six-day strike ended June 17 when the guild agreed to a new contract which covered news and editorial departments, advertising, circulation, and building maintenance employees. Workers will receive an average four percent salary increase each year during the three-year contract, and, for the first time, some will pay a percentage of the costs of their medical benefits.

In the third year of the contract, reporters with the daily and Sunday papers who have five years' experience will receive $790 a week. Top scale for suburban reporters will be $485. In the third year, editorial writers will receive $850 a week, advertising sales people, $745, and commercial artists, $515.

Chronology of *Sun* Ownership and Presidents

1836   A. S. Abell, Azariah H. Simmons, and William M. Swain found the *Philadelphia Public Ledger.*

1837   A. S. Abell is the prime mover in establishing the *Sun* with Simmons and Swain as partners.

1855   At Simmons's death, Abell and Swain purchase his interest in both the *Public Ledger* and the *Sun* from his estate.

1860   The partnership of Abell and Swain ends, Swain keeping the *Public Ledger,* Abell the *Sun.*

1887   The three sons of A. S. Abell—Edwin F. Abell, George W. Abell, and Walter Robert Abell—become partners in A. S. Abell & Company on the fiftieth anniversary of the *Sun.*

1887–1894 George W. Abell, who began directing the *Sun* in his father's last years, is publisher and editor.

1892   On the death of Walter Robert Abell (who never took an active role in managing the paper), A. S. Abell & Company is incorporated, becoming the A. S. Abell Company of Baltimore City. The incorporators are Edwin F. Abell, George W. Abell, Arunah S. Abell 2d (elder son of Edwin F.), Charles S. Abell (son of George W.), William H. Heindle, head bookkeeper of the *Sun,* and George H. Karsner, the cashier.

1894   Edwin F. Abell is elected president of the company, following the death of his brother George. Arunah S. Abell 2d becomes secretary-treasurer, and Walter W. (also son of Edwin F.) becomes a director. Charles S. Abell is named a director in 1898.

1904   Walter W. Abell is elected president of the company after the death of his father.

1909   In April, Walter W. Abell resigns as president and as a director of the company. Charles S. Abell is elected vice president (the office of president is not filled) and under the bylaws functions as general manager.

1910   In January, Charles S. Abell resigns as vice president and director of the A. S. Abell Company of Baltimore City. Charles H. Grasty takes control of the *Sun* and becomes president of the A. S. Abell Company, a new organization. Grasty's backers are H. Crawford Black, Robert Garrett, R. Brent Keyser, and John Campbell White. Charles S. Abell continues as a major stockholder.

1914   In September, Grasty resigns as president and general manager. Van-Lear Black, son of H. Crawford Black, becomes nominal head of the company while continuing as chairman of the board.

1919   In November, Paul Patterson is elected president of the company and serves until his retirement in January 1951.

1930   Harry C. Black, son of H. Crawford Black, becomes chairman of the board upon the death of his brother, Van-Lear, and serves until 1956.

1951–1960 William F. Schmick, Sr., is president of the company.

1956   Gary Black, son of Van-Lear Black, is named chairman of the board after the death of his uncle, Harry C. Black, and serves until 1984.

1960–1978 William F. Schmick, Jr., is president of the company.

1977   Donald H. Patterson is named publisher of the *Sunpapers*.

1979   Donald H. Patterson is president of the A. S. Abell Company and continues as publisher of the *Sunpapers*.

1981   On July 1, John R. (Reg) Murphy becomes publisher of the *Sunpapers* and a director of the A. S. Abell Company.

1982   The A. S. Abell Company, with Donald H. Patterson as president, forms two operating divisions: A. S. Abell Publishing Company, with Reg Murphy as president and publisher, and Abell Communications Company, with Stephen D. Seymour as president. On December 31, Donald H. Patterson retires as president of the A. S. Abell Company and is succeeded by William E. McGuirk, Jr., a member of the board since 1966.

1984–1986 William E. McGuirk, Jr., is chairman of the board.

1986   On October 27 the A. S. Abell Company merges with TMAC, Inc., a subsidiary of the Times Mirror Company, and *The Baltimore Sun* becomes a Times Mirror newspaper. The principal stockholders of the A. S. Abell Company were descendants of A. S. Abell, H. Crawford Black, Robert Garrett, and John Campbell White. They controlled 56 percent of the company stock.

Sources

Notes on the Sources

I am a collector at heart, and ever since I joined the *Sun* in 1940 I have been collecting material about the *Sun,* the *Evening Sun,* and the *Sunday Sun* and the men and women who have worked for the papers. I saved obituaries, bulletin board announcements, memoranda, edition and deadline schedules, office telephone directories, style books, letters to the editor commenting on and criticizing the papers and their policies, and blunders that were printed.

In 1976, William F. Schmick, Jr., president of the A. S. Abell Company, asked me to begin collecting information for the 1987 history of the *Sunpapers.* My collecting became more organized, and I began interviewing retired employees. Colleagues contributed keepsakes and odds and ends from the depths of desk drawers. One had a 1918 pass signed by the surveyor of customs for a 13-year-old *Sun* newsboy; it enabled him to sell papers on the waterfront, piers, and vessels during World War I.

A treasure of information—including a hand-drawn diagram of the *Evening Sun* news room in the 1930s—came from those who meet at an informal Thursday luncheon of *Sun* retirees (including former presidents of the company) and present employees held in the back room of the Downtown Athletic Club across from the *Sun* building. Another source of information was the Geritol Group, an annual spring luncheon of *Sun* men and women, started around 1960 by Roger S. Williamson, Jesse Glasgow, and John Ward.

The primary, and most important, sources used in preparing this history were:

- The pages of the *Sun,* the *Evening Sun,* and the *Sunday Sun.* The A. S. Abell Company's bound volumes are in the Library of the Univer- of Maryland Baltimore County campus, Catonsville. Billy R.

Wilkinson, library director, graciously let me borrow the volumes I needed.

- Personnel files of the A. S. Abell Company.
- A. S. Abell Company early minute books of the board of directors and meetings of stockholders.
- The *Baltimore Sun* Library.
- *The Sunpapers of Baltimore* by Gerald W. Johnson, Frank R. Kent, H. L. Mencken, and Hamilton Owens. (New York: Alfred A. Knopf, 1937).
- An invaluable source were the Date Books of James W. Dove, whose newspaper career began in 1896 on the Baltimore *Morning Herald* but who worked for the *Sunpapers* until 1950, retiring as assistant business manager. His three typed loose-leaf notebooks, meticulously kept, are filled with dates, facts, and figures on circulation and advertising, but more important, with a wealth of information about the *Sunpapers* and their personnel. In possession of author.
- The unpublished autobiographies of H. K. Fleming, Newton Aiken, and Miles H. Wolff were a major source of information. Wolff's autobiography was furnished by his son, Miles Wolff, Jr., publisher of *BaseBall America*, Durham, North Carolina. In possession of author.
- *Between Editions,* issued irregularly by the A. S. Abell Company for its employees. Sun Library.
- The Frank R. Kent Collection, Maryland Historical Society, Baltimore, Maryland.
- Unpublished letters and diaries of H. L. Mencken from the Mencken Collection of the Enoch Pratt Free Library, Baltimore, Maryland. Permission to quote from the diaries and letters was given by the Library.
- And, most of all, the information and reminiscences enthusiastically contributed in interviews, letters, and memoranda by more than seventy men and women who were or are part of the *Sun* papers.

1: THE BEGINNINGS, 1837–1839

Books, Periodicals, and Newspapers

Abell, Horace A., et al. *The Abell Family in America.* Rutland, Vt.: Tuttle Publishing Company, 1940.

Baltimore *Sun,* bound files, May 1837–December 1839. Sun Library.

The Biographical Cyclopedia of Representatives of Maryland and District of Columbia. Baltimore: National Biographical Publishing Company, 1879.

Forman, S. E. *Our Republic.* New York: Century Company, 1929.

Greene, Suzanne Ellery. *Baltimore: An Illustrated History.* Woodland Hills, Calif.: Windsor Publications, 1980.

Hewitt, John H. *Shadows on the Wall; or, Glimpses of the Past.* Baltimore: Turnbull Brothers, 1877.

Hiebert, Ray Eldon. *Mass Media: An Introduction to Modern Communication.* New York and London: Longman, 1982.

Hudson, Frederic. *Journalism in the United States, from 1690 to 1872.* New York: Harper & Brothers, 1873. Republished: Grosse Point, Mich.: Scholarly Press, 1968.

Isaacs, George A. *The Story of the Newspaper Printing Press.* London: Co-operative Printing Society, 1931.

Johnson, Gerald W., et al. *The Sunpapers of Baltimore.* New York: Alfred A. Knopf, 1937.

Keidel, G. C. "Early Maryland Newspapers." *Maryland Historical Magazine,* December 1933.

Mayer, Brantz. *Baltimore as It Was and as It Is Today: A Historical Sketch, 1729–1870.* Baltimore: Richardson & Bennett, 1871.

Mott, Frank Luther. *American Journalism: A History, 1690–1960.* Third edition. New York: Macmillan, 1962.

O'Brien, Frank M. *The Story of the [New York] Sun, 1833–1918.* New York: George H. Doran Company, 1918.

Olson, Sherry H. *Baltimore: The Building of an American City.* Baltimore: Johns Hopkins University Press, 1980.

"*Philadelphia Public Ledger.*" Part 3 of a "History of the *Philadelphia Inquirer.*" Supplement to the *Philadelphia Inquirer,* September 16, 1962.

Scharf, J. Thomas. *History of Baltimore City and County.* Philadelphia: Louis H. Everts, 1881.

Scharf, J. Thomas, et al. *History of Philadelphia.* Vol. 3. Philadelphia: L. H. Everts & Company, 1884.

West, Harold E. "History of the *Sun.*" Published on the *Sun's* 85th anniversary. *Sunday Sun,* May 14, 1922.

Other Sources

Baltimore City Directories, 1837–38, 1840–41.

Dove, James W. Date Books of the *Sunpapers.*

Library of Congress Information Circular no. 16. 1957.

"*Philadelphia Public Ledger.*" Memorandum of its founding. From the *Philadelphia Inquirer* and *Daily News* Library, Philadelphia, Pennsylvania, June 27, 1984. In possession of author.

Philadelphia Public Ledger, February 17, 18, and 21, 1868. Photocopies from the Free Library of Philadelphia. In possession of author.

2: Enterprise and the War, 1841–1858

Books, Periodicals, and Newspapers

Bauer, K. Jack. *The Mexican War, 1846–1848.* New York: Macmillan, 1974.

The Biographical Cyclopedia of Representatives of Maryland and District of Columbia. Baltimore: National Biographical Publishing Company, 1879.

Dufour, Robert. *"How N.H. Man Scooped World on Mexican War."* *New Hampshire Sunday News* (Manchester), February 1, 1953.

Gramling, Oliver. *AP: The Story of News.* New York: Farrar & Rinehart, 1940.

Huber, Leonard V., et al. *The Great Mail: A Postal History of New Orleans.* State College, Pa.: American Philatelic Society, 1949.

"James Bogardus." *Dictionary of American Biography.* 1957 edition.

Johnson, Gerald W., et al. *The Sunpapers of Baltimore.* New York: Alfred A. Knopf, 1937.

Levy, Lester S. "Music Inspired by the *Sun*'s Old 'Iron Building.'" *Sunday Sun Magazine,* February 4, 1973.

Mahoney, Thomas. "Our First Great War Correspondent." *American Legion Magazine,* December 1965.

Mott, Frank Luther. *American Journalism: A History, 1690–1960.* Third edition. New York: Macmillan, 1962.

Obituary of Charles Carroll Fulton. Baltimore *American,* June 6, 1883.

O'Brien, Frank M. *The Story of the [New York] Sun, 1833–1918.* New York: George H. Doran Company, 1918.

Papenfuse, Edward C., et al. Comps. and eds. *Maryland: A New Guide to the Old Line State.* Baltimore: Johns Hopkins University Press, 1976.

Ridgely, J. V. *John Pendleton Kennedy.* New Haven, Conn.: College & University Press, 1966.

Scharf, J. Thomas. *History of Baltimore City and County.* Philadelphia: Louis H. Everts, 1881.

Scheele, Carl H. *A Short History of the Mail Service.* Washington, D.C.: Smithsonian Institution Press, 1970.

Seitz, Don C. *The James Gordon Bennetts.* Indianapolis, Ind. Bobbs-Merrill, 1928.

Smith, Justin. *The War with Mexico.* 2 vols. New York: Macmillan, 1919.

Smith, Waddell F., ed. *The Story of the Pony Express.* San Francisco: Hesperion House, 1960.

West, Harold E. "History of the *Sun.*" Published on the *Sun*'s 85th anniversary. *Sunday Sun,* May 14, 1922.

Wright, David G. *Baltimore City Cast Iron.* Pamphlet published by Friends of Cast Iron Architecture (New York). February 1978.

Other Sources

Dove, James W. Date Books of the *Sunpapers.*

3: THE CIVIL WAR, 1859–1865

Books, Periodicals, and Newspapers

Andrews, J. Cutler. *The North Reports the Civil War.* Pittsburgh: University of Pittsburgh Press, 1955.

Andrews, Matthew Page. *History of Maryland, Province and State.* New York: Doubleday, Doran & Company, 1929.

The Biographical Cyclopedia of Representatives of Maryland and District of Columbia. Baltimore: National Biographical Publishing Company, 1879.

Bohner, Charles H. *John Pendleton Kennedy: Gentleman from Baltimore.* Baltimore: Johns Hopkins University Press, 1961.

Brown, George William. *Baltimore and the 19th of April, 1861.* Baltimore: Johns Hopkins University, 1887.

Browne, Gary. *Baltimore in the Civil War.* Pamphlet. Catonsville, Md.: University of Maryland Baltimore County, n.d.

Childs, George W. *Recollections.* Philadelphia: J. B. Lippincott, 1890.

Cuthbert, Norma B., ed. *Lincoln and the Baltimore Plot.* San Marino, Calif.: Huntington Library, 1949.

Hudson, Frederic. *Journalism in the United States, from 1690 to 1872.* New York: Harper & Brothers, 1873. Republished: Grosse Point, Mich.: Scholarly Press, 1968.

Johnson, Gerald W., et al. *The Sunpapers of Baltimore.* New York: Alfred A. Knopf, 1937.

Manakee, Harold R. *Maryland in the Civil War.* Baltimore: Maryland Historical Society, 1961.

Matthews, Sidney T. "Control of the Baltimore Press During the Civil War." *Maryland Historical Magazine,* June 1941.

Scharf, J. Thomas. *The Chronicles of Baltimore.* Baltimore: Turnbull Brothers, 1874.

———. *History of Maryland.* Vol. 3. Baltimore: John B. Piet, 1879.

Thomas, Benjamin P. *Abraham Lincoln.* New York: Alfred A. Knopf, 1952.

Trefousse, Hans L. *Ben Butler: The South Called Him a Beast.* New York: Twayne Publishers, 1957.

Walsh, Richard, et al., ed. *Maryland: A History, 1632–1974.* Baltimore: Maryland Historical Society, 1974.

4: THE LAST YEARS OF THE FOUNDER, 1865–1888

Books, Periodicals, and Newspapers

Abell, Arunah S. "Mr. A. S. Abell's Will." *Sun,* April 25, 1888.

Andrews, Matthew Page. *History of Maryland, Province and State.* New York: Doubleday, Doran & Company, 1929.

Crooks, James B. *Politics & Progress: The Rise of Urban Progressivism in Baltimore, 1895 to 1911.* Baton Rouge: Louisiana State University Press, 1968.

Essary, J. Frederick. *Washington Government Reflected to the Public in the Press, 1822–1926.* Boston: Houghton Mifflin Company, 1927.

Forman, S. E. *Our Republic.* New York: Century Company, 1929.

"Frank R. Kent Reflects on 'Good Old Days.'" *Editor & Publisher,* December 15, 1951.

Johnson, Gerald W., et al. *The Sunpapers of Baltimore.* New York: Alfred A. Knopf, 1937.

Lippman, Theo, Jr. "Notes & Comment" (column). *Sun,* April 11, 1983.

Obituary of Arunah S. Abell. *Sun,* April 20 and 21, 1888.

Obituary of Francis Asbury Richardson. *Sun,* February 2, 1926.

Richardson, Francis Asbury. "Recollections." *Washington Evening Star,* February 11, 1902. Frank R. Kent Collection, Maryland Historical Society, Baltimore, Maryland.

Scarborough, Katherine. "A Guilford That Is Gone." *Sunday Sun Magazine,* August 29, 1955.

Scharf, J. Thomas. *History of Maryland.* Vol. 3. Baltimore: John B. Piet, 1879.

Walsh, Richard, et al., eds. *Maryland: A History, 1632–1975.* Baltimore: Maryland Historical Society, 1974.

West, Harold E. "History of the Sun." Published on the *Sun's* 85th anniversary. *Sunday Sun,* May 14, 1922.

Other Sources

"A. S. Abell's estate, real and personal, set apart under order of Circuit Court of Baltimore City in care of E. F. Abell et al. vs. Walter R. Abell et al." January 12, 1895. Courtesy of William S. Abell.

5: SONS OF THE FOUNDER, 1888–1906

Books, Periodicals, and Newspapers

"Annie Oakley." *Dictionary of American Biography.* 1957 edition.

Crooks, James B. *Politics & Progress: The Rise of Urban Progressivism in Baltimore, 1895 to 1911.* Baton Rouge: Louisiana State University Press, 1968.

Dorsey, John. "Douglas Gordon: The Crusader of Charlcote Place." *Sunday Sun Magazine,* September 18, 1977.

"Grasty Buries Machine Politics." Baltimore *News,* January 25, 1895.

Jacobs, Bradford. *Thimbleriggers.* Baltimore: Johns Hopkins University Press, 1984.

Johnson, Gerald W., et al. *The Sunpapers of Baltimore.* New York: Alfred A. Knopf, 1937.

Manchester, William. *Disturber of the Peace: The Life of H. L. Mencken.* New York: Harper & Brothers, 1950.

Muller, Amelia. "Lady of the Press." *Sunday Sun Magazine,* January 5, 1947.

New Wings for Intelligence, Being a Tribute to the Life and Works of Ottmar Mergenthaler. Baltimore: Schneidereith & Sons, 1954.

Obituary of Walter R. Abell. *Sun,* January 3, 1891.

Obituary of Charles J. Bonaparte. *Sun,* June 28 and 29, 1921.

Obituary of Mrs. Alexander J. Dennistone. *Sun,* March 13, 1962.

Obituary of May Garrettson Evans. *Sun,* January 13 and 14, 1947.

Obituary of Walter Poole. *Sun,* October 20 and 21, 1953.

Obituary of Francis Asbury Richardson. *Sun,* February 2, 1926.

"Picture History of the Prep." *Johns Hopkins Peabody News.* April 1985.

Reynolds, William. "A Line of Type That Revolutionized Printing." *New York Times Magazine,* May 9, 1954.

Scarborough, Katherine. "At Side of Gutenberg." *Sunday Sun,* May 9, 1954.

Swanberg, W. A. *Citizen Hearst.* New York: Scribner, 1961.

West, Harold E. "History of the *Sun.*" Published on the *Sun*'s 85th anniversary. *Sunday Sun,* May 14, 1922.

When Denny Went to Towson. Brochure. Published by the *Sun,* 1922.

Wilkerson, Marcus M. *Public Opinion and the Spanish American War: A Study in Propaganda.* New York: Russell & Russell, 1967. Reprint of 1932 edition.

Winchester, Paul. *Newspapers and Newspapermen of Maryland.* Baltimore: Frank L. Sibley & Company, 1905.

Other Sources

A. S. Abell Company. Minute Books of the Board of Directors, 1892.

Dove, James W. Date Books of the *Sunpapers.*

6: THE GREAT FIRE OF 1904

Books, Periodicals, and Newspapers

Kelly, Jacques. "History of the *News American.*" "Extra" magazine. Baltimore *News American,* August 19, 1973.

Mencken, H. L. *Newspaper Days, 1899–1906.* New York: Alfred A. Knopf, 1941.
Obituary of Edwin F. Abell. *Sun,* February 29, March 2, 3, 12, 1904.
Obituary of Charles H. Grasty. *New York Times,* January 20, 1924.
Scharf, J. Thomas. *The Chronicles of Baltimore.* Baltimore: Turnbull Brothers, 1874.
The Sun Almanac, 1905.
West, Harold E. "History of the *Sun.*" Published on the *Sun*'s 85th anniversary. *Sunday Sun,* May 14, 1922.
Williams, Harold A. *Baltimore Afire.* Baltimore: Schneidereith & Sons, 1954. Reprinted 1979.

Other Sources

Baltimore City Directory, 1903.

7: SUN SQUARE DAYS, 1906–1910

Books, Periodicals, and Newspapers

"Charles H. Grasty." *Dictionary of American Biography.* 1957 edition.
Johnson, Gerald W., et al. *The Sunpapers of Baltimore.* New York: Alfred A. Knopf, 1937.
"Mark Twain Departs." *Sun,* May 12, 1907.
Mencken, H. L. "Walter Abell and The Sun." *Sun,* January 26, 1941.
Obituary of H. Crawford Black. *Sun,* March 23, 1921.
Obituary of Emily Emerson Lantz. *Sun,* March 23, 1931.
Obituary of Harry Martin Leitch. *Sun,* December 19, 1935.
Obituary of Folger McKinsey. *Sun,* July 23, 1950.
Obituary of John Campbell White. *Sun,* June 12, 1967.
"The Old Sun Building: A Memorial." *Sun,* October 1, 1964.
"*Sun* Square Building." Detailed description of the building and its operation. *Sun,* November 17, 1906.
Williams, Harold A. *Robert Garrett & Sons.* Baltimore: Schneidereith & Sons, 1965.

Other Sources

"A. S. Abell buildings, *Sun* Square. Prospectus." No date, probably 1954 or 1955. In possession of the author.
A. S. Abell Company. Minute Books of the Board of Directors, 1905, 1906.
A. S. Abell Company. Minutes of stockholders' meetings, 1908.

"An Appraisal" (of H. Crawford Black). Typed memorandum. August 1920. *Sun* Library.
Dove, James W. Date Books of the *Sunpapers.*

8: CHARLES H. GRASTY'S PAPER, 1910–1914

Books, Periodicals, and Newspapers

Berger, Meyer. *The Story of the New York Times, 1851–1951.* New York: Simon & Schuster, 1951.
"Charles H. Grasty." *Dictionary of American Biography.* 1957 edition.
Johnson, Gerald W., et al. *The Sunpapers of Baltimore.* New York: Alfred A. Knopf, 1937.
Link, Arthur S. *Wilson: The Road to the White House.* Princeton: Princeton University Press, 1974.
Obituary of Edwin L. James. *New York Times,* December 4, 1951.
Obituary of Felix Morley. *Sun,* March 18, 1982.
Obituary of Carr V. Van Anda. *Sun,* January 29, 1945.
The Sun Almanac, 1912.
Villard, Oswald Garrison. "The Baltimore *Suns:* A Notable Journalistic Resurrection." *The Nation,* April 5, 1922.

Interview

Douglas H. Gordon interview, September 29, 1983.

Other Sources

A. S. Abell Company. Minute Books of the Board of Directors, 1910, 1911, 1912.
"Charles H. Grasty, 1863–1924." Memorial brochure. Maryland Room, Enoch Pratt Free Library, Baltimore, Maryland.
Dove, James W. Date Books of the *Sunpapers.*
Obituary of McKee Barclay. No date. Diehlman files, Maryland Historical Society, Baltimore, Maryland.

9: THE *EVENING SUN* AND GRASTY, 1910–1914

Books, Periodicals, and Newspapers

Berger, Meyer. *The Story of the New York Times, 1851–1951.* New York: Simon & Schuster, 1951.

Britt, George. *Forty Years—Forty Million: The Career of Frank A. Munsey.* New York: Farrar & Rinehart, 1935.

"Charles H. Grasty." *Dictionary of American Biography.* 1957 edition.

The Evening Sun 75th Anniversary Magazine, April 18, 1985.

Johnson, Gerald W., et al. *The Sunpapers of Baltimore.* New York: Alfred A. Knopf, 1937.

Manchester, William. *Disturber of the Peace: The Life of H. L. Mencken.* New York: Harper & Brothers, 1950.

Mencken, H. L. "Adams as Editor." *Sun,* October 13, 1927.

Obituary of Mrs. John Haslup Adams. *Evening Sun,* August 20; *Sun,* August 21, 1929.

Obituary of Horatio Bottomley. *London Times,* May 27, 1933.

Obituary of Charles H. Grasty. *New York Times,* January 20, 1924.

Winchester, Paul. *Newspapers and Newspapermen of Maryland.* Baltimore: Frank L. Sibley & Company, 1905.

Other Sources

A. S. Abell Company. Minute Books of the Board of Directors, 1910, 1911, 1912, 1913, 1914.

Dove, James W. Date Books of the *Sunpapers.*

John E. Cullen personal file. August 10, 1936. *Sun* Library.

10: VAN-LEAR BLACK TAKES CHARGE, 1914–1919

Books, Periodicals, and Newspapers

"An American Newspaper Woman's Adventures in Soviet Russia." *Current Opinion,* May 1922.

Aunt Priscilla in the Kitchen. Baltimore: Aunt Priscilla Publishing Company, 1929.

Brewer, James H. Fitzgerald. *History of the 175th Infantry (Fifth Maryland).* Baltimore: Maryland Historical Society, War Records Division, 1955.

Britt, George. *Forty Years—Forty Million: The Career of Frank A. Munsey.* New York: Farrar & Rinehart, 1935.

Darin, Grace. "Reporting the News for 70 Years." *Evening Sun,* April 18, 1980.

A Gang of Pecksniffs and Other Comments on Newspapers, Publishers, Editors and Reporters, by H. L. Mencken. Selected, edited, and introduced with a profile on Mencken as newsman by Theo Lippman, Jr. New Rochelle, N.Y.: Arlington House, 1975.

Harrison, Marguerite. *There's Always Tomorrow.* New York: Farrar & Rinehart, 1935.

Sources

"Hospital Here Honors Marguerite Harrison, Colorful Woman of the Past."
Baltimore *News American,* September 15, 1975.
Johnson, Gerald W., et al. *The Sunpapers of Baltimore.* New York: Alfred A.
Knopf, 1937.
Kelly, Jacques. "History of the *News American.*" "Extra" magazine. Balti-
more *News American,* August 19, 1973.
———. "A Talent for Living." Baltimore *Messenger,* February 16, 1983.
Obituary of Van-Lear Black. *Sun,* August 20, 1930.
Obituary of Marguerite Harrison (Mrs. Arthur Blake). *Evening Sun,* July 17,
1967.
Obituary of Edwin L. James. *New York Times,* December 4, 1951.
Obituary of Stuart Olivier. *Evening Sun* and Baltimore *News American,* January
23, 1973.
Obituary of Eleanor Purcell. *Sun,* April 21, 1968.
Searl, Helen Hulett. "Marguerite Harrison: World Wanderer." *Woman Cit-
izen,* July 1926.
West, Harold E. "History of the *Sun.*" Published on the *Sun*'s 85th anni-
versary. *Sunday Sun,* May 14, 1922.

Interviews

Douglas H. Gordon.

Other Sources

A. S. Abell Company personnel records. Marguerite Harrison.
Biographical memorandum on Marguerite Harrison (Mrs. Arthur Blake),
December 5, 1958. *Sun* Library.
Dove, James W. Date Books of the *Sunpapers.*
Frank R. Kent Collection. Maryland Historical Society, Baltimore, Maryland.

11: The Beginning of the Modern Era, 1919–1930

Books, Periodicals, and Newspapers

"The Baltimore *Sunpapers.*" *The Quill,* December 1925.
Catledge, Turner. *My Life and The Times.* New York: Harper & Row, 1971.
Fielding, Geoffrey W. "The UP's Last Fling—But Maryland Lost at Aintree."
Evening Sun, March 30, 1983.
"From the Log of the Maryland Free State." *Sunday Sun,* May 18 and 25, 1930.
Grauer, Neil A. "Political Cartooning: From One Golden Age to Another."
Sun, November 27, 1980.

Hoopes, Roy. *Cain.* New York: Holt, Rinehart & Winston, 1982.

Johnson, Gerald W., et al. *The Sunpapers of Baltimore.* New York: Alfred A. Knopf, 1937.

Kelly, Jacques. "History of the *News American.*" "Extra" magazine. Baltimore *News American,* August 19, 1973.

Kidder, Key. "Baltimore Assembly." *Sun,* January 15, 1980.

Lunt, Richard L. *Law and Order vs. the Miners: West Virginia, 1907–1933.* Hamden, Conn.: Anchor Books, 1979.

MacColl, Rene. *A Flying Start: A Memory of the Nineteen Twenties.* London: Jonathan Cape, 1939.

Manchester, William. *Disturber of the Peace: The Life of H. L. Mencken.* New York: Harper & Brothers, 1950.

Miller, Nathan. *FDR: An Intimate History.* New York: Doubleday, 1983.

Neun, Johnny. "I Remember" (*Sun* Square Baseball Scoreboard). *Sunday Sun Magazine,* September 28, 1958.

Obituary of John Haslup Adams. *Sun,* October 14, 1927.

Obituary of Van-Lear Black. *Evening Sun,* August 19 and 22. *Sun,* August 20, 21, and 22, 1930.

Obituary of Lloyd B. Councill. *Sun,* May 21, 1971.

Obituary of George C. Dorsch. *Sun,* March 2, 1978.

Obituary of Gustafus Warfield Hobbs. *Sun,* April 25, 1957.

Obituary of Mrs. Banny McLean Near. *Sun,* December 17, 1963.

Obituary of Paul Patterson. *Sun,* April 22, 1952.

Obituary of Robert F. Sisk. *Sun,* March 6, 1964.

Obituary of Hendrik Willem van Loon. *New York Times,* March 12, 1944.

Obituary of Mark S. Watson. *Sun,* March 26, 1966.

Rose, Stuart. *The Maryland Hunt Cup.* New York: Huntington Press, 1931.

Swanberg, W. A. *Citizen Hearst.* New York: Scribner, 1961.

"Van-Lear Black's will." *Sun,* September 4, 1930.

Villard, Oswald Garrison. "The Baltimore *Suns:* A Notable Journalistic Resurrection." *The Nation,* April 5, 1922.

Interviews

Gary Black, Paul Broderick, George C. Dorsch (1976), Ernest B. Furgurson, Jr., Louis J. O'Donnell (conversations, 1941), Gwinn Owens, Mrs. Hamilton Owens, Donald H. Patterson.

Other Sources

A. S. Abell Company. Minute Books of the Board of Directors, 1920.

A. S. Abell Company. "An Editorial Memorandum" (The White Paper). 1919.

Dove, James W. Date Books of the *Sunpapers.*

Fleming, H. K. Letter to author. December 22, 1978.

Fleming, H. K. Unpublished autobiography. Excerpts in possession of author.

Frank R. Kent Collection. Maryland Historical Society, Baltimore, Maryland.

H. L. Mencken–John Owens correspondence. Paul Patterson Collection. Bettina Patterson Manheim, Brooklyn, New York.

Wolff, Miles H. Unpublished autobiography. Excerpts in possession of author.

Mrs. Donald H. Hooker file at *Sun* Library.

12: THE *EVENING SUN:* THE "ROLLICKING SON," 1922–1938

Books, Periodicals, and Newspapers

Beirne, Francis F. *The Amiable Baltimoreans.* New York: E. P. Dutton & Company, 1951.

_____. "The Paper That Won't Grow Old." *The Quill,* December 1925.

Bode, Carl. *Mencken.* Carbondale: Southern Illinois University Press, 1969.

A Gang of Pecksniffs and Other Comments on Newspapers, Publishers, Editors and Reporters, by H. L. Mencken. Selected, edited, and introduced with a profile on Mencken as newsman by Theo Lippman, Jr. New Rochelle, N.Y.: Arlington House, 1975.

Johnson, Gerald W., et al. *The Sunpapers of Baltimore.* New York: Alfred A. Knopf, 1937.

Lerner, Leon L. "A Long-Gone Tradition: 'Gob Humor.'" *Evening Sun,* June 11, 1985.

_____. ed. *Gob Humor.* Baltimore: I & M Ottenheimer, 1953.

Obituary of Bruce Earnest. *Evening Sun,* March 1; *Sun,* March 2, 1960.

Obituary of Mrs. Arthur B. Kinsolving. *Sun,* April 26, 1962.

Obituary of Lee McCardell. *Evening Sun,* February 7; *Sun,* February 8, 1963.

Obituary of J. Edwin Murphy. *Evening Sun,* March 29, 1943.

Obituary of Hamilton Owens. *Sun,* April 22, 1967.

Schoettler, Carl A. ". . . Sages of Legendary Newsmen." *Evening Sun,* April 24, 1984.

Villard, Oswald Garrison. "The Baltimore *Suns:* A Notable Journalistic Resurrection." *The Nation,* April 5, 1922.

Walsh, Richard, et al., eds. *Maryland: A History, 1632–1975.* Baltimore: Maryland Historical Society, 1974.

Interviews

Gary Black, James H. Bready, Paul Broderick, Robert B. Cochrane, Grace Darin, Dudley P. Digges, R. P. Harriss, Philip S. Heisler, Edgar L. Jones,

Michael Lhotsky, Lee McCardell (conversation, 1952), Nancy J. Oppel, John Stees, Clement G. Vitek, Philip M. Wagner, John Ward.

Other Sources

Dove, James W. Date Books of the *Sunpapers.*
Lund, Eric. "Letters from an American Mother." Magazine article on Holger A. Koppel (publication not named or dated). *Sun* Library.
Owens, Hamilton. Interview by Louis M. Starr of the Oral History Research Office, Columbia University, New York, July 23, 1958. In possession of Mrs. Hamilton Owens.
————. Letter to H. L. Mencken. Mencken files, Mencken Room, Enoch Pratt Free Library, Baltimore, Maryland.
Obituary of John Oldmixon Lambdin. Only date: 1923. Diehlman files, Maryland Historical Society, Baltimore, Maryland.
Ridgely, Janetta Somerset. Memorandum on Lee McCardell. January 7, 1984. In possession of author.

13: THE PAUL PATTERSON YEARS, 1930–1952

Books, Periodicals, and Newspapers

Ayerst, David. *Biography of a Newspaper [Manchester Guardian].* London: Collins, 1971.
Bready, James H. "The Bentztown Bard." *Sunday Sun Magazine,* August 28, 1949.
Edmund Duffy, as subject of "Uncle Dudley" column. *Union News* (Towson, Md.), September 20, 1962.
Fecher, Charles A. "Mencken and the Archbishop." *Menckeniana: A Quarterly Review,* Spring 1985.
————. "New Look at Old Media Flap. . . . Papers of H. L. Mencken." Baltimore *Catholic Review,* March 19, 1982.
"Hitler Described by Bouton. . . ." *Sun,* June 18, 1934.
Hohenberg, John, ed. *The Pulitzer Prize Story.* New York: Columbia University Press. 1959.
Johnson, Gerald W., et al. *The Sunpapers of Baltimore.* New York: Alfred A. Knopf, 1937.
Kent Cooper and the Associated Press: An Autobiography. New York: Random House, 1959.
Levine, Richard H. "Edmund Duffy, Political Cartoonist." *Johns Hopkins University Magazine,* July 1973.
Manchester, William. *Disturber of the Peace: The Life of H. L. Mencken.* New York: Harper & Brothers, 1950.

Maryland: A Guide to the Old Line State. New York: Oxford University Press, 1940.
"Mr. Bouton's Article—A Statement by the Sun." *Sun,* July 19, 1934.
Obituary of Price Day. *Sun,* December 10, 1978.
Obituary of Edmund Duffy. *Sun,* September 13, 1962.
Obituary of Lee McCardell. *Evening Sun,* February 7, 1963.
Obituary of Folger McKinsey. *Sun,* July 23, 1950.
Obituary of John W. Owens. *Sun,* April 25, 1968.
Obituary of Mark S. Watson. *Sun,* March 26, 1966.
Ridout, Mary McKinsey. "The Bentztown Bard as a Two-Finger Typist." *Sunday Sun Magazine,* May 10, 1970.
Snyder, Louis L. *Masterpieces of War Reporting.* New York: Julian Messner, 1962.
Time, November 16, 1942. In response to a reader's inquiry, *Time* editors pick nine top newspapers.
"Treasury Lists Highest Paychecks in U.S." *Evening Sun,* January 6, 1937.
"Treasury List of Md. Salaries Given." *Evening Sun,* January 9, 1937.

Interviews

William S. Abell, George T. Bertsch, Gary Black, James H. Bready, Robert B. Cochrane, Rodney Crowther, Grace Darin, Harrison Garrett, Gerald Griffin, R. P. Harriss, Philip S. Heisler, Bradford Jacobs, Edgar L. Jones, Thomas J. O'Donnell, Donald H. Patterson, Janetta Somerset Ridgely, Neil H. Swanson (1980), Philip M. Wagner, Carroll E. Williams.

Other Sources

Aiken, Newton. Unpublished autobiography. Photocopy in *Sun* Library.
Dove, James W. Date Books of the *Sunpapers.*
Fleming, H. K. Unpublished autobiography. Excerpts in possession of author.
Goodman, Julius B. Letter to author, February 20, 1986, about New Judea story in *Evening Sun,* May 12, 1948.
Harriss, R. P. Diary entry, August 30, 1946, with clipping of *New Yorker's* Department of Correction and Amplification statement regarding *Evening Sun* article on atomic bomb, September 1, 1946. Photocopy of entry and article in possession of author.
———. Diary entry, September 10, 1936. Photocopy in possession of author.
Johnson, Gerald W. Letter to Charles V. Flowers, July 25, 1972. In possession of author.
Mencken, H. L. Diary entry, July 16, 1946. Mencken Room, Enoch Pratt Free Library, Baltimore, Maryland.

Nelson, Frederic C. "Notes on My Tour at the *Sunpapers*." Manuscript. April 27, 1976. In possession of author.

Reporter's Notebook. Booklet of anecdotal memories printed for guests at the *Evening Sun*'s 75th anniversary banquet, April 19, 1985. Copy in *Sun* Library.

Wolff, Miles H. Unpublished autobiography. Photocopy of portion dealing with *Sunpapers* in possession of author.

14: The Washington Bureau, 1837–1987

Books, Periodicals, and Newspapers

Allen, Robert, and Drew Pearson. *Washington Merry-Go-Round.* New York: Horace Liveright, 1931.

Allen, Robert, and Drew Pearson. *More Washington Merry-Go-Round.* New York: Liveright, 1932.

"The Baltimore *Sunpapers*, Washington Bureau." *Editor & Publisher*, November 25, 1952.

Binder, Carroll. "The Press and the Pulitzer Prizes." *American Mercury*, April 1948.

Cooke, Alistair. *A Generation on Trial: U.S.A. vs. Alger Hiss.* New York: Alfred A. Knopf, 1952.

Essary, J. Frederick. *Covering Washington: Government Reflected to the Public in the Press, 1822–1924.* Boston and New York: Houghton Mifflin Company, 1927.

"Frank R. Kent Dies at 80: 'The Great Game Ends.'" *Editor & Publisher*, April 19, 1958.

"From a Window in Fleet Street: London Bureau of the Sun." *Sunday Sun Magazine*, January 15, 1950.

Furgurson, Ernest B., Jr. "Making a Move and Ending a Tradition in Washington." U.S.A. column. *Sunday Sun*, February 27, 1983.

Hess, Stephen. *The Washington Reporters.* Washington, D.C.: Brookings Institution, 1981.

Johnson, Gerald W., et al. *The Sunpapers of Baltimore.* New York: Alfred A. Knopf, 1937.

Jones, Carleton. "Restorers Make New Edition of *Sun*'s Old Building in D.C." *Sun*, October 5, 1982.

Lattimore, Owen. *Ordeal by Slander.* New York: Little, Brown & Company, 1950.

Manchester, William. *Disturber of the Peace: The Life of H. L. Mencken.* New York: Harper & Brothers, 1950.

Miller, Nathan. *FDR: An Intimate History.* New York: Doubleday & Company, 1983.

Nelson, Michael. "A New Look at 'The Great Game of Politics.'" *Sun,* April 23, 1978.

Obituary of George Washington Combs. *Sun,* December 6, 1958.

Obituary of J. Frederick Essary. *Evening Sun,* March 12, 1942.

Obituary of Dewey L. Fleming. *Sun,* May 5, 1955.

Obituary of Frank R. Kent. *Sun,* April 15, 1958.

Obituary of Paul W. Ward. *Sun,* November 25 and 26, 1976.

Pilat, Oliver. *Drew Pearson: An Unauthorized Autobiography.* New York: Harper's Magazine Press, 1973.

Recollections. Francis Asbury Richardson. *Sun,* February 11, 1902, and *Washington Evening Star,* February 11, 1902. Frank R. Kent Collection, Maryland Historical Society, Baltimore, Maryland.

Roberts, Chalmers M. *The Washington Post: The First 100 Years.* Boston: Houghton Mifflin Company, 1977.

TRB (Richard L. Strout). "Views from Backstage." *Sun,* April 7, 1983. Reprinted from The *New Republic.*

Interviews

Rodney Crowther, Muriel Dobbin, Ernest B. Furgurson, Jr., Edwin W. Goodpaster, Gerald Griffin, Frederic B. Hill, James I. Houck, Bradford Jacobs, James S. Keat, Frank R. Kent (1955), Peter J. Kumpa, Howard Norton, Philip Potter, Janetta Somerset Ridgely, Albert Sehlstedt, Jr., Frank C. Starr, Joseph R. L. Sterne.

Other Sources

Application for Historic Landmark Status, *Sun* Building, 1317 F Street, N.W., Washington, D.C. Copy in possession of author through courtesy of William S. Abell.

Houck, James I. (managing editor, the *Sun*). "Guidelines for the Washington Bureau of the *Sun.*" April 29, 1982.

Letters and related material on the career of Philip Potter, 1984–1985. In possession of author.

"Report of News Room Task Force," by Thomas Linthicum, Jr. chairman; Peter Behr, Kathy Lally, Robert DuPont, John M. McClintock, John Dorsey, Steve Luxenberg. December 14, 1978. In *Sun* managing editor's office.

Time magazine research memorandum on Philip Potter. 1964. Copy in possession of author.

"Washington Bureau History." Memorandum to H. L. Mencken from Washington Bureau, August 10, 1936. *Sun* Library.

15: Two Generations of Leadership, 1960–1983

Books, Periodicals, and Newspapers

Baker, Russell. *Growing Up.* New York: Congdon & Weed, 1982.
Carter, Bill. "Jim McKay [James McManus] Learns You Can Come Home." *Sun*, May 13, 1983.
Day, Price. "Spillway" column. *Sun*, April 24, 1956.
The Guild Reporter (Washington, D.C.), April 25, 1965.
Harriss, R. P. "Moco [Richard Q. Yardley]." *Gardens, Houses, and People*, August 1951.
Jacobs, Bradford. "Moco: A Big 'Little' Man." *Evening Sun*, November 26, 1979.
"John O'Ren." *Sun*, October 15, 1957.
"Letter from the Editor." *Sunday Sun*, August 8, 1982.
Lippman, Theo, Jr. Column on chronology of "Spillway" and "Notes & Comment." *Sun*, March 24, 1984.
Manchester, William. *Disturber of the Peace: The Life of H. L. Mencken.* New York: Harper & Brothers, 1950.
Obituary of J. Stephen Becker. *Sun*, June 21, 1976.
Obituary of Harry C. Black. *Sun* and *Evening Sun*, November 26, 1956.
Obituary of Price Day. *Sun*, December 10, 1978.
Obituary of Charles H. Dorsey, Jr. *Sun*, October 18, 1973.
Obituary of A. D. Emmart. *Evening Sun*, October 22, 1973.
Obituary of Rudolph J. Handel. *Sun*, December 18, 1986.
Obituary of C. P. Ives. *Sun*, March 11, 1982.
Obituary of W. Maclean Patterson. *Sun*, August 28, 1976.
Obituary of William J. Perkinson. *Sun*, August 2, 1969.
Obituary of William F. Schmick, Sr. *Sun*, March 15, 1963.
Obituary of Neil H. Swanson and editorial, *Evening Sun*, February 7, 1983.
Obituary of Charles G. Whiteford. *Sun*, January 16, 1982.
Obituary of Richard Q. Yardley. *Sun*, November 25, 1979.
Obituary of Edwin P. Young, Jr. *Sun*, December 14, 1982.
Schulian, John. "The *Evening Sun*'s Mike Lane." *Baltimore Magazine*, March 1975.
The Seybold Report: Harris 2500 at the Baltimore Sun. How to Do It Right. Media, Pa.: Seybold Publications, 1976.
"Sun Shine." *Newsweek*, May 6, 1963.
"Ten Best Newspapers." *Time*, January 10, 1964.

Terrill, Bramwell. "President: 'Young Bill' Schmick." *Editor & Publisher,* April 27, 1968.
Wells, Robert W. *The Milwaukee Journal, 1882–1982.* Milwaukee: Journal Publishing Company, 1982.
Wicker, Tom. "Russell Baker, the Observer, Wins Pulitzer Prize." [New York] *Times Talk,* May–June 1979.
Wilken, Earl. "All-Electronic Newsroom Will Become a Reality in Baltimore." *Editor & Publisher,* June 1, 1974.

Interviews

William S. Abell, Paul A. Banker, George T. Bertsch, Gary Black, James H. Bready, Paul Broderick, W. Stephens Broening, Jr., Bill Carter, Jesse T. Crowder, Jr., Sharon Dickman, Dudley P. Digges, Tom Flannery, Louis J. Franconeri, Ernest B. Furgurson, Jr., R. H. Gardner, Patrick M. Gilbert, Jesse E. Glasgow, Robert O. Grover, Gerald Griffin, Jean I. Hare, Louis Hatter, Philip S. Heisler, Bradford Jacobs, August J. Janos, Edgar L. Jones, James S. Keat, C. Ruth Kratz, Peter J. Kumpa, Patricia T. McLellan, Mary G. Myles, Jack W. Neely, Donald H. Patterson, John H. Plunkett, William Radford, Ruth E. Reimschissel, Janetta Somerset Ridgely, William F. Schmick, Jr., Howard W. Shank, Sr., Joseph R. L. Sterne, Richard Tucker, Philip M. Wagner, Carroll E. Williams.

Other Sources

A. S. Abell Company personnel records.
Agreements between the Baltimore Newspaper Guild, the Washington-Baltimore Newspaper Guild, and the A. S. Abell Company, 1952–1987. In private files.
Aiken, Newton. Unpublished autobiography. Photocopy in *Sun* Library.
"Baltimore *Sunpapers.*" Draft of article for *Time,* April 16, 1954. In possession of author.
Bertsch, George T. Memorandum on *Sunpapers,* December 12, 1976. In possession of author.
Biographical sketch of William F. Schmick, Jr. *Sun* Library.
Flores, Brian. *Washington-Baltimore Newspaper Guild Bulletin,* June 20, 1976.
"I Walk on Principle Only." Announcement prepared by Rudolph J. Handel, 1970 and 1973. Photocopy in possession of author.
"A New Dimension in the Production of Newspapers [Goss press and mailroom production system]." Brochure. No date, probably 1981.
' An Operating Guide to the [*Sun*] Op-Ed Page." April 1984. In editor's office.

Sunpaper strikes, 1965, 1970, 1978. Clippings in *Sun* Library.

Sun salary memorandum, including Russell Baker. No date (probably 1949). Courtesy of John H. Plunkett.

Task Force on Management Objectives of A. S. Abell Company. Minutes, memoranda, correspondence. Courtesy of James S. Keat.

"Toward Equality: Baltimore Progress Report, 1954–58." Pamphlet. Sidney Hollander Foundation, Baltimore, Maryland, 1958.

"Toward Equality," Supplement. Pamphlet. Sidney Hollander Foundation, Baltimore, Maryland, 1961.

16: THE *SUN* ABROAD, 1887–1987

Books, Periodicals, and Newspapers

Catling, Patrick Skene. *Better Than Working.* New York: Macmillan, 1960.

"From a Window in Fleet Street: London Bureau of the *Sun.*" Reminiscences on the 25th anniversary of the London bureau by James Bone, Rodney Crowther, A. D. Emmart, Dewey L. Fleming, Gerald Griffin, Frank R. Kent, Frank R. Kent, Jr., Lee McCardell, Thomas M. O'Neill, John W. Owens, Maclean Patterson, Philip M. Wagner, Paul W. Ward. *Sunday Sun Magazine,* January 15, 1950.

Graham, Joan. "From a Window in Fleet Street." *Sun,* June 3, 1956.

Johnson, Gerald W., et al. *The Sunpapers of Baltimore.* New York: Alfred A. Knopf, 1937.

McCardell, Lee. "Arabs' Arms Include U.S.-Made Weapons." *Sun,* September 5, 1957.

Norton, Howard. *Only in Russia.* New York. D. Van Nostrand, 1961.

Obituary of Robert P. Anderson. *Sun,* September 10, 1981.

Obituary of Felix Morley. *Sun,* March 3, 1982.

Obituary of Burwell C. Snyder. *Sun,* September 25, 1965.

Obituary of Paul W. Ward. *Sun,* November 25, 1976.

Obituary of Lord Winster (Reginald T. H. Fletcher). *Sun,* June 9, 1961.

Interviews

Judy Anderson, Paul A. Banker, Daniel Berger, Rodney Crowther, Dudley P. Digges, Robert A. Erlandson, Charles V. Flowers, Ernest B. Furgurson, Jr., Gerald Griffin, Frederic B. Hill, James I. Houck, Arnold R. Isaacs, Bradford Jacobs, James S. Keat, Peter J. Kumpa, Patricia T. McLellan, Nathan Miller, Howard Norton, Richard P. O'Mara, John H. Plunkett, Philip Potter, Janetta Somerset Ridgely, John Schidlovsky, Albert Sehlstedt, Jr., Matt Seiden, Joseph R. L. Sterne, Philip M. Wagner, Weldon Wallace, Davison D. White.

Other Sources

A. S. Abell Company personnel records.

McCardell, Lee. Letter to author, September 11, 1951.

Nelson, Frederic C. "Notes on My Tour at the *Sunpapers.*" April 27, 1976. Manuscript, in possession of author.

Norton, Howard. Letter to author, June 26, 1951.

"Report of News Room Task Force," Thomas Linthicum, chairman. December 14, 1978. In *Sun* managing editor's office.

Reports on *Sun* foreign bureaus. *Sun* Library.

Time magazine research memorandum on Philip Potter, 1964. Copy in possession of author.

17: REACHING 150 YEARS, 1981–1987

Books, Periodicals, and Newspapers

"Baltimore *Sunpapers* Are Not for Sale." *Editor & Publisher,* August 9, 1958.

"Baltimore *Sun* Case: Stock Value Gauged by Profit Factors." *Editor & Publisher,* October 15, 1960.

Bortz, Bruce. "John R. (Reg) Murphy: An Interview." *Baltimore Daily Record,* August 11, 1984.

Cook, Bruce. "Reg Murphy: 'Just-Folks' Publisher of the Baltimore *Sun.*" *Washington Journalism Review,* November 1983.

"Corporate Image Made Stronger, Logo Redesigned." *Between Editions* (the *Sun*), December 1982.

Douglas, Eric F. and Paul Mandelbaum. "The *Sun* Sells Out." *Baltimore Magazine,* July 1986.

"The Empire Builders" [Samuel I. Newhouse]. *Time,* August 11, 1958.

Latham, Aaron. "Can Reg Murphy Turn the *S. F. Examiner* Back into 'The Monarch of the Dailies?'" *New West Magazine,* November 22, 1976.

Mindus, Paul D. "Murphy Sets Goals for Next Five Years." *Between Editions* (the *Sun*), September 1981.

O'Connor, Bob. "Shades of the *Sun:* Reg Murphy Sets His Paper on a One-way Trip to Trendiness." *City Paper* (Baltimore), June 3–9, 1983.

Orrick, Phyllis. "Pressing Matters—Sales Talk." *City Paper* (Baltimore), November 1–7, 1985.

"Sun Vignette Redesigned." *Between Editions* (the *Sun*), March–April 1984.

Interviews

W. Shepherdson Abell, Jr., William S. Abell, Harold E. Archer, Marcia B. Bennett, Daniel Berger, James H. Bready, Bill Carter, John W. Cordes,

Sharon Dickman, Louis J. Franconeri, William E. N. Hawkins, James I. Houck, Imogene L. Hults, Ernest F. Imhoff, August J. Janos, Jacques Kelly, Kathleen Klein, John M. Lemmon, Thomas Linthicum, James P. McCrystal, Patricia T. McLellan, Carol A. Marks, Mary A. Maushard, Reg Murphy, Donald H. Patterson, John H. Plunkett, Nurite Rosin, Roger Simon, Gerald V. Smolinski, Charles E. Tait, Bill Tanton, Frank P. Wagner, Jr., Gilbert L. Watson 3d.

Other Sources

A. S. Abell Company Annual Report, 1985.
A. S. Abell Company personnel records.
A. S. Abell Company Proxy Statement, June 2, 1986.
Biographical sketch of Reg Murphy. *Sun* Library.
Bready, James H. Baltimore *Sun* memorandum for *Time* magazine. February 23, 1984. Copy in possession of author.
Mercantile–Safe Deposit & Trust Company. Federal transfer of funds wire from Morgan NYC/TMAC, Inc., October 27, 1986.

Index

Note: *Italic* page numbers refer to illustrations.

Abell, Arunah S.: beneficiaries of, 81, 370–71; biographical data, 3, 16; during Civil War, 52, 55, 61, 64; co-partnership of, with sons, 80; death of, 81; as editor, 11, 32, 34, 37, 71, 90, 95, 96; enterprise of, 1–2, 10–11, 17, 19, 23, 31, 36; and founding of *Sun*, 2, 6, 374; personal, 38–39, 79, 80–81; and *Philadelphia Public Ledger*, 5–6, 7, 38, 64; portraits of, *189, 372*; residences of, 15, 68, 80, 107, 130; association with Simmons and Swain, 3, 5–7, 38, 64

Abell, Arunah S., 2d, 89, 90, 115, 120–21, 126–27, 129, 130; death of, 147

Abell, Charles S., 84, 89, 90, 120–21, 125–26, 127, 130; biographical data, 121, 123–24; elected vice president and general manager, 121; resignations of, 123, 128, 129, 147

Abell, Edwin F., 80, 91, 92, 107, 113, 123; death of, 109–10; elected president, 90

Abell, George W.: changes by, to *Sun*, 69–71; death of, 89–90; elected president, 89; as founder of *Sun Almanac*, 70; as successor to father, 69, 75, 80, 84, 86, 92

Abell, W. Shepherdson, *209,* 366, 371

Abell, Walter R., 80, 88–89, 115, 120, 123

Abell, Walter R., 2d, 89, 116

Abell, Walter W., 90, 98, 123, 125, 148; and Baltimore fire, 101–2, 107; biographical data, 115; declined reelection as president, 121; and differences among Abells, 120

Abell, William S., 124, 263, 340; biographical data, 320

Abell Communications, 328, 348

Abell Foundation, 375

Abt, Sam, 266, 345

Adams, John Haslup, 140, 150, 168–69, 170, *195*; biographical data, 141–42; death of, 172; as editor, 146

Agnew, Spiro T., *212,* 286, 301, 336

Agnus, Felix, 127, 163, 226

Aiken, Newton, 231, 331; career of, 303–4

Albano, Donna L., 360

Allen, A. G., 269

Allen, Malcolm M., 2d, 361

Allen, Robert, 273; *Washington Merry-Go-Round* and *More Washington Merry-Go-Round,* 273

Alvarez, Rafael M., 360

American Newspaper Guild, 225, 266, 322

American Mercury, 275–76

American Party. *See* Know-Nothing Party

An American Mother. *See* Koppel, Holger A.

Anderson, Judy, 336

Anderson, Robert P., 345

Index

Index

Ridgely, Janetta Somerset, 295, 314, 323, 334, 335
Ridgely, Joseph, 314
Riggs, Lawrason, 106
Ringgold, Sam, 25, 32
Ritchie, Albert, 158
Roberts, Harold S., 361
Robinson, Boardman, 170, 236
Rodgers, George, 361
Rodricks, Dan, 298, 361
Roosevelt, Franklin D., 185, 186–87, 232–33, 240–42, 280
Roosevelt, Theodore R., 96, 130, 132
Ross, Harold, 175
Rousuck, J. Wynn, 361
Royal Dutch Airways, K.L.M., 186
Roylance, Frank, 361
Ruby, Robert, 344, 374
Rukeyser, Louis R., 315, 335, 340
Russell, William H., 52
Ryan, Thomas Fortune, 133–34

Sabalo (yacht), 160, 185, 186–87
Safe Deposit & Trust Company, 115, 120
Sage, Dewitt L., 326
St. Paul Dispatch, 122
St. Paul Pioneer Press, 122, 123, 127
Salganik, M. William, 325, 355
Samoa, 85–86
Sandler, Gilbert, 352
San Francisco Chronicle, 350
San Francisco Examiner, 349, 350, 352
Sarratt, Reed, 257
Sawyer, Kenneth, 313
Scarupa, Henry, 361
Schaefer, William Donald, 298
Scharf, J. Thomas, 19, 31, 55, 67–68; *History of Baltimore City and County,* 19; *History of Maryland,* 55, 67–68
Schidlovsky, John, 288, 343, 374
Schmick, William F., Jr., *205,* 285, 303, 341–42, 348, 372; advocates new editorial policy, 295–96, 299; biographical data, 291–92, 327; modernizes and expands *Sunpapers,* 321–22, 325, 336
Schmick, William F., Sr., 150–51, 152, 153, 168, *205,* 246, 262, 266, 320, 336, 348; biographical data, 142, 258, 290–93
Schmick, William F., 3d, 325, 339
Schoettler, Carl, 317, 361

Scholte, Johann B., 186, 187
Schumacher, Anne, 180
Schumann-Heink, Ernestine, 156
Schwerzler, Nancy J., 289
Scopes Trial, 181–82
Scott, C. P., 171
Scott, Winfield, 49
Scripps-Howard, 175–76
Scrivanish, Odette, 251
Sears, John, 362
Sedgwick, Ellery, 184
Sehlstedt, Albert, Jr., 286, 342, 360
Seiden, Matthew J., 311, 342–43
Semmes, John E., 235
Seymour, Stephen D., 348–49
Shaner, Joseph Jean, 246
Shapiro, Stephanie, 362
Shaw, James D., 353
Shelsby, Theodore F., 360
Sherman, William T., 55
Sherwin, Vernon, 315
Sherwood, Harry S., 222–23
Short, Joseph H., Jr., 278
Shuck, Henry, 69, 81
Shultz, Michael, 361
Sia, Richard H. P., 360
Sidney Hollander Foundation, 300
Siegel, Eric, 361
Simmons, Azariah H., 3, 5, 6, 38, 64, *189*
Simon, Roger, 298, 361
Simpson, Wallis Warfield, 332. *See also* Windsor, Duke and Duchess of
Singletary, Michelle, 361
Sisk, Robert F., 181
Six-penny papers, 4
Ski Racing International (magazine), 353
Slaves, 59
Smart Set (magazine), 165
Smith, Alfred E., 174
Smith, C. Fraser, 360
Smith, Linell, 361
Smith, Seymour, 361
Smith, Stuart, 323
Smolinski, Gerald V., 353
Snyder, Burwell, 178–79, 344–45
Snyder, Cameron, 345
Snyder, Dudley, 345
Somerset, Janetta. *See* Ridgely, Janetta Somerset
Somerville, Frank P. L., 360
Southern Mail, 24, 25, 26–27, 30
Spanish-American War, 95

Employees of the *Baltimore Sun* 150th Anniversary Year

A newspaper is only as good as its latest edition. The quality, integrity, and service expressed through the daily performance of its employees, however, is a lasting legacy, a proud tradition. Listed here are the 2,366 employees of the *Baltimore Sun* who continue to make ours one of the truly finest newspapers in publishing.

Robert B. Abell
Orem R. Abels
Claire A. Abt
Jon E. Ackerman
Kenneth S. Acton
Charles H. Adams
David D. Adams
Frederick M. Adams
Michael R. Adams
Harry C. Adamski
Dorothy D. Addington
Chandrae D. Adekoya
Anthony M. Adolfo
Elwood C. Agent
Bill Ahlfield
Henry L. Akins
Albert V. Alcarese
James H. Alexander
Barry J. Allen
Bobbie L. Allen
John F. Allen
Malcolm M. Allen
William M. Allred
Charles J. Alsruhe
George D. Altvater
Rafael M. Alvarez

Joseph L. Amereihn
Milton E. Amos
David N. Amtmann
Douglas D. Anderson
Gertrude S. Anderson
Judy Anderson
Linda D. Anderson
Lisa Anderson
Margaret T. Anderson
Nestor J. Aparicio
Jay Allen Apperson
Claudia S. Arbaugh
Raine G. Archer
Wayne W. Armstrong
Willie Armstrong
James T. Arnold
James W. Arther
Deborah A. Ashlock
B. Vance Askew
Duane R. Ather
Steven C. Auerweck
Dale A. Austin
Ann E. Ayers

David W. Backert
Emanuel Bacon

William A. Bacon
Sylvia H. Badger
Susan C. Baer
Bennie Bagby
Ramon R. Baier
Jerome H. Bailey
Paul T. Bailey
Stephen M. Bailey
William W. Bailey
George S. Bain
Austin H. Baker, Jr.
Bradley M. Baker
Donna M. Baker
Genice Baker
Jasper L. Baker
Kent Baker
Peter P. Baker
Ronald C. Baker
Sidney Baker
Maurice E. Baldwin
Warren R. Baldwin
Michael K. Ball
John J. Banach
Sujata C. Banerjee
Sandra A. Banisky
Eugene L. Bannister
Betty Lou Bannon
Bruce M. Barach
Joseph A. Baranowski
Fred C. Barantas
Anthony Barbieri
Charles W. Barksdale
Joan E. Barnes
Johnny Barnes
Nicholas E. Barnes
Richard J. Barnstein
Tonia L. Barnwell
John Barracate
Robert P. Bartlett
Elsie M. Barts
Joseph W. Barvir
Richard M. Basoco
George H. Bathon
Santo W. Battaglia
Jerry M. Bayne
Thomas L. Bazzell
Nancy Lea Bean
Charles B. Beaty
Elwood P. Beaty
Charles L. Beck
Myron Beckenstein
David Alan Becker

Ken S. Beckhardt
Gary Bell
Lorenzo Bell
Pamela M. Belt
Robert P. Belville
David R. Belz
Richard J. Belz
Jerry E. Bembry
Robert I. Benjamin
James G. Bennett
Marcia B. Bennett
William M. Bennett
Allen B. Benshoff
Gerald F. Beran
Rita G. Bergenstein
Daniel Berger
Linda L. Bernady
Richard J. Berquist
Charles F. Berry
Herbert D. Berry
Karin D. Berry
Joseph Bertorelli
Rogers Bess
Ralph W. Betz
Gary E. Bevans
Joseph V. Bianca
Lachelle B. Biddle
Robert G. Billingslea
Raymond C. Bingel
Doug M. Birch
George R. Bittner
Kenneth W. Blackburn
Warren J. Blackwell
Darlene R. Blaisdell
Paula S. Blank
James H. Blankenship
Robert A. Blankenship
W. DeWitt Bliss
Marc Sheldon Block
Denise Blount
Joseph Blount
David A. Bochenek
James K. Bock
Donald R. Boeshore
Ronald G. Bohn
Margaret U. Boles
Donna E. Boller
Mark W. Bomster
Anthony Boone
Eunetta T. Boone
Kevin A. Booth
James W. Born

Donald G. Bosley
Warren J. Bossalina
Joseph L. Boteler
Walter F. Boteler
Alfred D. Bouldin
Michael H. Bounan
Paul C. Bowen
Sharon M. Bowen
Frank L. Bowers
Larry R. Bowers
William L. Bowers
Elizabeth F. Bowie
Robert L. Bowings
Michael H. Bowler
Curtis W. Bowles
Marnon M. Bowles
Emma J. Bowman
Thomas M. Bowman
Cameron O. H. Boyd
Dan Boyd
Ernest Boyd
Rosetta Boyd
Sharon D. Boyd
Patricia A. Boykin
Gerald C. Brabham
William M. Bradford
Renee A. Branch
Charles W. Brandt
Edwin H. Brandt
Vera E. Braswell
Margaret C. Braun
Debra P. Braxton
James H. Bready
Richard E. Breen
Lloyd Brewington
Evon E. Briggs
Phyllis K. Brill
Earl A. Brinkmeyer
Edward W. Britain
Clarence Broady
Donald Brock
Joseph A. Brockmeyer
Peter S. Brodkin
Robert P. Brodowski
W. Stephens Broening
Robert C. Brookes
Jessica C. Brooks
John R. Brooks
Luther C. Brooks
A. Douglas Brown
Anntinett M. Brown
Clyde R. Brown

Edward M. Brown
George C. Brown
Holton F. Brown
James H. Brown
James J. Brown
Jerry W. Brown
Joseph M. Brown
Kenneth A. Brown
Kevin E. Brown
Kim C. Brown
Lee T. Brown
Leroy E. Brown
Melissa Ann Brown
Melvin C. Brown
Michael J. Brown
Reginald A. Brown
Robert C. Brown
Robert M. Brown
Ronald E. Brown
Thomas C. Brown
Thomas K. Brown
Thomas M. Brown
Robin L. Browning
Stephen H. Brozina
Frank J. Brulinski
Charles P. Bryant
Mary E. Bryant
John L. Buberl
Douglas R. Buckmeier
Jeffrey D. Buckmeier
Robert R. Buckmeier
Laverne A. Buckner
Wayne F. Buckner
Dorothy J. Budnichuk
James T. Buhl
Jason K. Bullard
Anthony G. Burdelas
Steve M. Burdusi
Arthur P. Burke
Donald G. Burke
Howard J. Burke
Judith E. Burke
James A. Burkey
Monica M. Burkhardt
Paula D. Burkholder
Godfrey W. Burns
James R. Burns
Leroy Burns
Michael K. Burns
Wendy L. Burns
Robert L. Burrell
Diana L. Burrows

Kathy Ann Burrows
Janice M. Burrus
Sharon A. Burrus
Kermit C. Burton
William J. Burton
William O. Burton
Joseph D. Bush
Lewis R. Bush
Robert H. Busick
Derek S. Butler
William D. Butler
John W. Byer
Wendell F. Byers
Karl G. Byrd
Robert P. Byrnes

Antonio A. Caesar
Calvin James Calhoun
Karen D. Calwrie
Donald E. Campbell
Janet Campbell
Michael A. Campbell
Douglas E. Canter
Eileen M. Canzian
Quinzel Capel
William P. Capo
Doris E. Carberry
Robert Carey
Rose L. Carnaggio
Joseph E. Carolan
William F. Carroll
Larry Carson
Fred R. Carter
William J. Carter
Raimon B. Cary
Padraic Cassidy
Randall M. Cathell
Wilbur A. Causion
Daniel P. Cavan
Charles I. Cayford
Louis R. Cedrone
Gerard A. Cegielski
Richard N. Celmer
Wayne E. Chalk
Zora A. Chambers
Donna S. H. Chan
John R. Chandler
Beverly A. Chaney
Alison M. Chaplin
James W. Chapman
Tracey L. Chapman
Laura L. Charles

Michele L. Chavis
Emory S. Chenoweth
Lawrence Chesla
Robert J. Chester
Tamera J. Chester
Sarah R. Chestnut
Francis J. Chilcoat
Michael A. Childs
Denise P. Chilson
Mary Jane Chirico
Elise T. Chisolm
Allen L. Chiveral
Warren E. Chiveral
Wayne Lee Christ
William F. Christopher
John C. Christopolus
John T. Christopoulos
Alice Ciano
Emma F. Cieri
Frank Cincotta
Loretta M. Claiborne
James Clark
Michael J. Clark
James R. Clarke
Clyde W. Clemens
William A. Clements
Jacob F. Clevenger
Marsha Y. Cliffton
Thomas L. Cline
Sherrie L. Clinton
Brian E. Clocker
Charles J. Close
Jennifer L. Coates
Leroy J. Coates
Robert R. Coates
David F. Cohn
Edward R. Colbert
Joann L. Cole
Richard D. Cole
Emerson L. Coleman
Harry C. Coleman
Marcian D. Coley
Kimberly M. Collins
William D. Collins
Marshall B. Commodari
John P. Conaboy
Alfred J. Conigliaro
Elizabeth A. Conley
John T. Conner
Edward Connolly
Darlene A. Connor
George C. Connor

Patrick C. Connors
Michael J. Conrad
James C. Conroy
Paul J. Conroy
J. D. Considine
James L. Conyers
Johnnie E. Conyers
Catherine P. Cook
Charles F. Cook
George H. Cook III
Marian F. Cook
Joanne M. Cooke
Edward R. Coombs
Alvesta Cooper
Catherine Cooper
Raymond E. Cooper
Anthony J. Coppolino
Kenneth J. Cora
Rebecca L. Corbett
Eunice M. Corbin
Joan E. Corcoran
Charles W. Corddry
Kathy G. Cordes
John W. Cordes
Mary J. Corey
Michael B. Cornell
Robert J. Cornish
M. Elizabeth Corrigan
Albert F. Costantino
Arthur Cote
Linda L. Cotton
Pantheria B. Council
Carl A. Covington
Donald B. Cowan
Martin E. Cowan
W. Kevin Cowherd
Carroll D. Cox
Thermon S. Cox
Gary J. Craft
Alphonso Craine
Elizabeth L. Cramer
Gene A. Crawford
Albert B. Crawley
Albert B. Crawley
John C. Creamer
Julia A. Cribbin
Felipe D. Crisostomo
Flordeliza Y. Crisostomo
Charles W. Critzer
Donna L. Crivello
Robert M. Crocco
Joseph F. Crocken

Sandra Crockett
Harry E. Cromer
Angela Y. Cromwell
Amor L. Crowe
Alvin L. Crowetz
Paul S. Crowl
Karen M. Culp
Michael W. Culver
Robert L. Culver
Michelle B. Cummings
Lawrence Cunningham
Walter F. Cwik

Joseph G. D'Adamo
Louis F. D'Adamo
Richard C. D'Agostino
Pietro D'Angelo
R. Scott Daeschner
Edward C. Dangerfield
Ann J. Daniells
Adolph L. Daniels
Kenneth A. Danzer
Sylvia L. Darden
Jeffrey L. Dauber
Louis A. Daubert
Sonceearay Davenport
Yvonne Davis-Robinson
Amy C. Davis
Antoinette S. Davis
Brenda J. Davis
Ellie Davis
Ervin Davis
Glenn W. Davis
Helen Davis
James F. Davis
Jesse W. Davis
John G. Davis
Lee H. Davis
Mattie B. Davis
Michael A. Davis
Phillip A. Davis
Richard W. Davis
Roslyn C. Davis
Samuel C. Davis
William N. Davis
Cecilia Dawkins
Herman L. Dawson
Robert A. Dawson
Sheri L. Dawson
James P. Day
Charles E. Dean
Edward T. Death

Dorothy L. Deaver
Francis J. Debinski
Luis R. Debriel
Eugene L. DeCarlo
William B. Decker
Antenor A. DeFeria
Brenda J. Delaney
Janice Delaney
Paul Delaney
Stephen L. Delaney
Bill H. Deloach
Raymond L. Dembeck
Lyle W. Denniston
Carmen A. DePaola
Michael J. DePasquale
Mark P. Derda
Vernon K. Desell
Charles H. Devaud
Janis E. Dice
K. Kareem Dickerson
Sharon A. Dickman
David S. Dickson
Joseph F. Dickson
Harry A. Dieter
Sharon Lea Dieter
Joseph M. Dieterich
George Dietze
Frank J. Dimeglio
Dorothy E. Dimick
Santo Dipasquale
Michael J. Dipinto
Carlton M. Dix
Barbara A. Dixon
Christine Dixon
Donald T. Dixon
Jeffrey L. Dixon
Shirley A. Dixon
Steve Dixon
Steven M. Dixon
Richard S. Dobyski
Diana M. Dodson
James D. Doged
Honora M. Dolan
Daniel L. Donahue
Teresa B. Donahue
Wilbert B. Doran
Charles C. Dorsey
Chesler T. Dorsey
John R. Dorsey
Carole L. Doughney
Robert B. Douglass
John L. Dowery

Bennett F. Downs
Katrina L. Drakeford
Deborah E. Dreer
Anne C. Dressel
Michael T. Dresser
Sheila McC. Dresser
Donald L. Driscoll
Eugene P. Driscoll
Michael R. Driscoll
Walter G. Driver
Donald R. Drumheller
Robert L. Drury
Harry M. Duckworth
Charles B. Dudley
Mary M. Dudley
John J. Dugan
Molly Dugan
Acquanetta Dukes
Antoinette L. Dukes
Henrietta Dukes
Calvin C. Duley
Scott R. Duncan
Lee J. Dunlap
Gregory J. Dupye
John W. Dwyer
Harry D. Dyer

Willie L. Eames
Charles M. Easter
Megan M. Easton
Thomas W. Easton
Earl W. Ebbert
Regina L. Ebsworth
Elvio Echart
Jerelyn Eddings
Mary Edmond
Francis A. Edwards
Robert G. Edwards
Jerry D. Einolf
John S. Eisenberg
Elizabeth A. Eldridge
Arthur M. Elliott
Lois J. Elliott
Barbara L. Ellis
Charles A. Ellis
Robert W. Ellison
Wilbert J. Elsroad
James R. Embrey
Edward E. Engel
Robert A. Engel
David J. Engelhardt
Thomas J. Engelmann

William A. Englund
Sara M. Engram
Ellsworth R. Ensey
Glenn L. Eppig
Patrick A. Ercolano
Kenneth P. Erisman
Robert A. Erlandson
David Michael Ettlin
Angela C. Evans
David W. Evans
John J. Evans
Joseph C. Evans
Leroy A. Evans
Martin C. Evans
Roy D. Evans
Frank Everhart

Charles W. Faber
John H. Fairhall
Sharon R. Faison
Vernon L. Faison
Andrew D. Faith
John O. Fajimolu
Lester J. Faltz
Tracey Y. Faltz
Patricia A. Fanning
Michael J. Farabaugh
Rosser S. Farley
William J. Farley
Bruce M. Farrell
Michael C. Farrell
Thomas J. Farrell
Arnel M. Faulkner
Walter J. Faulkner
Jerod Fauntleroy
Leon Faust
Richard A. Fava
Charles S. Fawcett
Donald A. Fawcett
Jack W. Fawcett
Richard L. Fawcett
Kenneth F. Feeley
Betty A. Feeley
Ann R. Feild
Thomas B. Feldmann
Johathan Fellner
Chinelle D. Fenwick
Bobbi L. Feraci
James M. Ferguson
Julie M. Ferguson
Richard A. Ferguson
Thomas N. Ferguson

Ywain B. Ferguson
Danilo Fernandez
Karl M. Ferron
Daniel L. Fesperman
David E. Fetters
Mary Anne Fieden
Joseph A. Fiedler
Joseph A. Fiedler
Lorraine W. Fiedler
Martha Fields
Marinaldo Figueiredo
David V. Filicko
John P. Filo
Irene M. Findlay
Daniel T. Finke
Nancy J. Finson
William M. Fiorito
Albert R. Fischer
David B. Fischer
Robert B. Fisher
D. F. Fitzgerald
William E. Fitzpatrick
Gregory A. Fitzwater
Raphael G. Fizer
Thomas F. Flannery
Dorothy S. Fleetwood
Mark B. Fleming
Calvin D. Fletcher
Constance A. Fletcher
Michael A. Fletcher
Saundra L. Fletcher
Faye C. Flythe
Edwin M. Foard
Michael B. Foard
Thomas L. Fogle
Edward J. Ford
Robert A. Ford
Robert E. Ford, Sr.
James Forsythe
Carolyn B. Foss
A. Barbara Fox
Darlene M. Fox
Raymond A. Frager
Betty J. Francis
Raymond L. Francis
Louis J. Franconeri
James B. Franczkowski
Michael J. Frangos
George V. Frank
Jonathan W. Frankton
John P. Frantz
Edwin K. Franze

Katherine A. Frazier
Francis J. Freburger
George H. Freburger
John W. Frece
Bill Free
Henry C. Freeman
Nora M. Frenkiel
Carol M. Frey
Maurice J. Fritz
Charles Frommelt
Vincent F. Fronczak
Warner R. Fryer
Samuel L. Fulwood III
Don R. Fuqua
Ernest B. Furgurson
Joan Helen Furton
Michael L. Futrell

Randy W. Gadsden
Curtis L. Gadson
Chester W. Gage
Barbara A. Gallagher
Ann T. Gallant
Patricia A. Galloway
Michael J. Galope
Bernard R. Galvin
Angela W. Gambill
Sylvia M. Gamble
David Gantt
Joseph Ganzzermiller
Robert W. Garber
Daryl P. Gardner
Joseph D. Gardner
Richard W. Gardner
Irving L. Garfinkle
Rita M. Garvey
Diane E. Gary
Julius Gasparik
Gary M. Gately
Thomas W. Gauger
John D. Gavounas
William R. Gay
Linda Anne Geeson
Lawrence E. Geho
Hilda R. Geiwitz
Charles R. Gentilcore
Melva A. George
Michael M. George
Phyllis M. George
Steven A. George
William C. George
Claudia A. Gerarde

Jack W. Germond
Thomas M. Germroth
Carol L. Gesser
Lucille F. Giacubeno
James J. Giannattasio
John J. Gibbons
Thomas M. Gibbons
Michelle Gibbs
Paul W. Gibbs
Elmer E. Gibson
Gene W. Gibson
Joseph J. Gibson
Kristy D. Gibson
Timmie Lee Gibson
Kelwin R. Gilbert
Patrick M. Gilbert
Sandra H. Gill
William C. Gindhart
Michael P. Giro
Paul S. Girvan
Robin Y. Gladden
Louis A. Glasser
Jesse E. Glasgow
Mary D. Glassman
William K. Glauber
Vincent Glorioso
Dennis J. Glowack
Melvin L. Gobrecht
Alice P. Goetke
Daniel P. Goguen
Leslie L. Gold
Peter C. Golden
David Goldman
Alan Goldstein
Amy E. Goldstein
Jerry L. Gollick
John H. Gollick
John A. Gonce
Edward L. Gonder
Andrew D. Gonzales
Lawrence B. Gonzales
Sally D. Goodhue
Carl R. Goodman
Edwin W. Goodpaster
Paul W. Goodwin
Alvin C. Goosman
John H. Gormley
Ray G. Gorschboth
John F. Gover
Robert T. Graf
John F. Graham
Phyllis A. Graham

Sammy Graham
Paul V. Grams
Eric L. Grandy
Joseph Granruth
Joseph S. Granruth
Emmanuel Grant
Pamela V. Grant
Aaron L. Gray
Jacquelyn C. Gray
Robert W. Gray
Mark F. Grayson
Kirk J. Greaver
Derrick V. Green
Ernest R. Green
Gregory C. Green
Herbert J. Green
Shelly L. Green
Vera J. Green
William L. Green
Deborah I. Greene
Marvin V. Greene
Ronald J. Greene
Michael Greenspun
D. Robert Greenwood
Acklima C. Greer
William T. Greeson
William B. Gregory
Helen C. Griffin
Raymond E. Griffin
Robert T. Griffin
Jerry H. Griffith
Janice L. Griggs
Janet K. Grigson
Clarence R. Grimes
James K. Grimes
Jimmie N. Grimes
Steven T. Groft
Lawrence L. Gross
Raymond E. Grove
George E. Gruebl
Nora Gruner
Paula B. Guest
Mary A. Gugliuzza
Michael A. Guidara
Mark G. Guidera
Vernon A. Guidry, Jr.
Felix J. Guinto
Eugene E. Gunter
Jody E. Gunter
Edward L. Gunts
Bruce G. Guthrie
Miles B. Gwyn

Audrey J. Haar
Barbara Haddock
Robert L. Hale
Glenn E. Hall
Leslie V. Hall
Mark S. Hall
Raymond D. Hall
Southern S. Hall
Terry E. Hall
Wiley A. Hall
John J. Hallameyer
Jean C. Halle
Denise L. Hamilton
Robert K. Hamilton
Deborah A. Hamlin
Moses Hammett
Dorothy M. Hammond
George A. Hammons
May M. Hancock
Robert J. Hand
Robert F. Hankey
Janet L. Hanna
S. Dwight Hanna
George H. Hanst
Michael J. Hardesty
C. Wayne Hardin
Carolyn J. Hardnett
Jean I. Hare
Marilyn N. Hare
Robert L. Hargrove
Thomas L. Harold
David W. Harp
Larry E. Harpster
Charles M. Harrington
Joseph L. Harrington
Barry M. Harris
Larry H. Harris
Leonard O. Harris
Patricia C. Harris
Ricky Harris
Kevin E. Harrison
Rochelle P. Harrison
Jonathan L. Harrod
Carl T. Harryman
Carroll L. Hart
Teresa A. Hartka
Marci L. Hartl
Ann F. Harvey
Bernard J. Haske
Melvin A. Haskett
Gregory N. Haskins
Clemie R. Haught

Nancy T. Hauswald
John P. Havrilak
Leslie S. Hawkins
William E. N. Hawkins
Ellen M. Hawks
Thomas J. Hayes
Helen I. Haynie
Charles R. Hazard
Michael J. Heid
John A. Heim
John L. Heimbach
Curtis E. Henderson
David K. Henderson
George J. Henderson
Harlow Henderson
Randi M. Henderson
Shirley A. Henderson
James F. Henneman
Diana S. Henry
Edward C. Hensler
William Herd
Richard F. Herda
Stephen G. Hertsch
Dennis W. Hess
Michael D. Hess
Joseph W. Hession
Ross L. Hetrick
Stephen B. Heuer
Edward D. Hewitt
Joann D. Hickman
Danny R. Hicks
William M. Higgins
Alvin Highkin
A. Michael Hill
Eileen O. Hill
Traci C. Hill
Robert C. Hilson, Jr.
Michael J. Himowitz
Richard C. Hinke
Richard D. Hoag
Edward J. Hoben
Karen B. Hodge
Brian W. Hoehn
H. Craig Hofferbert
Donald H. Hoffman
Elisabeth S. Hoffman
Gene E. Hoffman
George W. Hoffman
Harold K. Hoffman
Mark H. Hofmann
John C. Holdcraft
Earl T. Holland

Robin D. Holland
Timothy C. Holland
Brenda M. Holley
Angela D. Holmes
Joseph W. Holmes
George W. Holsey
Michael L. Holt
Franklin E. Holtman
Kimberly A. Holton
Eugene H. Holzapfel
John R. Holzinger
Holger K. Homann
Jake Honeycutt
Leroy H. Hood
Jack Hook
David M. Hopkins
Stephen A. Hopkins
William M. Hopkins
Richard H. Hoppert
R. Diane Horowitz
Thomas W. Horton
Karen A. Hosler
William G. Hotz
James I. Houck
Kenneth R. Hough
Phyllis N. Howard
George M. Hubbard
Frederick C. Huber
Elaine Hudgins
John J. Hudgins
Michael J. Hudlicka
Donnell D. Hudson
Margaret J. Huffman
Richard J. Huffman
Lorna V. Huggins
James M. Hughes
Thomas M. Hughes
David W. Hull
Imogene L. Hults
Mildred L. Humphrey
William A. Humphreys
Sonja K. Hunn
Alvin T. Hunnings
James A. Hunt
Steven B. Hunt
Robert H. Hunter
Stephen C. Hunter
Toni I. Hunter
George H. Huppman
Antonio D. Hutcherson
Paul H. Hutchins, Jr.
Kathleen Hutchinson

Genevieve D. Hutto
William J. Hyder
Mark S. Hyman
Gilbert E. Hynes

Ernest F. Imhoff
John R. Irwin
Gregory R. Isennock
Edward E. Itter

Philip J. Jackman
Charles E. Jackson
Freddie J. Jackson
James H. Jackson
Nancy M. Jackson
Shirley E. Jackson
Stephen V. Jackson
Ratan Jacob
Joan H. Jacobson
Benjamin F. James
Ellen L. James
Paul A. James
Rainer James
Sammie Lee James
John G. Jancuk
Clifton M. Janney
Richard E. Jeddock
Antoni Jefferson
Eric D. Jefferson
Horchell Jefferson
Joe R. Jefferson
Milton Jefferson
Glendora C. Jenifer
Bonnie L. Jenkins
C. Ray Jenkins
Clarence L. Jenkins
Robert L. Jenkins
Robert M. Jenkins
Thomas Jenkins
Vivian R. Jenkins
William F. Jenkins
Beverly A. Jennings
Moses Jennings
Peter E. Jensen
Robert Jimison
David R. Johns
Aaron W. Johnson
Alberta E. Johnson
Angela M. Johnson

Bradford R. Johnson
Cynthia D. Johnson
Elsie L. Johnson
Jereline Johnson
Joseph M. Johnson
Julie A. Johnson
Lenwood Johnson
Lonnie D. Johnson
Marvin A. Johnson
Olin D. Johnson
Robert C. Johnson
Samuel R. Johnson
Willamae Johnson
George J. Johnston
Arthur R. Jones
Beverly R. Jones
David R. Jones
David W. Jones
Dora D. Jones
Edward F. Jones
Edward T. Jones
Francis X. Jones
George E. Jones
Helen B. Jones
Joanette Jones
Carleton Jones
Joseph H. Jones
Kasey Jones
Leroy R. Jones
Leroy T. Jones
Marvina M. Jones
Sandra L. Jones
Sylvia Lee Jones
Francis E. Jordan
Raymond C. Jordan
Natalie L. Jowett
Dolores E. Joyce
Patrick V. Joyce
Carol Ann Julian

W. Martin Kaiser
Christopher Kaltenbach
George M. Kane
Gregory D. Kane
John T. Kane
Michael R. Kane
Michael S. Kane
Walter C. Kanter
Lois E. Kappel
William D. Karasek
Gary M. Karner

Abby Karp
Kirk T. Karwoski
Robert W. Kasper
Thomas M. Kavanagh
Donna M. Kearns
James S. Keat
Joseph R. Keaton
Irving Keener
Catherine Keiser
Paul D. Keith
Mervyn M. Keizer
Jacques S. Kelly
Jerome G. Kelly
Keiren O. Kelly
Michael T. Kelly
Neil T. Kelly
Suzanne P. Kelly
Toki S. Kelly
Dudley N. Kemp
Vicki A. Kemper
Paul Kendrick
Patterson N. Kennedy
Richard J. Kenney
Thomas L. Kenney
Milton D. Kent
Lionel J. Kenyon
Harry W. Kerber
Ned E. Kerfoot
Robert T. Kerfoot
Mary G. Kesting
John C. Ketchum
Judith Kay Keys
Pierce R. Keyser
Thomas F. Keyser
Rosy Liang Kiang
Francis K. Kidder
Gary F. Kidwell
John A. Kidwell
Charles Kilgour
Buddy J. Kinder
Shirley King
Stephen J. King
Roxanne Kirkland
Edward Kirschbaum
Calvin T. Kiser
William P. Kiser
Phyllis M. Kisner
Kathleen A. Klein
Stephanie W. Klein
Patricia A. Klemans
John J. Klima
Ronald C. Klima

John M. Klingaman
James W. Knapp
Leonard F. Knott
Wilmer J. Knott
Connie L. Knox
Mary A. Knudson
Gertrude A. Kobren
Michael A. Kobus
Catherine G. Kodat
Stan M. Kolb
Fransiscus Korstjens
Ludmila Kosenko
Brian T. Kowal
Peter Koziar
Ernest T. Kraft
Earl R. Krainer
Alan H. Krakovitz
Edward A. Kramer
Mary T. Kramer
Vivian L. Kramer
Shirley L. Kranz
Carolyn Krausch
Charles E. Krauss
James T. Krebs
Ronald E. Krebs
Lefty Kreh
John S. Kreiner
Joyce A. Kreutzer
Harry Krolus
Francis A. Kruml
Robert J. Kucharek
Richard M. Kucharski
Theresa A. Kuessner
Peter J. Kumpa
James M. Kunaniec
Steven Kunaniec
Steven R. Kunaniec
Louis W. Kupfer
Patricia C. Kupfer
Leslie S. Kurcz
Celia H. Kurisch
Timothy B. Kurkjian
Howard K. Kurman
Linda M. Kursch

Glenn G. Lacher
Andrew T. Lackey
Patrick J. LaForge
Wayne A. Laing
Kathleen J. Lally
Gary C. Lambrecht
Valerie A. Lambros

James S. Lamm
Fletcher Lance
Jeffrey M. Landaw
Frank V. Lane
Michael J. Lane
Mildred C. Lane
Martin M. Lang
Calvin R. Langford
Ursula M. Langston
Charles Lankford
Denise J. Lannon
Elizabeth D. Large
Harry J. Larkins
Albert F. Laro
Ronald C. Lattanzio
David E. Lau
Anthony J. Lawrence
Jodi A. Lawrence
Kevin L. Lawrence
Donnie M. B. Lawson
Irvin B. Lawson
Juanita T. Lawson
Terrence A. Layton
Carol J. Leake
Edward H. Lebon
Jack E. Lebon
John A. Leckliter
Brian L. Lee
Leonard Lee
Paul F. Lee
Wayne T. Lee
Willie H. Lee
Don R. Legeer
Dayle M. Lembach
John M. Lemmon
Regina M. Lentz
Rose Ann Leonard
Susan R. Leppert
Herman Lesser
Charles R. Lester
Russell J. Lester
James E. Lett
William C. Leuallen
Janet F. Leuthold
Jeffrey J. LeVan
Michael R. Levene
David M. Levy
Benjamin H. Lewis
Catherine J. Lewis
David M. Lewis
Donald C. Lewis
Jon P. Lewis

Joseph M. Lewis
Lloyd Lewis
Reginald G. Lewis
Shirley R. Lewis
Gilbert A. Lewthwaite
James W. Liberto
Karen M. Lich
Donald C. Liggins
Eva M. Liggins
Carl Lightner
Herbert Lindlaw
Dennis J. Lindsey
Thomas G. Linthicum , Jr.
Theo Lippman
Lillian A. Lipsky
Mary Lou List
Morgan J. Lister
Ernest M. Litrenta
Bobby J. Little
Christopher L. Little
Stephanie J. Little
D. Michael Littwin
Alfred M. Litz
Lorne J. Livingston
Alfred T. Lloyd
Lois A. Lockett
Lilah Lohr
Ann LoLordo
Dolores T. Lomax
William Lombardi
Francis J. Long
William Long III
Carol A. Longdon
Bruno A. Lopata
Maria C. Lopez
Margaret Lord
Laimute O. Loskarn
Charles H. Lottes
Joseph W. Lough
Darnetta L. Love
Mamie L. Love
Dora L. J. Lovell
Thomas F. Loverro
David R. Loving
Dewey E. Lowe
Steven A. Lowe
Beryl V. Lowensen
John R. Lowery
Charles W. Lowry
Fred A. Luc
Carl D. Lucas
Jack H. Luckhardt

Ronald Russell
Anthony J. Russo
Lawrence Rutherford
Carl D. Ryan

William H. Sachse
Ruth E. Sadler
Robert S. Safrit
Frank W. Salamone
Joseph Salamone
Michael A. Salamone
Steven J. Salembene
M. William Salganik
Dorothy P. Sallese
Fred L. Sammons
Thomas Samsel
Kathleen V. Sanders
Kimberly M. Sanders
Patrick J. Sandor
Joseph E. Sands
Robert E. Sands
Teresa C. Sands
Marina F. Sarris
Jo Ann Sasser
Sanford G. Satosky
Raymond W. Sauer
Robert S. Sauer
Marlene D. Saunders
Ronald E. Saunders
Billie B. Savage
Wendy A. Savage
James R. Sawyer
Lillian F. Sawyer
Robert A. Sawyer
Joseph J. Scarpulla
Henry P. Scarupa
Dorothea C. Schech
Elizabeth Scheminant
John Schidlovsky
Vernon L. Schlein
Merriel G. Schlicht
Meredith A. Schlow
George W. Schmidt
A. Michael Schneider
Deborah K. Schneider
Jane R. Schneider
Carl A. Schoettler
Leslie L. Scholl
John J. Scholz
Edward Schorr
Anna M. Schreiner
Leatrice H. Schroeder

Janice C. Schultz
Mary A. Schultz
Sandra L. Schultz
Charles J. Schwartz
Joan P. Schwartz
Edith E. Schwarz
Nancy J. Schwerzler
Francis X. Schwind
Antoinette Scopinich
Charles L. Scott
Kathy A. Scott
John E. Sears
Katherine A. Sears
Elmer G. Sease
George J. Sebree
George W. Sebree
John J. Seeberger
Albert Sehlstedt, Jr.
Arthur Seibel
Keith J. Sellman
Frank Serruto
Louis E. Setren
Martin L. Setren
Doris E. Setsor
Joseph R. Seubott
Wendell P. Seybolt
Richard J. Seymour
Edgar D. Shaffer
William M. Shanahan
Scott Shane
Howard W. Shank, Sr.
Harvey R. Shanklin
John R. Shanklin
Stephanie A. Shapiro
Kate M. Sharpless
Garland D. Shaw
James D. Shaw
Nathaniel Shaw
Guy H. Sheetz
Theodore F. Shelsby
Fern M. Shen
David W. Shifflett
Linwood Shiflett
Thomas A. Shilling
Amrut V. Shirodkar
Sangeeta A. Shirodkar
Howard L. Shoats
Catherine C. Shockney
Larry S. Shockney
Lawrence M. Short
Ruth G. Shortt
Jerome J. Shoul

Bruce C. McEntee
Letha Mae McFadden
Mary E. McGraw-Smith
Patrick A. McGuire
Dennis M. McGuirk
James L. McIntyre
John E. McIntyre
Sandra M. McKee
Colleen A. McKenna
Walter E. McKenzie
Stephen A. McKerrow
William E. McKewen
Wilson McKnight
Dennis P. McLaughlin
James H. McLaughlin
Patricia T. McLellan
Donald McLeod
Paul K. McMullen
James A. McNamara
Patrick McNaney
Glenn M. McNatt
James L. McNulty
Brian C. McTaggart
Gary D. Meador
Edwin C. Meadowcroft
Hugh B. Meadowcroft
Mary K. Meehan
Audrey T. Meekins
Deborah J. Meekins
Tina M. Meekins
Jerry Meeks
Pamela D. Mellison
Michael G. Memphis
Michael W. Menzel
Karol V. Menzie
John W. Mercer
Evangeline Meredith
Peter C. Meredith
John C. Merritt
Joan R. Messineo
Paul A. Mettille
Gilbert P. Meyer
Brendan P. Meyers
Catherine D. Meyers
Clifford R. Meyers
David M. Meyers
Kathleen M. Meyers
Robert A. Meyers
Suzanne M. Mianulli
Henry F. Michel
Francis Mikulski
Vincent M. Milando

Gene L. Miller
Leonard L. Miller
Lisa Y. Miller
Rosemary Miller
Sophia S. Miller
Stephen Miller
Stephen M. Miller
Timothy M. Miller
Helen L. Mims
Frank N. Minch
Catherine L. Minghini
Lawrence Leo Minghini
Leonard P. Mink
John L. Minter
Andy J. Mioduszewski
Lorraine Mirabella
Beverly Ann Miranto
Howard Mitchell
Thomas E. Mitchem
Cynthia D. Mobley
Maxine Mobley
Philip T. Moeller
Bernard J. Moll
Preston H. Moltz
John J. Monaghan
Michael T. Monaghan
Vernon R. Montague
David G. Moore
Ernest R. Moore
Felicia Moore
James H. Moore
John T. Moore
Perris W. Moore
Thomas C. Moore
William S. Moores
Linda G. Moran
Brian Lee Morgan
John R. Morgan
Jonathan C. Morgan
Francis J. Morgereth
Josephine P. Morman
Melvin Morning
Harold W. Morris
Jennifer B. Morris
Linda L. Morris
Ricky L. Morris
Harry L. Morrison
William G. Morrison
Charles P. Morrow
William H. Mortimer
Denies O. Moses
James O. Moudry

Jerome F. Mueller
Barbara J. Mulcahy
Marck O. Mulligan
John F. Mulqueen
William S. Mund
Jennifer M. Mundie
Floyd R. Munsey
Mary M. Murdock
Michelle D. Murdock
David C. Murphy
James M. Murphy
John R. Murphy
Marshall P. Murphy
Michael J. Murphy
Norma P. Murphy
Kenneth R. Murray
Edward G. Muse
Frank Musil
Glenda J. Myers
Mary G. Myles

Jack B. Naditch
John Naditch
Frank A. Nakuosas
Deborah V. Nash
Jerry E. Naylor
Alphonso L. Neal
W. James Neeld
Ruby C. Neely
Clarence Nelson
Frederick J. Nelson
Glenn J. Nelson
Sharon A. Nelson
Samuel N. Nemons
Diedre A. Nerreau
Carl C. Neuhaus
Donna M. Neuhaus
Carl E. Neville
Elaine C. Nichols
Dennis Nicholson
Onzalee Nickelson
Harold C. Neimeyer
M. A. Noppenberger
Robert I. Noppenberger
Ellsworth Nordbrook
James J. Nordbrook
Stephen E. Nordlinger
James A. Norris
John L. Norris
Raymond Lee Norris
Charles L. Norton
John C. Norwood

Andrew J. Novak
Frank C. Novotny
Frank J. Novotny
Douglas F. Nowakowski
Robert S. Nusgart
Harley E. Nussbaum

Dominic J. O'Brien
Gayle P. O'Brien
John B. O'Donnell
Patrick J. O'Malley
Richard P. O'Mara
Eddie G. O'Quinn
Joann H. Oberdalhoff
Bernard L. Oden
Raymond D. Odle
Charles H. Odom
Moses C. Ohale
Janice C. Ojason
Bart S. Olenik
Michael C. Olesker
John R. Olinger
Charles A. Oliver
George S. Oliver
Kenney Oliver
Thomas C. Oliver
Michael L. Ollove
Valerie Omisore
Catherine O'Neill
Nancy J. Oppel
Francis D. Orbin
Thomas E. Osborne
Martin T. Ostovitz
Gwinn F. Owens
Leonard V. Owings
Marilyn M. Ozsvath

Edward J. Pabst
Samuel P. Pace
Jean L. Packard
Martin T. Padden
David Page
Jean Marie Page
K. Kenneth Paik
Jack A. Paine
Thomas J. Palermo
David A. Palmer
Gary H. Palmer
Harold M. Paris
Sandra R. Paris
Alfred J. Parker
Regina M. Parks

William L. Parks
Elizabeth A. Parlett
James P. Parlett
Mark P. Parrent
Arch J. Parsons
Eric C. Parthree
Jan S. Pastor
John F. Patinella
Kenneth L. Patrick
Richard J. Patro
Dale D. Patton
Andrea G. Pawlyna
Ann Pearson
James E. Pearson
Ross D. Peddicord
Leroy A. Pendergast
William E. Perkowski
Gervin H. Perrine
Accie Perry
Clay C. Perry
Sarah Perry
Bruno J. Perseghin
Victor Persico
Charles F. Pessaro
Jeffrey W. Peters
Kaye T. Peters
Alfred J. Petersam
Thomas F. Peterson
Melvin T. Petty
Gregory Pfannenstein
Jack Pfeifer
Janet D. Pfeiffer
Irving H. Phillips
Leo M. Phillips
Ronald W. Phillips
James B. Phipps
Robert M. Pickering
Lisa A. Pierelli
Antero H. Pietila
Stan Pietrowski
Steven D. Pinder
Bernadine J. Pinkney
Kathleen W. Pinkney
Harold D. Piper
Anthony J. Pipitone
Nathan M. Pitts
Pauline Pitts
J. Kenneth Pivec
George W. Plant
Emory A. Plitt
Diana A. Plunkett
John H. Plunkett

Jack J. Poist
Stephen C. Pollock
Edwin S. Pomerantz
R. Timothy Pomeroy
Scott D. Ponemone
Amelia Pope
Vanessa S. Posey
John V. Poskocil
John M. Poteet
Madeline M. Potter
Jacqueline A. Powder
Todd W. Powell
Yolanda A. Powell
Deborah D. Powers
Mike Preston
Ellwod V. Price
G. Jefferson Price III
Robert T. Price
Robert G. Proctor
Stephen R. Proctor
James A. Propst
Gerald Pruchniewski
Ronald L. Pruitt
Juanita L. Pryor
Gary E. Puckett
James W. Pumphrey
Robert V. Pumphrey
John F. Purcell
Charles T. Pusey
Priscilla D. Putty

Joann R. Quattrochi
Don C. Queen
George F. Queen
Joseph L. Queen
Carroll R. Quinn
James R. Quinn

Edward R. Raab
Linda M. Racks
Corita E. Radcliffe
George Rader III
William B. Radford
John J. Radomski
Francis J. Rakowski
Herman E. Randall
Col L. Randolph
Dennis C. Rankin
Barbara J. Ranney
John E. Raschka
Barry C. Rascovar
Frederick Rasmussen

Joseph N. Rather
Andrew R. Ratner
John C. Rau
Robert V. Ray
George E. Raynor
Lawrence H. Raynor
Constance R. Raysor
Karen T. Reaves
Thomas L. Redd
Michael L. Redding
Ronald T. Reddish
Ann M. Redifer
Michael T. Reeb
Richard Lee Reed
Roger K. Reed
James C. Reeves
Isaac B. Rehert
Susan F. Reid
Wallace Reid
Patricia R. Reilly
Susan J. Reimer
Ruth E. Reimschissel
Albert Reinhardt
Joseph V. Reisler
Karin S. Remesch
Edwin H. Remsberg
Alphonse Renaud
Dolores A. Revis
Samuel B. Reyna
James D. Rhodes
Debbie A. Rice
Joseph M. Rice
Lucky Rich
Arthur J. Richardson
Dana A. Richardson
James A. Ricker
James C. Ricker
John W. Rickour
Julia L. Ridgell
Stephen L. Rifkin
Philip Rigney
Cynthia J. Riley
Robert A. Riley
John A. Ritter
Lois A. Ritter
Donna R. Rittermann
Geraldine Rittermann
Lola J. Rivers
Jacqueline V. Roane
Harold S. Roberts
Charles W. Robertson
Marie Robertson

William F. Robey
Barbara C. Robinson
Carroll E. Robinson
Charles E. Robinson
Deborah E. Robinson
Elmer E. Robinson
Francis B. Robinson
H. Darryl Robinson
Herbert Robinson
Josephine Robinson
Lynda Robinson
Michele D. Robinson
Nathaniel M. Robinson
Sharon C. Robinson
Ralph J. Rock
George G. Rodgers
John N. Rodgers
W. L. Rodgers
Wilbur E. Rodney
Daniel J. Rodricks
Jane P. Roesler
James J. Roles
Lee A. Roper
Antione L. Rose
Georgene B. Rose
Melody A. Rose
Vincent J. Rose
Harold Rosen
Jane L. Rosenberg
Donna L. Rosendale
David R. Rosenthal
Kenneth H. Rosenthal
Robert D. Rosier
Nurite L. Rosin
Dominic M. Ross
James J. Rossi
Judith W. Rousuck
Denise A. Rowland
Melvin E. Rowley
John C. Royer
Frank D. Roylance
Nathan L. Royster
Stephen W. Royston
Ludmila M. Rozanek
Kimberley A. Ruark
Robert S. Ruby
Gilbert Ruddie
Robert A. Ruff III
Michael P. Rumford
Robert J. Russ
Charles L. Russell
Edgar D. Russell

Thomas Ludd
Christine T. Lugat
Ananias Lumpkin
Michael S. Lurie
Frank J. Lynch
Raymond M. Lynch
Vanessa J. Lynch
Wayne Lynch
Dorothy B. Lyon
Donnalisa Lyons
Sheridan Lyons
Thomas C. Lyons

Irene M. MacDonald
Donald L. MacFarlane
Larry J. Machovec
Francis A. Maggitti
Albert E. Maher
Elmer M. Maher
Howard J. Maher
Kenneth T. Maher
Raymond P. Maher
Virginia F. Maher
Keith T. Mahone
Malisa Y. Mahone
Barbara J. Maiolatesi
Robert Lee Maisel
Robert Maivelett
Robert J. Maivelett
Richard E. Majewski
Sam Major
Leonard J. Makowski
Thomas D. Malenski
Locksley W. Mallett
Carol Mancini
John A. Mann, Jr.
Sangeeta Mann
Eddie M. Manning
John J. Manning
George J. Manns
Daniel S. Mantegna
Kathleen S. Mantegna
Deborah D. Marable
Louis A. Maranto
Michelle Marcellino
John V. Marchsteiner
Wayne M. Marcinko
Albert L. Marecki
Carolyn A. Marks
Donald G. Markus
Richard S. Markuson
Michael F. Marlow

James M. Marshall
John C. Marti
Brian L. Martin
Helen Martin
Joyce L. Martin
Robert W. Martin
Theresa A. Martin
Thomas F. Martin
Joseph J. Martini
Georgia C. Marudas
Deborah J. Marzan
Rajabali B. Masoudi
David L. Mather
Joseph P. Mathias
Amelia T. Mathison
Mark H. Matthews
Paul R. Mattix III
Andrew Matusky
Matthew Maulone
Mary A. Maushard
Frank McAllister
Jeanette McBride
Philip A. McCabe
Noami R. McCain
Rodney L. McCain
Dorothy McCall
Paul M. McCardell
Walter M. McCardell
Richard J. McCarren
Patricia M. McCarthy
George J. McCartney
Mary E. McCausland
Leona M. McClelland
John M. McClintock
Robert S. McClung
Joel S. McCord
Thomas G. McCormack
Richard G. McCotter
Raymond W. McCoy
Paul A. McCracken
James P. McCrystal
Robert McCullough, Jr.
Edgar J. McDaniel
Rikie K. McDaniels
Gary A. McDonald
Rico W. McDonald
William McDonald
Kelly A. McDonnell
Edward J. McDonough
Hamilton H. McDowell
Robert McDowell
Peter J. McElroy

Robert W. Shuey
Edward Shufford
Darryl G. Shuford
Michael L. Shultz
Edward H. Shur
Robert M. Shutt
Richard H. P. Sia
Louis Sieck
Eric C. Siegel
Silvio L. Sigismondi
Darrell Q. Simmons
Melody L. Simmons
Rosalind Simmons
William J. Simmons
Yvonne A. Simmons
Richard L. Simms
David J. Simon
Henry E. Simon
Leslie A. Simon
Roger M. Simon
Joseph W. Simpson
George F. Sims
George H. Sims
Michelle Singletary
Aldora M. Singleton
Frank G. Sisolak
Michael S. Sisson
Hyman H. Sitren
William E. Skuhr
Robert G. Slavin
Caryn B. Slotsky
Glenn M. Small, Jr.
James E. Smallwood, Jr.
Robert W. Smart
Erik A. Smist
Adrian M. Smith
Barbara H. Smith
C. Fraser Smith
Carol A. Smith
Dana L. Smith
Dawn L. Smith
Dorothy P. Smith
Douglas A. Smith
Eric I. Smith
Jane A. Smith
Jerald Smith
Joseph F. Smith
Kenneth E. Smith
Linell N. Smith
Maralee S. Smith
Mary C. Smith
Paul A. Smith

Philip L. Smith
Ronald S. Smith
Seymour S. Smith
Timothy A. Smith
Gerald V. Smolinski
George D. Smorse
Joseph R. Snair
Earl Sneed
Dudley C. Snyder
Joseph R. Snyder
Richard C. Sobus
John W. Sokolis
Jerome A. Solomon
Richard F. Solomon
Frederick W. Solowski
Frank P. L. Somerville
Kelvin W. Sorrell
Norman F. Spahn
Carol V. Spann
Lori S. Spann
Frank J. Speca
Kevin A. Spence
Kevin F. Spence
Angela M. Spencer
Carolyn M. Spencer
Raymond S. Spencer
William Spencer
Joseph P. Speranzella
John L. Sprigg
James H. Sprucebank
Benjamin Stachowski
Charles H. Stachowski
Lisa A. Stachowski
Harry N. Stadler
Ronald K. Staggs
Robert S. Stallings
Daniel Stamboni
Deborah C. Standiford
John L. Stark
Randolph Starks
C. G. Starner
Frank C. Starr
Clifford A. Staten
William E. Staubs
John F. Steadman
Alexa M. Steele
Barbara Stefanowitz
Phyllis A. Stefanski
William R. Steigerwald
Henry F. Steinacker
Alice C. Steinbach
Vito J. Stellino

Michael T. Stender
Edmund Stepniewski
Joseph R. L. Sterne
Clarence W. Stevens
Burton L. Stevenson
John W. Stewart
Martin E. Stewart
Russell Stewart
Patrick J. Stidham
George Stinebaugh
Antonio M. Stokes
Carl F. Stokes
John F. Stone
Thomas W. Stone
Pamela A. Stover
Michael J. Stracke
Diana M. Stratton
David M. Strickler
Irvin L. Strickler
Carl T. Strine
John L. Strosnider
Patrick H. Strow
Douglas W. Struck
Geraldine Stryjewski
Lloyd L. Stuart
Deborah J. Stubbs
Andrew F. Stubel
Fred Steuber
Mary Ann W. Stuller
Fred B. Sturgill
Granville Sturgill
Paul R. Sudbrook
Brian E. Sullam
Cathy H. Sullivan
Harry F. Sullivan
Richard B. Sullivan
Myer Summerfield
Lowell E. Sunderland
William E. Suter
Joseph D. Sutherland
Josephine Swagger
Weyman D. Swagger
Marlene V. Swan
Leonard H. Swarthout
Nancy Swartzendruber
Eugene M. Sweeney
N. Joseph Sweeney
John M. Sykes
Steven B. Sykes
Joseph L. Szymanski

Scott W. Taber

Charles E. Tait
William B. Talbott
Charmaine D. Tanner
G. William Tanton
Bernard Tassler
David R. Tate
Jon K. Tates
James L. Tawes
Benjamin F. Taylor
Brenda L. Taylor
Geoffrey R. Taylor
George B. Taylor
Larry A. Taylor
Purnell Arvell Taylor
Robert J. Taylor
Sannie M. Taylor
Sheri Taylor
Towanda P. Taylor
Vicki L. Taylor
George E. Teal
Karl T. Teel
Debra W. Temple
Ernest L. Temple
Alphonso A. Tenaglia
Wayne D. Tepper
Kim E. Testa
Sherrie J. Tewell
Alexandra Thomas
Barbara J. Thomas
David P. Thomas
Edwin H. Thomas
George R. Thomas
Judith A. Thomas
Kevin B. Thomas
Larry N. Thomas
Michael A. Thomas
Raymond E. Thomas
Charles A. Thompson
Edward F. Thompson
Garland L. Thompson
Gilbert A. Thompson
James E. Thompson
William L. Thompson
William F. Thomson
Larry M. Thornton
William C. Thorpe
Perry E. Thorsvik
James L. Thrower
Donald W. Thurlow
Edgar L. Tidwell
Gregory R. Tiller
Priscilla J. Tillman

Robert R. Timberg
Keith B. Titus
Robert S. Toelle
Charles W. Tolson
David C. Tolzmann, Jr.
Lorraine K. Tomsik
Dariel B. Torain
James R. Torrence
Robert L. Townes
Thomas M. Townsend
John F. Tracy
Andrew M. Trageser
John D. Trail
Joseph P. Trainor
Gene V. Travagline
Linda C. Trebes
Richard C. Trest
Charles A. Treuting
Martha S. Trotman
Thomas L. Tuck
John D. Tullier
Arlene K. Turner
David D. Turner
George E. Turner
Gerald G. Turner
Joseph F. Turner
Mary J. Turner
Paul E. Turner
Ronnie E. Turner
L. Roger Twigg
Danita L. Tyler
Donald L. Tyler
Joan D. Tyner
Irene S. Tyree

Frank R. Ulrich
Darryl W. Underwood
Gary L. Unglesbee
Rosanna R. Uranachek
Richard J. Utz
Ellen L. Uzelac

Oresti L. Valerio
Joel A. Vance
Lauren L. Vanhoy
Charlyne A. Varkonyi
Robert H. Vaughan
Steven P. Velte
Melvin W. Venable
Daniel Vereen
Norman D. Verill
Carolyn M. Vernon

Gary M. Vetter
Robert W. Vicarini
Jesse J. Vice
Patrick N. Vincent
Andrea J. Vissotzky
Michael P. Vitas
Marbury L. von Briesen
Frederick S. Vondy
Lewis G. vonLossberg
Marci M. Vorbach
Mark Vukov

Jack R. Wadsworth
Bruce W. Wagner
Frank P. Wagner
Judith I. Wagner
Richard L. Wagner
Helen L. Wah
Ralph Wainwright
Celeste A. Walatka
Edward Alan Waldman
Thomas W. Waldron
Cynthia M. Walins
Annie P. Walker
Clara M. Walker
Leslie A. Walker
Rosalind D. Walker
Stephen W. Walker
Darryl K. Wallace
James C. Wallace
Bernard M. Walsh
Winifred E. Walsh
Joseph P. Walter
John A. Waltermyer
George A. Walters
Janice L. Walters
Charles T. Wampler
James Paul Ward
Timothy E. Ward
Barney G. Ware
Karen E. Warmkessel
Lenora Warren
Marc E. Warren
Timothy P. Warren
Jan B. Warrington
Carol G. Washburne
Joann E. Washington
Randolph F. Washington
Rachel Wasserman
Franchester Waters
Arthur E. Watkins
Richard W. Watkins

Charles H. Watson
David Lee Watson
Donald L. Watson
Frank W. Watson
Gilbert L. Watson
James Watson
Marie G. Watson
Ralph G. Watson
Ronald G. Watts
Wayne A. Watts
Anthony Waytekunas
Octavia Weathington
Donna L. Weaver
Jerry Lee Weaver
Thomas E. Weber
Charles R. Wehnert
Francis C. Wehr
Joseph A. Weidner
Charles D. Weimer
Coleman J. Weiner
John F. Weis
Clay F. Welch
Evan W. Welch
John E. W. Welch
Lucy M. Wells
Darryl J. Welsh
Francis J. Welsh
George A. Welsh
Mary E. Welsh
Matthew F. Welsh
Tracy I. Welsh
Edward J. Wendel
Earl L. Wentz
Michael L. Wentzel
Edward W. Wernsing
Charles R. Wert
Donna B. Wertheimer
M. Delores West
Paul West
Jack Wetherson
Peter Wetmore
John L. Wetters
Michael S. Wheatley
Thomas R. Wheatley
Timonthy B. Wheeler
Brenda J. Whitaker
Brenda L. White
Constance M. White
Davison D. White
Joan E. White
John J. White
Wilbert N. White

William D. White
Bryan A. Whitehead
Sanora V. Whitehead
Willie Whitehead
Melvin L. Whiters
Thomas R. Whitten
Barbara M. Wiegel
Stephen Wigler
Joseph N. Wilderson
Louise Wiley
Clinton R. Wilkes
Anna M. Wilkinson
Paul O. Willhite, Jr.
Arvia M. Williams
Beverly A. Williams
Cornell F. Williams
Dana B. Williams
Daniel R. Williams
Dennis F. Williams
Earl L. Williams
John J. Williams
John L. Williams
Levey L. Williams
Lynn K. Williams
Margaret J. Williams
Michelle Williams
Milton J. Williams
Minnie C. Williams
Nancy L. Williams
Raymond E. Williams
Robert E. Williams
Robert L. Williams
Terry G. Williams
Toney I. Williams
Towanna L. Williams
Tracey Williams
Robert H. Willis
Walter L. Wilmer
Elizabeth B. Wilson
George C. Wilson
Gregory J. Wilson
John H. Wilson
Norman T. Wilson
Pamela L. Wilson
Paul B. Wilson
Terrance M. Wingert
Marva V. Wingfield
Vernon C. Winkler
Gabrielle D. Wise
Helena M. Wise
William J. Wise
Jules J. Witcover

Hubert H. Withrow
Richard D. Witler
John W. Wittman
Albert D. Woehlke
Herbert C. Wolfe
Yvonne E. Womack
Kimberly K. Wood
Rodney L. Wood
Cornell Woodard
James H. Wooden
John E. Woodruff
Raymond C. Woods
Norman G. Wooten
Suzanne W. Wooton
Charles A. Wright
James E. Wright
James H. Wright
James H. Wright
James S. Wright
John W. Wright
John F. Wrightson
Barbara L. Wrigley
Gary G. Wurzbacher

Richard P. Yancheski

Kofi Yirenkyi
George A. Yorkman
Lloyd S. Yost
Denise D. Young
Laverne B. Young
Luther O. Young
Tung Lin Yu
Jon C. Yuhn

Gerald C. Zakes
Mary S. Zamostny
Charles W. Zamzow
Basil G. Zarafonetis
Jill Zarend
Keefer F. Zeller
Joseph A. Zentgraf
David M. Zidek
Donald V. Zidek
Perry J. Ziegler
Carl G. Zigler
Roland F. Zimmerer
Diana M. Zinda
Joanne C. Zittle
William F. Zorzi
John N. Zurlo